Securing Development

Securing Development
Public Finance and the Security Sector

A Guide to Public Expenditure Reviews in the Security and Criminal Justice Sectors

Bernard Harborne
William Dorotinsky
Paul M. Bisca
Editors

ISBN (paper): 978-1-4648-0766-4
ISBN (electronic): 978-1-4648-0767-1
DOI: 10.1596/978-1-4648-0766-4

Cover photo: © Dimjul/Dreamstime.com. Used with the permission of Dimjul/Dreamstime.com.
Further permission required for reuse.

Cover design: Bill Pragluski, Critical Stages.

Library of Congress Cataloging-in-Publication data has been requested.

Contents

Selected Bibliography   477

Image Credits   489

Boxes

Figures

Maps

Tables

Preface

This book aims to highlight the role played by public finance in the delivery of security and criminal justice services. It seeks to strengthen the policy and operational dialogue on security sector issues by providing national and international stakeholders with key information on security expenditure policy. The book is part of a project undertaken by staff from the World Bank and the United Nations. The World Bank has a leading role in public finance as well as assistance to the public sector (including justice); this book will be its first step in bringing that expertise to the security sector. The United Nations generally, and specific actors such as the United Nations Department of Peacekeeping Operations (UNDPKO) and the United Nations Development Programme (UNDP), have sector expertise in security and justice. This book will thus integrate disciplines where each institution holds comparative advantage and a core mandate.

The primary audience includes government officials, staff of international organizations working on public expenditure management and security sector issues, and development practitioners working in an advisory capacity. The audience also includes World Bank staff who may be asked to assist in expenditure analysis related to the security sector; taking into account World Bank policy, the book clearly defines their role in the expenditure review process.

The interplay of security, justice, and public finance is still a relatively unexplored area of development. Security and criminal justice are fundamental public goods provided by governments, and they often have significant claims on national budgets. Informed discussions on security sector expenditure policy are an essential part of the national policy process, through which central finance agencies fulfill their function of contesting sector expenditure proposals in the planning and budgeting process. Dialogue on security expenditure policy also strengthens international partners' engagement on security issues, helping them make informed decisions regarding the appropriate level and form of external assistance. This book offers a framework for analyzing financial management, financial transparency, and oversight, as well as expenditure policy issues that determine how to most appropriately manage corruption risks. It also provides advice on entry points for integrating expenditure analysis into security sector and broader governance reform processes.

For a variety of reasons, a growing number of governments are requesting support from the World Bank and UN partners (whether working separately or jointly) in examining the effectiveness, efficiency, and sustainability of public spending in the sector. These have ranged from countries affected by high rates of crime and urban violence (such as El Salvador and Mexico), to countries undergoing fragile transitions with a large peacekeeping presence (such as Liberia and Somalia), to those affected by external threats and crisis (such as Mali and Niger). These case studies are now building up a body of experience on this work that feeds into this sourcebook on undertaking security sector public expenditure reviews.

Acknowledgments

This book is an outcome of a joint project between the World Bank and the United Nations (UN). It was conceived by a team led by Bernard Harborne and William Dorotinsky for the World Bank, and Adedeji Ebo and Alejandro Alvarez for the UN. Paul M. Bisca (World Bank), Thorodd Ommundsen (UN), and Christophe Pradier (UN) provided support.

The book was written by World Bank staff and consultants, with inputs from the United Nations Department of Peacekeeping Operations (UNDPKO) and the United Nations Development Programme (UNDP). Chapter 1, the introduction, is by Bernard Harborne; chapter 2, on public finance management, is by William Dorotinsky, Bernard Harborne, and Paul M. Bisca; chapter 3, on defense, is by Bradley Larson and Bernard Harborne; chapter 4, on policing, is by Antony Altbeker, Paul M. Bisca, and Erik Alda; and chapter 5, on criminal justice, is by Heike Gramckow, Fernando Fernandez-Monge, and Bernard Harborne. Contributions were also received from Nicole Ball (chapter 1), Giuseppe Manzillo (annex 3D, in chapter 3, on costing methodologies for defense), Rosemary Barberet (chapter 5), and the United Nations Police Division (chapter 4).

This book benefited at various stages from the guidance and comments of World Bank staff, including Alexandre Arobbio, Eric Brintet, James Brumby, Hassane Cisse, Klaus Decker, Adrian Fozzard (the original task manager of the initiative), Jimena Garrote, Maninder Gill, Luigi Giovine, Sudarshan Gooptu, Lewis Hawke, Deborah Isser, Sahr Kpundeh, Amit Mukherjee, Nadia Piffaretti, Vikram Raghavan, Carolina Renteria, Nicola Smithers, and Gert van der Linde. Suggestions were also received from Helen Olafsdottir and Christi Sletten (UNDP) and members of the United Nations Security Sector Reform Task Force.

The team also acknowledges the valuable insights offered by experts from academia, civil society, international organizations, and donor organizations who reviewed this work: Gordon Adams (Stimson Center), Louis-Alexandre Berg (Georgia State University), Mark Cancian (Johns Hopkins School of Advanced International Studies), Stephen Emasu (independent public finance consultant), Elizabeth Howe (International Association of Prosecutors), Eboe Hutchful (African Security Sector Network), Stuart Johnson (RAND Corporation), Seth Jones (RAND Corporation), Christian Mainzinger (German Federal Police), Peter Neyroud (Cambridge University), Mette Nielsen (U.K. Department for International Development), Wuyi Omitoogun (African Security Sector Network), Mark Pyman (Transparency International Defence Programme), Mark Sedra (Security Governance Group), Rodrigo Serrano-Berthet (Inter-American Development Bank), Victoria Walker (International Security Sector Advisory Team), and Vanessa Wyeth (Organisation for Economic Co-operation and Development Development Assistance Committee).

This book was made possible by grants from the Australian Partnership and Knowledge Trust Fund, the Bank-Netherlands Partnership Program Trust Fund, and the UN-World Bank Partnership Trust Fund (financed by the governments of Norway and Switzerland) as well as by support from the government of the United Kingdom's Stabilization Unit.

Last, the team thanks Anne Himmelfarb for editing and revising the book.

About the Editors

Bernard Harborne is the lead technical specialist on fragility, conflict, and violence in the Global Programs Unit for the Social, Urban, Rural, and Resilience Global Practice of the World Bank. He joined the World Bank in 2004 as the lead conflict adviser for Africa, serving as country manager in Côte d'Ivoire from 2007 to 2008. He has specialized in analytics, needs assessments, and strategies to address conflict, violence, and forced displacement, as well as led investment operations for the demobilization of ex-combatants, community-based development, and small-scale infrastructure. Before joining the World Bank, he worked for more than a decade in various roles, including as a human rights lawyer in Gaza and then in Cambodia, and for seven years in Africa for the United Nations, working on emergency relief and citizen protection, with his last post as head of the UN Coordination Office for Somalia. He then worked for two years with the U.K. government as the senior conflict adviser for Africa, managing the Africa Conflict Prevention Fund. He has a background in law, having worked as a criminal lawyer in London while he obtained a master's degree in international law from the London School of Economics. Harborne is an adjunct professor at The George Washington University.

William Dorotinsky is a global name in public finance, performance and results, and governance issues. He is currently responsible for knowledge, learning, and partnerships in the World Bank's Governance Global Practice. He previously served as acting director of the Governance Global Practice, founded the World Bank's global expert team on public sector performance, and was the driving force behind the Public Expenditure and Financial Accountability (PEFA) framework—the international standard for national public finance systems. He also served with the International Monetary Fund as a deputy division chief, with the U.S. Office of Management and Budget (where he held a secondment as deputy chief finance officer with the District of Columbia during its mid-1990s financial crisis), and with the Clinton administration's Health Care Reform Task Force. He was also a U.S. Treasury resident adviser to the governments of Argentina, Croatia, and Hungary. In 2014, Dorotinsky received the International Lifetime Achievement Award from the Association of Government Accountants for advancing public sector financial performance internationally.

Paul M. Bisca is a conflict and security analyst specializing in the intersection of security and development. He has previously led a public expenditure review of citizen security institutions in Mexico and has worked on World Bank social development projects in El Salvador, Indonesia, Liberia, and Rwanda. He has worked on developing strategies and financing instruments to enable the quick deployment of World Bank assistance to countries affected by conflict, fragility, and violence. Before joining the World Bank in 2010, he performed customized political risk assessments for firms specializing in business intelligence and corporate due diligence in Eastern Europe. He holds a master's degree in strategic studies and economics from The Johns Hopkins School of Advanced International Studies and a bachelor's degree in international studies from Macalester College in St. Paul, Minnesota.

Abbreviations

ABC	activity-based costing
ADB	Asian Development Bank
AfDB	African Development Bank
CARICOM	Caribbean Community Secretariat
CFAF	Central African CFA franc
COFOG	Classification of the Functions of Government
COIN	counterterrorism/counterinsurgency
COW	Correlates of War
CPA	Country Performance Assessment
CPIA	Country Policy and Institutional Assessment
CPS	Crown Prosecution Service
DAC	Development Assistance Committee
DDR	disarmament, demobilization, and reintegration
DMU	decision-making unit
DSR	defense sector reform
ECOWAS	Economic Community of West African States
FCS	fragile and conflict-affected states
FMIS	financial management information system
GDP	gross domestic product
GFS	government finance statistics
GFSM	*Government Finance Statistics Manual*
GNI	gross national income
IBRD	International Bank for Reconstruction and Development
IDA	International Development Association
IEP	Institute for Economics and Peace
IFMIS	integrated financial management information system
IGAN	Inspectorate General of the National Army
IMF	International Monetary Fund

IPSASB	International Public Sector Accounting Standards Board
ISSAT	International Security Sector Advisory Team
JC	judicial council
LAPOP	Latin American Public Opinion Survey
LNP	Liberia National Police
M&E	monitoring and evaluation
MDAs	ministries, departments, and agencies
NATO	North Atlantic Treaty Organization
NGO	nongovernmental organization
NISAT	Norwegian Initiative on Small Arms Transfers
O&M	operations and maintenance
ODA	official development assistance
OECD	Organisation for Economic Co-operation and Development
PEFA	Public Expenditure and Financial Accountability
PER	Public Expenditure Review
PFM	public financial management
PKO	peacekeeping operation
PNC	Congolese National Police
PPP	purchasing power parity
R&D	research and development
SAR	Special Administrative Region
SDC	Swiss Agency for Development and Cooperation
SICA	Security Commission of the Central American Integration System
SIPRI	Stockholm International Peace Research Institute
SSAPR	Security Sector Accountability and Police Reform Program
SSD	Security Sector Development
SSR	security sector reform
UEMS	unplanned explosions at munitions sites
UN	United Nations
UNDP	United Nations Development Programme
UNDPKO	United Nations Department of Peacekeeping Operations
UNMIL	United Nations Mission in Liberia
UNODC	United Nations Office on Drugs and Crime
UNPOL	United Nations Police
UNSG	United Nations Secretary General
UOR	urgent operational requirement
USAID	U.S. Agency for International Development
WAEMU	West African Economic and Monetary Union
WDI	World Development Indicators
WHO	World Health Organization

All dollar amounts are U.S. dollars unless otherwise indicated.

Overview

Introduction to *Securing Development*

We live in an insecure world, and some of the foremost public policy questions of our time address how we can strengthen our security and personal safety. Often those questions can be further broken down into what are the most affordable or cost-effective means of addressing insecurity.
These questions are critical in a variety of contexts.

- In late 2005, financial experts examined data at the Afghan Ministry of Finance to ascertain how much the security sector was costing. To their astonishment, they found that the sector cost some $1.3 billion per year, or 23 percent of gross domestic product (GDP), made up largely of donor contributions along with some government financing. Security spending therefore exceeded domestic revenues by over 500 percent.[1] Questions on the sustainability of security sector spending, and on the handover from international forces for policing and military functions, have been at the fore of policy making for the country ever since.[2]

- Central America, and particularly the northern triangle of El Salvador, Guatemala, and Honduras, is home to the highest homicide rates in the world. Interpersonal violence associated with gangs, drug trafficking, and weak criminal justice institutions has enormous costs in terms of health, economic growth, and people's overall well-being.[3] In El Salvador, official estimates show that crime costs 16 percent of GDP per year.[4] The governments in the region established the Security Commission of the Central American Integration System (known as SICA) in 1995 to harness their collective efforts to address these huge challenges, and donors have provided generous contributions to their security strategy.[5] Yet, the extremely high rates of crime and violence continue.

- Since 9/11, the U.S. and European governments have faced increasing costs for their counterterror measures. A central question is whether the gains in safety have been justified by the costs, which have run into the trillions of dollars.[6] When the surveillance of one individual associated with a radical political agenda can cost around $5.7 million per year,[7] governments must think about what price they are paying to keep their citizens safe, or feeling safe.

The need to understand security and justice systems in the context of the public expenditures they require is the subject of this sourcebook.[8] This is not a policy book that recommends different approaches to security threats and challenges. It is about numbers. Or more accurately, it is about helping governments and practitioners obtain a better picture of the money spent on security, including what it is spent on, and how. By providing a better analysis of such spending—through what is called a Public Expenditure Review (PER) of the security sector—a technical team of practitioners can facilitate better-informed decisions at the senior leadership level about policy and operational approaches to the sector.

The global context in which such decisions are made is constantly shifting. All the evidence suggests the nature of violence and conflict is changing,[9] presenting new challenges and threats. National and human security is now less concerned with conventional war than it was 30 years ago and more concerned with transnational political violence, drug trafficking, climate change, forced migration, slavery, urban crime and violence, pandemics, cybersecurity, and related threats and challenges.[10]

While the general historical patterns of war and violence may indicate that humankind is becoming less likely to resort to warfare than in the past,[11] the second decade of the 21st century suggests otherwise. Battle deaths have recently increased, largely due to protracted wars such as those in Afghanistan, Iraq, and the Syrian Arab Republic[12]; and far more homicides now take place, largely in cities of countries that are not at war but are subject to high rates of crime and violence.[13] Further, the consequences of that violence go far beyond excess mortality and include injury, poor health, and poverty. Above all, these recent trends have resulted in the largest refugee and internally displaced populations since World War II.[14]

The costs of such violence are enormous. According to a study by the Institute for Economics and Peace (IEP), the "economic cost of violence containment to the world economy in 2012 was estimated to be US$9.46 trillion or 11 percent of Gross World Product."[15] There are many different approaches to addressing both collective and interpersonal violence, ranging from coercive (e.g., military) to nonviolent (e.g., peacebuilding and violence prevention) to judicial (e.g., arrest and prosecution); and all these have their associated costs. This book focuses on the security and justice institutions, the instruments they use to contend with these challenges, and the cost of sustaining them. And according to the IEP study, these institutions and instruments take up the lion's share of the cost of violence containment: 51 percent of costs go to military expenditure, 14 percent to internal security, 6 percent to private security, and 4 percent to incarceration.[16]

In focusing on these institutions, we note that the public policy debate is no longer a binary one of whether money should be spent on these sectors or not (the guns versus butter argument).[17] Given that resources will be allocated to the security sector, the important question for policy makers is how resources can be used to ensure effective, professional, modern, and accountable institutions that provide security and justice services for citizens.

The aim of this overview is to provide policy makers and practitioners with useful tools for answering this question about strengthening the performance and accountability of security and justice institutions. The overview is structured as follows. This section concludes with an examination of the security-development nexus and security sector reform (SSR). The second section outlines what a PER is, explains the rationale and potential entry points for undertaking such an exercise, and provides a simple checklist for the PER process. The third section focuses on how to understand political, security, macroeconomic, gender, and institutional contexts. The fourth section applies a public finance framework for the security sector. The fifth section offers some final conclusions.

The Security-Development Nexus

In recent years, security challenges have moved from the margin to the mainstream of the development agenda. Security is now recognized as essential for citizens' livelihoods and access to services, and for the free exercise of civil, political, social, and economic rights. Security is particularly important for the poor and other vulnerable groups, who suffer disproportionately from fear, loss of property, and violence.[18] Moreover, insecurity is the principal development challenge in fragile and conflict-affected states (FCS). In 2005, the report of the UN Secretary General (UNSG) emphasized that longer-term development demands a sufficient degree of security to facilitate poverty reduction and shared prosperity.[19]

These themes are picked up in the 2011 *World Development Report*, which calls for a shift in the development community's work on security. The report argues that fragility and violence arise when countries are exposed to economic, political, or security stresses that they are institutionally unable to cope with.[20] Figure O.1 shows that poverty trends are directly proportional to the degree of intensity of violence: countries suffering from a significant level of violence tend to see poverty increase, while those experiencing little or no violence see the share of the population below the poverty line decrease significantly.[21] Moreover, countries affected by conflict—including middle- and lower-income countries—risk entering a vicious cycle of repeated conflict.

Figure O.1   **Negative Effect of Violence on Development**

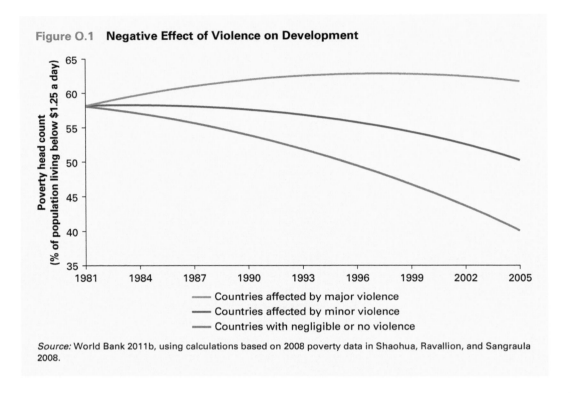

Source: World Bank 2011b, using calculations based on 2008 poverty data in Shaohua, Ravallion, and Sangraula 2008.

Security also has a direct impact on the growth of investment, social and human capital, public institutions, and distribution of resources. Insecurity weakens the investment climate by making investment incentives scarcer and destroying material assets and human capital.[22] It subjects the private sector both to higher costs in the form of security taxes—i.e., the additional costs associated with negative externalities as a result of instability—and to disorganized markets. Violence and insecurity harm human and social capital, particularly among the most vulnerable segments of the population; their effects are evident in physical and psychological damage, migration, deteriorating living standards, and interruptions in public services. Insecurity also weakens the legitimacy of public institutions and creates points of entry for corruption. Finally, growing insecurity can be both the cause and the consequence of skewed distribution of national resources, which, in turn, weakens the overall security sector apparatus of the society.

For these reasons, security and development have increasingly been seen as inextricably linked, and development actors have progressively engaged in the sector with aspirations for promoting change and reform.

Security Sector Reform

Change within the military structure and the broader security sector has historically been an essential part of state formation. This is reflected in the social and political transformations effected by demilitarization and democratization processes in Latin America, as well as in the changes in Eastern Europe after the fall of the Soviet Union.[23]

However, the involvement of international donors and agencies in security and justice service provision is still relatively new.[24] In the late 1990s, a number of key bilateral donors, undertaking a whole-of-government approach to development aid, began integrating security into development programming. This effort culminated in the work at the Organisation for Economic Co-operation and Development (OECD) Development Assistance Committee (DAC), which led to donor consensus around what was termed "security system reform" (now more commonly called "security sector reform," or SSR) and policy development through the 2000s.[25]

These advances have been mirrored by the United Nations' (UN) increasing role in SSR, particularly but not exclusively within the parameters of peacekeeping operations. The UNSG's first report on SSR was *Securing Peace and Development: The Role of the United Nations in Supporting Security Sector Reform*, issued in 2008.[26] The UNSG subsequently reported on various UN initiatives, including strengthened approaches to supporting the police as well as civilian capacities, such as for the criminal justice sector.[27] An Inter-Agency Security Sector Reform Task Force cochaired by the United Nations Development Programme (UNDP) and the United Nations Department of Peacekeeping Operations has brought together 14 UN entities to promote an integrated approach to SSR support. In addition to handling operational and training aspects of SSR, the task force has conducted wide-ranging consultations to develop SSR guidelines, including the Integrated Technical Guidance Notes issued in 2012.[28] These initiatives were followed by the UNSG's second report on SSR in 2013,[29] and were endorsed in 2014 by the UN Security Council in Resolution 2151, the first stand-alone resolution on SSR. These efforts reiterated the centrality of national ownership of SSR, recognizing that such processes need to support and be informed by the broader national political context, and they underlined the importance of strengthening support to sectorwide initiatives that aim to enhance the governance and overall performance of the security sector.

Extensive programmatic work on SSR in various countries has evolved in parallel to these policy developments. Examples include the rebuilding and reform of national armies in Afghanistan, Burundi, Iraq, Liberia, and Sierra Leone; the demobilization and reintegration of over 400,000 ex-combatants in Africa's Great Lakes region; the democratizing of security sector governance in Ghana, South Africa, and Latin America; and the building of capacity in criminal justice to address burgeoning rates of crime and violence in Central America. National and international expertise in SSR has also grown and now covers strategic and policy advice, arms control, governance and oversight, and criminal justice support. Further, various networks and nongovernmental organizations are being formed at the global, regional, and national levels in this area.[30] However, the literature suggests that while the policies and norms associated with the SSR framework have been increasingly accepted, more can be done to improve its impact.[31]

Largely missing from this growing body of policy and practice has been the link between public finance and the security sector. While general aspirations for affordability are often stressed with regard to SSR, there has been little guidance to support governments in better understanding whether security sector costs are within a sustainable macrofiscal envelope, let alone efficiently and effectively allocated. Development practitioners have worked with governments for some time on improving national budgetary processes. After all, national budgets are the most important policy vehicle for putting a country's priorities into effect within the scarce resources that are available to a government for public expenditure; it is through the policy and budget processes that competing priorities are reconciled and implemented. However, there often remains a gap between the national budgeting process and the financing of the security sector.

More specifically, little work has been undertaken to date on the composition of security sector budgets, or on the processes by which they are planned and managed. Ultimately, sound fiscal management of the security sector is essential if a country is to have effective, efficient, and professional security organizations that are capable of protecting the state and its population against internal and external threats. Integrated systems for planning, policy making, and budgeting are necessary to achieve an appropriate allocation of public sector resources and to manage those resources effectively and efficiently.[32]

Currently, public finance practitioners have little or no experience in working with the security sector. In turn, security institutions may not consult the ministry of finance on security sector expenditures and allocations. Even where security sector expenditures and financial management are addressed, a firewall of security classification often prevents practitioners from applying good public finance principles to the security sector, and also prevents their sharing with other sectors the lessons on public finance learned in the security sector.[33]

A further difficulty is that in many countries, the security sector is treated uniquely, with few or no standard oversight and accountability practices in place to assure value for money. External auditors may not be empowered to examine security sector spending. Parliaments may similarly not be permitted to engage in oversight, or they may simply have little capacity to undertake it. Procurement may be secret, with no process for assuring proper pricing of bids. Internal auditors may not exist, or they may be compromised by lacking the authority or ability to share their findings with civilian policy officials nominally in charge of the security sector.

One important effect of applying the principles of sound public finance to the security sector would be to improve mobilization of resources, which is a challenge in developed and developing countries alike. An emphasis on financial probity, integrity, and transparency would encourage the efficient, effective, and accountable allocation of resources to the security sector. External financing of the sector has been a process of trial and error for development actors, particularly in terms of how to engage with the sector, which has traditionally been outside most development programming. According to the OECD, "aid to the security sector comprises a small amount of all sector-allocated aid" (some 1.4 percent for security and 3.1 percent for related justice). In 2012, aid allocated to building the security sector in fragile states totaled only $858 million.[34]

These figures do not include direct military assistance, which runs into several billions of dollars (and as yet is not globally measured).[35] However, they confirm the assumption that the primary actors responsible for providing security to citizens will remain national governments (as well as other formal and informal actors working at the subnational and local levels). This finding parallels the general work on financing for development, which has emphasized that in fact "for most countries, domestic resource mobilization is the largest resource available to fund their national development plans. A country's ability to mobilize domestic resources and spend them *effectively* . . . lies at the crux of financing for development."[36]

Given that governments play this primary role in providing security, the PER represents a powerful tool for them, one that can help them strengthen the legitimacy, effectiveness, accountability, and modernization of their security services.

Public Expenditure Reviews

What Is a PER?

A PER is an analytical instrument that examines government resource allocations within and among sectors, assessing the equity, efficiency, and effectiveness of those allocations in the context of a country's macroeconomic framework and sectoral priorities. In addition, a PER identifies the reforms needed in budget processes and administration in order to improve the efficiency of public spending. PERs may focus on critical economic policy questions, such as affordability and sustainability, or they may focus on public financial management (PFM) and assess the quality of budget execution. The latter highlights the control and management functions and mechanisms in place to ensure that public monies are used correctly for their intended purposes, are deployed quickly and efficiently, and are properly accounted for.

Governments and donor partners are increasingly using security and justice sector PERs to inform their decisions about sectoral development. Security and justice sector issues have traditionally been addressed from strategic, policy, and operational perspectives; examining these sectors through the public finance lens serves a number of important purposes that might otherwise not be met:

- A PER usually starts with an institutional mapping that throws light on the security sector management structure, the key actors and their functions, and the way in which the political economy of the sector affects the quantity and quality of resource allocation.
- A public finance perspective addresses the question of whether programs have adequate and sustainable resourcing, without which they are at best ineffective and at worst likely to create additional sources of conflict and violence.
- Where security forces seek the necessary finance for modernization and professionalization, a public finance perspective accounts for value for money and so can justify additional resources from national budgets and development partners.
- A PER can make explicit the resource allocation trade-offs underlying different policy options; in particular, it can help address the tendency of security sector resourcing to absorb a huge share of scarce public resources and crowd out other activities required to rebuild the nation politically, socially, and economically.
- A PER can address the way that financial management of the security sector reflects on the legitimacy of governments to both domestic and external stakeholders. Security and justice service provision are the fundamental public goods that states are expected to provide their citizens; and sustained and accountable financing of the sectors is a critical ingredient for that role.

In other words, the PER integrates the security sector within the overall public sector by way of the budget process. The national budget provides the financial basis for the delivery of government functions and the implementation of public policies. By balancing competing objectives, it allows the government to strategically allocate scarce public resources to achieve the greatest public good. It also promotes accountability by associating public funds with specific government services.

Figure O.2 describes the relationship between the preparation of a security strategy, in this case for defense, and the wider government budgetary process. The two processes are essentially parallel to each other, and while some special considerations apply to sensitive issues such as secret budgets, security sector budgeting should follow the same path as other public sector entities. Once the budget is formulated, that is, it follows the standard procedure for all sectors and goes through execution, oversight, and performance.

There are, however, potential points in the budget cycle where the security sector may be treated differently from other government sectors and line ministries. These are summarized in table O.1.

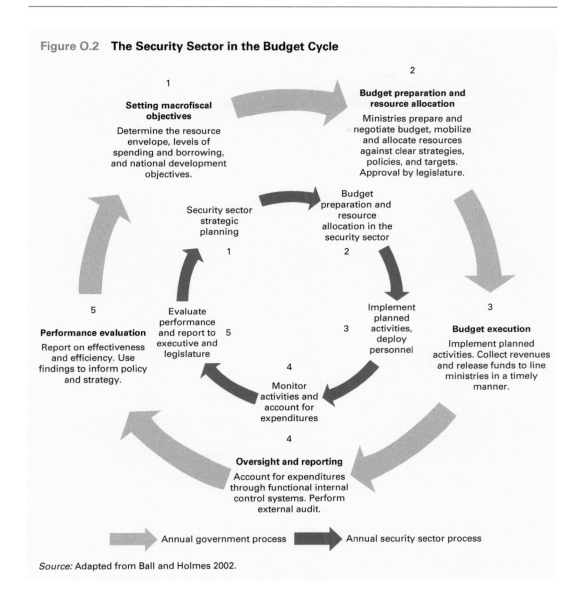

Figure O.2   **The Security Sector in the Budget Cycle**

Source: Adapted from Ball and Holmes 2002.

Obviously, full integration of the military sector into the national budget process requires that the military be subject to the same regulations as other line ministries. In most countries, these regulations are issued by the ministry of finance, which is responsible for regulating and administering the budget process.

What Is the Rationale for Doing a PER?

The PER should be regarded as a tool to assist governments and donor partners in making key "over the horizon" policy and operational decisions in the security sector, through the particular perspective of

Table O.1   The Budget Cycle and the Security Sector: Defense Compared with Standard Practice

Budget cycle phase	International practice	Defense treated differently?
Budget planning and formulation	Sector strategies are developed.	Defense strategies may be kept secret, or official strategies may differ from strategies actually followed. Thus it can be difficult to assess the relationship between strategy and budget.
	Medium-term expenditure estimates are formulated.	No
	All sectors compete for funding based on priority and performance at cabinet level.	Treatment of defense is highly dependent on context; need for funding could be assessed by a security subcommittee.
	Budget proposals are all subject to the same scrutiny by the budget office.	Security clearances are required for budget staff dealing with defense budget.
	Funding set aside for specific contingencies is subject to clear criteria.	There may be a rationale for a separate security contingency fund, although sudden events are usually met by a general government contingency budget.
Legislative scrutiny	All spending is subject to the same scrutiny through the committee system.	Issues of national security can be handled in closed committee hearings.
	Information should be sufficiently detailed to allow the legislative to call the executive to account.	Scrutiny depends on the security context: the more insecure the country, the more secret legislative scrutiny is. It also depends on the political regime: many developing countries give a minor role to Parliament in the budget process, especially for defense.
Budget execution	Funds are released to departments in accordance with budget appropriations; clear rules exist for addressing shortfalls.	Budget execution sometimes obeys specific procedures, as for global grants, escrow accounts, absence of complete reporting, etc.
Monitoring and reporting	All expenditures are reported along appropriation lines to (i) accounting office and (ii) legislature.	No
	End-of-year financial statements are available in a timely manner.	No
	Annual reports on operations, including performance, are published.	Reporting is modified to reflect legitimate national security considerations.
External audit	All expenditures are subject to an external audit: • Financial statements are given to legislature. • Legislative committee system acts upon recommendations of audit reports. • Legislature has the capacity to call executive to account on audit recommendations.	Auditing of sensitive issues in defense needs appropriate security clearance, and legislative meetings may be closed. Sometimes, the weakness or absence of external audit can be replaced by a strong internal audit or inspection reporting to the highest defense authority.

public finance. Historical and current data and analysis may be used to make future projections and provide decision makers with key options on critical issues in national defense as well as criminal justice, public order, and policing.

The rationale for undertaking a PER will vary according to context and the government's preferred focus. However, a PER in the security sector can generally signal a number of objectives on the government's part, including the modernization and professionalization of the sector; it can also signal the possibility of some movement toward cost-effectiveness, even if actual budget cuts are not envisaged. In this way, the rationale of a PER in the sector is aligned with the generic objectives of sound public expenditure management, as follows:

- *Fiscal stability and affordability*. The objective is to maintain control of a country's overall fiscal position. To this end, government budgets need to be realistic and affordable. Thus "the security sector should be fully incorporated into the annual budget formulation process, subject to aggregate fiscal constraints and sector ceilings like any other sector and fully incorporated in medium-term fiscal projections and planning."[37]

- *Allocative efficiency*. The objective is to balance competing demands and allocate scarce public resources where they will have the greatest benefit. This is one of the most difficult tasks of the ministry of finance; the security sector in general usually takes a large share of the national budget. The government therefore has to offset demands from the military against those of other sectors. In turn, within other sectors—for example, criminal justice—there must be a well-balanced prioritization between the competing subsectors, in this case crime prevention, police, judiciary, prosecution and legal aid, and corrections. It is also important here to analyze all sources of revenue and types of expenditure broken down into assets as well as recurrent costs.

- *Operational efficiency and effectiveness*. The objective is to achieve outputs and outcomes that are economical, efficient, and effective and so get the most out of all funds expended. This aim applies to the security sector just as it does to other sectors. Value for money and achievement of targets can be difficult to measure, particularly in a potentially "static" sector such as the military, where nonperformance may be in fact a sign of good performance (i.e., deterrence of any external threats).

- *Fiscal transparency and accountability*. The objective is to provide open and transparent access to financial decisions and data so that government officials can be held accountable for their actions. Governance, oversight, and civilian control of the security sector are often the rationale for SSR as a whole, and they are particularly important in terms of accounting for public expenditures in an area that often presents itself as a "black box" to public scrutiny.

The state-owned enterprises that operate in the security sector may use noncommercial accounting principles with unclear accountability structures, making their impact on the treasury or fiscal balance similarly unclear.

- *Reporting on external assistance.* The objective is particularly important for low-income countries and those emerging out of conflict, whose governments may be in receipt of significant external support from donor partners, as well as revenues from peacekeeping operations or hardware sales. Often such support can be ad hoc and off budget, and a PER is a useful mechanism by which to obtain a better picture of that support and its sustainability.

Ultimately, the reasons for undertaking a PER have to be drawn from a dialogue with the government, including the key stakeholders within the security and justice sectors. Such a dialogue can only be built upon trust between the different stakeholders and the pursuit of key benefits that may arrive with public financial reform, such as greater external on-budget financing or savings from better efficiency and effectiveness in service delivery.

What Are the Entry Points for a PER?

Like the rationale, the specific triggers for undertaking a PER vary subject to context; these are summarized in table O.2.

Given the sensitive and confidential nature of security sector spending, a successful PER will be contingent on trusted relationships—either between government actors (such as principals in ministries, departments, and agencies), or between the government and external partners. This is true regardless of the specific entry point for the PER.

How Is a PER for Security Conducted?

There is no fixed methodology for undertaking a security sector PER because the scope of a PER is so dependent on context. A potential outline of steps is shown in table O.3.

It needs to be emphasized that the issues raised by a PER can be very sensitive for a government, particularly when international partners are involved in the review. SSR is thus intensely political, involving differing and sometimes competing national interests. As the OECD explains:

> Experience shows that reform processes will not succeed in the absence of commitment and ownership on the part of those undertaking reforms. Assistance should be designed to support partner governments and stakeholders as they move down a path of reform, rather than determining that path and leading them down it. A major problem in the area of security system reform in some regions . . . has been a lack of local input to and ownership of the emerging reform agenda. This issue is most significant in "difficult partnership" countries.[38]

Table O.2   Entry Points for a Security Sector Public Expenditure Review

Type of change	Examples
Political: changes in political conditions at home, among key allies, or among adversaries	Elections or change in administration
	Change in public opinion
	Legislative scrutiny or change in legislative attitudes
	Peace accord implementation
	Implementation of international obligations, such as European Union accession requirements
	Human rights review
Economic: changes in expenditure caused by macroeconomic or fiscal shocks, or changes in the way economic resources are allocated and controlled	Change in the fiscal space or resource envelope available due to changes in revenue
	Realignment of national spending priorities
	Reduction in defense expenditure by allies
	Response to increased defense spending by neighbors or adversaries
	Macroeconomic shocks
	Adoption of medium-term expenditure framework
	Institutional or process reforms to strengthen government-wide financial management
Security: changes in national, regional, or international security context	Security sector reform program sponsored by the domestic government or an international partner
	Strategic shock resulting in the redefinition of security threats
	Adoption of a sectorwide all-inclusive approach to government
	Internal security challenges, including civil unrest
	Public safety and security pressures created by organized crime and violence
	Border tensions
	Implementation of arms control, transnational crime, or other international obligations
	Arrival or withdrawal of international military or peacekeeping force
	Updated defense/criminal justice planning assumptions following fragility analysis or threat assessment
	Defense review initiating either defensewide or individual service reform
	Accountability and military effectiveness issues
	Major equipment procurement decisions
	Interservice rivalries, including redefinition of investment priority

Table O.3   Key Steps for Undertaking a Security Sector Public Expenditure Review (PER)

Step	Key issues
Preliminary steps	
1. Government consultation and ownership	There must be traction within security sector ministries, departments, and agencies as well as finance ministries. Clarity should be achieved on the following issues: (i) scope—e.g., whether to include both economic policy and public financial management (PFM) issues, whether to include all security actors or focus on one subsector (defense or criminal justice); (ii) legal restrictions on freedom of information; (iii) the PER's focal points; and (iv) the existence of an explicit request for assistance (where international partners are involved).
2. Establishing a PER team	A government or international practitioner team—one with the skills needed to cover both the political/security and public financial aspects of the review—is selected to carry out the PER. The team should be given an appropriate time frame for the work and should be properly resourced.
Analysis of context	
3. Political security context	The team analyzes the political, security, social, and economic contexts, including the relevant international treaties (peace agreements, sanction regimes, etc.), participation in regional organizations, and key security threats, challenges, and patterns over time. This effort should include aspects of gender as well as analysis of underlying drivers of fragility if appropriate.
4. Macrofiscal context	The team describes and analyzes the various macrofiscal scenarios (overall government revenues versus expenditures, economic growth potential and risks) in the short, medium, and long term as well as the budgetary implications of the macrofiscal context for the different sectors (not only the security sector).
Understanding the sector	
5. Institutional and functional mapping	The team examines the key institutions (state and nonstate) and their functions at all levels (central down to local), along with the key actors and their relationships and interests.
6. Strategic and policy objectives	The team identifies the sector or subsector national strategy, related policy papers, and key documents for the various subsectors and related legislation.
Analysis of the key economic policy and PFM issues	
7. Public expenditure policy	The team analyzes the situation of the security sector within the overall fiscal framework; the realism and affordability of the overall envelope; the efficiency of subsector allocations; the effectiveness and efficiency of operations; and the systems for strengthening civilian oversight, accountability, and governance.
8. Scenarios	In light of the macroeconomic framework, available resources, political security context, and security objectives, the team determines financing scenarios for the government going forward.
9. Public financial management	The team analyzes the systems and processes in place for budget credibility, comprehensive and transparent budgeting, policy-based budgeting, predictable and controlled budget execution, recording and reporting, and external scrutiny and audit.
Conclusions	
10. Options and recommendations	The team describes options and makes potential recommendations. A process should be devised to ensure incremental implementation of the recommendations and continuing buy-in from the various line ministries.

Consequently, early consultation within the government about the objectives of a security sector PER—and the role of international partners—is essential to the success of a PER exercise. National owner-ship is central to the "aid effectiveness" policy of donor countries; but it is important to move beyond the rhetoric to ensure that such ownership exists.[39] Further, if international partners are involved, they may call for rapid results and timelines, and these may be difficult to impose on a political context that requires time for consultation and client feedback. In many instances, despite the presence of significant levers such as international support, local political interest does not allow for reform to take place.[40]

Understanding Context

The Security Context

The term "security" is ambiguous, difficult to define, contested, and subject to wide treatment in the literature.[41] It is thus "a powerful political tool in claiming attention for priority items in the competition for government attention."[42] A PER team will need to review government documents and consult with key interlocutors to determine what those priority items are. Typically they cover a number of different security dimensions, including the following:

- *National security.* This dimension involves the protection of the sov-ereign state, including territorial borders and population, from exter-nal threats; it is further elaborated to include both objective measures (e.g., the absence of threats) and a subjective sense (e.g., the absence of fear of attack).[43]
- *Individual or citizen security.* Originally outlined by the UNDP in 1994,[44] this dimension is now more narrowly defined by the 2011 *World Development Report* as "freedom from physical violence and freedom from the fear of violence. Applied to the lives of all the mem-bers of a society (whether nationals of the country or otherwise), it encompasses security at home, in the workplace and in the political, social, and economic interactions with the state and other members of society."[45]
- *Terrorism/political violence.* UN Security Council Resolution 1566 (2004) defines terrorism as "criminal acts, including against civil-ians, committed with the intent to cause death or serious bodily injury, or taking of hostages, with the purpose to provoke a state of terror in the general public or in a group of persons or particular persons, intimidate a population or compel a government or an international organization to do or to abstain from doing any act."
- *Economic security.* This dimension involves threats to economic, financial, and commercial systems.

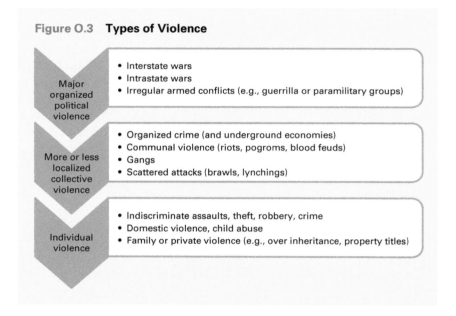

Figure O.3   Types of Violence

Major organized political violence
- Interstate wars
- Intrastate wars
- Irregular armed conflicts (e.g., guerrilla or paramilitary groups)

More or less localized collective violence
- Organized crime (and underground economies)
- Communal violence (riots, pogroms, blood feuds)
- Gangs
- Scattered attacks (brawls, lynchings)

Individual violence
- Indiscriminate assaults, theft, robbery, crime
- Domestic violence, child abuse
- Family or private violence (e.g., over inheritance, property titles)

- *Cybersecurity.* This dimension involves threats to national information systems, technology breaches, and virus attacks.
- *Environmental security.* This dimension involves threats related to human-made disasters, including dumping of toxic waste, as well as the global implications of climate change.
- *Criminal security.* This dimension involves threats arising from organized crime, including trafficking in drugs, people, arms, or contraband goods.

Another useful typology of security challenges distinguishes between major organized political violence, localized collective violence, and individual violence. Breaking these categories down (see figure O.3) demonstrates the variety of risks that societies and communities face, and the diversity of the challenges to which security sector agencies may be expected to respond.[46]

The PER undertaken in Liberia in 2012 offers an example of how a PER takes the security context into account. Here, although an army was in the process of being rebuilt with international support, the focus for the government was on internal security challenges around public order and localized conflict (see box O.1).

The Macroeconomic Context

Another important context for a security sector PER is the wider macroeconomic context, which includes the general drivers of growth and sources of domestic and external revenue. Using current economic and fiscal data to make projections contingent on different variables, the PER

Box O.1   Liberia—National Security Strategy Focused on Internal Threats

According to the security sector Public Expenditure Review (PER) carried out by the World Bank and the United Nations during Liberia's security transition, the country had been generally stable since the deployment of the United Nations Mission in Liberia (UNMIL) in 2003, but peace remained fragile in 2012. Many of the remaining security threats were internal, including the tendency of minor incidents to escalate into large-scale violent confrontations beyond the response capability of the national police. High crime, an inadequate justice system, youth alienation, and land disputes remained serious conflict triggers. Moreover, structural conditions—including economic inequality, corruption, political exclusion, human rights violations, ineffective accountability mechanisms, and weak state institutions—heightened the risk that conflicts would escalate.

All of Liberia's neighboring countries were undergoing some form of internal transition. Liberia remained vulnerable to disruption by regional political tensions or insecurity due to highly porous borders. Networks persisted for the illegal exploitation of natural resources and transnational crime, including the trafficking of drugs and other goods. Finally, the influx of refugees following the contested 2011 elections in Côte d'Ivoire strained the state, and sizable refugee populations remained in volatile border areas.

Liberia's 2008 National Security Strategy orients the country's security sector. It defines national security in a holistic manner, incorporating issues ranging from democracy and rule of law to reconciliation and the professionalism of security actors. The strategy identifies numerous internal threats, including poor rule of law and poverty; the large numbers of deactivated ex-servicemen (17,000) and ex-combatants (103,019 demobilized and an estimated 9,000 who did not benefit from reintegration programs); illegally held arms; land and property disputes; and ethnic tensions. The strategy's objectives include consolidating peace; developing a coordinated national security system; avoiding duplication of roles; recruiting staff in a transparent manner; conducting gender-responsive reform initiatives; establishing county and district security councils; creating democratic civilian oversight mechanisms; safeguarding the integrity, sovereignty, and political independence of Liberia; participating in regional security forces; establishing economic security and reducing poverty; and managing the environment and resources.

Although the National Security Strategy and sector-specific reform strategies are well designed, reform of Liberia's security sector is undermined by deficiencies in coordination, oversight, and financial sustainability. While the national security strategy emphasizes the need for accountable and democratic security architecture, reform of the sector has so far focused on developing the operational effectiveness of the security institutions. Mechanisms for accountability and coordination remain weak, and civilian oversight of the security sector is ineffective. Moreover, the PER noted that given the prevalence of internal security threats and the military's external security remit, reforming the Liberia National Police and the border police was more critical than reforming the Armed Forces of Liberia in the short run.

Source: World Bank and United Nations 2012.

will need to estimate state revenues as well as other competing claims on state resources.

Historically there has been some consideration of the link between military expenditures and growth, and in particular the idea of setting parameters around expenditure/growth ratios.[47] In turn, there is a debate about the relationship between growth and such expenditures, although the evidence of either a negative or positive impact is mixed. This book takes no position on this question, favoring more a value-for-money approach: the critical question is not how much money is spent, but rather how well the money is spent.

As part of the effort to understand the macroeconomic context, the PER team will need to run a number of projections, particularly focusing on overall GDP growth, government revenue, and expenditure. This can be done even in data-poor environments such as Somalia (see box O.2).

The Fragility Context

The security and justice sectors in fragile and conflict-affected states (FCS) present particular challenges. The international community, notably the UN (and other actors such as the African Union), may be the main provider of security and justice services for these countries—for example, where a noninclusive peace agreement is in effect.[48] Such contexts also include countries that are beset by urban crime and violence, a large part of which may be associated with organized crime, as in Central America.

Our general view here is that the findings and recommendations of the PER process are as valid in FCS as they are in normal states, although a number of caveats apply. PER teams in FCS face some real challenges, ranging from scarce data to limited access to certain parts of the country (see table O.4 for a summary of issues specific to FCS). These obstacles highlight the importance of the process aspects of the PER exercise; the PER team may need a longer time frame than usual in order to ensure that minimal objectives for policy and system reform are achieved.

Box O.2   Somalia—Security and Justice Public Expenditure Review: Revenue Projections

A 2015 security and justice Public Expenditure Review (PER) undertaken in Somalia—a country that has not had a solid set of public statistics and national accounts since 1990—required revenue projections to compare with future security costs. For the purposes of the PER, projections were based on a set of preliminary national accounts built from household surveys undertaken by the World Bank and the International Monetary Fund.[a] The three revenue scenarios were primarily modeled using the ratio of revenue to GDP, changing under different assumptions in order to separate out the effects of the broader economy from the improvements in tax administration and policy that could lead to greater revenue for the public sector in Somalia. These were also compared with benchmark values of postconflict states and other states in Sub-Saharan Africa.

It is important to note that the levels of revenue collected in Somalia were extremely low compared to those in other postconflict settings, not to mention in broader Sub-Saharan Africa (see figure BO.2.1).

(Box continues on next page)

Box O.2   Somalia—Security and Justice Public Expenditure Review: Revenue Projections *(continued)*

Figure BO.2.1   Somalia's Projected Revenue Paths Compared with Postconflict and Sub-Saharan African Benchmarks

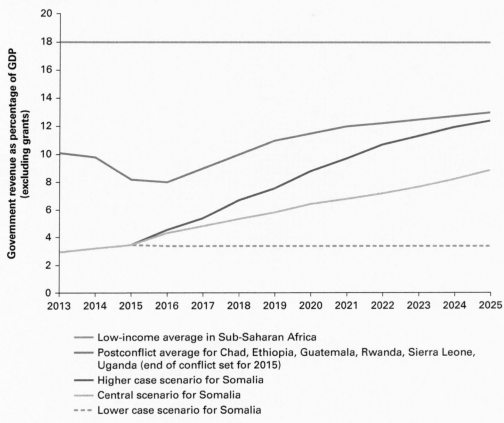

Low-income average in Sub-Saharan Africa

Postconflict average for Chad, Ethiopia, Guatemala, Rwanda, Sierra Leone, Uganda (end of conflict set for 2015)

Higher case scenario for Somalia

Central scenario for Somalia

Lower case scenario for Somalia

Source: World Bank and United Nations, forthcoming.

This can be explained primarily by the fact that most conflict incidences in the benchmark last about a year, whereas conflict in Somalia has lasted over 25 years. This lengthy conflict has considerably hampered the ability to structure and fund a state, as large parts of the population have no recollection of paying taxes to a central government. Moreover, Somalia is distinctive in that even prior to the fall of the Barre regime in 1991, it had exceptionally low revenue collection rates, relying instead on its geostrategic importance to the Cold War superpowers to fund its sustained deficits.[b]

The process of building an internally funded and sustainable financing model for the Somali state is likely to be a prolonged endeavor, in part because the population has not come to expect the level of services that most governments deliver in Sub-Saharan Africa. While this situation has resulted in other benefits, such as a relatively thriving private sector, it represents a particular governance and legitimacy challenge.

a. See further discussion in World Bank 2015.
b. World Bank 1990.

Table O.4   Issues of Relevance for Fragile and Conflict-Affected States (FCS)

FCS factors	Impact upon the security sector
Type of political settlement	A weak political settlement may be characterized by a weak political bargain between the competing stakeholders. This will affect decision making and coherence at the national level and in turn will impact the rationalization of security forces.
	A military victory, of one party over another, may privilege the security forces to such an extent that it will be difficult to incorporate the sector into the public financial management system and strengthen accountability and oversight systems.[a]
Weak institutional capacity	Relevant challenges include the paucity of data and analysis on the sector, weak systems and controls in place, and the expectation that public sector reform results will take time.
Limited oversight capacity	Weak institutions both inside the state and outside mean that there is weak oversight and citizen control of the security sector.
Legacies of conflict and violence	Armed conflict and violence may have resulted in extensive social trauma, including displacement, casualties, and physical destruction. A traumatized population possibly bearing continued grievances will require specific and carefully considered security and justice provision, including potential mechanisms for transitional justice.[b]
Role of the security sector	FCS are characterized by the absence of rule of law, impunity of security services, and prevailing insecurity. On one hand, governments and partners will want to prevent the security services from preying on civilians; on the other hand, functioning police and criminal justice institutions are needed to support governments in addressing violence and crime.
Weak macroeconomic position	Armed conflict most likely results in increased borrowing and greater debt combined with increased expenditures on the sector. In turn, a widespread conflict will likely harm the economy, prospects for growth, and revenue projections.
External financing	The financing of the security sector by external donors can lead to distortions and questions about sustainability and about recording of external funds (that is, whether on or off budget).[c]
Cost drivers	Conflict or violent settings will result in several potentially high cost drivers for the sector, including (i) integration of armed groups into one army financed by the state, (ii) demobilization and reintegration of ex-combatants, and (iii) establishment of transitional justice mechanisms such as special courts.

a. Adejumobi and Binega 2006.
b. Transitional justice traditionally comprises a number of components, such as (i) rehabilitation of the public sector, including criminal justice institutions; (ii) accounting for past crimes through prosecutions, truth telling, and reparations; and (iii) vetting of security sector personnel.
c. World Bank 2005a.

Gender and Security

The provision of personal security is highly gendered.[49] Women's and men's security and justice needs—and their perceptions of the public services provided—can differ significantly. It is well known that in armed conflict the main casualties are women (and children),[50] whereas in gang violence the main casualties are young men 15–24 years old.

> ## Box O.3   Examples of Gender Issues in a Security Sector Public Expenditure Review
>
> - *Recognition in government strategic priorities.* The government may be seeking to respond to a number of specific concerns that relate to gender differentiations in violence and security, such as increases in gender-based sexual violence or in violence among youth around schools.
> - *Representation through governance and accountability.* Auditory, judicial, and legislative accountability mechanisms, both internal and external, may include women to a greater or lesser extent; and the gender aspects of security and justice provision may be more or less a part of the normal sector discourse.
> - *Redress through personnel recruitment and prevention.* The government may have a general priority to increase female enrollment in the armed forces or the police, or it may have specific targets to address specific needs, such as increasing women's presence at control points on borders or seaports/airports (to check men and women), increasing specific female-staffed sexual crime units, or ensuring that particular security and criminal justice policies pay attention to gender issues such as sexual violence.

In turn, security services are generally dominated by men: in Canada women make up only some 18 percent of the police force; in the United States the share is smaller, at 12–14 percent. At high levels of government, women's representation in the security sector is very low: in 2008, women held 1,022 ministerial portfolios across 185 countries, but only 6 of these were in areas of defense and veterans' affairs.[51] It is thus important for the PER team to examine the particular aspects of gender from the strategic to the operational level. Some examples are outlined in box O.3.

Understanding Security and Justice Institutions

There are many tools available that can assist a PER team in assessing the security sector and in understanding its place within the country and government contexts.[52] The security sector is most commonly defined by the types of institutions it encompasses. The two main international sources, the UN and the OECD DAC, define the security sector in similar, institution-based terms (see box O.4).[53] Their examples of institutions comprising the security sector are illustrative; in reality, there are a wide variety of institutions that fit into these broad categories, and the exact configuration of institutions varies by context.

A useful graphic (figure O.4) is used by the International Security Sector Advisory Team (ISSAT) in its assessment toolkit to set out the various components of the sector and their interconnections.

In many societies, a number of institutions that are not funded through public revenues may also deliver public security and justice. These institutions include traditional, nonstatutory police as well as courts whose operations are either only partly or not at all codified in law and which are not funded through the tax system; examples are private security and community responses to criminality. While it is often assumed that the

Box O.4   **Definitions of "Security Sector"**

UN Definition

"The 'security sector' is a broad term often used to describe the structures, institutions and personnel responsible for the management, provision and oversight of security in a country. It is generally
accepted that the security sector includes defense, law enforcement, corrections, intelligence
services and institutions responsible for border management, customs and civil emergencies.
Elements of the judicial sector responsible for the adjudication of cases of alleged criminal conduct
and misuse of force are, in many instances, also included. Furthermore, the security sector includes
actors that play a role in managing and overseeing the design and implementation of security, such
as ministries, legislative bodies and civil society groups. Other non-State actors that could be considered part of the security sector include customary or informal authorities and private security
services."[a]

**Organisation for Economic Co-operation and Development (OECD) Development Assistance
Committee (DAC) Definition**

"The OECD DAC Guidelines on Security System Reform and Governance agreed by ministers
in 2004 define the security system as including: core security actors (e.g., armed forces, police,
gendarmerie, border guards, customs and immigration, and intelligence and security services); security management and oversight bodies (e.g., ministries of defense and internal
affairs, financial management bodies and public complaints commissions); justice and law
enforcement institutions (e.g., the judiciary, prisons, prosecution services, traditional justice
systems); and non-statutory security forces (e.g., private security companies, guerrilla armies
and private militia)."[b]

a. UNSG 2008, 5; and UN Security Council Resolution 2151.
b. OECD 2007, 5.

processes of social and economic development will lead to an increase in
formal responses to insecurity and a decrease in informal (nonstatutory)
responses, in fact this has not always been the case, and many developing societies continue to have strong nonstate responses to crime and
insecurity.[54]

Some Examples of Criminal Justice Institutions

Undertaking a security sector PER often entails understanding the various
institutions that make up the criminal justice system. The police, prosecution service, criminal courts, and corrections are the core agencies of the
institutional framework that most countries have adopted to respond to
crime through investigation and prosecution of criminal activities, adjudication of criminal cases, and incapacitation and/or rehabilitation of
offenders. At the same time, a range of other entities delivers important
criminal justice services that have to be funded from the government's
budget. Legal aid and criminal defense services are among the more costly
of these services—and they often remain underfunded, with serious consequences for individual rights and justice system operations. Particularly as

Figure O.4   State and Nonstate Institutions of the Security and Justice Sectors

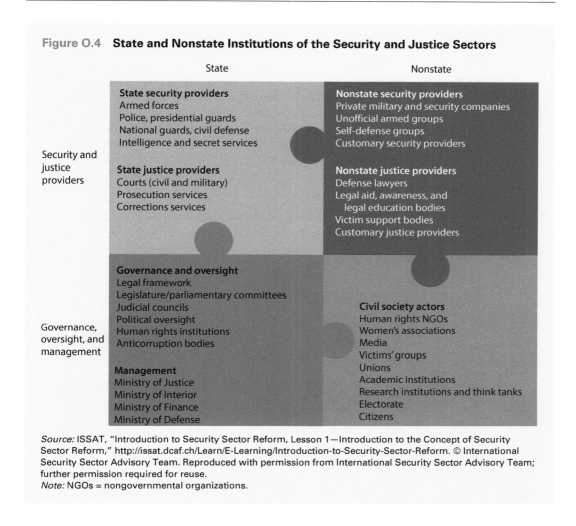

State   Nonstate

State security providers
Armed forces
Police, presidential guards
National guards, civil defense
Intelligence and secret services

Nonstate security providers
Private military and security companies
Unofficial armed groups
Self-defense groups
Customary security providers

Security and justice providers

State justice providers
Courts (civil and military)
Prosecution services
Corrections services

Nonstate justice providers
Defense lawyers
Legal aid, awareness, and
    legal education bodies
Victim support bodies
Customary justice providers

Governance and oversight
Legal framework
Legislature/parliamentary committees
Judicial councils
Political oversight
Human rights institutions
Anticorruption bodies

Governance, oversight, and management

Civil society actors
Human rights NGOs
Women's associations
Media
Victims' groups
Unions
Academic institutions
Research institutions and think tanks
Electorate
Citizens

Management
Ministry of Justice
Ministry of Interior
Ministry of Finance
Ministry of Defense

Source: ISSAT, "Introduction to Security Sector Reform, Lesson 1—Introduction to the Concept of Security Sector Reform," http://issat.dcaf.ch/Learn/E-Learning/Introduction-to-Security-Sector-Reform. © International Security Sector Advisory Team. Reproduced with permission from International Security Sector Advisory Team; further permission required for reuse.
Note: NGOs = nongovernmental organizations.

societies increasingly recognize the importance of crime prevention, additional institutions join the criminal justice sector, such as services for youth at risk, school crime prevention services, employment and treatment services for offenders, child protective services, and a range of public education efforts along with research and evaluation efforts—and all require funding.

Examining this complex institutional terrain will require an inventory of the organizations and actors involved. There is no standard institutional typology, and there is variation between common and civil law systems, depending on the legal framework. A PER needs to examine what links form the institutional chain, how the different institutions work together, and above all whether individual resource allocations add up to an effective systemwide whole. This was the approach taken by the World Bank in El Salvador, as detailed in box O.5.

Box O.5   Police and Criminal Justice Institutions in El Salvador

In June 2012, the World Bank completed a Public Expenditure Review of the security and justice sectors in El Salvador. This was the first comprehensive assessment of the sector's resource allocation, efficiency, and effectiveness. The analysis divided the security and justice institutions according to the main tasks they fulfill, and sought to evaluate the allocation of inputs (resources), outputs (specific services), and outcomes (citizen security). In El Salvador, several state institutions that are located under different branches of government execute five main tasks: (i) crime and violence prevention; (ii) police patrolling; (iii) crime investigation and formal indictment; (iv) presentation to court and judicial resolution; and (v) sentencing, supervision, imprisonment, and rehabilitation (see figure BO.5.1).

Figure BO.5.1   Security and Justice Sectors: Tasks and Institutions

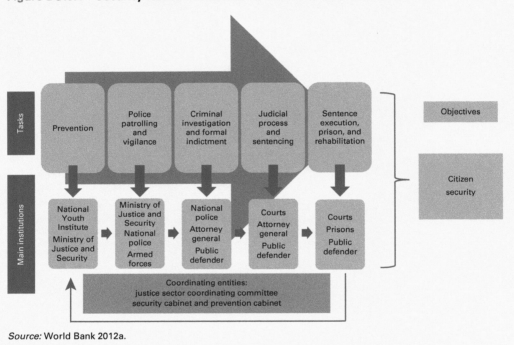

Source: World Bank 2012a.

Integrating Public Finance, Security, and Criminal Justice

Public Finance Policy

Over the last 20 years there has been a concerted push among both developed and developing countries to standardize and improve measures around PFM.[55] The focus of that effort has been the strengthening of public budgeting in connection with two key elements of government:

1. *Public expenditure policy*, particularly as it relates to fiscal stability, efficiency, and effectiveness
2. *PFM* around functional aspects of budget implementation and systems.

Public expenditure policy (also termed macroeconomic and fiscal policy) concerns the overarching balance sheet of the government—that is, its revenues and its expenditures. The goal of macroeconomic and fiscal policy is to achieve potential output, full employment, and macroeconomic stability, which together provide the economic foundation for sustainable growth.[56] Of central importance is the fiscal deficit: the government cannot spend more than it collects through taxation and borrowing beyond the short run. High debts and high inflation are destabilizing. The government must therefore set and adhere to fiscal targets related to debt sustainability and fiscal balance. Doing so requires reasonably accurate revenue projections and a comprehensive process for estimating current and potential expenditures. The framework for analyzing public finance is based upon existing World Bank tools (as well as those of the International Monetary Fund) that focus on critical economic policy issues.[57]

PFM is concerned with the management and controls around the use of public funds. PFM particularly focuses on the budget process, resource allocation, the way expenditures are made (such as for public service payroll or capital investments), and the way public funds are accounted for. The Public Expenditure and Financial Accountability (PEFA) framework is now the internationally recognized tool for assessing and measuring budget planning, implementation, and control along a series of indicators, including (i) budget reliability, (ii) transparency of public finances, (iii) management of assets and liabilities, (iv) policy-based fiscal strategy and budgeting, (v) predictability and control in budget execution, (vi) accounting and reporting, and (vii) external scrutiny and audit.[58]

There is considerable overlap between these two areas of public finance. However, ultimately the former concentrates on the big policy questions that concern the national budget, and the latter focuses on how the system is run. We can see this difference in the variety of security and criminal justice PER examples in this book, which include some that emphasize policy issues relating to the affordability and sustainability of the security sector, and others that emphasize questions of efficiency control and oversight.

The Security Sector and the National Budget System

The key question for government decision makers is to what degree the security sector is subject to the same budget policy and management standards as any other sector. The general trend in international practice is for the security sector to be treated differently, for these reasons:

- Many governments do not include security expenditures in their budgets, and where budgets are included, they tend not to be disaggregated (studies have shown a discrepancy between official statistics and actual expenditures).[59]

- Key security actors, such as the military, are concerned about secrecy and confidentiality, which can impede attempts to strengthen transparency and accountability and the undertaking of any kind of review.
- In the defense sector, and particularly in the military, oversight by external auditors is very limited during operations. Robust internal audit mechanisms can compensate, but normal practices used for other public sectors are not appropriate.

However, in most ways the security sector should not be treated differently from other sectors; with certain modifications, it should be incorporated into the regular government PFM system. The comprehensive integration of the sectors into the budgetary and public finance system is key to the creation of democratically accountable, modern, and professional security and justice services.

This integration can be prompted by undertaking a PER for the sector or part of the sector. Subject to the right conditions and incentives within government, it can be a very useful tool for finance agencies as well as for defense and interior ministries. The PER can serve as a platform to bring together security and other ministries and public agencies to discuss, negotiate, and assess issues of resource allocation, institutional efficiency, and effectiveness on the basis of a numerate understanding of security sector costs and challenges.

We now discuss a number of these critical economic policy and PFM issues and see how they have been dealt with in PERs that have been undertaken to date.

Affordability and Sustainability

The national budget must be affordable in the short and long run to be credible and ensure macroeconomic stability. Meeting this goal requires full integration of the security sector.[60] The security sector often comprises the largest or one of the largest shares of the national budget; the question is how these expenditures equate with government revenues, including external aid. This question is particularly important for low-income countries, and it is critical for low-income countries transitioning from war to peace, since these countries often have extremely limited domestic revenues and may also be facing peacebuilding challenges that come with significant price tags, such as army integration or demobilization (see box O.6).

Once sustainable aggregate spending levels are determined, government priorities—including defense, public order, and justice—can be weighed, current policies reviewed, and the budgetary impact of policy changes estimated. To facilitate these steps, security sector expenditures should be fully incorporated into medium-term fiscal projections based on life-cycle costing of defense capabilities. For example, too often the military sector's recurrent operation and maintenance costs are neglected, especially in fragile and conflict-prone states. If the national budget is not

> **Box O.6   Affordability Questions for Countries Emerging from Conflict**
>
> The government may face existential trade-offs between peacebuilding priorities and fiscal stability. A few examples are given below:
>
> - *Political versus fiscal stability.* A government established under a peace agreement after conflict may seek to integrate ex-belligerents into one national army. This can be a very expensive exercise that is at odds with the demands for fiscal stability, but it may be justified in order to maintain political stability and keep the former warring factions at peace.[a]
> - *Transition from peacekeeping to government security provision.* Some war-to-peace transitions are accompanied by a UN Security Council–endorsed peacekeeping mission that provides basic security services during the life of the mission. As these peacekeeping forces depart, the government is expected to increase its own capacity to provide potentially expensive security and justice services for the population.[b]
> - *Transition from external assistance to domestic revenues.* Some war-to-peace transitions have been internationalized in character; in these cases, external actors as well as national actors are engaged in military interventions (as in Afghanistan or Somalia). Such external intervention can be accompanied by (at times significant) external financing to government security forces. The question is how long these external finances can be sustained and what happens when they diminish.[c]
>
> a. See for example World Bank 2012b.
> b. See for example World Bank and United Nations 2012.
> c. See for example World Bank 2005b; World Bank and United Nations Assistance Mission in Somalia 2016.

realistic in its estimation of government expenditures, it will be irrelevant and never implemented. Moreover, if line ministries are allowed to spend indiscriminately, the result may be a "tragedy of the commons" scenario, where unrestrained revenue collection, deficits, and debt lead to adverse economic outcomes.[61]

Confronted with the challenges of tight resources, policy makers can use the PER exercise to identify potential savings and in certain instances realize increases in public expenditure. These increases can result from the following: (i) bringing off-budget expenditures into the budget; (ii) consolidating all security-related expenditures under the appropriate functional headings; (iii) including adequate operation and maintenance costs for equipment; (iv) setting appropriate salary and wage scales; (v) taking account of costs associated with downsizing, such as disbursement of pensions or settlements; and (vi) changing the shape of the military or police (for example, into a force reliant on smaller numbers of personnel with greater mobility).[62] Issues of this kind concerned Liberia's Ministries of Finance and Interior as the UN peacekeeping mission drawdown approached; a PER focusing on affordability questions helped to clarify what Liberia's costs going forward would be (see box O.7).

Box O.7   Liberia—Cost of Transitioning and Maintaining Security

According to the security sector Public Expenditure Review carried out by the World Bank and the United Nations during Liberia's security transition, the United Nations Mission in Liberia (UNMIL) contributed to Liberia's security reform efforts, helped establish the conditions for peaceful democratic elections and the transfer of power in 2011, and contributed to economic growth by reestablishing peace and security, thereby allowing development opportunities to emerge.

Total UNMIL spending steadily declined from $723 million in FY2004/2005 to $512 million in FY2010/2011. These funds covered expenses related to military contingents, international civilian salaries, information technology and communications infrastructure, and air transportation; personal allowances not spent within Liberia; mission funds spent in country on imported goods and services; and spending on locally produced goods and services. At the beginning of the mission, it was estimated that local spending did not exceed 10 percent of the total but still boosted local income—primarily in Monrovia—by almost 10 percent of GDP.

It is expected that the ongoing provision of security services will cost Liberia significantly less than the costs incurred by UNMIL because not all functions will need to be replaced. Among the costs that can be eliminated are salaries and costs for UNMIL civilian personnel and the costs associated with protecting UNMIL personnel and assets. Moreover, the costs of Liberian security personnel and recurrent items are substantially lower than those under UNMIL. The average salary of a Liberian police officer, for example, is approximately $150 per month—much lower than that of a UN police officer, which is based on international standards. The total projected cost of providing security services in 2012–2019 is $712 million—less than the costs incurred by the UN in the first year of its mission. Of this total, ongoing security services are estimated to cost $546 million over the seven years projected, with the annual cost increasing at the average inflation rate of 4 percent per year through 2019. The remainder comprises the transfer of security functions from UNMIL over the seven-year drawdown—including costs associated with the Liberia National Police and the Bureau of Immigration and Naturalization—and recurring costs for proposed regional hubs under the Justice and Security Joint Program (see table BO.7.1). In the final analysis, the PER found that there would be a fiscal gap of some $86 million over the 2012–2019 period.

Table BO.7.1   Liberia's Projected On-Budget Costs for Security Services, 2012–2019
$ million

		2012/ 2013	2013/ 2014	2014/ 2015	2015/ 2016	2016/ 2017	2017/ 2018	2018/ 2019	Total
Ongoing security services		69	72	75	78	81	84	87	**546**
UNMIL transition costs	Liberia National Police	11	12	14	6	7	8	10	**68**
	Bureau of Immigration and Naturalization	4	3	4	3	4	4	5	**27**
	Regional hubs	1	1	2	2	2	2	2	**10**
	Other transition costs	23	8	7	4	5	6	6	**61**
	Subtotal	**39**	**24**	**27**	**15**	**18**	**20**	**23**	**166**
Total		**108**	**96**	**102**	**93**	**99**	**104**	**110**	**712**

Source: World Bank and United Nations 2012.
Note: UNMIL = United Nations Mission in Liberia.

Budget Credibility

A realistic and credible budget is fundamental for establishing fiscal stability. In terms of PFM, there are two ways that management of the security sector often undermines budget credibility:

- *Financial deviations.* There is often a significant gap between approved budgets and actual expenditures of the security sector: "Systematic deviations are a sign of poor or deceptive budgeting [and] reduce the credibility of the budget hence weakening its role as a policy tool."[63] Like planners in other sectors, security planners should provide for contingencies that can be exceptionally expensive (for example, armed conflict). In resource-constrained countries, actual expenditures may deviate significantly from the approved budget. In addition to providing insight into priorities, clarity on why deviations occur can help make the budgetary process more predictable. The reasons for deviation may vary over time.[64]
- *Confidentiality and moving off-budget.* The degree of external scrutiny of the security sector is often limited by legal and policy procedures related to freedom of information, confidentiality, and transparency. On national security grounds it can be difficult to ascertain accurate budget details for the sector. This challenge is compounded when donor assistance is also given off-budget. In Sierra Leone, for example, more than half the total security sector expenditure in 2005 was reported to be off-budget.[65] Studies have found that deviations shielded by confidentiality can include significant security finances kept off-budget, revenues that are secretly banked, and accounts held overseas.[66]

Off-budget revenues were the subject of concerns raised by the Ministry of Finance in the PER for the Central African Republic in 2009 (see box O.8).

Efficiency of Sector Allocations

Once a country has determined its overall resource envelope, the most difficult set of decisions then needs to be made about how to allocate those resources according to the different security sector priorities. At this point, internal government competition is inevitable and will lead to extensive negotiation within the different subsectors—e.g., between the army and air force or between the various components of the criminal justice system (police, judiciary, and corrections). A well-informed and empowered ministry of finance can play a useful role in mediating these discussions and assisting in decision making about final allocations. But such an exercise is challenging for a ministry of finance for a number of reasons:

- *The budget may be held hostage.* The security sector, particularly the military, may have a politically prominent position in government and therefore may demand high allocations without a solid justification.

Box O.8   **Central African Republic—Off-Budget Revenues**

According to the World Bank's 2009 financial management assessment of the Central African Republic, defense services generated considerable income in 2008, but the revenues were badly organized in their identification, legal framework, and budgeting.

One source of income was the sale of escort or guard services to private companies and international organizations (soldiers accompany people in unsafe areas in the provinces). Extrapolating from payments for security services by the Bank of Central African States, the United Nations Development Programme, and the International Monetary Fund, the Public Expenditure Review team estimated that total revenues generated amounted to the equivalent of $680,000 in 2008.

Another source of income was fines issued by the gendarmerie; in the Bangui region, these came to $160,000 in 2008. According to legislation then in force, 30 percent of proceeds accrued to the Ministry of Defense and 70 percent to the Treasury. The Ministry of Defense was to split its share between the gendarmerie (25 percent to be managed by the *régisseur* to cover miscellaneous items) and the army (75 percent to be managed by the national army's treasury outside of any accounting cycle and without any form of accounts management). Theoretically, fines collected by the gendarmerie in the provinces should flow to the national Treasury via Treasury special agents, but the central government has limited visibility and the amount collected is unknown.

Finally, the Battalion for the Protection and Security of Institutions, part of the Republican Guard reporting to the president and under the administrative control of the General Staff of the Armies, collected the airport security tax. This generated the equivalent of $260,000 in 2008.

In total, the Ministry of Defense generated the equivalent of $1.1 million in 2008. This is a significant sum relative to the $16.2 million the ministry received in appropriations for 2009, and to the entire state budget of $78.3 million. To the extent these payments do not figure in the state budget, the revenues generated remain extrabudgetary income, or indeed secret income.

Source: World Bank 2009.

- *There may be ideological differences over security and justice provision.* The intense debates over what works in providing security are reflected in how governments prioritize their budgets. An example of this debate is the gradual shift in Central America away from *mano dura* policies, which use heavy, coercive measures to combat crime and violence,[67] toward more preventive (and cheaper) interventions.
- *International comparisons are not possible.* The security sector is unlike other sectors in that very few international comparisons or standards are available to support decision makers in addressing critical questions, such as unit costs or numbers of personnel. This is partly due to the fact that financial and staffing figures are rarely disclosed publicly, and that when disclosed they rarely follow common rules that could allow comparisons. The UN has some helpful guidance, particularly on population-based ratios for police and other criminal justice personnel.[68] In addition, comparisons can be made with neighboring countries, particularly those with similar population sizes, income per capita, and sources of revenue.

The following inputs are useful for the process of making decisions about security sector allocations: (i) a well-articulated strategy setting out key targets; (ii) measures of good past performance; (iii) indications of how subsectors relate to other subsectors (particularly important in the criminal justice sector); and (iv) empirical evidence from global experience on what interventions work in security and justice provision. In contexts affected by fragility or conflict, the PER team will confront a number of particular challenges and issues where allocative efficiency is concerned. These are described in box O.9.

These discussions about allocation are where expenditure and security policy converge; and in light of sovereignty or mandate issues, there may be a limited role for external actors such as the UN or the World Bank.[69] For matters relating to national security, the appeal to confidentiality and sovereignty is understandable. However, as governments increasingly recognize the close relationship between security and development outcomes, they are increasingly seeking policy advice from multilateral partners, particularly on matters relating to internal security and justice provision (such as what policies work, how to prioritize them, and what costs are involved). Two particular policy aspects are worth briefly considering here:

1. *Policy alternatives.* Responses to insecurity and violence are usually broken down into the following components:

   - *Suppression,* or the direct exercise of force (through the use of military, paramilitary, or police) in response to instances of crime or violence

---

Box O.9 Key Strategic Issues in Fragile and Conflict-Affected States

Countries facing high rates of crime or violence or coming out of conflict face a number of particular challenges that need to be addressed in formulating security and justice strategies and in setting priorities for allocations:

- *Contending domestic and international objectives of governments and partners.* These objectives may not be coherent—e.g., counterterrorism, counterinsurgency, and counternarcotics objectives may outweigh peacebuilding and efforts to provide individual security and justice.
- *Peace agreements.* Peace agreements may comprise the bulk of security objectives and in fact replace a national security strategy by setting out priorities and key targets over a specific time frame. What is important here is that questions about affordability and costing are inserted during the peace process so that agreements are realistic and implementable. Here, the report on security sector reform (SSR) by the Secretary General of the United Nations (2008)[a] can be helpful in emphasizing that SSR issues should be addressed as early as possible in the peace process.
- *Governance and accountability.* In the drive to consolidate state authority (including by strengthening command and control over the security services), issues around accountability and governance may be ignored, which creates the possibility of dangers down the road in terms of governance and citizen oversight.

a. UNSG 2008.

- *Deterrence*, or the use of military, paramilitary, or police in order to intimidate and discourage potential perpetrators
- *Incapacitation*, or the policy of taking offenders out of society through judicial means (such as imprisonment) or administrative means (such as internment during rebellion)
- *Rehabilitation*, or the process of reforming those who have been associated with crime and violence, such as those in prison or heavy drug users
- *Prevention*, including an array of interventions intended to prevent people from entering a life of crime and violence, from the systemic (such as reducing inequality) to the specific (such as job creation).

2. *Institutional alternatives.* An important policy question concerns what institutions most effectively provide security and justice. Increasingly, the private sector plays a significant role in security provision, particularly in urban areas for commercial and individual residences. The private sector, including nonprofit organizations, is also involved in other areas of security provision such as demining. Private alternatives may be cheaper than public, although their use raises other regulatory and policy challenges.[70]

As a PER is carried out, intragovernmental discussions about allocations and sector ceilings can expand to a more comprehensive policy discussion about what security sector policies are appropriate in general, what are most effective, and what may be cheapest.[71] These debates are held in developed as well as developing countries and involve the ideological contests referred to above.

Policy-Based Budgeting

A sound budget system is related to credible sector strategies, including a security sector strategy that (i) is based in context; (ii) relates to other government security actors (e.g., within the criminal justice chain); (iii) links with other relevant line ministries, departments, and agencies within government outside the sector; and (iv) has realistic and affordable targets. As important as the sector strategy is the process that produced it—a process that should allow for consultation and debate, ensuring links to key actors within the government (including the legislature) and outside the government (including civil society).

However, few countries have formal security sectorwide policies, and even fewer have undertaken the broad security evaluation that ideally underpins policy and strategy development. Recent UN policy guidance emphasizes the importance of building a common national security vision and strategy in order to create sustainable and nationally owned security institutions.[72]

Although it is true that policy is ultimately what government does (not what it says it wants to do), formal policies and plans that articulate a course of action are important. Clearly articulated policies make it possible to manage the finances of the security sector in a cost-effective manner. In the absence of such policies, budgeting aims to maintain the previous year's level of expenditure without assessing whether the configuration of that expenditure will help to meet government's priorities or deliver services needed by the population. Performance benchmarks are difficult to develop, and without them it is hard to monitor the use of security-related resources and assess the efficiency and effectiveness of the security sector. In the absence of a strategic plan tied to policy, countries risk not obtaining a level of security and justice commensurate with their financial outlays.

In an examination of government policy in the security sector (written or unwritten), there is no exhaustive checklist of issues to watch out for. Some critical issues that can arise concerning efficiency and effectiveness in the sector include the following:

- *Sectorwide approaches.* When subsectors of the security sector (military, intelligence, police, judiciary, etc.) submit their own priorities unrelated to those of other subsectors, the result is fragmented approaches to common challenges and an absence of complementarities and coherence.
- *Recurrent versus capital costs.* In low-income countries, the largest share of the security sector budget goes to recurrent costs, particularly personnel and equipment. A critical part of recurrent costs, operations and maintenance, is often overlooked or not budgeted for in the acquisition of new vehicles, weaponry, etc.
- *Training and personnel.* Low-income countries often prioritize personnel recruitment over training for professional induction into the security sector or capacity building for training institutions.
- *Demobilization and pensioning.* Policy may not account for the aging of the workforce or provide for pensions that are in line with generic civil service guidelines and standards. In turn, there may be little robust calculation of the costs of demobilization (particularly after a peace agreement) or military retrenchment in peacetime.

Some of the difficulties that arise when budgeting is not grounded in sector policy and strategy were identified in the 2013 PER in Niger (box O.10).

Operational Efficiency and Effectiveness

Under ideal circumstances, once funds have been appropriated for the various sectors, according to their strategies and priorities, they are used efficiently and effectively for their intended purposes. *Efficiency* in budget execution involves PFM systems and processes, including procurement, payroll, audit, and accounting, whereas *effectiveness* relates to the measurement of performance against targets/indicators of progress for the sector.

Box O.10   Niger—Security Strategy and Funding Mismatch

The World Bank's security sector Public Expenditure Review (PER) in Niger identified multiple domestic and external security challenges. The post-electoral crisis in Côte d'Ivoire in 2010, the war in Libya in 2011, the crisis in Mali in 2012–2013, deteriorating security in Algeria in 2013, and ongoing political-religious tensions in northern Nigeria have combined to make the Sahara-Sahel region turbulent and conflict prone. Niger's domestic risk factors include an immense territory with uneven distribution of population, endemic poverty, a high degree of political instability, and occasionally violent conflicts between the northern and southern areas of the country. In recent years, these risks have been manifested in increased terrorist threats, kidnappings, and trafficking in drugs and other contraband.

In response, the Nigerien government increased security spending significantly, incorporated security in its planning processes, and introduced new border control measures. As a share of public spending, security spending increased from 13.8 percent in 2010 to 16.1 percent in 2012. This increase is generally consonant with other countries in the region. The composition of the security budget has changed to favor capital expenditure, which became the largest component in 2012, at 55 percent of the total. Personnel expenditure continued to comprise a large portion of the budget that same year, while funding for operations was reduced. However, the PER found the accuracy of Niger's security budgets to be precarious. Numerous supplementary budget laws since 2009 revealed a lack of spending predictability, although this is justified by the deteriorating security situation.

Overall, the PER determined Niger lacked a genuine sectoral strategy that sets clear priorities. The multiyear security sector estimates were not realistic or achievable over indicated periods: "All things being equal, and without taking personnel expenditures into account, it would have taken over 30 years to respond to the needs that were deemed priority needs." Among the particular shortcomings of the multiyear sectoral estimates were the failure to include appropriations to compensate increased staffing levels; the absence of a detailed, transparent breakdown of security sector spending; the multiplicity of objectives and lack of forecasting of total costs; and a disconnect between the armed forces' estimates of their requirements and the formalized sector strategy.

Source: World Bank 2013b.

Measuring effectiveness in the security sector is not an easy task; hence more often the focus is on input and output indicators such as unit costs, personnel trained and equipped, and the number of forces ready for deployment. As explained in more detail in the substantive chapters on defense, policing, and criminal justice, a disaggregated approach, treating each subsector separately, is important here:

- *Defense/military.* Most often this security component is measured in peacetime based on the "state of readiness" to meet external threats, measured in terms of output indicators such as soldiers trained and vehicles or aircraft on standby. Evaluating performance of the military is a sensitive area and usually left to ministries of defense and their bilateral partners.
- *Criminal justice and policing.* Performance standards across the developing and developed world are increasingly being used to measure performance in this subsector; standards range from measurement of crime and violence rates to public opinion and perception surveys.[73]

Measuring efficiency is a well-standardized practice under PFM. Particular aspects relating to the security sector are outlined in box O.11.

How to strengthen the efficient use of financial resources in the security sector was an important consideration in Mali after the Tuareg rebellion and coup d'état of March 2012. The coup by mid-ranking military

---

Box O.11   Components of Efficiency

To strengthen the efficient utilization of financial resources in the security sector, it is important to address the following issues:

- *Sustainability.* Over time, an unsustainable sector plan and programs will lead to ineffective capabilities. Sustainability will be achieved only if governments commit themselves to the approved plan, if all planning is done on full life-cycle costing, and if the defense budget is expended in the most efficient manner possible. Care must also be taken in planning to accurately evaluate the effect of currency fluctuations on the life-cycle cost of capital equipment.

- *Contingency funding of operations.* It is not desirable to budget for the execution of operations other than those that are routine and can be accurately planned well ahead of time. Most military operations come at short notice and in the financial year for which the budget was developed and approved many months ago. Examples are peace-support missions, major disaster relief missions, and even limited war. Trying to budget for the unforeseeable runs a strong risk of misappropriating funds. It is preferable for the finance ministry to maintain a central contingency fund that could be tapped into as needed. For large-scale contingencies exceeding the capacity of such a contingency fund, governments should revise the total budget both for departmental allocations and income.

- *Tooth-to-tail ratios.* Particularly in the military, efforts should be made to ensure the optimal tooth-to-tail ratio. All too often supporting structures and headquarters are bloated at the cost of operational capabilities. The size and capacity of support structures can be determined only once the force design has been agreed. Business process reengineering techniques can assist in solving this problem, but they will be effective only if top management is committed to this cause and ruthless in its application.

- *Direct client/supplier relationships.* In many defense forces certain structures exist for historic reasons only. Either because of the organizational culture or other interests, the client (e.g., a combat service) is forced to use the services of a certain organization and not allowed to shop for this service elsewhere. Clients should be allowed freedom of choice and be able to establish direct client/supplier relationships. If governments are under threat, however, then it may be in their interests to organize their support in house and to militarize all or part of the supply chain. Choices between these extremes may also vary depending on history and on the degree of readiness defined by the government.

Other potential solutions for the improvement of efficiency include outsourcing and public-private partnerships, improved collaboration between services, improved management information through better information technology, use of reserves, use of civilians in defense ministries, and improved management and leadership through education, training, and development. Of these, the use of better information technology for strengthening information management systems might be the most crucial way to improve efficiency in defense organizations.

Source: Ball and le Roux 2006.

Box O.12   Mali—Budget Requests for Force Provision and Support

The World Bank's 2013 report on financial management in Mali's defense and police forces found that these forces were significantly underequipped, but noted that they were undergoing a massive program of reequipping. In 2012 alone, the Malian armed forces acquired approximately 160 troop-carrying vehicles, five tank carriers, two reservoirs for the air force, five power generators, communications equipment, light and heavy weapons, and some T-55 tanks. In total, the Ministry of Defense's budget request estimated that, based on assessed requirements, 300 billion Central African CFA francs (CFAF) was needed to rebuild the army alone.

Resources for maintenance and upkeep were even scarcer than for rebuilding, and the weak budgetary system and heterogeneity of management methods did not facilitate optimal allocation of maintenance funds. The majority of funds were centrally managed by the Finance and Equipment Directorate, which decided on a case-by-case basis whether to honor requests for repairs or parts that were too costly for the various security forces. This practice caused delays detrimental to the training and operation of security forces. Annual allocations to the security forces themselves included less than CFAF 50 million for the army, CFAF 30 million for the police, CFAF 25 million for the gendarmerie, CFAF 12 million for the national guard, and no funds at all for the air force. A supplementary appropriation for the army provided no more than CFAF 500 million. Inadequate as they were, these allocations were often channeled to other uses, exacerbating the degradation of matériel. Overall, the inadequacy of follow-up and funds for effective upkeep and maintenance threatened the usability and sustainability of new investments provided for in the Ministry of Defense's budget request.

Source: World Bank 2013a.

---

officers highlighted the deficiencies and inadequacies of the Malian army. At the request of the new Ministry of Finance, which was seeking to rectify these failures, a PER was carried out that same year and identified practices and policies that were contributing to inefficient budget execution (see box O.12).

Governance and Accountability

PFM principles call for civilian oversight of the security sector and the sector's increasing accountability to citizens, as represented by the executive and legislature specifically as well as the general public. Such oversight is needed because the instruments and agencies of the security sector designed to improve security can themselves be sources of insecurity unless kept in check. An important aspect of that oversight is financial accountability and the capacity of civilian institutions to carry out a sound budget process, expenditure tracking, anticorruption measures, fair and competitive procurement procedures, and proper auditing and accounting.

A PER in the Central African Republic looked at these issues in relation to the auditing processes for the Ministry of Defense and found multiple problems (box O.13).

Box O.13   Central African Republic—Internal Audit Does Not Meet Standards

The World Bank's 2009 financial management assessment of the Central African Republic found that internal audit for the Ministry of Defense failed to meet international standards of professionalism and independence. In 2005, the Inspectorate General of the National Army (IGAN)—the main agency for internal audit in the Ministry of Defense—was attached directly to the defense minister's departmental staff. The office was led by a lieutenant, had a staff of five, and received operational resources from the defense minister. Its oversight authority depended on the trust of the minister, and was limited to the administrative and financial control of management; the office may also have exercised some control over exceptional revenues derived from benefits granted to private actors. The chief weaknesses of the IGAN were its precarious legal authority, funding, and stature within the military hierarchy. Its existence and resources derived from the defense minister and were not provided for in law. And even with the support of the minister, it was difficult for a lieutenant to stand his ground during audits and command respect from officers three or four levels his superior in the normal hierarchy.

The IGAN reflected a broader trend in the security sector, where presidential, interministerial, and ministerial general inspections had been replaced with new authorities in which the executive had more faith. The result was a mix of small inspection or auditing departments with no link between them and without any guarantee of compliance with international standards. This trend created a number of weaknesses, including auditors' lack of independence from the executive hierarchy; the absence of an auditing approach based on thorough and objective risk analysis; the absence of planning and approval for annual audit plans by a higher echelon; a lack of professionalism and training among auditors; and the absence of respect for adversarial proceedings. These weaknesses, in turn, made detecting fraud and irregularities more difficult, and increased the risk that members of the defense hierarchy would use internal inspection and audit offices for personal or political purposes, and not to improve defense efficiency or outcomes.

Source: World Bank 2009.

Management of Assets and Liabilities

Managing assets and liabilities is particularly complex when the security sector is directly involved in running parts of the economy, either to provide an input into defense or for profit.[74] For the purposes of the current review, asset management is considered the more important of the two concerns.

The operation and maintenance of equipment used to execute various functions ranging from personnel transport (cars and trucks; aircraft) to combat (light weapons, munitions, and complex weapon systems) will be at a premium in the military, and the processes and resources in place for the maintenance and operations of such assets are fundamental. One study found that "armed forces can improve both the efficiency and effectiveness of their maintenance repair and overhaul function by as much as 60 percent, but doing so requires fundamental changes to organization, processes, and mindsets."[75] Even in the least-resourced security sector institutions, where most assets do not have a high capital value, basic systems (e.g., vehicle fleet management) are important for maximizing efficiency and reducing corruption.

In certain countries, particularly where there has been internal armed conflict (or the risk of it), arms management and destruction is a key issue. A number of agencies support the improved storage, securing, and management of weapons and munitions, including weapon-marking programs and the destruction of surplus, obsolete, or unstable weapons and munitions. This support may enable security forces to professionalize and modernize their weaponry, as well as to manage both the risks of unplanned explosions at munitions sites (UEMS) and the risks associated with diverting arms to the illicit market.[76] Assistance programs specific to national context and developed with national authorities might include systematic assessments, technical guidance and advice, operations in response to assessed priorities, and training and capacity building.

Certain challenges entailed in managing security sector assets were identified during a security sector PER in Niger in 2013; they are described in box O.14.

Box O.14   Niger—Asset Management Institutions and Practices

According to the World Bank's 2013 Public Expenditure Review of Niger's security sector, asset management is a major challenge following the country's fivefold increase in security investments in 2010–2012. These investments have an enduring financial impact. Unless they are maintained, the investments will not be available for use, but maintaining them requires recurrent expenditures for supplies and human resources that could result in cuts to other sectors. A strong asset management capacity has two advantages: it helps ensure that equipment is efficiently allocated to operational units, and it helps reduce transparency risks and prolong the life of the equipment, which contributes to a better economic return on the investments.

Several departments in the Nigerien Armed Forces are responsible for managing equipment: the Central Department of Military Intendance, the Central Department of Equipment, and the Department of Infrastructure. The Central Department of Military Intendance purchases, transports, stores, and distributes equipment procured from the civilian market and also audits expenditures and stocks accounts. The Central Department of Equipment is responsible for armored cars and vehicles, munitions, and the supply and accounting of equipment. Finally, the Department of Infrastructure is responsible for the supply, storage, and distribution of hydrocarbons. The police and gendarmerie have separate asset management and logistics departments, and pooled asset management between the security forces is not common. Overall, the personnel in charge of equipment are insufficiently trained, and departments could benefit from procedure manuals.

Internal control of asset management is largely on paper, and given the regular power outages and limited backup capacities, the weakly computerized system is likely to persist. When procured equipment is received and accepted, it is recorded in a central equipment registry; the Nigerien Armed Forces records its equipment in spreadsheets, while the national guard uses a Microsoft

(Box continues on next page)

Box O.14   Niger—Asset Management Institutions and Practices *(continued)*

Word file. Depending on the type, the equipment is kept in central stocks until deployed or distributed directly to individual units. Recurrent needs, such as spare vehicle parts, are kept in stock and made available when requested. Other equipment is stocked on a quarterly basis or procured as needed. Inspections of equipment and stocks are usually conducted annually, but shortage of personnel means the planned periodicity is not always respected. Vehicle disposal is controlled by the Ministry of Finance, with revenues accruing to the Treasury. Weapons disposal is under the control of the Commission on Illegal Arms of the Economic Community of West African States. Finally, the responsibility for repair and maintenance depends on the degree of specialization required, ranging from the user of the matériel, to the company level, battalion level, centralized repair, and finally an external vendor. Maintenance of aircraft and armored vehicles is done by international service providers, whereas lighter vehicles are repaired domestically subject to public procurement rules.

Source: World Bank 2013b.

Predictability and Control in Budget Execution

A critical part of the public financial dimension of security is ensuring that the expenditures are used efficiently and for their intended purposes. Budget execution covers a number of PFM areas ranging from internal controls over payroll, for example, to procurement procedures, and is at the heart of understanding the coherence between a planned and actual budget. This is the part of a PER analysis that potentially comes the closest to an audit in terms of understanding how security sector institutions spend their allocations. Two issues are highlighted here, payroll/corruption and procurement.

The payroll system (including personnel registration and verification of payments and allowances) is often one of the largest shares of the security budget and is a regular source of corruption. Typically, a percentage of salary payments to lower ranks is misappropriated, or "ghosts" are created and their wages embezzled. One of the more notable examples of efforts to discourage corruption—the European Union's work in the Democratic Republic of Congo—is described in box O.15.

Where procurement is concerned, there should be little difference between public expenditure management in general and public expenditure management in the military sector.[77] Defense procurement and acquisition should be carried out according to the same principles that guide public sector procurement in nonmilitary areas: fairness, impartiality, transparency, cost-effectiveness and efficiency, and openness to competition.[78] In addition, it is essential that all major projects for all forms of public sector procurement and acquisition be subject to high-level consultation and evaluation. Box O.16 presents a generic procurement process, applicable to all sectors of government.

Box O.15   Democratic Republic of Congo—Chain of Payments Project to Discourage Corruption

The European Union mission to provide assistance for security sector reform (SSR) in the Democratic Republic of Congo was established in 2005. It was originally mandated to assist in the process of integrating the various armed groups into the national army and to support good governance in the field of security. One of its first initiatives was the Chain of Payments project aimed at rehabilitating the salary system and delinking the wage distribution lines from the official chain of command. A biometric census was undertaken (finding 120,000 soldiers instead of the official count of 190,000); army IDs were issued; and a central database and payroll system were created (the salaries of lowest ranks increased from $10 to $40/month). This intervention was credited with cleaning up a part of the financial management system commonly associated with embezzlement and a preponderance of "ghost soldiers"; however, it did not manage to lead to longer-term structural reform in the sector.

Source: More and Price 2011.

Box O.16   A Generic Procurement Process

A generic procurement process includes the following:

- A clear definition of the requirement
- Clear technical quality specifications and standards
- An open request for proposals and tenders
- Tender adjudication according to set criteria
- Selection of a preferred bidder
- Drawing up of a contract
- Placing the contract or order
- Monitoring progress
- Reception of goods
- Quality assurance checks on goods received
- Acceptance or rejection of goods
- Payment
- Distribution of goods.

Source: Ball and le Roux 2006, 40.

Procurement decision processes may fall outside regular frameworks and processing. Ad hoc exceptions to normal procedures can include direct government-to-government weapons deals, sole-sourcing of contracts, secrecy surrounding tender requirements, and preference for certain domestic suppliers.

At the same time, except for procurement of nonlethal works and commodities (such as clothing, food, fuel, etc.), defense procurement does exhibit some distinctive characteristics. These include (i) the relative importance of cost in determining which bid is accepted, (ii) the confidentiality associated with national security considerations, (iii) the time frame for major weapons procurement, (iv) the complexity of defense procurement, and (v) the existence of international arms control treaty regimes and national legislation governing arms procurement. These distinctive characteristics—discussed below—are deviations in scale rather than principle. For example, adequate levels of confidentiality can be maintained without violating basic public expenditure management principles. There certainly should be skepticism about any claims that procurement of relatively standard materials, services, and commodities for the military should be subject to different rules.

Cost considerations in bidding. Standard procurement practice in non-military sectors emphasizes value for money, but in the defense sector other factors, such as national interest and defense industry promotion, are often cited as more important than cost in accepting a bid for weapons procurement projects. Defense analysts point out, however, that national legislation can influence the part that cost plays in weapon procurement processes. In South Africa, for example, the 1998 defense review and the 1999 white paper on defense-related industries spell out which technologies are considered "strategically essential capabilities" and thus exempt from lowest-cost considerations.[79] The South African Parliament approved both documents.

Confidentiality. Transparency in defense procurement must be limited by national security interests. Confidentiality clauses are required in the arms procurement process; these, too, can be regulated by national legislation. The South African defense review lists a number of reasons for confidentiality in defense procurement, including the protection of third-party commercial information; national security; prevention of harm to South Africa's ability to conduct international relations; and the protection of South Africa's economic interests and the commercial activities of government bodies.[80]

Time frame for major weapons procurement. From inception to final acceptance of the product, procurement of major weapon systems may take as long as 15 years. Some flexibility needs to be built into the procurement process to take account of contingencies such as fluctuations in currency exchange rates. This long time frame also necessitates quality control throughout the procurement process, not just when the product is ready for delivery. In addition, it requires efforts to forecast spending farther into the future than in nondefense sectors; the United Kingdom, for example, has a 10-year "long-term costing" system for defense.[81] Finally, arms procurement projects should take into account full life-cycle costs and support for the acquired systems.

The complexity of arms procurement. Because of the complexity of arms procurement, sound management of the procurement process requires interdisciplinary project teams with expertise in engineering, resource management, contracting, quality assurance, and design assurance. The particular complexity of major weapon systems procurement, which can involve a substantial number of subcontractors, creates significant opportunities for corruption. These projects therefore require the highest level of management and scrutiny by government accountability mechanisms. For example, South Africa has three levels of approval for major arms procurement projects within its Department of Defence. For other major projects, parliamentary approval may also be required.

International arms control treaty regimes and national legislation governing arms procurement. Procurement in the military sector is distinct from general government procurement in being subject to international treaties and specific national legislation. Some defense budgeting specialists suggest that the oversight mechanisms associated with this national and international regulation increase transparency.

Recording and Reporting in Accounting

The assumption is that the security sector is part of the government's financial management information system (FMIS), which is central to the running of public finance. The FMIS in turn requires a high quality of data and accounting in order to be effective in capturing useful information. The kind of information an FMIS captures is listed in box O.17.

However, many countries have no FMIS, or at least none used by security line ministries, departments, and agencies. Many countries have to contend with weak human and institutional capacity for finance management in the security sector. Sometimes this weak capacity reflects a desire to shroud in secrecy decision making, levels of expenditure, and the way in which resources are allocated; but it also can simply reflect the nature of the general public finance system. Throughout the public sector, linkages between policy, planning, budget development and execution, and oversight may be inadequate; and the individual components of that chain are often weak. Thus the capacity to generate the type of information that is required for evidence-based diagnosis and policy making is limited.

Box O.17   Information Captured by a Financial Management Information System

- Approved budget allocations for both recurrent and capital outlays
- Sources of financing for programs and projects
- Budget transfers
- Supplementary allocations
- Fund releases against budgetary allocations
- Data on commitments and actual expenditures against budgeted allocations.

Source: World Bank 1998.

> ## Box O.18   El Salvador—Weak Capacity to Generate Information
>
> A 2012 Public Expenditure Review undertaken in El Salvador found that the "lack of reliable and comparable statistics makes it challenging to measure efficiency of spending. El Salvador has no unified system of crime statistics integrating the arrests by the police and citizens' complaints to the Police and Attorney General's Office. Consequently, crime statistics vary in the country (sometimes significantly) depending on the source consulted, not only in terms of numbers, but also in the definition and classification of crimes."[a]
>
> a. World Bank 2012a, 11.

A PER of the criminal justice sector in El Salvador offers an example of such limited capacity (box O.18).

In many countries, basic systems of security sector data and expenditure classification do not exist, or they may require significant reform to provide the type of information policy makers and budget holders require. Under these circumstances, it is unrealistic to assume that practices in the security sector will meet a high standard or that the security sector will necessarily advance more rapidly than other parts of the public sector. A general need to strengthen public finance systems therefore provides an opportunity to strengthen the security sector specifically.

External Scrutiny and Audit

The final aspect of the PFM system is ensuring external audit and oversight, which—accounting for national security considerations—should be the same for the security sector as for any other.[82] The auditor general should have sufficient access to transactions and performance indicators in the security sector and to audit reports discussed in Parliament (if need be, discussions can be in closed committee and include only those individuals with the necessary security clearance).

Activities aimed at improving the capacity of legislative bodies to perform their mandated public expenditure oversight offer another avenue for engaging with the security sector. Legislatures are often constitutionally mandated to authorize and scrutinize security expenditures. Figure O.5 shows the potential roles legislatures can play during an annual budget cycle in democratic systems. In reality, of course, the actual responsibilities and level of authority vary among countries, as does the capacity of legislators to authorize and scrutinize government budgets. Legislatures frequently benefit from capacity-building activities. Activities aimed at public accounts committees can examine the specificities of security budgeting, while activities aimed at defense, security, or intelligence committees can incorporate finance

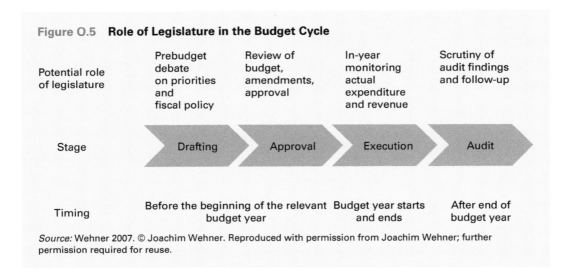

Figure O.5   **Role of Legislature in the Budget Cycle**

Source: Wehner 2007. © Joachim Wehner. Reproduced with permission from Joachim Wehner; further permission required for reuse.

management issues. It is important to note, however, that legislatures may need to strengthen their overall capacity to engage in financial oversight before they are able to address the specific challenges of engaging with the security sector.

The following are some helpful questions for assessing external scrutiny of the security sector[83]:

- Are there clearly defined executive and legislative responsibilities for external and internal security?
- Are the security forces subject to democratic citizen control?
- Are parliamentarians, the media, and civil society free and able to participate in the security debate?
- Are the security forces able to exercise political influence?
- Are the security services open to unnecessary political interference through political reach into the promotion system?
- Are the security forces more loyal to the regime or to the people?
- Are there budgetary checks, balances, and internal and external audit, and are these transparent?
- Are the duties and responsibilities of the security services enshrined in legal statutes, military law, and codes of conduct?

Answers to these questions can be further corroborated by government-led surveys and opinion polls seeking public perceptions of the military, police, criminal justice institutions, and other actors. This information will shed light on the nature of state-society linkages in the sector.[84]

In fragile and conflict-prone states, external oversight institutions will likely not be robust. Weak audit institutions identified by a 2013 PER in Mali are described in box O.19.

> **Box O.19   Mali—Security Forces Not Subject to External Oversight**
>
> According to the World Bank's 2013 financial management assessment, Mali's military and internal security forces are in practice not subject to external oversight; all of the external monitoring bodies avoid using their oversight powers for issues related to the security forces. The review determined that this situation encouraged the development of "extra-procedural practices" and should therefore be redressed.
>
> The Office of the General Auditor, created in 2004, had never carried out a compliance verification in the Ministry of Defense, despite its large size and the fact that all other important departments had been the subject of such missions. One of the obstacles to external oversight, according to the General Auditor, was uncertainty surrounding the concept of an "official secret."
>
> The accounts section of Mali's Supreme Court is responsible for assessing accounts maintained by the government accountants and determining whether they conform to the country's finance laws. The office is understaffed, with only 13 counselors for more than 1,000 accounts per year. Moreover, personnel in the accounts section do not have the status of a judge and the wages are not attractive. In recent years, the accounts section has not specifically reviewed Ministry of Defense accounts, and only an aggregate administrative account is transmitted by the Ministry of Finance to the court when the finance law is examined. Even so, the accounts section was able to determine that CFAF 2 billion paid by the Ministry of Defense in 2011 was not supported by documentary evidence.
>
> Parliament was similarly ineffective. Staffing is inadequate, with only one staff assistant for the defense commission. Moreover, a request for an on-site oversight mission in 2011 was rejected by the Office of the President. Finally, the General Inspectorate of Finances, which has 17 agents and is tasked with monitoring the accountants and administrators, has not recently inspected the military or internal security forces, according to the best knowledge of the chief inspector.
>
> *Source:* World Bank 2013a.

Conclusions

This overview has offered a brief outline of the role of security and justice institutions in a changing global context, and it has further pointed to a practical application of the security-development nexus—specifically, the emerging practice of including the public finance dimension in the policy dialogue on security and justice, generally by means of a PER. This approach is by no means the norm, but it has utility in addressing critical sector issues such as the affordability, effectiveness, efficiency, and accountability of services delivered.

A number of potential entry points are available for raising the public finance perspective in policy dialogue, with the expectation that over time the security actors (ministries, departments, and agencies) will participate in the regular budgetary process. In many countries, however, this path remains unlikely, and then the decision about whether to undertake a PER carries with it certain risks that need to be assessed and discussed with the government concerned. Ultimately, the conditions under which a PER proceeds will be contingent on the levels of trust among the key stakeholders, and their confidence that the PER will provide favorable outcomes for all involved.

In opening the dialogue among government stakeholders, most PER processes have followed some kind of road map. This overview considered context (political, security, gender, and economic) and institutional architecture before covering economic management policy issues and the principles and methodologies relating to PFM. This discussion lays the foundation for considering the three main subsystems of the security sector: defense, policing, and criminal justice.

Staff from the World Bank as well as from the UN have applied the framework described here to an evolving body of PERs undertaken in the last 10 years in about 20 countries. These PERs have varied in context (from rich and middle-income countries to those undergoing war-to-peace transitions), scope (from defense to justice), time frame (a few months to three years), cost (from one individual's time for a few staff weeks to a large team of experts and several hundred thousand dollars), and impact.

A number of lessons can be taken from this work:

- *Undertaking a process of engagement is critical to securing buy-in from the various stakeholders involved in the PER and hence to ensuring access to the right and most relevant counterparts and the best data.* This process may involve relatively high up-front transaction costs, such as holding a number of "expert workshops" with invitations to people from around the country, the region, and beyond, in order to share experience and expertise on the sectors, the issues related to confidentiality, and the objectives and expected outcomes of the exercise.
- *It is important to obtain a relatively good idea of the scope of work early on, given that the issues concerning security and justice can be so enormous.* A wide scope encompassing both the military and criminal justice sectors provides policy makers with an overview of all instruments available for delivering security and justice services. This wide scope is particularly important when examining critical questions about the balance between the military and the police, or about the criminal justice chain linking policing, judicial, and corrections functions. However, such a wide scope can be costly and take time, requiring the necessary expertise to cover all these subsectors. A narrow scope can be more manageable and produce more rapid results, though it risks missing links with other subsectors. Given the range of potential issues, an early agreement on the key questions that counterparts want help in answering is critical to defining the scope and ultimately the success of the PER.
- *The sharing of data can be challenging, particularly because much of the material may be sensitive if not confidential, and in some contexts there may be very little data to share.* What can help data exchange is a sharing of preliminary "stock-take notes" with key interlocutors that set out what is known; this can prompt a more intense sharing of information.

One final lesson is that a PER should be seen as the start of a process of engagement on public finance and the security and justice sectors, and not a one-off event. Some issues might be dealt with relatively immediately, such as determining the fiscal gap on various options for the composition and structure of the sector. But addressing issues where adaptation and reform are sought, such as those relating to PFM and integration into the national budget process, will take time. It is to these issues that we turn in the chapters of *Securing Development*.

Notes

1. World Bank, *Improving Public Financial Management in the Security Sector*, vol. 5 of *Afghanistan: Managing Public Finances for Development* (Washington, DC: World Bank, 2005).
2. Currently the Afghanistan National Defense and Security Forces cost international partners about $5.1 billion per year. See Franz-Stefan Gady, "Afghanistan Won't Be Able to Pay for Its Military Until 2024 (At Least)," *The Diplomat*, February 4, 2016.
3. World Bank, "Crime and Violence in Central America: A Development Challenge" (World Bank, Washington, DC, 2011).
4. "The Gangs that Cost 16% of GDP," *The Economist*, May 21, 2016.
5. Congressional Research Service, "Central America Regional Security Initiative: Background and Policy Issues for Congress" (Congressional Research Service, Washington, DC, December 2015).
6. John Mueller and Mark Stewart, *Terror, Security, and Money: Balancing the Risks, Benefits, and Costs of Homeland Security* (New York: Oxford University Press, 2011).
7. John Mueller and Mark Stewart, "Fear and Budgets: Scrutinising the Costs of Counterterrorism," *Canberra Times*, March 2, 2015.
8. The focus of the book is on the security sector as defined by the Organisation for Economic Co-operation and Development (OECD) and the United Nations, which includes the military and criminal justice institutions such as the police, prosecutors, and courts working under the criminal or penal laws of a country; it does not include wider justice or legal institutions.
9. World Bank, *World Development Report 2011: Conflict, Security, and Development* (Washington, DC: World Bank, 2011); and OECD, *Violence and Fragility: States of Fragility Report 2016* (Paris: OECD, forthcoming).
10. Paul Jackson, ed., *Handbook of International Security and Development* (Northampton, MA: Edward Elgar Publishing, 2015).
11. Stephen Pinker, *The Better Angels of Our Nature: Why Violence Has Declined* (New York: Penguin, 2011).
12. Battle deaths increased from 56,000 in 63 conflicts in 2008 to 180,000 in 42 conflicts in 2014. International Institute for Strategic Studies (IISS), *Armed Conflict Survey* (Routledge, 2015).

13. On average 508,000 died violently every year in the period 2007–2012, the majority outside conflict zones. Geneva Declaration Secretariat, *The Global Burden of Armed Violence 2015: Every Body Counts* (Cambridge, U.K.: Cambridge University Press, 2015).

14. UN Refugee Agency (UNHCR), "World at War: Global Trends in Forced Displacement" (UNHCR, 2014).

15. Violence containment spending is defined as economic activity that is related to the consequences or prevention of violence where the violence is directed against people or property. IEP, "The Economic Cost of Violence Containment (IEP, 2015), 4, http://economicsand peace.org/wp-content/uploads/2015/06/The-Economic-Cost-of -Violence-Containment.pdf.

16. Ibid.

17. See for example Robert S. McNamara, "Reducing Military Expenditures in the Third World," *Finance and Development* 28, no. 3 (September 1991).

18. Deepa Narayan, Raj Patel, Kai Schafft, Anne Rademacher, and Sarah Koch-Schulte, *Can Anyone Hear Us? Voices from 47 Countries,* vol. 1 of *Voices of the Poor* (Washington, DC: World Bank, 1999).

19. UN Secretary General, *In Larger Freedom: Towards Development, Security and Human Rights for All* (United Nations, A/59/2005, March 21, 2005).

20. World Bank, *World Development Report 2011: Conflict, Security, and Development* (Washington, DC: World Bank, 2011).

21. For every three years that a country is affected by major violence (battle deaths or excess deaths from homicide equivalent to a major war), poverty reduction lags by 2.7 percentage points. Ibid., based on 2008 poverty data in Chen Shaohua, Martin Ravallion, and Prem Sangraula, "Dollar a Day Revisited," *World Bank Economic Review* 23, no. 2 (2008): 163–84. Data are available on POVCALNET, http:// iresearch.worldbank.org.

22. See William Byrd and Stephane Guimbert, "Public Finance, Security, and Development: A Framework and an Application to Afghanistan" (Policy Research Working Paper, World Bank, Washington, DC, 2009).

23. See for example John Samuel Fitch, *The Armed Forces and Democracy in Latin America* (Baltimore: Johns Hopkins University Press, 1998); and Anton Bebler, *Civil-Military Relations in Post-Communist States: Central and Eastern Europe in Transition* (Abingdon, U.K.: Routledge, 1997).

24. See for example Nicole Ball, "Spreading Good Practices in SSR: Policy Options for the British Government" (Saferworld, 1998), http://www .ciponline.org/images/uploads/publications/Spreading_Good _Practices_in_SSR_NB_Saferworld_1998.pdf.

25. Significant milestones include OECD, "The 2001 DAC Guidelines: Helping Prevent Violent Conflict" (OECD, Paris, 2001); UNDP, *Human Development Report 2002: Deepening Democracy in a Fragmented*

World (New York: Oxford University Press, 2002); the revised 2004 OECD guidelines, published in "Security System Reform and Governance: Policy and Good Practice" (OECD, Paris, 2004); the inclusion of several SSR elements in the definition of official development assistance in 2005; and the publication of the *OECD DAC Handbook on Security System Reform: Supporting Security and Justice* (Paris: OECD Publishing, 2007).

26. UN Secretary General, *Securing Peace and Development: The Role of the United Nations in Supporting Security Sector Reform* (United Nations, A/62/659; S/2008/39, January 2008).

27. See for example UN Secretary General, *Civilian Capacity in the Aftermath of Conflict* (United Nations, A/67/312–S/2012/645, August 2012); UN Secretary General, *Peacebuilding in the Immediate Aftermath of Conflict* (United Nations, A/63/881-S/2009/304, June 2009).

28. United Nations SSR Task Force, "Security Sector Reform Integrated Technical Guidance Notes" (United Nations, New York, 2012), http://unssr.unlb.org/Portals/UNSSR/UN%20Integrated%20Technical%20Guidance%20Notes%20on%20SSR.PDF.

29. UN Secretary General, *Securing States and Societies: Strengthening the United Nations Comprehensive Support to Security Sector Reform* (United Nations, A/67/970–S/2013/480, August 2013).

30. These organizations include (among others) the Geneva Centre for the Democratic Control of Armed Forces and its attached International Security Sector Advisory Team (ISSAT), the Centre for Governance and Security, and the African Security Sector Network.

31. See for example Louise Andersen, "Security Sector Reform and the Dilemmas of Liberal Peacebuilding" (DIIS Working Paper 2011:31, Danish Institute for International Studies, Copenhagen, 2011); and Paul Jackson, "Security Sector Reform and State Building," *Third World Quarterly* 32, no. 10 (2011).

32. Nicole Ball and Jay Kayode Fayemi, eds., *Security Sector Governance in Africa: A Handbook* (Centre for Democracy and Development, 2003).

33. For example, the capacity-based budgeting approach used by some advanced-country defense ministries is an advanced form of program and performance budgeting, with object metrics of "capacility." This approach might be used to inform other sectors, but is often "secured" within the defense sector.

34. OECD, *States of Fragility 2015: Meeting Post-2015 Ambitions* (Paris: OECD Publishing, 2015), doi:10.1787/9789264227699-en. The quotation is on p. 74.

35. See the Security Assistance Monitor, which tracks U.S. military assistance, at www.securityassistance.org.

36. African Development Bank, Asian Development Bank, European Bank for Reconstruction and Development, European Investment Bank,

Inter-American Development Bank, International Monetary Fund, and World Bank Group, "From Billions to Trillions: Transforming Development Finance," April 2, 2015, 7, http://siteresources.worldbank.org/DEVCOMMINT/Documentation/23659446/DC2015-0002(E) FinancingforDevelopment.pdf. Emphasis is added.

37. William Byrd, "The Financial Dimension of Security Sector Reform," in *The Future of Security Sector Reform*, ed. Mark Sedra (Waterloo, Ontario: Centre for International Governance Innovation, 2010), 305.

38. OECD, "Security System Reform and Governance" (OECD, Paris, 2004).

39. Laurie Nathan, ed., "Local Ownership of Security Sector Reform: A Guide for Donors" (U.K. Global Conflict Pool, 2007), http://www.lse.ac.uk/internationalDevelopment/research/crisisStates/download/others/SSRReformNathan2007.pdf.

40. See for example Daniel Brumberg and Hesham Sallam, "The Politics of SSR in Egypt" (U.S. Institute of Peace, Washington, DC, 2012).

41. See for example Paul D. Williams, ed., *Security Studies: An Introduction* (Abingdon, U.K.: Routledge, 2008); and Christopher H. Hughes and Lai Yu Meng, *Security Studies: A Reader* (Abingdon, U.K.: Routledge, 2011).

42. Barry Buzan, *People, States and Fear* (Harvester Wheatsheaf, 1991); cited in Paul D. Williams, ed., *Security Studies: An Introduction* (Abingdon, U.K.: Routledge, 2008), 2.

43. Arnold Wolfers, "National Security as an Ambiguous Symbol," in *Discord and Collaboration* (Baltimore: Johns Hopkins University Press, 1962).

44. UNDP, *Human Development Report* (New York: Oxford University Press, 1994).

45. World Bank, *World Development Report 2011: Conflict, Security, and Development* (Washington, DC: World Bank, 2011), 116.

46. Patti Petesch, "How Communities Manage Risks of Crime and Violence" (*World Development Report 2014* background paper, World Bank, Washington, DC, 2014).

47. See for example Robert S. McNamara, "The Post–Cold War World: Implications for Military Expenditures in Developing Countries," in *Proceedings of the World Bank Annual Conference on Development Economics 1991*, ed. Lawrence H. Summers and Shekhar Shah (Washington, DC: World Bank, 1992), 95–125.

48. Hans Born and Albrecht Schnabel, eds., *Security Sector Reform in Challenging Environments* (Geneva Centre for the Democratic Control of Armed Forces, 2009).

49. See Megan Bastick and Kristin Valasek, eds., "Gender and Security Sector Reform Toolkit" (Geneva Centre for the Democratic Control of Armed Forces, 2008); and Jennifer Erin Salahub and Krista Nerland, "Just Add Gender? Challenges to Meaningful Integration of Gender in SSR Policy and Practice," in *The Future of Security Sector Reform*, ed. Mark Sedra (Waterloo, Ontario: Centre for International Governance Innovation, 2010), 263–80.

50. See for example Olara A. Otunnu, "'Special Comment' on Children and Security," *Disarmament Forum* 3 (2002).

51. Inter-Parliamentary Union and UN Division for the Advancement of Women, "Women in Politics, 2008," http://www.ipu.org/pdf/publications /wmnmap08_en.pdf.

52. See for example the resources of the UN Security Sector Reform Task Force (www.unssr.unlb.org/) and those of the International Security Sector Advisory Team (www.issat.dcaf.ch).

53. The OECD speaks of the "security system" rather than the "security sector."

54. A. Adeyemi, "Crime and Development in Africa: A Case Study of Nigeria," in *Essays on Crime and Development*, ed. U. Zvekic (UN Interregional Crime and Justice Research Institute, 1990).

55. Richard Allen, Salvatore Schiavo-Campo, and Thomas Columkill Garrity, *Assessing and Reforming Public Financial Management: A New Approach* (Washington, DC: World Bank, 2004).

56. Richard Hemming, "The Macroeconomic Framework for Managing Public Finances," in *The International Handbook of Public Financial Management*, ed. Richard Allen, Richard Hemming, and Barry Potter (New York: Palgrave Macmillan, 2013), 17–37.

57. The World Bank and the International Monetary Fund have developed a number of instruments for assessing and improving budget planning, implementation, and control. These include (i) PERs, (ii) Country Procurement Assessment Reviews and the OECD DAC MAPS (Methodology for Assessing Procurement Systems), (iii) Medium-Term Expenditure Frameworks, (iv) Review of the Observance of Standards and Codes, (v) Public Expenditure Tracking Surveys, (vi) Institutional and Governance Reviews, and (vii) Functional Reviews. Relevant materials include Allen Schick, *A Contemporary Approach to Public Expenditure Management* (Washington, DC: World Bank, 1998); Richard Allen and Daniel Tommasi, *Managing Public Expenditure: A Reference Book for Transition Countries* (Paris: OECD, 2001); and World Bank, *Tools for Evaluating Public Expenditures: Benefit Incidence Analysis* (Washington, DC: World Bank, 2010), http://wbi .worldbank.org/boost/tools-resources/topics/sector-analysis/benefit -incidence-analysis.

58. PEFA, "Framework for Assessing Public Financial Management" (PEFA Secretariat, Washington, DC, 2016), http://www.pefa.org/en /content/pefa-2016-framework.

59. Michal Brzoska, "World Military Expenditures," in *Handbook of Defence Economics*, ed. Keith Hartley and Todd Sandler (Amsterdam: Elsevier, 1995); Stockholm International Peace Research Institute, Military Expenditure Database, https://www.sipri.org/databases/milex.

60. The question of the size of the overall defense budget has been a contentious one in relation to its overall impact on economic growth as well as its relationship with armed conflict. The PER policy outline

does not take a position on the recommended macroceilings for the security sector, but some of the current debates on these issues are outlined in annex 1B in the introduction.

61. Richard Hemming, "The Macroeconomic Framework for Managing Public Finances," in *The International Handbook of Public Financial Management*, ed. Richard Allen, Richard Hemming, and Barry Potter (New York: Palgrave Macmillan, 2013), 34.

62. Adapted from Nicole Ball and Malcolm Holmes, "Integrating Defense into Public Expenditure Work" (DFID, London, 2002), http://www.gsdrc.org/docs/open/ss11.pdf.

63. William Byrd, "The Financial Dimension of Security Sector Reform," in *The Future of Security Sector Reform*, ed. Mark Sedra (Waterloo, Ontario: Centre for International Governance Innovation, 2010).

64. Some of the main reasons for deviations in public sector financing are identified in World Bank, *Public Expenditure Management Handbook* (Washington, DC: World Bank, 1998).

65. Peter J. Middlebrook and Sharon M. Miller, *Sierra Leone Security Expenditure Review* (London: DFID, 2006).

66. Dylan Hendrickson and Nicole Ball, "Off-Budget Military Expenditure and Revenue: Issues and Policy Perspectives for Donors" (CSDG Occasional Paper 1, International Policy Institute, King's College London, 2002), https://www.ciponline.org/images/uploads/publications/OP1_OffBudget_Military_Expenditure.pdf.

67. For more on *mano dura*, see for example Niels Uildriks, ed., *Policing Insecurity: Police Reform, Security and Human Rights* (Lanham, MD: Lexington Books, 2009).

68. United Nations Office on Drugs and Crime (UNODC) Statistics, "Data," http://www.unodc.org/unodc/en/data-and-analysis/statistics/data.html.

69. See World Bank, "Management Note (1991 Guidelines), SecM91-1563, Military Expenditure," December 1991.

70. See for example Rita Abrahamsen and Michael C. Williams, *Security beyond the State: Private Security in International Politics* (Cambridge, U.K.: Cambridge University Press, 2011).

71. See for example Mitchell Polinsky and Steven Shavell, "The Theory of Public Enforcement of the Law" (NBER Working Paper 11780, National Bureau of Economic Research, Cambridge, MA, 2005), which suggests that lower enforcement costs and higher fines would lead to less expensive but equally effective deterrence.

72. See the UN Integrated Technical Guidance Note on National Ownership of SSR, 2012, https://unssr.unlb.org/Portals/UNSSR/UN%20Integrated%20Technical%20Guidance%20Notes%20on%20SSR.PDF.

73. See chapter 4 on policing for a detailed discussion of measuring police performance.

74. See for example "Khaki Capitalism," *The Economist*, December 3, 2011, http://www.economist.com/node/21540985.

75. Colin Shaw, *Mastering Military Maintenance* (London: McKinsey, 2010).
76. See for example the MAG (Mines Advisory Group) website at http://www
    .maginternational.org/ (and contact MAG at info@maginternational.org
    for further information).
77. The discussion of procurement is adapted from Nicole Ball and
    Malcolm Holmes, "Integrating Defense into Public Expenditure Work"
    (DFID, London, 2002), http://www.gsdrc.org/docs/open/ss11.pdf.
78. Some countries distinguish between the "procurement" of commercial
    goods and services and the "acquisition" of armaments. Others use
    the term "procurement" for both commercial goods and services and
    weapons or weapon systems. This discussion follows the latter
    practice.
79. South African Department of Defence, "Defence in a Democracy:
    South African Defence Review 1998" (Pretoria, 1998), http://www
    .dod.mil.za/documents/defencereview/defence%20review1998.pdf;
    and South African National Conventional Arms Control Committee,
    "White Paper on the South African Defence Related Industries,"
    Pretoria, December 1999, http://www.dod.mil.za/documents/White
    PaperonDef/white%20paper%20on%20the%20SA%20defence%
    20related%20industries1999.pdf.
80. South African National Conventional Arms Control Committee,
    "White Paper on the South African Defence Related Industries," par. 68.
81. See British Army, *Design for Military Operations: The British Military
    Doctrine* (London: Ministry of Defence, 1996), http://www.army.mod
    .uk/doctrine/branches/doc.htm.
82. See Geneva Centre for the Democratic Control of Armed Forces
    (DCAF), "International Standards for Financial Oversight in the
    Security Sector" (DCAF, Geneva, 2015).
83. Gregory F. Treverton and Robert Klitgaard, "Enhancing Security
    through Development: Probing the Connections" (paper presented at
    the Annual Bank Conference on Development Economics, Amsterdam,
    May 23–24, 2005).
84. See for example Nawaf Wasfi Tell, "Public Opinion, Terrorism and
    the Jordanian Security Sector" (Center for Strategic Studies, Jordan,
    July 2008), http://www.arab-reform.net/sites/default/files/Article_Nawaf
    _el_Tell.pdf.

References

Abrahamsen, Rita, and Michael C. Williams. 2011. *Security beyond
    the State: Private Security in International Politics.* Cambridge, U.K.:
    Cambridge University Press.

Adejumobi, Said, and Mesfin Binega. 2006. "Ethiopia." In *Budgeting for the
    Military Sector in Africa*, edited by Wuyi Omitoogun and Eboe Hutchful,
    48–71. Oxford, U.K.: Oxford University Press.

Adeyemi, A. 1990. "Crime and Development in Africa: A Case Study of Nigeria." In *Essays on Crime and Development*, edited by U. Zvekic. UN Interregional Crime and Justice Research Institute.

AfDB (African Development Bank), ADB (Asian Development Bank), EBRD (European Bank for Reconstruction and Development), EIB (European Investment Bank), IADB (Inter-American Development Bank), IMF (International Monetary Fund), and World Bank Group. 2015. "From Billions to Trillions: Transforming Development Finance." April 2. http://siteresources.worldbank.org/DEVCOMMINT/Documentation /23659446/DC2015-0002(E)FinancingforDevelopment.pdf.

Allen, Richard, Salvatore Schiavo-Campo, and Thomas Columkill Garrity. 2004. *Assessing and Reforming Public Financial Management: A New Approach*. Washington, DC: World Bank.

Allen, Richard, and Daniel Tommasi. 2001. *Managing Public Expenditure: A Reference Book for Transition Countries*. Paris: OECD.

Andersen, Louise. 2011. "Security Sector Reform and the Dilemmas of Liberal Peacebuilding." DIIS Working Paper 2011:31, Danish Institute for International Studies, Copenhagen.

Ball, Nicole. 1998. "Spreading Good Practices in SSR: Policy Options for the British Government." Saferworld. http://www.ciponline.org /images/uploads/publications/Spreading_Good_Practices_in_SSR_NB _Saferworld_1998.pdf.

Ball, Nicole, and Jay Kayode Fayemi, eds. 2003. *Security Sector Governance in Africa: A Handbook*. Centre for Democracy and Development.

Ball, Nicole, and Malcolm Holmes. 2002. "Integrating Defense into Public Expenditure Work." DFID, London. http://www.gsdrc.org/docs /open/ss11.pdf.

Ball, Nicole, and Len le Roux. 2006. "A Model for Good Practice in Budgeting for the Military Sector." In *Budgeting for the Military Sector in Africa*, edited by Wuyi Omitoogun and Eboe Hutchful. Oxford, U.K.: Oxford University Press for SIPRI.

Bastick, Megan, and Kristin Valasek, eds. 2008. "Gender and Security Sector Reform Toolkit." Geneva Centre for the Democratic Control of Armed Forces.

Bebler, Anton. 1997. *Civil-Military Relations in Post-Communist States: Central and Eastern Europe in Transition*. Abingdon, U.K.: Routledge.

Born, Hans, and Albrecht Schnabel, eds. 2009. *Security Sector Reform in Challenging Environments*. Geneva Centre for the Democratic Control of Armed Forces.

British Army. 1996. *Design for Military Operations: The British Military Doctrine*. London: Ministry of Defence. http://www.army.mod.uk /doctrine/branches/doc.htm.

Brumberg, Daniel, and Hesham Sallam. 2012. "The Politics of SSR in Egypt." U.S. Institute of Peace, Washington, DC.

Brzoska, Michal. 1995. "World Military Expenditures." In *Handbook of Defence Economics*, edited by Keith Hartley and Todd Sandler. Amsterdam: Elsevier.

Buzan, Barry. 1991. *People, States and Fear*. Harvester Wheatsheaf.

Byrd, William. 2010. "The Financial Dimension of Security Sector Reform." In *The Future of Security Sector Reform*, edited by Mark Sedra. Waterloo, Ontario: Centre for International Governance Innovation.

Byrd, William, and Stephane Guimbert. 2009. "Public Finance, Security, and Development: A Framework and an Application to Afghanistan." Policy Research Working Paper, World Bank, Washington, DC.

Congressional Research Service. 2015. "Central America Regional Security Initiative: Background and Policy Issues for Congress" (Congressional Research Service, Washington, DC, December).

DCAF (Geneva Centre for the Democratic Control of Armed Forces). 2015. "International Standards for Financial Oversight in the Security Sector." DCAF, Geneva.

Economist. 2011. "Khaki Capitalism." December 3. http://www.economist .com/node/21540985.

———. 2016. "The Gangs that Cost 16% of GDP." May 21.

Fitch, John Samuel. 1998. *The Armed Forces and Democracy in Latin America*. Baltimore: Johns Hopkins University Press.

Gady, Franz-Stefan. 2016. "Afghanistan Won't Be Able to Pay for Its Military Until 2024 (At Least)." *The Diplomat*, February 4.

Geneva Declaration Secretariat. 2015. *The Global Burden of Armed Violence 2015: Every Body Counts*. Cambridge, U.K.: Cambridge University Press.

Hemming, Richard. 2013. "The Macroeconomic Framework for Managing Public Finances." In *The International Handbook of Public Financial Management*, edited by Richard Allen, Richard Hemming, and Barry Potter, 17–37. New York: Palgrave Macmillan.

Hendrickson, Dylan, and Nicole Ball. 2002. "Off-Budget Military Expenditure and Revenue: Issues and Policy Perspectives for Donors." CSDG Occasional Paper 1, International Policy Institute, King's College London. https://www.ciponline.org/images/uploads/publications/OP1 _OffBudget_Military_Expenditure.pdf.

Hughes, Christopher H., and Lai Yu Meng. 2011. *Security Studies: A Reader*. Abingdon, U.K.: Routledge.

IEP (Institute for Economics and Peace). 2015. "The Economic Cost of Violence Containment." IEP.

IISS (International Institute for Strategic Studies). 2015. *Armed Conflict Survey.* Routledge.

Jackson, Paul. 2011. "Security Sector Reform and State Building." *Third World Quarterly* 32 (10): 1803–22.

Jackson, Paul, ed. 2015. *Handbook of International Security and Development.* Northampton, MA: Edward Elgar Publishing.

McNamara, Robert S. 1991. "Reducing Military Expenditures in the Third World." *Finance and Development* 28 (September): 26–30.

———. 1992. "The Post–Cold War World: Implications for Military Expenditures in Developing Countries." In *Proceedings of the World Bank Annual Conference on Development Economics 1991*, edited by Lawrence H. Summers and Shekhar Shah, 95–125. Washington, DC: World Bank.

Middlebrook, Peter J., and Sharon M. Miller. 2006. *Sierra Leone Security Expenditure Review.* London: DFID.

More, Sylvie, and Megan Price. 2011. "The EU's Support to Security System Reform in the Democratic Republic of Congo: Perceptions from the Field." Netherland Institute of International Relations, The Hague.

Mueller, John, and Mark Stewart. 2011. *Terror, Security, and Money: Balancing the Risks, Benefits, and Costs of Homeland Security.* New York: Oxford University Press.

———. 2015. "Fear and Budgets: Scrutinising the Costs of Counterterrorism." *Canberra Times,* March 2.

Narayan, Deepa, Raj Patel, Kai Schafft, Anne Rademacher, and Sarah Koch-Schulte. 1999. *Can Anyone Hear Us? Voices from 47 Countries.* Vol. 1 of *Voices of the Poor.* Washington, DC: World Bank.

Nathan, Laurie, ed. 2007. "Local Ownership of Security Sector Reform: A Guide for Donors." U.K. Global Conflict Pool. http://www.lse.ac.uk/internationalDevelopment/research/crisisStates/download/others/SSRReformNathan2007.pdf.

OECD (Organisation for Economic Co-operation and Development). 2001. "The 2001 DAC Guidelines: Helping Prevent Violent Conflict." OECD, Paris.

———. 2004. "Security System Reform and Governance: Policy and Good Practice." OECD, Paris.

———. 2007. *OECD DAC Handbook on Security System Reform: Supporting Security and Justice.* Paris: OECD Publishing.

———. 2015. *States of Fragility 2015: Meeting Post-2015 Ambitions.* Paris: OECD Publishing. doi:10.1787/9789264227699-en.

———. Forthcoming. *Violence and Fragility: States of Fragility Report 2016.* Paris: OECD.

Otunnu, Olara A. 2002. "'Special Comment' on Children and Security." *Disarmament Forum* 3.

PEFA (Public Expenditure and Financial Accountability). 2016. "Framework for Assessing Public Financial Management." PEFA Secretariat, Washington, DC. http://www.pefa.org/en/content/pefa-2016-framework.

Petesch, Patti. 2014. "How Communities Manage Risks of Crime and Violence." *World Development Report 2014* background paper, World Bank, Washington, DC.

Pinker, Stephen. 2011. *The Better Angels of Our Nature: Why Violence Has Declined.* New York: Penguin.

Polinsky, Mitchell, and Steven Shavell. 2005. "The Theory of Public Enforcement of the Law." NBER Working Paper 11780, National Bureau of Economic Research, Cambridge, MA.

Salahub, Jennifer Erin, and Krista Nerland. 2010. "Just Add Gender? Challenges to Meaningful Integration of Gender in SSR Policy and Practice." In *The Future of Security Sector Reform*, edited by Mark Sedra, 263–80. Waterloo, Ontario: Centre for International Governance Innovation.

Schick, Allen. 1998. *A Contemporary Approach to Public Expenditure Management.* Washington, DC: World Bank.

Shaohua, Chen, Martin Ravallion, and Prem Sangraula. 2008. "Dollar a Day Revisited." *World Bank Economic Review* 23 (2): 163–84.

Shaw, Colin. 2010. *Mastering Military Maintenance.* London: McKinsey.

South African DoD (Department of Defence). 1998. "Defence in a Democracy: South African Defence Review 1998." Pretoria. http://www.dod.mil.za/documents/defencereview/defence%20review1998.pdf.

South African NCACC (National Conventional Arms Control Committee). 1999. "White Paper on the South African Defence Related Industries." Pretoria. http://www.dod.mil.za/documents/WhitePaperonDef/white%20paper%20on%20the%20SA%20defence%20related%20industries1999.pdf.

Stockholm International Peace Research Institute. Military Expenditure Database. https://www.sipri.org/databases/milex. Accessed June 30, 2016.

Tell, Nawaf Wasfi. 2008. "Public Opinion, Terrorism and the Jordanian Security Sector." Center for Strategic Studies, Jordan. http://www.arab-reform.net/sites/default/files/Article_Nawaf_el_Tell.pdf.

Treverton, Gregory F., and Robert Klitgaard. 2005. "Enhancing Security through Development: Probing the Connections." Paper presented at the Annual Bank Conference on Development Economics, Amsterdam, May 23–24.

Uildriks, Niels, ed. 2009. *Policing Insecurity: Police Reform, Security and Human Rights.* Lanham, MD: Lexington Books.

UNDP (United Nations Development Programme). 1994. *Human Development Report.* New York: Oxford University Press.

———. 2002. *Human Development Report 2002: Deepening Democracy in a Fragmented World.* New York: Oxford University Press.

UNHCR (UN Refugee Agency). 2014. "World at War: Global Trends in Forced Displacement." UNHCR.

United Nations SSR Task Force. 2012. "Security Sector Reform Integrated Technical Guidance Notes." United Nations, New York.

UNODC (United Nations Office on Drugs and Crime) Statistics. "Data." http://www.unodc.org/unodc/en/data-and-analysis/statistics/data.html. Accessed June 30, 2016.

UNSG (United Nations Secretary General). 2005. *In Larger Freedom: Towards Development, Security and Human Rights for All.* United Nations, A/59/2005, March 21.

———. 2008. *Securing Peace and Development: The Role of the United Nations in Supporting Security Sector Reform.* United Nations, A/62/659; S/2008/39, January.

———. 2009. *Peacebuilding in the Immediate Aftermath of Conflict.* United Nations, A/63/881-S/2009/304, June.

———. 2012. *Civilian Capacity in the Aftermath of Conflict.* United Nations, A/67/312–S/2012/645, August.

———. 2013. *Securing States and Societies: Strengthening the United Nations Comprehensive Support to Security Sector Reform.* United Nations, A/67/970–S/2013/480, August.

Wehner, Joachim. 2007. "Strengthening Legislative Financial Scrutiny in Developing Countries: Report Prepared for the U.K. Department for International Development." London School of Economics and Political Science, London.

Williams, Paul D., ed. 2008. *Security Studies: An Introduction.* Abingdon, U.K.: Routledge.

Wolfers, Arnold. 1962. *Discord and Collaboration: Essays on International Politics.* Baltimore: Johns Hopkins University Press. Chapter 10: "National Security as an Ambiguous Symbol." 147–66.

World Bank. 1990. "Somalia Country Economic Memorandum." World Bank, Washington, DC.

———. 1991. "Management Note (1991 Guidelines), SecM91-1563, Military Expenditure." World Bank, Washington, DC.

———. 1998. *Public Expenditure Management Handbook.* Washington, DC: World Bank.

————. 2005a. *Afghanistan: Managing Public Finances for Development.* Washington, DC: World Bank.

————. 2005b. *Improving Public Financial Management in the Security Sector.* Vol. 5 of *Afghanistan: Managing Public Finances for Development.* Washington, DC: World Bank.

————. 2009. "Report on the Assessment of the Financial Management of the Defense and Security Forces in the Central African Republic." World Bank, Washington, DC.

————. 2010. *Tools for Evaluating Public Expenditures: Benefit Incidence Analysis.* Washington, DC: World Bank. http://wbi.worldbank.org/boost/tools-resources/topics/sector-analysis/benefit-incidence-analysis.

————. 2011a. "Crime and Violence in Central America: A Development Challenge." World Bank, Washington, DC.

————. 2011b. *World Development Report 2011: Conflict, Security, and Development.* Washington, DC: World Bank.

————. 2012a. "El Salvador Security and Justice Public Expenditure and Institutional Review: Decision Document." World Bank, Washington, DC.

————. 2012b. "Republic of Burundi Public Expenditure Review: Fiscal Challenges, Security, and Growth in Burundi." Report no. ACS3988, World Bank, Washington, DC.

————. 2013a. "Malian Security Forces: Financial Management Assessment Report." World Bank, Washington, DC.

————. 2013b. "Niger Security Sector Public Expenditure Review." Report no. 83526-NE, World Bank, Washington, DC.

————. 2015. "Transition amid Risks with a Special Focus on Intergovernmental Fiscal Relations." *Somalia Economic Update* 1, October. http://documents.worldbank.org/curated/en/2015/11/25468667/somalia-economic-update-transition-amid-risks-special-focus-intergovernmental-fiscal-relations.

World Bank and United Nations. 2012. "Liberia Public Expenditure Review Note: Meeting the Challenges of the UNMIL Security Transition." World Bank, Washington, DC.

————. Forthcoming. "Security and Justice Public Expenditure Review for Somalia." World Bank, Washington, DC.

World Bank and United Nations Assistance Mission in Somalia. 2016. "Security and Justice Public Expenditure Review." June.

CHAPTER 1

Introduction to *Securing Development*

Why This Book?

We live in an insecure world, and some of the foremost public policy questions of our time address how we can strengthen our security and personal safety. Often those questions can be further broken down into what are the most affordable or cost-effective means of addressing insecurity.

These questions are critical in a variety of contexts.

- In late 2005, financial experts examined data at the Afghan Ministry of Finance to ascertain how much the security sector was costing. To their astonishment, they found that the sector cost some $1.3 billion per year, or 23 percent of gross domestic product (GDP), made up largely of donor contributions along with some government financing. Security spending therefore exceeded domestic revenues by over 500 percent.[1] Questions on the sustainability of security sector spending, and on the handover from international forces for policing and military functions, have been at the fore of policy making for the country ever since.[2]

- Central America, and particularly the northern triangle of El Salvador, Guatemala, and Honduras, is home to the highest homicide rates in the world. Interpersonal violence associated with gangs, drug trafficking, and weak criminal justice institutions has enormous costs in terms of health, economic growth, and people's overall well-being.[3] In El Salvador, official estimates show that crime costs 16 percent of GDP per year.[4] The governments in the region established the Security Commission of the Central American Integration System (known as SICA) in 1995 to harness their collective efforts to address these huge challenges, and donors have provided generous contributions to their security strategy.[5] Yet the extremely high rates of crime and violence continue.

- Since 9/11, the U.S. and European governments have faced increasing costs for their counterterror measures. A central question is whether the gains in safety have been justified by the costs, which have run into the trillions of dollars.[6] When the surveillance of one individual associated with a radical political agenda can cost around $5.7 million per year,[7] governments must think about what price they are paying to keep their citizens safe, or feeling safe.

The need to understand security and justice systems in the context of the public expenditures they require is the subject of this sourcebook.[8] This is not a policy book that recommends different approaches to security threats and challenges. It is about numbers. Or more accurately, it is about helping governments and practitioners obtain a better picture of the money spent on security, including what it is spent on, and how. By providing a better analysis of such spending—through what is called a Public Expenditure Review (PER) of the security sector—a technical team of practitioners can facilitate better-informed decisions at the senior leadership level about policy and operational approaches to the sector.

The global context in which such decisions are made is constantly shifting. All the evidence suggests the nature of violence and conflict is changing,[9] presenting new challenges and threats. National and human security is now less concerned with conventional war than it was 30 years ago and more concerned with transnational political violence, drug trafficking, climate change, forced migration, slavery, urban crime and violence, pandemics, cybersecurity, and related threats and challenges.[10]

While the general historical patterns of war and violence may indicate that humankind is becoming less likely than in the past to resort to warfare,[11] the second decade of the 21st century suggests otherwise. Battle deaths have recently increased, largely due to protracted wars such as those in Afghanistan, Iraq, and the Syrian Arab Republic;[12] and far more homicides now take place, largely in cities of countries that are not at war but are subject to high rates of crime and violence.[13] Further, the consequences of that violence go far beyond excess mortality and include injury, poor health, and poverty. Above all, these recent trends have resulted in the largest refugee and internally displaced populations since World War II.[14]

The costs of such violence are enormous. According to a study by the Institute for Economics and Peace (IEP), the "economic cost of violence containment to the world economy in 2012 was estimated to be US$9.46 trillion or 11 percent of Gross World Product."[15] There are many different approaches to addressing both collective and interpersonal violence, ranging from coercive (e.g., military) to nonviolent (e.g., peacebuilding and violence prevention) to judicial (e.g., arrest and prosecution); and all these have their associated costs. This book focuses on the security and justice institutions, the instruments they use to contend with these challenges, and the cost of sustaining them. And according to the IEP study, these institutions and instruments take up the lion's share of the cost of violence containment: 51 percent of costs go to military expenditure, 14 percent to internal security, 6 percent to private security, and 4 percent to incarceration.[16]

In focusing on these institutions, we note that the public policy debate is no longer a binary one of whether or not money should be spent on these sectors (the guns versus butter argument).[17] Given that resources will be allocated to the security sector, the important question for policy makers is how resources can be used to ensure effective, professional, modern, and accountable institutions that provide security and justice services for citizens.

In turn, as the debates have changed so have the orthodox barriers between different policy arenas. No longer does the discussion take place among security actors alone; it now includes other players such as ministries of finance and development organizations.

Security and Development

In recent years, security challenges have moved from the margin to the mainstream of the development agenda. Security is now recognized as essential for citizens' livelihoods and access to services, and for the free exercise of civil, political, social, and economic rights. Security is particularly important for the poor and other vulnerable groups, who suffer disproportionately from fear, loss of property, and violence.[18] Moreover, insecurity is the principal development challenge in fragile and conflict-affected states (FCS). In 2005, the report of the UN Secretary General (UNSG) emphasized that longer-term development demands a sufficient degree of security to facilitate poverty reduction and shared prosperity.[19]

These themes are picked up in the 2011 *World Development Report*, which calls for a shift in the development community's work on security. The report argues that fragility and violence arise when countries are exposed to economic, political, or security stresses that they are institutionally unable to cope with.[20] Figure 1.1 shows that poverty trends are directly proportional to the degree of intensity of violence: countries suffering from a significant level of violence tend to see poverty increase, while those experiencing little or no violence see the share of the population below the poverty line decrease significantly.[21] Moreover, countries affected by conflict—including middle- and lower-income countries—risk entering a vicious cycle of repeated conflict.

Security also has a direct impact on the growth of investment, social and human capital, public institutions, and distribution of resources. Insecurity weakens the investment climate by making investment incentives scarcer

Figure 1.1   Negative Effect of Violence on Development

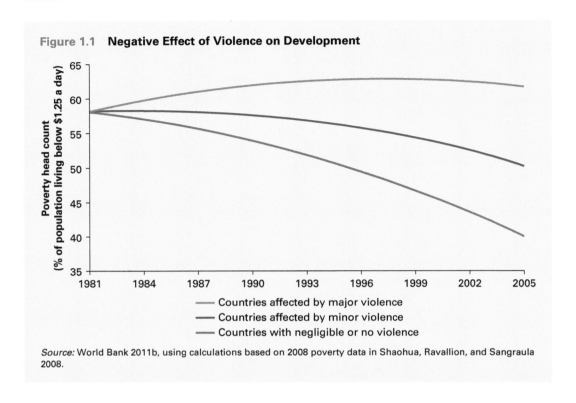

Countries affected by major violence
Countries affected by minor violence
Countries with negligible or no violence

Source: World Bank 2011b, using calculations based on 2008 poverty data in Shaohua, Ravallion, and Sangraula 2008.

and destroying material assets and human capital.[22] It subjects the private sector both to higher costs in the form of security taxes—i.e., the additional costs associated with negative externalities as a result of instability—and to disorganized markets. Violence and insecurity harm human and social capital, particularly among the most vulnerable segments of the population; their effects are evident in physical and psychological damage, migration, deteriorating living standards, and interruptions in public services. Insecurity also weakens the legitimacy of public institutions and creates points of entry for corruption. Finally, growing insecurity can be both the cause and the consequence of skewed distribution of national resources, which, in turn, weakens the overall security sector apparatus of the society.

For these reasons, security and development have increasingly been seen as inextricably linked, and development actors have progressively engaged in the sector with aspirations for promoting change and reform.

Security Sector Reform

Change within the military structure and the broader security sector has historically been an essential part of state formation. This is reflected in the social and political transformations effected by demilitarization and democratization processes in Latin America, as well as in the changes in Eastern Europe after the fall of the Soviet Union.[23]

However, the involvement of international donors and agencies in security and justice service provision is still relatively new.[24] In the late 1990s, a number of key bilateral donors, undertaking a whole-of-government approach to development aid, began integrating security into development programming. This effort culminated in the work at the Organisation for Economic Co-operation and Development (OECD) Development Assistance Committee (DAC), which led to donor consensus around what was termed "security system reform" (now more commonly called "security sector reform," or SSR) and policy development through the 2000s.[25]

These advances have been mirrored by the United Nations' increasing role in SSR, particularly, but not exclusively, within the parameters of peacekeeping operations. The UNSG's first report on SSR was *Securing Peace and Development: The Role of the United Nations in Supporting Security Sector Reform,* issued in 2008.[26] The UNSG subsequently reported on various UN initiatives, including strengthened approaches to supporting the police as well as civilian capacities, such as for the criminal justice sector.[27] An Inter-Agency Security Sector Reform Task Force cochaired by the United Nations Development Programme (UNDP) and the United Nations Department of Peacekeeping Operations has brought together 14 UN entities to promote an integrated approach to SSR support. In addition to handling operational and training aspects of SSR, the task force has conducted wide-ranging consultations to develop SSR guidelines, including the Integrated Technical Guidance Notes issued in 2012.[28] These initiatives were followed by the UNSG's second report on SSR in 2013,[29] and were endorsed in 2014 by the UN Security Council in Resolution 2151, the first stand-alone resolution on SSR. These efforts reiterated the centrality of national ownership of SSR, recognizing that such processes need to support and be informed by the broader national political context, and they underlined the importance of strengthening support to sectorwide initiatives that aim to enhance the governance and overall performance of the security sector.

Extensive programmatic work on SSR in various countries has evolved in parallel to these policy developments. Examples include the rebuilding and reform of national armies in Afghanistan, Burundi, Iraq, Liberia, and Sierra Leone; the demobilization and reintegration of over 400,000 ex-combatants in Africa's Great Lakes region; the democratizing of security sector governance in Ghana, South Africa, and Latin America; and the building of capacity in criminal justice to address burgeoning rates of crime and violence in Central America. National and international expertise in SSR has also grown and now covers strategic and policy advice, arms control, governance and oversight, and criminal justice support. Further, various networks and nongovernmental organizations are being formed at the global, regional, and national levels in this area.[30] However, the literature suggests that while the policies and norms associated with the SSR framework have been increasingly accepted, more can be done to improve its impact.[31]

Largely missing from this growing body of policy and practice has been the link between public finance and the security sector. While general aspirations for affordability are often stressed with regard to SSR, there has been little guidance to support governments in better understanding whether security sector costs are within a sustainable macrofiscal envelope, let alone efficiently and effectively allocated. Development practitioners have worked with governments for some time on improving national budgetary processes. After all, national budgets are the most important policy vehicle for putting a country's priorities into effect within the scarce resources that are available to a government for public expenditure; it is through the policy and budget processes that competing priorities are reconciled and implemented. However, there often remains a gap between the national budgeting process and the financing of the security sector.

More specifically, little work has been undertaken to date on the composition of security sector budgets, or on the processes by which they are planned and managed. Ultimately, sound fiscal management of the security sector is essential if a country is to have effective, efficient, and professional security organizations that are capable of protecting the state and its population against internal and external threats. Integrated systems for planning, policy making, and budgeting are necessary to achieve an appropriate allocation of public sector resources and to manage those resources effectively and efficiently.[32]

Currently, most public finance practitioners have little or no experience in working with the security sector. In turn, security institutions may not consult the ministry of finance on security sector expenditures and allocations. Even where security sector expenditures and financial management are addressed, a firewall of security classification often prevents practitioners from applying good public finance principles to the security sector, and also prevents their sharing with other sectors the lessons on public finance learned in the security sector.[33]

A further difficulty is that in many countries, the security sector is treated uniquely, with few or no standard oversight and accountability practices in place to assure value for money. External auditors may not be empowered to examine security sector spending. Parliaments may similarly not be permitted to engage in oversight, or they may simply have little capacity to undertake it. Procurement may be secret, with no process for assuring proper pricing of bids. Internal auditors may not exist, or they may be compromised by lacking the authority or ability to share their findings with civilian policy officials nominally in charge of the security sector.

One important effect of applying the principles of public finance to the security sector would be to improve mobilization of resources, which is a challenge in developed and developing countries alike. An emphasis on financial probity, integrity, and transparency in how resources are spent would encourage allocation of resources to the security sector. External financing of the sector has been a process of trial and error for development actors, particularly in terms of how to engage with the sector, which traditionally has been outside most development programming. According to the OECD, "aid to the security sector comprises a small amount of all sector-allocated aid" (some 1.4 percent for security and 3.1 percent for related justice). In 2012, aid allocated to building the security sector in fragile states totaled only $858 million.[34]

These figures do not include direct military assistance, which runs into several billions of dollars (and as yet is not globally measured). However, they confirm the assumption that the primary actors responsible for providing security to citizens will remain national governments (as well as other formal and informal actors working at the subnational and local levels). This finding parallels the general work on financing for development, which has emphasized that in fact "for most countries, domestic resource mobilization is the largest resource available to fund their national development plans. A country's ability to mobilize domestic resources and spend them *effectively* . . . lies at the crux of financing for development."[35]

Given that governments play this primary role in providing security, the PER represents a powerful tool for them, one that can help them strengthen the legitimacy, effectiveness, accountability, and modernization of their security services.

Public Expenditure Reviews

Governments and donor partners are increasingly using security and justice sector PERs to inform their decisions about sectoral development. Security and justice sector issues have traditionally been addressed from strategic, policy, and operational perspectives; examining these sectors through the public finance lens serves a number of important purposes that might otherwise not be met.

- A PER usually starts with an institutional mapping that throws light on the security sector management structure, the key actors and their functions, and the way in which the political economy of the sector affects the quantity and quality of resource allocation.
- A public finance perspective addresses the question of whether programs have adequate and sustainable resourcing, without which they are at best ineffective and at worst likely to create additional sources of conflict and violence.
- Where security forces seek the necessary finance for modernization and professionalization, a public finance perspective accounts for value for money and so can justify additional resources from national budgets and development partners.
- A PER can make explicit the resource allocation trade-offs underlying different policy options; in particular, it can help address the tendency of security sector resourcing to absorb a huge share of scarce public

resources and crowd out other activities required to rebuild the nation politically, socially, and economically.

- A PER can address the way that financial management of the security sector reflects on the legitimacy of governments to both domestic and external stakeholders. Security and justice service provision are the fundamental public goods that states are expected to provide for their citizens; and sustained and accountable financing of the sectors is a critical ingredient for that role.

Integrating the security sector into standard thinking on public finance and development policy is important but challenging. One aim of this book is to strengthen the ability of national actors to develop and manage security expenditure policy, and to build the capacity of their international partners to support them in these efforts. It does so by providing a framework for the analysis of finance management, financial oversight, and expenditure policy issues in the security sector.

The book will be of interest to practitioners working on public expenditure management and to those working on security sector issues. For public finance specialists, it will help clarify the similarities and differences between the security sector and the rest of the public sector and will demonstrate how commonly used analytic tools can be applied in the security sector; it will also describe what the main security institutions are, how they relate to each other, and how the security sector is governed. For security specialists, it will clarify critical aspects of finance management and the place of the security institutions in that process. It will also explain how adhering to finance management processes helps governments achieve their objectives and provides them with a comprehensive view of the sector (one that shows how their particular portion of the sector fits into the whole).

At the national level, the book is aimed at high-level government officials in relevant ministries (finance, public safety, interior, justice, and defense) and in intelligence services, as well as at parliamentarians. It is expected to reach a broader audience through the process of policy dialogue and training. Among international actors, the audience includes World Bank and UN staff and other development officials asked to assist in expenditure analysis related to the security sector. In particular, the book responds to demand from international organizations and practitioners working in conflict-affected countries, particularly those with UN peace support operations.

The remainder of this chapter consists of (i) an outline of the public expenditure and budgeting process, including a rationale for including the security sector as well as entry points and risks; (ii) the key steps in a security sector PER, including consultations with government, analysis of general context, and the main issues raised by a PER and by public financial management (PFM) analysis more generally; and (iii) the potential conclusions and processes that can follow such a sector analysis. Following this introduction, the book describes public finance management and its application to the security sector (chapter 2), and then looks in detail at defense (chapter 3), policing services (chapter 4), and the criminal justice sector (chapter 5).

Reasons for Conducting a Security Sector Public Expenditure Review

Over the last 20 years, both developed and developing countries have made a concerted push to standardize and improve measures around PFM.[36] The focus of that effort has been on the systems and processes that run the national budget. Efforts to strengthen public budgeting have focused on two areas: (i) improved public expenditure policy, particularly policy relating to fiscal stability, efficiency, and effectiveness; and (ii) improved PFM relating to the functional aspects of budget implementation and systems.

Effective budget planning, implementation, and control have been codified in a set of internationally accepted rules, including rules related to the following:

- *Comprehensiveness or completeness.* All government income and expenditure are linked.
- *Sustainability.* Expenditure and income must be balanced in the medium term.
- *Competition between categories of expenditures.* Decisions on allocation of resources within the budget, including capital versus recurrent spending, must be well founded.
- *Transparency.* Information must be given on expenditures and income.
- *Accountability.* Inefficient and unintended expenditure of funds should be accounted for.[37]

General Trends in Public Finance and Security

The Public Expenditure and Financial Accountability (PEFA) framework is now the internationally recognized tool for assessing and measuring budget planning, implementation, and control along a series of indicators, including (i) budget reliability, (ii) transparency of public finances, (iii) management of assets and liabilities, (iv) policy-based fiscal strategy and budgeting, (v) predictability and control in budget execution, (vi) accounting and reporting, and (vii) external scrutiny and audit.[38] Although designed to assess countrywide PFM practice, the majority of indicators are applicable to the security sector as well, and they have been included in the questions-to-ask diagnostics that are part of this book.[39]

The key question is to what degree the security sector is subject to the same budget policy and management standards as other sectors.

The general trend in international practice is for the security sector to be treated differently, for these reasons:

- Many governments do not include security expenditures in their budgets; where they are included, they tend not to be disaggregated (studies have shown a discrepancy between official statistics and actual expenditures).[40]
- Key security actors, such as the military, have concerns about secrecy and confidentiality, which can impede attempts to strengthen transparency and accountability and the undertaking of any review of expenditures.
- In the defense sector, and particularly in the military, oversight by external auditors is very limited during operations. Robust internal audit mechanisms can compensate, but normal practices used for other public sectors are not appropriate.

In many ways, however, the security sector should not be treated differently from other sectors and should be incorporated—with certain modifications—into the government's regular PFM system. Part of this process can be prompted by undertaking a PER for the sector or part of the sector. Subject to the right conditions and incentives within government, a PER can be a very useful tool for finance agencies and for defense and interior ministries alike. The PER can serve as a platform to bring together security and nonsecurity ministries and public agencies to discuss, negotiate, and assess issues of resource allocation, institutional efficiency, and effectiveness on the basis of a numerate understanding of security sector costs and challenges.

The Rationale for Undertaking a PER in the Security Sector

The PER should therefore be regarded as a tool to assist governments and donor partners in making key "over the horizon" policy and operational decisions in the security sector, through the particular perspective of public finance. Historical and current data and analysis may be used to make future projections and provide decision makers with key options on critical issues in national defense as well as criminal justice, public order, and policing.

The rationale for undertaking a PER will vary according to context and the government's preferred focus. However, a PER in the security sector can generally signal a number of objectives on the government's part, including the modernization and professionalization of the sector; it can also signal the possibility of some movement toward cost-effectiveness, even if actual budget cuts are not envisaged. In this way, the rationale of a PER in the sector is aligned with the generic objectives of sound public expenditure management, as follows:

- *Fiscal stability and affordability.* The objective is to maintain control of a country's overall fiscal position. To this end, government budgets need to be realistic and affordable. Thus "the security sector should be fully incorporated into the annual budget formulation process, subject to aggregate fiscal constraints and sector ceilings like any other sector and fully incorporated in medium-term fiscal projections and planning."[41]

- *Allocative efficiency.* The objective is to balance competing demands and allocate scarce public resources where they will have the greatest benefit. This is one of the most difficult tasks of the ministry of finance; the security sector in general usually takes a large share of the national budget. The government therefore has to offset demands from the military against those of other sectors. In turn, within other sectors—for example, criminal justice—there must be a well-balanced prioritization between the competing subsectors, in this case crime prevention, police, judiciary, prosecution and legal aid, and corrections. It is also important here to analyze all sources of revenue and types of expenditure broken down into assets as well as recurrent costs.

- *Operational efficiency and effectiveness.* The objective is to achieve outputs and outcomes that are economical, efficient, and effective and so get the most out of all funds expended. This aim applies to the security sector just as it does to other sectors. Value for money and achievement of targets can be difficult to measure, particularly in a potentially "static" sector such as the military, where nonperformance may be in fact a sign of good performance (i.e., deterrence of any external threats). As noted elsewhere in this book, much more work is being done in terms of the performance indicators for policing (chapter 4) and criminal justice (chapter 5).

- *Fiscal transparency and accountability.* The objective is to provide open and transparent access to financial decisions and data so that government officials can be held accountable for their actions. Governance, oversight, and civilian control of the security sector are often the rationale for security sector reform as a whole, and they are particularly important in terms of accounting for public expenditures in an area that often presents itself as a "black box" to public scrutiny. The state-owned enterprises that operate in the security sector may use noncommercial accounting principles with unclear accountability structures, making their impact on the treasury or fiscal balance similarly unclear.

- *Reporting on external assistance.* The objective is particularly important for low-income countries and those emerging out of conflict, whose governments may be in receipt of significant external support from donor partners, as well as revenues from peacekeeping operations or hardware sales. Often such support can be ad hoc and off budget, and a PER is a useful mechanism by which to obtain a better picture of that support and its sustainability.

Entry Points for Undertaking a PER

Like the rationale, the specific triggers for undertaking a PER vary subject to context. Chapter 3 on defense sets out a number of possible entry points that can apply to the whole sector. These are summarized in table 1.1.

Given the sensitive and confidential nature of security sector spending, a successful PER will be contingent on trusted relationships—either between

Table 1.1   Entry Points for a Security Sector Public Expenditure Review

Type of change	Examples
Political: changes in political conditions at home, among key allies, or among adversaries	Elections or change in administration
	Change in public opinion
	Legislative scrutiny or change in legislative attitudes
	Peace accord implementation
	Implementation of international obligations, such as European Union accession requirements
	Human rights review
Economic: changes in expenditure caused by macroeconomic or fiscal shocks, or changes in the way economic resources are allocated and controlled	Change in the fiscal space or resource envelope available due to changes in revenue
	Realignment of national spending priorities
	Reduction in defense expenditure by allies
	Response to increased defense spending by neighbors or adversaries
	Macroeconomic shocks
	Adoption of medium-term expenditure framework
	Institutional or process reforms to strengthen government-wide financial management
Security: changes in national, regional, or international security context	Security sector reform program sponsored by the domestic government or an international partner
	Strategic shock resulting in the redefinition of security threats
	Adoption of a sectorwide all-inclusive approach to government
	Internal security challenges, including civil unrest
	Public safety and security pressures created by organized crime and violence
	Border tensions
	Implementation of arms control, transnational crime, or other international obligations
	Arrival or withdrawal of international military or peacekeeping force
	Updated defense/criminal justice planning assumptions following fragility analysis or threat assessment
	Defense review initiating either defensewide or individual service reform
	Accountability and military effectiveness issues
	Major equipment procurement decisions
	Interservice rivalries, including redefinition of investment priority

government actors (such as principals in ministries, departments, and agencies), or between the government and external partners. This is true regardless of the specific entry point for the PER.

Risks and Risk Management

The combination of security and financial analysis entailed in a security sector PER is relatively new. Conducting such a PER involves certain risks, though there are also risks involved in failing to conduct one. Both sets of risks are summarized in table 1.2.

A number of measures can be taken to manage these risks. The starting points are a rigorous analysis of context and consultations with the key stakeholders, particularly inside the government. Such steps are outlined in table 1.3.

Table 1.2 Public Expenditure Review (PER) versus No PER in the Security Sector

Risks of conducting a PER	The PER may provide endorsement to security sector services when such endorsement is not timely or appropriate.
	The PER may alienate the security services, which see in it potential threats (e.g., breach of confidentiality, retrenchment, reduction in resources).
	The PER may jeopardize support to general financial management reform.
Risks of not conducting a PER	The security sector may remain overresourced compared to other priorities.
	The credibility of defense budgeting—and therefore the budget process as a whole—may be undermined.
	Accountability mechanisms—related not only to financial management but also to overall civilian governance—may be weakened.
	Opportunities to improve efficiencies and effectiveness within the sector may be missed.

Sources: Adapted from Ball and Holmes 2002; Jacquand and Ranii 2014.

Table 1.3 Approaches to Managing Risks Arising from a Security Sector Public Expenditure Review (PER)

Approach	Description
Defer the review	Hold off on the PER and instead engage key stakeholders from finance and the security sector in peer exchanges, in the region or elsewhere, on the lessons of other PERs.
Use a whole-of-government approach	Without undertaking a specific "vertical" PER involving the line ministries in the security sector, ensure that "horizontal" public financial management processes engage those line ministries.[a]
Conduct a partial PER	Undertake an incremental PER that examines only certain less-sensitive sectors, such as the police or criminal justice (rather than the military).
Focus on systems, not policy	Undertake a PER that focuses more on the control aspects of public financial management—systems and processes—rather than on the policy questions associated with effectiveness and affordability.

a. A "vertical" process is a detailed public sector reform in one particular sector or line ministry; a "horizontal" process is a whole-of-government approach that includes all line ministries in public sector reform.

Notwithstanding the sensitivities and obstacles noted here, in general there can be no justification for not fully incorporating the security sector into the annual budget formulation. But whether, and how, this takes place ultimately depend on the context and on the views of the government concerned.

Undertaking a PER: Context and Institutional Architecture

It is possible—and useful—to list key steps involved in undertaking a PER, along with the types of sectoral and financial issues that PERs typically confront (see annex 1A). But in fact there is no fixed methodology for undertaking a security sector PER because the scope and direction of a PER are so dependent on context. A variety of contexts—including security, macrofiscal, fragility, and gender—are discussed in this section, along with the key issues relating to security and justice institutions and institutional arrangements, which also help to determine how a PER will proceed. For more detail on the public financial and economic policy contexts, see chapter 2.

First, it needs to be emphasized that the issues raised by a PER can be very sensitive and difficult for a government, particularly when international partners are involved in the review. Security sector reform is thus intensely political, involving differing and sometimes competing national interests. As the OECD explains:

> Experience shows that reform processes will not succeed in the absence of commitment and ownership on the part of those undertaking reforms. Assistance should be designed to support partner governments and stakeholders as they move down a path of reform, rather than determining that path and leading them down it. A major problem in the area of security system reform in some regions . . . has been a lack of local input to and ownership of the emerging reform agenda. This issue is most significant in "difficult partnership" countries.[42]

Consequently, early consultation within the government about the scope and objectives of a security sector PER—and about the role of international partners—is essential to the success of a PER exercise. National ownership is central to the "aid effectiveness" policy of donor countries; but it is important to move beyond the rhetoric to ensure that such ownership exists.[43] Further, if international partners are involved, they may call for rapid results, timelines, and deliverables, and these may be difficult to impose on a political context that requires time for consultation and client feedback. In many instances, despite the presence of significant levers such as international support, local political interest does not allow for reform to take place.[44]

Neither the UN nor the World Bank works in the security sector without an explicit request from the client government. Even with a written request, however, it is incumbent on the international partners to facilitate an early multistakeholder consultation with all the relevant ministries and departments in order to test both the "ownership" of the process and the various interests behind the request.

Understanding Context

The Security Context

The term "security" is ambiguous, difficult to define, contested, and subject to wide treatment in the literature.[45] It is thus "a powerful political tool in claiming attention for priority items in the competition for government attention."[46] A PER team will need to review government documents and consult with key interlocutors to determine what those priority items are. Typically they cover a number of different security dimensions, including the following:

- *National security.* This dimension involves the protection of the sovereign state, including territorial borders and population, from external threats; it is further elaborated to include both objective measures (e.g., the absence of threats) and a subjective sense (e.g., the absence of fear of attack).[47]

- *Individual or citizen security.* Originally outlined by the UNDP in 1994,[48] this dimension is defined by the 2011 *World Development Report* as "freedom from physical violence and freedom from the fear of violence. Applied to the lives of all the members of a society (whether nationals of the country or otherwise), it encompasses security at home, in the workplace and in the political, social, and economic interactions with the state and other members of society."[49]

- *Terrorism/political violence.* UN Security Council Resolution 1566 (2004) defines terrorism as "criminal acts, including against civilians, committed with the intent to cause death or serious bodily injury, or taking of hostages, with the purpose to provoke a state of terror in the general public or in a group of persons or particular persons, intimidate a population or compel a government or an international organization to do or to abstain from doing any act."

- *Economic security.* This dimension involves threats to economic, financial, and commercial systems.

- *Cybersecurity.* This dimension involves threats to national information systems, technology breaches, and virus attacks.

- *Environmental security.* This dimension involves threats related to human-made disasters, including dumping of toxic waste, as well as the global implications of climate change.

- *Criminal security.* This dimension involves threats arising from organized crime, including trafficking in drugs, people, arms, or contraband goods.

Another useful typology of security challenges distinguishes between major organized political violence, localized collective violence, and individual violence. Breaking these categories down (see figure 1.2) demonstrates the variety of risks that societies and communities face, and the diversity of the challenges to which security sector agencies may be expected to respond.[50]

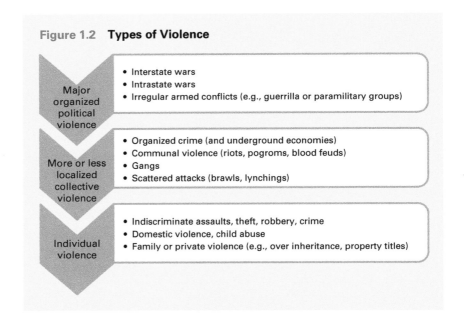

Figure 1.2   **Types of Violence**

Major organized political violence
- Interstate wars
- Intrastate wars
- Irregular armed conflicts (e.g., guerrilla or paramilitary groups)

More or less localized collective violence
- Organized crime (and underground economies)
- Communal violence (riots, pogroms, blood feuds)
- Gangs
- Scattered attacks (brawls, lynchings)

Individual violence
- Indiscriminate assaults, theft, robbery, crime
- Domestic violence, child abuse
- Family or private violence (e.g., over inheritance, property titles)

The Macroeconomic Context

The PER should also consider the macroeconomic context, which includes the general drivers of growth and sources of domestic and external revenue. Using current economic and fiscal data to make projections contingent on different variables, the PER will need to estimate state revenues as well as other competing claims on state resources (examined in chapter 2).

Historically there has been some consideration of the link between military expenditures and growth, and in particular the idea of setting parameters around expenditure/growth ratios.[51] In turn, there is a debate about the relationship between growth and such expenditures, although the evidence of either a negative or positive impact is mixed (see annex 1B). This sourcebook takes no position on this question, favoring more a value-for-money approach: the critical question is not how much money is spent, but rather how well the money is spent.

As part of the effort to understand the macroeconomic context, the PER team will need to run a number of projections, particularly focusing on overall GDP growth, government revenue, and expenditure.

The Fragility Context

The security and justice sectors in fragile and conflict affected states (FCS) present particular challenges. The international community, notably the UN (and others such as the African Union), may be the main provider of security and justice services for these countries—for example, where a noninclusive peace agreement is in effect.[52] Such contexts also include countries that are beset by high rates of urban crime and violence, a large part of which may be associated with organized crime, as in Central America.

Our general view here is that the findings and recommendations of the PER process are as applicable in FCS as they are in middle-income countries, although a number of caveats apply. PER teams in FCS face some real challenges, ranging from scarce data to limited access to certain parts of the country (see table 1.4 for a summary of issues specific to FCS). These obstacles highlight the importance of the *process* aspects of the PER exercise;

Table 1.4　Issues of Relevance for Fragile and Conflict-Affected States (FCS)

FCS factors	Impact upon the security sector
Type of political settlement	The political settlement may be characterized by a weak political bargain between the competing stakeholders. This will affect decision making and coherence at the national level and in turn will impact the rationalization of security forces.
	A military victory, of one party over another, may privilege the security forces to such an extent that it will be difficult to incorporate the sector into the public financial management system and strengthen accountability and oversight systems.[a]
Weak institutional capacity	Relevant challenges include the paucity of data and analysis on the sector, weak systems and controls in place, and the expectation that public sector reform results will take time.
Limited oversight capacity	Weak institutions both inside the state and outside mean that there is weak oversight and citizen control of the security sector.
Legacies of conflict and violence	Armed conflict and violence may have resulted in extensive social trauma, including displacement, casualties, and physical destruction. A traumatized population possibly bearing continued grievances will require specific and carefully considered security and justice provision, including potential mechanisms for transitional justice.[b]
Role of the security sector	FCS are characterized by the absence of rule of law, impunity of security services, and prevailing insecurity. On one hand, governments and partners will want to prevent the security services from preying on civilians; on the other hand, functioning police and criminal justice institutions are needed to support governments in addressing violence and crime.
Weak macroeconomic position	Armed conflict most likely results in increased borrowing and greater debt combined with increased expenditures on the sector. In turn, a widespread conflict will likely harm the economy, prospects for growth, and revenue projections.
External financing	The financing of the security sector by external donors can lead to distortions and questions about sustainability and about recording of external funds (that is, whether on or off budget).[c]
Cost drivers	Conflict or violent settings will result in several potentially high cost drivers for the sector, including (i) integration of armed groups into one army financed by the state, (ii) demobilization and reintegration of ex-combatants, and (iii) establishment of transitional justice mechanisms such as special courts.

a. Adejumobi and Binega 2006.
b. Transitional justice traditionally comprises a number of components, such as (i) rehabilitation of the public sector, including criminal justice institutions; (ii) accounting for past crimes through prosecutions, truth telling, and reparations; and (iii) vetting of security sector personnel.
c. World Bank 2005.

Box 1.1   Examples of Gender Issues in a Security Sector Public Expenditure Review

- *Recognition in government strategic priorities.* The government may be seeking to respond to a number of specific concerns that relate to gender differentiations in violence and security, such as increases in gender-based sexual violence or in violence among youth around schools.
- *Representation through governance and accountability.* Auditory, judicial, and legislative accountability mechanisms, both internal and external, may include women to a greater or lesser extent; and the gender aspects of security and justice provision may be more or less a part of the normal sector discourse.
- *Redress through personnel recruitment and prevention.* The government may have a general priority to increase female enrollment in the armed forces or the police, or it may have specific targets to address specific needs, such as increasing women's presence at control points on borders or seaports/airports (to check men and women), increasing specific female-staffed sexual crime units, or ensuring that particular security and criminal justice policies pay attention to gender issues such as sexual violence.

the PER team may need a longer time frame than usual in order to ensure that minimal objectives for policy and system reform are achieved.

Gender and Security

The provision of personal security is highly gendered.[53] Women's and men's security and justice needs—and their perceptions of the public services provided—can differ significantly. It is well known that in armed conflict the main casualties are women (and children),[54] whereas in gang violence the main casualties are young men 15–24 years old. In turn, security services are generally dominated by men: in Canada women make up only some 18 percent of the police force; in the United States the share is smaller, at 12–14 percent. At high levels of government, women's representation in the security sector is very low: in 2008, women held 1,022 ministerial portfolios across 185 countries, but only 6 of these were in areas of defense and veterans' affairs.[55] It is thus important for the PER team to examine the particular aspects of gender from the strategic to the operational level. Some examples are outlined in box 1.1.

The Security Sector: Institutional and Functional Mapping

Security Institutions

There are many tools available that can assist a PER team in assessing the security sector and in understanding its place within the country and government contexts.[56] The security sector is most commonly defined by the types of institutions it encompasses. The two main international sources, the UN and the OECD DAC, define the security sector in similar, institution-based terms (see box 1.2).[57] Their examples of institutions comprising the security sector are illustrative; in reality, there are a wide variety of institutions that fit into these broad categories, and the exact configuration of institutions varies by context.

Box 1.2   Definitions of "Security Sector"

UN Definition

"The 'security sector' is a broad term often used to describe the structures, institutions and person- nel responsible for the management, provision and oversight of security in a country. It is generally accepted that the security sector includes defense, law enforcement, corrections, intelligence services and institutions responsible for border management, customs and civil emergencies. Elements of the judicial sector responsible for the adjudication of cases of alleged criminal conduct and misuse of force are, in many instances, also included. Furthermore, the security sector includes actors that play a role in managing and overseeing the design and implementation of security, such as ministries, legislative bodies and civil society groups. Other non-State actors that could be con- sidered part of the security sector include customary or informal authorities and private security services."[a]

Organisation for Economic Co-operation and Development (OECD) Development Assistance Committee (DAC) Definition

"The OECD DAC Guidelines on Security System Reform and Governance agreed by ministers in 2004 define the security system as including: core security actors (e.g., armed forces, police, gendarmerie, border guards, customs and immigration, and intelligence and security ser- vices); security management and oversight bodies (e.g., ministries of defense and internal affairs, financial management bodies and public complaints commissions); justice and law enforcement institutions (e.g., the judiciary, prisons, prosecution services, traditional justice systems); and non-statutory security forces (e.g., private security companies, guerrilla armies and private militia)."[b]

a. UNSG 2008, 5; and UN Security Council Resolution 2151.
b. OECD 2007, 5.

A useful graphic (figure 1.3) is used by the International Security Sector Advisory Team (ISSAT) in its assessment toolkit to set out the various com- ponents of the sector and their interconnections.

In many societies, a number of institutions that are not funded through public revenues may also deliver public security and justice. These insti- tutions include traditional, nonstatutory police and courts whose opera- tions are either only partly or not at all codified in law and which are not funded through the tax system; examples are private security and com- munity responses to criminality. While it is often assumed that the pro- cesses of social and economic development will lead to an increase in formal responses to insecurity and a decrease in informal (nonstatutory) responses, in fact this has not always been the case, and many develop- ing societies continue to have strong nonstate responses to crime and insecurity.[58]

A valid critique of the SSR approach is therefore that it tends to be "Weberian" in its conception of the state, identifying and analyzing institu- tions that replicate the European-state model. In many countries, these sys- tems are neither historically appropriate nor affordable; thus the degree of

Figure 1.3   State and Nonstate Institutions of the Security and Justice Sectors

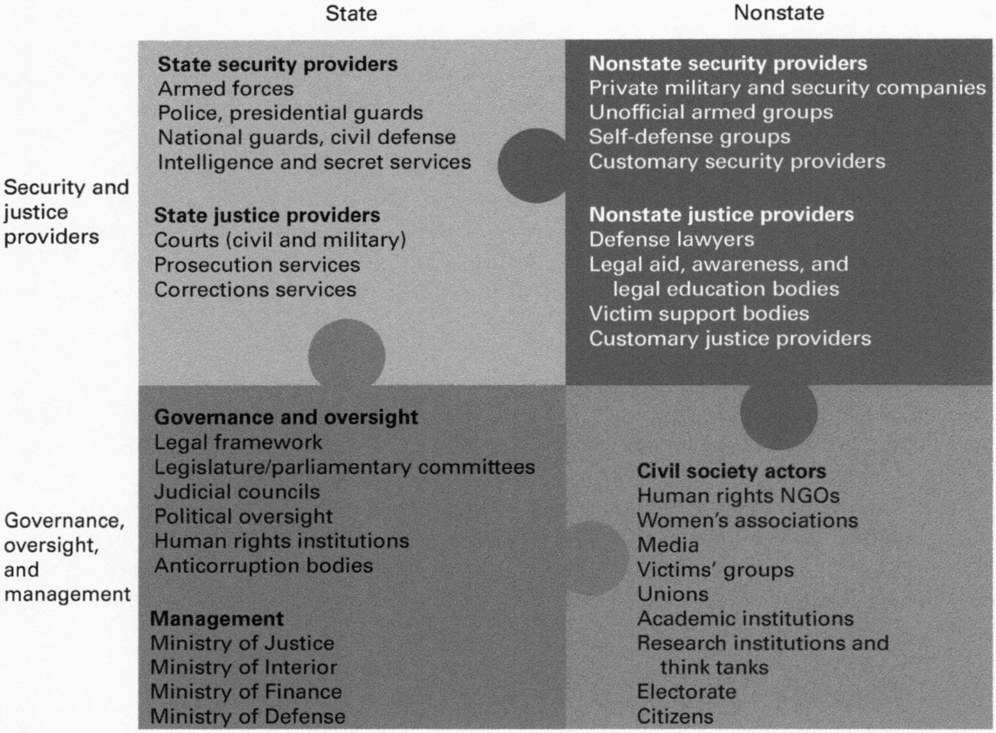

	State	Nonstate
Security and justice providers	**State security providers** Armed forces Police, presidential guards National guards, civil defense Intelligence and secret services **State justice providers** Courts (civil and military) Prosecution services Corrections services	**Nonstate security providers** Private military and security companies Unofficial armed groups Self-defense groups Customary security providers **Nonstate justice providers** Defense lawyers Legal aid, awareness, and legal education bodies Victim support bodies Customary justice providers
Governance, oversight, and management	**Governance and oversight** Legal framework Legislature/parliamentary committees Judicial councils Political oversight Human rights institutions Anticorruption bodies **Management** Ministry of Justice Ministry of Interior Ministry of Finance Ministry of Defense	**Civil society actors** Human rights NGOs Women's associations Media Victims' groups Unions Academic institutions Research institutions and think tanks Electorate Citizens

Source: ISSAT, "Introduction to Security Sector Reform, Lesson 1—Introduction to the Concept of Security Sector Reform," http://issat.dcaf.ch/Learn/E-Learning/Introduction-to-Security-Sector-Reform. © International Security Sector Advisory Team. Reproduced with permission from International Security Sector Advisory Team; further permission required for reuse.
Note: NGOs = nongovernmental organizations.

informality or formality of institutions and the share between public and private service provision will vary hugely depending on country context. In countries where public institutions may be nascent, governments and citizens rely heavily on informal governance structures to exercise security and justice functions. This critique is examined in box 1.3.

The operations and activities of these entities may complement those of the public institutions. But if these entities compete with (or are even in conflict with) public institutions, a number of issues may arise:

- It may not be clear what the jurisdictional boundaries are between various entities; role definitions (or their absence), including in relation to command and control over non-national forces, may likewise be unclear.
- It may not be clear to what extent these entities exist because of public bodies' failures (real or perceived) or their lack of social and political legitimacy.

Box 1.3   **Nonstate Actors and Informal Institutions**

As many have noted, most poor people rely on nonstate actors or so-called hybrid political orders for the provision of basic security and justice services.[a] These nonstate actors include vigilance groups formed to combat local crime; religious police; ethnic or clan militias; civil defense forces; semicommercial anticrime groups; autonomous local government security structures; customary institutions such as elders exercising judicial functions; restorative justice community-based organizations; and locally formed peace committees.[b]

Such bodies rarely have formal budgetary processes that can be incorporated into a Public Expenditure Review (PER) and for which specific costs can be determined. They are by nature individual or informal collective responses to a perceived or actual failure by public bodies to exercise security and justice functions, and they are therefore not likely to include financial management systems. However, they could be part of a security sector PER for two reasons: First, if they provide security and justice in parallel to public institutions, then it may be in the government's interest to consider their policy, legal, and financial implications. Second, many of these bodies function by exacting informal "taxation" upon local communities, so that a better understanding of these revenue systems could also show governments some innovative options for affordable service provision.

a. See Luckham and Kirk 2012; and OECD 2007, which states that "in sub-Saharan Africa at least 80 percent of justice services are delivered by non-state providers" (17).
b. Baker 2010. The list was compiled for Africa but is more widely applicable.

- It may not be clear to what extent their operational ethos accords with the legal restrictions placed on the conduct of statutory institutions (e.g., in relation to the use of force or the securing of due process and rights for suspects and accused persons).

It can be useful for analytical purposes to break up the sector into subsystems. For the purposes of this sourcebook, there are essentially three subsystems: defense, police, and criminal justice. A more expansive PER, however, could include other subsectors, such as the intelligence system (comprising the police, intelligence collection agencies, strategic analysis organizations, military, and oversight institutions).[59] We have chosen to focus on the core subsystems but the same principles of approach and analysis can be applied to these other subsectors.

Security Functions

The most commonly used functional classification of government activities is the UN Classification of the Functions of Government.[60] The composition of the "defense" and "public order and safety" functions as defined by the UN and the International Monetary Fund (IMF) are shown in box 1.4.[61] These systems provide a useful basis for countries establishing their own classification systems. However, countries often adapt these systems to their own program structures, and many countries have likely adjusted the standard classification for security-related functions, as it is incomplete. Specifically, it excludes intelligence services that are not directly linked to the defense forces or the police, as well as the myriad of special security

---

Box 1.4   **Functions of Security Institutions**

International Monetary Fund Functional Breakdowns of Defense and Public Order and Safety
Defense: military defense, civil defense, foreign military aid, military R&D, other defense
Public order and safety: police services, fire protection services, law courts, prisons, public order
    R&D, other public order and safety

UN Classification of Defense and Public Order

02	Defense
02.1	Military defense
02.2	Civil defense
02.3	Foreign military aid
02.4	R&D defense
02.5	Defense (n.e.c.)
03	Public order and safety
03.1	Police services
03.2	Fire protection services
03.3	Law courts
03.4	Prisons
03.5	R&D public order and safety
03.6	Public order and safety (n.e.c.)

Sources: United Nations Statistics Division; IMF 2014, table 6.1.
Note: n.e.c. = not elsewhere classified; R&D = research and development.

services that typically exist in most countries. It also mixes institutions with functions (law courts and prisons versus the various functions that law courts and prisons fulfill, for example).

What is more, there is often crossover in terms of functions. Defense forces are viewed in most OECD countries as intended to protect countries from external threats; however, in many countries, the military plays a critical domestic role. Further, there may be other institutions that play a role in the security sector (or that are deemed to do so). These might include the authorities responsible for managing borders and border posts, the revenue authorities, and various independent and specialized law enforcement agencies, including those focused on combating corruption, policing money laundering, and enforcing traffic laws. In addition, some jurisdictions may impose noncustodial sentences that require convicted offenders to obtain alcohol or drug rehabilitation or engage in some form of public service. As they are public, the mandates and operations of these institutions are codified in law, while their resources are supplied from public revenues.

Conclusion

This introductory chapter has offered a brief overview of the role of security and justice institutions in a changing global context. It has further pointed to a practical application of the security-development nexus—specifically, the emerging practice of including the public finance dimension in the policy dialogue on security and justice. This approach is by no means the norm, but it has utility in addressing critical sector issues such as the affordability, effectiveness, efficiency, and accountability of services delivered.

A number of potential entry points are available for raising the public finance perspective, with the expectation that over time the security actors (ministries, departments, and agencies) will participate in the regular budgetary process. In many countries this path may be unlikely, however, and then the decision about whether to undertake a PER carries with it certain risks that need to be assessed and discussed with the government concerned.

In opening the dialogue among government stakeholders, most PER processes have followed some kind of road map (outlined in annex 1A); this chapter considered two important aspects of the PER process, context (political, security, and economic) and institutional architecture. Chapter 2 goes into more detail about economic management policy issues as well as the principles and methodologies relating to PFM. That discussion lays the foundation for the consideration of the three main subsystems of the security sector in the respective chapters on defense, policing, and criminal justice.

Staff from the World Bank as well as from the UN have applied this framework to an evolving body of PERs undertaken in the last 10 years in about 20 countries. These PERs have varied in context (from rich middle-income countries to those undergoing war-to-peace transitions), scope (from defense to justice), time frame (a few months to three years), cost (from one individual's time for a few staff weeks to a large team of experts and several hundred thousand dollars), and impact.

A number of lessons can be taken from this work.

Undertaking a process of engagement is critical to securing buy-in from the various stakeholders involved in the PER and hence to ensuring access to the right and most relevant counterparts and the best data. This process may involve relatively high up-front transaction costs, such as holding a number of "expert workshops" with invitations to people from around the country, the region, and beyond, in order to share experience and expertise on the sectors, the issues related to confidentiality, and the objectives and expected outcomes of the exercise.

It is important to obtain a relatively good idea of the scope of work early on, given that the issues concerning security and justice can be so enormous. A wide scope encompassing both the military and criminal justice sectors provides policy makers with an overview of all instruments available for delivering security and justice services. This wide scope is particularly important when examining critical questions about the balance between the military and the police, or about the criminal justice chain linking policing, judicial, and corrections functions. However, such a wide scope can be costly and take time, requiring the necessary expertise to cover all these subsectors. A narrow scope can be more manageable and produce more rapid results, though it risks missing links with other subsectors. Given the range of potential issues, an early agreement on the key questions that counterparts want help in answering is critical to defining the scope and ultimately the success of the PER.

The sharing of data can be challenging, particularly because much of the material may be sensitive, if not confidential, and in some contexts there may be very little data to share. What can help data exchange is a sharing of preliminary "stock-take notes" with key interlocutors that set out what is known; this can prompt a more intense sharing of information.

Finally, a PER should be seen as the start of a *process* of engagement on public finance and the security and justice sectors, and not a one-off event. Some issues might be dealt with relatively immediately, such as determining the fiscal gap on various options for the composition and structure of the sector. But addressing issues where adaptation and reform are sought, such as those relating to PFM and integration into the national budget process, will take time. It is to these issues that we turn in the next chapters.

Annex 1A: Key Steps for Undertaking a Security Sector PER

Table 1A.1   Key Steps for Undertaking a Security Sector Public Expenditure Review (PER)

Step	Key issues
Preliminary steps	
1. Government consultation and ownership	There must be traction within security sector ministries, departments, and agencies as well as finance ministries. Clarity should be achieved on the following issues: (i) scope—e.g., whether to include both economic policy and public financial management (PFM) issues, whether to include all security actors or focus on one subsector (defense or criminal justice); (ii) legal restrictions on freedom of information; (iii) the PER's focal points; and (iv) the existence of an explicit request for assistance (where international partners are involved).
2. Establishing a PER team	A government or international practitioner team—one with the skills needed to cover both the political/security and public financial aspects of the review—is selected to carry out the PER. The team should be given an appropriate time frame for the work and should be properly resourced.
Analysis of context	
3. Political security context	The team analyzes the political, security, social, and economic contexts, including the relevant international treaties (peace agreements, sanction regimes, etc.), participation in regional organizations, and key security threats, challenges, and patterns over time. This effort should include aspects of gender as well as analysis of underlying drivers of fragility if appropriate.
4. Macrofiscal context	The team describes and analyzes the various macrofiscal scenarios (overall government revenues versus expenditures, economic growth potential and risks) in the short, medium, and long term as well as the budgetary implications of the macrofiscal context for the different sectors (not only the security sector).

(Table continues on next page)

Table 1A.1   Key Steps for Undertaking a Security Sector Public Expenditure Review (PER) *(continued)*

Step	Key issues
Understanding the sector	
5. Institutional and functional mapping	The team examines the key institutions (state and nonstate) and their functions at all levels (central down to local), along with the key actors and their relationships and interests.
6. Strategic and policy objectives	The team identifies the sector or subsector national strategy, related policy papers, and key documents for the various subsectors and related legislation.
Analysis of the key economic policy and PFM issues	
7. Public expenditure policy	The team analyzes the situation of the security sector within the overall fiscal framework; the realism and affordability of the overall envelope; the efficiency of subsector allocations; the effectiveness and efficiency of operations; and the systems for strengthening civilian oversight, accountability, and governance.
8. Scenarios	In light of the macroeconomic framework, available resources, political security context, and security objectives, the team determines financing scenarios for the government going forward.
9. Public financial management	The team analyzes the systems and processes in place for budget credibility, comprehensive and transparent budgeting, policy-based budgeting, predictable and controlled budget execution, recording and reporting, and external scrutiny and audit.
Conclusions	
10. Options and recommendations	The team describes options and makes potential recommendations. A process should be devised to ensure incremental implementation of the recommendations and continuing buy-in from the various line ministries.

Annex 1B: Literature Review on the Nexus between Military Expenditure and Growth

In theory, military spending can affect economic growth in a variety of ways. On the positive side, studies have suggested that higher military spending increases economic growth through improved security, direct benefits (feeding, housing, and training), positive spin-offs (dual-use infrastructure, modernization, efficiency), and increased aggregate demand. On the negative side, studies have suggested that higher military spending decreases economic growth through misallocation of resources and crowding out of productive investments. However, as noted by Heo: "No political or economic theory surveyed is applicable to all the countries all the time. Because of the complicated nature of the relationship between military spending and economic growth, considerable disagreement still exists. Consequently, the impact of defense spending on economic growth is an empirical question rather than a theoretical one."[62]

Unfortunately, the empirical relationship between military spending and economic growth is ambiguous and inconclusive. Citing previous studies, Dunne[63] provided a useful overview of the mixed results to date: in a survey of literature on military spending growth, Chan[64] found a lack of consistency in the results, while a review by Ram of 29 studies[65] found little evidence of either a positive or negative effect of defense outlays on growth. Dunne[66] covered 54 studies and concluded that military spending had at best no effect on growth and was likely to have a negative effect. Smith[67] concluded that the large literature did not indicate any robust empirical regularity, positive or negative; he suggested there is a small negative effect in the long run, but one that requires considerably more sophistication to find. In a review of Africa, Smaldone[68] considered military spending relationships to be heterogeneous, elusive, and complex, but concluded that variations can be explained by intervening variables; the effects can be both positive and negative but are usually not pronounced, although the negative effects tend to be wider and deeper in Africa and to be most severe in countries experiencing legitimacy/security crises and economic/budgetary constraints. Dunne and Uye,[69] who surveyed 102 studies on the economic effects of military spending, reported that almost 39 percent of the cross-country studies and 35 percent of the case studies find a negative effect of military spending on growth, with only around 20 percent finding a positive effect for both types of studies. Models allowing for a demand side, and hence the possibility of crowding out investment, tend to find negative effects, unless there is some reallocation to other forms of government spending; those with only a supply side find positive, or positive but insignificant, effects. That the supply-side models find a positive effect is not a surprise, given that the models are inherently structured to find such a result (Brauer and Dunne[70]). Thus the fact that over 40 percent of the studies found unclear results could actually be interpreted as providing further evidence against there being a positive impact of military spending on the economy.

The early literature mainly applied cross-sectional analysis to estimate the average effect of military spending on economic growth. The results were mixed, suggesting there is no average effect or that it is highly conditional on sample, period, and model specification. Accordingly, some studies attempted to classify countries by economic or regional characteristics, and indeed found conditional effects. Although there was no consensus, the preponderance of evidence showed that increased military spending negatively affected (or at least did not encourage) economic growth during the Cold War period. This view was taken up by the development community, which generally advocated that countries reduce their military burden.

Benoit[71] was the first to apply econometric analysis to the growth effects of military spending, sparking a dense and still active literature. He applied correlation analysis to a 44-country sample (covering about three-quarters of the developing world's population), gross national product, and defense expenditures outside of China. The study investigated the effect of the defense burden on economic growth in the civilian (nondefense) sector.

Contrary to expectations, it found that when military dictatorships were excluded and the effects of foreign assistance and the investment rate were controlled for, the countries with the highest defense burdens typically grew the fastest. Reverse causality was discounted on grounds of theory: political and military leaders' threat perceptions were thought to determine the size of the military burden, not economic variables like income per capita or tax receipts. To explain these findings, Benoit hypothesized that a higher defense burden attracted bilateral economic assistance; that defense spending increased aggregate demand; and that the civilian economy might benefit from military expenditures on food, education and training, the construction of public works, and various scientific and technical services.

Frederiksen and Looney[72] posited that Benoit[73] had neglected countries' financial resource constraints. A severely resource-constrained country is likely to cut development projects to maintain defense spending. These cuts will inhibit growth directly and also lead to a simultaneous decrease in private investment. In contrast, relatively resource-unconstrained countries can afford growth-oriented projects while sustaining (or increasing) defense expenditures. To test their hypothesis, they divided countries into two groups—resource constrained and resource unconstrained—and used Lim's[74] specification of the military-expenditure-growth relationship. Their empirical results confirmed their hypothesis: military expenditure was found to have a positive and statistically significant effect for the unconstrained group, and a negative but not significant effect for the constrained group. In response, Ball[75] pointed to a number of methodological and interpretational problems shared by Frederiksen and Looney[76] and Benoit[77] (which were known to the former), including a lack of political analysis, failure to consider the effects of corruption, and a theoretical uncertainty about the impact of external resource flows.

Landau[78] (1993) hypothesized that the impact of military expenditures on growth was a combination of three effects: (i) increased security (positive), (ii) pressure for government efficiency (positive), and (iii) diversion of resources from productive investments (negative). Moreover, the net effect would be nonlinear: at low levels of military expenditure, security and efficiency effects would predominate and thus promote growth, but at higher levels "the negative resource-use impact will lead to lower growth." His regression analysis used a sample of 71 countries with a population of 2 million or more covering the time period 1969–1989. Control variables were selected on the basis of data availability, demonstrated influence on economic growth, and exogeneity with regard to military expenditure; they included the growth rate of developed countries, debt burden, average life expectancy, political condition variables (including the existence of civil or interstate war), and the share of fuel exports in national product. Growth variables were lagged to assess the long-term impact of the regressions and to control for endogeneity (because future growth could not explain past military expenditures). As expected, the analysis showed a nonlinear relationship, with statistically significant positive effects at low levels and statistically significant negative effects at higher levels. The results were not sensitive to changes in specification, but regional variation was observed that suggested the full sample results were being driven by Asia, the Middle East and North Africa, and southern Europe. The relationship did not hold for Latin America or Sub-Saharan Africa in isolation. As the study noted, Latin American countries did not generally face significant threats from one another, whereas in Sub-Saharan countries not at war, there was an observed pattern of low per capita output and small size. In both cases, the result was relatively low military spending by world standards—too low to adequately test the inverted-U relationship because higher levels of military spending were not observed.

Landau[79] also tested the specific channels through which military spending affected growth. His analysis found no evidence that security or diversion of resources was significant, but it did provide support for the efficiency argument. Finally, Landau also tested the economic impacts of military expenditure beyond growth, and found that a higher military burden "does not reduce expenditure on education, health, and infrastructure as shares of GDP in developing countries in general." Instead, as the military burden increases, overall government spending increases to keep social and infrastructure spending from declining as a share of GDP. Similarly, he found no significant negative impact of increased military burden on measures of inflation, education, investment, balance of trade, official transfers, or the overall balance of current and capital accounts.

Knight, Loayza, and Villanueva[80] determined that military spending was growth retarding because of its adverse effects on capital formation (crowding out) and resource allocation. Using a sample of 79 countries over the period 1971–1985 and averaging growth over five-year periods to lessen the effect of short-run fluctuations, they applied a standard neoclassical growth model to cross-sectional and panel data to simulate the links between military spending, productive investment, and the long-run growth of per capita capacity output. They then used the estimated model to simulate the long-run effects of the expected post–Cold War "peace dividend," which they defined as the percentage difference in real capacity output per capita resulting from a reduction in military spending compared to a baseline absent such reductions. For both the investment and the growth equations, the estimated coefficients were significant and of the expected sign. According to their analysis, the direct effect of higher military spending on growth was "unambiguously negative and large," and the indirect effect, through the impact of military spending on productive investment, was also statistically significant and negative. Their simulation indicated that if peace and associated military spending cuts could be sustained, they would result in substantial gains in capacity output over the long run.

Heo[81] (1999) used a three-sector production function where inputs of capital and labor produce output in the military, nonmilitary governmental, and private sectors. The analysis covered 80 countries over the period 1961–1990. He found that "approximately 60 percent of both developing and developed countries showed a negative elastic relationship between economic outputs and an increase in the defense burden." He noted that the difference with the Benoit study might be in research design (linear versus nonlinear) or in Benoit's inclusion of technology in the production function. Interestingly, an increase in nonmilitary government spending was found to be even worse for growth, with 70 percent of developing countries and 82 percent of developed countries showing negative elasticity with respect to an increase in nonmilitary government spending.

Early comments on the literature offered useful critiques of the theory and econometric techniques being used, but did little on their own to explain the growth effects of military spending. For example, Ball[82] broadly questioned the value of regression analysis in illuminating complex issues like armament and economic growth, and noted that rapid rates of economic growth do not imply equitable distribution of wealth, social equality, or self-sustaining economic growth. Ball questioned Benoit's (1978) definition of foreign assistance and Benoit's interpretation of the relationship between economic growth and military expenditure, and contended that the quantified relationship did not address the presumed growth-enhancing contributions made by military expenditure. In particular, Ball argued that by excluding foreign private investment, multilateral aid, and military assistance, Benoit "stack[ed] the deck in favor of the defense burden." Ball maintained more generally that the inflow of foreign resources cannot "automatically be equated with an increase in domestic investment rates or with increased economic growth," nor can the supposed benefits of military spending be presumed to operate simultaneously or effectively in individual countries without careful examination.

Meanwhile, advocacy in the development community generally reflected the negative empirical results. Most prominently, McNamara[83] proposed that worldwide defense expenditures be cut in half to roughly 2 percent of GDP. Writing in response to a radical change in Soviet policy under Gorbachev and the prospect of an enduring end to the Cold War, McNamara proposed a transition away from power politics and the use of national militaries as the ultimate guarantor of security to a system of collective security managed by the United Nations Security Council and led by the United States. He asserted that worldwide military expenditures would decrease by a quarter relative to 1989 levels due to the termination of ongoing conflicts and easing of tensions between the United States and the Soviet Union; he said expenditures could (and should) be reduced by half if arms-producing countries limited exports, budget-support policies considered the fungibility of resources, and a system of collective security guaranteed the territorial integrity of states. Although conceding that "the role of the military is the prerogative of each government," McNamara further advocated conditioning financial assistance on progress toward "optimal" levels of military expenditure in developing countries.

More recent contributions to the literature better assess heterogeneity among countries, regions, and income groups. Among them are case studies of individual countries, which provide econometric and political analysis to explain country-specific effects. Other studies apply recently developed and more advanced econometric techniques to determine the growth effects of military spending on finer subsets of countries, including regional and income groups.

Antonakis[84] asserted that the ambiguous evidence from prior cross-sectional studies was mainly due to "differences in the specificational choices and time periods examined and the different databases used across the various studies," a point made earlier by Ball[85] and others. Following Deger[86] and Kusi,[87] Antonakis noted that the effects of military expenditure cannot be generalized across all countries because of different—and dynamic—structural factors, namely in countries' natural environments and socioeconomic structures. He therefore advocated a case-study method using time-series data on individual countries. In this study, Antonakis analyzed Greece—which had the highest military burden among NATO and European Union countries in the post-war period—using a simultaneous-equation model "to capture the multiple conduits through which one variable affects another." He identified three mechanisms through which military expenditure can affect growth: (i) direct and indirect spin-offs (increased aggregate demand and modernization); (ii) reallocation of resources (trade-offs between military spending and investment); and (iii) the creation of new resources (increased profitability through inflation, which leads to higher investment and thus growth). He concluded that "the effect of military expenditure on economic growth in Greece is significantly negative," with a unit percent increase in the military burden reducing the output growth rate by 0.413 percent—comparable to the effect Deger[88] found for his sample of 50 countries.

In a similar vein, Caruso and Francesco[89] analyzed the growth effects of military spending in Italy. Specifically, they tested the effect of military expenditure on productivity, which was interpreted as a long-run determinant of economic growth. Their production function used labor and capital as inputs, augmented total-factor productivity by the military burden to assess its impact, and lagged the dependent variable to account for dynamic adjustment. When estimated, their model showed that the "military sector indeed imposes a real cost in terms of overall growth and productivity," and concluded that "if military expenditures are substituted by civilian expenditures, Italian overall productivity would be expected to improve."

For a sample of 170 countries over the period 1988–2006, Dunne[90] used a fixed-effects model to test the effect of military spending on capital accumulation and thus economic growth. For the sample as a whole, his model showed a "clear negative effect of the change in military burden, but not the lagged level," suggesting "evidence of short run negative effects of military spending, but not long run." Estimates for the subsample of nondeveloped (low- and middle-income) countries were remarkably similar. Long-run negative effects were significant only for low-income countries. According to his analysis, this finding could be caused by the level of conflict—particularly civil conflict—in poor countries, which would be most prevalent in the Sub-Saharan Africa region. However, estimates for "major conflict" countries were not significant, although this could be due to the small subsample of eight countries. He concluded that conflict could be an important determinant (fundamental or intervening), but that further research was necessary to assess its impact on the growth effects of military spending.

Finally, Chang et al.[91] used a newly developed bootstrap approach that incorporates time-series and cross-sectional dimensions to assess the impact of military expenditure on growth for China and the G7 countries for the period 1988–2010. This approach allowed them to capture cross-country interrelations (through globalization, international trade, and financial integration) and heterogeneity between countries in economic and institutional terms. Empirical tests confirmed dependency and heterogeneity; this result "implies that a shock occur[ing] in a country is quickly transmitted to other countries," but also that "the direction [of] causal linkages among the variables of interest may differ across countries." This finding confirms the intuition of Antonakis[92] and others that the effect of military spending on growth is country specific, but suggests that some common patterns might be identified. Indeed, according to the analysis, "like" countries had similar outcomes: military spending had a negative effect on economic growth in the United Kingdom and Canada; military spending had no discernible effect on economic growth in France, Germany, and Italy; there was a bidirectional (feedback) relationship between military spending and economic growth in Japan and the United States (showing a negative reinforcement in both directions for Japan and mixed effects for the United States, with increased expenditures negatively affecting growth but increased growth positively affecting military expenditures); and one-way (reversed) causality in China, where higher economic growth resulted in higher military expenditures.

Notes

1. World Bank, *Improving Public Financial Management in the Security Sector*, vol. 5 of *Afghanistan: Managing Public Finances for Development* (Washington, DC: World Bank, 2005).
2. Currently the Afghanistan National Defense and Security Forces cost international partners about $5.1 billion per year. See Franz-Stefan Gady, "Afghanistan Won't Be Able to Pay for Its Military Until 2024 (At Least)," *The Diplomat*, February 4, 2016.
3. World Bank, "Crime and Violence in Central America: A Development Challenge" (World Bank, Washington, DC, 2011).

4. "The Gangs that Cost 16% of GDP," *The Economist*, May 21, 2016.

5. Congressional Research Service, "Central America Regional Security Initiative: Background and Policy Issues for Congress" (Congressional Research Service, Washington, DC, December 2015).

6. John Mueller and Mark Stewart, *Terror, Security, and Money: Balancing the Risks, Benefits, and Costs of Homeland Security* (New York: Oxford University Press, 2011).

7. John Mueller and Mark Stewart, "Fear and Budgets: Scrutinising the Costs of Counterterrorism," *Canberra Times*, March 2, 2015.

8. The focus of the book is on the security sector as defined by the Organisation for Economic Co-operation and Development (OECD) and the United Nations, which includes the military and criminal justice institutions such as the police, prosecutors, and courts working under the criminal or penal laws of a country; it does not include wider justice or legal institutions.

9. World Bank, *World Development Report 2011: Conflict, Security, and Development* (Washington, DC: World Bank, 2011); and OECD, *Violence and Fragility: States of Fragility Report 2016* (Paris: OECD, forthcoming).

10. Paul Jackson, ed., *Handbook of International Security and Development* (Northampton, MA: Edward Elgar Publishing, 2015).

11. Stephen Pinker, *The Better Angels of Our Nature: Why Violence Has Declined* (New York: Penguin, 2011).

12. Battle deaths increased from 56,000 in 63 conflicts in 2008 to 180,000 in 42 conflicts in 2014. International Institute for Strategic Studies (IISS), *Armed Conflict Survey* (Routledge, 2015).

13. On average 508,000 died violently every year in the period 2007–2012, the majority outside conflict zones. Geneva Declaration Secretariat, *The Global Burden of Armed Violence 2015: Every Body Counts* (Cambridge, U.K.: Cambridge University Press, 2015).

14. UN Refugee Agency (UNHCR), "World at War: Global Trends in Forced Displacement" (UNHCR, 2014).

15. Violence containment spending is defined as economic activity that is related to the consequences or prevention of violence where the violence is directed against people or property. IEP, "The Economic Cost of Violence Containment (IEP, 2015), 4, http://economicsandpeace.org/wp-content/uploads/2015/06/The-Economic-Cost-of-Violence-Containment.pdf.

16. Ibid.

17. See for example Robert S. McNamara, "Reducing Military Expenditures in the Third World," *Finance and Development* 28, no. 3 (September 1991).

18. Deepa Narayan, Raj Patel, Kai Schafft, Anne Rademacher, and Sarah Koch-Schulte, *Can Anyone Hear Us? Voices from 47 Countries*, vol. 1 of *Voices of the Poor* (Washington, DC: World Bank, 1999).

19. UN Secretary General, *In Larger Freedom: Towards Development, Security and Human Rights for All* (United Nations, A/59/2005, March 21, 2005).

20. World Bank, *World Development Report 2011: Conflict, Security, and Development* (Washington, DC: World Bank, 2011).

21. For every three years that a country is affected by major violence (battle deaths or excess deaths from homicide equivalent to a major war), poverty reduction lags by 2.7 percentage points. Ibid., based on 2008 poverty data in Chen Shaohua, Martin Ravallion, and Prem Sangraula, "Dollar a Day Revisited," *World Bank Economic Review* 23, no. 2 (2008): 163–84. Data are available on POVCALNET, http://iresearch .worldbank.org.

22. See William Byrd and Stephane Guimbert, "Public Finance, Security, and Development: A Framework and an Application to Afghanistan" (Policy Research Working Paper, World Bank, Washington, DC, 2009).

23. See for example John Samuel Fitch, *The Armed Forces and Democracy in Latin America* (Baltimore: Johns Hopkins University Press, 1998); and Anton Bebler, *Civil-Military Relations in Post-Communist States: Central and Eastern Europe in Transition* (Abingdon, U.K.: Routledge, 1997).

24. See for example Nicole Ball, "Spreading Good Practices in SSR: Policy Options for the British Government" (Saferworld, 1998).

25. Significant milestones include OECD, "The 2001 DAC Guidelines: Helping Prevent Violent Conflict" (OECD, Paris, 2001); UN, *Human Development Report 2002: Deepening Democracy in a Fragmented World* (New York: Oxford University Press, 2002); the revised 2004 OECD guidelines, published in "Security System Reform and Governance: Policy and Good Practice" (OECD, Paris, 2004); the inclusion of several SSR elements in the definition of official development assistance in 2005; and the publication of the *OECD DAC Handbook on Security System Reform: Supporting Security and Justice* (Paris: OECD Publishing, 2007).

26. UN Secretary General, *Securing Peace and Development: The Role of the United Nations in Supporting Security Sector Reform* (United Nations, A/62/659; S/2008/39, January 2008).

27. See for example UN Secretary General, *Civilian Capacity in the Aftermath of Conflict* (United Nations, A/67/312–S/2012/645, August 2012); UN Secretary General, *Peacebuilding in the Immediate Aftermath of Conflict* (United Nations, A/63/881-S/2009/304, June 2009).

28. United Nations SSR Task Force, "Security Sector Reform Integrated Technical Guidance Notes" (United Nations, New York, 2012), http:// unssr.unlb.org/Portals/UNSSR/UN%20Integrated%20Technical%20 Guidance%20Notes%20on%20SSR.PDF.

29. UN Secretary General, *Securing States and Societies: Strengthening the United Nations Comprehensive Support to Security Sector Reform* (United Nations, A/67/970–S/2013/480, August 2013).

30. These organizations include (among others) the Geneva Centre for the Democratic Control of Armed Forces and its attached International Security Sector Advisory Team (ISSAT), the Centre for Governance and Security, and the African Security Sector Network.

31. See for example Louise Andersen, "Security Sector Reform and the Dilemmas of Liberal Peacebuilding" (DIIS Working Paper 2011:31, Danish Institute for International Studies, Copenhagen, 2011); and Paul Jackson, "Security Sector Reform and State Building," *Third World Quarterly* 32, no. 10 (2011).

32. Nicole Ball and Jay Kayode Fayemi, eds., *Security Sector Governance in Africa: A Handbook* (Centre for Democracy and Development, 2003).

33. For example, the capacity-based budgeting approach used by some advanced-country defense ministries is an advanced form of program and performance budgeting, with object metrics of "capacility." This approach might be used to inform other sectors, but is often "secured" within the defense sector.

34. OECD, *States of Fragility 2015: Meeting Post-2015 Ambitions* (Paris: OECD Publishing, 2015), doi:10.1787/9789264227699-en. The quotation is on p. 74.

35. African Development Bank, Asian Development Bank, European Bank for Reconstruction and Development, European Investment Bank, Inter-American Development Bank, International Monetary Fund, and World Bank Group, "From Billions to Trillions: Transforming Development Finance," April 2, 2015, 7, http://siteresources.worldbank .org/DEVCOMMINT/Documentation/23659446/DC2015-0002(E) FinancingforDevelopment.pdf. Emphasis is added.

36. Richard Allen, Salvatore Schiavo-Campo, and Thomas Columkill Garrity, *Assessing and Reforming Public Financial Management: A New Approach* (Washington, DC: World Bank, 2004).

37. International Monetary Fund and World Bank, "Code of Good Practices on Transparency in Monetary and Financial Policies, Declaration of Principles" (IMF, September 1999).

38. PEFA, "Framework for Assessing Public Financial Management" (PEFA Secretariat, Washington, DC, 2016), http://www.pefa.org/en /content/pefa-2016-framework.

39. The World Bank and the International Monetary Fund have also developed a number of instruments for assessing and improving budget planning, implementation, and control. These include (i) PERs, (ii) Country Procurement Assessment Reviews and the OECD DAC MAPS (Methodology for Assessing Procurement Systems), (iii) Medium-Term Expenditure Frameworks, (iv) Review of the Observance of Standards and Codes, (v) Public Expenditure Tracking Surveys, (vi) Institutional and Governance Reviews, and (vii) Functional Reviews. Relevant materials include Allen Schick, *A Contemporary Approach to Public Expenditure Management*

(Washington, DC: World Bank, 1998); Richard Allen and Daniel Tommasi, *Managing Public Expenditure: A Reference Book for Transition Countries* (Paris: OECD, 2001); and World Bank, "Tools for Evaluating Public Expenditures: Benefit Incidence Analysis" (World Bank, Washington, DC, 2010), http://wbi.worldbank.org /boost/tools-resources/topics/sector-analysis/benefit-incidence-analysis.

40. Michal Brzoska, "World Military Expenditures," in *Handbook of Defence Economics*, ed. Keith Hartley and Todd Sandler (Amsterdam: Elsevier, 1995); and Stockholm International Peace Research Institute Military Expenditures Database, http://www.sipri.org/research /armaments/milex/milex_database.

41. William Byrd, "The Financial Dimension of Security Sector Reform," in *The Future of Security Sector Reform*, ed. Mark Sedra (Waterloo, Ontario: Centre for International Governance Innovation, 2010), 305.

42. OECD, "Security System Reform and Governance" (OECD, Paris, 2004), 14.

43. Laurie Nathan, ed., "Local Ownership of Security Sector Reform: A Guide for Donors" (U.K. Global Conflict Pool, 2007), http://www .lse.ac.uk/internationalDevelopment/research/crisisStates/download /others/SSRReformNathan2007.pdf.

44. See for example Daniel Brumberg and Hesham Sallam, "The Politics of SSR in Egypt" (U.S. Institute of Peace, Washington, DC, 2012).

45. See for example Paul D. Williams, ed., *Security Studies: An Introduction* (Abingdon, U.K.: Routledge, 2008); and Christopher H. Hughes and Lai Yu Meng, *Security Studies: A Reader* (Abingdon, U.K.: Routledge, 2011).

46. Barry Buzan, *People, States and Fear* (Harvester Wheatsheaf, 1991); cited in Paul D. Williams, ed., *Security Studies: An Introduction* (Abingdon, U.K.: Routledge, 2008), 2.

47. Arnold Wolfers, "National Security as an Ambiguous Symbol," in *Discord and Collaboration* (Baltimore: Johns Hopkins University Press, 1962).

48. UNDP, *Human Development Report* (New York: Oxford University Press, 1994).

49. World Bank, *World Development Report 2011: Conflict, Security, and Development* (Washington, DC: World Bank, 2011), 116.

50. Patti Petesch, "How Communities Manage Risks of Crime and Violence" (*World Development Report 2014* background paper, World Bank, Washington, DC, 2014).

51. See for example Robert S. McNamara, "The Post–Cold War World: Implications for Military Expenditure in the Developing Countries," in *Proceedings of the World Bank Annual Conference on Development Economics 1991*, ed. Lawrence H. Summers and Shekhar Shah (Washington, DC: World Bank, 1992), 95–125.

52. Hans Born and Albrecht Schnabel, eds. *Security Sector Reform in Challenging Environments* (Geneva Centre for the Democratic Control of Armed Forces, 2009).

53. See Megan Bastick and Kristin Valasek, eds., "Gender and Security Sector Reform Toolkit" (Geneva Centre for the Democratic Control of Armed Forces, 2008); and Jennifer Erin Salahub and Krista Nerland, "Just Add Gender? Challenges to Meaningful Integration of Gender in SSR Policy and Practice," in *The Future of Security Sector Reform*, ed. Mark Sedra (Waterloo, Ontario: Centre for International Governance Innovation, 2010), 263–80.

54. See for example Olara A. Otunnu, "'Special Comment' on Children and Security," *Disarmament Forum* 3 (2002).

55. Inter-Parliamentary Union and UN Division for the Advancement of Women, "Women in Politics, 2008," http://www.ipu.org/pdf/publications/wmnmap08_en.pdf.

56. See for example the resources of the UN Security Sector Reform Task Force (www.unssr.unlb.org/) and those of the International Security Sector Advisory Team (www.issat.dcaf.ch).

57. The OECD speaks of the "security system" rather than the "security sector."

58. A. Adeyemi, "Crime and Development in Africa: A Case Study of Nigeria," in *Essays on Crime and Development*, ed. U. Zvekic (UN Interregional Crime and Justice Research Institute, 1990).

59. OECD, *OECD DAC Handbook on Security System Reform: Supporting Security and Justice* (Paris: OECD Publishing, 2007).

60. United Nations Statistics Division, "COFOG (Classification of the Functions of Government)," http://unstats.un.org/unsd/cr/registry/regcst.asp?Cl=4.

61. The UN classification is the basis of the IMF's government finance statistics (GFS) classification system. According to the IMF's *Government Finance Statistics Manual* (Washington, DC: IMF, 2001), "The GFS analytic framework can be used to analyze the operations of a specific level of government and transactions between levels of government as well as the entire general government or public sector" (2).

62. U. Heo, "Defense Spending and Economic Growth in South Korea: The Indirect Link," *Journal of Peace Research* 36, no. 6 (1999): 699–708.

63. J. Paul Dunne, "Military Spending, Growth, Development and Conflict" (University of the West of England and University of Cape Town, 2011).

64. Steve Chan, "Military Expenditures and Economic Performance," in *World Military Expenditures and Arms Transfers* (Washington, DC: U.S. Arms Control and Disarmament Agency, 1987).

65. Rati Ram, "Defense Expenditures and Economic Growth," in *Handbook of Defense Economics*, ed. T. Sandler and K. Hartley (Amsterdam: Elsevier, 1995).

66. J. Paul Dunne, "The Economic Effects of Military Spending in LDCs: A Survey," in *The Peace Dividend*, ed. N. P. Gleditsch et al. (Amsterdam: Elsevier, 1996).

67. R. P. Smith, "Defense Expenditure and Economic Growth," in *Making Peace Pay: A Bibliography on Disarmament and Conversion*, ed. N. P. Gleditsch et al. (Claremont, CA: Regina Books, 2000).

68. Joseph Smaldone, "African Military Spending: Defence versus Development?" *African Security Review* 15, no. 4 (2006): 17–32.

69. J. Paul Dunne and Mehmet Uye, "Military Spending and Development," in *The Global Arms Trade: A Handbook*, ed. Andrew T. H. Tan (London: Routledge, 2010).

70. J. Brauer and J. P. Dunne, *Arming the South: The Economics of Military Expenditure, Arms Production and Arms Trade in Developing Countries* (New York: Palgrave Macmillan, 2002).

71. Emile Benoit, "Growth and Defense in Developing Countries," *Economic Development and Cultural Change* 26, no. 2 (January 1978): 271–80.

72. P. C. Frederiksen and Robert E. Looney, "Another Look at the Defense Spending and Development Hypothesis," *Defense Analysis* 1, no. 3 (1985): 205–10.

73. Emile Benoit, "Growth and Defense in Developing Countries," *Economic Development and Cultural Change* 26, no. 2 (January 1978): 271–80.

74. David Lim, "Another Look at Growth and Defense in Less Developed Countries," *Economic Development and Cultural Change* 31, no. 2 (January 1983): 377–84.

75. Nicole Ball, "Defense and Development: A Critique of the Benoit Study," *Economic Development and Cultural Change* 31, no. 3 (April 1983): 507–24.

76. P. C. Frederiksen and Robert E. Looney, "Another Look at the Defense Spending and Development Hypothesis," *Defense Analysis* 1, no. 3 (1985): 205–10.

77. Emile Benoit, "Growth and Defense in Developing Countries," *Economic Development and Cultural Change* 26, no. 2 (January 1978): 271–80.

78. Daniel Landau, "The Economic Impact of Military Expenditures" (Policy Research Working Paper WPS 1138, World Bank, Washington, DC, 1993).

79. Ibid.

80. Malcolm Knight, Norman Loayza, and Delano Villanueva, "The Peace Dividend: Military Spending Cuts and Economic Growth" (Policy Research Working Paper 1577, World Bank, Washington, DC, 1996).

81. U. Heo, "Defense Spending and Economic Growth in South Korea: The Indirect Link," *Journal of Peace Research* 36, no. 6 (November 1999): 699–708.

82. Nicole Ball, "Defense and Development: A Critique of the Benoit Study," *Economic Development and Cultural Change* 31, no. 3 (April 1983): 507–24.

83. Robert S. McNamara, "The Post–Cold War World: Implications for Military Expenditure in the Developing Countries," in *Proceedings of the World Bank Annual Conference on Development Economics 1991*, ed. Lawrence H. Summers and Shekhar Shah (Washington, DC: World Bank, 1992), 95–125.

84. Nicholas Antonakis, "Military Expenditure and Economic Growth in Greece, 1960–1990," *Journal of Peace Research* 34, no. 1 (1997): 89–100.

85. Nicole Ball, "Defense and Development: A Critique of the Benoit Study," *Economic Development and Cultural Change* 31, no. 3 (April 1983): 507–24.

86. Saadet Deger, *Military Expenditure in Third World Countries: The Economic Effects* (London and Boston: Routledge & Kegan Paul, 1986).

87. N. K. Kusi, "Economic Growth and Defense Spending in Developing Countries: A Causal Analysis," *Journal of Conflict Resolution* 38, no. 1 (March 1994): 152–59.

88. Saadet Deger, *Military Expenditure in Third World Countries: The Economic Effects* (London and Boston: Routledge & Kegan Paul, 1986).

89. Raul Caruso and Addesa Francesco, "Country Survey: Military Expenditure and Its Impact on Productivity in Italy, 1988–2008," *Defence and Peace Economics* 23, no. 5 (2012): 471–84.

90. J. Paul Dunne, "Military Spending, Growth, Development, and Conflict," *Defence and Peace Economics* 23, no. 6 (2012): 549–57.

91. Tsangyao Chang, Chien-Chiang Lee, Ken Hung, and Kuo-Hao Lee, "Does Military Spending Really Matter for Economic Growth in China and G7 Countries: The Roles of Dependency and Heterogeneity," *Defence and Peace Economics* 25, no. 2 (2014): 177–91.

92. Nicholas Antonakis, "Military Expenditure and Economic Growth in Greece, 1960–1990," *Journal of Peace Research* 34, no. 1 (1997): 89–100.

References

Adejumobi, Said, and Mesfin Binega. 2006. "Ethiopia." In *Budgeting for the Military Sector in Africa*, edited by W. Omitoogun and E. Hutchful, 48–71. Oxford, U.K.: Oxford University Press.

Adeyemi, A. 1990. "Crime and Development in Africa: A Case Study of Nigeria." In *Essays on Crime and Development*, edited by U. Zvekic, UN Interregional Crime and Justice Research Institute.

African Development Bank, Asian Development Bank, European Bank for Reconstruction and Development, European Investment Bank, Inter-American Development Bank, International Monetary Fund, and World Bank Group. 2015. "From Billions to Trillions: Transforming Development Finance." April 2, 7, http://siteresources.worldbank.org/DEVCOMMINT /Documentation/23659446/DC2015-0002(E)FinancingforDevelopment.pdf.

Allen, Richard, Salvatore Schiavo-Campo, and Thomas Columkill Garrity. 2004. *Assessing and Reforming Public Financial Management: A New Approach*. Washington, DC: World Bank.

Allen, Richard, and Daniel Tommasi. 2001. *Managing Public Expenditure: A Reference Book for Transition Countries*. Paris: OECD.

Andersen, Louise. 2011. "Security Sector Reform and the Dilemmas of Liberal Peacebuilding." DIIS Working Paper 2011:31, Danish Institute for International Studies, Copenhagen.

Antonakis, Nicholas. 1997. "Military Expenditure and Economic Growth in Greece, 1960–1990." *Journal of Peace Research* 34 (1): 89–100.

Baker, B. 2010. "The Future Is Non-State." In *The Future of Security Sector Reform*, edited by M. Sedra, 208–28. Waterloo, Ontario: Centre for International Governance Innovation.

Ball, Nicole. 1983. "Defense and Development: A Critique of the Benoit Study." *Economic Development and Cultural Change* 31 (3): 507–24.

———. 1998. "Spreading Good Practices in SSR: Policy Options for the British Government." Saferworld. http://www.ciponline.org/images/uploads/publications/Spreading_Good_Practices_in_SSR_NB_Saferworld_1998.pdf.

Ball, Nicole, and Jay Kayode Fayemi, eds. 2003. *Security Sector Governance in Africa: A Handbook*. Centre for Democracy and Development.

Ball, Nicole, and Malcolm Holmes. 2002. "Integrating Defense into Public Expenditure Work." U.K. Department for International Development, January 11. http://www.gsdrc.org/document-library/integrating-defence-into-public-expenditure-work/.

Bastick, Megan, and Kristin Valasek, eds. 2008. "Gender and Security Sector Reform Toolkit." Geneva Centre for the Democratic Control of Armed Forces.

Bebler, Anton. 1997. *Civil-Military Relations in Post-Communist States: Central and Eastern Europe in Transition*. Abingdon, U.K.: Routledge.

Benoit, Emile. 1978. "Growth and Defense in Developing Countries." *Economic Development and Cultural Change* 26 (2): 271–80.

Born, Hans, and Albrecht Schnabel, eds. 2009. *Security Sector Reform in Challenging Environments*. Geneva Centre for the Democratic Control of Armed Forces.

Brauer, J., and J. P. Dunne. 2002. *Arming the South: The Economics of Military Expenditure, Arms Production and Arms Trade in Developing Countries*. New York: Palgrave Macmillan.

Brumberg, Daniel, and Hesham Sallam. 2012. "The Politics of SSR in Egypt." U.S. Institute of Peace, Washington, DC.

Brzoska, Michal. 1995. "World Military Expenditures." In *Handbook of Defence Economics*, edited by Keith Hartley and Todd Sandler. Amsterdam: Elsevier.

Buzan, Barry. 1991. *People, States and Fear*. Harvester Wheatsheaf.

Byrd, William. 2010. "The Financial Dimensions of Security Sector Reform." In *The Future of Security Sector Reform*, edited by Mark Sedra, 305. Waterloo, Ontario: Centre for International Governance Innovation.

Byrd, William, and Stephane Guimbert. 2009. "Public Finance, Security, and Development: A Framework and an Application to Afghanistan." Policy Research Working Paper, World Bank, Washington, DC.

Caruso, Raul, and Addesa Francesco. 2012. "Country Survey: Military Expenditure and Its Impact on Productivity in Italy, 1988–2008." *Defence and Peace Economics* 23 (5): 471–84.

Chan, Steve. 1987. "Military Expenditures and Economic Performance." In *World Military Expenditures and Arms Transfers*. Washington, DC: U.S. Arms Control and Disarmament Agency.

Chang, Tsangyao, Chien-Chiang Lee, Ken Hung, and Kuo-Hao Lee. 2014. "Does Military Spending Really Matter for Economic Growth in China and G7 Countries: The Roles of Dependency and Heterogeneity." *Defence and Peace Economics* 25 (2): 177–91.

Congressional Research Service. 2015. "Central America Regional Security Initiative: Background and Policy Issues for Congress." Congressional Research Service, Washington, DC, December.

Deger, Saadet. 1986. *Military Expenditure in Third World Countries: The Economic Effects*. London and Boston: Routledge & Kegan Paul.

Dunne, J. Paul. 1996. "The Economic Effects of Military Spending in LDCs: A Survey." In *The Peace Dividend*, edited by N. P. Gleditsch, O. Bjerkholt, A. Cappelen, R. Smith, and J. P. Dunne. Amsterdam: Elsevier.

———. 2011. "Military Spending, Growth, Development and Conflict." University of the West of England and University of Cape Town.

———. 2012. "Military Spending, Growth, Development, and Conflict." *Defence and Peace Economics* 23 (6): 549–57.

Dunne, J. Paul, and Mehmet Uye. 2010. "Military Spending and Development." In *The Global Arms Trade: A Handbook*, edited by Andrew T. H. Tan. London: Routledge.

Economist. 2016. "The Gangs that Cost 16% of GDP." May 21.

Fitch, John Samuel. 1998. *The Armed Forces and Democracy in Latin America*. Baltimore: Johns Hopkins University Press.

Frederiksen, P. C., and Robert E. Looney. 1985. "Another Look at the Defense Spending and Development Hypothesis." *Defense Analysis* 1 (3): 205–10.

Gady, Franz-Stefan. 2016. "Afghanistan Won't Be Able to Pay for Its Military Until 2024 (At Least)." *The Diplomat*, February 4.

Geneva Declaration Secretariat. 2015. *The Global Burden of Armed Violence 2015: Every Body Counts*. Cambridge, U.K.: Cambridge University Press.

Heo, U. 1999. "Defense Spending and Economic Growth in South Korea: The Indirect Link." *Journal of Peace Research* 36 (6): 699–708.

Hughes, Christopher H., and Lai Yu Meng. 2011. *Security Studies: A Reader*. Abingdon, U.K.: Routledge.

IEP (Institute for Economics and Peace). 2015. "The Economic Cost of Violence Containment." http://economicsandpeace.org/wp-content/uploads/2015/06/The-Economic-Cost-of-Violence-Containment.pdf.

IISS (International Institute for Strategic Studies). 2015. *Armed Conflict Survey*. Routledge.

IMF (International Monetary Fund). 2001. *Government Finance Statistics Manual* (Washington, DC: IMF), http://www.imf.org/external/np/sta/gfsm/index.htm.

———. 2014. *Government Finance Statistics Manual 2014*. Washington, DC: IMF. http://www.imf.org/external/np/sta/gfsm/index.htm.

IMF (International Monetary Fund) and World Bank. 1999. "Code of Good Practices on Transparency in Monetary and Financial Policies, Declaration of Principles" (IMF, September).

Jackson, Paul. 2011. "Security Sector Reform and State Building." *Third World Quarterly* 32 (10): 803–22.

———, ed. 2015. *Handbook of International Security and Development*. Northampton, MA: Edward Elgar Publishing.

Jacquand, Mark, and Shelley Ranii. 2014. "UN Development System Risk Management in Fragile States." New York University Center on International Cooperation, New York.

Knight, Malcolm, Norman Loayza, and Delano Villanueva. 1996. "The Peace Dividend: Military Spending Cuts and Economic Growth." Policy Research Working Paper 1577, World Bank, Washington, DC.

Kusi, N. K. 1994. "Economic Growth and Defense Spending in Developing Countries: A Causal Analysis." *Journal of Conflict Resolution* 38 (1): 152–59.

Landau, Daniel. 1993. "The Economic Impact of Military Expenditures." Policy Research Working Paper WPS 1138, World Bank, Washington, DC.

Lim, David. 1983. "Another Look at Growth and Defense in Less Developed Countries." *Economic Development and Cultural Change* 31 (2): 377–84.

Luckham, Robin, and Tom Kirk. 2012. "Security in Hybrid Political Contexts: An End-User Approach." JSRP Paper 2, Justice and Security Research Program, London.

McNamara, Robert S. 1991. "Reducing Military Expenditures in the Third World." *Finance and Development* 28 (3): 26–30.

———. 1992. "The Post–Cold War World: Implications for Military Expenditure in the Developing Countries." In *Proceedings of the World Bank Annual Conference on Development Economics 1991*, edited by Lawrence H. Summers and Shekhar Shah, 95–125. Washington, DC: World Bank.

Mueller, John, and Mark Stewart. 2011. *Terror, Security, and Money: Balancing the Risks, Benefits, and Costs of Homeland Security*. New York: Oxford University Press.

————. 2015. "Fear and Budgets: Scrutinising the Costs of Counterterrorism." *Canberra Times*, March 2.

Narayan, Deepa, Raj Patel, Kai Schafft, Anne Rademacher, and Sarah Koch-Schulte. 1999. *Can Anyone Hear Us? Voices from 47 Countries,* vol. 1 of *Voices of the Poor*, Washington, DC: World Bank.

Nathan, Laurie, ed. 2007. "Local Ownership of Security Sector Reform: A Guide for Donors." U.K. Global Conflict Pool. http://www.lse.ac.uk /internationalDevelopment/research/crisisStates/download/others /SSRReformNathan2007.pdf.

OECD (Organisation for Economic Co-operation and Development). 2001. "The 2001 DAC Guidelines: Helping Prevent Violent Conflict." OECD, Paris.

————. 2004. "Security System Reform and Governance: Policy and Good Practice." OECD, Paris.

————. 2007. *OECD DAC Handbook on Security System Reform: Supporting Security and Justice.* Paris: OECD Publishing.

————. 2015. *States of Fragility 2015: Meeting Post-2015 Ambitions.* Paris: OECD Publishing. doi:10.1787/9789264227699-en.

————. Forthcoming. *Violence and Fragility: States of Fragility Report 2016.* Paris: OECD.

Otunnu, Olara A. 2002. "'Special Comment' on Children and Security." *Disarmament Forum* 3.

PEFA (Public Expenditure and Financial Accountability). 2016. "Framework for Assessing Public Financial Management." PEFA Secretariat, Washington, DC, http://www.pefa.org/en/content/pefa -2016-framework.

Petesch, Patti. 2014. "How Communities Manage Risks of Crime and Violence." *World Development Report 2014* background paper, World Bank, Washington, DC.

Pinker, Stephen. 2011. *The Better Angels of Our Nature: Why Violence Has Declined.* New York: Penguin.

Ram, Rati. 1995. "Defense Expenditures and Economic Growth." In *Handbook of Defense Economics*, edited by T. Sandler and K. Hartley. Amsterdam: Elsevier.

Salahub, Jennifer Erin, and Krista Nerland. 2010. "Just Add Gender? Challenges to Meaningful Integration of Gender in SSR Policy and Practice." In *The Future of Security Sector Reform*, edited by Mark Sedra, 263–80. Waterloo, Ontario: Centre for International Governance Innovation.

Schick, Allen. 1998. *A Contemporary Approach to Public Expenditure Management.* Washington, DC: World Bank.

Shaohua, Chen, Martin Ravallion, and Prem Sangraula. 2008. "Dollar a Day Revisited." *World Bank Economic Review* 23 (2): 163–84.

Smaldone, Joseph. 2006. "African Military Spending: Defence versus Development?" *African Security Review* 15 (4): 17–32.

Smith, R. P. 2000. "Defense Expenditure and Economic Growth." In *Making Peace Pay: A Bibliography on Disarmament and Conversion*, edited by N. P. Gleditsch, G. Lindgren, and N. Mouhleb. Claremont, CA: Regina Books.

Stockholm International Peace Research Institute Military Expenditures Database. http://www.sipri.org/research/armaments/milex/milex_database.

UN (United Nations). 2002. *Human Development Report 2002: Deepening Democracy in a Fragmented World*. New York: Oxford University Press.

UNDP (United Nations Development Programme). 1994. *Human Development Report*. New York: Oxford University Press.

UNHCR (UN Refugee Agency). 2014. "World at War: Global Trends in Forced Displacement." UNHCR.

United Nations SSR Task Force. 2012. "Security Sector Reform Integrated Technical Guidance Notes." United Nations, New York. http://unssr.unlb .org/Portals/UNSSR/UN%20Integrated%20Technical%20Guidance %20Notes%20on%20SSR.PDF.

United Nations Statistics Division. "COFOG (Classification of the Functions of Government)." http://unstats.un.org/unsd/cr/registry /regcst.asp?Cl=4.

UNSG (United Nations Secretary General). 2005. *In Larger Freedom: Towards Development, Security and Human Rights for All*. United Nations, A/59/2005, March 21.

———. 2008. *Securing Peace and Development: The Role of the United Nations in Supporting Security Sector Reform*. United Nations, A/62/659; S/2008/39, January.

———. 2009. *Peacebuilding in the Immediate Aftermath of Conflict*. United Nations, A/63/881-S/2009/304, June.

———. 2012. *Civilian Capacity in the Aftermath of Conflict*. United Nations, A/67/312–S/2012/645, August.

———. 2013. *Securing States and Societies: Strengthening the United Nations Comprehensive Support to Security Sector Reform*. United Nations, A/67/970–S/2013/480, August.

Williams, Paul D., ed. 2008. *Security Studies: An Introduction*. Abingdon, U.K.: Routledge.

Wolfers, Arnold. 1962. "National Security as an Ambiguous Symbol." In *Discord and Collaboration*. Baltimore: Johns Hopkins University Press.

World Bank. 2005. *Improving Public Financial Management in the Security Sector*. Vol. 5 of *Afghanistan: Managing Public Finances for Development*. Washington, DC: World Bank.

————. 2010. "Tools for Evaluating Public Expenditures: Benefit Incidence Analysis." World Bank, Washington, DC. http://wbi.worldbank.org /boost/tools-resources/topics/sector-analysis/benefit-incidence-analysis.

————. 2011a. "Crime and Violence in Central America: A Development Challenge." World Bank, Washington, DC.

————. 2011b. *World Development Report 2011: Conflict, Security, and Development.* Washington, DC: World Bank.

CHAPTER 2

The Basics of Public Finance and the Security Sector

Introduction

This chapter brings together the two perspectives that lie at the core of this book: that of public finance, on the one hand, and that of the security sector on the other. This chapter serves as a guide to security sector practitioners on the key principles and issues relating to the budgetary process. As such, it focuses on explaining how the national budget can be an instrument for discussing, negotiating, and reconciling security and economic policy considerations, so that governments can meet their defense and criminal justice objectives within their fiscal parameters and according to general public financial management (PFM) standards.

The chapter starts with basic definitions of budget principles and classification and shows how the security sector is integrated into a government's budget cycle. It then highlights ways in which good expenditure planning and management practices can be applied to security institutions in order to ensure both the sustainability of security spending and the functioning of a country's PFM systems.

Budgeting and the Security Sector: Key Concepts

The National Budget

The national budget provides the financial basis for the delivery of government functions and the implementation of public policies. By balancing competing objectives, it allows the government to strategically allocate scarce public resources to achieve the greatest public good. It also promotes accountability by associating public funds with specific government services.

Particularly given the size of its spending, integrating the security sector into the national budget is essential for meeting the four overriding fiscal goals of: (i) macroeconomic stability, (ii) allocative efficiency, (iii) operational efficiency, and (iv) fiscal transparency and accountability. A security sector that is too large to be sustainable will promote macroeconomic instability, which directly harms poverty reduction and economic development efforts and which may itself become a source of conflict.[1] Meanwhile, funds dedicated to the security system need to be expended effectively and efficiently to best provide defense, ensure internal public order, deliver justice functions, and promote and lay the foundation for broad-based poverty reduction and economic development. Money that is wasted on unnecessary weapon systems or inappropriate force structures, or that is lost to corruption, undermines the purpose for which it was intended and can promote insecurity. Finally, fiscal transparency is essential to holding the government accountable for the use of public resources.

Ultimately it is important to recognize that budget formulation is a political process, and it is not reducible to technical means. It necessarily requires trade-offs between diverse policy objectives, the relative merits of which are a matter of interpretation. For instance, this sourcebook argues that defense is a necessary government function and that security is a precondition for poverty reduction and economic development. That does not mean, however, that the military sector should enjoy special status beyond what is actually necessary. Competing on a level playing field, through a formal process, is the surest means to achieve optimal results for the military sector and the country as a whole.

Budgetary Principles

There has been long-standing agreement on basic budgetary principles, which codify characteristics of a budget to fulfill their functions.[2] The exact formulation of these principles varies by source, but each set incorporates principles for the composition and character of the budget (comprehensiveness, discipline, specification, periodicity, accuracy, predictability), as well as for the budget formulation process and its relevance to society (legitimacy, contestability, transparency, accountability). A typical, contemporary list of budget principles is provided in table 2.1.

These principles are a guide; no PFM system in the world is perfect, and actual budgetary conditions might deviate significantly. In conflict-affected or fragile states, the Public Expenditure Review (PER) team should expect serious weaknesses, and application of budgetary principles will likely be especially difficult. But every PFM system can be improved incrementally, and these principles can provide a framework or set of objectives for the PER team's "best fit" reform plan. For example, these budgetary principles stipulate that public budgets should be comprehensive. A PER that identified off-budget revenue generation or expenditure for the military sector would therefore recommend that it be incorporated into the national budget.

Table 2.1   **Budgetary Principles**

Principle	Description
Comprehensiveness	The budget must encompass all government revenues and expenditures to prevent off-budget items from undermining planning, control, and oversight. All budgetary operations should be covered in a single document, draw from a common pool of resources, and employ a single reporting system to avoid duplication and fragmentation.
Discipline	Payments must be balanced against receipts, and expenses must be balanced against revenues, financing, or external assistance. Countries should adopt a hard budget constraint, whereby policy decisions with financial implications are made in competition with other demands and there is no medium-term fiscal gap in the approved budget.
Specification	The budget must specify detailed revenues and expenditures against standard budget codes, and must spend public resources only for the specified purpose and in the specified amount. If mid-cycle reallocations are necessary, they should be made according to established laws and regulations and approved by the legislature or fiscal authority.
Periodicity	Budgets should be formulated and approved for a specific time period— usually annually, but possibly less often in countries that have adopted a medium-term fiscal framework. Authorized and approved exceptions could be made for multiyear appropriations or end-of-year carryovers, but all transactions should be estimated for their periodic effect.
Accuracy	Budgets must be derived from honest, unbiased, and credible projections of revenue and expenditures in order to maintain the hard budget constraint, facilitate strategic priority setting, and promote efficiency. Accurate and timely information on costs, outputs, and outcomes is essential. Political and technical bias should also be controlled.
Predictability	The budget must provide for a fair degree of stability in fiscal conditions, national policy objectives, and program funding in order to support efficient and effective policy implementation and ensure that policy commitments are met.
Legitimacy	Policy makers who can change budget policies during implementation must take part in their original formulation and authorization. This constraint ensures that the line agencies with the greatest information on cost requirements and relative utility of public funds can influence the de jure policy process, and it reduces the likelihood that de facto spending decisions will deviate from the agreed budget.
Contestability	All sectors (and programs within sectors) must compete on an equal footing for funding during budget planning and formulation to ensure the best use of public funds. This requirement subjects existing policies to evaluation and reform and encourages continuous improvement of line agency performance. It also requires that policy makers be fully aware of all relevant issues and information.
Transparency	Information should be readily available regarding the roles and responsibilities of all public bodies and the bases on which budget decisions are made. This principle requires prompt publication of all budget documents, public deliberation of budget matters, and broad dissemination of budget information. In addition, the budget should be presented in an understandable way that leaves little room for misinterpretation and that allows for comparability over time.
Accountability	All expenditures (and often revenues) must be voted for and authorized by competent authorities before execution; the executive must clearly define and enforce rules for budget managers and periodically report to the legislature on fiscal performance; and an independent audit body must periodically report to the legislature on budget execution. Holding decision makers accountable maintains the separation of powers and ensures that public funds support the public interest.

Sources: Lienert 2013; de Renzio 2013.

The military, police, and courts are not much different from other sectors in PFM terms, and there is no valid reason why they should violate any of the basic budgetary principles. Limited considerations have to be made for legitimately secret policies, like defense plans. Public budgets might also legitimately include relatively small allocations to secret activities, but these activities should, in principle, be disclosed to legislative defense committees and be subject to some oversight.

Budget Classification

Budget classification is a coding system for revenues and expenditures at all stages of the budget process. By necessity, it must be comprehensive and internally consistent. It must cover all government activities and address similar activities in a similar manner. The budget classification system should also allow for aggregation, so that generalizations can be made about a collection of budget activities. This is especially important in the budget formulation process. For example, reporting each individual transaction in the military sector to the ministry of defense and the legislature would be unwieldy and infeasible. But aggregated army or navy program budgets could be formulated under the direction of the ministry of defense and presented to the legislature for approval. Subsequently, those aggregates could be used for oversight and accountability purposes. Finally, a budget classification scheme should be made adaptable; threat assessments, police deployments, and force structures are constantly evolving, and the budget classification scheme must keep pace.

Budget classification lies at the heart of the fundamental budgetary principles listed in table 2.1, and it is usually considered a precondition for major PFM reform. Without a clear and consistent framework for classifying budgetary transactions, it is simply impossible to be comprehensive, specific, or accurate in the national budget. Systematic budget classification provides a way to categorize and structure budgetary information so that it can be interpreted and used by defense and finance officials, the legislature, and the general public. It also enables transparency, so that the military can be held accountable for delivering defense services. On the other hand, it is important to be cautious when introducing new classification schemes. Governments require sufficient institutional capacity, discipline, and time to successfully implement a budget classification scheme, and inappropriate or overly complex schemes can result in information overload.

There are several classification systems in use, each providing different views of budget information and useful for different purposes. The most commonly used scheme is classification by administrative unit; this was the original form of classification, deriving from accounting systems, and it enables basic accountability by indicating what unit and officials are responsible for fund use. Classification schemes are set out in more detail in annex 2A.

The Budget Cycle and the Security Sector

The budget cycle should be periodic, predictable, and sufficient in length for each stage to be completed satisfactorily. Overall, budget formulation can be broken down into four main stages, each of which requires security sector participation or consideration of security concerns:

1. *Setting fiscal objectives.* The government establishes the fiscal policy framework and determines aggregate public spending, the council of ministers agrees to preliminary sectoral allocations, and the ministry of finance issues a budget circular containing budgetary guidelines to the ministries of defense, interior, and justice as well as other line ministries.
2. *Preparing budget requests.* The security services under the policy command of relevant ministries prepare budget requests based on assessed requirements and in line with the sectoral ceiling specified by the ministry of finance.
3. *Negotiating allocations.* Central finance officials determine whether the defense, security, or justice budget submission conforms to spending limits and other guidelines; necessary modifications are made based on changes in the macroeconomic and fiscal environment; and the defense, security, and justice budget is consolidated with other sectoral budgets.
4. *Reviewing and approving the budget.* The legislature reviews the consolidated budget, collects additional information as necessary through reports or testimony, makes agreed changes to allocations where necessary, and approves the consolidated budget when satisfied.

The core task of this initial stage is setting a hard ceiling on aggregate and sectoral spending. Giving the security sector a hard constraint from the beginning of the process shifts the focus from a *needs-based* mentality, where budgets are built from the ground up according to assessed military requirements, to an *availability* mentality, where those defense requirements are defined within agreed economic constraints determined at the top. Of course, fiscal discipline is weak in many developing countries, and the military in particular frequently enjoys a privileged position that allows it to flout macroeconomic and fiscal strictures. However, by failing to provide sectoral limits—or by failing to accurately and comprehensively record sectoral expenditures—governments risk fiscal deficits and macroeconomic instability.

All else being equal, fiscal or economic instability makes revenue projections more tenuous, and under these circumstances the ministry of defense or interior might require extra time to make programmatic trade-offs and prepare budget submissions. Yet, a timeline that becomes too long might prevent the security ministries and central finance officials from fully exploiting the lessons learned in executing the previous year's budget. The PER team should note that some security functions are more amenable than others to these instability-induced trade-offs. For example, defense administration and force employment can be modified on a year-to-year basis, but force structure and procurement decisions have budgetary implications that can last for decades. It is therefore essential that the budget cycle for defense be firmly rooted in the priorities derived from the country's defense policy objectives and military strategy (as discussed in the substantive chapter on defense).

The ministry of finance and the security sector ministries and agencies must therefore discuss their strategic priorities over the short to medium term as well as the related expenditures. A critical part of that exchange is having a clear security sector strategy; more usually this is outlined in the sector's constituent parts (i.e., defense, police, criminal justice). Ideally such a strategy should have the following components: (i) an evaluation of the country's security context, external and/or internal depending on the relevant component; (ii) broad policy guidelines based upon the legal and political consensus on how security operates in the particular context; and (iii) a detailed elaboration of mission, doctrine, force structures, and human resource and capital needs.

Public Expenditure and Financial Accountability

The framework for analyzing public finance is based upon existing World Bank tools that focus on critical policy issues,[3] as well as on the well-established methodology of Public Expenditure and Financial Accountability (PEFA), a multi-agency partnership program created around the seven critical dimensions of a PFM system.[4] These are (i) budget reliability, (ii) transparency of public finance, (iii) management of assets and liabilities, (iv) policy-based fiscal strategy and budgeting, (v) predictability and control in budget execution, (vi) accounting and reporting, and (vii) external scrutiny and audit.

Figure 2.1 describes the relationship between the preparation of a security strategy, in this case for defense, and the wider government budgetary process. The two processes are essentially parallel to each other, and while some special considerations apply to sensitive issues such as secret budgets, security sector budgeting should follow the same path as other public sector entities. In other words, once the budget is formulated, it follows the standard procedure for all sectors and goes through execution, oversight, and performance.

There are potential points in the budget cycle where the security sector may be treated differently from other government sectors and line ministries. These are summarized in table 2.2.

Obviously, full integration of the military sector into the national budget process requires that the military be subject to the same regulations as other line ministries. In most countries, these regulations are issued by the ministry of finance, which is responsible for regulating and administering the budget process. The ministry of finance issues budget circulars that stipulate

Figure 2.1   The Security Sector in the Budget Cycle

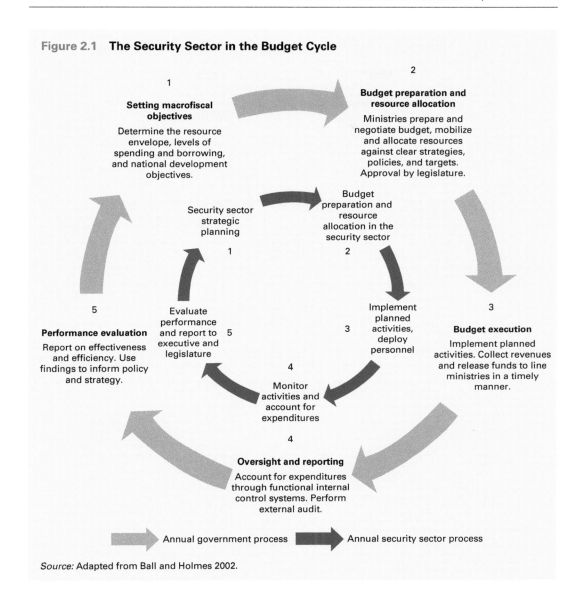

Source: Adapted from Ball and Holmes 2002.

deadlines, rules, and expectations. More specifically, these circulars typically include the following:

- *Budget calendar*, specifying budget activities, due dates, and responsible stakeholders
- *Statement of the macroeconomic and fiscal situation*, including key assumptions related to inflation, the exchange rate, unemployment, and other variables
- *Estimate of expected tax revenues and other financial resources* from internal and external sources

Table 2.2   The Budget Cycle and the Security Sector: Defense Compared with Standard Practice

Budget cycle phase	International practice	Defense treated differently?
Budget planning and formulation	Sector strategies are developed.	Defense strategies may be kept secret, or official strategies may differ from strategies actually followed. Thus it can be difficult to assess the relationship between strategy and budget.
	Medium-term expenditure estimates are formulated.	No
	All sectors compete for funding based on priority and performance at cabinet level.	Treatment of defense is highly dependent on context; need for funding could be assessed by a security subcommittee.
	Budget proposals are all subject to the same scrutiny by the budget office.	Security clearances are required for budget staff dealing with defense budget.
	Funding set aside for specific contingencies is subject to clear criteria.	There may be a rationale for a separate security contingency fund, although sudden events are usually met by a general government contingency budget.
Legislative scrutiny	All spending is subject to the same scrutiny through the committee system.	Issues of national security can be handled in closed committee hearings.
	Information should be sufficiently detailed to allow the legislative to call the executive to account.	Scrutiny depends on the security context: the more insecure the country, the more secret legislative scrutiny is. It also depends on the political regime: many developing countries give a minor role to Parliament in the budget process, especially for defense.
Budget execution	Funds are released to departments in accordance with budget appropriations; clear rules exist for addressing shortfalls.	Budget execution sometimes obeys specific procedures, as for global grants, escrow accounts, absence of complete reporting, etc.
Monitoring and reporting	All expenditures are reported along appropriation lines to (i) accounting office and (ii) legislature.	No
	End-of-year financial statements are available in a timely manner.	No
	Annual reports on operations, including performance, are published.	Reporting is modified to reflect legitimate national security considerations.
External audit	All expenditures are subject to an external audit: • Financial statements are given to legislature. • Legislative committee system acts upon recommendations of audit reports. • Legislature has the capacity to call executive to account on audit recommendations.	Auditing of sensitive issues in defense needs appropriate security clearance, and legislative meetings may be closed. Sometimes, the weakness or absence of external audit can be replaced by a strong internal audit or inspection reporting to the highest defense authority.

- *Fiscal targets*, including those for debt reduction
- *Policy and budget priorities*
- *Sectoral spending ceilings*
- *Guidance on the required format for budget submissions,* including the presentation of major expenditure items like personnel, investment projects, and entitlement programs.

Annual budget cycles are most common, but the optimal cycle length depends on country circumstances. In many Organisation for Economic Co-operation and Development countries, the budget circular is distributed shortly after the start of the fiscal year, meaning that the actual process of budget formulation spans 9 or 10 months. More advanced systems might employ a medium-term framework of several years and update program effectiveness and efficiency information as new data become available to inform annual or multiyear resource allocations. At a minimum, a developing country probably requires at least six months between the finance ministry's publication of proposed sectoral spending ceilings and the final submission of the consolidated budget to the legislature for approval.

Budgets and the Goals of Fiscal Policy

Macroeconomic Stability and Fiscal Affordability

The budget formulation process starts with the government establishing the macroeconomic and fiscal policy framework. Whereas PFM is primarily concerned with the management of public funds—particularly budgeting, resource allocation, and expenditure—macroeconomic and fiscal policy is concerned with government revenues as well. The goal of macroeconomic and fiscal policy is to achieve potential output, full employment, and macroeconomic stability, which together provide the economic foundation for sustainable growth.[5] Of central importance is the fiscal deficit: the government cannot spend more than it collects through taxation and borrowing beyond the short run. High debts and high inflation are destabilizing. The government must therefore set and adhere to fiscal targets related to debt sustainability and fiscal balance. Doing so requires reasonably accurate revenue projections, which are especially difficult in fragile and conflict-prone states. It also requires a comprehensive, rational process for estimating current and potential expenditures.

Essentially, the national budget must be affordable in the short run and the long run; and meeting this goal requires full integration of the security sector.[6] The security sector often comprises the largest or one of the largest shares of the national budget; the question is how these expenditures equate with government revenues, including external aid. This question is particularly important for low-income countries, and it is critical for countries transitioning from war to peace, since these countries often have limited domestic revenues and may also be facing peacebuilding challenges that come with significant price tags, such as army integration or demobilization (see box 2.1).

Box 2.1   Affordability Questions for Countries Emerging from Conflict

The government may face existential trade-offs between peacebuilding priorities and fiscal stability. A few examples are given below:

- *Political versus fiscal stability.* A government established under a peace agreement after conflict may seek to integrate ex-belligerents into one national army. This can be a very expensive exercise that is at odds with the demands for fiscal stability, but it may be justified in order to maintain political stability and keep the former warring factions at peace.[a]
- *Transition from peacekeeping to government security provision.* Some war-to-peace transitions are accompanied by a UN Security Council–endorsed peacekeeping mission that provides basic security services during the life of the mission. As these peacekeeping forces depart, the government is expected to increase its own capacity to provide potentially expensive security and justice services for the population.[b]
- *Transition from external assistance to domestic revenues.* Some war-to-peace transitions have been internationalized in character; in these cases, external actors as well as national actors are engaged in military interventions (as in Afghanistan or Somalia). Such external intervention can be accompanied by (at times significant) external financing to government security forces. The question is how long these external finances can be sustained and what happens when they diminish.[c]

a. See for example World Bank 2012b.
b. See for example World Bank and United Nations 2012.
c. See for example World Bank 2005a; World Bank and United Nations Assistance Mission in Somalia 2016.

Once sustainable aggregate spending levels are determined, government priorities—including defense, public order, and justice—can be weighed, current policies reviewed, and the budgetary impact of policy changes estimated. To facilitate these steps, security sector expenditures should be fully incorporated into medium-term fiscal projections based on life-cycle costing of defense capabilities. For example, too often the military sector's recurrent operation and maintenance costs are neglected, especially in fragile and conflict-prone states. If the national budget is not realistic in its estimation of government expenditures, it will be irrelevant and never implemented. Moreover, if line ministries are allowed to spend indiscriminately, the result may be a "tragedy of the commons" scenario, where unrestrained revenue collection, deficits, and debt lead to adverse economic outcomes.[7]

Confronted with the challenges of tight resources, policy makers can use the PER exercise to identify potential savings and in certain instances realize increases in public expenditure. These increases can result from the following: (i) bringing off-budget expenditures into the budget; (ii) consolidating all security-related expenditures under the appropriate functional headings; (iii) including adequate operation and maintenance costs for equipment; (iv) setting appropriate salary and wage scales; (v) taking account of costs associated with downsizing, such as disbursement of pensions or settlements; and (vi) changing the shape of the military or police (for example, into a force reliant on smaller numbers of personnel with greater mobility).[8]

Allocative Efficiency

Once the overall resource envelope has been determined, the most difficult set of decisions then needs to be made about how to allocate those resources according to the different security sector priorities. At this point, internal government competition is inevitable and will lead to extensive negotiation within the different subsectors—e.g., between the army and air force or between the various components of the criminal justice system (police, judiciary, and corrections). A well-informed and empowered ministry of finance can play a useful role in mediating these discussions and assisting in decision making about final allocations. But such an exercise is challenging for a ministry of finance for a number of reasons:

- *The budget may be held hostage.* The security sector, particularly the military, may have a politically prominent position in government and therefore may demand high allocations without a solid justification.
- *There may be ideological differences over security and justice provision.* The intense debates over what works in providing security are reflected in how governments prioritize their budgets. An example of this debate is the gradual shift in Central America away from *mano dura* policies, which use heavy, coercive measures to combat crime and violence,[9] toward more preventive (and cheaper) interventions.
- *International comparisons are not always possible.* The security sector is unlike other sectors in that very few international comparisons or standards are available to support decision makers in addressing critical questions, such as unit costs or numbers of personnel. This is partly due to the fact that financial and staffing figures are rarely disclosed publicly, and that when disclosed they rarely follow common rules that could allow comparisons. The UN has some helpful guidance, particularly on population-based ratios for police and other criminal justice personnel.[10] In addition, comparisons can be made with neighboring countries, particularly those with similar population sizes, income per capita, and sources of revenue (see annex 3D in the defense chapter for more information).

The following inputs are useful for the process of making decisions about allocations: (i) a well-articulated strategy setting out key targets; (ii) measures of good past performance; (iii) indications of how subsectors relate to other subsectors (particularly important in the criminal justice sector); and (iv) empirical evidence from global experience on what interventions work in security and justice provision. In contexts affected by fragility or conflict, the PER team will confront a number of particular challenges and issues. These are described in box 2.2.

These discussions about allocation are where expenditure and security policy converge; and in light of sovereignty or mandate issues, there may be a limited role for external actors such as the UN or the World Bank.[11] For matters relating to national security, the appeal to confidentiality and

---

Box 2.2   Key Strategic Issues in Fragile and Conflict-Affected States

Countries facing high rates of crime or violence or coming out of conflict face a number of particular challenges that need to be addressed in formulating security and justice strategies and in setting priorities for
allocations:

- *Contending domestic and international objectives of governments and partners.* These objectives
  may not be coherent—e.g., counterterrorism, counterinsurgency, and counternarcotics objectives
  may outweigh peacebuilding and efforts to provide individual security and justice.
- *Peace agreements.* Peace agreements may comprise the bulk of security objectives and in fact
  replace a national security strategy by setting out priorities and key targets over a specific time
  frame. What is important here is that questions about affordability and costing are inserted during
  the peace process so that agreements are realistic and implementable. Here, the report on security
  sector reform (SSR) by the Secretary General of the United Nations (2008)[a] can be helpful in
  emphasizing that SSR issues should be addressed as early as possible in the peace process.
- *Governance and accountability.* In the drive to consolidate state authority (including by strengthening command and control over the security services), issues around accountability and governance
  may be ignored, which creates the possibility of dangers down the road in terms of governance
  and citizen oversight.

a. UNSG 2008.

---

sovereignty is understandable. However, as governments increasingly recognize the close relationship between security and development outcomes,
they are increasingly seeking policy advice from multilateral partners, particularly on matters relating to internal security and justice provision (such
as what policies work, how to prioritize them, and what costs are involved).
Two particular policy aspects are worth briefly considering here:

1. *Policy alternatives.* Responses to insecurity and violence are usually
   broken down into the following components (more fully outlined in
   annex 4A of the chapter on police in this sourcebook):

   - *Suppression,* or the use of military, paramilitary, or police in order
     to intimidate and discourage potential perpetrators
   - *Deterrence,* or the capacity of the state to identify, prosecute, and
     punish criminal and violent offenders with a view to deterring others
   - *Incapacitation,* or the policy of taking offenders out of society
     through judicial means (such as imprisonment) or administrative
     means (such as internment during rebellion)
   - *Rehabilitation,* or the process of reforming those who have been
     associated with crime and violence, such as those in prison or heavy
     drug users
   - *Prevention,* including an array of interventions intended to prevent
     people from entering a life of crime and violence, from the systemic
     (such as reducing inequality) to the specific (such as job creation).

2. *Institutional alternatives.* An important policy question concerns what institutions most effectively provide security and justice. Increasingly, the private sector plays a significant role in security provision, particularly in urban areas for commercial and individual residences. The private sector, including nonprofit organizations, is also involved in other areas of security provision such as demining. Private alternatives may be cheaper than public, although their use raises other regulatory and policy challenges.[12]

As a PER is carried out, intragovernmental discussions about allocations and sector ceilings can expand to a more comprehensive policy discussion about what security sector policies are appropriate in general, what are most effective, and what may be cheapest.[13] These debates are held in developed as well as developing countries and involve the ideological contests mentioned at the beginning of this section.

In sum, particularly in poorer countries, the majority of security and justice service providers are informal institutions. These may present both a challenge and an opportunity to governments with scarce resources; better regulation and building of capacity of informal institutions might be preferable to establishing expensive centralized alternatives.[14]

Operational Efficiency and Effectiveness

Under ideal circumstances, once funds have been appropriated for the various sectors, according to their strategies and priorities, they are used efficiently and effectively for their intended purposes. *Efficiency* in budget execution involves PFM systems and processes, including procurement, payroll, audit, and accounting, whereas *effectiveness* relates to the measurement of performance against targets/indicators of progress for the sector.

Measuring effectiveness in the security sector is not an easy task; hence more often the focus is on input and output indicators such as unit costs, personnel trained and equipped, and the number of forces ready for deployment. As explained in more detail in the substantive chapters on defense, policing, and criminal justice, a disaggregated approach, treating each subsector, is important here.

- *Defense/military.* Most often this security component is measured in peacetime based on the "state of readiness" to meet external threats, measured in terms of output indicators such as soldiers trained and vehicles or aircraft on standby. Evaluating performance of the military is a sensitive area and usually left to ministries of defense and their bilateral partners.
- *Criminal justice and policing.* Performance standards across the developing and developed world are increasingly being used to measure performance in this subsector; standards range from measurement of crime and violence rates to public opinion and perception surveys.[15]

Measuring efficiency is a well-standardized practice under PFM. Particular aspects relating to the security sector are outlined in box 2.3.

Box 2.3 **Components of Efficiency**

To strengthen the efficient utilization of financial resources in the security sector, it is important to address the following issues:

- *Sustainability.* Over time, an unsustainable sector plan and programs will lead to ineffective capabilities. Sustainability will be achieved only if governments commit themselves to the approved plan, if all planning is done on full life-cycle costing, and if the defense budget is expended in the most efficient manner possible. Care must also be taken in planning to accurately evaluate the effect of currency fluctuations on the life-cycle cost of capital equipment.

- *Contingency funding of operations.* It is not desirable to budget for the execution of operations other than those that are routine and can be accurately planned well ahead of time. Most military operations come at short notice and in the financial year for which the budget was developed and approved many months prior. Examples are peace-support missions, major disaster relief missions, and even limited war. Trying to budget for the unforeseeable runs a strong risk of misappropriating funds. It is preferable for the finance ministry to maintain a central contingency fund that could be tapped into as needed. For large-scale contingencies exceeding the capacity of such a contingency fund, governments should revise the total budget both for departmental allocations and income.

- *Tooth-to-tail ratios.* Particularly in the military, efforts should be made to ensure the optimal tooth-to-tail ratio. All too often supporting structures and headquarters are bloated at the cost of operational capabilities. The size and capacity of support structures can be determined only once the force design has been agreed. Business process reengineering techniques can assist in solving this problem, but they will be effective only if top management is committed to this cause and ruthless in its application.

- *Direct client/supplier relationships.* In many defense forces certain structures exist for historic reasons only. Either because of the organizational culture or other interests, the client (e.g., a combat service) is forced to use the services of a certain organization and not allowed to shop for this service elsewhere. Clients should be allowed freedom of choice and be able to establish direct client/supplier relationships. If governments are under threat, however, then it may be in their interests to organize their support in house and to militarize all or part of the supply chain. Choices between these extremes may also vary depending on history and on the degree of readiness defined by the government.

Other potential solutions for the improvement of efficiency include outsourcing and public-private partnerships, improved collaboration between services, improved management information through better information technology, use of reserves, use of civilians in defense ministries, and improved management and leadership through education, training, and development. Of these, the use of better information technology for strengthening information management systems might be the most crucial way to improve efficiency in defense organizations.

Source: Ball and le Roux 2006.

Governance and Accountability

A normative aspect of security sector reform more generally is the principle of civilian oversight of the sector and the sector's increasing accountability to citizens, as represented by the executive and legislature specifically as well as the general public. Such oversight is needed because the instruments and agencies of the security sector designed to improve security can themselves be sources of insecurity unless kept in check. An important aspect of that oversight is financial accountability and the capacity of civilian institutions to carry out a sound budget process, expenditure tracking, anticorruption measures, fair and competitive procurement procedures, and proper auditing and accounting. Many of these aspects are discussed in the following section on PFM.

Public Financial Management in the Security Sector

Managing public finance involves a wide range of functions (see box 2.4). Establishing the requisite PFM systems and capacities, and ensuring that they perform effectively and efficiently so that the entire PFM system achieves its objectives, is a complex process, one that is generally accomplished incrementally over a period of time. It is essential that government-wide systems and procedures operate well if there is to be fiscal discipline, strategic allocation of resources, and efficient service delivery in the security sector.

National authorities take the lead in efforts to strengthen the public finance management system, both across government and in specific sectors; and they may be supported in these endeavors by international partners. In the nonsecurity sectors, assistance often goes beyond supporting the development of systems and processes to making recommendations on how resources should be allocated and budgets structured. But making recommendations for the security sector—for example, on the share of national resources allocated to the security sector, the composition of that

---

Box 2.4   An Illustrative Disaggregation of a Typical Public Finance Management System

1. Macro forecasting and fiscal envelope (revenues and expenditures)
2. Revenue management
3. Sectoral allocation
4. Capital budgeting
5. Sectoral planning and budgeting
6. In-year fiscal adjustment
7. Treasury, cash management
8. Procurement
9. Payroll and human resource management
10. Management control and internal audit
11. Accounting and reporting
12. Debt and aid management
13. External audit
14. The legislature, accountability, and transparency.

Source: World Bank 2005b, 7.

expenditure, the size of the wage bill, and the like—is much more sensitive. Some development actors, including the World Bank, are expressly forbidden from providing this type of advice in the security sector.[16] This sourcebook focuses on how to strengthen governments' capacity to make sound decisions on resource allocation; it takes no position on the size or structure of the security budget.

More specifically, both the International Monetary Fund (IMF) and the World Bank have standard frameworks that the PER team can use to assess PFM practices in the country of interest. The World Bank's PEFA framework in particular can be a valuable tool for assessing PFM in developing countries, including fragile and conflict-prone states. High-level PFM indicators from this framework are shown in table 2.3. Although designed to assess countrywide PFM practices, many of the indicators are also applicable to the defense sector. How these indicators are useful will depend on the context of the PER; for example, subnational transfers are not relevant for assessing the military, but they are important in examining the police and judiciary.

The seven dimensions of PFM provide a framework for assessing budget management and systems related to the security sector. The starting

Table 2.3   World Bank Public Financial Management Indicators

Category	Indicator
1. Budget reliability	Aggregate expenditure out-turn
	Expenditure composition out-turn (compared to original approved budget)
	Revenue out-turn (compared to original approved budget)
2. Transparency of public finances	Budget classification
	Budget documentation
	Central government operational outside financial reports
	Transfers to subnational governments
	Performance information for service delivery
	Public access to fiscal information
3. Management of assets and liabilities	Fiscal risk reporting
	Public investment management
	Public asset management
	Debt management
4. Policy-based fiscal strategy and budgeting	Macroeconomic and fiscal forecasting
	Fiscal strategy
	Medium-term perspective in expenditure budgeting
	Budget preparation process
	Legislative scrutiny of budgets

(Table continues on next page)

Table 2.3 **World Bank Public Financial Management Indicators** *(continued)*

Category	Indicator
5. Predictability and control in budget execution	Revenue administration
	Accounting for revenue
	Predictability of in-year resource allocation
	Expenditure arrears
	Payroll controls
	Procurement management
	Internal controls on nonsalary expenditure
	Internal audit
6. Accounting and reporting	Financial data integrity
	In-year budget reports
	Annual financial reports
7. External scrutiny and audit	External audit
	Legislative scrutiny of audit reports

Source: PEFA Secretariat 2011, 9.

point for any assessment is to ascertain to what degree security sector policy and planning are integrated into the government's normal public finance system.

With regard to external financial support, under an earlier PEFA framework, donor indicators were included; but these have been either subsumed under the existing framework or linked to the Global Partnership for Effective Development Co-operation diagnostics.[17] Particularly for countries where the security sector receives substantial external support (for example, where conflict is internationalized, such as Afghanistan, Iraq, and Somalia), the PER should assess (i) predictability, (ii) levels of financial information given with such aid, and (iii) the proportion of aid that is managed through national systems.

The chapter now examines in greater detail the seven PEFA categories and their relevance to security.

1. Budget Reliability

A realistic and credible budget is fundamental for establishing fiscal stability. In terms of PFM, there are two ways that management of the security sector often undermines budget credibility:

1. *Financial deviations.* There is often a significant gap between approved budgets and actual expenditures of the security sector: "Systematic deviations are a sign of poor or deceptive budgeting [and] reduce the credibility of the budget hence weakening its role as a policy tool."[18]

Like planners in other sectors, security planners should provide for contingencies that can be exceptionally expensive (for example, armed conflict). In resource-constrained countries, actual expenditures may deviate significantly from the approved budget. In addition to providing insight into priorities, clarity on why deviations occur can help make the budgetary process more predictable. The reasons for deviation may vary over time.[19] Some deviations relating to both expenditures and revenues are explained in box 2.5.

2. *Confidentiality and moving off-budget.* The degree of external scrutiny of the security sector is often limited by legal and policy procedures related to freedom of information, confidentiality, and transparency. On national security grounds it can be difficult to ascertain accurate budget details for the sector. This challenge is compounded when donor assistance is also given off-budget. In Sierra Leone, for example, more than half the total security sector expenditure in 2005 was reported to be off-budget.[20] Studies have found that deviations shielded by confidentiality can include significant security finances kept off-budget, revenues that are secretly banked, and accounts held overseas.[21]

Box 2.5   Mechanisms for Off-Budget Military Expenditures and Revenue

The following examples of off-budget military spending and revenue were derived from the countries examined in a study conducted for the U.K. Department for International Development in 2001. Although the study focused on military expenditure and revenue, many of these mechanisms can be, and have been, used by other security institutions.

Budgetary mechanisms for disguising military spending include the following:

- *Contingency funds.* Reserve budget lines for emergencies are used to pay military "debts" and to fund establishment of "urgent" military commissions to resolve border disputes, pay defecting soldiers from antigovernment forces, care for refugees in conflict zones, or repair military hardware (substantiation of spending rarely provided by the military).
- *Supplementary budgets.* Government can top up this budget line during the year by passing a new subdecree; money is taken from other budget lines that have not disbursed funds due to lack of "absorptive capacity." Government justifies spending to Parliament at year's end in vague terms.
- *Spending under nondefense budget lines.* Examples include (i) military units commissioned to build roads which either are not built or serve primarily military commercial interests (logging); disbursements under public works/rural development budget lines; (ii) defense spending (for the Home Guards, a form of territorial army) placed under police budget line; (iii) army pay increases kept off budget because too sensitive; (iv) military involvement in administering social "safety net" during times of crisis, including provision of disaster relief, running hospitals, etc.; (v) personnel costs (military wages) run through nonsecurity ministries; (vi) rice supplements for military monetized and counted as "civilian wages"; (vii) spending for military vehicles recorded in "social budgets," for instance as "ambulances" or for use in "peace operations."

(Box continues on next page)

Box 2.5   **Mechanisms for Off-Budget Military Expenditures and Revenue** *(continued)*

- *Nontransparent or highly aggregated budget categories (budget lines for debt repayment, public investment/capital, presidential offices, etc.).* Examples include (i) repair of military equipment paid for by nonconcessional loans and funds recorded under public investments; (ii) government bailout of highly indebted banking sector covering many military businesses unable to repay massive preferential loans; and (iii) accumulation of wage arrears, including military salaries, covered under a nondefense budget line.
- *Diversion of resources from social budget lines after budget approved.* Examples include (i) diversion of unused funds to military spending due to lack of absorptive capacity in social sectors; (ii) freeing up of counterpart funding for military uses when donor funding for a development program requiring counterpart funding does not materialize; and (iii) paying salaries of military personnel working on development projects through the investment (development) budget.
- *Procurement of military matériel.* Examples include (i) procurement of military equipment funded through nondefense budget lines or not accounted for in the budget; and (ii) procurement of military equipment through supplier credit terms without prior scrutiny by appropriate authorities to ensure funds are available.
- *Undervaluation of economic resources.* For example, use of forced labor to construct military infrastructure, a practice that does not adequately reflect the true opportunity cost to society or the level of resources consumed by the military.

Extrabudgetary sources of military revenue include the following:

- *Parastatals.* Nonmilitary groups (including companies owned by ruling parties) are used to fund security services. State-owned enterprises are decapitalized to release funds for the military, and then recapitalized the following year; or governments simply bail out enterprises that have become heavily indebted due to the diversion of resources for military purposes.
- *Military-owned businesses/involvement in nonmilitary activity.* Examples include (i) "charitable" status tax-exempt foundations that serve as holding groups for commercial enterprises or cooperatives that are used to fund the military; leakage from military-owned business is very high; (ii) military interests that run private security companies and serve as suppliers of various matériel to the military and other government departments for which they receive state subsidies; and (iii) police units that have a financial interest in private security firms; both military and police personnel work in private security firms to supplement salaries.
- *Creation of funds.* Examples include (i) petroleum fund that is entirely off-budget, with reportedly 20–50 percent of income allocated to the armed forces; (ii) cocoa board funds that are used to finance president's special forces; (iii) reforestation fund (fed by logging fees) and under military control, which ostensibly served to replant trees/build roads, though funds were allegedly diverted; and (iv) fund ostensibly created to assist the unemployed that was used to divert resources to the Ministry for War Veterans, undermining International Monetary Fund austerity targets.
- *Barter trade.* For example, barter of agricultural commodities for military equipment.
- *Direct financing of military in field through extraction of natural resources.* Examples include (i) the use of state/military organizational structures, though levels of leakage are typically very high, for exploitation of diamonds, precious stones, timber, fisheries, oil, etc.; (ii) granting concessions and access to mineral and other natural resources to their allies by both the government and the rebel forces; (iii) the government's signing over of control of all timber

(Box continues on next page)

> **Box 2.5** **Mechanisms for Off-Budget Military Expenditures and Revenue** *(continued)*
>
> revenue to the military, during a war against an insurgency movement; and (iv) use of revenue from sales of natural resources as collateral to finance short-term borrowing in order to procure military equipment.
>
> - *Avoidance of taxes.* For example, military-run casinos and unused land purchased for purposes of speculation by the military are regularly exempt from taxation; a region settled by former rebel soldiers is officially exonerated from paying tax on all business activities and imports from neighboring countries in order to "avoid destabilizing the peace process" (the government army is also heavily involved in this trade).
> - *Mortgaging of national resources.* For example, the government grants long-term concessions to foreign oil companies in exchange for advance payments in annual fees, which are then used to fund the war effort.
> - *War levies.* Examples include (i) use of 10 percent (revenue of firms, tax on citizens) to fund the government's war effort; the process is largely ad hoc, not recorded in the budget; (ii) a "voluntary" security levy is raised from citizens and recorded in the budget under nontax revenue and defense spending.
> - *Foreign military assistance.* Examples include (i) failure to record military equipment received as a foreign grant in the capital budget; and (ii) underreporting of income from donors, suggesting possible diversion of resources to the military.
> - *Donor assistance for demobilization.* Donor assistance provided to support military demobilization and reintegration programs is not recorded in the defense budget.
> - *Assistance from multinational companies.* Examples include an oil company's provision of assistance to the government to procure arms and pay salaries of state security personnel protecting its operations.
> - *Informal/criminal activities.* Examples include fuel smuggling; operating casinos; trafficking in drugs, humans, arms, timber, precious stones; kidnapping; protection rackets; prostitution; printing of money; piracy.
>
> *Source:* Adapted from Hendrickson and Ball 2002.

2. Transparency of Public Finances

Transparency relates to the need for a comprehensive and sectorwide incorporation of security into the budgeting process that includes various institutional components (military, policing, border management, criminal justice, etc.) as well as domestic revenues and external finance.

Transparency can sit at odds with the general confidentiality that is associated with the security sector. However, various steps and processes—such as closed committee hearings and security-cleared budgeting staff—can help to maintain the integrity of serious national security matters. Transparency results in better outcomes for the planning and implementation process: sharing information allows for better political participation and better policy decisions; it fosters coordination with other sectors, which is important particularly for domestic security and its relationship with other sectors; and it promotes monitoring to ensure accountability, encourages self-restraint, and in general supports better implementation.[22]

Finally, fiscal transparency is one component of the IMF's Reports on Observance of Standards and Codes (ROSC) program, which summarizes countries' compliance with certain codes and standards, including some relating to defense.[23] The program is voluntary but countries are encouraged to comply.

3. Management of Assets and Liabilities

Managing assets and liabilities is particularly complex when the security sector is directly involved in running parts of the economy, either to provide an input into defense or for profit.[24] For the purposes of this review, asset management is the more important of the two issues.

The operation and maintenance of equipment used to execute various functions ranging from personnel transport (cars and trucks; aircraft) to combat (light weapons, munitions, and complex weapon systems) will be at a premium. The processes and resources in place for the maintenance and operations of such assets are fundamental. One study found that "armed forces can improve both the efficiency and effectiveness of their maintenance repair and overhaul function by as much as 60 percent, but doing so requires fundamental changes to organization, processes, and mindsets."[25] Even in the least-resourced security sector institutions, where most assets do not have a high capital value, basic systems (e.g., vehicle fleet management) are important for maximizing efficiency and reducing corruption.

In certain countries, particularly where there has been internal armed conflict (or the risk of it), arms management and destruction is a key issue. A number of agencies support the improved storage, securing, and management of weapons and munitions, including weapon-marking programs and the destruction of surplus, obsolete, or unstable weapons and munitions. This support may enable security forces to professionalize and modernize their weaponry, as well as to manage both the risks of unplanned explosions at munitions sites (UEMS) and the risks associated with diverting arms to the illicit market.[26] Assistance programs specific to national context and developed with national authorities might include systematic assessments, technical guidance and advice, operations in response to assessed priorities, and training and capacity building.

4. Policy-Based Fiscal Strategy and Budgeting

A sound budget system is related to credible sector strategies, including a security sector strategy that (i) is based in context; (ii) relates to other government security actors (e.g., within the criminal justice chain); (iii) links with other relevant line ministries, departments, and agencies (MDAs) within government outside the sector; and (iv) has realistic and affordable targets. As important as the sector strategy is the process that produced it—a process that should allow for consultation and debate, ensuring links to key actors within the government (including the legislature) and outside the government (including civil society).

However, few countries have formal security sectorwide policies, and even fewer have undertaken the broad security evaluation that ideally underpins policy and strategy development. Recent UN policy guidance emphasizes the importance of building a common national security vision and strategy in order to create sustainable and nationally owned security institutions.[27] Some policy makers may resist policy development, particularly in fragile and conflict-affected countries, where the security sector may be highly contested. The political consensus on the way forward that is necessary to develop viable policies may simply be lacking. In aid-dependent countries, therefore, efforts by external partners to promote policy development without corresponding efforts to build consensus and a national security vision will likely be unsuccessful.

Although it is true that policy is ultimately what government does (not what it says it wants to do), formal policies and plans that articulate a course of action are important. Clearly articulated policies make it possible to manage the finances of the security sector in a cost-effective manner. In the absence of such policies, budgeting aims to maintain the previous year's level of expenditure without assessing whether the configuration of that expenditure will help to meet government's priorities or deliver services needed by the population. Performance benchmarks are difficult to develop, and without them it is hard to monitor the use of security-related resources and assess the efficiency and effectiveness of the security sector. In the absence of a strategic plan tied to policy, countries risk not obtaining a level of security and justice commensurate with their financial outlays.

In an examination of government policy in the security sector (written or unwritten), there is no exhaustive checklist of issues to watch out for. Some critical issues that can arise concerning efficiency and effectiveness in the sector include the following:

- *Sectorwide approaches.* When subsectors of the security sector (military, intelligence, police, judiciary, etc.) submit their own priorities unrelated to those of other subsectors, the result is fragmented approaches to common challenges and an absence of complementarities and coherence.
- *Recurrent versus capital costs.* In low-income countries, the largest share of the security sector budget goes to recurrent costs, particularly personnel and equipment. A critical part of recurrent costs, operations and maintenance, is often overlooked or not budgeted for in the acquisition of new vehicles, weaponry, etc.
- *Training and personnel.* Low-income countries often prioritize personnel recruitment over training for professional induction into the security sector or capacity building for training institutions.
- *Demobilization and pensioning.* Policy may not account for the aging of the workforce or provide for pensions that are in line with generic civil service guidelines and standards. In turn, there may be little robust calculation of the costs of demobilization (particularly after a peace agreement) or military retrenchment in peacetime.

5. Predictability and Control in Budget Execution

A critical part of the public financial dimension of security is ensuring that the expenditures are used efficiently and for their intended purposes. Budget execution covers a number of PFM areas ranging from internal controls over payroll, for example, to procurement procedures, and is at the heart of understanding the coherence between a planned and actual budget. This is the part of a PER analysis that potentially comes the closest to an audit in terms of understanding how security sector institutions spend their allocations. Two issues are highlighted here, payroll and procurement:

Payroll (Including Personnel Registration and Verification of Payments and Allowances)

A regular source of corruption is the payroll system, which is often one of the largest shares of the security budget. Typically, a percentage of salary payments to lower ranks is misappropriated, or "ghosts" are created and their wages embezzled. One of the more notable examples of efforts to discourage corruption—the European Union's work in the Democratic Republic of Congo—is described in box 2.6.

Procurement

There should be little difference between public expenditure management in general and public expenditure management in the military sector.[28] Defense procurement and acquisition should be carried out according to the same principles that guide public sector procurement in nonmilitary areas: fairness, impartiality, transparency, cost-effectiveness and efficiency, and openness to competition.[29] In addition, it is essential that all major projects for all forms of public sector procurement and acquisition be subject to high-level consultation and evaluation. Box 2.7 presents a generic procurement process, applicable to all sectors of government.

Box 2.6   Chain of Payments: Discouraging Corruption in the Democratic Republic of Congo

The European Union mission to provide assistance for security sector reform in the Democratic Republic of Congo was established in 2005. It was originally mandated to assist in the process of integrating the various armed groups into the national army and to support good governance in the field of security. One of its first initiatives was the Chain of Payments project aimed at rehabilitating the salary system and delinking the wage distribution lines from the official chain of command. A biometric census was undertaken (finding 120,000 soldiers instead of the official count of 190,000); army IDs were issued; and a central database and payroll system were created (the salaries of lowest ranks increased from $10 to $40/month). This intervention was credited with cleaning up a part of the financial management system commonly associated with embezzlement and a preponderance of "ghost soldiers"; however, it did not manage to lead to longer-term structural reform in the sector.

Source: More and Price 2011.

Box 2.7   A Generic Procurement Process

A generic procurement process includes the following:

- A clear definition of the requirement
- Clear technical quality specifications and standards
- An open request for proposals and tenders
- Tender adjudication according to set criteria
- Selection of a preferred bidder
- Drawing up of a contract
- Placing the contract or order
- Monitoring progress
- Reception of goods
- Quality assurance checks on goods received
- Acceptance or rejection of goods
- Payment
- Distribution of goods.

Source: Ball and le Roux 2006, 40.

Procurement decision processes may fall outside regular frameworks and processing. Ad hoc exceptions to normal procedures can include direct government-to-government weapons deals, sole-sourcing of contracts, secrecy surrounding tender requirements, and preference for certain domestic suppliers.

At the same time, except for procurement of nonlethal works and commodities (such as clothing, food, fuel, etc.), defense procurement does exhibit some distinctive characteristics: (i) the relative importance of cost in determining which bid is accepted, (ii) the confidentiality associated with national security considerations, (iii) the time frame for major weapons procurement, (iv) the complexity of defense procurement, and (v) the existence of international arms control treaty regimes and national legislation governing arms procurement. These distinctive characteristics are deviations in scale rather than principle. For example, adequate levels of confidentiality can be maintained without violating basic public expenditure management principles. There certainly should be skepticism about any claims that procurement of relatively standard materials, services, and commodities for the military should be subject to different rules.

Cost Considerations in Bidding. Standard procurement practice in nonmilitary sectors emphasizes value for money, but in the defense sector other factors, such as national interest and defense industry promotion, are often cited as more important than cost in accepting a bid for weapons procurement projects. Defense analysts point out, however, that national legislation can influence the part that cost plays in weapon procurement processes. In South Africa, for example, the 1998 defense review and the 1999 white paper on defense-related industries spell out which technologies are considered "strategically essential capabilities" and thus exempt from lowest-cost considerations.[30] The South African Parliament approved both documents.

Confidentiality. Transparency in defense procurement must be limited by national security interests. Confidentiality clauses are required in the arms procurement process; these, too, can be regulated by national legislation. The South African defense review lists a number of reasons for confidentiality in defense procurement, including the protection of third-party commercial information, national security, prevention of harm to South Africa's ability to conduct international relations, and the protection of South Africa's economic interests and the commercial activities of government bodies.[31]

Time Frame for Major Weapons Procurement. From inception to final acceptance of the product, procurement of major weapon systems may take as long as 15 years. Some flexibility needs to be built into the procurement process to take account of contingencies such as fluctuations in currency exchange rates. This long time frame also necessitates quality control throughout the procurement process, not just when the product is ready for delivery. In addition, it requires efforts to forecast spending farther into the future than in nondefense sectors; the United Kingdom, for example, has a 10-year "long-term costing" system for defense.[32] Finally, arms procurement projects should take into account full life-cycle costs and support for the acquired systems.

The Complexity of Arms Procurement. Because of the complexity of arms procurement, sound management of the procurement process requires interdisciplinary project teams with expertise in engineering, resource management, contracting, quality assurance, and design assurance. The particular complexity of major weapon systems procurement, which can involve a substantial number of subcontractors, creates significant opportunities for corruption. These projects therefore require the highest level of management and scrutiny by government accountability mechanisms. For example, South Africa has three levels of approval for major arms procurement projects within its Department of Defence. For other major projects, parliamentary approval may also be required.

International Arms Control Treaty Regimes and National Legislation Governing Arms Procurement. Procurement in the military sector is distinct from general government procurement in being subject to international treaties and specific national legislation. Some defense budgeting specialists suggest that the oversight mechanisms associated with this national and international regulation increase transparency.

6. Accounting and Reporting

The assumption is that the security sector is part of the government's "financial management information system" (FMIS), which is central to the running of public finance. The FMIS in turn requires a high quality of data

---

> **Box 2.8   Information Captured by a Financial Management Information System**
>
> • Approved budget allocations for both recurrent and capital outlays
> • Sources of financing for programs and projects
> • Budget transfers
> • Supplementary allocations
> • Fund releases against budgetary allocations
> • Data on commitments and actual expenditures against budgeted allocations.
>
> *Source:* World Bank 1998.

and accounting in order to be effective in capturing useful information. The kind of information an FMIS captures is listed in box 2.8.

However, many countries have no FMIS, or at least none used by security MDAs. Many countries have to contend with weak human and institutional capacity for finance management in the security sector. Sometimes this weak capacity reflects a desire to shroud in secrecy decision making, levels of expenditure, and the way in which resources are allocated; but it also can simply reflect the nature of the general public finance system. Throughout the public sector, linkages between policy, planning, budget development and execution, and oversight may be inadequate; and the individual components of that chain are often weak. Thus the capacity to generate the type of information that is required for evidence-based diagnosis and policy making is limited.

The 2012 PER of the criminal justice sector in El Salvador offers an example of such limited capacity. It found that the "lack of reliable and comparable statistics makes it challenging to measure efficiency of spending. El Salvador has no unified system of crime statistics integrating the arrests by the police and citizens' complaints to the Police and Attorney General's Office. Consequently, crime statistics vary in the country (sometimes significantly) depending on the source consulted, not only in terms of numbers, but also in the definition and classification of crimes."[33] In many countries, basic systems of security sector data and expenditure classification may not exist, or they may require significant reform to provide the type of information policy makers and budget holders require.

Under these circumstances, it is unrealistic to assume that practices in the security sector will meet a high standard or that the security sector will necessarily advance more rapidly than other parts of the public sector. A general need to strengthen public finance systems therefore provides an opportunity to strengthen the security sector specifically.

7. External Scrutiny and Audit

The final aspect of the PFM system is ensuring external audit and oversight, which—accounting for national security considerations—should be the same for the security sector as for any other.[34] The auditor general should

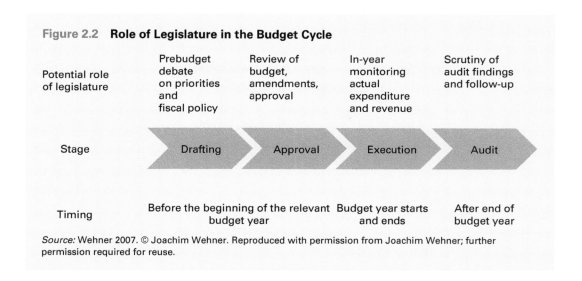

Figure 2.2   **Role of Legislature in the Budget Cycle**

Source: Wehner 2007. © Joachim Wehner. Reproduced with permission from Joachim Wehner; further permission required for reuse.

have sufficient access to transactions and performance indicators in the security sector and to audit reports discussed in Parliament (if need be, discussions can be in closed committee and include only those individuals with the necessary security clearance).

Activities aimed at improving the capacity of legislative bodies to perform their mandated public expenditure oversight offer another avenue for engaging with the security sector. Legislatures are often constitutionally mandated to authorize and scrutinize security expenditures. Figure 2.2 shows the potential roles that legislatures can play during an annual budget cycle in democratic systems. In reality, of course, the actual responsibilities and level of authority vary among countries, as does the capacity of legislators to authorize and scrutinize government budgets. Legislatures frequently benefit from capacity-building activities. Activities aimed at public accounts committees can examine the specificities of security budgeting, while activities aimed at defense, security, or intelligence committees can incorporate finance management issues. It is important to note, however, that legislatures may need to strengthen their overall capacity to engage in financial oversight before they are able to address the specific challenges of engaging with the security sector.

Treverton and Klitgaard have proposed a number of helpful questions for assessing external scrutiny of the security sector[35]:

- Are there clearly defined executive and legislative responsibilities for external and internal security?
- Are the security forces subject to democratic citizen control?
- Are parliamentarians, the media, and civil society free and able to participate in the security debate?
- Are the security forces able to exercise political influence?
- Are the security services open to unnecessary political interference through political reach into the promotion system?

- Are the security forces more loyal to the regime or to the people?
- Are there budgetary checks, balances, and internal and external audit, and are these transparent?
- Are the duties and responsibilities of the security services enshrined in legal statutes, military law, and codes of conduct?

Answers to these questions can be further corroborated by government-led surveys and opinion polls seeking public perceptions of the military, police, criminal justice institutions, and other actors. This information will shed light on the nature of state-society linkages in the sector.[36]

Conclusion

The goal of this chapter was to introduce key concepts in public finance and security that facilitate integration of the security sector within the broader scope of public sector governance analysis. The basis for the dialogue between security sector practitioners and economists/finance specialists is the national budget, which provides the financial basis for the delivery of government functions and the implementation of public policies. The chapter thus attempted to present the basics of public expenditure and PFM, and to identify the space where security services such as the military, police, and the criminal justice system fit within these processes.

Including the security sector in the national budget is essential for ensuring macroeconomic stability, allocative and operational efficiency, fiscal transparency, and accountability. Indeed, the military, police, and courts are no different from any other sector in PFM terms, and there is no valid reason why they should violate any PFM principles. Limited considerations have to be made for legitimately secret policies, like war plans. But in general security actors should follow the same budget process as other public sector entities, from formulation to execution and performance monitoring, and adhere to the same PFM standards of budget credibility, predictability, transparency, and so on.

At a minimum, then, the core task of a PER team is to elicit a sound analytical product that makes public finance professionals more aware of security sector needs, and that makes security sector practitioners more cognizant of the fiscal and governance rigors by which they must abide. However, a security sector PER should be just a stepping stone to institutionalizing this dialogue. The chapters that follow delve deeper into how these goals might be achieved in the military, police, and criminal justice system.

Annex 2A: UN and IMF Classifications of the Functions of Government: Defense

Schemes for budget classification, including (i) functional, (ii) economic, and (iii) programmatic classification schemes, have evolved over time to serve different purposes. These schemes are not mutually exclusive, and combinations of two or more enable more complex analysis of units and programs. However, introducing new classification schemes is not a small exercise; it places significant accounting and data demands on public institutions and in weak capacity settings may take some time to be implemented and yield reliable information.

Functional classification categorizes government activities based on their broad policy objectives—such as defense, justice, or public order—and so facilitates the analysis of resource allocation between government functions and sectors. It is important for the PER team to remember that there is not a one-to-one mapping between functions and institutions. Countries differ in the way they organize institutionally to provide security services, including defense; and defense sector institutions can provide nondefense services in addition to their core defense function. The United Nations' Classification of the Functions of Government (COFOG)[37] scheme provides an international standard that is comprehensive and facilitates cross-country comparisons. It comprises 10 major government functions and their subfunctions. Those comprising the defense function are provided in table 2A.1 as an example. One downside to the UN COFOG scheme is that certain expenditures related to veterans' benefits are included under a nondefense heading, which could frustrate a sectoral approach in postconflict situations where veterans' benefits are used to further demobilization efforts or are otherwise a significant part of the defense budget.[38]

It is common to combine the functional classification scheme with administrative and economic classification schemes to meet country needs. (See table 2A.2 for a sampling of the diversity of classification schemes.) Organizing economic transactions by function, for example, facilitates a sectoral approach while revealing intrasectoral imbalances. This can be especially important in the military sector, which often fails to account sufficiently for the long-term impact of major weapons procurements or force modifications. Similarly, the functional classification for defense is often subdivided into distinct defense programs. This method enables a sectoral approach to national budgeting, where the military sector competes with other sectors on a level playing field, but also allows the government to establish output and outcome goals for specific defense sector expenditures. This approach can help improve military effectiveness if the government establishes and implements effective performance metrics and holds program managers accountable for results.

Whatever classification scheme is adopted, budget categories for the defense, public safety, and justice sectors need to be comprehensive, internally consistent, and coherent with the rest of the national budget. Given the impact of security spending on macroeconomic stability and the importance of security provision to poverty reduction and economic development, it is crucial that the military, police, and judicial institutions be included in any process that updates central finance systems. If the PER team is involved in creating or reforming the defense sector classification scheme, for instance, it could be useful to consider the military budget from

Table 2A.1   UN Classification of the Functions of Government (COFOG): Defense Sector and Subsectors

Code	Title	Description
02	Defense	• Includes all subdivisions of defense
02.1	Military defense	• Administration of military defense affairs and services • Operation of land, sea, air, and space defense forces; operation of engineering, transport, communication, intelligence, personnel, and other noncombat defense forces; operation or support of reserve and auxiliary forces of the defense establishment • Includes offices of military attachés stationed abroad; field hospitals • Excludes military aid missions (02.3.0); base hospitals (07.3); military schools and colleges where curricula resemble those of civilian institutions even though attendance may be limited to military personnel and their families (09.1), (09.2), (09.3), or (09.4); pension schemes for military personnel (10.2)
02.2	Civil defense	• Administration of civil defense affairs and services; formulation of contingency plans; organization of exercises involving civilian institutions and populations • Operation or support of civil defense forces • Excludes civil protection services (03.2.0); purchase and storage of food, equipment, and other supplies for emergency use in the case of peacetime disasters (10.9.0)
02.3	Foreign military aid	• Administration of military aid and operation of military aid missions accredited to foreign governments or attached to international military organizations or alliances • Military aid in the form of grants (cash or in kind), loans (regardless of interest charged), or loans of equipment; contributions to international peacekeeping forces including the assignment of manpower
02.4	R&D defense	• Administration and operation of government agencies engaged in applied research and experimental development related to defense • Grants, loans, or subsidies to support applied research and experimental development related to defense undertaken by nongovernment bodies such as research institutes and universities • Excludes basic research (01.4.0)
02.5	Defense n.e.c.	• Administration, operation, or support of activities such as formulation, administration, coordination, and monitoring of overall policies, plans, programs, and budgets relating to defense; preparation and enforcement of legislation relating to defense; production and dissemination of general information, technical documentation, and statistics on defense; etc. • Includes defense affairs and services that cannot be assigned to (02.1), (02.2), (02.3), or (02.4) • Excludes administration of war veterans' affairs (10.2)

Source: United Nations Statistics Division, "Detailed Structure and Explanatory Notes," http://unstats.un.org/unsd/cr/registry/regcst.asp?Cl=4.
Note: n.e.c. = not elsewhere classified; R&D = research and development. The excluded budget codes refer to other sections of the UN COFOG scheme not included in this table.

Table 2A.2   Budget Classification Schemes

Resource	Description
United Nations Classification of the Functions of Government (UN COFOG) http://unstats.un.org/unsd/cr/registry /regcst.asp?Cl=4	Provides an international standard for functional classification
National Classifications http://unstats.un.org/unsd/cr/ctryreg /default.asp?Lg=1	Provides national classification schemes, where available, including each country's classification structure; the classification scheme's relationship to international standards; how and by whom it is used within government; its revision status; a summary of supporting documents; and contact information for the office responsible for maintaining the scheme
International Monetary Fund Government Finance Statistics Manual http://www.imf.org/external/np/sta/gfsm /index.htm	Provides an international standard for economic classification; chapter 6 focuses on government expenses and includes an annex discussing cross-classification with the UN COFOG to Government Finance Statistics reporting (where section "702 Defense" is analogous to the functions provided in table 2A.1).

the national perspective by asking what information is necessary to assess military budget requests and balance them against budget requests from other government sectors. The result might be an administrative, economic, functional, or program classification scheme, or some combination. Provisions must, of course, be made for legitimately secret budgets. Special codes could allow aggregation to a nonsensitive level for public disclosure, but could also enable specially cleared executive officials and legislative members to view budgets in more detail. The biggest challenge will likely be institutional resistance by the military or police to being integrated into the national budget process. Budget classification facilitates integration, and might be resisted for that reason.

An economic classification scheme groups expenditures by type, including compensation of employees; use of goods and services; consumption of fixed capital, interest, subsidies, and social benefits; and other expenses. The budget can incorporate economic categories for each institution and its subdivisions. In the army, for example, economic categories could be provided for each unit within the infantry, armor, special forces, civil affairs, and other subcommands. Combining an administrative and economic classification enables examination of personnel and capital spending by unit, for example, and highlights the production function for the units' outputs. The IMF's *Government Finance Statistics Manual* (GFSM) provides useful guidance for economic classification of expenses.[39] In addition to providing a classification scheme for revenues and expenses, the GFSM discusses institutional units and sectors; defines economic flows, stock positions, and accounting rules; and distinguishes between transactions in financial and nonfinancial assets and liabilities. It is important to note that GFSM 2014 covers accrual-based concepts, which may not be relevant or useful in many countries. A simplified version of the IMF's scheme for expense classification is provided in table 2A.3.

Programmatic classification specifies distinct programs—groupings of relatively homogenous policy objectives—with their associated expenditures. In this scheme, defense programs constitute the building blocks of the military budget, and include diverse activities such as procuring missiles for fighter aircraft, feeding troops in battle, or providing benefits to widows and orphans. In contrast to the functional classification, the program classification focuses on specific policy objectives and how they are going to be implemented. It can thus support performance evaluation and performance-based budgeting by linking economic inputs to program outputs (and potentially to program outcomes).

Program classification is the least common classification system, and it is especially challenging to implement in capacity-constrained environments.

Table 2A.3 IMF Economic Classification of Expenses

Expense category		Expense subcategory	
21	Compensation of employees	211	Wages and salaries
		212	Employers' social contributions
22	Use of goods and services		n.a.
23	Consumption of fixed capital		n.a.
24	Interest	241	To nonresidents
		242	To residents other than general government
		243	To other general government units
25	Subsidies	251	To public corporations
		252	To private enterprises
		253	To other sectors
26	Grants	261	To foreign governments
		262	To international organizations
		263	To other general government units
27	Social benefits	271	Social security benefits
		272	Social assistance benefits
		273	Employment-related social benefits
28	Other expense	281	Property expense other than interest
		282	Transfers not elsewhere classified
		283	Premiums, fees, and claims related to non-life insurance and standardized guarantee schemes

Source: Adapted from IMF 2014, table 6.1.
Note: IMF = International Monetary Fund; n.a. = not applicable. The actual *Government Finance Statistics Manual* scheme further delineates expense subcategories.

The original concept of program budgeting arose from applications in the U.S. Department of Defense in the 1950s and 1960s, and the approach was subsequently applied government-wide. Variations of program budgeting most recently have been at a level of aggregation below functions, sometimes below sectors, but covering larger policy areas of importance for a country's national objectives. A recent variation of this approach, specifically in defense, is capability-based planning,[40] where a specific functional capability is defined (for example, securing national borders from illegal or uncontrolled traffic), and all military services necessary for achieving that capability are considered, whether ground, air, or maritime/naval. The budget process within defense would seek to identify the most cost-effective combination of forces needed to achieve the objective along with the required funds.

Notes

1. World Bank, *Breaking the Conflict Trap: Civil War and Development Policy* (Washington, DC: World Bank and Oxford University Press, 2003).
2. See the website of the Public Expenditure and Financial Accountability (PEFA) initiative (launched in 2001) at www.pefa.org.
3. World Bank, *Public Expenditure Management Handbook* (Washington, DC: World Bank, 1998).
4. See the PEFA program website at www.pefa.org.
5. Richard Hemming, "The Macroeconomic Framework for Managing Public Finances," in *The International Handbook of Public Financial Management*, ed. Richard Allen, Richard Hemming, and Barry Potter (New York: Palgrave Macmillan, 2013), 17–37.
6. The question of the size of the overall defense budget has been a contentious one in relation to its overall impact on economic growth as well as its relationship with armed conflict. The PER policy outline does not take a position on the recommended macro-ceilings for the security sector, but some of the current debates on these issues are outlined in annex 1B in the introduction.
7. Richard Hemming, "The Macroeconomic Framework for Managing Public Finances," in *The International Handbook of Public Financial Management*, ed. Richard Allen, Richard Hemming, and Barry Potter (New York: Palgrave Macmillan, 2013), 34.
8. Adapted from Nicole Ball and Malcolm Holmes, "Integrating Defense into Public Expenditure Work" (U.K. Department for International Development, London, 2002), http://www.gsdrc.org/docs/open/ss11.pdf.
9. For more on *mano dura*, see for example Niels Uildriks, ed., *Policing Insecurity: Police Reform, Security and Human Rights* (Lanham, MD: Lexington Books, 2009).
10. United Nations Office on Drugs and Crime (UNODC) Statistics, "Data," http://www.unodc.org/unodc/en/data-and-analysis/statistics/data.html.

11. See World Bank, "Management Note (1991 Guidelines), SecM91-1563, Military Expenditure," December 1991.

12. See for example Rita Abrahamsen and Michael C. Williams, *Security beyond the State: Private Security in International Politics* (Cambridge, U.K.: Cambridge University Press, 2011).

13. See for example Mitchell Polinsky and Steven Shavell, "The Theory of Public Enforcement of the Law" (NBER Working Paper 11780, National Bureau of Economic Research, Cambridge, MA, 2005), which suggests that lower enforcement costs and higher fines would lead to less expensive but equally effective deterrence.

14. Robin Luckham and Tom Kirk, "Security in Hybrid Political Contexts: An End-User Approach" (London School of Economics, October 2012).

15. See the chapter on policing for a detailed discussion of measuring police performance.

16. World Bank, "Management Note (1991 Guidelines), SecM91-1563, Military Expenditure," December 1991.

17. The Global Partnership for Effective Development Co-operation works to strengthen aid effectiveness for developing countries; see the organization's website at http://effectivecooperation.org/.

18. William Byrd, "The Financial Dimensions of Security Sector Reform," in *The Future of Security Sector Reform*, ed. Mark Sedra (Waterloo, Ontario: Centre for International Governance Innovation, 2010), 21.

19. Some of the main reasons for deviations in public sector financing are identified in World Bank, *Public Expenditure Management Handbook* (Washington, DC: World Bank, 1998).

20. Peter J. Middlebrook and Sharon M. Miller, *Sierra Leone Security Expenditure Review* (London: U.K. Department for International Development, 2006).

21. Dylan Hendrickson and Nicole Ball, "Off-Budget Military Expenditure and Revenue: Issues and Policy Perspectives for Donors" (CSDG Occasional Paper 1, International Policy Institute, King's College London, 2002), https://www.ciponline.org/images/uploads/publications/OP1_OffBudget_Military_Expenditure.pdf.

22. Alasdari Roberts, "Transparency in the Security Sector," in *The Right to Know: Transparency for an Open World*, ed. Ann Florini (New York: Columbia University Press, 2007), 309–36; quoted in William Byrd, "The Financial Dimensions of Security Sector Reform," in *The Future of Security Sector Reform*, ed. Mark Sedra (Waterloo, Ontario: Centre for International Governance Innovation, 2010).

23. See the ROSC webpage at https://www.imf.org/external/NP/rosc/rosc.aspx.

24. See for example "Khaki Capitalism," *The Economist*, December 3, 2011, http://www.economist.com/node/21540985.

25. Colin Shaw, *Mastering Military Maintenance* (McKinsey, 2010), 28.

26. See for example the MAG (Mines Advisory Group) website at http://www.maginternational.org/ (and contact MAG at info@maginternational.org for further information).

27. See the UN Integrated Technical Guidance Note on National Ownership of SSR, 2012, https://unssr.unlb.org/Portals/UNSSR/UN%20Integrated%20Technical%20Guidance%20Notes%20on%20SSR.PDF.

28. This section is adapted from Nicole Ball and Malcolm Holmes, "Integrating Defense into Public Expenditure Work" (U.K. Department for International Development, London, 2002), http://www.gsdrc.org/docs/open/ss11.pdf.

29. Some countries distinguish between the "procurement" of commercial goods and services and the "acquisition" of armaments. Others use the term "procurement" for both commercial goods and services and weapons or weapon systems. This discussion follows the latter practice.

30. South African Department of Defence, "Defence in a Democracy: South African Defence Review 1998" (Pretoria, 1998), http://www.dod.mil.za/documents/defencereview/defence%20review1998.pdf; and South African National Conventional Arms Control Committee, "White Paper on the South African Defence Related Industries," Pretoria, December 1999, http://www.dod.mil.za/documents/WhitePaperonDef/white%20paper%20on%20the%20SA%20defence%20related%20industries1999.pdf.

31. South African National Conventional Arms Control Committee, "White Paper on the South African Defence Related Industries," par. 68.

32. See British Army, *Design for Military Operations: The British Military Doctrine* (London: Ministry of Defence, 1996), http://www.army.mod.uk/doctrine/branches/doc.htm.

33. World Bank, "El Salvador Security and Justice Public Expenditure and Institutional Review: Decision Document" (World Bank, Washington, DC, June 2012), 11.

34. See Geneva Centre for the Democratic Control of Armed Forces (DCAF), "International Standards for Financial Oversight in the Security Sector" (DCAF, Geneva, 2015).

35. Gregory F. Treverton and Robert Klitgaard, "Enhancing Security through Development: Probing the Connections" (paper presented at the Annual Bank Conference on Development Economics, Amsterdam, May 23–24, 2005).

36. See for example Nawaf Wasfi Tell, "Public Opinion, Terrorism and the Jordanian Security Sector" (Center for Strategic Studies, Jordan, July 2008), http://www.arab-reform.net/sites/default/files/Article_Nawaf_el_Tell.pdf.

37. The UN systems and procedures related to government statistics are on the United Nations Statistics Division website at http://unstats.un.org/unsd/default.htm.

38. United Nations Statistics Division, "Detailed Structure and Explanatory Notes," http://unstats.un.org/unsd/cr/registry/regcst.asp?Cl=4. A further weakness of the UN COFOG scheme from the perspective of this sourcebook is that the public order and safety function includes "fire

protection services," which are not directly related to the broader security and justice function defined here.

39. IMF, *Government Finance Statistics Manual 2014* (Washington, DC: International Monetary Fund, 2014), http://www.imf.org/external /np/sta/gfsm/index.htm.

40. For a readable treatise on the concept, see Colonel Stephen K. Walker, "Capabilities-Based Planning: How It Is Intended to Work and Challenges to Its Successful Implementation" (U.S. Army War College Strategic Research Project, 2005).

References

Abrahamsen, Rita, and Michael C. Williams. 2011. *Security beyond the State: Private Security in International Politics*. Cambridge, U.K.: Cambridge University Press.

Ball, Nicole, and Malcolm Holmes. 2002. "Integrating Defense into Public Expenditure Work." U.K. Department for International Development, London. http://www.gsdrc.org/docs/open/ss11.pdf.

Ball, Nicole, and Len le Roux. 2006. "A Model for Good Practice in Budgeting for the Military Sector." In *Budgeting for the Military Sector in Africa*, edited by W. Omitoogun and E. Hutchful. Oxford, U.K.: Oxford University Press for SIPRI.

British Army. 1996. *Design for Military Operations: The British Military Doctrine*. London: Ministry of Defence. http://www.army.mod.uk /doctrine/branches/doc.htm.

Byrd, William. 2010. "The Financial Dimensions of Security Sector Reform." In *The Future of Security Sector Reform*, edited by M. Sedra. Waterloo, Ontario: Centre for International Governance Innovation.

DCAF (Geneva Centre for the Democratic Control of Armed Forces). 2015. "International Standards for Financial Oversight in the Security Sector." DCAF, Geneva.

de Renzio, Paolo. 2013. "Assessing and Comparing the Quality of Public Financial Management Systems: Theory, History, and Evidence." In *The International Handbook of Public Financial Management*, edited by Richard Allen, Richard Hemming, and Barry Potter, 137–60. New York: Palgrave Macmillan.

Economist. 2011. "Khaki Capitalism." December 3. http://www.economist .com/node/21540985.

Hemming, Richard. 2013. "The Macroeconomic Framework for Managing Public Finances." In *The International Handbook of Public Financial Management*, edited by Richard Allen, Richard Hemming, and Barry Potter, 17–37. New York: Palgrave Macmillan.

Hendrickson, Dylan, and Nicole Ball. 2002. "Off-Budget Military Expenditure and Revenue: Issues and Policy Perspectives for Donors." CSDG

Occasional Paper 1, International Policy Institute, King's College, London. https://www.ciponline.org/images/uploads/publications/OP1_OffBudget_Military_Expenditure.pdf.

IMF (International Monetary Fund). 2014. *Government Finance Statistics Manual 2014*. Washington, DC: IMF. http://www.imf.org/external/np/sta/gfsm/index.htm.

Lienert, Ian. 2013. "The Legal Framework for Public Finances and Budget Systems." In *The International Handbook of Public Financial Management*, edited by Richard Allen, Richard Hemming, and Barry Potter, 63–83. New York: Palgrave Macmillan.

Luckham, Robin, and Tom Kirk. 2012. "Security in Hybrid Political Contexts: An End-User Approach." London School of Economics.

Middlebrook, Peter J., and Sharon M. Miller. 2006. *Sierra Leone Security Expenditure Review*. London: U.K. Department for International Development.

More, Sylvie, and Megan Price. 2011. "The EU's Support to Security System Reform in the Democratic Republic of Congo: Perceptions from the Field." Netherlands Institute of International Relations, The Hague.

PEFA (Public Expenditure and Financial Accountability) Secretariat. 2011. "Annex 1: The PFM High-Level Performance Indicator Set." In *Public Financial Management Performance Measurement Framework*. Washington, DC: PEFA. http://www.pefa.org/sites/pefa.org/files/attachments/PMFEng-finalSZreprint04-12_1.pdf.

Polinsky, Mitchell, and Steven Shavell. 2005. "The Theory of Public Enforcement of the Law." NBER Working Paper 11780, National Bureau of Economic Research, Cambridge, MA.

Roberts, Alasdari. 2007. "Transparency in the Security Sector." In *The Right to Know: Transparency for an Open World*, edited by A. Florini, 309–36. New York: Columbia University Press.

Shaw, Colin. 2010. *Mastering Military Maintenance*. McKinsey.

South African Department of Defence. 1998. "Defence in a Democracy: South African Defence Review 1998." Pretoria. http://www.dod.mil.za/documents/defencereview/defence%20review1998.pdf.

South African National Conventional Arms Control Committee. 1999. "White Paper on the South African Defence Related Industries." Pretoria. http://www.dod.mil.za/documents/WhitePaperonDef/white%20paper%20on%20the%20SA%20defence%20related%20industries1999.pdf.

Tell, Nawaf Wasfi. 2008. "Public Opinion, Terrorism and the Jordanian Security Sector." Center for Strategic Studies, Jordan. http://www.arab-reform.net/sites/default/files/Article_Nawaf_el_Tell.pdf.

Treverton, Gregory F., and Robert Klitgaard. 2005. "Enhancing Security through Development: Probing the Connections." Paper presented at the Annual Bank Conference on Development Economics, Amsterdam, May 23–24.

Uildriks, Niels, ed. 2009. *Policing Insecurity: Police Reform, Security and Human Rights*. Lanham, MD: Lexington Books.

United Nations Office on Drugs and Crime (UNODC) Statistics. "Data." http://www.unodc.org/unodc/en/data-and-analysis/statistics/data.html.

United Nations Statistics Division. "Detailed Structure and Explanatory Notes." http://unstats.un.org/unsd/cr/registry/regcst.asp?Cl=4.

UNSG (United Nations Secretary General). 2008. *Securing Peace and Development: The Role of the United Nations in Supporting Security Sector Reform*. United Nations, A/62/659; S/2008/39.

Walker, Colonel Stephen K. 2005. "Capabilities-Based Planning: How It Is Intended to Work and Challenges to Its Successful Implementation." U.S. Army War College Strategic Research Project.

Wehner, Joachim. 2007. *Strengthening Legislative Financial Scrutiny in Developing Countries: Report Prepared for the U.K. Department for International Development*. London School of Economics and Political Science.

World Bank. 1991. "Management Note (1991 Guidelines), SecM91-1563, Military Expenditure."

———. 1998. *Public Expenditure Management Handbook*. Washington, DC: World Bank.

———. 2003. *Breaking the Conflict Trap: Civil War and Development Policy*. Washington, DC: World Bank and Oxford University Press.

———. 2005a. *Improving Public Financial Management in the Security Sector*. Vol. 5 of *Afghanistan: Managing Public Finances for Development*. Washington, DC: World Bank.

———. 2005b. "Public Financial Management (PFM) Work Staff Guidance." http://www1.worldbank.org/publicsector/pe/StrengthenedApproach /3StaffGuidance.pdf.

———. 2012a. "El Salvador Security and Justice Public Expenditure and Institutional Review: Decision Document." World Bank, Washington, DC.

———. 2012b. "Republic of Burundi Public Expenditure Review: Fiscal Challenges, Security, and Growth in Burundi." Report no. ACS3988. World Bank, Washington, DC.

World Bank and United Nations. 2012. "Liberia Public Expenditure Review Note: Meeting the Challenges of the UNMIL Security Transition." World Bank, Washington, DC.

World Bank and United Nations Assistance Mission in Somalia. 2016. *Security and Justice Public Expenditure Review*.

CHAPTER 3

Public Expenditure Reviews in the Defense Sector

Introduction

This chapter examines the potential role of a Public Expenditure Review (PER) in the defense sector, which is usually among the most sensitive areas of government in developing and developed countries alike. The basic analytical framework for a defense sector PER is the same as for any other sector, and the PER team can employ many of the same techniques to assess overall fiscal sustainability, the role of various military and policy-making institutions, the strategic allocation of resources, and the efficiency and effectiveness of government spending in providing defense services.

The scope and methodology of a defense sector PER depend on the nature of the government's request and subsequent discussions. But in all cases, a successful PER will require buy-in from relevant officials. These officials will almost certainly include the ministers of defense and finance, and senior military officers, but also senior executive officials, personnel from oversight agencies, and lower-level military officers.

Whatever motivates the request (the potential reasons are explored in this chapter), trust between stakeholders is critical given the sensitivities of the issues involved. Without such trust, a PER in the defense sector is not going to get very far. In 2005, for example, the heads of the World Bank, the United Nations Department of Peacekeeping, and the European Commission jointly agreed that a review of expenditures in the Democratic Republic of Congo would be a very worthwhile exercise. However, the government was not party to this agreement and therefore the recommended PER was never initiated.

The goals of a defense sector PER are to shed light on public spending decisions in the military sector by (i) assessing the extent to which the military budget is prepared against a clear, nationally determined security strategy; (ii) analyzing the affordability of defense sector policies and expenditures in a macroeconomic context; (iii) helping policy makers determine the appropriateness of resource allocations given the security sector trade-offs available and the specific strategies adopted; and (iv) measuring the efficiency and effectiveness of overall military expenditures. In carrying out these aims, the PER can help establish objective standards and an inclusive national process for allocating scarce public resources among various policy options, and in turn improve service delivery, not just in the security sector but more broadly across government.

A defense sector PER can also help build public trust by promoting transparency and accountability, which are essential to the long-term sustainability and success of the military and other government institutions. Successfully connecting informed policy to reliable, sufficient resourcing can help improve overall military effectiveness, thus providing an essential supply-side boost to security. Similarly, improving perceptions of military accountability can help build trust and mitigate social cleavages, thus providing an essential demand-side boost.

This chapter proceeds in five parts:

1. The introduction provides an overview of defense sector PERs. It discusses possible entry points for a PER and describes possible methodologies, which vary depending on the composition of the PER team and the nature of the client request.
2. The section on defense functions and military institutions defines the broad functions expected of the sector and describes how they are organized.
3. The section on budgeting in defense applies universal budgetary principles (enumerated in chapter 2) to the military sector's budget formulation process. It also looks at specific concerns for military budgets and outlines a standard annual budget cycle.
4. The section on budget execution discusses budget authority, the budget execution cycle, and internal controls in the defense sector.
5. The section on performance measurement and oversight offers a broad view of these functions in the military sector, with a focus on the importance of fiscal transparency and the role of oversight agencies.

Entry Points and Methodology for Defense Sector PERs

There are many possible entry points for defense sector PERs (see table 3.1). In some instances, a PER might be motivated by factors that do not originate in the security sector but still affect it, such as changes in government or the political environment, the country's strategic context, or macroeconomic or financial conditions. Other entry points may relate to the state of

Table 3.1   Entry Points for a Defense Sector Public Expenditure Review

Type of change	Examples
Political: changes in political conditions at home, among key allies, or among adversaries	Elections or change in administration
	Change in public opinion
	Legislative attitudes and scrutiny
	Peace accord implementation
	Implementation of international obligations, such as European Union accession requirements
	Human rights review
Economic: changes in expenditure caused by macroeconomic or fiscal shocks, or in the way economic resources are allocated and controlled	Changes in the fiscal space or resource envelope available due to changes in revenue
	Realignment of national spending priorities
	Reduction in defense expenditure by allies
	Response to increased defense spending by neighbors or adversaries
	Macroeconomic shocks
	Medium-term expenditure framework process
	Institutional or process reforms to strengthen government-wide financial management
Security: impact of national, regional, or international security developments	Security sector reform program sponsored by the domestic government or an international partner
	Strategic shock resulting in the redefinition of security threats
	Adoption of a security sector approach
	Internal security challenges, including civil unrest
	Public safety and security pressures from organized crime and violence
	Border tensions
	Implementation of international obligations (e.g., relating to arms control or transnational crime)
	Arrival or withdrawal of international military force
Military: changes in military capabilities to reflect political, economic, or security context	Updated defense planning assumptions following fragility analysis or threat assessment
	Defense review initiating either defensewide or individual service reform
	Accountability and military effectiveness issues
	Major equipment procurement decisions
	Interservice rivalries, including redefinition of investment priority

the civil-military relationship or external shocks such as insecurity in the region or a successful peace process.

Given the range of entry points and topics, and given the different mandates of the actors that might conduct such a study, there is no standard methodology for a defense sector PER. Since 2005, the World Bank has worked with the United Nations or partners on PERs relevant to the military in various countries, including Afghanistan (2005 and 2010), the Central African Republic (2009), Liberia (2012), Burundi (2012), Mali (2013), and Niger (2013); all varied in scope (see table 3.2) and in how they applied PER methodologies and public financial management (PFM) principles.[1] Case studies drawn from these PERs are used throughout this chapter to illustrate general observations.

A defense sector PER typically includes a functional mapping of the military sector that provides the basis for determining whether military spending actually addresses security needs. If public funds are optimally allocated, there will be a clear link between security threats, defense policy objectives, military strategy, and military institutions. Defense policy objectives must address the country's threat perceptions to mitigate risks and provide the necessary conditions for peace, economic development, and poverty reduction; military strategy must explicitly define how military forces will achieve defense policy objectives; and decisions about force structure, equipping, training, and employment must fulfill the military strategy. A functional mapping will therefore review the country's defense policy objectives and map service delivery responsibilities to specific military institutions; the goal is to identify the military sector's prescribed functions and policy objectives and to assess the extent to which coherent strategies guide public expenditure allocations. Generally, roles and responsibilities are a key determinant of funding and staffing requirements.

The following institutional actors are included in a functional mapping of the military sector:

- *Policy and administration agencies:* the chief executive, legislature, defense council, ministry of defense, joint chiefs of staff, and ministry of finance, which determine defense policy objectives and military strategy
- *Armed services:* the army, navy, air force, and other branches depending on country context, which train, equip, and maintain military forces
- *Operational military forces:* joint commands of military units from the various branches that are operationally employed to deliver security services
- *Oversight agencies:* internal and external oversight bodies that monitor and report on defense sector efficiency and performance.

On the basis of this mapping exercise, a defense sector PER will typically survey the existing level and structure of security expenditures, as well as recent trends and likely future expenditure requirements. This type of analysis should cover recurrent expenses and a full costing of major procurement, capital expenditures, and force modifications in order to determine resource requirements and assess whether funds are allocated efficiently. If military institutions are not mapped, assessing the disposition and use of funds for the defense function is difficult, if not impossible.

Table 3.2 Coverage of UN, World Bank, and Bilateral Public Expenditure Reviews of the Defense Sector, 2005–2013

	Security context	Economic or fiscal context	Security institution mapping	Survey resource allocation	Budget formulation	Budget execution	Personnel	Procurement	Asset management	Oversight and audit
Afghanistan World Bank, *Improving Public Financial Management in the Security Sector* (2005 and 2010)	✓	✓	✓	✓	✓	✓				
Burundi World Bank, "Republic of Burundi Public Expenditure Review: Fiscal Challenges, Security, and Growth in Burundi" (2012)	✓	✓	✓							
Central African Republic World Bank, "Report on the Assessment of the Financial Management of the Defense and Security Forces in the Central African Republic" (2009)			✓	✓	✓	✓	✓			✓

(Table continues on next page)

Table 3.2 Coverage of UN, World Bank, and Bilateral Public Expenditure Reviews of the Defense Sector, 2005–2013 *(continued)*

	Security context	Economic or fiscal context	Security institution mapping	Survey resource allocation	Budget formulation	Budget execution	Personnel	Procurement	Asset management	Oversight and audit
Liberia										
World Bank and United Nations, "Liberia Public Expenditure Review Note: Meeting the Challenges of the UNMIL Security Transition" (2012)	✓		✓	✓						
Mali										
World Bank, "Malian Security Forces: Financial Management Assessment Report" (2013)		✓			✓	✓	✓	✓		✓
Niger										
World Bank, "Niger Security Sector Public Expenditure Review" (2013)	✓	✓	✓	✓	✓	✓	✓		✓	

Source: World Bank data.

Thus under most circumstances, a defense sector PER implicitly includes the more narrowly defined functional mapping. In any case, it is good practice for a PER to define the universe or scope of the topic addressed, and specify which parts of that universe the subsequent review will analyze.

A defense sector PER also typically seeks to apply internationally accepted PFM principles and practices to the defense function and military institutions. Applying these principles and practices improves budget formulation, budget execution, and oversight practices, and in turn supports four overriding goals of sound macrofiscal management:

1. *Macroeconomic and fiscal stability*, which involves maintaining control of a country's overall fiscal position
2. *Allocative efficiency*, which involves balancing competing demands and allocating scarce public resources where they will have the greatest benefit (as well as assessing whether allocations match government sectoral policy priorities)
3. *Operational efficiency*, which involves achieving outputs and outcomes that are economical, efficient, and effective to get the most out of all funds expended
4. *Fiscal transparency and accountability*, which involves providing open and transparent access to financial decisions and data so that government officials can be held accountable for their actions.

Fiscal stability and allocative efficiency are largely achieved through an effective national budget process. The national budget is therefore considered the government's single most important policy instrument from a PFM perspective. Through the national budget, competing policy objectives are reconciled and specific government initiatives are supported by means of a deliberate, informed, and competitive process of resource allocation. A defense sector PER will likely review the processes for determining funding levels, allocating resources to the military sector, executing defense budgets, and providing ex post oversight and impact assessment. The goal is to assess the equity, efficiency, and effectiveness of resource allocations in the context of the country's macroeconomic constraints, defense policy, and other sectoral priorities. An essential element of fiscal sustainability is managing multiyear and long-term commitments to ensure that both the capital expenditure itself and associated operating and maintenance costs are affordable and sustainable. This is most often associated with capital investment and constructions, but also encompasses large multiyear procurements.

Operational efficiency depends on the country's internal control environment and practices, as well as its systems of performance measurement and oversight. Under the great majority of circumstances, internationally accepted PFM principles apply to the military sector as well as any other sector. Limited special considerations have to be made for secret activities, operational uncertainties, and the long time horizon of many force structuring and procurement decisions, as well as for the difficulty of measuring defense outcomes. But overall, there is no reason the military sector should be held to weaker standards than the rest of government. Moreover, the military sector potentially has much to gain from a PER, which will likely improve not only efficiency and accountability but also performance. Typically, a defense sector PER (i) surveys internal controls for human resources, procurement, asset management, and other aspects of budget execution; (ii) assesses the effectiveness of financial management and financial oversight practices and their impact on service delivery; and (iii) identifies necessary financial management reforms to improve the effectiveness and efficiency of public spending. A defense sector PER will also likely assess the capacity and effectiveness of the country's legislature and its internal and external oversight institutions. In doing so, it will identify and incorporate indicators to assess institutional performance and service delivery.

Finally, fiscal transparency and accountability are especially important for the military sector. Often, public perceptions about military exceptionalism, the military's predominance in domestic politics, or the military's operational control of deadly force make this sector particularly prone to waste, fraud, and abuse. The public services delivered by the military sector are intended to be a source of security, but the military can be a source of insecurity if its coercive powers are exercised to advance its own interests. Moreover, as a classic public good, defense is noncontested, meaning that individuals have no effective way to deny payment for substandard service. The only way of ensuring that the military serves the national interest and promotes security, not insecurity, is through the "long route" of democratic accountability: the military must receive policy guidance from, and answer to, elected civilian leaders.[2] For those elected civilian leaders to fulfill their role, they need information about military activities and spending decisions, which is facilitated by fiscal transparency.

A PER's specific methodology and focus depend on the context and country request. Generic guidance is outlined in the introduction to this book, and this chapter considers the potential spectrum of issues to be covered in defense. The work undertaken by the United Nations Development Programme (UNDP) and Interpeace in Guatemala (box 3.1) offers an interesting example of how these issues have been approached. How a PER is conducted, and how the results are used and disseminated, can vary depending on its objectives. Most PERs are at a minimum an analytic piece covering policy, funding, institutions, and impact/outcomes, with the objective of providing information about economic and policy issues and facilitating government deliberations and decisions. Some PERs engage multiple domestic and international stakeholders in order to clarify issues, develop options, and build consensus for the sector. The PER's focus and methodology shape the work program and its timing and should be understood from the start.

> **Box 3.1   Guatemala—A Security Policy for Democracy**
>
> From 1999 to 2002, the United Nations Development Programme and Interpeace supported a civil society–led policy dialogue in Guatemala on the security sector. This exercise, called POLSEDE ("toward a security policy for democracy"), brought together civil society, military, intelligence, and political actors at the end of the civil war to examine the role and potential reform of the armed forces and intelligence services. The initiative started with three criteria: (i) the agenda was open, (ii) the agenda was defined by the participants, and (iii) recommendations were nonbinding in nature. The research-oriented open agenda encouraged key participants to engage in a potentially threatening dialogue about comprehensive reform. In turn, the extended timeline allowed reform alliances to be built around key areas in the defense sector and its links to civilian oversight and accountability.
>
> *Source:* Arevalo de Leon 2007.

Country Contexts

Countries vary significantly in the orientation, composition, and resourcing of their military sectors. As the "Defense Functions and Military Institutions" section of this chapter will explain, the specific functions fulfilled by the military sector vary based on national priorities, perceived security threats, military strategy, tradition, and other factors. Resource allocations should be determined based on several interrelated factors: nationally determined defense policy objectives and military strategy, assessed resource requirements to meet those objectives, and a centrally determined resource constraint set to maintain fiscal and macroeconomic stability. Security threats, functional organization, and resource allocations vary across countries and across time, so it is difficult to make generalizations and there is no universal formula that can be applied.

Even so, three factors are especially important to defining country context: (i) institutional strength, (ii) vulnerability to conflict, and (iii) the country's level of economic development. Together, they condition the objectives, standards, and practices of a country's defense policy, military strategy, and resource allocation. They should therefore guide the PER team's analysis and its development of "best fit" reforms. The team might also compare the country of interest to international standards—or to other countries with similar institutional, conflict, and economic profiles—in order to further highlight areas of concern and suggest possible reforms.

Institutional Strength

Institutions, in the classic definition, are "humanly devised constraints that structure political, economic, and social interactions."[3] Strong institutions are those that promote desired outcomes, and the World Bank has identified numerous institutions important for economic development. To monitor policy and institutional quality and to help allocate concessional lending and grants for low-income countries, the World Bank uses a Country Policy and Institutional Assessment (CPIA). The CPIA uses a six-point scale to score 16 relevant institutions organized into four clusters:

- *Economic management,* comprising monetary and exchange rate policies, fiscal policy, and debt policy and management
- *Structural policies,* relating to trade, the financial sector, and the business regulatory environment
- *Policies for social inclusion/equity,* relating to gender equality, equity of public resource use, human resources development, social protection and labor, and policies and institutions for environmental sustainability
- *Public sector management and institutions,* relating to property rights and rule-based governance, quality of budgetary and financial management, efficiency of revenue mobilization, quality of public administration, and transparency, accountability, and corruption in the public sector.[4]

The World Bank defines a fragile state (or "situation") as one that has a harmonized CPIA score of 3.2 or less (on the six-point scale) or that has hosted a UN or regional peacekeeping or peacebuilding mission in the last three years.[5] Among them are some of the world's poorest countries, including the four poorest in per capita (purchasing power parity) terms—the Democratic Republic of Congo, Burundi, Eritrea, and Liberia.[6] The list of fragile states also includes Timor-Leste and Zimbabwe, which are "blend" countries eligible for concessional and nonconcessional lending, as well as Bosnia and Herzegovina, Iraq, Lebanon, Libya, and the Syrian Arab Republic, which are middle-income countries (and therefore not scored by the CPIA). For each of the World Bank–designated fragile situations, average CPIA scores and indicators for the presence of peacekeeping or peacebuilding missions are shown in table 3.3.

Institutional strength in the military sector is determined by the accountability, effectiveness, and efficiency of the country's policy and administrative agencies, armed services, operational military forces, and oversight agencies. Democratic accountability and effective service delivery have long been commonly accepted criteria in the security sector reform (SSR) community (see box 3.2 for an example). More recently, efficiency—including the transparency of finances and the rationalization of budgets—has been identified as another key indicator of strength.[7] Means to assess accountability, effectiveness, and efficiency in the context of a defense sector PER are discussed in the "Performance Measurement and Oversight" section of this chapter.

Table 3.3   **World Bank–Designated Fragile Situations, 2016**

	CPIA cluster averages			Presence of mission	
	World Bank	AfDB/ADB	Harmonized	Peacekeeping	Political
IDA eligible					
Afghanistan	2.65	2.80	2.7		X
Burundi	3.26	3.37	3.3		X
Central African Republic	2.43	2.28	2.4		X
Chad	2.69	3.24	3.0		
Comoros	2.71	2.46	2.6		
Congo, Dem. Rep.	2.97	3.29	3.1	X	
Côte d'Ivoire	3.25	3.49	3.4	X	
Eritrea	1.99	2.14	2.1		
Gambia, The	3.14	3.20	3.2		
Guinea-Bissau	2.50	2.67	2.6		X
Haiti	2.85	—	2.9	X	
Kiribati	2.95	3.05	3.0		
Kosovo	3.55	—	3.6	X	
Liberia	3.10	3.49	3.3	X	
Madagascar	3.13	3.19	3.2		
Mali	3.36	3.65	3.5	X	
Marshall Islands	2.64	2.90	2.8		
Micronesia, Fed. Sts.	2.73	2.95	2.8		
Myanmar	3.05	3.13	3.1		
Sierra Leone	3.26	3.36	3.3		X
Solomon Islands	2.93	3.30	3.1		
Somalia	—	1.10	1.1		X
South Sudan	2.00	2.21	2.1	X	
Sudan	2.42	2.56	2.5	X	
Togo	2.99	3.20	3.1		
Tuvalu	2.79	2.97	2.9		
Yemen, Rep.	2.97	—	3.0		
Territories					
West Bank and Gaza	—	—	—		X
Blend					
Timor-Leste	3.05	3.39	3.2	X	
Zimbabwe	2.65	2.20	2.4		
IBRD only					
Bosnia and Herzegovina					X
Iraq					X
Lebanon					X
Libya					X
Syrian Arab Republic					X

Sources: World Bank; Asian Development Bank 2013; African Development Bank Group.
Note: — = not available. ADB = Asian Development Bank; AfDB = African Development Bank; CPA = Country Performance Assessment; CPIA = Country Policy and Institutional Assessment; IBRD = International Bank for Reconstruction and Development; IDA = International Development Association. Numbers are affected by rounding. Middle-income countries (Bosnia and Herzegovina, Iraq, Lebanon, Libya, and the Syrian Arab Republic) are not scored by the CPIA. CPIA uses a six-point scale, with 1 being the least institutionally developed and 6 being the most institutionally developed. The Asian Development Bank uses the CPA as its indicator.

> **Box 3.2   Indonesia—Internal Institutional Reform and Civil Society Capacity**
>
> After the fall of Suharto in 1998, Indonesia installed a civilian minister of defense as a signal that the military was prepared to come under civilian oversight. In turn, the reform process was supported by a very strong civil society platform, the Indonesian Working Group on Security Sector Reform. Over the next four years and with very little external support, national institutions reformed military procurement, established parliamentary oversight commissions, and produced a defense white paper.
>
> *Source:* Muna 2008.

There is no standard index of institutional strength for national militaries, and developing one is probably impossible because the broad range of defense policy objectives prevents cross-country comparisons of service-delivery effectiveness. However, Transparency International has developed a typology of 28 defense sector corruption risks (see annex 3B). Using this index, Transparency International ranked 82 economies on a 100-point scale. Nearly 70 percent had high to critical risk of corruption in the military sector. Among them were the majority of the world's major arms importers and exporters, as well as all of the fragile states assessed. All the countries that scored within the top 10 percent are classified as high-income by the World Bank: Germany (88), Australia (86), Norway (82), the United States (81), the United Kingdom (77), Taiwan, China (75), Sweden (75), and Austria (72). All the countries that scored in the bottom 10 percent are located in the Middle East and North Africa or Sub-Saharan Africa: the Syrian Arab Republic (3), Libya (5), Eritrea (7), the Republic of Yemen (8), Angola (8), the Arab Republic of Egypt (11), Algeria (12), and the Democratic Republic of Congo (14).[8] Integrity scores for assessed fragile states and average integrity scores by income group and region are provided in annex 3C. In most cases, defense sector corruption risks are caused or exacerbated by weaknesses in PFM principles and practices. The PER team can therefore use this typology, and the data collected by Transparency International, to benchmark defense sector corruption risks for the country of interest. In terms of economic output, Transparency International's corruption-risk index covers a wider range of countries than does the CPIA. That makes it more useful for benchmarking middle- or upper-income countries, but somewhat less helpful for fragile states. Even so, there is a strong positive correlation between the two indexes for the 25 countries they share in common, as shown in figure 3.1. Where data availability is limited, therefore, the PER team might consider the CPIA index of government-wide institutions as indicative of institutional quality within the military sector.[9]

Figure 3.1 Transparency International and Country Policy and Institutional Assessment Indicators of Institutional Quality

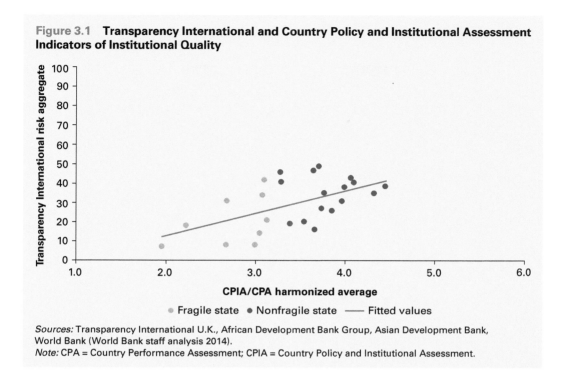

Sources: Transparency International U.K., African Development Bank Group, Asian Development Bank, World Bank (World Bank staff analysis 2014).
Note: CPA = Country Performance Assessment; CPIA = Country Policy and Institutional Assessment.

Vulnerability to Conflict

Armed conflict is obviously directly relevant for the military sector. The level of civil unrest and external threat will determine the structure and disposition of the country's security forces, including the military. Active conflict takes a toll on military forces: it depletes the country's stock of ammunition and supplies; wears out weapons and other defense matériel; damages transport, physical infrastructure, and other assets; and—perhaps most important—exhausts military personnel and prevents or delays their training. Finally, conflict often implicates the security forces in human rights abuses; in addition to the direct harm this causes to the populace, human rights abuses indicate weak military accountability.

Data on the incidence of civil wars and interstate conflicts at the national level are well developed, but data availability is more limited for the effects of civil conflict and criminal violence (on lives and the economy), and for subnational geographical areas. Moreover, data are particularly weak for fragile and low-income states. Nonetheless, data on battle deaths and homicide rates are widely used for cross-country comparisons and for determining if a state is conflict prone, and both indicators are available from the World Bank's World Development Indicators Database (see table 3A.1 in annex 3A). These data can be used by the PER team to benchmark the country of interest and to roughly determine whether security spending is adequate to meet the evident security challenges. Conflict indicators for fragile states are listed in table 3.4. In addition to providing valuable comparative statistics, this table

Table 3.4   Conflict Indicators in Selected Fragile States

	Annual averages over designated period			
	Homicides per 100,000 people		Battle deaths	
	10-year	20-year	10-year	20-year
Afghanistan	2.4	2.4	3,503.6	3,994.1
Bosnia and Herzegovina	1.8	1.8	—	4,064.0
Burundi	21.7	21.7	516.0	555.0
Central African Republic	29.3	29.3	71.6	98.7
Chad	15.8	15.8	411.6	396.7
Comoros	12.2	12.2	—	56.0
Congo, Dem. Rep.	21.7	21.7	556.1	1,301.9
Côte d'Ivoire	56.9	56.9	211.0	211.0
Eritrea	17.8	17.8	57.0	11,460.2
Guinea-Bissau	20.2	20.2	—	234.7
Haiti	5.8	5.8	244.0	244.0
Iraq	2.0	2.0	2,806.0	1,546.4
Kiribati	7.3	7.3	—	—
Liberia	10.1	10.1	1,118.5	658.8
Libya	2.9	2.9	1,928.0	1,928.0
Madagascar	8.1	8.1	—	—
Mali	8.0	8.0	64.6	71.5
Micronesia, Fed. Sts.	0.9	0.9	—	—
Myanmar	10.2	10.2	221.0	318.7
Sierra Leone	14.9	14.9	—	578.5
Solomon Islands	4.7	4.7	—	—
Somalia	1.6	1.6	1,326.0	819.9
South Sudan	—	—	216.0	216.0
Sudan	24.2	24.2	1,275.9	1,751.7
Syrian Arab Republic	2.4	2.3	842.0	842.0
Timor-Leste	7.0	7.0	—	—
Togo	10.9	10.9	—	—
West Bank and Gaza	3.7	2.7	—	—
Yemen, Rep.	4.0	4.0	349.8	578.0
Zimbabwe	14.3	14.3	—	—

Source: World Bank data.
Note: Annual 10-year (2002–2011) and 20-year (1992–2011) averages are based on the most recent available data. — = not available.

makes clear the effect of data constraints. Burundi, for example, has homicide data only for 2008; annual 10- and 20-year averages are therefore the same.[10] Conflict indicators by geographical region and income group are provided in table 3.5. According to the available data, homicide rates are high in Latin America and the Caribbean and Sub-Saharan Africa, and remarkably

Table 3.5   Conflict Indicators, by Region and Income Group

		Annual averages over designated period			
		Homicides per 100,000 people		Battle deaths	
		10-year	20-year	10-year	20-year
Region	East Asia and Pacific	4.0	4.1	210.5	223.9
	Europe and Central Asia	3.4	3.9	207.9	677.9
	Latin America and Caribbean	20.7	19.8	241.8	223.0
	Middle East and North Africa	2.0	1.9	757.9	535.8
	North America	4.6	4.4	—	233.0
	South Asia	3.5	3.6	2,383.4	1,723.5
	Sub-Saharan Africa	18.3	18.5	345.7	936.3
Income group	High income	5.0	4.9	296.5	213.3
	Lower middle income	13.2	13.4	694.5	636.3
	Upper middle income	10.9	10.9	561.2	765.4
	Low income	14.3	14.4	546.8	1,013.7
World		10.1	10.1	581.4	744.4

Source: World Bank data.
Note: — = not available. Annual 10-year (2002–2011) and 20-year (1992–2011) averages based on most recent data.

low in the Middle East and North Africa and South Asia. In contrast, recorded battle deaths are much higher in the Middle East and North Africa and South Asia than in other geographical regions. For the most part, higher income is associated with fewer homicides and battle deaths.[11]

Finally, conflict and weak institutions are part of a vicious cycle. This is evident in figure 3.2, which plots homicide rates against Transparency International's aggregate defense sector integrity scores. In general, institutionally weak countries—particularly fragile countries—suffer from higher levels of conflict. Institutions shape the incentives for violence in at least three ways:

1. Higher institutional capacity, particularly strong policing and prevention capabilities, deters violent crime and makes it less likely that the populace will turn to nonstate groups for protection.
2. Inclusive institutions ensure that all ethnic, social, and religious groups feel equally served, mitigating social fragmentation and increasing the costs of resorting to crime and rebellion.
3. Accountable institutions help prevent active abuse by the security services.[12]

That said, there is not perfect correlation: fragile and conflict-affected countries do not always have weak institutions, and countries with weak institutions are not always prone to or affected by conflict. Consequently, in

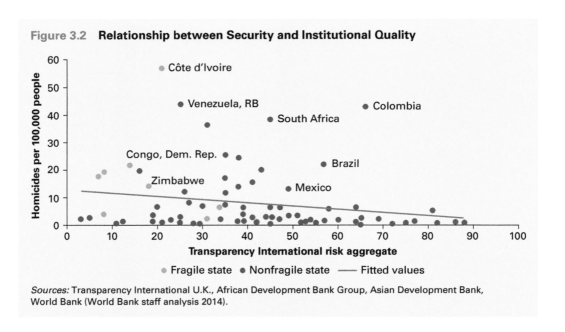

Figure 3.2   **Relationship between Security and Institutional Quality**

Sources: Transparency International U.K., African Development Bank Group, Asian Development Bank, World Bank (World Bank staff analysis 2014).

the context of a defense sector PER, it might be helpful to consider institutional strength and the level of conflict on two separate dimensions. When military institutions are accountable, there is less risk that increased funding for defense will be lost to corruption or adversely strengthen abusive military forces. Thus in a country affected by fragility, conflict, and violence, but which has well-developed institutions, increasing budgetary allocations to the military sector might be a feasible way of improving the delivery of security services; examples of such countries are South Africa, Mexico, Brazil, and Colombia (figure 3.2). Of course, this option is feasible only if fiscal constraints allow. On the other hand, a fragile state that also has weak institutions should give relatively more attention to transparency, accountability, and operational efficiency for funds that are already committed; examples of such countries are the Democratic Republic of Congo, Zimbabwe, Côte d'Ivoire, and República Bolivariana de Venezuela (figure 3.2).

Economic Development

In general, lower-income countries are more resource constrained. Consequently, the military—and other elements of the public sector—face tighter fiscal constraints. Military spending must conform to spending limits if macroeconomic and fiscal stability is to be maintained. There will therefore be a tension between providing defense services and maintaining economic stability. Under extreme circumstances, excessive military spending can crowd out spending in productive sectors, exacerbating economic development challenges. On the other hand, budget restrictions could starve the military of resources and leave it incapable of providing defense services.

The appropriate level of military spending depends on country-specific circumstances. Military spending should be based on the country's threat perceptions, defense policy objectives, and military strategy. Reference to international patterns can indicate whether military spending in the country of interest deviates significantly from the norm. As shown in table 3.6, the worldwide average for military spending is 2.0 percent of gross domestic product (GDP) and 7.9 percent of the overall government budget. In North America, the Middle East and North Africa, and South Asia, military spending tends to be higher as a percentage of GDP and the government budget. Military spending is also higher as a percentage of the government budget in lower-income countries. Military spending per capita is far higher in North America than in any other region, and is very low in lower-income countries and in Sub-Saharan Africa.[13]

While useful, geographical and income-group averages can obscure important differences between countries. These individual differences can help illuminate factors driving defense policy decisions or the effect of those policy decisions. As shown in table 3.7, the United States spends far more than any other country in absolute terms; at more than $676 billion, its spending is higher than that of the next 14 countries combined. But when military spending is calculated as a percentage of GDP, seven other countries outrank the United States, with Saudi Arabia and Oman exceeding 8 percent of GDP. In comparing country population size and numbers of military personnel, it should be noted that some large militaries reflect regional strategic threats; examples include the Democratic People's Republic of Korea, the Republic of Korea, Egypt, and Iraq. When military size is ranked

Table 3.6   Average Military Spending Relative to Economic Output and Population

		GDP		Military expenditure		
		$ billion	Per capita, PPP ($)	Per capita	% of GDP	% of budget
Region	North America	6,024	47,141	1,379	2.9	12.8
	East Asia and Pacific	633	18,679	296	1.7	9.4
	Europe and Central Asia	375	25,594	353	1.8	5.9
	South Asia	286	4,136	30	2.5	13.2
	Latin America and Caribbean	161	12,348	94	1.4	6.5
	Middle East and North Africa	159	21,165	559	3.7	12.4
	Sub-Saharan Africa	28	4,249	44	1.8	7.3
Income group	High income	724	37,125	673	2.2	6.8
	Upper middle income	321	12,176	122	1.9	8.0
	Lower middle income	100	4,039	39	1.9	7.9
	Low income	14	1,320	12	1.9	10.3
World		354	15,777	256	2.0	7.9

Source: World Bank, World Development Indicators database, http://data.worldbank.org/data-catalog/world-development-indicators.
Note: PPP = purchasing power parity. Expenditure data are averaged over the last five years of available data.

Table 3.7   **Military Spending and Force Size, by Selected Category**

		Military expenditure			Military personnel	
		Total, $ billions	% of GDP	% of budget	Total	% of labor force
Highest absolute military spending	United States	676.38	4.5	18.3	1,549,703	0.98
	China	127.90	2.1	16.1	2,921,000	0.36
	Russian Federation	70.56	4.3	16.1	1,448,200	1.91
	France	63.18	2.4	5.0	344,437	1.16
	United Kingdom	60.54	2.5	5.7	167,628	0.53
	Japan	54.17	1.0	5.5	252,970	0.38
	Germany	47.08	1.4	4.5	237,386	0.56
	Saudi Arabia	46.00	8.2	—	244,600	2.66
	India	42.02	2.6	16.5	2,611,265	0.56
	Italy	37.39	1.8	4.2	385,173	1.53
Highest military spending per GDP	Saudi Arabia	46.00	8.2	—	244,600	2.66
	Oman	4.57	8.1	31.7	47,000	4.20
	Israel	14.35	6.4	15.8	184,730	5.98
	South Sudan	0.85	6.1	—	175,000	—
	Jordan	1.37	5.3	18.2	110,700	7.04
	United Arab Emirates	15.52	5.1	—	51,000	1.04
	Georgia	0.61	4.8	17.4	32,612	1.40
	United States	676.38	4.5	18.3	1,549,703	0.98
	Russian Federation	70.56	4.3	16.1	1,448,200	1.91
	Lebanon	1.51	4.1	14.2	78,040	5.34
Largest military, by personnel	China	127.9	2.1	16.1	2,921,000	0.36
	India	42.02	2.6	16.5	2,611,265	0.56
	United States	676.38	4.5	18.3	1,549,703	0.98
	Russian Federation	70.56	4.3	16.1	1,448,200	1.91
	Korea, Dem. People's Rep.	—	—	—	1,345,400	9.22
	Pakistan	6.05	3.2	18.1	931,000	1.61
	Egypt, Arab Rep.	4.19	2.0	7.0	853,700	3.35
	Brazil	30.84	1.5	5.8	716,488	0.72
	Korea, Rep.	28.12	2.8	13.6	672,500	2.72
	Iraq	4.28	2.7	—	640,639	8.70
Largest military, by personnel per labor force	Korea, Dem. People's Rep.	—	—	—	1,345,400	9.22
	Iraq	4.28	2.7	—	640,639	8.70
	Eritrea	—	—	—	201,850	7.56
	Jordan	1.37	5.3	18.2	110,700	7.04
	West Bank and Gaza	—	—	—	56,000	6.37
	Syrian Arab Republic	2.23	3.8	—	357,200	6.25
	Israel	14.35	6.4	15.8	184,730	5.98
	Singapore	8.10	3.7	26.7	155,320	5.79
	Lebanon	1.51	4.1	14.2	78,040	5.34
	Brunei Darussalam	0.39	2.8	—	9,150	4.80

Source: World Bank, World Development Indicators database, http://data.worldbank.org/data-catalog/world-development-indicators.
Note: — = not available. Expenditures are averaged over the last five years of available data.

as a percentage of the total labor force, the effect of threatening neighbors and recent conflict is even more apparent.[14] Finally, the military may also have purposes unrelated to security, such as reduction of unemployment, training and education, or indeed the integration of diverse social groups.

Fragile states exhibit a wide range of military-spending and force-size patterns, although data are not comprehensive. As shown in table 3.8,

Table 3.8   Military Expenditures and Force Size, Selected Fragile and Conflict-Affected States

	Military expenditure				Military personnel	
	$ billions	Per capita ($)	% of GDP	% of budget	Total	% of labor force
Afghanistan	0.53	17.76	3.3	6.1	209,579	2.94
Bosnia and Herzegovina	0.23	59.67	1.3	3.2	9,941	0.68
Burundi	0.05	5.22	2.6	—	51,030	1.24
Central African Republic	0.04	8.77	2.0	—	3,090	0.16
Chad	0.38	30.44	3.7	—	34,946	0.83
Congo, Dem. Rep.	0.20	3.08	1.4	7.5	149,250	0.64
Côte d'Ivoire	0.39	19.57	1.6		18,850	0.27
Eritrea	—	—	—	—	201,850	7.56
Guinea-Bissau	0.02	9.76	1.9	—	6,873	1.06
Haiti	—	—	—	—	25	0.00
Iraq	4.28	131.27	2.7		640,639	8.70
Liberia	0.01	2.26	0.7	3.6	2,026	0.15
Libya	1.10	178.73	1.2	—	76,000	3.42
Madagascar	0.07	3.34	0.8	9.3	21,760	0.22
Mali	0.15	10.02	1.6	11.3	12,090	0.32
Myanmar	—	—	—	—	513,150	1.73
Sierra Leone	0.03	4.20	0.9	5.1	10,700	0.49
Somalia	—	—	—	—	2,400	0.08
South Sudan	0.85	78.09	6.1	—	175,000	—
Sudan	—	—	—	—	154,380	1.42
Syrian Arab Republic	2.23	99.69	3.8	—	357,200	6.25
Timor-Leste	0.03	25.23	3.2	—	1,199	0.36
Togo	0.06	8.67	1.7	11.8	9,480	0.33
West Bank and Gaza	—	—	—	—	56,000	6.37
Yemen, Rep.	1.24	52.14	4.0	—	137,940	2.26
Zimbabwe	0.20	14.92	2.3	—	50,880	0.78
Average	**0.54**	**35.04**	**2.2**	**7.5**	**105,918**	**1.79**

Source: World Bank, World Development Indicators database, http://data.worldbank.org/data-catalog/world-development-indicators.
Note: — = not available. Expenditures are averaged over the last five years of available data.

military spending ranges from a high of nearly $4.3 billion per year in Iraq to a low of approximately $10 million per year for Liberia (averaged over the last five years of available data). Libya spends the most in per capita terms, followed by Iraq and the Syrian Arab Republic. Yet no fragile state ranks in the top 50 countries worldwide in per capita spending. For some fragile states, relatively low per capita spending on the military might be a function of low economic output. South Sudan, for example, spends more than 6 percent of its GDP on the military. However, when military spending is measured as a percentage of the government budget, fragile states display a broad range, and none is exceptionally high. Togo and Mali top the list, at 11.8 percent and 11.3 percent of the budget, respectively, but neither ranks in the top 20 worldwide. Iraq has the largest military in absolute terms and as a percentage of the labor force. Myanmar and the Syrian Arab Republic also have large armies in absolute terms. Finally, when the military is measured as a percentage of the total labor force, four of the world's top-10 largest militaries belong to fragile states: Iraq, Eritrea, West Bank and Gaza, and Syrian Arab Republic. In sum, these statistics suggest fragile states have relatively large militaries that are relatively underresourced.[15]

Challenges and Opportunities

In conducting a PER, the PER team should be aware of several challenges specific to the military sector.

Challenge 1: Multilateral development institutions have historically been reluctant to work with the military on PFM issues.

A distinguishing feature of the military sector is that it may threaten or use deadly force to implement policy objectives. This inherently violent and destructive modality has made multilateral institutions reluctant to engage on military issues. This PER sourcebook, however, takes for granted that military organizations exist to secure countries from external aggression, advance the national interests of the state, and protect the state's citizens. It accepts the fact that war and violence have affected livelihoods and shaped institutions throughout history and that security is a primary development challenge today. Finally, it recognizes that national militaries have become the standard, internationally sanctioned institutions responsible for fulfilling the defense function. Dealing with militaries is unavoidable, and it can have profound benefits for institutional reform, economic development, and poverty reduction.

Challenge 2: The military is often understood as exceptional in its relation to society and in its operating requirements, and therefore it is not subject to the same standards of performance and accountability as the rest of government—particularly with regard to secrecy.

The military does, in fact, have a special role in society, safeguarding the state and securing citizens' welfare and livelihoods. To fulfill that role, some of the military's activities and policy decisions need to remain confidential. War plans, for example, should be tightly guarded. However, it is possible to retain confidentiality in highly sensitive areas without undermining the principle of democratic accountability. PFM practices can be modified to satisfy confidentiality concerns when necessary, but not in ways that undermine fundamental accountability to civil authorities. In practice, this means that small portions of the military budget might be classified as secret, but that the legislature—or a designated committee of the legislature—would be fully informed of secret-budget activities, capable of influencing policy and reallocating budgets, and empowered to hold military officials accountable. The need for confidentiality and reluctance to share information may present an obstacle to the PER team. First and foremost this is overcome by an explicit directive from the government to the relevant ministries and line agencies, requesting them to share data with the PER team. Second, a brief security classification analysis may be needed to indicate what specific data can be used by the PER team, particularly if the findings are to be published.

Challenge 3: Militaries often exercise de facto dominance among government institutions.

This dominance is a function of militaries' long-standing or founding roles in modern nation states, the often highly political nature of defense sector expenditure decisions, and the military's operational control of deadly force. It can result in a lopsided distribution of political influence, in which military leaders have special access to the chief executive or exercise relative autonomy in revenue collection, budgeting, and expenditure. Accepting this de facto dominance insulates the military sector from the trade-offs and oversight mechanisms inherent to a formal budget process and can lead to the misallocation of public resources or outright corruption. On the other hand, integrating the military sector into the national budget process provides an opportunity to redress disproportionate military influence. As will be discussed, a formalized national budget process encourages trade-offs between and within sectors to maximize allocative efficiency.

Challenge 4: There are often significant asymmetries in the knowledge, skills, and incentives of professionals in the finance and military sectors.

To the extent that the military operates outside the formal budget process, military leaders will remain ignorant of the country's macroeconomic context and its capacity to support their chosen military strategy. Similarly, to the extent that legislators and ministry of finance officials are excluded from the military's strategy deliberations, they will remain ignorant of security threat assessments, resource requirements, and long-term financial implications of military decisions. The result is bad policy: unsustainable, unrealistic, and insufficient to address the country's security challenges. This gap in understanding is especially problematic for major military procurements, which have long-term financial and military consequences that are difficult to project. The gap is exacerbated when civil-military institutions are absent or weak. Without an effective defense council or defense ministry, there is no institutional home where financial and military matters can be jointly decided. The connection between the effective deployment of resources to defense and the level of economic development, revenues, and quality of fiscal institutions should be an obvious and natural one, though it often fails in practice. A weak economy, the inability to collect domestic revenues, and the inability to deploy resources effectively can themselves pose a threat to security.[16] When these elements are absent, more basic collaboration can be encouraged through the PER process itself. Simply convening the interested parties and providing a platform for dialogue and trade-offs can be a significant improvement over prevailing practices.

Challenge 5: Defense policy and military strategy are not always formally defined, making decisions about resource allocation difficult.

Achieving the defense function is at the heart of the military enterprise, and a PER is meant to assess the reasonableness and efficiency of government efforts toward that end. In situations where there is no formal defense policy or military strategy, the PER team can use certain techniques to identify the essential purpose and objectives of the military forces. These techniques—described in detail in the next section, on functions and institutions—include analyzing the regional context, existing military force structures and resource allocations, and current and anticipated military commitments. These de facto policies and strategies can guide the expenditure analysis and should be updated as the PER progresses.

Challenge 6: The military sector's weak financial management and oversight practices expose it to numerous corruption risks, which undermine accountability, effectiveness, and efficiency.

This is especially true for fragile and conflict-affected states. The PER team should determine how these corruption risks affect the overall budget process, resource allocation, and accountability and oversight mechanisms, and should identify specific institutional or process reforms to strengthen PFM policies and practices.

Defense Functions and Military Institutions

The primary function of a modern military sector is national defense: protecting citizens and preserving domestic peace and order, ensuring the sovereignty of the state and its territorial integrity, and pursuing the national interest in the international arena. The defense function, as it is treated in this sourcebook, is generally comparable to the United Nations' definition; it comprises administration of military defense affairs and services; operation of land, sea, air, and space defense forces; operation of engineering, transport, communication, intelligence, personnel, and other noncombat defense forces; and operation or support of reserve and auxiliary forces of the defense establishment. This view of the defense function is through a service-delivery lens: the state is responsible for setting defense policy and holding service providers accountable; the nation's military forces are responsible for devising military strategy and providing defense services; and the public consumes those defense services, elects representatives to the state to secure their interests, and advocates for specific policies. By analyzing the defense function in this manner, this sourcebook seeks to connect specific defense policy objectives to resource allocations and the defense services they support, and then to measure the results in terms of accountability, effectiveness, and efficiency. This approach elucidates necessary institutional relationships and information requirements. It also facilitates a broader "security and justice sector" approach to PERs if used alongside the police and criminal justice chapters in this volume.

In military parlance, functions are often referred to as "missions." A security sector PER may therefore address the defense mission, the law enforcement mission, the counternarcotics mission, or the like. In this section, the term "function" is used in place of "mission," but they mean essentially the same thing.

In addition to carrying out the defense function, defense sector institutions have any number of other purposes. Table 3.9 provides a list of possible defense sector activities, which vary on a country-by-country basis. A common responsibility for the military sector outside of the defense function is supporting domestic police forces in maintaining public security. A domestic focus might result from insecurity and civil strife, as in the

Table 3.9 Range of Possible Defense Sector Activities

Function	Activity
Defense	Defend national citizens at home and abroad
	Project power strategically or in expeditionary interventions
	Engage in stability or peacekeeping operations as part of a UN mission or ad hoc coalition
	Support diplomacy and protect diplomatic missions
	Provide nuclear deterrence
	Provide defense and strategic intelligence
Public security	Provide domestic counterinsurgency services
	Conduct counternarcotics operations
	Support police activities through the provision of paramilitary forces
Other	Support civil emergency organizations during crises
	Provide airlift capacity or other transportation services for nondefense purposes
	Provide engineering or construction services

formation of high-capacity counterinsurgency forces, or from the particular historical development of a country's military forces, as in the European-style gendarmerie. For practical purposes, the focus in this chapter is on the defense function as just defined. The public security function is addressed in the chapter on the police.

The military sector is influenced by the police and criminal justice sectors even if its mandate has strictly to do with defense. A highly effective and accountable military sector might still fail to ensure security if domestic institutions are weak, illegitimate, or otherwise incapable of controlling domestic criminality and preserving order. In these cases, there are potentially important trade-offs between military and police institutions in fulfilling security functions, and analyzing the military or police sectors in isolation would be insufficient. Instead, the PER team should adopt an explicitly comprehensive security sector approach, and should draw on considerations presented in the chapter on the police.

Defense sector institutions and capacities vary greatly across countries. Consequently, the PER team should map functions against institutions in the specific country context. Table 3.10 provides a generic overview of typical defense sector institutions involved in the defense function. It is important to reiterate that the military sector is just one part of the security and justice sector. Institutions listed—particularly those at more senior levels—likely have functional responsibilities outside of defense or citizen security. Moreover, most of the institutions listed coordinate or interact with institutions outside of the military sector to fulfill the defense function.

To fulfill its primary function of defense, the military sector requires centralized control and a hierarchical structure. Thus in contrast to the police and criminal justice sectors, the military sector is relatively isolated from local affairs and subnational levels of government. This comparative isolation simplifies analysis to the extent that the military sector's policies and activities are transparent and that data are available to the PER team. On the other hand, deviations from the norm are likely cause for concern. In addition to frustrating a defense sector PER, the absence of centralized command and control or clear lines of policy guidance and oversight will exacerbate problems of accountability, effectiveness, and efficiency.

In the great majority of conceivable circumstances, there is no good alternative to a national military for pursuing the defense function. The exceptions to this rule are illustrative. The majority of countries without militaries are microstates or island nations whose defense requirements are guaranteed by neighbors, by security partners, or by the "global public goods" provided by multilateral institutions and international policing of the high seas. Even then, many countries that nominally have no military still field heavily armed police or paramilitary units that report to intelligence agencies or the ministry of interior. In other words, the necessity of the defense function still prevails, but it is fulfilled by foreign militaries or by domestic nonmilitary statutory forces.

Table 3.10   Generic Defense Sector Security Architecture

Function	Institution	Typical tasks
Management and oversight	Chief executive	Commander in chief of the military; principle decider of political objectives for the security sector
	Defense council	Integrates and coordinates security sector policies
	Legislature	Provides authorization, funding, and oversight; may provide policy guidance
	Ministry of defense	Provides policy guidance and support functions for military services
	Ministry of finance	Allocates funding across sectors, pays bills, and provides financial oversight
Service delivery	Army, navy, air force	Organizes, trains, and supplies military forces; employs military forces in offensive and defensive operations; defines and costs military requirements
	Coast guard	Organizes, trains, and supplies coast guard elements; provides emergency response and regulatory services
	Paramilitary police forces	Work with local security services (police) to employ military tactics and capacity for public security
	Border control	Provides border security and border control services
	Presidential guards	Protect executives
	Defense intelligence	Provides strategic intelligence related to other countries' military capacity and operational intelligence related to adversary's force status, location, and condition
	National intelligence	Provides strategic intelligence to inform defense policy
Nonstatutory service delivery	Guerillas	Advance sectarian, national, revolutionary, or insurrectionary interests through the threat or use of force; organized and equipped along military lines
	Armed wings of political parties	Advance political interests through threat or use of force; informally organized
	Ethnic and religious militias	Provide local population security and advance sectarian interests through threat or use of force; informally organized
	Private security companies	Hired to provide security services in support of statutory security forces or other institutions

Countries host to weak, unaccountable, or inefficient militaries are unfortunately much more common than those entirely without them. These inadequate militaries are either unable or unwilling to provide fair, equitable, and effective defense services, which can result in a security vacuum. In these situations, local populations will likely seek to promote citizen security through alternative institutions, including nonstatutory security forces (sectarian militias, for example) or local statutory forces (police). Both alternatives provide a poor substitute for a national military, especially when sectarian divisions are severe or violence is prevalent. Nonstatutory forces are inherently less accountable to national interests. Frequently they prey on, rather than protect, the local populations from which they emerge. At worst, police forces might be no better than the militaries they are supplanting. But assuming they are representative of and accountable to their communities, the police function still requires substantially different skills, capacity, and reporting practices than does the defense function. Police tactics might be appropriate for some dimensions of defense, including the investigatory elements of counterterrorism or cybersecurity, but they would be inappropriate for others, including deterrence and defense against opposing national militaries. Moreover, mixing the police and military functions threatens the important divide between civil and military spheres.

The Defense Function: Policy, Strategy, and Operations

The defense function can be analyzed in a hierarchy comprising three tiers: (i) defense policy, (ii) military strategy, and (iii) military operations. This generally accepted scheme encapsulates the functionally specific defense sector activities and provides a rough guide for institutional mapping. At the top of this hierarchy, at the level of defense policy, civilian and military officials decide broad national objectives that bear on defense, foreign affairs, public security, trade, and other national concerns. Consequently, there are potentially significant trade-offs between the various functions and institutions of government, and it is here that a broad security sector approach is most relevant and helpful. At the bottom of this hierarchy, the functional range is much narrower. Military institutions are predominant, tasks are highly specialized, and there are few trade-offs with other functions and institutions of government. That is not to say that other functions do not affect the military sector's activities at the operational and tactical levels. Instead, it means that other functions are exogenous to operational and tactical choices.

Defense planning, programming, and budgeting constitute the process by which the defense function is made manifest in government institutions and services. This process aligns defense policy objectives with specific military programs designed to meet them, and allocates public resources to their support. Policy direction and budget guidelines flow from the top of the hierarchy down. Assessments of military requirements flow from the bottom up. Programs and budgets result from a negotiation between these inputs. This process is at the heart of defense sector PFM and is discussed in greater depth in the "Budget Formulation Cycle" section in this chapter.

Defense Policy

Defense policy defines a country's security challenges and identifies the ways in which that country will address them.[17] It is the central mechanism through which security concerns across government are integrated, interests rationalized, rivalries resolved, and common policy objectives developed and disseminated. A "successful" defense policy is (i) coherent in reflecting all valid concerns and providing for a common response, (ii) adequate in

> **Box 3.3   South Africa—The Defense White Paper**
>
> After the fall of the apartheid regime and the election of the Mandela govern-
> ment in 1994, many questions were asked about the function and role of the
> South African National Defense Forces. In 1996, with a view toward significant
> defense reform, the Ministry of Defense prepared a white paper designed to
> articulate a defense policy appropriate for the new regime. This underwent sig-
> nificant public consultation and parliamentary consideration. In preparing the
> final defense review in response to the white paper, the government had to
> "ensure that the document was technically sound from a military perspective,
> conformed to constitutional principles, captured the values and priorities of the
> new government, honored the government's commitment to national reconcili-
> ation, and enjoyed the support of senior officers, the majority of whom were
> apartheid-era officials" (97). This was a time-consuming and expensive exer-
> cise, but one that was acclaimed for navigating a break with South Africa's past.
>
> *Source:* Nathan 2007.

addressing each security challenge according to its likelihood and expected impact, and (iii) accomplishable with the country's unique set of capacities and constraints. South Africa offers a good example of how defense policy can be integral to generic political reform (see box 3.3).

Under ideal circumstances, defense policy

- Is established through a formal, regular process that incorporates all legitimate concerns and relevant information from across government
- Is realistic in its assumptions and analysis
- Incorporates trends-based analysis of the current and future strategic context, including risk-weighted analysis of potential shocks
- Identifies the defense implications of trends and potential shocks, including their budgetary impact
- Is disseminated in a comprehensive public document that informs national institutions, allies, and adversaries alike of the country's threat perceptions and planned response.

Countries face diverse threats and exhibit a range of capabilities. The focus, scope, and content of defense policies are therefore unique for each country. In fragile states, for example, domestic insecurity could pose a greater or more immediate threat to the sovereignty of the state and the welfare of the population than do external threats. In these cases, heavily armed constabulary forces—provided with military training and exercising military tactics—might work with police in providing local security. Thus the dividing line between internal and external security duties might be arti-ficial, and a broad security sector approach would be more appropriate than one focusing narrowly on defense. An example taken from Liberia is provided in box 3.4.

Box 3.4   Liberia—National Security Strategy Focused on Internal Threats

According to the security sector Public Expenditure Review (PER) carried out by the World Bank and the United Nations during Liberia's security transition, the country had been generally stable since the deployment of the United Nations Mission in Liberia (UNMIL) in 2003, but peace remained fragile in 2012. Many of the remaining security threats were internal, including the tendency of minor incidents to escalate into large-scale violent confrontations beyond the response capability of the national police. High crime, an inadequate justice system, youth alienation, and land disputes remained serious conflict triggers. Moreover, structural conditions—including economic inequality, corruption, political exclusion, human rights violations, ineffective accountability mechanisms, and weak state institutions—heightened the risk that conflicts would escalate.

All of Liberia's neighboring countries were undergoing some form of internal transition. Liberia remained vulnerable to disruption by regional political tensions or insecurity due to highly porous borders. Networks persisted for the illegal exploitation of natural resources and transnational crime, including the trafficking of drugs and other goods. Finally, the influx of refugees following the contested 2010 elections in Côte d'Ivoire strained the state, and sizable refugee populations remained in volatile border areas.

Liberia's 2008 National Security Strategy orients the country's security sector. It defines national security in a holistic manner, incorporating issues ranging from democracy and rule of law to reconciliation and the professionalism of security actors. The strategy identifies numerous internal threats, including poor rule of law and poverty; the large numbers of deactivated ex-servicemen (17,000) and ex-combatants (103,019 demobilized and an estimated 9,000 who did not benefit from reintegration programs); illegally held arms; land and property disputes; and ethnic tensions. The strategy's objectives include consolidating peace; developing a coordinated national security system; avoiding duplication of roles; recruiting staff in a transparent manner; conducting gender-responsive reform initiatives; establishing county and district security councils; creating democratic civilian oversight mechanisms; safeguarding the integrity, sovereignty, and political independence of Liberia; participating in regional security forces; establishing economic security and reducing poverty; and managing the environment and resources.

Although the National Security Strategy and sector-specific reform strategies are well designed, reform of Liberia's security sector is undermined by deficiencies in coordination, oversight, and financial sustainability. While the national security strategy emphasizes the need for accountable and democratic security architecture, reform of the sector has so far focused on developing the operational effectiveness of the security institutions. Mechanisms for accountability and coordination remain weak, and civilian oversight of the security sector is ineffective. Moreover, the PER noted that given the prevalence of internal security threats and the military's external security remit, reforming the Liberia National Police and the border police was more critical than reforming the Armed Forces of Liberia in the short run.

Source: World Bank and United Nations 2012.

Another challenge for defense policy is that it is usually based on imperfectly framed perceptions of risk, not on clearly defined and measurable risk factors. Strategic thinking in the military sector is suffused with contingency planning and risk management. Planners assume that adversaries are trying to deceive them, that war is chaotic and impossible to control, and that policies will be difficult to implement even in the best of circumstances.

The challenge, in the view of some commentators, is that there is no way to identify the correct level of defense expenditure, or exactly which forces should be acquired and when.[18]

Even technically proficient and well-resourced defense sectors struggle to correctly assess risks and capacities and to survey, let alone reach agreement between, the many relevant national interests and perspectives. Success requires political will, a high degree of institutional capacity, routine and effective coordination, and reliable feedback mechanisms. For example, the United States completed its first "Bottom-Up Review" as recently as the end of the Cold War, and it became a regular endeavor only after the U.S. Congress passed a law mandating institutional reforms to make it possible.

Understanding a country's formal or de facto defense policy is critically important to a defense sector PER because it drives the major decisions on force structure, capital investment, and procurement. Consequently, the PER team should seek to understand country perceptions of the most immediate and important security threats and trends; identify defense policy objectives and security sector policies established to meet them; and assess the current and budgetary implications of those policies. Understanding a country's defense policy will also help the PER team situate the military in the broader security and justice sector, alongside police and criminal justice institutions.

Even when there is no formal defense policy, a country faces security challenges, is subject to binding capacities and constraints, and makes policy decisions to reach certain objectives. The outcome might not be coherent, adequate, or accomplishable, but the amalgamation of these activities still comprises a de facto defense policy. Where the defense policy is de facto rather than formal, the PER team can employ several methods to identify the essential purpose and objectives of the country's military forces:

- Analyze the security and military context in the region, including the defense policy and military strategy of neighbors, to acquire some sense of the country's security challenges and how they are addressed in the regional setting
- Survey existing military force structures, which will indicate the relative strength and influence of the army, navy, air force, and other units
- Review current and recent military operations, including what units of the military structure are involved and what programs are implemented, which will indicate the country's de facto military strategy
- Analyze the current and recent military budgets and expenditure rates to identify relative resource requirements and efficiency
- Meet with foreign security officials involved with the country's military sector who may have insight into the likely military strategy or policy.

The PER team should exercise caution when trying to identify the de facto defense policy. An informal policy will probably not fully reflect current or future security needs, nor is it likely to be realistic in fiscal terms. The de facto defense policy should therefore serve as only a rough guide or reference point when assessing resource allocations for defense provision. In the medium to long term, low- and middle-income countries, as well as those in transition from conflict, must ensure that defense policy is not merely a replication of past practices, but is conditioned on anticipated security challenges and is affordable given the country's fiscal constraints.

Military Strategy
Different from defense policy, military strategy details the security challenges that drive (i) the capabilities the military requires; (ii) the current and future commitments of these capabilities; and (iii) the personnel, capital investment, and operating costs of the military institutions. By interpreting defense policy objectives in military terms, strategy also provides focus for operational planning and employment of military forces. Military strategy should be stable from year to year to accommodate the long lead times necessary for force development and weapons procurement and to provide sufficient guidance for military officers in conducting operations. However, it must also be flexible enough to accommodate evolving threats, advances in technology, and other factors.

Military strategy is developed in response to a "threat assessment," which determines the defense capabilities required to meet security threats and hence is the main driver of defense costs. Defense capabilities incorporate all aspects of quantity and quality in the military sector: military units; weapons, transport, and real estate; equipment and defense matériel; unit readiness levels; and other factors. Defense capabilities are thus the instruments with which the military executes its strategy to fulfill defense policy objectives. These capabilities should be defined and costed in the defense plan, which is negotiated between political leaders, defense planners, and financial officials. The PER team cannot advise the government on military strategy, but it must be capable of assessing the appropriateness of resource allocations given the existing military strategy and probable medium-term adjustments. For this reason it must have access to the defense plan (and basic information about the plan), and it must understand the defense planning, programming, and budgeting process. Allocative efficiency suffers when there is an undefined military strategy, or when resource allocations are divorced from strategic planning. This problem is illustrated in box 3.5, which describes the World Bank's PER of Niger's security sector.

Military Operations
An operation is a military action to implement the overarching military strategy or to fulfill some other military function (such as a maintenance, training, or administrative task). It comprises a series or

Box 3.5   Niger—Security Strategy and Funding Mismatch

The World Bank's security sector Public Expenditure Review (PER) in Niger identified multiple domestic and external security challenges. The post-electoral crisis in Côte d'Ivoire in 2010, the war in Libya in 2011, the coup d'etat and rebellion in Mali in 2012–2013, deteriorating security in Algeria in 2013, and ongoing political-religious tensions in northern Nigeria have combined to make the Sahara-Sahel region turbulent and conflict prone. Niger's domestic risk factors include an immense territory with uneven distribution of population, endemic poverty, a high degree of political instability, and occasionally violent conflicts between the northern and southern areas of the country. In recent years, these risks have been manifested in increased terrorist threats, kidnappings, and trafficking in drugs and other contraband.

In response, the Nigerien government increased security spending significantly, incorporated security in its planning processes, and introduced new border control measures. As a share of public spending, security spending increased from 13.8 percent in 2010 to 16.1 percent in 2012. This increase is generally consonant with other countries in the region. The composition of the security budget has changed to favor capital expenditure, which became the largest component in 2012, at 55 percent of the total. Personnel expenditure continued to comprise a large portion of the budget that same year, while funding for operations was reduced. However, the PER found the accuracy of Niger's security budgets to be precarious. Numerous supplementary budget laws since 2009 revealed a lack of spending predictability, although this is justified by the deteriorating security situation.

Overall, the PER determined that Niger lacked a genuine sectoral strategy that sets clear priorities. The multiyear security sector estimates were not realistic or achievable over indicated periods: "All things being equal, and without taking personnel expenditures into account, it would have taken over 30 years to respond to the needs that were deemed priority needs." (179) Among the particular shortcomings of the multiyear sectoral estimates were the failure to include appropriations to compensate increased staffing levels; the absence of a detailed, transparent breakdown of security sector spending; the multiplicity of objectives and lack of forecasting of total costs; and a disconnect between the armed forces' estimates of their requirements and the formalized sector strategy.

Source: World Bank 2013b.

collection of tactical actions that share a common, unifying theme. In a literal sense, an operation is a time- and area-bound application of military means to achieve strategic ends. In contrast to defense policy objectives and military strategy, which are always in place to guide and shape military activities, an operation is a discrete event. As such, the decision to conduct an operation is contingent on exogenous factors as well as on existing policy objectives and military capabilities. A series (or collection) of major operations to achieve a particular political goal is referred to as a campaign. The details of campaign plans are likely secret, but they must be costed to sustain combat operations over the medium run.

Overall, operations are inherently unpredictable, difficult to execute successfully, and uncertain in their consequences. The prevalence of threats as defined in the country's defense policy and defense strategy can suggest an operation's requirements and tempo, but by definition operations are not regular, recurrent activities amenable to standard budgetary principles.

Contingency funds, supplementary budgets, and "deployable" financial management systems—with their added complexity and risks—are commonly employed to fund operations. Uncertainty, error, miscommunication, and strategic resistance by an adversary can nullify operational assumptions, including those related to financial costs. Moreover, operations can have serious unintended consequences. Countries can win a war, but so-called Pyrrhic victories can prove strategically or financially ruinous. Finally, because operations are the context in which military activities are most visible to the civilian population, the military's good conduct in carrying out operations is crucial to maintaining public trust.[19] Although difficult to ensure, efficiency and accountability are of paramount importance during operations.

In conducting the PER, it might be useful to distinguish between three types of operations: (i) defense commitments, (ii) contingency operations, and (iii) crisis operations. These range from the most predictable to the least predictable: the PER team should incorporate resource allocations for defense commitments into the PER, make allowances for probable contingency operations, and be aware that crisis operations could require special budgetary exceptions.

Defense commitments are short- to medium-term operational outputs that the military definitely intends to implement. They are determined through a military operational assessment based primarily on the country's defense and foreign policy objectives, as conditioned by intelligence forecasts of the internal and external security environment. Resource allocations for known commitments should include all employment costs, including increased maintenance, fuel, ammunition, rations, and operational allowances.[20]

Contingency operations are those that arise given a certain set of conditions and interests. Contingency plans are operational options that could be implemented in the event of a crisis if implementation is in the national interest. Accordingly, contingency planning seeks to identify operational requirements ahead of time to determine how the military will respond and to prepare that response. Contingency plans are primarily intelligence driven, although broad defense policy objectives are used to define planning parameters. Given their conditional nature, determining resource requirements for contingency operations is more difficult than for defense commitments. If probabilities are applied, a certain level of resources for contingency operations can be built into the defense budget. Militaries almost always reserve uncommitted military capacity for this type of operation, and use contingency funds or supplementary budgets to fund incidental expenses.

Crisis operations are quickly planned and implemented military outputs that respond to emerging issues. They are determined and directed by the political leadership, and the lead-up time could range from a year to a matter of hours. By definition, it is difficult or impossible to sufficiently program and budget for crisis operations, and the military must rely on contingency and supplemental budgets to cover expenses.

Box 3.6   Burundi—Reasons to Contribute to Peacekeeping Operations

According to the World Bank's 2012 Public Expenditure Review for Burundi, the country has sent troops to support UN or African Union peacekeeping operations (PKOs) in the Central African Republic, Chad, Somalia, and Sudan, and has contributed police to PKOs in the Central African Republic, Chad, Côte d'Ivoire, Haiti, and Sudan, despite itself hosting a UN peacekeeping mission as recently as 2007 and suffering endemic poverty. Burundi contributes to these missions for several reasons: PKOs provide a significant source of revenue for the government and reduce the cost of the wage bill; they reduce the number of soldiers operating inside the country and thereby relieve internal tensions; they provide training and capacity building for the troops abroad; and they are an important source of income for the troops themselves, because wages are significantly higher for PKOs than for nationally based troops. More specifically: Burundi earns approximately $20 million per year for its support of PKOs; the United States provides training to Burundi military personnel engaged in PKOs, as well as those nationally based; and the government collects $100 in taxes from the $750 per month that the African Union pays to each Burundi peacekeeper.

Source: World Bank 2012.

Finally, peacekeeping operations (PKOs) represent a special type of military operation, with special PFM concerns. PKOs differ from normal military operations in that they require the consent of the conflicting parties, they are politically impartial, and they use force only in self-defense or defense of the mandate. Still, PKOs are staffed by military personnel and rely on the threat of force to compel parties to support the mandate and to engage in nonviolent political dialogue. Member countries perform the force provision function and are compensated by the international community for the troops they provide. The great majority of troops participating in PKOs are provided by countries with relatively poor PFM practices at home, which increases the risk of corruption in the field. In countries where a PKO is in place, the PER team should be mindful of how the operation's presence distorts or undermines domestic PFM practices. It should also be mindful that payments for the provision of peacekeeping forces go directly to contributing governments. Although these payments should be counted as general government revenue and used to support the cost of force provision, payments have in some cases been captured by corrupt central government officials or senior military officers. If the country of interest is contributing troops to a PKO, the PER team should note the disposition and use of compensation payments. Often these compensation payments are well above standard for troop-contributing countries, as indicated by the Burundi case study (box 3.6).

Institutional Mapping

At a minimum, fulfilling the defense function means having sufficient capacity to deter enemy attack and maintain citizen security or, if at war, effectively employ forces to defend citizens and reach strategic decisions. Establishing, maintaining, and employing military capacity involves substantial institutional requirements, including extensive and potentially expensive systems of policy making and strategy; administration; recruitment and training; intelligence; procurement, logistics, and maintenance; and learning and doctrine. Institutional patterns vary considerably from country to country, reflecting the nature and scope of security threats; financial, personnel, and defense matériel constraints; and tradition.

There are three ways to divide tasks among civilian and military members of the defense establishment: (i) parallel structures, (ii) parallel hierarchies, and (iii) integrated hierarchies.[21] Under a parallel structure, civilian officials in the defense ministry are in charge of policy, strategy, and finance, and a separate national military headquarters handles military technicalities and operational command and control. Under a parallel hierarchy, distinct military and civilian structures exist within the ministry of defense, and a separate military headquarters is responsible only for policy implementation. Under an integrated hierarchy, the ministry of defense is functionally organized into offices staffed by a mix of civilian and military officials. In each of these schemes, there is a relationship between institutions involved in defense policy making and administration at the top, military strategy and force provision in the middle, and operations and program implementation at the bottom. In most cases, the ministry of defense oversees all defense sector activities. A generic institutional framework is provided in figure 3.3.

The PER team should be careful to identify defense sector institutions as they exist formally and in practice. To that end, the PER team should be mindful that a military's function can be more broadly (or narrowly) defined, and that how it is defined affects the institutional composition of the country's military sector. Moreover, in countries where there is an active peacekeeping mission, external actors might constitute a significant part of the overall security sector.

Defense Policy Institutions

Defense policy is determined at the nexus of civilian and military leadership. Under the direction of the chief executive (head of state or head of government), the defense council or its equivalent works with policy units from the ministry of defense and military services to assess the country's strategic situation, identify threats and challenges, and determine what national capacities can and should be used to address them. These deliberations are informed by defense and national intelligence, open-source information on economic and security trends, and requirements defined at lower echelons of the military hierarchy or by specialized commands (such as training and doctrine, logistics, or finance) with unique insight into their fields.

The chief executive establishes or oversees the development of defense policy. In most cases, the chief executive is the only individual in government with authority over the full range of security and financial matters. Under ideal circumstances, the chief executive can balance perspectives

Figure 3.3   Defense Sector Institutional Framework

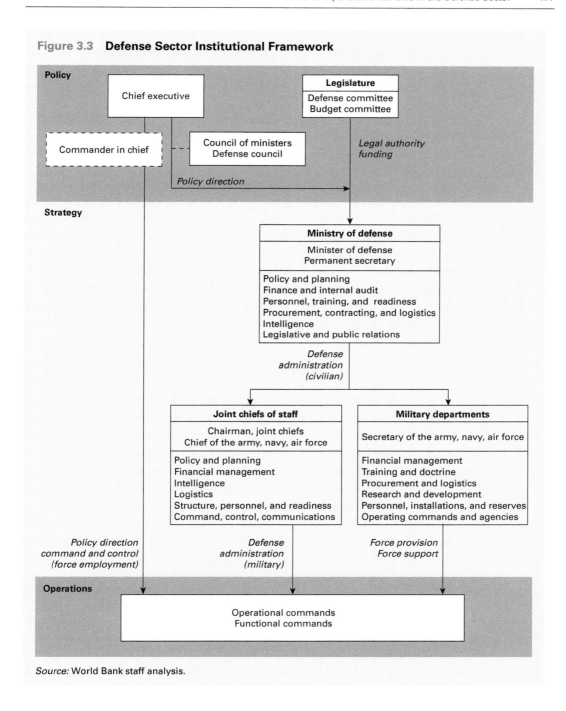

Source: World Bank staff analysis.

and generate or facilitate defense policy objectives that are responsive to all valid concerns and that are widely viewed as legitimate and accomplishable. In fulfilling his or her policy responsibilities, the chief executive is assisted on defense issues primarily by the defense council and secondarily by civilian officials from the ministry of defense and military officials from the joint staff or equivalent. In addition, the chief executive may receive independent intelligence and analysis from national intelligence services. He or she will also oversee the activities of the ministry of finance or treasury and might receive independent economic advice from a council of economic advisers.

The commander in chief of the armed forces exercises supreme operational command of the country's military forces. Often, this authority is exercised directly by the chief executive, and in democratic countries, civilian control of operations is the most direct mechanism for promoting military accountability. In other contexts, commander-in-chief authority might reside with the minister of defense, cabinet of ministers, or military officer subordinate to the chief executive. In military dictatorships, the commander in chief is a military officer who also controls the other functions of government.

The role of the defense council (or national security council) is to integrate and coordinate all elements of defense policy. The defense council typically comprises the chief executive's security advisers, members of the cabinet in charge of security-related ministries and agencies (including foreign affairs, defense, interior, and the like), representatives from the military services and intelligence agencies, and the minister of finance. The defense council may be executive in nature—that is, with the authority to allocate security budgets and task security sector officials—or it may be merely advisory, serving as a coordinator or clearinghouse of policies formulated and implemented elsewhere. In either case, the defense council is typically the forum with the broadest representation of security sector interests within government. It therefore facilitates information sharing and can help reduce confusion and rivalry among security sector institutions. It is also the best place to decide resource allocation trade-offs between security sector functions and institutions.

Not all countries have a defense council. Where they are absent, the council of ministers, council of state, military council, or an ad hoc or informal body of government and military personnel might serve the same purpose and integrate security sector interests, mitigate rivalries, and establish priorities. The task for the PER team is first to determine what body performs such tasks in a given country; then to survey its authority, policymaking process, and feedback mechanisms; and finally to use the insights gleaned to inform the analysis of the country's institutional framework and resource allocation practices.

Legislatures commonly perform a number of key tasks related to the authorization, funding, and oversight of the military sector, which are especially relevant and influential at the level of defense policy:

- *Legislatures authorize military sector activities by establishing the legal basis on which the armed forces, intelligence services, border guards, and police operate.* Constitutional law likely provides the foundation for civil-military relations and the existence and operation of military institutions, but the particular size, shape, and character of a country's military sector is typically defined by statutory law.

- *Legislatures authorize much of the PFM framework, including the budget process, through legislation that elaborates and clarifies constitutional and common law.* Effective PFM law will provide a comprehensive legal framework that specifies a balanced division of responsibilities among the main actors in the budget process—including the legislature itself.

- *Legislatures appropriate funds for military operations, scrutinize agency budgets and procurement decisions, and review how appropriated money was spent.* Best-practice standards stipulate that budget review and appropriations should be regular, recurrent, and predictable, with no intra-year (or intra-period) changes unless a major contingency—like war—arises. To meet these standards, budgets submitted to the legislature must be legitimate and realistic, and there must be sufficient revenue to cover necessary and approved activities.

- *Legislatures provide oversight in two ways: by examining processes and outcomes, and by holding civilian officials and senior military officers accountable for how approved policies are implemented.* Legislatures exercise oversight by holding hearings or inquiries where military officials testify; by investigating allegations of policy failure, abuses by the defense and security sector, and financial malfeasance; by requesting documents from the executive; and by directing or requesting audits of military institutions. The legislature's oversight authority ensures defense sector accountability to the public interest and promotes efficiency.

- *Strong legislatures might also provide policy guidance on the use of force and deployment of troops, as well as on international commitments and treaties.* This function creates an obvious tension between the legislative and executive branches that has historically proved difficult to maintain in wartime. In more benign threat environments, however, it can provide a useful and beneficial check on executive power.

- *Finally, legislatures can be reservoirs of useful knowledge, especially if specialized defense and finance committees are in place.* Long-serving legislators who work on defense sector issues can draw on a wider and longer scope of experience than can many military officers themselves, especially with regard to civil-military relations and the military sector's contribution to public service provision. In developing countries, on the other hand, there might be a gap in legislative knowledge and expertise, particularly on military and security issues.

The ministry of defense is a cabinet-level agency that is responsible for matters of defense, including formulating defense policy and regulating the military services. It is typically headed by a politically appointed civilian defense minister, who also serves as a close adviser to the chief executive on matters of defense. In parliamentary systems, a permanent secretary (or director general) might serve as the defense minister's deputy. In functional terms, defense ministries bridge the gap between defense policy and military strategy. Along with the national military headquarters, they seek to translate defense policy objectives into actionable military strategy. This entails interpreting broadly defined goals with detailed planning and budgeting. In organizational terms, defense ministries bridge the gap between civilian and military spheres. They are usually staffed by civilian and military officials who collaborate to direct and enable military functions. A well-functioning defense ministry clearly defines organizational roles and functions; minimizes overlap, duplication, and rivalry; and facilitates unity of purpose and unity of effort.

The minister of defense heads the defense ministry, serves on the defense council (if it exists), and influences national policy as an important member of the executive cabinet. Thus the minister of defense is usually the second-most powerful individual in the military sector after the chief executive, and could serve as commander in chief. The defense minister's diverse responsibilities include handling the defense budget; dealing with Parliament, the media, and the public; negotiating with other government agencies; and heading defense relations with other countries.

The permanent secretary (if such a position exists) serves as the head of the professional ministry staff. Like the defense minister, the permanent secretary is typically a civilian. However, the permanent secretary is not politically appointed; rather, the position is filled by a senior member of the civil service and does not automatically rotate with a change in administration. The permanent secretary serves as the ministry's chief accounting officer and answers to the Parliament on the ministry's budget and expenditures. In cases where there is adequate democratic oversight, this might entail frequent reports and testimony before the legislature's defense committee. The permanent secretary is also responsible for the day-to-day operations of the ministry, including issues like human resources, payroll, and asset management. In cases where there is no permanent secretary, administrative and policy activities at the ministry of defense might be overseen by military or civilian officials who answer to the minister of defense.

Defense ministries are typically organized along functional lines. Common schemes include dedicated offices for the following: policy and planning; defense intelligence; research and engineering; procurement and contract management; logistics; personnel, training, and readiness; security cooperation and international defense relations; financial management and accounting; internal audit and oversight; human resources; legal counsel; technology and physical security; and public relations. In addition, there are often dedicated offices within the defense ministry for the respective armed services, headed by civilian secretaries. Given the broad range of tasks and actors involved, designing and operating an effective defense ministry is difficult.

From Policy to Strategy

Military forces (or armed services) are organized into distinct elements (army, navy, and air force, for example)—each with its own command structure, culture, and doctrine—or into a combined armed forces with a single command structure and integrated capabilities. Most military forces engaged in the defense function will likely be readily identifiable for the PER team, but the task becomes more difficult when the military sector assumes internal security responsibilities or other nondefense functions. The most common military forces are the army, navy, and air force. A country might also have military police, national police, coast guard, border guard, special forces, marines, air defense, paramilitary, strategic defense, joint support, or joint medical forces. In addition, there might be reserve or national guard forces that can be called upon during war to support the main military forces. Outside of the defense function, military forces might be used for disaster response, engineering, construction, or any of the other activities listed in table 3.9.

Military forces are led by senior military officers, known as service chiefs or chiefs of staff, who are the program managers for the force provision element of the defense function. These officers are responsible for establishing, developing, and maintaining combat-ready forces as stipulated by the national military strategy. These force provision requirements exist whether or not military forces are operationally employed. When employed, military forces are usually under a different command structure. Thus there is a critical difference between the "institutional" military forces under the command of the service chiefs, which are focused on force provision, and the "operational" military force, under the command of combatant or joint-force commanders, which is focused on force employment. Force provision subprograms are headed by subordinate general officers. In the army, for example, the army chief of staff might oversee separate commands for infantry, armor, special forces, civil affairs, and other technical specialties.

In contrast to civilian organizations, militaries are organized hierarchically, in a system of formalized ranks. This provides clear lines of accountability for policy implementation. However, formal ranks can encourage insularity and make whistle-blowing difficult. Adequate protections should be provided to military personnel who report corrupt practice. Otherwise, it will be difficult to enforce PFM principles. The system of formalized ranks also influences how internal control for PFM is structured in military institutions. Best practice stipulates that the command hierarchy should be distinct from the payments hierarchy, so that payments can be reviewed and commanders prevented from abusing their power for financial gain.

The composition of a country's military (including whether it is organized into distinct elements) is largely determined by its defense policy objectives and the military strategy devised to meet them. In general, the structure of military forces reflects country-specific security challenges. For example, light infantry counterinsurgency forces are appropriate for

Afghanistan's current security challenges, but a coast guard would be useless. Similarly, large nuclear powers might have a distinct strategic command, but countries without nuclear weapons or a deterrence policy would not need such an organization, and one would not exist. Military forces in many fragile countries, including most African countries, largely consist of light infantry. The specific ways in which defense policy objectives are met—force design, structure, and readiness requirements—are negotiated between the service chiefs, the defense ministry, and the chief executive. Stability is important, and these requirements cannot change radically with each new budget given the huge scale and long time horizons of military personnel and equipment investments. As part of the national military strategy, however, military requirements are subject to revision over the medium run based on evolving security threats and budget constraints.

Military systems also broadly reflect the political orientation of the national government, the institutions of contemporary allies, and the influence of former colonizers. For example, the influence of French and British military institutions can be seen respectively in Francophone and Anglophone countries in Africa. Military assistance missions and military equipment imports also exert an influence. Thus military institutions in Afghanistan and Iraq today are much more similar to the U.S. system than they are to their Soviet-style predecessors.

Finally, a country's military institutions directly reflect country capacity. Smaller countries, or countries with smaller military budgets, might have a combined armed forces with a single command structure that integrates land, sea, air, and other elements simply because it is cheaper and there are no efficiency gains to specialization at that scale. Country capacity also affects how military personnel are recruited. Countries that are less resource constrained—with larger military-age populations and military budgets, or with less-expansive defense policy objectives—typically have professional militaries, in which service is voluntary. In contrast, countries that are more resource constrained often have conscription militaries, in which service is compulsory. Conscription militaries are usually less expensive on a per-unit basis, because personnel can be compensated at less than the market rate. On the other hand, they are often of poorer quality because recruiters cannot be as selective and because compulsory service erodes purpose-driven esprit de corps. Conscription also raises the risk of corruption; individuals might pay bribes to avoid service, or commanders might use conscripts for private ends, including protection services for private corporations or labor in commercial enterprises.

From Strategy to Operations

The senior military officer in the operational chain of command, known as the chairman of the joint chiefs of staff, heads the national military headquarters and serves as the program manager for defense employment. Like the defense ministry, the joint staff is typically organized along functional lines, with offices for policy and planning, intelligence, foreign relations, financial management, strategic communication, and internal auditing and inspection. Depending on economies of scale and efficiencies of centralization, the joint staff might administer services to support service chiefs, including personnel management, logistics, acquisition and procurement, or health services. As the title implies, the chairman of the joint chiefs chairs a committee composed of the chief officers of the various armed services. The chairman also serves as an important adviser to the chief executive on military matters.

The military's operational commands are responsible for implementing policy; they command combat, combat-support, and service-support forces to achieve a policy objective. In modern militaries, forces from the various military branches are employed in "joint" operational task forces. Thus complementary elements from the army, navy, air force, etc., are combined under a single commander from one of those services. Table 3.11 lists typical operational military units, by size and level of command. At the lower end of the spectrum, units usually consist of single-service personnel who make tactical decisions, at most. At the higher end of the spectrum, vast numbers of military personnel can be employed across all of the military services. At this scale, operational (or strategic) decisions can have considerable budgetary impact.

The commander is the central figure in defining and directing military operations, and defense activities related to force employment are determined and managed largely by the joint operations division at defense headquarters. The resources allocated to these activities depend on the scale, duration, and intensity of operations. It is important for the PER team to note any interdepartmental transfers between operational commands and the military services for the provision of forces, weapons,

Table 3.11 Typical Operational Military Units

Unit	Personnel (no.)	Commander
Fire team	4	Noncommissioned officer/subofficer (corporal or sergeant)
Squad/section	8–13	Squad leader (noncommissioned officer/subofficer)
Platoon	26–64	Platoon leader/commander (typically a lieutenant, but a captain may serve for special forces)
Company	80–225	Captain or major
Battalion	300–1,300	Lieutenant colonel/colonel
Regiment/brigade	3,000–5,000	Lieutenant colonel/colonel/brigadier/brigadier general
Division	10,000–30,000	Major general, or two-star general
Corps	40,000–80,000	Lieutenant general, or three-star general
Army	100,000–200,000[a]	General, army general, colonel general, or four-star general

Source: World Bank staff analysis.
a. In many countries the army may be much smaller.

equipment, and other defense matériel used in the course of force employment, as discussed in the "Budget Execution" section of this chapter.

An overriding goal for contemporary militaries, particularly in operations, is to increase the "tooth-to-tail" ratio—the number of combat
troops relative to troops conducting support operations. Consequently,
many of the tasks that used to be "military"—including supply, logistics,
and maintenance—are now contracted to the private sector. This approach
could create corruption risks in operations if proper PFM controls are not
in place.

Budgeting in Defense

This section applies the universal budgetary principles enumerated in chapter 2 to the military sector's budget formulation process. It discusses the
composition and character of military budgets, with special attention to
corruption risks and the challenges faced by fragile and conflict-affected
states. It also outlines a standard annual budget cycle, highlighting the
respective roles of the ministry of defense, ministry of finance, military services, and the legislature.

The Basics

The national budget should comprehensively cover all military expenditures, regardless of financing source, and categorize those expenditures in a
way that is useful to policy makers and policy implementers. Below, budget
composition and budget classification concepts are discussed in relation to
the military sector. Following that, two common defense sector challenges—
off-budget activities and secret budgets—are discussed.[22]

In general, the national budget must provide for the following defense
sector activities, although the specific way in which they are classified
will vary:

- *Defense administration*, which includes political direction, day-to-
  day operations, policy development, departmental planning, strategic
  intelligence, defense foreign-relations, financial management, strategic communication, and internal auditing and inspection
- *Force provision*, which includes recruiting, training, equipping, and
  maintaining combat forces, including service- or capability-specific
  activities (infantry, armor, artillery, anti-aircraft, engineering, special
  forces, fighter aircraft, air reconnaissance, helicopters, air transport,
  surface combat ships, maritime surveillance, etc.)
- *Force support*, which includes personnel management, facilities management, capital acquisition, procurement, logistics, and health
  services
- *Force employment*, which includes military operations (command
  and control, operational intelligence and counterintelligence, war
  gaming, and joint exercises).

A central objective of a defense sector PER is to gain as complete an understanding as possible of the current level and structure of security expenditures, recent trends in expenditures, and likely future expenditure requirements based on current plans. Understanding a country's budget composition and classification scheme is therefore crucial for accurately assessing its past, current, and future allocations to the defense function.

Budget Composition and Classification

Although budgets should cover all spending, irrespective of financing sources, in countries where foreign donors finance a large portion of government expenditures, a distinction can be made between the core budget and the external budget. The core budget is the product of the normal national budget process. As such, it covers government revenues and expenditures, including those for the military sector. The external budget, if it exists, supports donor-directed projects and is likely wholly or substantially donor financed. Many countries receive some form of military assistance, and they often fail to report that assistance as revenue or record the projects it supports as expenditures. For the country to fully adhere to universal budgetary principles, external revenues and expenditures would have to be integrated into the national budget. Some countries distinguish between the operating (annual) budget under the domain of a ministry of finance, and a capital or investment budget, often under a separate planning ministry (which may include capital and recurrent spending deemed a development investment). In the latter cases, both parallel budgets are under national procedures, but may follow different calendars and processes, and often are poorly integrated. The PER team should identify all relevant planning and budgeting processes and spending that affect the defense sector.

In fragile states, the external budget could constitute the majority of the military sector's overall budget. In these countries, existing security forces are usually too weak or too unaccountable to effectively provide security. Donor-directed projects will therefore likely focus on basic security force provision or on a more comprehensive SSR program. Basic security-force provision entails building, training, and equipping statutory security forces, often at a rudimentary level. SSR will couple security force provision projects with efforts to establish defense administration capabilities and accountability and efficiency mechanisms.

It is important for the PER team to remember that the external budget is not the product of the national budget process, and could therefore violate many of the core budgetary principles by its very nature. In addition to compromising comprehensiveness and predictability, a predominant external budget also undermines (i) *legitimacy*, if domestic implementers are not involved in its formulation; (ii) *contestability*, in the likely event that the domestic government cannot reallocate external security funding to other budget priorities; (iii) *transparency*, especially if donors do not coordinate or do not publish budget details, or if they support secret activities; (iv) *accountability* to the domestic government and population, as spending allocations are largely determined by donors, and donor-country personnel are often immune from domestic sanction; and (v) *periodicity*, by the temporary status of external intervention.

Even so, external support to the military sector is often the only thing preventing a slide back into conflict. In countries that host a PKO or otherwise receive significant external support to the security sector, the PER team should therefore concentrate on sustainability issues. This focus requires identifying what defense services are being provided, and how much they would cost if provided nationally. Often, national provision of defense services is less costly because of lower relative wages and greater familiarity with the country's security threats and political objectives. Moreover, the longer peace is sustained—and the more conflict can be channeled into nonviolent political discourse—the lower the "demand" for defense services. Domestic governance problems and sectarian rivalries, however, could introduce costs and constraints not binding on international forces. Eventually the country will have to provide defense services on its own, but in the immediate future international support mitigates costs. The external security umbrella should therefore be treated as a window of opportunity for reforms to be carried out. An example taken from Liberia is provided in box 3.7.

Box 3.7   Liberia—Cost of Transitioning and Maintaining Security

According to the security sector Public Expenditure Review carried out by the World Bank and the United Nations during Liberia's security transition, the United Nations Mission in Liberia (UNMIL) contributed to Liberia's security reform efforts, helped establish the conditions for peaceful democratic elections and the transfer of power in 2011, and contributed to economic growth by reestablishing peace and security, thereby allowing development opportunities to emerge.

Total UNMIL spending steadily declined from $723 million in FY2004/2005 to $512 million in FY2010/2011. These funds covered expenses related to military contingents, international civilian salaries, information technology and communications infrastructure, and air transportation; personal allowances not spent within Liberia; mission funds spent in country on imported goods and services; and spending on locally produced goods and services. At the beginning of the mission, it was estimated that local spending did not exceed 10 percent of the total but still boosted local income—primarily in Monrovia—by almost 10 percent of GDP.

It is expected that the ongoing provision of security services will cost Liberia significantly less than the costs incurred by UNMIL because not all functions will need to be replaced. Among the costs that can be eliminated are salaries and costs for UNMIL civilian personnel and the costs associated with protecting UNMIL personnel and assets. Moreover, the costs of Liberian security personnel and recurrent items are substantially lower than those under UNMIL. The average salary of a Liberian police officer, for example, is approximately $150 per month—much lower than that of a UN police officer, which is based on international standards. The total projected cost of providing security services in 2012–2019 is $712 million—less than the costs incurred by the UN in the first year of its mission. Of this total, ongoing security services are estimated to cost $546 million over the seven years

(Box continues on next page)

Box 3.7   Liberia—Cost of Transitioning and Maintaining Security (*continued*)

projected, with the annual cost increasing at the average inflation rate of 4 percent per year through 2019. The remainder comprises the transfer of security functions from UNMIL over the seven-year drawdown—including costs associated with the Liberia National Police and the Bureau of Immigration and Naturalization—and recurring costs for proposed regional hubs under the Justice and Security Joint Program (see table B3.7.1). In the final analysis, the PER found that there would be a fiscal gap of some $86 million over the 2012–2019 period.

Table B3.7.1   Liberia's Projected On-Budget Costs for Security Services, 2012–2019
$ million

		2012/ 2013	2013/ 2014	2014/ 2015	2015/ 2016	2016/ 2017	2017/ 2018	2018/ 2019	Total
Ongoing security services		69	72	75	78	81	84	87	546
UNMIL transition costs	Liberia National Police	11	12	14	6	7	8	10	68
	Bureau of Immigration and Naturalization	4	3	4	3	4	4	5	27
	Regional hubs	1	1	2	2	2	2	2	10
	Other transition costs	23	8	7	4	5	6	6	61
	Subtotal	**39**	**24**	**27**	**15**	**18**	**20**	**23**	**166**
Total		**108**	**96**	**102**	**93**	**99**	**104**	**110**	**712**

Source: World Bank and United Nations 2012.
Note: UNMIL = United Nations Mission in Liberia.

Off-Budget Revenues and Expenditures

The military sector is especially prone to off-budget revenues and expenditures, which by definition are not reported to central finance officials and not included in the national budget process. The most common techniques and mechanisms for keeping defense sector revenues and expenditures off budget are shown in table 3.12 and table 3.13, respectively. These tables are not exhaustive, and actual conditions vary on a case-by-case basis.

Off-budget activities are prevalent in the military sector for a number of reasons, ranging from the benign to the nefarious. Perhaps the most common reason is a desire for military secrecy, which was identified at the outset as one of the main challenges for defense sector PERs. Another motivation is a failure on the part of the national government to sufficiently support military requirements. Under these circumstances, the military could engage in commercial activities or natural resource extraction to raise funds to support its defense provision responsibilities. Similarly, national governments in fragile or conflict-prone states might simply lack the expertise or capacity to introduce and adhere to PFM standards. Integrating a significant portion of off-budget defense sector revenues and expenditures into the national budget during the course of a defense sector PER would

Table 3.12   Off-Budget Defense Sector Revenues

Type	Description
State- or military-owned businesses	The government, dominant political party, or the military itself may own businesses and use their profits to support defense sector activities. Alternatively, these businesses might be decapitalized to release funds for the military and later recapitalized at public expense.
Donor assistance for procurement, training, or demobilization	Most developed countries provide some form of military assistance to allied and friendly countries. Types of support include training and equipping to enhance military capacity for internal and external security missions; training in human rights and civil-military relations to improve accountability; cash transfers to procure weapons; and payments to support disarmament, demobilization, and reintegration (DDR). When the recipient country lacks funds or institutional capacity (as in postconflict situations, for example), external support can comprise a large portion of the total military budget. External assistance is especially problematic if it is not transparent, since in these cases it might be subject to some hidden quid pro quo arrangement that undermines accountability and hinders effective achievement of the military's given defense function.
Extraction or mortgaging of natural resources	The government or military might illegally extract or grant long-term concessions to natural resources—including oil, gems, fisheries, or timber—to support military procurement, personnel payments, or operations.
Sale or barter of equipment and commodities	The sale or barter of military equipment, legal or not, can be used to raise funds outside of the national budget process. Alternatively, the military could barter agricultural commodities for military equipment and matériel.
Payments from multinational companies	Payments from multinational companies to offset major procurements or compensate military forces for protection services could be a significant source of military revenues, especially for large aid recipients or in resource-rich but institutionally weak states. Among the more prevalent examples are donor-supported weapons procurements that include rebates, or "offsets," which channel funds back to officials in the recipient country. Many oil companies are also known to pay the salaries of military personnel guarding their operations.
Payments for peacekeeping operations	Peacekeeping forces are typically provided by resource-constrained countries, and compensation can sometimes comprise a significant portion of their military budgets. Often, these payments are made directly to the ministry of defense or military services and not recorded as general government revenue. Worse, they are sometimes illegally distributed as bonuses to senior military officers.
Informal or corrupt activities	The control of deadly force gives military institutions considerable scope to abuse their mandate if accountability mechanisms are not in place. Militaries have been known to engage in numerous informal or criminal activities, including smuggling fuel; operating casinos; trafficking in drugs, humans, arms, and natural resources; kidnapping and extortion; running protection rackets; counterfeiting money; and engaging in or supporting piracy.

Source: Ball and Holmes 2002.

therefore be a huge boost to the integrity and utility of the national budget as a whole, and could very well establish the necessary foundation for longer-term reforms to improve military capacity and effectiveness. Finally, off-budget revenues and expenditures might serve illicit purposes such as masking corruption by defense officials and military officers.

Table 3.13   Off-Budget Defense Sector Expenditures

Type	Description
Contingency funds and supplemental budgets	In-year additions to the defense sector budget might not be subject to the same fundamental principles of comprehensiveness and contestability as the regular national budget. Contingency funds and supplemental budgets are often used when there is a major change in perceived security threats or defense policy objectives—such as the outbreak of war—that must be addressed immediately.
Spending under nondefense budget lines	Defense spending under nondefense budget lines includes military units commissioned to build roads (which do not serve primarily military purposes); internal defense spending budgeted under the police function; military involvement in administering disaster relief or running hospitals; and funds for vehicle procurement supplied under social budgets, including ambulances used for military operations.
Nontransparent or highly aggregated budget categories	Nontransparent and highly aggregated budget categories include budget lines for debt repayment, public investment or capital acquisition, presidential offices, and the like. This method also comprises government bailouts for highly indebted lenders to the military sector and payment of compensation arrears for military personnel through social budget provisions.
Diversion of resources from social budgets	The lack of state capacity in many developing countries means that social sector budgets are often not executed over the course of the budget cycle. Unexpended funds can be diverted to military spending. In addition, military personnel working on development projects are sometimes paid out of development budgets.
Procurement of military matériel	Military matériel might be procured through nondefense budget lines and supplier credit, which were not scrutinized or approved by government authorities.
Undervaluation of economic resources	Undervaluation of economic resources includes the use of conscripted military personnel for forced labor to construct military infrastructure or to staff commercial operations. By definition, these practices do not adequately reflect the true opportunity cost to society.

Source: Adapted from Ball and Holmes 2002.

Whatever the motivation and technique, off-budget revenues and expenditures violate sound budgetary principles. If off-budget military revenues or expenditures are substantial (see box 3.8), they can undermine the budget process; they make it difficult to ensure an optimal allocation of public resources, to limit budget deficits, and to maintain macroeconomic stability. Moreover, without knowing the military sector's ongoing expenditures—or the mechanisms by which they are financed—it is difficult to develop a realistic sense of the defense function's actual resource requirements. Finally, significant levels of off-budget revenue and expenditures create substantial corruption risks, and point to serious problems of accountability.

Secret Budgets

Some small percentage of the core budget might legitimately be dedicated to secret activities, such as specific intelligence activities or weapons procurements in cases where public exposure would grant an adversary a strategic military advantage. However, in many countries, the criteria for secret

Box 3.8   **Central African Republic—Off-Budget Revenues**

According to the World Bank's 2009 financial management assessment of the Central African Republic, defense services generated considerable income in 2008, but the revenues were badly organized in their identification, legal framework, and budgeting.

One source of income was the sale of escort or guard services to private companies and international organizations (soldiers accompany people in unsafe areas in the provinces). Extrapolating from payments for security services by the Bank of Central African States, the United Nations Development Programme, and the International Monetary Fund, the Public Expenditure Review team estimated that total revenues generated amounted to the equivalent of $680,000 in 2008.

Another source of income was fines issued by the gendarmerie; in the Bangui region, these came to $160,000 in 2008. According to legislation then in force, 30 percent of proceeds accrued to the Ministry of Defense and 70 percent to the Treasury. The Ministry of Defense was to split its share between the gendarmerie (25 percent to be managed by the *régisseur* to cover miscellaneous items) and the army (75 percent to be managed by the national army's treasury outside of any accounting cycle and without any form of accounts management). Theoretically, fines collected by the gendarmerie in the provinces should flow to the national Treasury via Treasury special agents, but the central government has limited visibility and the amount collected is unknown.

Finally, the Battalion for the Protection and Security of Institutions, part of the Republican Guard reporting to the president and under the administrative control of the General Staff of the Armies, collected the airport security tax. This generated the equivalent of $260,000 in 2008.

In total, the Ministry of Defense generated the equivalent of $1.1 million in 2008. This is a significant sum relative to the $16.2 million the ministry received in appropriations for 2009, and to the entire state budget of $78.3 million. To the extent these payments do not figure in the state budget, the revenues generated remain extrabudgetary income, or indeed secret income.

Source: World Bank 2009.

classification are unclear or too broad and thus encourage corruption. Of the 82 countries Transparency International assessed, 75 percent do not publicly reveal the percentage of defense spending dedicated to secret activities; 50 percent do not audit secret expenditures or do not provide legislators with audit reports; and 40 percent do not provide the legislative defense committee with any secret-budget details.[23]

The need for secrecy does not mean the military sector should be free of democratic oversight and accountability. Both are critical for ensuring that the military sector serves the national interest, that public funds are used efficiently, and ultimately that the military sector is effective in fulfilling its functional responsibilities. As discussed, effective budgeting requires comprehensiveness, transparency, and contestability. If the legislature cannot review and modify the military sector's secret budget, then trade-offs between and within sectors are not possible, and public funds will not be put to best use. Moreover, if the public is not informed of at least aggregate secret spending amounts, it cannot hold the legislature accountable.

Instead of unclear or overly broad criteria for secret classification, the government needs to establish (i) appropriate and effective systems of security clearance, (ii) procedures for ensuring competent and effective legislative and audit oversight, and (iii) means to provide the public with enough information to ensure accountability. Legislative defense committees, and possibly "select" committees for intelligence, should be granted the security clearance necessary to review secret defense budgets. Furthermore, they should be empowered to comment on and make changes to those budgets. Without this authority, the defense sector can act with impunity, and is vulnerable to waste or capture by special or criminal interests. Finally, secret-budget aggregates, at a minimum, should be shared with the public. Sharing these aggregates can occur in the normal process of publishing the budget and disseminating budget information; it typically entails divulging a line item amount within the broader security budget that combines all secret activities. This information must be accurate and comparable over time.

The Budget Formulation Cycle

The PER team should note that the national budget cycle is a recurring process. In each period, objectives are set, the ministry of finance publishes sectoral spending limits, the ministry of defense and military services assess requirements and draft their budget requests, the military budget request is reviewed and consolidated with other sectoral budgets, and the consolidated budget is presented to the legislature for review and approval.

The PER team should also note that defense policy development and strategic planning are ongoing processes that feed into the national budget cycle. Decisions about major weapons procurements or force structure modifications should be sensitive to spending restrictions established each cycle, but must necessarily have a longer time horizon than the annual, or at most medium-term, fiscal policy framework. Defense policy development and strategic planning are specialized military activities. Through the national budget process they are rationalized with the rest of government policy.

Similarly, defense expenditures are ongoing, although funds allocated must typically be expended (or obligated) within a certain period of time. As in all sectors, optimal budgeting in the military sector requires that performance information about current expenditures be used to inform future spending decisions. This step is especially important in fragile or conflict-prone states, which likely do not have the capacity to engage in regular strategic reviews. Measuring security outcomes is particularly difficult, but a focus on outputs—particularly military readiness or capability—can be beneficial.[24]

The four stages involved in this process are discussed next. They are (i) setting national fiscal objectives, (ii) preparing defense budget requests, (iii) negotiating allocations, and (iv) reviewing and approving the national budget.

Stage 1: Setting National Fiscal Objectives

Cutting military budgets is not always the best option if the government wants to reduce poverty and encourage economic development. In some countries, particularly where military institutions are disproportionately strong or after periods of civil conflict, the military sector might receive too great a share of public resources. In these cases, there is scope for reducing security sector expenditures and reallocating those funds to productive sectors. Conversely, resource allocations to the security sector might be too small if the state has insufficient capacity to maintain law and order or if adverse exogenous shocks have increased the risk of conflict. In these cases, it might be necessary to increase security sector expenditures, or reallocate funds within the security sector. In any case, simply integrating all off-budget and secret defense sector expenditures into the national budget will increase overt military spending.

There is no best-practice formula that governments can use in determining fiscal objectives and sectoral allocations, but there are general guidelines that might help a defense sector PER. Four abstract security contexts and their general implications for defense sector expenditures and expenditure analysis are provided in table 3.14. A more rigorous approach was employed in the World Bank's 2012 PER for Burundi, described in box 3.9.

Table 3.14   Security Contexts and Implications for Military Expenditures and Expenditure Analysis

Context	Expenditure implications	Analysis implications
Instability and tension	Defense sector expenditures should remain unchanged as required investments are identified and costed, but they might increase beyond the short run.	The military will likely wish to prepare contingency plans for urgent additional investment. These investments should focus on resolving military capacity gaps related to emerging security challenges.
Conflict	Defense sector spending ceilings should be increased to encourage successful conflict resolution, including provisions for additional personnel, equipment, supplies, and weapons.	Revised fiscal targets and policies will need to be developed to balance immediate operational requirements and long-term fiscal sustainability. The Public Expenditure Review team should note that military expenditure, as a percentage of GDP, can double during conflict.
Postconflict reconstruction	Defense sector expenditures should decline in parallel with implementation of peace agreement, and provisions should be made for disarmament, demobilization, and reintegration (DDR) and defense sector reform (DSR).	Establishing a baseline early in the postconflict period will ensure accurate expenditure estimates. These will include numbers and readiness of military personnel, the condition of military equipment and assets, and the stock of military supplies. Expenditure estimates should also be derived for likely DDR and DSR programs.
Stability	Defense sector expenditures should be regularly rebalanced according to security threat assessments and changes in defense policy objectives and military strategy.	The focus will be on the implementation of agreed reform plans to promote fiscal sustainability, allocative and operational efficiency, and fiscal transparency. Accordingly, defense sector expenditures should be kept under regular review.

> ## Box 3.9   Burundi—Simulating Trade-Offs between Security and Productive Sectors
>
> The World Bank's 2012 Public Expenditure Review (PER) for Burundi analyzed trade-offs between security spending and spending in the productive sectors. The PER used a macroeconomic model to estimate the marginal benefits of decreasing security sector expenditures under three simulations.
>
> The first simulation contracted the level of total spending while maintaining the share of security spending at the 2011 level. In this simulation, the contraction of overall spending reduced the fiscal deficit but also limited the capacity of government to undertake the ambitious programs required to lay the foundation of a strong economy. The available fiscal space was insufficient to meet the basic needs of the civilian population or provide for basic security requirements. As a result, expected GDP growth was slow, and persisting insecurity undermined the nascent private sector.
>
> The second simulation reduced total expenditures and reallocated funds from the security sector to the productive sectors. This approach provided some impetus to economic activity, but contracting total spending reduced aggregate demand and economic growth in the short run. Moreover, if the private sector was assumed to be highly sensitive to the security situation, the economic growth rate would be weaker still.
>
> The third simulation increased overall spending while reallocating funds from the security sector to the productive sectors. This approach encouraged growth through increased public demand, which had spillover effects for the private sector. Moreover, increased public spending would enable demobilization to proceed more quickly.
>
> In each simulation, the model distinguished between productive and nonproductive sectors, estimated medium-term growth prospects, and attempted to account for the endogenous relationship between security and economic output. The first simulation, where spending was reduced but the security sector's share remained constant, had the worst estimated growth outcomes; the third had the best. Whatever the approach used, the PER team should be mindful that there are trade-offs between sectors, and no single policy prescription applies to all cases.
>
> *Source:* World Bank 2012.

Stage 2: Preparing Defense Budget Requests

The ministry of defense is responsible for preparing its budget request to meet defense policy objectives according to established military strategy and within the spending constraints specified by the ministry of finance. The full budgetary impact of ongoing and proposed programs should be provided in the budget submissions, including estimates for operation and maintenance. This step requires comprehensive costing methodologies for personnel, equipment, operations, and other activities as well as a competent staff and a level of transparency that is often lacking in the military sector's budget activities. (Annex 3D includes further detail on how to approach defense costing in low-capacity countries.) Throughout the process, the ministry of defense plays a leadership role: it provides policy guidance and support to the military services, resolves any conflicts or rivalries that arise, and ensures that the consolidated budget request meets the core fiscal requirement of allocative efficiency by focusing on the most valued programs and projects.

Ideally, the ministry of defense's budget request will include the following:

- A brief policy statement describing defense policy objectives and expected outputs and outcomes
- An elucidation of the military strategy developed to meet those defense policy objectives in terms that the ministry of finance, chief executive, and legislature can understand
- Key performance indicators for policy outputs and outcomes, preferably by program and activity
- Current- and future-year expenditure estimates by program and activity, as compared with actual expenditure data for previous years.

Given the diffuse and contingent qualities of security threats, the difficulty of measuring security outcomes, and the long time horizon of many force structure and procurement decisions, defining defense policy objectives and the national military strategy is crucial. Without a clear statement of what the military sector is meant to accomplish—and, more generally, what is included in the defense function—it is impossible to adequately plan, program, or fully understand the costs associated with defense provision. It is also difficult to establish benchmarks and assess the efficiency and effectiveness of defense expenditures.[25] The PER team must be able to understand a country's defense policy objectives to adequately assess the extent to which those objectives are supported in the defense budget request.

It is essential to base defense sector resource allocations on a formal defense plan derived from the country's defense policy objectives and military strategy. It is theoretically easier to assess trade-offs within the military sector than between government sectors, because the range of policy objectives and options is smaller. However, those trade-offs must be made on the basis of promoting optimal outcomes for society at large. Together, defense policy objectives and military strategy define the country's national interests and strategic imperatives. By definition, allocative efficiency requires that they be used to allocate public resources within the military sector. Misallocation, where military expenditures are determined on a nonstrategic basis, can starve high-priority activities of needed funds while wasting resources on low-priority activities. Over time, misallocation will leave the military incapable of responding to security threats and therefore unable to fulfill the defense function, or will lead to unconstrained budget growth that threatens a country's macroeconomic and fiscal stability.

Force provision and force support are the main cost drivers of defense and therefore require deliberate and systematic planning. Together they comprise the defense capabilities that the military sector is responsible for defining, supplying, and maintaining. Investments related to weapon systems, infrastructure, or force structure and readiness should therefore be based on sound methodology that covers the entire life cycle of the investment—including the concept, development, production, utilization, support, and retirement stages. This approach requires collecting, interpreting, and analyzing data and applying quantitative methods and techniques to estimate the future resources that will be required. The World Bank's 2013 financial management assessment of Mali's security forces (box 3.10) demonstrated the necessity of fully costing force provision and force support programs, as well as the value of PERs in identifying equipment gaps and budgetary anomalies that could undermine the efficient and effective provision of security services.

Every defense investment entails some uncertainty and risk, so a range of cost estimates is appropriate. Nor is the cheapest option necessarily the best: achieving value for money requires attention to economy (the cost of inputs), efficiency (the ratio of outputs to inputs), and effectiveness (the value of outcomes from outputs).[26] Life-cycle cost estimates should be used in conjunction with assessments of operational requirements and fiscal constraints when determining resource allocations. This approach can help evaluate alternative policy options, assess the affordability of defense programs, manage existing budgets, develop future expenditure profiles, evaluate cost reduction opportunities, improve business processes, and analyze capability portfolios. Various defense-costing methods are outlined in table 3.15; related PER resources are in annex 3A

Table 3.15   Defense-Costing Methods

Method	Description
Analogy	The analogy method compares new systems (or subsystems) with one or more existing systems (or subsystems) for which there are accurate cost and technical data. This method assumes that no program is entirely new or without precedent and that useful comparisons can be made. The major disadvantage is that finding a good analogy can be difficult, and estimators must be sensitive to the context of prior usage.
Parametric	Parametric methods estimate costs based on measurable attributes or characteristics, and assume a causal relationship between these parameters and life-cycle costs. Examples include estimating costs as a function of equipment weight, payload, number of military personnel, or any other variable for which historical data are available for regression analysis.
Bayesian	Bayesian techniques build on parametric techniques by modifying estimates as additional information becomes available. Bayesian techniques take a weighted average of the available estimates, based on their level of uncertainty. These can be valuable as new data become available during the regular planning and budgeting cycle or as the development process for specific weapon systems or force modifications progresses.
Engineering	Engineering, or bottom-up, methods are the most detailed and costly to implement. They build up cost estimates from the lowest level of definable work to create an aggregate life-cycle cost. Engineering cost estimates developed by the contractor are usually more accurate in program-specific details, but typically neglect the system integration or other out-year costs on which government estimates must focus.
Catalog	Catalog, or handbook, estimates use published reference books that contain lists of off-the-shelf or standard items, with unit or total cost estimates. The U.S. Excess Defense Articles Database, referenced in table 3A.2 (annex 3A), is a readily accessible example.
Heuristics	Heuristics methods use standardized rules of thumb repeated many times to produce a "good enough" solution. They are less precise than some methods, but easier to apply. In general, they should be used at early stages of the program when specifications and requirements are poorly defined, but they could be of more general value in fragile or conflict-prone states where data quality is low.
Expert opinion	An expert opinion is the informed judgment of a defense expert. It can be used when the data required for other techniques are not available, or to confirm cost estimates derived from other techniques. Usually multiple experts should be surveyed, and a consensus estimate established.

Source: NATO Research and Technology Organization 2007.
Note: The applicability and usefulness of these methods will depend on data availability and the life-cycle stage at which a particular investment is being assessed.

(table 3A.2) as well as a costing methodology in annex 3D. Further details about costing DDR (disarmament, demobilization, and reintegration) and defense sector reform (DSR)—both vitally important topics for fragile and conflict-prone states—are provided at the end of this section. It is important to remember that defense requirements will be different for each country. These tools can help the PER team, but each PER must ultimately be grounded in the defense policy objectives, military strategy, and force structure and readiness practices of the country of interest.

Within the context of a medium-term expenditure framework, the current and near-term budgetary impact of force provision and support must be included in the normal budget request.[27] The budget request should include:

- Personnel expenditures, with a statement of the number of staff positions and separately identified expenditure estimates for compensation, bonuses, and special allowances
- Entitlement and subsidy expenditures, such as the number of beneficiaries and the key assumptions used in the calculation
- Investment expenditures above a specified size, separately identified by program or project, including necessary current-year and future-year commitments
- Weapons and equipment procurement expenditures above a specified size, with full life-cycle costing, separately identified expenditure estimates by unit or objective, and a statement of the items' utility for meeting defense policy objectives
- Estimated proceeds from the disposal of state assets.

If the country lacks the data required to perform detailed risk analysis for defense equipment procurement or for significant force modifications, estimates should be adjusted upward based on past experience in related projects.

Finally, the PER team should note that force structure and force readiness are two separate but related issues. Force structure refers to combat-capable manpower, organization, weapons, and equipment, and how they are expected to be used. Readiness refers to the ability of a given force structure to meet the strategic objectives outlined in national defense policy and military strategy and to accomplish the missions for which it was designed. The cost of maintaining a given force structure will vary depending on its level of readiness. It is less expensive to maintain reserve forces than active-duty forces, but sufficient time must be allowed for training and deployment before reserves are fully ready to supply defense services.

Compared to force provision and force support, defense administration and force employment have less consequential long-term implications. These activities are based mostly on current or medium-term requirements, and can therefore be modified in the future at comparatively low cost. They are thus amenable to a medium-term expenditure framework of three to five years. Allowances for force employment, in particular, might be provided in contingency or supplementary budgets because they depend on exogenous factors that are difficult to predict. It should be noted that force employment is not synonymous with operations. Defense operations are essentially unexpected mandates that must be handled outside the normal budget process. It is possible to have contingency funds for operations, but this arrangement involves financial risks and program risks. To provide some control of these risks, the country could use supplemental funding appropriations. On the other hand, unless the country has a fiscal cushion—which is unlikely in developing countries—supplemental funding is not likely provided for in the medium-term expenditure framework. Consequently, too much expenditure on military operations could threaten macroeconomic and fiscal sustainability. Finally, during operations, personnel and matériel will be lost, damaged, or expended; restoring defense capabilities can have major cost implications more appropriately requested under headings for force provision and support than headings for force employment.

The ministry of defense is responsible for coordinating the preparation of military budgets with the military services and their subordinate commands, which have the expertise and information necessary to assess military requirements and estimate program expenditures. The ministry must provide top-down budget constraints for each component of the military sector that when combined will match the sectoral spending ceiling. The military services and their subordinate commands then build up their budget requests, by program and activity, conditional on their respective ceilings. Optimal methods vary by the type and status of individual programs. New programs, including proposed weapons procurements, might use zero-based budgeting. Ongoing programs, like those for personnel compensation, might employ incremental budgeting. The expenditure estimates that result are then fed up the chain, and there is an iterative negotiation within the ministry of defense to determine the final military budget request. If the military's assessed requirements cannot be fulfilled within the budget envelope, possible efficiency improvements should be identified. In their absence, adjustments are necessary in the defense policy objectives, force structure, or program resourcing. Budget requests from the military services and subordinate commands should meet the same criteria as the consolidated military budget, as defined in the ministry of finance's budget circular. The obvious difference is that budget requests from the military services and subordinate commands will be narrower in scope.

Stage 3: Negotiating Allocations

After the ministry of defense submits its budget request, the ministry of finance reviews it for conformity to legal requirements, spending limits, and other guidelines set out in the budget circulars, and then negotiates final defense sector allocation requests with the ministry of defense. In reviewing the defense sector budget request, central finance officials discuss the budget submission with senior defense officials and military officers, and may make site visits or question subordinate program managers directly. In countries where central finance officials lack defense sector expertise, this step can be challenging, and capacity building might be required before negotiations can be effective. Major disagreements between finance and defense officials should be referred upward to the council of ministers or chief executive for arbitration.

During the negotiation stage, officials should account for any changes in the macroeconomic, fiscal, program, and strategic environment since initial spending ceilings were set, and make necessary modifications. Revenue projections could be amended; if the fiscal space shrinks, then defense programs have to be trimmed or eliminated. At this stage, more data are available regarding expenditure rates and program performance for the budget currently in force, which could impact budget formulation for future periods. This stage also needs to take account of any exogenous factors that have intervened. The most significant would be the onset of war or a major change in the security environment that requires force employment. Operational costs could be covered by supplemental or contingency funding, but there would be indirect effects for defense administration, force provision, and force support that would have to be accounted for in the regular defense budget. Other exogenous factors include policy revisions, changes in legislation, and litigation that results in claims against the government. Box 3.11 on Burundi suggests how a country's macroeconomic and fiscal environment can be affected by war.

Finally, the ministry of finance consolidates the military budget request with budget requests from other government sectors and submits the consolidated budget to the legislature for review and approval. The entire package must be subject to aggregate spending limits and designed to efficiently meet national policy objectives, including fiscal targets for debt reduction. The council of ministers or the chief executive is normally responsible for final approval of the consolidated budget before it is submitted to the legislature.

Stage 4: Reviewing and Approving the National Budget

In a system of democratic accountability, the legislature is responsible for reviewing and enacting the national budget. In general, the legislature has the most contact with, and accountability to, the public. Given that the budget is the mechanism through which national policy priorities are established and supported, it is appropriate that the legislature be empowered to ultimately determine whether the budget optimally matches national needs with available resources.

Ideally, the legislature is authorized and empowered to review and challenge defense sector budget requests, as it is for other sectors. For the legislature to be effective in this regard, it must meet several requirements:

* It must be recognized in law and practice as the ultimate arbiter of budgetary matters in the constitution and legal framework for public finance.
* It must be capable of accessing and questioning defense and finance officials on matters of strategy, policy, and programming.
* It must have sufficient time and budgetary resources of its own to review the government's budget request at the conclusion of the budget cycle.
* It must develop well-defined internal rules and procedures to carry out this work. The precise role of the legislature in the budget process varies from country to country based on legislative capacity and authority. In less democratic countries, legislatures might be little

Box 3.11   Burundi—Macroeconomic and Fiscal Impact of Civil War

According to the World Bank's 2012 Public Expenditure Review for Burundi, the country's 1993–2005 civil war led to a precipitous drop in its gross national income (GNI) per capita (see figure B3.11.1). The civil war destroyed capital resources, repressed investment, and seriously damaged the capacity of the public sector to provide basic public services.

More recent data from the World Bank's World Development Indicators further demonstrate the impact of conflict on economic output and public spending. As shown in figure B3.11.1, GNI per capita fell by 45 percent between 1992—the year before the war started—and its low point in 2003, before rebounding in 2004. The civil war had the opposite effect on military spending; it increased by 83 percent as a percentage of GDP between 1992 and its high point in 1998 before declining again.

Figure B3.11.1   GNI per Capita and Military Expenditure in Burundi, 1990–2012

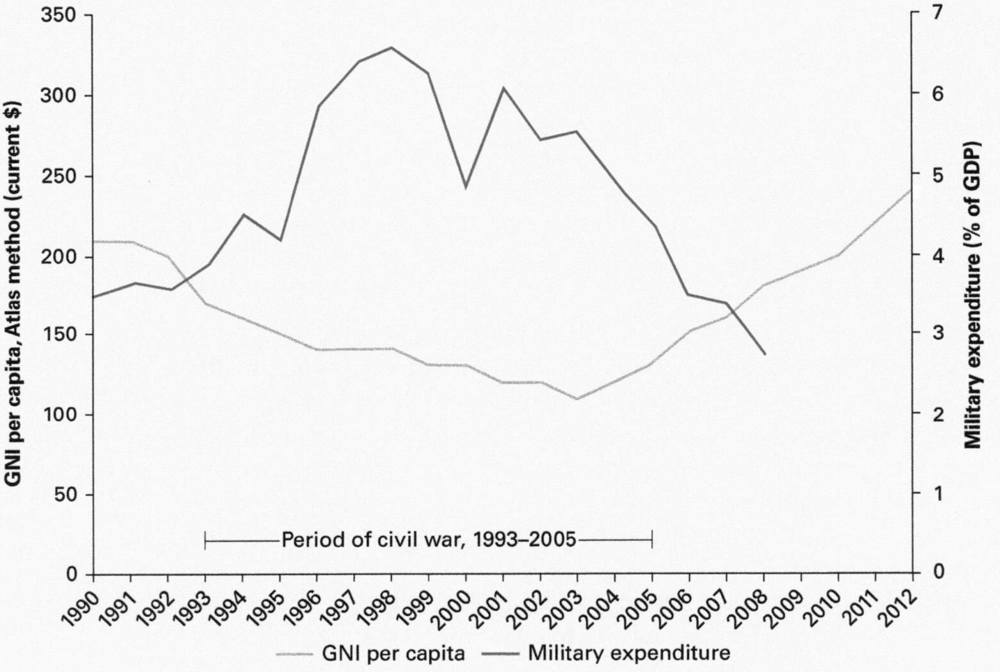

Sources: World Bank 2012; World Bank data.
Note: GDP = gross domestic product; GNI = gross national income. In calculating GNI in U.S. dollars for certain operational and analytical purposes, the World Bank uses the Atlas conversion factor instead of simple exchange rates in order to reduce the impact of exchange rate fluctuations in the cross-country comparison of national incomes. See World Bank Data Compilation Methodology: https://datahelpdesk.worldbank.org /knowledgebase/articles/378832-the-world-bank-atlas-method-detailed-methodology.

more than a rubber stamp for executive decrees, especially those related to the military sector. Even when democratic accountability is greater, legislatures might lack practical influence over military matters because of knowledge gaps, lack of access to secret information or relevant officials, or the special status of the military sector. Finally, in the more democratic and developed countries of the Organisation for Economic Co-operation and Development, and in many countries of the former Soviet Union, the legislature exercises a huge authority over the national budget and PFM matters.

Many national legislatures have a budget or appropriations committee that coordinates the legislature's amendments to the budget and leads legislative discussions with central finance officials on budget issues. To satisfactorily review and approve the military budget, committee members (or staff) have to be sufficiently knowledgeable of military issues and authorized to review secret budgets, plans, and other documents. This work might be conducted by a subcommittee of the budget committee or by members who also serve on the defense policy committee. In practice, legislative authority over the budget is exercised through formal or informal amendments to the appropriations bill or by simply refusing to enact the proposed budget.

As a rule, the budget should be presented to the legislature two to four months before the start of the fiscal year to allow time for consultations with defense and finance officials and for deliberations within the legislative body. Since the legislature is not always capable of enacting a budget law on time, the budget law should include provisions for the executive to commit expenditures before the budget is approved. In most countries, these "continuing resolutions" authorize new spending based on budget allocations from the previous year, not on budget allocations in the current, disputed budget request. This approach can be problematic for the military sector, however, particularly if perceptions of strategic threats or defense policy objectives have changed during the course of the year. The budget law should also include provisions authorizing the legislature to approve agreed portions of the national budget request in the absence of full approval. Such an approach might allow the military sector (or other sectors) to be funded even if legislators cannot agree on the full package. Both continuing resolutions and independently approved sectoral budgets violate fundamental budgetary principles, so they should be avoided. But they are preferable to a government shutdown or failure to provide defense services.

Planning for DDR and DSR

Disarmament, demobilization, and reintegration and defense sector reform are common postconflict activities for the military sector, particularly in fragile and conflict-prone states where there is a substantial international presence. DDR is intended to contribute to postconflict security and stability by physically removing weapons and ammunition, disbanding armed groups, and reintegrating former combatants into civilian society. DSR is a broader initiative, intended to reform, restructure, or otherwise develop accountable, effective, and efficient military institutions that operate fairly and that fully respect human rights. Of the two, DDR is the more immediate postconflict concern, whereas DSR often has a broader remit and longer-term focus on the nation's formal military institutions.

DDR and DSR have significant—but different—implications for public expenditure and financial management. A central goal of DSR is creating an efficient and affordable military sector that will be sustainable and effective beyond the short run. In programmatic terms, the integration or regularization of nonstatutory forces is most appropriately handled within a DSR program. Transition planning for national replacement of an international peace mission would also fall under the DSR remit. DDR, on the other hand, usually entails more upfront costs, but financial assistance is often available from the international community. Whereas DSR entails a PER followed by PFM reforms, DDR programs typically do not lead to the reform of related PFM and budgetary systems.

The main expenditure requirements of DDR are related to the short-term funding and implementation of disarmament and demobilization programs and the longer-term poverty reduction and civilian employment activities related to reintegration. Immediate needs are likely to be funded from a combination of international budgetary sources, including UN trust funds, World Bank trust funds, and direct bilateral support. The longer-term reintegration component of DDR should be fully incorporated into the country's poverty reduction and development strategies. To that end, the ministry of defense and former combatants should be consulted when identifying national development priorities. In all cases, the PER team should estimate any associated costs or long-term financial commitments that will have to be covered by the national budget.

It is important to note that financial management for DDR programs, like international assistance more broadly, might be conducted outside of the normal national budget process. While such an arrangement undermines the national budget's comprehensiveness and transparency, it might be a practical compromise reflecting the complexity of funding sources, the mix of supporting international partners, and the supported country's capacity to manage funding and implement programs. Additional details and guidance are offered by the UN's Disarmament, Demobilization, and Reintegration Resource Center (see table 3A.3 in annex 3A).

DSR is intended to fundamentally redefine the military sector's role in providing security services. Good practice requires that policy makers consider related reform processes under way in the security and justice sector, including DDR, to develop a shared assessment of threats, national interests, and policy objectives. Specific DSR policy objectives will then determine how to modify the military's strategic, operational, and tactical capabilities to meet these newly agreed security requirements within the available fiscal space. Areas to be reformed could include structure; function and human capacity; infrastructure and assets; legislation, policy, or doctrine; or some combination. It is practically guaranteed that a DSR program will reallocate resources between public sector institutions, which could entail a downsizing of the military in favor of the police or a reallocation from the security sector to the productive sectors. Given its far-reaching implications, DSR must be a nationally owned process.

Expenditure implications for DSR are shaped by the security environment and the condition of existing military institutions. In general, there are five categories within which defense sector institutions can be classified, ranging from least challenging and expensive to reform to most challenging and expensive:

1. Military institutions fully in place and organized
2. Military institutions partially disabled by the withdrawal of relevant agencies or personnel, with dysfunctional or parallel chains of command
3. Military institutions dismantled and providing defense services only sporadically
4. Military institutions only on paper, with no authorized or funded programs
5. Nonexistent military institutions, with no legal authorities or funding in place.

To ensure an affordable and sustainable outcome, policy makers need to condition the DSR program on available resources. Clear top-down direction on the immediate and medium-term fiscal space should be provided early in the process. This is not unlike the standard, best-practice national budget process, and establishing this requirement in the DSR program can serve as a valuable precedent for civilian control of the military and for an integrated, efficient national budget process over the long run. In contrast, a largely bottom-up process might lead to accurate costing of future force structures; but it is unlikely to reflect national political priorities or budget constraints. This initial work also provides an excellent opportunity to establish productive working relationships and mutual understanding between officials of the ministries of finance and defense and military officers. Additional details and guidance can be found in the UN Department of Peacekeeping Operation's policy for DSR (see table 3A.3 in annex 3A).

Budget Execution

Budget execution is the exercise of budget authority in pursuit of a plan: the approved national budget is the plan; legislative appropriation of public funds provides the legal authority; and the ministry of defense exercises that authority through the budget execution cycle. In PFM terms, the provision of defense services is thus a matter of executing the defense budget. At this point, defense policy objectives and military strategy have been established based on the threat perceptions of the national leadership and military professionals, and resources have been allocated according to strategic priorities and fiscal constraints. For the budget to be a useful policy tool—and for defense services to be delivered as intended—the budget must be properly executed as provided for in law. Specifically, budget inputs must be applied as directed.

Program execution, on the other hand, is more appropriately focused on defense outputs and outcomes than on budgetary inputs. Program execution may entail a trade-off between control and efficiency. Itemized budgets require defense program managers to obtain central approval before they can hire personnel, acquire matériel, or otherwise spend public funds. Controlling inputs in this way does not give defense program managers incentives to economize and diverts attention from defense outputs. In theory, it could be possible to achieve the same (or greater) outputs at less cost than estimated in the budget. In these cases, there is greater scope for flexibility in budget execution, and program managers should be granted greater discretion provided there is sufficient institutional strength and oversight to guarantee beneficial outcomes.

The PER team should be aware of the trade-offs between budget execution and program execution. While there is no universal rule, past experience suggests that in most countries where a defense sector PER is likely to be performed, institutional capacity is weak and fiscal constraints severe. In most cases, therefore, the PER team should give greater attention to budget execution and the operational control of appropriated funds than to program execution and its attendant systems of management control. Accordingly, this sourcebook focuses primarily on budget execution, not program execution. Outputs and outcomes are still important measures of success in delivering defense services—as discussed in detail in the "Performance Measurement and Oversight" section of this chapter—but this approach gives program managers less flexibility to decide how those outputs and outcomes will be achieved once the national budget is adopted.

Budget execution is chiefly concerned with operational efficiency—achieving defense outputs and outcomes that are economical, efficient, and effective in order to get the most out of all funds expended and thus maximize public utility. Operational efficiency requires expending funds in conformity with the authorizations provided by law; exercising flexibility when unexpected security threats emerge or the macroeconomic context changes so that defense programming reflects updated defense priorities; monitoring program implementation to ensure that funds are used for the purposes intended and achieve the outputs expected; and controlling the risks associated with implementing defense programs.

Budget Authority

Legislative approval of the military budget through the appropriations process, described in the "Budget Formulation Cycle" section of this chapter, grants the ministry of defense legal authority to obligate public resources for defense provision. During the budget execution cycle, this legal authority—also called "budget authority"—flows from the ministry to subordinate spending units within the ministry and the military services. Budget authority gives program managers the power to legally bind, or obligate, the government to make a payment in exchange for assets, goods, or services supplied by vendors. Accordingly, an obligation is a legal reservation of government funds that must be paid if the contracted party delivers as promised. The ministry of defense exercises its budget authority to hire personnel, acquire goods and services, and pay for operation and maintenance to meet the nationally determined defense policy objectives. As discussed, these services fall into the generic categories of defense administration, force provision, force support, and force employment, but the specific formulation will vary by country.

Appropriations define the purpose, amount, and time period of defense spending:

- *Purpose.* The purposes for which funds can be obligated are typically provided in the budget law. Under most circumstances the PER team can expect the budget request to be fairly similar to the approved budget bill, provided that the budget request reflected fiscal constraints and agreed policy objectives. Less frequently, the legislature might mandate spending on alternative or additional items that the ministry of defense has not requested to satisfy constituent demands or compel defense reforms. Changes of this kind can have beneficial effects where budget requests were outdated or the military has resisted necessary changes, but only if democratic accountability is adequate and the legislature's actions reflect security concerns or defense priorities. Alternatively, legislative changes that are motivated by sectional interests undermine allocative efficiency. In less developed countries, and for items or programs of special interest, spending categories might be narrowly defined. In more developed countries, or countries that have a performance-based budget, program managers might be given more latitude.
- *Amount.* Appropriations almost always provide an upper limit on the amount the ministry of defense can spend for any given purpose defined in the budget. The legislature might also stipulate that "no less than" a certain amount can be spent. The result is a narrow range or specific amount to be spent, and budget execution is measured in terms of the ministry's ability to spend the prescribed amount, as will be discussed.
- *Time period.* For most types of spending, appropriations will define the period of availability for funds made available. Accordingly, the ministry of defense must make obligations before the appropriation expires. This helps ensure that the mandated defense services will be provided in a timely fashion and helps maintain fiscal balance over the medium term. After the appropriation expires, no new obligations

---

Box 3.12   Mali—Cash Account for Operations Vulnerable to Fraud, Waste, and Abuse

According to the World Bank's 2013 financial management assessment of Mali's military, the maintenance of a special account for operations in the country's "Northern Zone" was a major source of vulnerability. In this case, there was no de facto spending ceiling, the purpose and operating conditions of the special account were not adhered to, budget charges displayed anomalies and lacked transparency, and the controls performed on expenditures from the special account were less rigorous than the country's normal budget procedures.

Source: World Bank 2013a.

---

can be made, although some adjustments might be permitted. The period of availability can vary, from one (annual) cycle for the acquisition of simple goods and services to several budget cycles for major infrastructure or weapon system procurements. Contingency funds, which are common in the military sector, can be open-ended. They exist to be used in times of emergency (not by a certain date) and are replenished as necessary.

A warrant is the financial control document that establishes the amount of funds authorized to be withdrawn from treasury accounts for each appropriation title. Once funds are appropriated by the legislature, the ministry of finance or the treasury will issue a warrant to the ministry of defense to grant it budget authority for defense provision. Similarly, the ministry of defense's finance office or comptroller will issue subwarrants to transfer budget authority to the military services and subordinate spending units. Through this legal mechanism, budget authority is provided to the spending units according to the approved budget.

There are circumstances in many developing countries where cash literally flows from the treasury to the military sector. Where electronic banking does not exist, for example, payrolls are often disbursed in this way. Direct cash payments to the military sector are most likely in conflict settings, where normal infrastructure may not be functional. In these cases, it is harder to effectively manage government funds, and a de facto corruption risk arises, as the example of Mali suggests (box 3.12).

The Budget Execution Cycle

In a fully developed PFM framework, there are four main stages to budget execution:

1. *Apportionment* of funds appropriated to the sector, and their release by the ministry of finance to the ministry of defense
2. *Commitment* of funds by program managers to particular activities in support of defense provision
3. *Acquisition* of goods or services, and certification that they have been provided as agreed
4. *Payment* to suppliers for the goods or services provided.

The military sector should be fully integrated into the standard budget execution cycle (and indeed into all the PFM practices discussed in this sourcebook), and should abide by the laws and regulations prevailing for the rest of government. In practice, however, the military sector often has off-budget revenues and expenditures. By definition, there will be no apportionment of those funds by the ministry of finance. In developing countries more broadly—particularly fragile or conflict-prone states—the process might be considerably less rigorous. For example, there might be no obligation phase. Instead, ministry of defense officials or military officers might simply pay for goods after they are delivered, without any prior commitment or obligation for either the provider or the defense program manager.

Stage 1: Apportionment

Apportionment is the distribution of budget authority for specified activities and time periods. Once a warrant is received for defense spending, the ministry of finance or treasury—working with information provided by the ministry of defense finance office—can release tranches of budget authority to the ministry of defense, which will then distribute it through subwarrants to ministry of defense offices and the military services. Each major command will further distribute budget authority to subordinate commands, program offices, or installations, depending on the level of decentralization provided for in the country's institutional framework. The goal is to ensure that the ministry of defense and its subordinate spending units do not obligate funds so rapidly that they exhaust available funds before the end of the fiscal year or endanger the country's cash balances and fiscal stability. Generally, apportionments are cumulative, so there could still be a "rush to obligate" at the end of year if the ministry of defense spending units do not stay on schedule. Apportionments should be made in accordance with military units' expenditure, or "phasing," plans. These are typically month-to-month projections of the rate at which funds will be obligated, built from expectations about payroll, contract award dates, and the timing of intra-governmental purchases. As it does in the budget formulation process, the ministry of defense should consolidate subordinate agencies' projections for a sectorwide phasing plan, which is submitted to the ministry of finance. In many countries, the first and last months of the fiscal year have the highest obligation rates: in the first month, annual contracts are agreed; in the last month, there is a rush to obligate remaining budget authority before it expires at the end of the fiscal year.[28] In developing countries, particularly fragile and conflict-prone states, obligation and expenditure rates are typically better for the military sector than for other sectors of government. Given capacity constraints, however, it is still possible that obligation rates will lag behind schedule or that funds will be obligated to activities that were not authorized by the legislature. Sectorwide management of defense funding and support for effective internal controls across all military activities will be undermined if there is no single person accountable for military appropriations.

The ministry of finance could freeze approved appropriations by not issuing warrants, and thereby not apportioning funds. This might be a prudent measure to maintain fiscal balance if the macroeconomic or fiscal conditions have changed or if other unfunded mandates—like war—have emerged. Where cash flow issues and weak treasury management are present, it is not uncommon for a finance ministry to withhold some percentage of budget allocation as a hedge against cash flow or revenue shortfalls. If revenues materialize, these resources may be released late in the fiscal year to spending ministries, potentially creating a wasteful year-end spending situation.

Stage 2: Commitment

In the commitment stage, the future obligation to pay for goods or services acquired is incurred. Depending on the country context, legally binding agreements are called obligations or, simply, commitments. An administrative commitment (also called "budgetary commitment" or "accounting commitment") by which apportioned funds are set aside for a specific purpose might precede the legal commitment. Administrative commitments are useful for managing defense activities and cash flow, but the practice is not universal. Contracts defining the obligation are common with private sector vendors. If goods or services are acquired from other government institutions, within the military sector or not, a formal interdepartmental purchase request is used instead. These could be used, for example, for defense services provided by the military services to the operational commands.

Expenditures can be committed in a variety of ways, depending on their nature:

- *Defense matériel, transport, and other short-term or recurrent goods and services.* Goods and services that can be completed within one fiscal year should usually be committed through annual contracts. Alternatively, routine activities—like payment for utilities—might be subject to less formal rules. These commitments must not exceed the appropriations allocated to them.
- *Large investment projects.* Large projects, particularly procurement of major weapon systems, will likely require several years to be completed, and thus will be committed through multiyear contracts. The total cost of these multiyear contracts will likely exceed the annual appropriations provided for the activity. Consequently, obligations of this type will be liquidated incrementally over multiple annual budgets or through capital investment appropriations that have extended periods of availability. It is important that countries engage in full life-cycle costing of large procurements, as already described in the "Budget Formulation Cycle" section of this chapter, to ensure that money is not wasted on projects that cannot be completed due to future fiscal constraints.
- *Personnel expenditures and other mandatory expenditures related to interest and entitlements.* Expenditures of this type are often legally committed through prior legislation or executive decisions.

Consequently, these obligations will predate the current fiscal year, but must still be covered with available funds in any given fiscal year.[29]

The program manager is responsible for implementing the commitment stage of the budget execution process. Alternatively called the "spending agent" or "authorizing officer," the program manager has the authority to obligate funds and authorize payments. For defense administration programs, the program manager is likely an official in the ministry of defense or in the joint chiefs of staff. For force provision and force support programs, the program manager is likely a military officer serving at defense headquarters or at the headquarters of one of the military services. For force employment programs, the program manager is likely a military officer deployed in one of the operational or functional commands. The program manager should be held accountable for failure to comply with financial regulations, and may be held financially liable for fraud or error. Key controls to be exercised by the program manager include verifying that the proposed expenditure is provided for in the appropriation, ensuring that sufficient funds remain available in the relevant category of expenditure, and ensuring that the expenditure is classified correctly.[30]

Stage 3: Acquisition and Verification

Goods and services should be accepted by the authorizing officer, who should then immediately verify that they are consistent with the contract or interdepartmental purchase request and generate documentary evidence for payment and audit purposes. If the country has an accrual accounting system, the expenditure is also recorded at this stage. Verification for payroll purposes requires determining the eligibility of the recipient, which can be difficult in defense situations where there are variable hardship or danger pay allowances, and in fragile or conflict-prone situations where recordkeeping is lax. Moreover, many payroll requirements are provided for in statutory law or prior regulations, not individual contracts or agreements. Particular problems related to "ghost soldiers," undermanning, and payment arrears are discussed in the "Military Payroll" subsection that follows. Verification for the procurement of defense matériel and other goods can range from the relatively simple (verification of the delivery of bulk commodities in the quantities agreed upon) to the more detailed and difficult (verification of the performance of bespoke weapon systems against agreed-upon specifications).

Stage 4: Payment

Once delivery is verified, the authorizing agent sends a payment order to the accountant responsible for making the payment. The accountant may be an official at the ministry of defense, a military officer, or a ministry of finance official seconded to the ministry of defense, depending on the country's institutional framework. In principle, the accountant is the only person empowered to handle cash and other assets, and is financially liable in cases of procedural error or fraud. At this stage, it is important to verify that

(i) the expenditure was properly committed, (ii) a competent person verified that the goods or services were received as expected, (iii) the invoice and other documents supporting payment are complete and correct, and (iv) the creditor is identified correctly.[31] Once paid, an obligation is said to be liquidated. If the country has a cash accounting system, the expenditure is also recorded at this stage.

The PER team should be aware that payment systems, like all systems of accountability, can break down in a conflict setting. Even when there is no open conflict, deployed forces may not have adequate controls in place—because the required personnel or hardware is located at defense headquarters or on base, or there is not sufficient time to establish or implement controls in the field, or operational commanders do not make financial management a priority. Still, segregation of duties is perhaps the single most important internal control for financial management. The PER team should determine whether it is exercised in practice by identifying the authorizing agents and accountants for all major programs and by ensuring that an adequate system of reporting is in place.

Under ideal circumstances, payment is made from a Treasury Single Account by electronic funds transfer, check, or cash. Use of a single account facilitates control of expenses and cash and helps maintain adequate fiscal balances, which can be particularly important in developing countries. Alternatively, the ministry of finance or treasury could transfer funds to the ministry of defense's bank accounts, from which payment is then made to the vendor. Meanwhile, petty expenditures might be paid from an imprest account or cash advance that resides at the ministry of defense or subordinate military unit and is replenished as needed. Where institutions are weak, a broader range of activities might use imprest accounts and cash advances, but this practice creates corruption risks by reducing the number of people who have to sign off on any given expenditure.

Internal control is a practice designed to provide reasonable assurance of the effectiveness and efficiency of operations, the reliability of financial reporting, and compliance with laws and regulations. It comprises several features:

- *The control environment*, which establishes the basic structure and tone for the organization. In the military sector, it is heavily influenced by the country's level of economic development and the outlook and behavior of senior ministry of defense and military officials.
- *Control activities*, which are specific policies and procedures that help ensure policy directives are implemented. In the military sector, control activities related to payroll and procurement are particularly important.
- *Accounting and reporting systems*, which support the timely identification, capture, and sharing of information to enable policy makers and program managers to carry out their responsibilities. A modern

financial management information system (FMIS) can automate many of these tasks.

- *Risk management*, which is the systematic identification, analysis, and mitigation of program, operational, and financial management risks.

Internal Control

There are two main models that define the structure of internal control: (i) a centralized system characterized by ex ante control of expenditures by ministry of finance officials, called the Francophone system; and (ii) a decentralized system in which ministry of defense officials and military officers control expenditures subject to ex post monitoring, called the Westminster system. The country's level of institutional development, its colonial legacy, and other factors influence which system it uses. In less developed countries, the centralized Francophone approach, with its ex ante controls, may make sense until the ministry of defense has established sufficient capacity to efficiently manage its own finances, and there is greater trust, transparency, and accountability in the management of public finances. Given the prevalence of off-budget revenues and expenditures, integrating the military sector into national PFM practices would imply greater central control of program implementation, at least in the short run. More developed countries likely use the decentralized Westminster model of control, in which there is ex post monitoring of expenditures through internal audit and other techniques. Decentralized systems are more compatible with a "managerial" approach to public administration, in which program managers are given discretion over how to achieve intended outputs within specific budget categories. An example from Mali is provided in box 3.13.

Control activities refer to a broad collection of specific policies and procedures that help ensure that policy directives are implemented in a cost-effective and efficient way. In general, financial controls seek to

- Establish responsibility for budget execution decisions to promote accountability
- Segregate duties related to authorization, payment, and recordkeeping to reduce the risk of fraud or error
- Monitor transactions, either before or after obligations are made, to safeguard funds and ensure they are used for the purposes intended
- Document procedures and retain records, so that transactions can be audited and substantiated.

As with all the other PFM principles and practices discussed in this sourcebook, the military sector should be just as rigorous as the rest of government in financial control activities. Financial control activities should be practiced at each stage of the budget execution cycle, as described earlier (and shown in figure 3.4). That said, payroll and procurement require some

---

Box 3.13   **Mali—Highly Formalized Control Environment**

According to the World Bank's 2013 report on financial management in Mali's security forces, Mali's expenditure chain is highly formalized, but provides little autonomy to the technical directorates to exercise managerial authority. It is patterned on the Francophone model, with a four-step procedure: (i) expenditure commitment, (ii) validation, (iii) payment order, and (iv) payment. In this system, only the public accountant can handle funds or securities. The public accountant is under the oversight of the Ministry of Finance and is personally and financially responsible for funds or securities missing from his or her till. The only senior account manager is the minister of finance; in the security sector, the only delegated secondary account manager is the director of the Finance and Equipment Directorate (DFM).

The technical directorates' lack of autonomy in financial matters results in considerable inefficiencies. All commitments and payments must pass through the DFM, unless paid from special imprest accounts. "Thus, when the Air Force wants to acquire a spare part for an aircraft, the request has to go first to the Air Force Chief of Staff, who passes the request to the Armed Forces Chief of Staff, who then submits the request to the DFM. Even if the appropriation is ultimately released, the decision-making process takes weeks, and the airplane remains grounded the entire time." Purchasing is similarly inefficient: the DFM is responsible for developing a procurement plan and monitoring its execution, and the technical directorates are only marginally involved. "Thus, the director of the Army Supplies Directorate, specifically charged with providing uniforms to the troops, has never been involved in developing the specifications, nor in selecting the suppliers who provide camouflage uniforms to the forces. This results in inefficient spending: despite repeated requests each year by the Directorate, the same blue camouflage uniform is ordered year after year for the Air Force, even though it fades very rapidly and quickly becomes unusable or unpresentable." Finally, even the technical directorates themselves are highly centralized. For example, a purchase request for a vehicle tire in the gendarmerie goes all the way up to the director general.

Source: World Bank 2013a, 35–36.

special considerations, discussed below, given the unique aspects of the military sector and defense function.

Military Payroll

Military payroll must be sensitive to the heightened security and corruption risks unique to the military sector. Payroll arrears are a particular concern; failing to compensate or adequately supply organized, armed personnel risks insurrection or predatory acts, including the collection of illegal "taxes" from the population. Military forces are meant to provide defense services and thereby promote security, but weak PFM can make military forces a source of insecurity. The relatively closed nature of the military hierarchy can also invite abuse. Chains of command should be separate from chains of payment, so that commanders cannot withhold pay or divert funds to illicit purposes. Finally, it is important to establish oversight mechanisms that prevent the use of conscripted (or volunteer) military personnel as labor for commercial or private enterprises.

Figure 3.4   Budget Execution Controls

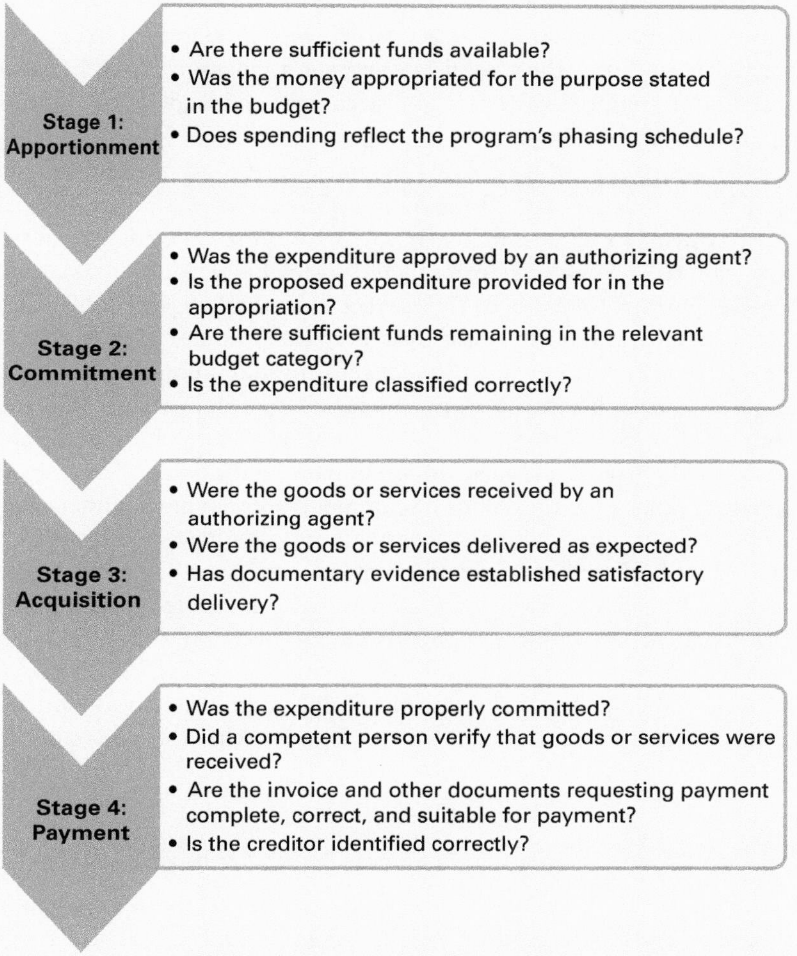

Stage 1: Apportionment	• Are there sufficient funds available? • Was the money appropriated for the purpose stated in the budget? • Does spending reflect the program's phasing schedule?
Stage 2: Commitment	• Was the expenditure approved by an authorizing agent? • Is the proposed expenditure provided for in the appropriation? • Are there sufficient funds remaining in the relevant budget category? • Is the expenditure classified correctly?
Stage 3: Acquisition	• Were the goods or services received by an authorizing agent? • Were the goods or services delivered as expected? • Has documentary evidence established satisfactory delivery?
Stage 4: Payment	• Was the expenditure properly committed? • Did a competent person verify that goods or services were received? • Are the invoice and other documents requesting payment complete, correct, and suitable for payment? • Is the creditor identified correctly?

Two problematic personnel practices have been repeatedly observed in the military sector: (i) undermanning of military forces to achieve budget savings, and (ii) keeping "ghost soldiers" on the military payroll to divert appropriated funds. Undermanning occurs when the military services fail to recruit sufficient officers and enlisted men and women to meet the requirements of the defense provision program. This can save money, assuming the full budgeted amount is not spent. However, the extra funds are often diverted to illicit or illegitimate ends, such as bonuses paid to general officers or senior defense officials. "Ghost soldiers" are military force personnel who exist only on paper; who are not trained or equipped to fulfill their roles; or who simply do not show up for work. These nonexistent forces obviously contribute nothing to the provision of defense services, but are allocated salary payments that are then diverted to other, possibly illicit, purposes. In countries that lack veterans', death, or disability benefits, payments to ghost soldiers can provide legitimate, if not officially authorized, relief. Often, however, payments to ghost soldiers enrich corrupt military or government officials. In any case, ghost soldiers represent a violation of the budgetary principles of comprehensiveness and accuracy, and undermine allocative and operational efficiency.

Systematic methods of verifying the number of personnel employed by the ministry of defense and the military services, and of linking salary and wage payments to actual employees, can help control related program and corruption risks. Possible reforms include using biometric identification to ensure payments are made to the correct individuals. However, ensuring that those individuals are sufficiently prepared and are present to fulfill their duties also requires institutional reforms and a commitment on the part of leaders to better outcomes. Segregation of duties is perhaps more important (see box 3.14 on the Central African Republic). In addition to mitigating the risk that troops will go unpaid (and perhaps revolt in consequence), separating the chains of command and payment eliminates the risk that illicit gain—through undermanning or ghost soldiers—can be achieved without collusion. Another reform is to issue payments through electronic funds transfer to mitigate the risks associated with handling large amounts of cash, although this can be done only if the country's treasury and banking systems are sufficiently developed, and if cultural norms allow. Finally, the relatively simple administrative control of comparing unit rosters and payment requests with the personnel files

---

Box 3.14   Central African Republic—Failure to Segregate Duties Creates Payroll Risk

According to the World Bank's 2009 financial management assessment of the Central African Republic, the military's personnel and salaries management chain is not fully computerized, and effective mechanisms have not been established to verify the authenticity or accuracy of personnel files and payrolls. As a result, there is considerable risk that funds will be lost to mismanagement or corruption. Salaries are paid in cash to nearly 70 percent of military personnel. Under this system, cash is sent from the Treasury of the Directorate General of National Army Administration to the relevant directorate; it is then distributed to intermediaries known as "payeurs," who are soldiers drawn from the units; finally, these payeurs redistribute the cash to the final beneficiaries without any supervision by competent accountants. Moreover, the state treasury receives no checklists from this practice.

The Ministry of Defense has established an antifraud committee and payroll monitoring committee to verify salaries based on documentary evidence, which has made it possible to clean up the files pertaining to military personnel strength and reduce the ministry's payroll. Additional reforms are under way to ensure greater involvement of the banking sector. Despite these improvements, the system runs counter to the fundamental principle of segregating the duties of authorizer and accountant. The assessment therefore concludes that it should not be maintained and that the management of public funds should fall within the sole competence of the state treasury.

Source: World Bank 2009.

maintained by ministry of defense personnel offices or the ministry of finance can prevent gross abuse while promoting managerial control, information gathering, and allocative efficiency in addition to promoting more immediate operational efficiency. To determine if undermanning or ghost soldiers are a concern, the PER team should itself compare staffing and payment data from various sources.

Defense Procurement

Procurement is the second area of special concern in defense sector budget execution. Like any other sector, the defense sector should require a full accounting of procurement transactions, and its records should be open to public scrutiny. As noted, goods and services procured should reflect the perceived security threat and support agreed-upon defense policy objectives. Beyond that, special consideration might be necessary for the sensitive nature or complexity of some defense sector items, and the country will have to abide by international laws that restrict certain types of defense spending.

The overriding objective of a public procurement system is to deliver value for money in the use of public funds, while adhering to principles of fairness, nondiscrimination, impartiality, openness to competition, and transparency. A generic procurement process therefore involves the following steps:

- Defining clear requirements for the desired goods or services
- Defining clear technical quality specifications and standards
- Requesting proposals and tenders
- Adjudicating tenders according to preestablished criteria
- Selecting a preferred bidder
- Drawing up of a contract
- Placing the order
- Monitoring progress
- Receiving goods or services
- Verifying the quality of goods or services received
- Paying for goods or services
- Distributing goods or services to the relevant defense programs.

Defense procurement should follow standard government-wide practices for all nonsensitive items, including construction, clothing, food, fuel, vehicles, and other equipment and defense matériel necessary to support military forces and defense administration. These nonsensitive items meet the great majority of defense needs. Integrating procurement on a sectorwide basis, or with other sectors of the government, could enable the military sector to increase monopsony power, consolidate and exploit government-wide procurement expertise, and take advantage of corruption control mechanisms that already exist in other sectors or at the central procurement agency. As in any other government sector, major procurements in the defense sector should be subject to high-level consultation and legislative approval.

Sensitive defense items might require special considerations unique to the military sector. Sensitive items include any of the goods and services provided for under secret budgets, such as those supporting intelligence operations, as well as strategically important weapon systems that if denied by a foreign supplier would harm national security. In these cases, the military sector should focus less on minimizing the price it pays, and more on minimizing the risk that goods or services will not be delivered and that follow-up support and maintenance will be denied. If procurement is meant to be secret, the military sector will also have to curtail normal transparency requirements. If large enough, secret procurement should still be reviewed by tender boards and be subject to high-level consultation and legislative approval, but this oversight can be accomplished in the confidential manner already described for budget formulation.

Among the defense procurements that require special considerations are major weapon systems, which from inception to final acceptance can take as long as 15 years. Given this long time frame, officials should devise means of controlling currency and economic risks to protect against adverse contingencies. Given the size of such procurements, there are likely to be multiple customers spanning numerous domestic military services (and potentially those of international partners as well); multiple contractors and subcontractors are almost guaranteed. To promote operational efficiency and accountability, the authorities should establish rigorous oversight and anticorruption mechanisms with the authority and resources to review all parties involved. Given their complexity, such procurements should be overseen by interdisciplinary teams, including engineering, resource management, contracting, and quality assurance experts. Furthermore, quality control mechanisms should be established for each stage of development. Finally, defense procurement must consider the full life-cycle costs of procured weapon systems, including the specialized personnel needed to operate them and regular maintenance and upkeep costs. Major weapon systems can remain in service for decades, and defense budget projections must reflect their true costs if macroeconomic and fiscal stability is to be achieved.

Defense procurement is constrained legally by international arms control regimes and strategically by the practices of international security partners. It is illegal to traffic in many types of arms, including nuclear, chemical, and biological weapons. Specific countries might also be subject to sanctions on small arms or dual-use technologies. Obviously, defense procurement should be bound by these strictures, and must necessarily be so if it is open and transparent. For strategic reasons, a country should procure weapon systems that are similar to those employed by its security partners, all else equal. Using the same ammunition or radar systems, for example, allows for interoperability. This will improve defense outcomes when national military forces operate in coalition with those of other countries.

Accounting, Asset Management, and Reporting

Accounting, asset management, and reporting are necessary to ensure that funds are being spent for the purposes and in the manner intended, and to avoid loss of defense articles, which can undermine security. In terms of financial accounting, the military sector is similar to other government sectors. Limited resources must be applied in accordance with the law in order to achieve allocative and operational efficiency. In terms of asset management, however, the military sector is somewhat different from other sectors: because the tools with which it delivers defense services can also promote insecurity, defense program managers controlling stocks of arms and ammunition must adhere to more demanding asset-control standards than those prevailing elsewhere in government. Finally, in terms of financial reporting, the military sector should meet the same requirements as the rest of government. Special provisions might be made for secret-budget categories, but budgetary aggregates can and should be publicly released.

A core assumption in the national budget process is that military professionals have accurately, or at least reasonably, estimated the actual cost of providing the defense services covered in the budget. It is therefore expected that funds will be fully expended in the time allotted as the defense function is fulfilled. Here the difference between program execution and budget execution alluded to at the outset of this section is clear. For the purposes of program execution, it makes no difference if the military sector finds a way to provide the required level of defense services at a lower cost (through improved operational efficiency or other savings). For the purposes of budget execution, however, any savings the military sector achieves should be translated into more defense services than initially agreed—up to the amount that the appropriation can afford. The ultimate objective is the same from a PFM perspective: full obligation of the appropriation by its expiration date, and liquidation of obligations as goods or services are delivered. If the budget estimates were accurate and savings were achieved, then the military will have supplied more defense services than planned. This could result in decreased budget allocations for defense in subsequent years if national policy makers determine that funds can be optimally allocated elsewhere. Conversely, if there are cost overruns or if the ministry of defense fails to expend the entirety of its budget allocation, then defense services will be underprovided. In that case, the military sector may need additional funds in subsequent years to fulfill the defense function, or it may need to implement PFM reforms to achieve allocative and operational efficiency. Finally, if budget estimates were wrong, effective accounting and reporting practices will be necessary to identify mistakes and make corrections so that defense policy objectives can be reasonably aligned with resource requirements.

The most common measures of budget execution are the obligation and expenditure rates. The PER team should assess the extent to which the government monitors obligation and expenditure rates in the military sector, which agencies have access to the relevant reports, and how they are used in policy making and budgeting. The PER team should also undertake independent analysis of obligation and expenditure rates over time and between institutional units within the military sector to compare them against similar calculations for other sectors of government. This type of deviation analysis will illuminate areas of weakness in PFM practices and institutional capacity and will also help explain the quality of defense service delivery. Additional means by which to measure performance in the military sector are provided in the "Performance Measurement and Oversight" section of this chapter.

Accounting and reporting systems allow the ministry of defense to measure progress toward its prescribed budget execution goals, and allow the central government to manage its finances and overall fiscal balance. They also provide generalized and comparable information about the extent and efficiency of program implementation that can help the commander in chief, defense council, minister of defense, and other administrators manage the defense function, and that can enable the chief executive, council of ministers, and legislature to make informed judgments about trade-offs within the broader security and justice sector.

The military sector should meet the same standards of accounting as other government sectors do; standards will vary across countries depending on the level of economic development. Most developing countries continue to rely on cash-basis accounting systems, while many middle-income and developed countries have accrual-basis accounting systems. Accrual-basis accounting is superior in several ways, but more difficult to implement:

- *Cash-basis accounting* relies on the manual recording of transactions as they occur, which requires no estimation and limited contract management. It is thus simpler than accrual-based accounting and can be more easily applied in countries where there are human capital constraints. But cash-based accounting provides no means of recording commitments or obligations, and therefore makes planning and cash management difficult. Moreover, it can be easily manipulated by changing the timing of transactions so that they fall within a particular budget period, thus increasing corruption and mismanagement risks.
- *Accrual-basis accounting* records revenues when funds are earned and records expenses when the funds are committed or obligated. This approach provides several distinct advantages for the ministry of defense, and should be encouraged when possible. Accrual-basis accounting requires the valuation of assets and liabilities; depreciating assets, particularly weapon systems that last for decades, can more realistically portray military capabilities. This method also allows ministry of defense officials to report their net financial position, inclusive of commitments, when financial statements are prepared, regardless of whether debts were

actually paid in that respective period. Finally, it facilitates a comprehensive chart of accounts that records the assets and liabilities of all defense sector entities, which can help protect against the illegal sale of military equipment and the "hollowing out" of military forces.

A well-functioning FMIS can be useful for monitoring and reporting budget implementation, if the underlying systems of budget classification and accounting are in place. An FMIS can be broadly defined as a set of automation solutions that enable governments to plan, execute, and monitor the budget. Information typically captured by an FMIS includes approved budget allocations for both recurrent and capital expenditures; sources of financing for programs and projects; budget transfers; supplementary allocations; funds released against budgetary allocations; and data on commitments and actual expenditure against budgeted allocations. If the FMIS is integrated with other management systems—such as payroll—the database can be used to generate consolidated daily reports on transactions and the ministry of defense's financial standing.

In general, funds should be expended for the purpose and in the amounts provided for in the appropriations act. As discussed, the national budget formulation process is intended to promote allocative efficiency, and the allocations provided in law reflect agreed-upon defense priorities and military requirements. Stability in funding is important not only for macroeconomic and fiscal sustainability, but also for defense program performance. Unplanned transfers of money out of military training, for example, will undermine force readiness, directly reducing defense outputs and potentially hurting defense outcomes.

In-year modifications to approved defense sector budget allocations should be subject to the same standards and procedures as similar modifications in other government sectors. These standards and procedures should be defined in law and regulation, and the PER team should identify the extent to which they are applied. Some issues which the PER team might encounter include the following:

- Arrears, or unpaid obligations, can occur if the government faces a cash shortage. The consequences can be severe in the military sector if troops go unpaid or service providers stop delivering matériel. Overall, it is a damaging way to effect budgetary "savings," and should be avoided.

- Carryovers to the next budget cycle indicate the opposite problem of inadequate or slow budget execution. At the very least, excessive carryovers violate the budgetary principle of periodicity, but also likely mean that defense services are not being delivered at optimum levels.

- Virement, or transfers between budget categories, can be common in the military sector, depending on country context. Typically, the ministry of defense has a higher execution rate than other sectors of government. Unspent allocations from other sector budgets might therefore be applied to the military sector, especially in times of war. The government might also use unspent funds from other sectors to pay its military arrears, which can create corruption risks and which almost certainly undermines allocative efficiency.

Specification and *predictability* are very important budgetary principles, specifically in developing countries where the resource envelope is tight and institutions lack the capacity to sufficiently review and approve extraordinary requests. Too many amendments to the military budget during the budget execution cycle will weaken the credibility of the budget, but precluding all amendments is impractical for most developing-country contexts. To maintain flexibility, the ministry of defense should be free to reallocate within program activities as it sees fit, contingent on legislative reporting. Reallocating between programs or economic categories (from salaries to operations and maintenance, for example) may or may not require prior legislative approval depending on the country, but the legislature should always be notified on a timely basis and have the opportunity to raise questions or objections.

In terms of asset management, the military sector is unique: weapons, ammunition, and other sector-specific matériel are obviously dangerous to the health and welfare of the general public if they are not strictly controlled. Defense matériel must also be available at the time and place required for military operations if defense services are to be effectively provided. Logistics is therefore a core military activity, and the PER team should assess the quality and appropriateness of logistics institutions, policies, and procedures, as well as defense sector systems of asset control. Whereas control activities in other government sectors have gradually moved away from physical assets toward financial assets over the last few centuries, physical assets remain critically important for the military (see box 3.15).

Finally, as in any sector, measuring performance and feeding that information back into the budget cycle is essential. These steps can be taken by the military hierarchy or by the specialized oversight agencies discussed at length in the "Performance Measurement and Oversight" section of this chapter.

Risk Management

Risks related to budget execution fall into two broad categories: operational risks and financial management risks. Military institutions should establish control activities targeted at each, based on methods used elsewhere in government. These activities should balance the expected costs of identified risks with the costs of controlling them. Operational

Box 3.15   Niger—Asset Management Institutions and Practices

According to the World Bank's 2013 Public Expenditure Review of Niger's security sector, asset management is a major challenge following the country's fivefold increase in security investments in 2010–2012. These investments have an enduring financial impact. Unless they are maintained, the investments will not be available for use, but maintaining them requires recurrent expenditures for supplies and human resources that could result in cuts to other sectors. A strong asset management capacity has two advantages: it helps ensure that equipment is efficiently allocated to operational units, and it helps reduce transparency risks and prolong the life of the equipment, which contributes to a better economic return on the investments.

Several departments in the Nigerien Armed Forces are responsible for managing equipment: the Central Department of Military Intendance, the Central Department of Equipment, and the Department of Infrastructure. The Central Department of Military Intendance purchases, transports, stores, and distributes equipment procured from the civilian market and also audits expenditures and stocks accounts. The Central Department of Equipment is responsible for armored cars and vehicles, munitions, and the supply and accounting of equipment. Finally, the Department of Infrastructure is responsible for the supply, storage, and distribution of hydrocarbons. The police and gendarmerie have separate asset management and logistics departments, and pooled asset management between the security forces is not common. Overall, the personnel in charge of equipment are insufficiently trained, and departments could benefit from procedure manuals.

Internal control of asset management is largely on paper, and given the regular power outages and limited backup capacities, the weakly computerized system is likely to persist. When procured equipment is received and accepted, it is recorded in a central equipment registry; the Nigerien Armed Forces records its equipment in spreadsheets, while the national guard uses a Microsoft Word file. Depending on the type, the equipment is kept in central stocks until deployed or distributed directly to individual units. Recurrent needs, such as spare vehicle parts, are kept in stock and made available when requested. Other equipment is stocked on a quarterly basis or procured as needed. Inspections of equipment and stocks are usually conducted annually, but shortage of personnel means the planned periodicity is not always respected. Vehicle disposal is controlled by the Ministry of Finance, with revenues accruing to the Treasury. Weapons disposal is under the control of the Commission on Illegal Arms of the Economic Community of West African States. Finally, the responsibility for repair and maintenance depends on the degree of specialization required, ranging from the user of the matériel, to the company level, battalion level, centralized repair, and finally an external vendor. Maintenance of aircraft and armored vehicles is done by international service providers, whereas lighter vehicles are repaired domestically subject to public procurement rules.

Source: World Bank 2013b.

risks result from the increased use of supplies, equipment, and personnel during military operations; examples and possible mitigation measures are presented in table 3.16. Financial management risks depend largely on the overall quality of internal control measures already described, the availability of competent staff, the quality of accounting practices and FMIS, and the priority given to anticorruption and integrity-development initiatives. Examples and possible mitigation measures are presented in table 3.17.

Table 3.16   Sources of Defense Sector Operational Risk and Potential Mitigation Measures

Operational risk	Potential mitigation measures
Increased rate of resource consumption	Maintaining military units on operations or at increased levels of readiness increases consumption of all associated support costs, such as food, fuel, ammunition, clothing, and personal allowances. These additional costs should be identified and calculated for each military unit involved to determine in advance the expected overall increase.
Urgent operational requirements (UORs) for new equipment	Requests for UORs should be subject to the same scrutiny as that given to equipment in the main equipment program; processing should be faster and more streamlined, but involve similar financial rigor. Where possible, UOR purchases should replace an item already identified on the equipment program in order to bring forward a purchase rather than add a purchase.
Repair or replacement of damaged military equipment and facilities	At appropriate junctures, condition surveys of military equipment and facilities should be completed to determine the size of the repair liability. The survey should trigger critical analysis to decide if the equipment or facility should be repaired, disposed of, or replaced. To complete this analysis effectively may require a rapid review of the defense strategy in order to ensure the strategic context is still relevant.
Remediation costs of military conflict	Postconflict remediation is a whole-of-government effort, and the first important control is to determine the extent of the military's liability. In addition to those for repair and replacement, costs include medical treatment for injured soldiers and compensation payments to injured soldiers and those killed in action. These policies should be costed (if costing has not already taken place) and should be subject to tight deadlines for claims to ensure efficient verification.
Participation in an alliance, international military, or international peacekeeping operation	Contributing nations receive payment for the military forces they deploy. Transparent calculation of this payment and monitoring to ensure that it has been fully settled are necessary to prevent any misuse of funds. Generally, these revenues should be paid directly to the ministry of finance or treasury, not the ministry of defense.

Table 3.17   Sources of Defense Sector Financial Management Risk and Potential Mitigation Measures

Financial management risk	Potential mitigation measures
Excessive use of cash	Military organizations with low-control environments may wish to use cash for payments, especially for operational reasons. The use of cash as a payment method should be minimized in favor of more secure and traceable payment methods. Where operational requirements necessitate cash, robust accounting, reporting, and security controls should be in place to prevent the misuse of the funds.
Asset management, including security of weapons and ammunition, military vehicles, food, office supplies	Military organizations hold high volumes of equipment that need to be accounted for in robust ways to minimize loss. Robust equipment accounting procedures should be in place with controls for write-offs of equipment, especially specialized and high-value equipment.
Asset transfer from international security force, including UN peacekeeping forces	Transfer of assets may present the military with a substantial repair and maintenance liability for which it has neither the budget nor the expertise. Proposed asset transfers should be reviewed in the context of their fit with the stated defense strategy and supporting equipment program, available skilled personnel to operate and maintain the assets, and clear calculation of future maintenance costs and available budget.

(Table continues on next page)

Table 3.17   Sources of Defense Sector Financial Management Risk and Potential Mitigation Measures *(continued)*

Financial management risk	Potential mitigation measures
Disposal of military equipment, assets, and facilities	Clear authority and procedures for the disposal of military assets is necessary to avoid misuse of funds from the receipt of proceeds.
Role of the military in civil contingencies, including disaster relief, infrastructure development, public service strike	Military support to other government departments may result in some form of cross-charging to meet the military's costs. Transparent calculation of this payment and monitoring to ensure that it has been fully settled are necessary to prevent any misuse of funds.
Contingent liabilities, including cleanup of military training areas and contaminated land in military bases	Military organizations can harm the environment by occupying base locations, conducting training, and carrying out military operations. Cleanup and restoration may be required when the military leaves land mines, ammunition-related debris, and stocks used in training and operations, or when land is contaminated by fuel spillage. In certain countries, stocks of nuclear, biological, and chemical weapons represent a safety and security risk as well as a substantial financial burden.
Fragmented (or insufficient) financial management information systems	This risk varies depending on the extent to which a military institution works jointly across organizational boundaries. Substantial duplication is possible where there are low levels of coordination and limited understanding of modern integrated systems. A strategic information technology development road map would chart the required information technology applications and indicate how they should be integrated and interoperate. This charting would include the core functions of accounting, budgeting, and commitment systems, along with human resources, payroll, pensions, and asset management. Coherent and comprehensive systems are a particular challenge for the military because of the geographic distribution of units and locations, mobility of soldiers transferred between units, and information security. Reconciliation checks should be used to ensure that the human resources list matches the payroll and that only retiring soldiers identified on that list are transferred to the pension list.

Performance Measurement and Oversight

Performance measurement and oversight of the defense sector are the means by which the public and the state determine whether the military sector is effectively and efficiently meeting nationally determined defense policy objectives. Performance measurement is a means to objectively, or at least systematically, assess the military sector's proficiency in providing the defense function at an acceptable cost and to the benefit of society at large. Oversight is the process through which military performance is observed, interpreted, and reported to policy makers and the public. It is important to note that a PER team should use performance information if available, but not seek to generate that information. In some cases, expert assessments by specialists might substitute for numeric performance information.

The first half of this section discusses performance measurement in the military sector and provides performance indicators that can be used to assess military accountability, effectiveness, and efficiency in terms of inputs, outputs, and outcomes. This sourcebook departs from the standard treatment of performance metrics by including accountability as an element that should be independently and systematically assessed. This approach is necessitated by the special requirements of defense, which is a pure public good, and of the military sector, which has operational control over deadly force. The effectiveness metrics presented are more classic means to measure sectoral performance and can be used in cost-benefit analysis. They are meant to provide insight into how well defense sector institutions are fulfilling the defense functions assigned to them. Finally, the efficiency metrics are meant to provide insight into how well defense sector institutions incorporate and exercise PFM principles and practices known to promote economy and operational efficiency across the whole of government. These indicators are not universally applicable, but rather should guide the development of indicators appropriate to the country of interest.

The second half of this section describes oversight of the military sector, with special attention to transparency requirements and the nonmilitary institutions involved. The central theme is that the military sector should be subject to the same standards as other sectors of government. Effective oversight requires transparency, which can be difficult to achieve in the military sector. It also requires an established framework of empowered, resourced institutions that can observe, understand, and share information about the military—a framework that is difficult to create in fragile and conflict-prone states. Secret information may require special consideration, but the ambit of what is considered secret should be well defined and relatively small. Importantly, nonmilitary institutions, including the supreme audit authority and the legislature, must have access to all relevant information, including secret information under special arrangements.

If performance measurement and oversight are successfully implemented, the information gleaned can be a valuable input for the policy-making process. Performance measurement and oversight are therefore intimately related with budget formulation and budget execution. The PER team should think in terms of an ongoing cycle in which the central government allocates resources based on policy objectives and past performance, the military sector uses those funds to implement programs in pursuit of established objectives, and the military's performance in meeting those objectives is measured and reported to help decide the next round of resource allocations.

Performance Measurement

Three criteria for measuring military performance are commonly used[32]:

1. *Accountability* to a sovereign, elected civilian authority
2. *Effectiveness* in achieving prescribed defense policy objectives or identified capabilities
3. *Efficiency* in managing and using scarce public resources.

An overview of performance metrics for accountability, effectiveness, and efficiency is provided in table 3.18. This collection of indicators is not meant to be exhaustive, but it should provide the PER team with a good basis on which to build a country-specific framework. Importantly, it features metrics for inputs, outputs, and outcomes to facilitate cost-benefit analysis and strategic allocation of resources. Like any set of performance metrics, these are obviously limited by data availability. Measuring performance can be especially challenging in conflict-prone and fragile states where data are scarce or unreliable.

These performance metrics are closely interrelated in the military sector, and weaknesses in one will lead to weaknesses in another. An unaccountable military can become a cause unto itself, using public and off-budget funds to enrich its members and employing force to decrease, rather than increase, public security. An ineffective military is one that fails to achieve its politically determined defense policy objectives, either because those goals are not coherent enough or otherwise adequate to appropriately address the

Table 3.18   Overview of Performance Metrics

	Inputs	Outputs	Outcomes
Accountability	• De jure civil authority over the military • Established policy process with institutional checks and balances • Strategically informed resource allocation • Free elections for legislative and executive posts	• Adherence to established budgetary principles • Internal controls and external review for expenditure • External scrutiny of defense sector audit reports	• Change in perceptions of defense sector corruption and security service delivery • De facto civil authority
Effectiveness	• Defense sector budget (aggregate, per capita, and as a share of GDP and government receipts) • Personnel authorized and resourced • Security threats reasonably assessed	• Troops: recruited, trained, equipped, on duty (and interactions) • Unit readiness assessments • Tooth-to-tail ratio • Hierarchy/rank balance • (Specialized) training hours completed	• Ongoing conflict • Homicide rates • Country-led security provision • Capability achieved
Efficiency	• Quality of PFM regulations • Adherence to budget execution principles • Institutional framework for oversight • FMIS integration	• Budget execution rates, with seasonal and program variability • Unit costs • Audit reports released to the legislature and public	• Fiscally sustainable defense provision

Note: FMIS = financial management information system; PFM = public financial management.

country's security threats, or because they are not accomplishable with the resources available. Finally, an inefficient military is one in which resource shortages result from fraud, waste, or abuse. Put simply, the military sector needs to be both accountable and effective to provide the defense function. To be accountable and effective consistently and at a sustainable and publicly acceptable cost, the military sector must also be efficient.

These performance metrics relate to broadly applicable PFM policies and practices, as well as defense-specific concerns. Many of the institutions and metrics discussed below will be familiar from a generic PFM perspective—particularly those related to efficiency—and can be usefully applied in any public sector. A central theme in this chapter is that the military sector should not be exempt from government-wide PFM principles and practices, and performance measurement and oversight are no exception. Other institutions and metrics discussed below are more specific to the military's ability to provide the defense function. By definition, most of these are related to military effectiveness, including force provision and readiness. Finally, accountability encompasses both PFM and functional aspects, but in different ways. The military sector should be held as accountable as any other sector for meeting its PFM obligations, and common measures and diagnostics can be used for this purpose. However, functional accountability in the military sector requires special treatment. The military is unique in that the services it provides can be a source of both security and insecurity, and national defense is unique in that it is a pure public good.

Accountability

Accountability integrates the military sector into the broader political economy of a country, thereby ensuring that it fulfills its defense function rather than pursuing special interests or private gain. Military accountability requires that defense policy objectives are formulated at the highest levels of government; that those objectives are implemented reliably by an organized, hierarchical military institution; that the military chain of command ultimately reports to a civilian chief executive; and that the chief executive is elected by and answerable to the nation. The military's subordination to civilian leadership is commonly reflected in constitutional law, but de jure protections are insufficient if the military sector subverts its role de facto. The concentration of deadly force in the military sector makes accountability mechanisms especially important. The control of deadly force can allow military officers to intimidate civilian monitors, subvert financial management and anticorruption mechanisms, dismantle systems of accountability, or compel the government to exempt the military from government-wide rules and regulations. In ethnically, linguistically, or religiously diverse countries, accountability is buttressed if the military is broadly representative of the national population.

Military accountability can be explained using a standard public service framework comprising three main actors: (i) the state, (ii) the service providers, and (iii) the public. As shown in figure 3.5, the state includes the

Figure 3.5 Service Delivery Framework for Defense

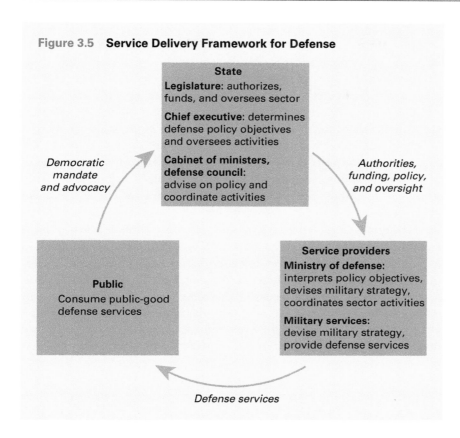

Democratic mandate and advocacy

State

Legislature: authorizes, funds, and oversees sector

Chief executive: determines defense policy objectives and oversees activities

Cabinet of ministers, defense council: advise on policy and coordinate activities

Authorities, funding, policy, and oversight

Public
Consume public-good defense services

Service providers
Ministry of defense: interprets policy objectives, devises military strategy, coordinates sector activities

Military services: devise military strategy, provide defense services

Defense services

legislature and the chief executive, and could include advisory and coordinating bodies like the cabinet of ministers and the defense council; service providers include defense policy and administration institutions and the military services; and the public are the nation's consumers of defense services. There are two ways to hold service providers accountable in this framework: the "short route," through which the people interact directly with service providers, and the "long route," through which the people interact with service providers via the state. For many private and some public services, the people can directly influence service providers through selection, voicing complaints, or withholding compensation. However, national defense is a pure public good—with no legitimate competitors and no way to assign costs directly to beneficiaries—so the short route is not viable for the military sector. Instead, the public must rely on the long route, wherein the state is an essential intermediary.[33]

For the long route of accountability to work, the military must answer to civilian authorities, which is a sector-specific way to say that there should be a clear separation between policy makers and service providers within government. Civilian authorities must decide policy to ensure that defense policy objectives and resource allocations are oriented to national interests, not the military's corporate interests. This separation is evinced in the military sector through historically grounded and internationally recognized norms, including the use of uniforms, the military's hierarchical structure, and its unique professional standards. Problems arise when identities and incentives are mixed. An extreme but all-too-common example occurs when a military officer is raised to a position of national leadership because of his ties with the military. If that officer and his supporters fail to hold elections or "doff the uniform," the result is state capture by the military and the imposition of a military regime. These regimes are often justified on the basis of gross insecurity or institutional weakness in the rest of government. In the long run, however, military control of the state undermines defense provision by distracting military institutions from their sole legitimate objective, increases the risk of corruption by eliminating institutional checks on military activities, weakens provision of public services across government by subverting accountability mechanisms, and ultimately undermines both defense provision and the strength of nonmilitary government institutions. The failure to effectively separate military and civilian spheres is also detrimental in less extreme scenarios, including when preferential treatment is granted to the military sector during the budget formulation process. Only when policy maker and service provider are distinct can the policy maker direct service provision policies, review outputs and outcomes, and punish wrongdoing.

A second requirement for the long route of accountability is that the people be able to influence policy makers' decisions and actions regarding security provision through voting and advocacy. The state can have effective control over the military and still fail to have defense provision that benefits the public; totalitarian regimes of the 20th century are powerful examples. Democratic accountability means that the public can hold the state to account for its policy decisions, administration practices, and program outcomes. Unfortunately, democratic accountability is often lacking in the developing world, particularly in fragile and conflict-prone states, where weak institutions or unrest might prevent elections or limit the remit of the central government. Even when the state has control over all its territory and there is a well-functioning electoral system, significant swathes of the public—especially the poor and vulnerable—might not be able to influence political discourse regarding public services, including defense. This situation can occur when citizens vote along ethnic or ideological lines (irrespective of public service provision), when they lack information on the quality of public services provided to them or others in the country, or when they do not trust that candidates can deliver on promises of better public services for lack of time or state capacity. The risk that the public will be unable to influence policy is elevated where the military is concerned, given its traditionally secretive nature and its control of deadly force, which enable it to contribute as much to insecurity as to security and to intimidate civilian monitors and the public more broadly. Only when policy makers answer to the public can the public ensure that defense services are provided to their benefit.

A third requirement for the long route of accountability is the free flow of information, without which the state and the people are limited in their capacity to make informed decisions about the quality of security service provision. This is another way of saying that accountability for the provision of defense services requires an accounting of the defense services provided. When insecurity is severe—as in war or civil strife—the costs for society are abundant and pervasive. But security outcomes are more difficult to observe and measure in times of peace. In such periods, performance metrics that focus on military readiness, cost efficiency, and institutional checks and balances are more useful. A list of such metrics for use by the PER team is provided in this section. Also provided in this section are profiles of oversight institutions and processes that should be in place to promote transparency, the free flow of information, and the use of information to improve service provision. Only when such information is available to the state and the public can both actors fulfill their roles.

Finally, it should be noted that donors can be significant actors in the provision of security services in developing countries, particularly in fragile and conflict-prone states. Donors influence security provision through dialogue with the central government and the military, through the projects they choose to support, and through their own PFM practices. It is therefore important for donors to promote good practice on governance, policy, and PFM if security service provision is to improve. Donors can undermine accountability if they make direct payments to the military—for example by paying military salaries or funding weapons procurement—without conditioning that assistance on nationally determined defense policy objectives or on military accountability to civil control. The PER team should also note that donors fall outside the standard public service framework. They are potentially major contributors to the short-run provision of defense services, and their policies and actions must be taken into account, but they are not a substitute for long-run defense provision by the national government or for effective national-level accountability.

Specific measures of accountability inputs include the following:

- De jure civil authority over the military, reflected in constitutional and statutory law
- Established policy process with institutional checks and balances, reflected in the strength of policy-making and oversight institutions and the manner in which they interact
- Strategically informed resource allocation, reflected in how faithfully defense sector resource allocations reflect nationally determined defense policy objectives.

Specific measures of accountability outputs include the following:

- Adherence to established budgetary principles, described in chapter 2 of this sourcebook
- Internal controls and external review for expenditure, including an adequate control framework, effective systems for accounting and reporting, and sufficient transparency
- External scrutiny of defense sector audit reports, which presupposes that oversight institutions are sufficiently resourced and empowered and is determined by the extent to which oversight institutions can share findings with policy makers and the public.

Finally, specific measures of accountability outcomes include changes in perceptions of defense sector corruption and the delivery of security services. These are best measured through regular public opinion polls issued before and after reforms.

Effectiveness

Military effectiveness is a measure of the military sector's ability to provide the defense function as defined by the nation's defense policy. It is thus similar to the generic notion of sectoral performance found in the PFM literature, and performance-based budgeting would use measures of effectiveness to guide resource allocation. Military effectiveness is determined by the appropriateness of military strategy to achieving defense policy objectives, and by the resources—personnel and matériel—the military sector has to implement its strategy.

Measuring military effectiveness is extremely difficult because security requirements are different for each country and across time. As discussed, strategic interests and threat perceptions vary widely, depending on the behavior of a country's neighbors and competitors, its economic constraints and goals, and its diplomatic agenda. At best, threat perceptions are risk-weighted estimates of the impact of potential security-related events. But given the complexity of making such estimates, threat perceptions are often defined on a much less rigorous basis.

Defense outcomes are notoriously difficult to observe, let alone compare to inputs. Outcomes are most apparent when the military sector fails to adequately provide defense services, as in situations of chronic low-level insecurity, civil strife, or war. In such situations, the costs of insecurity to society are multifarious and potentially severe; people may avoid business investments for fear of expropriation, for example, or in the worst cases suffer outright destruction of property and loss of life. On the other hand, it is difficult to attribute a benign security environment to any particular government program. Measuring benefits for the defense function involves a host of low-risk but high-cost (even catastrophic) events. Beneficial outcomes result from a composite of defense programs. Moreover, as a public good, defense benefits are diffuse across society. Counterfactuals that try to determine what outcomes could be achieved if a specific defense program were eliminated or modified are therefore difficult to posit with any confidence.

Given these difficulties, cross-country comparisons for the military sector will be problematic and should be used only to make broad generalizations or identify gross outliers. As noted, the optimum level and distribution of resource inputs varies across countries and across time. Moreover, the quality of military expenditure data is often poor, especially in fragile and conflict-prone states. Even if optimum inputs could be identified, it is difficult to determine whether resources are used as intended. Nonetheless, comparative statistics can help identify what is relatively normal given country characteristics. If the country of interest is well out of the ordinary, cross-country comparisons could highlight policies and institutions to reform or areas where the reallocation of public resources is necessary.

Country-specific assessments of military effectiveness should be firmly rooted in the country's defense policy objectives and its military strategy. As discussed, there is no universal standard for military performance, and defense objectives and military strategy vary on a case-by-case basis. As conditions change, so too must the way in which military performance is assessed. The PER team must be able to identify the nationally derived defense policy objectives and military strategy, whether they exist formally or not. The PER team must then help program managers design performance measures that are appropriate to the country's current and future security threats and its particular capacities and strategy.

In weighing costs and benefits to assess military effectiveness, it will likely be easier and more helpful to focus on outputs rather than outcomes. In contrast to outcomes, specific outputs can be associated with specific inputs. For example, the number of army soldiers trained and equipped is a function of the resources allocated to army force provision and support programs. This approach avoids the difficulty of associating a security outcome—such as border security or conventional deterrence—to the army force provision and support programs, or any other program. It also obviously highlights problems at the output stage, where progress might be challenging enough for fragile and conflict-prone states, instead of waiting until a later stage, when reform is even more difficult.

Finally, it is important to remember that complementarities are critically important factors in determining military performance. Put simply, a trained force that is not equipped will not be effective. Effective defense provision depends on a host of interactions among measurable (and perhaps nonmeasurable) security outputs. At the most basic level, effective force provision requires success in recruiting, training, equipping, supplying, and life support, and weaknesses in any one of those areas will undermine program performance. Likewise, effective force employment requires sufficient command and control, operational intelligence, logistics, and maintenance capabilities. Finally, effective strategy making and defense administration requires advanced systems of threat assessment, strategic intelligence, civil-military relations, policy planning, and defense budgeting. Output metrics should therefore be assessed in conjunction with one another, and never in isolation.

Specific measures of effectiveness inputs include budget and staff resources allocated to defense programs. Defense sector budgets can be analyzed in numerous ways: in aggregate, per capita, as a share of GDP, as a share of government receipts, or as a share of government expenditures. Resource allocations to specific programs must be analyzed so that imbalances can be identified and program inputs can be measured against program outputs. Variation over time should also be assessed. Unpredictable budgets undermine service delivery; without a hard "floor" for resource allocations, shortages can hollow out military capacity or encourage military institutions to look for extrabudgetary sources of revenue. Finally, personnel inputs can be measured in terms of authorized and resourced personnel for administrative, management, service support, and service delivery (military force) functions.

Specific measures for effectiveness outputs cover actual force strength, unit readiness assessments, and training hours completed. Force strength can be measured in many ways, and complementarities must be considered. Force strength is provided by the number of troops recruited, trained, equipped, and on duty, and the interactions of those terms. To determine the extent to which the military sector is meeting its force provision goals, these measures can be compared against the numbers authorized. They can also be compared against program budgets to identify resource shortages, which further investigation might link to incorrect resource assessments, waste, fraud, or abuse. Unit readiness assessments are used to determine how ready specific military units are to fulfill their function. In some sense, then, they are a composite of measures focused on individual personnel. However, they also include an assessment of how well a unit's members work together and the quality of leadership. Unit readiness assessments are thus more subjective, but also more comprehensive and potentially useful, than individual counts of troop numbers. Finally, it might be useful to measure how many hours of training have been provided, or how many personnel have completed full training courses, in specialized subjects. This information can be especially helpful when new functional requirements are identified and forces to fulfill them must be developed, as is common in postconflict or SSR scenarios.

Specific measures for effectiveness outcomes refer to the scale and character of ongoing conflict, homicide rates, or the status of country-led security provision. As discussed, measuring outcomes is difficult. However, the scale and character of any ongoing conflict can point to material or accountability weaknesses in the military sector that must be addressed. One approach used by studies of state fragility is to treat homicide rates as proxies for general security conditions. In transitional countries, where defense services are provided by external actors or not at all, it is also helpful to devise some measure of a state's progress in consolidating its monopoly of legitimate force. This can be done on a territorial basis, for example, where progress is registered when provinces are transferred to sovereign control as the nation's military becomes capable of providing defense services.

Efficiency

Military efficiency is a measure of the military's ability to achieve intended outputs and outcomes in the most economical way possible, so that maximum utility can be gained from the scarce public resources allocated to the military sector. Efficiency is therefore chiefly focused on budget implementation, or how proficient the military is at carrying out agreed plans. Focusing on this aspect highlights the principal-agent dilemma of public service provision. Because efficiency is potentially less political than accountability or effectiveness, there should be less resistance from the central government and military leadership to devising and incorporating performance measures for it. There might, however, be resistance from military units and other service providers to fully accounting for the use and disposition of public funds, especially where corruption is prevalent.

Military efficiency is promoted by applying PFM principles and practices in the military sector, so the subject overlaps considerably with that of budget formulation and budget execution already discussed. Indeed, much of the data necessary for measuring military efficiency can be collected through the comprehensive national budget process already described. This information can then feed into audit and oversight reports. Efficiency suffers when resources are lost to fraud, waste, or abuse; all else equal, weaker technical capacity and greater corruption risks will be correlated with less efficiency. Measures of corruption risk outlined in annex 3B can therefore also be used to illuminate areas where reforms are needed.

Deviation analysis and public expenditure tracking surveys are two particularly useful techniques for assessing sectorwide or program-specific efficiency problems. Both techniques derive from PFM analyses of other government sectors, but like many PFM methods, they are perfectly applicable to the military sector as well. Deviation analysis looks at the difference between budgeted and actual expenditures to identify cases in which funds are not being used for their intended purposes. Deviations might be explained by institutional capacity weaknesses and the inability to execute programs, or they could signal fraud, waste, or abuse. In either case, operational efficiency requires correcting the problem so that funds can be expended as planned. Box 3.16 describes an analysis of Niger's efforts to improve efficiency and increase budget execution rates.

Public expenditure tracking surveys can be used to measure and improve the flow of budgeted funds from the central government to the ministry of defense, military services, and operational commands. These surveys can thus provide a way to check the accuracy and validity of centrally collected data used in deviation analysis. They might also be used to encourage full military participation in the PER process. Increasing operational efficiency will increase military readiness, and therefore military effectiveness. This connection should provide a powerful incentive for professional leaders whose main challenge is implementation, not intent.[34]

Specific measures for efficiency inputs include the quality of the country's PFM regulations, and in particular the military's adherence to budget

Box 3.16   Niger—Expenditure Rates for the Security Sector

According to the World Bank's 2013 Public Expenditure Review of Niger's security sector, the executed budgets in the security sector were smaller than the approved budgets in the 2003–2012 fiscal years, although the last two years analyzed for the ministry of defense showed improvement. For the entire period, 2003–2012, budget execution averaged 85 percent (see table B3.16.1). It declined in 2010, especially for the ministry of interior, because spending did not keep pace with the very large increase in the approved investment budget for that year. For the ministry of defense, budget execution improved remarkably to 93 percent in 2011 and 97 percent in 2012. Budget execution improved for the ministry of interior as well, but was more erratic—at 106 percent in 2011 and 96 percent in 2012. Overexecution in the ministry of interior was due to personnel spending, which was 132 percent of the approved budget in 2011 and 137 percent of the budget in 2012, while investment spending achieved just 55 percent and 57 percent, respectively. Details of budget execution rates for Niger's ministry of defense and ministry of interior are provided in table B3.16.1.

Table B3.16.1   Budget Execution Rates for Niger's Ministries of Defense and Interior
percent

Sector	Category	2010	2011	2012	Average 2003–2012	Average 2010–2012
Defense	Personnel	98	93	97	—	96
	Operations	75	97	95	—	89
	Transfers and subsidies	89	91	100	—	93
	Investments	79	94	98	—	90
	Treasury and special accounts	65	83	74	—	74
	Total	**83**	**93**	**97**	**87**	**91**
Interior	Personnel	97	132	137	—	122
	Operations	90	94	94	—	93
	Transfers and subsidies	100	100	76	—	92
	Investments	13	55	57	—	42
	Total	**45**	**106**	**96**	**84**	**83**
Security sector	**Total**	**63**	**98**	**97**	**85**	**86**

Source: World Bank 2013b.
Note: — = not available.

execution principles. PFM principles apply at each stage of the policy and budget process. Military efficiency inputs depend in large part on how these principles are reflected in government regulations.

Specific measures for efficiency outputs include FMIS integration, deviation analysis, and unit costs. FMIS integration requires a full accounting of defense sector assets using standard codes, which may or may not be linked to budget classification codes used in the national budget formulation process. Full accounting reduces the risks of fraud, waste, and abuse. Accessible data also increase policy makers' ability to make rational decisions regarding the application of public resources as threat perceptions and defense requirements evolve. Deviation analysis can be used to determine whether funds are being used for their intended purposes. Comparing the results for the military sector against other sectors within the country and against military sectors in other countries can highlight areas of concern. Finally, analysis of unit costs, particularly unexpected operation, sustainment, or maintenance costs, can give a fuller picture of defense costs for ongoing and future programs.

One measure of efficiency outcomes is fiscally sustainable defense provision. Public services require public resources to supply and maintain them. This is especially true of defense, given that it is a pure public good. Defense can be extremely expensive in fragile and conflict-prone states, where fiscal bases are weak and there are aggravated security threats. In those cases, it is difficult to significantly modify assessments of security threats or resource requirements. The most feasible means to increase resource allocations to meet prescribed defense policy objectives is by improving efficiency. Achieving macroeconomic and fiscal stability while adequately providing defense services will require concerted application of PFM principles and timely correction of exposed efficiency problems.

Oversight

Effective oversight requires fiscal transparency and the free flow of information so that policy makers can make informed policy and budgetary decisions. This applies to the military as well; the assumption that the military must keep its budget secret or free of political interference in order to effectively provide the defense function is unfounded. Insufficient transparency or access to information undermines policy makers' ability to make competent decisions and thereby hurts military effectiveness. Special considerations can be made for confidential information, but exceptional treatment for the military sector as a whole is not justified.

Effective oversight also requires a framework of empowered, resourced, and competent institutions to monitor, analyze, and report fiscal and performance data, and to hold service providers accountable for fulfilling their mandate. Without oversight institutions—namely internal and external audit and the legislature—there is no independent means to assess probity and performance, and service delivery problems will likely remain hidden. Likewise, without an ultimate accountability institution—the legislature—it is impossible to guarantee that identified problems will be resolved.

Fiscal Transparency

Fiscal transparency is essential to holding the government accountable for the use of public resources. That includes funds allocated to the defense function, which can comprise a substantial part of the national budget in fragile and conflict-prone states. Ensuring that public funds support nationally determined defense policy objectives mitigates many of the corruption risks common to the military sector and prevents its capture by malign interests.

Fiscal transparency is usually defined and assessed in terms of the availability and quality of information about the public sector's past, current, and future fiscal activities, and the institutional arrangements that determine fiscal policies and outcomes.[35] The benefits of transparency for society as a whole are widely cited; cross-sectional analyses have shown that countries whose public finances are more transparent have better fiscal discipline, a lower perceived level of corruption, better credit ratings, and lower public sector borrowing costs. Defense is a core government function, and the military is an integral and costly part of the state. Standards of fiscal transparency are therefore just as crucial for the military sector as for any other public sector if the country is to meet its basic fiscal policy objectives of macroeconomic stability, allocative efficiency, and operational efficiency, discussed in the introduction to this chapter. More specifically:

- Macroeconomic stability can be guaranteed only if the national budget is comprehensive, accurate, and disciplined. Given the impact of military expenditures on fiscal sustainability and the importance of security for poverty reduction and economic development, it is important for the public to know aggregate spending in the military sector, and what these expenditures are expected to accomplish for the defense function.
- Allocative efficiency requires that policy makers base resource allocation decisions on agreed policy objectives. Divulging defense policy objectives through policy statements or white papers allows the public (and the PER team) to determine the reasonableness of allocations and hold service providers accountable through the "long route" described earlier.
- Operational efficiency requires that service providers make the most of the scarce public resources appropriated to them. To this end, the military and the state must share information on the fiscal transactions conducted to meet those defense policy objectives, including tax revenues, borrowing, and income from commercial activities, as well as budget allocations, actual expenditures, and the disposition of unspent funds. The state also needs to keep a comprehensive chart of accounts to record the assets and liabilities of government entities, including the military services, to protect against the illegal sale of military equipment and the hollowing out of military forces.

Transparency is important to the extent that it promotes accountability, effectiveness, and efficiency in the military sector. The PER team should therefore focus on transparency's instrumental value, not its intrinsic value. Divulging information—even accurate information—that undermines operational effectiveness or adversely distorts the incentives of military officials is harmful. As noted previously, war plans, intelligence operations, and some small percentage of the military budget might legitimately be kept secret.

When assessing transparency, it is therefore necessary to distinguish between core PFM concerns and matters that are more purely military in nature. The planning and conduct of military operations and the assessment of military requirements are best addressed by military professionals, and will likely suffer from full transparency. But that does not mean there should be no accountability. It is possible to implement a classification system that restricts legitimately sensitive information to those with a "need to know," including select members of the legislature and other oversight institutions, so that accountability can be guaranteed through the "long route" discussed earlier.

Transparency obviously requires that information be made accessible to policy makers and the public. The PER team should assess the extent to which standard budget, fiscal, and oversight reports are routinely generated and disseminated. Examples of such reports are provided in table 3.19. Advances in technology and PFM practices have made it easier and less costly to share this information across government, including in the military sector. An FMIS, for example, can provide a wide range of disaggregated data on underlying defense transactions at a very low marginal cost. Similarly, publishing defense expenditure plans, budget proposals, and

Table 3.19 Standard Budget and Oversight Products

Category	Representative proposal, statute, or report
Budget formulation	**Expenditure plans,** including the medium-term expenditure framework and the economic development plan
	Prebudget statement, presenting assumptions used in preparing the budget, fiscal aggregates, and sectoral allocations
	Aggregated budget proposal, which lays out the policies and priorities for the fiscal year, including macroeconomic assumptions, revenue targets, expenditure allocations, and financing requirements according to established budget classifications, together with accumulated debt and state assets; might also include performance information
	Budget as approved by the legislature, which incorporates any amendments made to policies and appropriations
Budget execution	**Budget execution reports,** which provide information of actual against planned revenue, expenditures, and financing; should be published within one month of the close of the period to ensure timeliness
	Mid-year budget reviews, where produced, including adjustments in resource allocations
	Year-end financial statements, providing information on actual revenue, expenditure, and financing against the adjusted budget plan
	Public procurement reports, including procurement plans, bidding opportunities, contract awards, and data on the resolution of procurement complaints
Performance measurement	**Performance reports,** which include information about policy objectives and resource inputs, along with the outputs and outcomes achieved by military services
	Audit reports, prepared by the internal auditor or the supreme audit authority and made available to the legislature and the public

budget laws on the Internet can greatly reduce costs associated with printing and distributing hard copies and provide the public with more timely access.

There could be legitimate reasons to restrict public dissemination of budget details or audit results if the underlying program is secret, but at a minimum the military must fully disclose information to relevant executive branch policy makers at the ministry of defense, defense council, and office of the chief executive and to cleared members the legislature. Restricting information to the military hierarchy alone undermines the service provider's accountability to the state. In the great majority of cases where the underlying military program is not secret, there should be full public dissemination of audit results so that the military can benefit from the insight of civil society and multilateral actors and so that the public has the means to hold the state accountable. Outsized budgets, critical audit reports, negative performance reviews, and any other potentially embarrassing information should not be suppressed simply because it is harmful to defense sector interests. For the military to be effective in providing security services to the public, it must be accountable. Accountability requires the free flow of information—especially when there are problems with performance or efficiency.

To facilitate accountability, the information made accessible must be timely, relevant, and reliable. Information is timely if it is accessible when necessary to influence the decision-making process or monitor progress in implementation. Long delays can prevent learning and necessary corrections in policy objectives, resource allocation, and program implementation. In fragile and conflict-prone countries, conditions can change rapidly, and policy makers and the public must be kept abreast. Information is relevant if it is presented in a way that meets the needs of users, which vary based on institutional role and context. Standard budget documents and audit reports will cover most needs, but policy makers in particular might need more detailed or topical information. Finally, information is reliable if it accurately and comprehensively represents the government's policy objectives, revenue projections, and expenditure estimates. The reliability of budgets in particular will be undermined if the government or military services fail to adhere to the budgetary principles discussed in the chapter 2.

Importantly, the public must also be able to understand the available information.[36] Ensuring that fiscal information is understood can be especially problematic in fragile and conflict-prone states where human capital is low. In these cases, the role of donors in supporting good PFM practices—and setting a good example in their own conduct—is even more significant. More generally, understanding can be promoted by the limited use of jargon and the publication of "citizen budgets" that use simple language to describe defense policy, military strategy, and resource allocations. The PER team should also be mindful that a lack of human capital within government could undermine the processes described in the pages that follow, because those institutions require staff knowledgeable of fiscal and military matters to fulfill their roles. Means to improve human capital are beyond the scope of this sourcebook and largely irrelevant to the conduct of a defense sector PER. Nevertheless, acknowledging this constraint illustrates the endogenous relationship between security and development and the long-term importance of improving PFM practices in the military sector, thereby encouraging accountability, effectiveness, and efficiency in service delivery.

Finally, it should be reiterated that security is a public good, and military accountability therefore depends on the ability of the public to act through their legislature. An informed public is still powerless if the legislature is not democratically accountable or if the military is not subject to civilian oversight.

The Legislature

In a functioning democracy, the legislature is the most representative governance institution, with the most direct connection to the citizenry. If the executive is inattentive or unresponsive to the public interest, there is a risk that military power will be abused. Moreover, the public cannot act directly to ensure military accountability, because defense is a pure public good. A legislature that is properly empowered, resourced, and motivated is therefore an essential check on executive power and a critically important anchor for military accountability. More specifically, the legislature needs to have the sovereign authority to make laws and see them enforced. Without this authority, the legislature cannot punish illegal or abusive behavior or remedy wasteful practices.

Especially in fragile and conflict-prone countries, the executive often lacks accountability and can be repressive in the exercise of its powers. In these cases the legislature might be unable or unwilling to provide oversight of the defense sector. This lack of oversight can undermine public trust in formal security institutions, thereby undermining the state's monopoly of force. If major security sector or financial management reforms are to succeed, it is essential to support legislative capacity and effectiveness and to build political will to engage on military issues. The consequences of weak legislative oversight in Liberia are described in box 3.17.

The legislature is responsible for establishing the legislative framework for oversight and for reviewing and acting on oversight products. The legislative framework for oversight builds on the legislative framework for budget and PFM (discussed earlier) through an audit law (or equivalent), which authorizes audit institutions and sets auditing and reporting requirements; an anticorruption law (or equivalent), which authorizes anticorruption institutions and sets standards; and an access-to-information law (or equivalent), which authorizes information commissions and establishes transparency requirements. In addition to authorizing and mandating the supreme audit institution, the legislature also approves the appointment and removal of its head, approves its budget, and oversees its performance. In a well-functioning system, there is regular coordination between the

Box 3.17   Liberia—Weak Legislative Oversight

According to the security sector Public Expenditure Review (PER) carried out by the World Bank and United Nations during Liberia's security transition, legislative oversight of the security sector is weak.

In the Senate, the Committee on National Defense, Intelligence, Security and Veteran Affairs is responsible for common defense, including arms, armament, recruitment, promotion, service pay and other benefits of military members, and the size and composition of the Armed Forces; the Ministry of Defense and all military activities; strategic and critical materials, including weaponry necessary for common defense and military functions; and the Ministry of National Security, National Security Agency, National Bureau of Investigation, and all other security services/agencies installations. The Senate committee includes subcommittees on defense, intelligence and security, and veteran affairs.

In the House of Representatives, the Committee on National Defense is responsible for common defense, including arms, armament, recruitment, and service; the Ministry of Defense and all military activities; pay, promotions, retirement, and other military benefits; the size and composition of the Armed Forces; military installations and strategic and critical materials and weaponry; and military dependents and war veterans. Meanwhile, the House of Representatives Committee on National Security and Intelligence is responsible for the national intelligence activities of all ministries and agencies of government, as well as matters related to checkpoints in the country and international arms control and disarmament.

The joint PER found these committees to be weak and ineffective in exercising authority due to a lack of permanent staff, poor capacity, and weak governance. The PER concluded that the lack of civilian oversight contributed to informal or facilitation payments and corruption, which in turn reduced public access to security and justice services, undermined public trust in security personnel, and limited public recourse to the formal justice system.

Sources: World Bank and United Nations 2012; Legislature of Liberia, Senate; Legislature of Liberia, House of Representatives; Legislature of Liberia, House of Representatives.

legislature and the supreme audit institution on substantive matters as well. The legislature receives and reviews financial, compliance, and performance audits; refers matters to the supreme audit institution for investigation; and fosters cooperation between the supreme audit institution and other government entities, including the military. As with all of the PFM practices discussed in this sourcebook, the military should be subject to the provisions of oversight legislation, and audits of the military sector should be regularly reviewed by the legislature.

In less democratic countries, exceptions might be made for the military sector in legislation or oversight practice. This double standard undermines the comprehensive approach advocated above, and thereby hurts accountability, effectiveness, and efficiency. There is no legitimate reason why the military should receive exceptional treatment, aside from the limited provisions for secret information already discussed. Even then, the audit and anticorruption agencies should be able to review and report on military activities, and legislative oversight is necessary to ensure accountability.

Finally, the legislature should as a matter of course conduct oversight of the military sector itself, as it would for any other government sector. This core responsibility of the legislative branch is intended to ensure that the government and its agents use their powers and resources in ways that respond to the needs and interests of all members of the nation. Legislative oversight of the military sector should be similar to that for other sectors, with special considerations made for secret programs. In all cases, the executive branch and public officials should be obligated to provide justifications for and information about their policy decisions and activities—through mandatory reporting, response to public questioning of defense officials and military officers on defense administration and program performance, and provision of testimony or documentation during investigations of the military sector. Secret information should not be shared in an open format, but rather reviewed by cleared members of the legislature in closed hearings, confidential reports, or confidential annexes to publicly available reports. Such reviews will most likely be done by the legislature's defense committee, or equivalent. Budget matters might be overseen by the finance committee, or equivalent, as well as the defense committee.

External Audit

Most countries have supreme audit institutions that are mandated to independently review the central government's fiscal accounts. Variously called auditors general, boards of supreme audit, or the like, supreme audit institutions provide a valuable external oversight role—monitoring, assessing, and reporting on defense sector issues related to accountability, effectiveness, efficiency, and whatever else is within their mandate. The specific institutional form varies by country. In the United States, for example, the Government Accountability Office reports directly to the U.S. Congress. In the United Kingdom and many Commonwealth countries, the Auditor General is usually an officer of Parliament. In Central Europe, the Court of Accounts has audit authority, as well as judicial and prosecutorial powers.

Audits generally fall into one of three categories: (i) financial audits, (ii) compliance audits, and (iii) performance audits. Financial audits review agencies' financial statements to provide reasonable assurance that they are true and fair according to national standards. Compliance audits review agencies' adherence to established regulations, and can thus be particularly helpful in fragile states. And performance audits review management systems and processes to determine how economical and effective agencies are in meeting their assigned policy objectives. If other aspects of the PFM system are strong, supreme audit institutions can diagnose problems, identify systemic issues, and focus on materiality and risk. If PFM systems are weak, supreme audit institutions that are appropriately empowered and resourced can support reform, especially in areas such as accounting and reporting.

According to the Open Budget Initiative, in most countries the supreme audit institution has de jure authority to audit the military sector.[37] This is not a new phenomenon for more developed countries. Indeed, there is a long tradition of auditing the military sector, dating back to 17th-century Europe, when militaries consumed the bulk of government resources and state survival depended on improving efficiency. Given the institutional weaknesses of fragile and conflict-prone states, the PER team will probably not encounter robust external audit institutions. Weak audit institutions in Mali are described in box 3.18.

External audit standards are set by an international body known as the International Organization of Supreme Audit Institutions, and national regulations are established in statutory law or regulation on a country-by-country basis. Audit standards, like those in the U.S. government's "Yellow Book," provide an objective, transparent methodology for collecting and analyzing information. More information can be found at the International Organization of Supreme Audit Institutions' website (see table 3A.4 in annex 3A). These standards do not guarantee legality and accuracy of the transactions audited, but they do provide some level of

---

Box 3.18   Mali—Security Forces Not Subject to External Oversight

According to the World Bank's 2013 financial management assessment, Mali's military and internal security forces are in practice not subject to external oversight; all of the external monitoring bodies avoid using their oversight powers for issues related to the security forces. The review determined that this situation encouraged the development of "extra-procedural practices" and should therefore be redressed.

The Office of the General Auditor, created in 2004, had never carried out a compliance verification in the Ministry of Defense, despite its large size and the fact that all other important departments had been the subject of such missions. One of the obstacles to external oversight, according to the General Auditor, was uncertainty surrounding the concept of an "official secret."

The accounts section of Mali's Supreme Court is responsible for assessing accounts maintained by the government accountants and determining whether they conform to the country's finance laws. The office is understaffed, with only 13 counselors for more than 1,000 accounts per year. Moreover, personnel in the accounts section do not have the status of a judge and the wages are not attractive. In recent years, the accounts section has not specifically reviewed Ministry of Defense accounts, and only an aggregate administrative account is transmitted by the Ministry of Finance to the court when the finance law is examined. Even so, the accounts section was able to determine that CFAF 2 billion paid by the Ministry of Defense in 2011 was not supported by documentary evidence.

Parliament was similarly ineffective. Staffing is inadequate, with only one staff assistant for the defense commission. Moreover, a request for an on-site oversight mission in 2011 was rejected by the Office of the President. Finally, the General Inspectorate of Finances, which has 17 agents and is tasked with monitoring the accountants and administrators, has not recently inspected the military or internal security forces, according to the best knowledge of the chief inspector.

Source: World Bank 2013a.

assurance, especially when applied in a risk management approach. Unfortunately, international standards are frequently not met in the military sector, especially in fragile and conflict-prone countries. In these countries, military secrecy and the military sector's disproportionate political influence may make it difficult to gain access to necessary information, to publicly disseminate audit reports in a timely manner, and to ensure the political independence of external audits.

Internal Audit

Internal audit is an independent, systematic evaluation and assurance practice that is intended to improve an agency's risk management, control, and governance processes. In contrast to the systems of internal control discussed earlier, internal audit is conducted after expenditure has been incurred. In contrast to external audit, internal audit reports to the minister of finance or the minister of defense, not the legislature. The objective of internal audit is to improve agency performance and efficiency, not necessarily to find fault or facilitate democratic accountability. Internal audit's more circumscribed mandate and reporting requirements might therefore make it more palatable than external audit to defense sector leadership. However, for internal audit to improve efficiency and effectiveness, there must be efficient and reliable systems of accounting and financial reporting and a clearly defined management structure within the ministry of defense. Internal audit will not be effective in a country that lacks internal controls or managerial accountability. Ultimately, only accountability to the legislature and the public—facilitated by external audit and financial and performance reporting—can ensure optimal outcomes.

There are two basic models for internal audit in the public sector: centralized and decentralized. In the centralized model, the chief internal auditor reports to the minister of finance, and ministry of finance personnel—seconded to the ministry of defense and military services or centrally located—conduct internal audit activities for defense programs. In the decentralized model, the ministry of defense and military services have their own internal audit departments reporting to the minister of defense. Centralized internal audit is more common in Francophone and Central European countries, whereas the decentralized model is common in Anglophone countries.

Internal audit standards are set by an international body known as the Institute of Internal Auditors, and national regulations are established in statutory law or regulation on a country-by-country basis. The ministry of finance generally has more influence over internal audit regulations and practices than it does over external audit—especially in the centralized model, since it provides the audit staff. More information can be found on the Institute of Internal Auditors' website (see table 3A.4 in annex 3A). A case in which internal audit did not meet international standards is described in box 3.19.

Box 3.19   Central African Republic—Internal Audit Does Not Meet Standards

The World Bank's 2009 financial management assessment of the Central African Republic found that internal audit for the Ministry of Defense failed to meet international standards of professionalism and independence. In 2005, the Inspectorate General of the National Army (IGAN)—the main agency for internal audit in the Ministry of Defense—was attached directly to the defense minister's departmental staff. The office was led by a lieutenant, had a staff of five, and received operational resources from the defense minister. Its oversight authority depended on the trust of the minister, and was limited to the administrative and financial control of management; the office may also have exercised some control over exceptional revenues derived from benefits granted to private actors. The chief weaknesses of the IGAN were its precarious legal authority, funding, and stature within the military hierarchy. Its existence and resources derived from the defense minister and were not provided for in law. And even with the support of the minister, it was difficult for a lieutenant to stand his ground during audits and command respect from officers three or four levels his superior in the normal hierarchy.

The IGAN reflected a broader trend in the security sector, where presidential, interministerial, and ministerial general inspections had been replaced with new authorities in which the executive had more faith. The result was a mix of small inspection or auditing departments with no link between them and without any guarantee of compliance with international standards. This trend created a number of weaknesses, including auditors' lack of independence from the executive hierarchy; the absence of an auditing approach based on thorough and objective risk analysis; the absence of planning and approval for annual audit plans by a higher echelon; a lack of professionalism and training among auditors; and the absence of respect for adversarial proceedings. These weaknesses, in turn, made detecting fraud and irregularities more difficult, and increased the risk that members of the defense hierarchy would use internal inspection and audit offices for personal or political purposes, and not to improve defense efficiency or outcomes.

Source: World Bank 2009.

Annex 3A: Public Expenditure Review (PER) Resources

Table 3A.1   PER Resources 1: Military, Defense, and Development Data Sets

Resource	Description
World Bank World Development Indicators (WDI) http://databank.worldbank.org/data/	The World Bank's WDI contains 1,300 indicators and spans every country in the world. Public sector indicators focus on conflict and fragility, defense and the arms trade, and policy and institutions, and they can facilitate country comparisons (in total armed force personnel, for example); sustainability assessments (such as military spending as a percentage of gross national income or revenues); and state fragility (as measured by the strength of institutions).
World Bank Country Policy and Institutional Assessment (CPIA) http://data.worldbank.org/indicator/IQ.CPA.PUBS.XQ	The CPIA data set (also available in the broader WDI) rates how conducive countries' policies and institutional arrangements are to sustainable growth and poverty reduction. The World Bank classifies a situation as "fragile" if the average CPIA score is less than 3.2 or if a UN or multilateral peacekeeping or peacebuilding force was present during the last three years.

(Table continues on next page)

Table 3A.1   **PER Resources 1: Military, Defense, and Development Data Sets** *(continued)*

Resource	Description
Stockholm International Peace Research Institute (SIPRI) Data portal http://www.sipri.org/databases	The SIPRI data portal includes a military expenditure database for 172 countries since 1988, allowing comparison of countries' military spending.
Correlates of War (COW) Data sets http://www.correlatesofwar.org/	COW data sets include lists of interstate, intrastate, and nonstate wars; national military capabilities; formal alliances; and other topics related to military power, conflict, and international affairs.
Uppsala University Department of Peace and Conflict Research, Uppsala Conflict Data Program (UCDP) Battle-Related Deaths Data Set http://ucdp.uu.se/	The UCDP data set includes conflict-year and dyad-year information on the number of battle-related deaths in conflicts from 1989 to 2012.
Transparency International Government Defence Anti-Corruption Index http://government.defenceindex.org/	This index of defense sector corruption risks is based on a sample of 82 countries in response to a 77-question questionnaire. The website includes the questionnaire, data, and country-specific reports.

Table 3A.2   **PER Resources 2: Defense Costing**

Resource	Description
North Atlantic Treaty Organization (NATO) "Methods and Models for Life Cycle Costing" http://www.cso.nato.int/Pubs/RDP .asp?RDP=RTO-TR-SAS-054	This technical report, prepared by NATO's Research and Technology Organization, provides a comprehensive review of life-cycle costing methodologies, from the conceptual phase through disposal.
U.K. Ministry of Defense "Guide to Investment Appraisal and Evaluation" https://www.gov.uk/government /uploads/system/uploads/attachment data/file/27385/jsp507.pdf	This guide assists practitioners in appraising and evaluating defense investments; it includes advice on building a business case, forms and models of appraisal and evaluation, cash-flow models, hidden costs, and cost-effectiveness analysis, as well as separate chapters on fixed assets, personnel, and other operating costs.
U.S. Defense Security Cooperation Agency Excess Defense Articles Database http://www.dsca.mil/programs/eda	This database of over 10,000 defense-related items authorized for sale by the U.S. military can be used by the Public Expenditure Review team to estimate the acquisition costs of specific items.
Norwegian Initiative on Small Arms Transfers (NISAT) Small Arms Trade Database http://legacy.prio.no/nisat	NISAT's database includes over 1 million records of weapons imports, including unit cost where available. In addition, the website hosts a large collection of articles on small-arms issues.

Table 3A.3 PER Resources 3: Planning for DDR and DSR

Resource	Description
UN Disarmament, Demobilization, and Reintegration [DDR] Resource Center Integrated DDR Standards http://www.unddr.org/iddrs.aspx	This website hosts the integrated DDR standards (IDDRS), operational guide, and briefing note for senior managers. Section 3.41 of the operational guide addresses finance and budgeting.
Geneva Centre for the Democratic Control of Armed Forces (DCAF) The DDR-SSR Nexus http://www.dcaf.ch/Project /The-DDR-SSR-Nexus	This website provides analysis of the intersection of DDR and security sector reform, including a module designed for the IDDRS and applications to Afghanistan and Africa.
UN Department of Peacekeeping Operations Policy: Defense Sector Reform [DSR] http://www.un.org/en/peacekeeping /documents/2011.17_Defence_Sector_Reform _Policy.pdf	This policy is intended to guide UN DSR efforts. It outlines parameters and components of DSR support and highlights linkages to security sector reform and other public reform initiatives.
Organisation for Economic Co-operation and Development-Development Assistance Committee (OECD-DAC) *International Support to Post-conflict Transition* http://www.oecd.org/dac/incaf /internationalsupporttopost-conflicttransition.htm	This guidance provides recommendations to improve the speed, flexibility, predictability, and risk management of transition assistance.

Table 3A.4 PER Resources 4: International Standards for External and Internal Audit

Resource	Description
International Organization of Supreme Audit Institutions http://www.intosai.org/	This website provides standards for external audit agencies and hosts a journal covering external audit issues.
Institute of Internal Auditors https://na.theiia.org/Pages/IIAHome.aspx	This website provides more information on internal auditing, including standards and practice guides.

Annex 3B: Defense Sector Corruption Risks

Table 3B.1 Defense Sector Corruption Risks

Type of risk	Indicators
Political	**Defense and security policy:** ability of individuals or groups to manipulate the policy process for illicit enrichment
	Defense budgets: lack of transparency and openness for defense budgets; lack of effective internal and external auditing; lack of clarity on revenue sources and expenditures
	Natural resources: improper exploitation of natural resources by the military
	Organized crime: penetration by organized crime of defense sector institutions; lack of policing or awareness of the threat by the government
	Intelligence services: inability to hold intelligence services accountable; nonobjective selection criteria for senior appointments
	Export controls: lack of transparent or well-scrutinized arms control policies and practices

(Table continues on next page)

Table 3B.1   Defense Sector Corruption Risks *(continued)*

Type of risk	Indicators
Financial	**Asset disposal:** lack of effective controls, transparency, or independent scrutiny of asset disposals and proceeds of sale
	Secret budgets: large percentage of defense budgets dedicated to secret spending; inability of the legislature to review secret expenditures; lack of auditing or legislative review of audit reports; prevalence of off-budget expenditures
	Military-owned businesses: prevalence of beneficial ownership by the military of commercial businesses; lack of independent scrutiny of the military's business activities
	Illegal private enterprise: illicit use of public funds or service personnel for private gain; payoffs from private enterprises to military services for protection services
Personnel	**Leadership behavior:** failure to publicly commit to anticorruption measures; absence of visible disciplinary sanctions for corruption; lack of whistle-blowing incentives and protections; failure to sufficiently vet or rotate personnel in sensitive positions
	Payroll, promotions, appointments, rewards: lack of accuracy or transparency in personnel numbers, pay rates, and allowances; failure to provide full timely payment; absence of an objective, transparent process for senior appointments and promotion
	Conscription and recruitment: evidence of accepting bribes to avoid conscription or to secure preferred placement; lack of policies or sanctions to deal with observed instances
	Salary chain: evidence of "ghost soldiers"; failure to separate chains of command from chains of payment
	Values and standards: nonexistent or noncomprehensive code of conduct; failure to enforce the code of conduct or to provide evidence that breaches are sanctioned; lack of regular anticorruption training
	Small bribes and favors: failure to discourage facilitation payments
Operations	**Disregard of corruption in country:** absence of anticorruption measures in military doctrine; lack of training for commanders on corruption issues in deployment
	Corruption within mission: failure to deploy trained professionals to monitor conduct
	Contracting: lack of guidelines and training in contracting corruption risks
	Private security companies: prevalence of private security companies; lack of standards and oversight
Procurement	**Government policy:** unclear procurement legislation or military exemptions; failure to disclose needs assessment, implementation, or asset disposal procedures; absence of oversight mechanisms, standards for military suppliers, or public disclosure of purchases
	Capability gap and requirements definition: procurements not derived from a transparent, audited defense strategy or from clearly identified and quantified requirements
	Tender solicitation, assessment, and contract award: lack of competition in procurement; failure to regulate or audit tender boards; failure to outlaw collusion
	Contract delivery and in-service support: failure to train or empower procurement staff or to sanction corrupt practices; absence of complaint mechanisms for suppliers
	Offset contracts: failure to explicitly address corruption risks in offset contracts; lack of transparency or competition in offset contracts
	Agents/brokers: lack of policies regarding the use of procurement intermediaries
	Subcontractors: lack of requirements that subcontractors adopt anticorruption program
	Seller influence: evidence of political influence in procurement decisions

Source: Adapted from Transparency International U.K., Defence and Security Programme 2013.

Annex 3C: Integrity Scores for Geographic Regions, Income Groups, and Selected Fragile and Conflict-Affected States, 2013

Table 3C.1   Integrity Scores for Geographic Regions, Income Groups, and Selected Fragile and Conflict-Affected States, 2013

		Integrity score					
		Political	Financial	Personnel	Operations	Procurement	Overall
Region	North America	83	73	91	70	77	81
	Europe and Central Asia	58	57	59	39	51	55
	East Asia and Pacific	54	44	59	38	49	52
	Latin America and Caribbean	54	51	54	29	50	51
	South Asia	32	33	51	27	35	37
	Sub-Saharan Africa	26	21	36	18	26	27
	Middle East and North Africa	23	21	36	15	25	26
Income group	High income	58	59	64	40	54	57
	Upper middle income	39	34	45	26	37	38
	Low income	29	24	41	23	29	31
	Lower middle income	27	20	35	15	25	26
Fragile state	Bosnia and Herzegovina	47	45	53	55	41	47
	West Bank and Gaza	37	23	50	19	45	39
	Afghanistan	39	22	34	35	17	31
	Iraq	26	7	28	5	28	23
	Côte d'Ivoire	17	14	34	5	23	21
	Zimbabwe	14	5	29	20	18	18
	Congo, Dem. Rep.	11	0	19	10	21	14
	Yemen, Rep.	9	0	14	5	9	8
	Eritrea	3	5	14	13	3	7
	Libya	9	3	6	0	0	5
	Syrian Arab Republic	1	0	6	10	3	3
Fragile states average		21	15	29	17	21	22
World average		42	39	49	28	40	42

Source: Transparency International U.K., Defence and Security Programme 2013.
Note: Transparency International reviewed 82 countries in 2013, and not all fragile states identified by the World Bank were assessed. The overall integrity score is calculated from the scores for individual questions, and is not equal to the average of the five categories.

Annex 3D: Methodology for Costing Defense Operations in Low- and Lower-Middle-Income Countries

Introduction: Methodology and Assumptions

This analysis provides general guidance on how to approach the fixed, variable, and procurement costing for national defense operations. Unlike upper-middle- and high-income economies, where defense and finance ministries can leverage historical data and sophisticated methodologies acquired over time to realistically determine security sector costing with a certain degree of accuracy, countries with less experience or just coming out of fragility may find such an exercise very challenging, if not impossible, mainly due to lack of data or capacity.

In such circumstances, ministers of finance or defense will likely have questions about how best to cost the performance of smaller-scale contingency operations and other military operations besides war.[38] Acknowledging that there is no perfect science for answering these questions, this annex aims to serve as a reference for defense budgeting processes. In particular, for international development professionals and policy makers engaged in evaluating or planning a country's defense budget, it offers analysis and benchmarking of established and functional defense systems that are part of economies at various levels of development.

Controlling for income-level classification, the analysis undertaken here estimates median defense operating costs in low-income and lower-middle-income countries at 1.5 percent and 1.8 percent of GDP, respectively. Procurement costs are covered in a separate analysis, given that prices of weapon systems and other technological equipment are internationally fixed and cannot be adjusted for a country's price index.[39]

The annex is organized in three sections. The first section covers operating costs by area of expenditure—personnel, operations and maintenance (O&M), and investments. The second section specifies procurement costs for providing a unit with basic equipment and logistics in order to make it operationally ready. The third section describes how military compensation is reflected in the national budgeting process and public wage bill. It also compares personnel costs across countries and further compares these costs with the cost of living in selected countries.

The analysis uses data from economies at various levels of income (following the World Bank's income-level classification)[40] that have decent defense capabilities and data availability on military spending, cost of living, and public sector compensation.

In order to make the study useful to low- and lower-middle-income countries, defense spending is expressed as a share of GDP. The study also breaks down total operating costs by area of expenditure—personnel, O&M, and investments—as a share of total operating costs.

To estimate as realistically as possible the cost of military personnel, stipends and other allowances in selected countries are benchmarked against respective cost of living. The goal is to show how much of a burden cost of living is to military compensation, on average, so that planners have a consistent rationale in determining how much to compensate their military.

Figures and costs estimated in this annex should be considered as indicative only.

Operating costs refer to a basic defense system, used for conventional operations only (i.e., no nuclear weapons, no cyber activity, no unmanned systems, etc.) in a context of peace and daily routine activities, such as scheduled training, administrative tasks, and normal work time, usually in line with other sectors of the public administration, except for those on duty for force protection (e.g., headquarters and compound guards, 24-hour on-site patrolling, etc.).

A typical defense system is made up of several branches, such as army, navy (except for landlocked countries), and air force. In some countries, armed forces also include military police (e.g., gendarmerie, carabinieri, etc.) and special operation forces (e.g., U.S. Marines). In this annex the armed forces consist only of a land component, with its typical assets, such as tanks and armored vehicles; consideration of an air component is limited to support and logistics operations (as opposed to offensive capabilities, not covered here). However, the principles can apply to other branches of the military, albeit the cost ratios may significantly differ (in both the navy and air force, for example, expenditure is skewed more toward equipment and weapon systems—warships, aircraft, and their weapons and communication/identification systems—than to personnel).

How a land component is formed depends on the country's geostrategic and regional contexts. These contexts may skew choices for weapon systems and organization. For example, a country facing a possible threat mainly composed of tanks may create an army whose anti-tank assets are more substantial than its infantry or motorized transportation. On the other hand, if a state mainly needs to counter terrorism, it may opt for an organization dominated by infantry and fast, motorized armored vehicles, and so on. At the same time, an organization type is also shaped by a country's national strategy, which can be primarily defensive, primarily offensive, almost neutral (Switzerland), or somewhere in between. A state may prefer protection over rapidity or vice versa, may want to limit its operational sphere to domestic territory or have expeditionary ambitions, etc.

Defense's Operating Costs

Based on data on military spending[41] and GDP, and controlling for income level, median operating costs for defense in low- and lower-middle-income countries are estimated at 1.5 percent and 1.8 percent of GDP, respectively[42] (figure 3D.1 and figure 3D.2).

Defense Budget

The budget allocated to the defense sector is entirely sustained by a government because defense is a pure public good[43] and cannot be privatized (privatization of defense would fail because of the free-rider issue).

The annual budget for defense is determined on the basis of the following:

- Medium- to long-term planning based on perceived threats to national security and consequent need to adapt the military instrument
- National strategy
- Need to be competitive in the job market to attract qualified candidates

Figure 3D.1   Defense Spending as a Share of GDP in Low-Income Countries, 2005–2014 Average

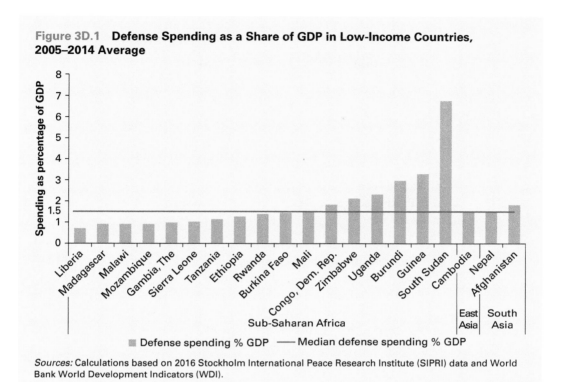

Sources: Calculations based on 2016 Stockholm International Peace Research Institute (SIPRI) data and World Bank World Development Indicators (WDI).

Figure 3D.2   Defense Spending as a Share of GDP in Lower-Middle-Income Countries, 2005–2014 Average

Sources: Calculations based on 2016 Stockholm International Peace Research Institute (SIPRI) data and World Bank World Development Indicators (WDI).

- Need to retain high-quality employees through benefits and other advantages (compared to those offered by other sectors of the economy, including the private sector)
- Geopolitical context
- International obligations to neighbors (bilateral obligations) and to multilateral organizations.

Defense appropriations are normally constrained by a country's development objectives in other sectors, such as health, education, social protection, and infrastructure, among many others.

Composition of Defense's Operating Costs

The defense sector's operating costs are allocated to three different areas of expenditure:

1. *Compensation for personnel*, which comprises base pay plus other extras, and in some countries pensions (in other countries pensions are managed by the ministry of defense)
2. *O&M*, which takes into account operations, training (initial and recurrent), logistics, and maintenance
3. *Investments* in infrastructure, equipment, transportation, weapon systems, and warfare doctrine[44] (figure 3D.3).

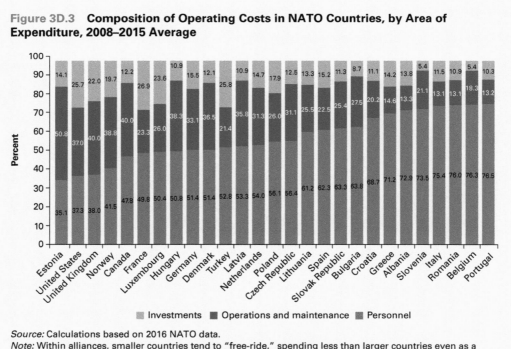

Figure 3D.3   Composition of Operating Costs in NATO Countries, by Area of Expenditure, 2008–2015 Average

Source: Calculations based on 2016 NATO data.
Note: Within alliances, smaller countries tend to "free-ride," spending less than larger countries even as a fraction of GDP. Iceland does not have defense forces and is not included. Albania, Bulgaria, Romania, and Turkey are upper-middle-income countries; the rest are high-income. Albania and Croatia joined NATO in 2009 (a factor accounted for in the analysis).

The allocation of funds over the three areas of expenditure is decided (and proposed) each fiscal year by a country's ministry of defense and generally depends on the following:

- The defense budget as negotiated with the ministry of finance
- The country's national strategy, defense policy, and planned future use of the armed forces
- The requirements for membership in international organizations[45]
- The need to keep the stock of weapons and equipment up to date and operational
- Security considerations mainly associated with the changing geopolitical context (real or perceived) and equilibria, geography,[46] etc.

Normally, personnel costs constitute the bulk of defense spending, unless a country is involved in high-intensity operations, in which case O&M could actually trump the other two areas of expenditure.[47] Figure 3D.3 shows operating costs for NATO countries by expenditure type.

Personnel Costs

Personnel costs include compensation and allowances for military employees. As figure 3D.4 shows, the share of total military compensation decreases from the "officer" down to the "enlisted" category. Despite being fewer in number, officers usually receive the largest share of total compensation, mainly due to higher per capita pay and higher allowances. Figure 3D.4 also includes compensation for generals within the officer category, though given the substantial gap between colonels (the most senior commanding officers) and generals (who are categorized as "general officers"), generals' compensation could be considered an outlier. Notwithstanding their large numbers, enlisted receive the smallest share of compensation, likely because their unitary allowances and bonuses are lower in monetary terms, but also because their per capita base pay is relatively much smaller.

Operations and Maintenance Costs

Costs for O&M—that is, employment and use of the organization—represent the second component of the total operating costs. They include both initial training for new entries (schools, academy, training centers, etc.) and recurrent training for active duty personnel, which is normally conducted each fiscal year in order to keep units operationally ready and prepared for real-world operations. As mentioned, the budget for this type of activity is set annually, based on previous fiscal year reports on results and estimated future needs. O&M costs also cover maintenance and logistics, works on infrastructure (such as maintenance, repairs, remodeling, new construction, etc.), funds to compensate for overtime and other engagements that affect personnel's normal daily activity (including relocation), cleaning (usually by private companies), and other contingencies. Finally, costs for injuries and accidents occurring while on duty are also included in this category. All these components of O&M costs are shown in table 3D.1.

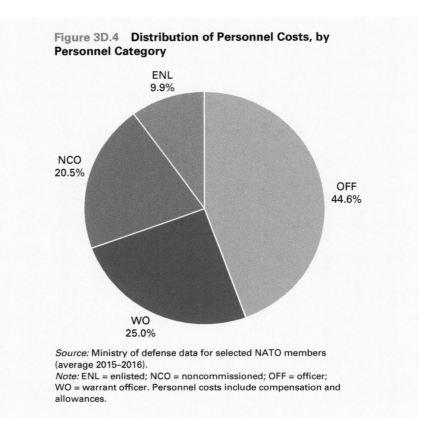

Figure 3D.4   **Distribution of Personnel Costs, by Personnel Category**

Source: Ministry of defense data for selected NATO members (average 2015–2016).
Note: ENL = enlisted; NCO = noncommissioned; OFF = officer; WO = warrant officer. Personnel costs include compensation and allowances.

Table 3D.1   **Operations and Maintenance Costs as a Share of Total, by Component**

Component	Percentage
Basic training and military exercises	4.7
Maintenance and support	48.0
Infrastructure	2.5
Miscellaneous[a]	43.3
On-duty accidents fund	1.5

Source: Calculations based on ministry of defense data from European Union countries (average).
a. Category includes personnel relocation, overtime, manual labor, cleaning, and other contingencies.

Investment Costs

Investment costs are the third area of expenditure for operating the defense sector. They are further split into research and development (R&D), which constitute only 2.5 percent of investment costs, and modernization and renovation, which constitute 97.5 percent. Specifically, modernization refers to maintenance of the defense's stock (i.e., vehicles, equipment, technology)

Table 3D.2   Investments by Operational Capacity as a Share of Total

Operational capacity	Percentage
C4-ISTAR	14.3
Deployment and mobility	7.7
Accuracy and effectiveness of engagements, survival, and force protection	26.9
Logistics sustainability and general support	49.4
Scientific research	1.7

Source: Calculations based on ministry of defense data for European Union countries (average).
Note: C4-ISTAR = command, control, communications, computers, intelligence, surveillance, target acquisition, and reconnaissance.

to keep it efficient while not being used (this is done to maximize resources' return on investment, while minimizing economic losses due to nonuse). Renovation refers to new acquisitions, particularly of new technology and more advanced equipment systems.

Investments comprise several areas meant to maintain the military at a high level of operational readiness and efficacy, including command, control, and communications, which allow political/military decision makers to direct and manage operations based on their objectives, as well as areas related to mobility, logistics, and overall efficacy (table 3D.2).

Equipment and Unit Procurement Costs for Light Infantry

The list of equipment, vehicles, weapons, and communications systems presented in table 3D.3 is for a light infantry organization, which also includes artillery, combat service support, logistics, and other supporting units.

The weapons shown for infantry are standard, whereas those for artillery include just mortars, tactical anti-tank missiles, tanks, and other light mechanized vehicles. The transport vehicles category covers only armored vehicles, both mechanized and wheeled, and anti-explosive ordnance utility vehicles. In addition, given its undeniable importance, a possible air service support—comprising standard transport helicopters only, mainly for transport of troops/supply and medical evacuations—is also part of the list. Finally, the command and control network is assumed to integrate all defensive elements into one command center at the national level. Notably, the list does not include acquisition of spare parts or manufacturer support plans (usually sold with systems).

Strategic systems such as an army's combat air support, medium/heavy artillery batteries, satellite communications and mapping, missiles, and many other technologically advanced weapon and communications systems have not been included. In addition, there is no army aviation combat support wing in the table of equipment. Finally, cost of equipment for specific counterterrorism/counterinsurgency is presented at the level of the battalion (about 300 troops).

Table 3D.3   **Table of Equipment for a Light Infantry: Unitary Costs**

Weapon systems and equipment	Unitary cost (2015 $)
Infantry weapons	
Gun	460
Rifle	160
Light machine gun	4,890
Medium machine gun	6,600
Heavy machine gun	14,000
Artillery weapons	
Anti-tank missiles (1 launcher, 24 missiles)	402,733
81 mm mortar	91,669
120 mm mortar	115,067
Tank destroyer	2,215,032
Howitzer	4,500,000
Main battle tank	3,912,264
Vehicles	
APC/AFV	9,870,000
Infantry fighting vehicle	7,200,000
Light multirole vehicle	3,340,000
Cavalry	
Helicopter (reconnaissance/transport)	3,567,065
Operational equipment	
C4I[a]	3,600,000
Weapon systems and equipment for COIN operations[b]	56,285
Individual combat system[c]	1,150

Source: Data from NATO member countries, 2015.
Note: The prices shown are international prices. APC/AFV = armored personnel carrier/armored fighting vehicle; C4I = command, control, communications, computers, and intelligence.
a. C4I is meant here as one system for the entire organization and is considered as centralized at the national/government level.
b. This item includes special equipment for COIN (counterterrorism/counterinsurgency) operations, including special combat vest, vehicle protection, MOOTW (military operations other than war) weapons, special ammunition and explosives, night goggles, urban combat equipment, and precision systems for sniper.
c. This item includes regular combat uniforms, combat and bullet-proof vests, and other regular equipment for conventional operations, including chemical, biological, radiological, and nuclear defense. The unitary cost reflects the fact that some equipment (such as types of night goggles, flashlights, grenade launchers, and anti-explosive systems) is included at the squad level (7–8 troops).

Military Compensation

Military compensation is a component of personnel costs and is normally included in the central government public wage bill.[48] Like compensation in any other sector of the public administration, military compensation is regulated and established through a concerted agreement involving the relevant ministries (in this case defense and finance/treasury) and the executive.

More specifically, the ministry of defense and the ministry of finance (or any other government agency in charge of determining budget appropriations) determine a certain base pay and other benefits and allowances, in a concerted agreement, usually valid for one fiscal year.[49]

Notwithstanding a rather large number of military unions (some 32 associations or unions represent military personnel in over 24 European countries),[50] few if any governments permit military collective bargaining on matters concerning salaries.[51] There are, however, extensive mechanisms to facilitate joint consultation on virtually all factors that affect military work and conditions of employment. These are mainly for the sake of military discipline and operational efficiency.

Unfortunately, systematic and comparable information on public sector employment and wages, and on how they are regulated, is not easy to come by, both because of issues with data availability and because of the different terminology used by governments to indicate the same category. These problems are especially evident in the defense sector. One difficulty is that some countries include paramilitary personnel among civilian employees, while others consider them part of the military. Some countries consider local government employees paid from the central budget as local government staff, whereas others designate these as central government staff. Finally, it is not possible to consider nonwage allowances and other monetary benefits uniformly because certain countries include them in the wage package while others include only the basic salary.[52] Figure 3D.5 shows a generic representation of a country's public sector structure.

Finally, in an organization made up of professional volunteers,[53] the compensation regime is primarily based on the attempt to match to the extent possible the armed forces' manpower requirements with the national supply of human capital. A compensation regime has the objective of being competitive relative to other sectors of the economy so as to increase the quality of the workforce. It can also be adjusted by manipulating personnel intake (such as by retirements) to increase the per capita share, all else equal.

Military Compensation and Organizational Structure

Compensation reflects the workforce structure (hierarchy) and depends on rank, tenure (seniority), specialty, location, and employment type (routine versus deployment).

Personnel employed in the army are grouped in three categories in function of their role. Each of the categories includes a subhierarchy of different ranks.[54] These are mainly determined by tenure and level of education.

Commissioned officers have a leadership role and operate as commanding officers at various levels of the organization. Warrant officers include middle-level personnel, primarily with a managerial role to provide coordination and management of troops. In some instances, high levels of seniority make a warrant office more important than an inexperienced junior officer. Enlisted personnel and noncommissioned officers represent the operational workforce that undertakes most of the organization's several activities.

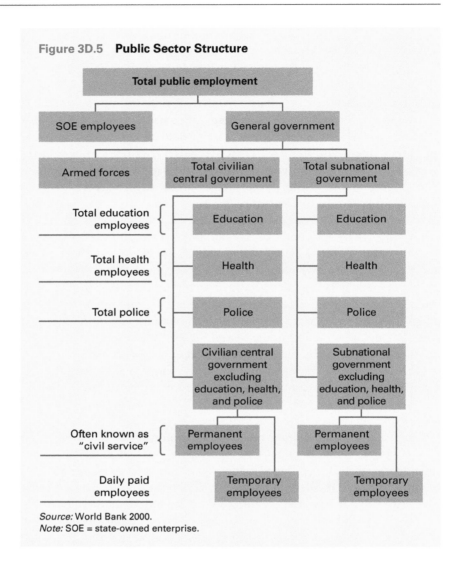

Figure 3D.5   **Public Sector Structure**

Source: World Bank 2000.
Note: SOE = state-owned enterprise.

The organization is pyramidal, with most employees at the "enlisted" level (table 3D.4 and figure 3D.6).

Compensation Structure and Salary Payment Types

Military compensation typically includes basic pay, allowances, and benefits. Basic pay depends solely on rank and years of service (experience). In some countries, allowance is not considered as income and is therefore nontaxable. The most important allowances are for subsistence and housing. The sum of basic pay, allowances, and tax advantage from the nontaxable status of allowances is called "regular military compensation." This may be supplemented by specialty pay—explained further on—or (in some countries, including the United States), by incentive pay for reenlistment, which seeks to minimize turnover and retain experienced personnel.

Table 3D.4   **Army Personnel, by Category, Rank, and Function**

Category	Rank	Main role
Officers	General	Command units and provide leadership
	Colonel	
	Lieutenant colonel	
	Major	
	Captain	
	Lieutenant	
Warrant officers	Warrant officer 1	Provide overall management and coordination
	Warrant officer	
Noncommissioned officers	Staff sergeant	Manage personnel, mainly enlisted and new entrants
	Sergeant	
	Corporal	
Enlisted	Private	Perform various tasks, depending on skill and specialization

Figure 3D.6   **Light Infantry's Composition, by Category**

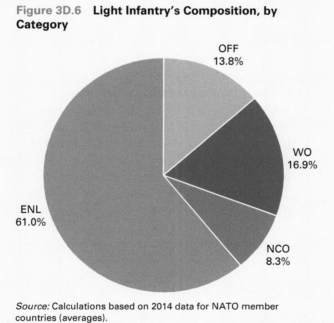

Source: Calculations based on 2014 data for NATO member countries (averages).
Note: ENL = enlisted; NCO = noncommissioned; OFF = officer; WO = warrant officer.

In addition to the base pay, military personnel at all levels receive other direct and indirect economic compensation.[55]

Types of direct monetary compensation include the following[56]:

- *Specialty pay.* This is pay for dangerous or risky specialties, such as tank officer or rotating/fixed-wing pilot; artillery, cavalry, or infantry; paratrooper, submariner, special forces, etc. The more technologically skilled, dangerous, and challenging the job, the higher the specialty pay.
- *Bonus.* Each rank gets a bonus, depending on the years spent in that rank: e.g., a major who has held that rank for three years gets the same pay as a major of two years, plus a bonus for the additional year at that rank. A major of four years gets a higher bonus, etc. When the major is promoted to lieutenant colonel, the cycle starts over.

Types of indirect monetary compensation (benefits) include the following:

- *Housing allowance.* When personnel move anywhere in the world, the administration pays an amount to cover housing. For example, if a staff member buys a property, the administration covers the mortgage up to the amount meant to be given to that individual for housing. That is also true for rent and any other accommodation.
- *Health care and insurance.* These are provided for personnel and family members.
- *Fuel.* For U.S. military personnel and NATO personnel of any nationality, fuel for personal/household consumption is paid for at the same cost as in the United States. In some cases the administration provides coupons to buy gas at a lower price (gas is subsidized by the government).
- *Grocery.* In commissaries, military malls, and post exchanges, military personnel can buy goods and services (food, clothes, jewelry, cars, vacation, education, etc.) subsidized by the administration and hence pay a much lower price than the actual market (civilian) price.
- *Pensions/retirement benefits.* These are paid by the government, but the paying agency varies across countries and could include the defense administration, treasury, or social security administration. These benefits are activated when retirement age is achieved (60–65) or after a certain number of years of active duty (20 in the United States, 40 in Italy), whatever comes first.
- *Widows' benefits.* Surviving spouses inherit benefits, in full or partially, depending on various circumstances (e.g., cause of death, seniority, whether the country is at peace or war). Governments' decisions about extending these benefits are extremely variable and incidental. For this reason they are not addressed in this analysis.

Military Compensation in Selected Countries

Compensation of armed forces personnel for a group of selected countries is shown in table 3D.5. Israel is included as an example of a high-income economy in a constant state of conflict.

Table 3D.5 Average Army Net Monthly Basic Pay in Selected Countries, by Rank ($)

	High income							Upper middle income				Lower middle income		
	Australia	Canada	France	Germany	Israel	Italy	United Kingdom	Azerbaijan	Belarus	Kazakhstan	Armenia	India	Kyrgyz Republic	Ukraine
Brig. general	—	11,694	9,575	—	11,000	3,258	7,311	1,200	—	1,100	—	358	—	—
Colonel	8,925	9,620	7,607	—	—	3,080	6,312	—	675	—	—	324	300	350
Lt. colonel	—	—	—	—	—	2,915	5,335	—	—	—	—	—	—	—
Major	5,324	6,320	3,589	—	—	2,915	3,886	—	—	—	—	249	—	—
Captain	4,171	4,694	2,708	4,163	—	2,813	3,098	—	—	—	—	206	—	300
Lieutenant	—	—	—	—	2,400	2,711	2,387	600	475	470	—	—	200	190
Junior lt.	—	—	—	—	—	2,601	—	—	—	—	—	—	—	—
Officers average	—	—	—	—	—	—	—	—	730	700	450	—	—	—
Chief WO	—	—	—	—	—	2,709	—	—	—	—	—	—	—	—
Senior WO	—	—	—	—	—	2,600	3,168	—	—	—	—	—	—	—
Mid-level WO	—	—	—	—	—	2,505	—	—	—	—	—	—	—	—
Ordinary WO	4,722	5,941	2,130	—	—	2,429	—	—	—	—	—	—	—	—
Staff sergeant	—	—	—	—	—	2,367	2,841	—	400	—	285	—	—	—
Sergeant	—	—	—	—	—	—	2,481	—	—	—	—	—	—	—
Corporal	3,758	4,895	1,637	2,126	—	1,741	2,936	—	—	—	—	—	—	—
Soldier	2,626	2,536	1,532	1,872	400	2,207	2,207	40	330	300	230	—	70	—

Sources: Ministry of defense in selected countries (2014 data); *Pravda* for former Soviet countries (2014 data), http://www.pravdareport.com/world/ussr/01-05-2015/113579-military_life-0/.

Note: brig. = brigadier; lt. = lieutenant; WO = warrant officer; — = not available.

Cost of Living and Military Compensation Regimes

On average, the cost of living captures about 67 percent of median military compensation (figure 3D.7). (The analysis refers to an individual with a standardized lifestyle—no gym, no smoking, no extra activities, etc.—and military stipends do not include extra working time or specialty pay.)

Figure 3D.7   Cost of Living as Share of Military Stipends: Comparison in Selected Countries

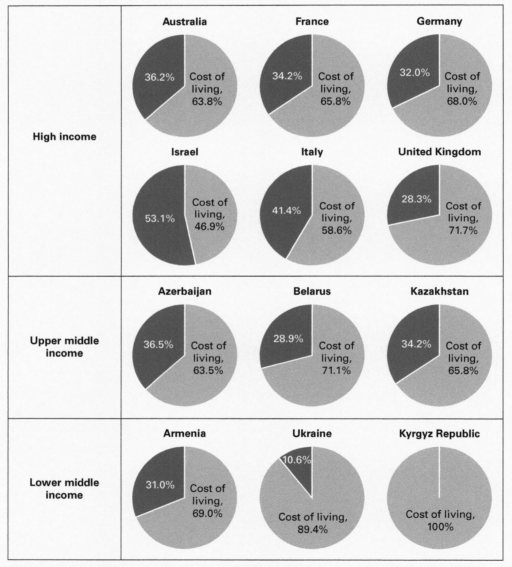

Sources: Calculations based on 2016 data from ministry of defense (for high-income countries); 2015 data from *Pravda* (for former Soviet economies), http://www.pravdareport.com/world/ussr/01-05-2015/113579-military _life-0/. Cost of living index as reported by Numbeo database, 2016, http://www.numbeo.com/cost-of-living/.
Note: Israel is included as an example of a high-income country engaged in combat operations.

As mentioned, this statistic has the unique purpose of providing practitioners and decision makers with a realistic reference point when determining a possible compensation regime for personnel employed in the defense sector.

Notes

1. Information on these PERs can be found at World Bank, "Governance and Public Sector Management," http://search.worldbank.org/per.
2. World Bank, *World Development Report 2004: Making Services Work for the Poor* (Washington, DC: World Bank, 2003); World Bank, *Improving Public Financial Management in the Security Sector*, vol. 5 of *Afghanistan: Managing Public Finances for Development* (Washington, DC: World Bank, 2005).
3. Douglas North, "Institutions," *Journal of Economic Perspectives 5*, no. 1 (Winter 1991): 97.
4. World Bank, "International Development Association Resource Allocation Index—2011," http://www.worldbank.org/ida/IRAI-2011 .html; World Bank, "CPIA Public Sector Management and Institutions Cluster Average," http://data.worldbank.org/indicator/IQ.CPA.PUBS .XQ; and World Bank, "International Development Association (IDA)—Country Policy and Institutional Assessment," http://go .worldbank.org/EEAIU81ZG0.
5. World Bank, "Harmonized List of Fragile Situations FY16," http:// pubdocs.worldbank.org/pubdocs/publicdoc/2015/7 /700521437416355449/FCSlist-FY16-Final-712015.pdf. The World Bank's list of fragile situations averages CPIA cluster scores from the World Bank, the Asian Development Bank, and the African Development Bank to produce a harmonized average. Peacekeeping and peacebuilding missions exclude border-monitoring operations. The Asian Development Bank's overall CPIA score weights governance indicators more heavily under the assumption that governance is particularly important for economic development. In contrast, the African Development Bank gives zero weight to governance indicators in producing its composite score. For the purposes of defining state fragility, the World Bank weights all clusters equally.
6. World Bank, "GDP per Capita, PPP (current international $)," 2014, http://data.worldbank.org/indicator/NY.GDP.PCAP.PP.CD. Calculation is based on the most recent available data.
7. Organisation for Economic Co-operation and Development, *OECD DAC Handbook on Security System Reform: Supporting Security and Justice* (Paris: OECD Publishing, 2007); Mark Sedra, "Introduction: The Future of Security Sector Reform," in *The Future of Security Sector Reform*, ed. Mark Sedra (Waterloo, Ontario: Centre for International Governance Innovation, 2010), 16–27; and Nicole Ball, "The Evolution of the Security Sector Reform Agenda," in *The Future of Security Sector Reform*, 29–44.

8. Transparency International U.K., Defence and Security Programme, "Government Defence Anti-Corruption Index 2013," January 2013, http://transparencyschool.org/wp-content/uploads/GI-main-report.pdf. Transparency International used the World Bank's definition of "fragile state" from the FY2012 "Harmonized List." The fragile states it assessed were Afghanistan, Angola, Bosnia and Herzegovina, Democratic Republic of Congo, Côte d'Ivoire, Eritrea, Iraq, Libya, Nepal, the Syrian Arab Republic, West Bank and Gaza, the Republic of Yemen, and Zimbabwe.

9. Transparency International U.K., Defence and Security Programme, "Government Defence Anti-Corruption Index 2013," January 2013, http://transparencyschool.org/wp-content/uploads/GI-main-report.pdf; Asian Development Bank, "Country Performance Assessment," 2013, http://www.adb.org/site/adf/country-performance-assessment; African Development Bank Group, "Country Policy and Institutional Assessment (CPIA)," http://www.afdb.org/en/documents/project-operations/country-performance-assessment-cpa/country-policy-and-institutional-assessment-cpia/; World Bank, World Development Indicators, CPIA cluster averages, http://data.worldbank.org/indicator.

10. World Bank, World Development Indicators Database, http://data.worldbank.org/data-catalog/world-development-indicators.

11. World Bank, *World Development Report 2011: Conflict, Security, and Development* (Washington, DC: World Bank, 2011); see in particular the overview on p. 279.

12. World Bank, *World Development Report 2011: Conflict, Security, and Development* (Washington, DC: World Bank, 2011).

13. World Bank, World Development Indicators Database, http://data.worldbank.org/data-catalog/world-development-indicators.

14. Ibid.

15. Ibid.

16. For a thorough treatment of the connection in an earlier period, see John Brewer, *The Sinews of Power: War, Money, and the English State, 1688–1783* (Abingdon, U.K.: Routledge, 1989).

17. As previously stated, the guidance for World Bank staff conducting a PER is that they not evaluate defense policy; their focus should be on the alignment between policy and budgetary allocation. For this reason, working in partnership has been the most effective form of support to client governments in analyzing this sector.

18. Colin S. Gray, "Strategic Thoughts for Defence Planners," *Survival: Global Politics and Strategy* 52, no. 3 (2010): 159–78.

19. Transparency International U.K., Defence and Security Programme, "Government Defence Anti-Corruption Index 2013," January 2013, http://transparencyschool.org/wp-content/uploads/GI-main-report.pdf.

20. Nicole Ball and Len le Roux, "A Model for Good Practice in the Military Sector," in *Budgeting for the Military Sector in Africa:*

The Processes and Mechanisms of Control, ed. Wuyi Omitoogun and Eboe Hutchful (New York: Oxford University Press, 2006), 14–47.

21. David Chutter, *Governing and Managing the Defense Sector* (Pretoria, South Africa: Institute for Strategic Studies, 2011). https://www .issafrica.org/uploads/Book2011GovManDefSec.pdf.

22. Generic information on the budget cycle was drawn and adapted from the World Bank's internal Public Financial Management Training Program manual.

23. Transparency International U.K., Defence and Security Programme, "Government Defence Anti-Corruption Index 2013," January 2013, http://transparencyschool.org/wp-content/uploads/GI-main-report.pdf.

24. Nicole Ball and Len le Roux, "A Model for Good Practice in the Military Sector," in *Budgeting for the Military Sector in Africa: The Processes and Mechanisms of Control*, ed. Wuyi Omitoogun and Eboe Hutchful (New York: Oxford University Press, 2006), 14–47.

25. Ibid.

26. United Kingdom Ministry of Defense, "JSP 507: MOD Guide to Investment Appraisal and Evaluation (Version 5.0)," April 2011, https://www.gov.uk/government/publications/jsp-507-mod-guide-to -investment-appraisal-and-evaluation.

27. Nicole Ball and Len le Roux, "A Model for Good Practice in the Military Sector," in *Budgeting for the Military Sector in Africa: The Processes and Mechanisms of Control*, ed. Wuyi Omitoogun and Eboe Hutchful (New York: Oxford University Press, 2006), 14–47.

28. L. R. Jones, Philip J. Candreva, and Marc R. Devore, *Financing National Defense: Policy and Process* (Charlotte, NC: Information Age Publishing, 2012).

29. Ibid.; Daniel Tommasi, "The Budget Execution Process," in *The International Handbook of Public Financial Management*, ed. Richard Allen, Richard Hemming, and Barry Potter (New York: Palgrave Macmillan, 2013), 285–311.

30. Tommasi, "The Budget Execution Process."

31. Ibid.

32. Under a "threat-based" defense planning and budgeting system, some argue, performance can be "measured" only if a conflict occurs and the military is engaged. This is a specious argument, given that in any sector, intermediate measures such as "readiness" suffice to provide some assessment of performance. In the more recent capability-based planning model (introduced in the United States around 2001 and subsequently into the Australia, New Zealand, United States Security Treaty [ANZUS], Canada, and NATO), some sense of performance can be measured or tested with respect to capability, far short of open conflict.

33. World Bank, *World Development Report 2004: Making Services Work for the Poor* (Washington, DC: World Bank, 2003); World Bank,

Improving Public Financial Management in the Security Sector, vol. 5 of *Afghanistan: Managing Public Finances for Development* (Washington, DC: World Bank, 2005).

34. Nicole Ball and Malcolm Holmes, "Integrating Defense into Public Expenditure Work," U.K. Department for International Development, January 11, 2002.

35. International Monetary Fund (IMF), "Fiscal Transparency," May 2015, http://www.imf.org/external/np/fad/trans/.

36. David Heald, "Strengthening Fiscal Transparency," in *The International Handbook of Public Financial Management,* ed. Richard Allen, Richard Hemming, and Barry Potter (New York: Palgrave Macmillan, 2013), 711–41.

37. Open Budget Initiative, "Guide to the Open Budget Questionnaire: An Explanation of the Questions and the Response Options" (Open Budget Initiative, Washington, DC, July 2011), http://internationalbudget.org/wp-content/uploads/Guide-OBS2012_English-Final.pdf.

38. Military operations other than war include peace support operations, arms control, humanitarian assistance, and disaster relief. Smaller-scale contingency operations include deterrence and limited interventions, noncombatant evacuation operations, no-fly-zone enforcement, and counterterrorism/counterinsurgency (COIN) operations.

39. They have the same price across countries.

40. Income-level classifications for 2016 are explained in World Bank, "Country and Lending Groups," http://data.worldbank.org/about/country-and-lending-groups.

41. The analysis includes countries that also operate a navy and an air force. However, spending allocated to both maritime and air branches can be considered negligible compared to ground force appropriations.

42. Average costs are 1.8 percent and 2.0 percent of GDP, respectively. However, a median value is reported to account for outliers, such as Georgia, South Sudan, and the Republic of Yemen (figure 3D.1 and figure 3D.2).

43. Being nonexcludable and nonrivalrous, defense benefits everybody, including free riders, and the marginal cost to include one more user is zero.

44. A warfare doctrine provides a frame of reference across the military to standardize operations, promote interoperability among units, and facilitate readiness by establishing common ways of accomplishing military tasks.

45. For example, NATO suggests a minimum of 20 percent of total operating costs for investments and a minimum of 2 percent of GDP for total defense spending. NATO, "Defence Expenditures of NATO Countries (2008–2015)," 2016, http://www.nato.int/nato_static_fl2014/assets/pdf/pdf_2016_01/20160129_160128-pr-2016-11-eng.pdf. The first requirement can be met by the ministry of defense, whereas

the other concerns defense budget allocation by the ministry of finance/government, rather than ministry of defense policy.

46. Geography plays a role because (for example) island, mountainous, or remote countries are easier to defend and can spend less on defense.

47. Cases in point are Estonia, which has extensively participated in coalition activities in Afghanistan and Iraq since 2004; and the United Kingdom and United States, which have been conducting a long-standing "War on Terror."

48. The wage bill represents the sum of wages and salaries paid to civilian central government and the armed forces. World Bank, "Measuring Government Employment and Wages," 2000. Wages and salaries consist of all payments in cash (no other forms of payment, such as in-kind, are considered) to employees in return for services rendered, before deduction of withholding taxes and employee pension contributions. Monetary allowances (e.g., for housing or transportation) are also included in the wage bill.

49. This process may vary across countries. Clearly, the ministry of defense advocates for higher compensation levels, whereas its counterpart needs to address other sectors of the economy, such as health, education, etc.

50. Those European countries that have not granted military personnel the right to freedom of association are under pressure to do so.

51. Lindy Heinecken, "Ban Military Unions, They're a Threat to National Security! So Where to from Here?" *Strategic Review for Southern Africa* 31 (November 2009), https://www.questia.com/read/1G1 -220202630/ban-military-unions-they-re-a-threat-to-national; EU Parliament, "Military Unions and Associations," chapter 9 of the *Handbook on Human Rights and Fundamental Freedoms of Armed Forces Personnel* (OSCE/ODIHR, DCAF, 2014), http://www.europarl .europa.eu/meetdocs/2009_2014/documents/sede/dv/sede291111 odihrhandbook_/sede291111odihrhandbook_en.pdf.

52. World Bank, "Measuring Government Employment and Wages," 2000.

53. Conscription (draft) is not covered in this analysis due to its decreasing use, for which there are two reasons: (i) it entails high turnover, which negatively affects expertise (the organization does not invest much in draftees' training considering they are not a long-term resource), and hence outcomes; and (ii) those drafted may not want to fight, hence either are ineffective or cause morale issues. However, an advantage of conscription is costs, as draftees receive a very low pay; it allows for an inexpensive military apparatus, but at the expense of quality.

54. Categories and ranks are standard across branches, even though ranks may have different denominations and names for historical or traditional reasons, particularly in the navy.

55. This is true for the U.S. military, but it applies to other countries as well, although the amounts paid vary.

56. In some countries (for example, the United States and the United Kingdom), the forms of direct compensation discussed here (bonuses and specialty pay) are nontaxable because they are not considered as salary; in other countries they are taxed as regular income.

References

African Development Bank. n.d. "Country Policy and Institutional Assessment (CPIA)." http://www.afdb.org/en/documents/project -operations/country-performance-assessment-cpa/country-policy-and -institutional-assessment-cpia.

Arevalo de Leon, Bernardo. 2007. "Guatemala Case Study, Inter-Sectoral Dialogue on SSR." In *No Ownership, No Commitment: A Guide to Local Ownership of Security Sector Reform*, edited by Laurie Nathan, 68–77. 2nd ed. University of Birmingham.

Asian Development Bank. 2013. "Country Performance Assessment." http://www.adb.org/site/adf/country-performance-assessment.

Ball, Nicole. 2010. "The Evolution of the Security Sector Reform Agenda." In *The Future of Security Sector Reform*, edited by Mark Sedra, 29–44. Waterloo, Ontario: Centre for International Governance Innovation.

Ball, Nicole, and Malcolm Holmes. 2002. "Integrating Defense into Public Expenditure Work." U.K. Department for International Development, January 11.

Ball, Nicole, and Len le Roux. 2006. "A Model for Good Practice in the Military Sector." In *Budgeting for the Military Sector in Africa: The Processes and Mechanisms of Control*, edited by Wuyi Omitoogun and Eboe Hutchful, 14–47. New York: Oxford University Press.

Brewer, John. 1989. *The Sinews of Power: War, Money, and the English State, 1688–1783*. Abingdon, U.K.: Routledge.

Chutter, David. 2011. *Governing and Managing the Defense Sector*. Pretoria, South Africa: Institute for Strategic Studies. https://www.issafrica.org /uploads/Book2011GovManDefSec.pdf.

EU Parliament. 2014. "Military Unions and Associations." Chapter 9 of the *Handbook on Human Rights and Fundamental Freedoms of Armed Forces Personnel*. OSCE/ODIHR, DCAF. http://www.europarl.europa.eu /meetdocs/2009_2014/documents/sede/dv/sede291111odihrhandbook _/sede291111odihrhandbook_en.pdf.

Gray, Colin S. 2010. "Strategic Thoughts for Defence Planners." *Survival: Global Politics and Strategy* 52 (3): 159–78.

Heald, David. 2013. "Strengthening Fiscal Transparency." In *The International Handbook of Public Financial Management*, edited by Richard Allen, Richard Hemming, and Barry Potter, 711–41. New York: Palgrave Macmillan.

Heinecken, Lindy. 2009. "Ban Military Unions, They're a Threat to National Security! So Where to from Here?" *Strategic Review for Southern Africa* 31 (November). https://www.questia.com /read/1G1-220202630/ban-military-unions-they-re-a-threat-to -national.

IMF (International Monetary Fund). 2015. "Fiscal Transparency." http:// www.imf.org/external/np/fad/trans/.

Jones, L. R., Philip J. Candreva, and Marc R. Devore. 2012. *Financing National Defense: Policy and Process.* Charlotte, NC: Information Age Publishing.

Legislature of Liberia, House of Representatives. n.d. "Committee on National Defense." http://legislature.gov.lr/committees/committee-national-defense, accessed June 30, 2014.

Legislature of Liberia, House of Representatives. n.d. "Committee on National Security." http://legislature.gov.lr/committees/committee-national-security, accessed June 30, 2014.

Legislature of Liberia, Senate. n.d. "Committee on National Defense, Intelligence, Security and Veteran Affairs." http://legislature.gov.lr /content/committee-national-defense-intelligence-security-and-veteran -affairs, accessed June 30, 2014.

Muna, Riefqi. 2008. "Local Ownership and the Experiences of SSR in Indonesia." In *Local Ownership and Security Sector Reform*, edited by Timothy Donais, 233–52. Geneva: Geneva Centre for the Democratic Control of Armed Forces.

Nathan, Laurie, ed. 2007. "South Africa Case Study: Inclusive SSR and Design and the White Paper on Defence." In *No Ownership, No Commitment: A Guide to Local Ownership of Security Sector Reform*, 94–99. 2nd ed. Edgbaston, Birmingham, U.K.: University of Birmingham.

NATO. 2016. "Defence Expenditures of NATO Countries (2008–2015)." http://www.nato.int/nato_static_fl2014/assets/pdf/pdf_2016_01 /20160129_160128-pr-2016-11-eng.pdf.

NATO Research and Technology Organization. 2007. "TR-SAS-054: Methods and Models for Life Cycle Costing." June. https://www .cso.nato.int/pubs/rdp.asp?RDP=RTO-TR-SAS-054.

North, Douglas. 1991. "Institutions." *Journal of Economic Perspectives* 5 (1): 97.

OECD (Organisation for Economic Co-operation and Development). 2007. *OECD DAC Handbook on Security System Reform: Supporting Security and Justice.* Paris: OECD Publishing.

Open Budget Initiative. 2011. "Guide to the Open Budget Questionnaire: An Explanation of the Questions and the Response Options." Open Budget Initiative, Washington, DC. http://internationalbudget.org /wp-content/uploads/Guide-OBS2012_English-Final.pdf.

Sedra, Mark. 2010. "Introduction: The Future of Security Sector Reform." In *The Future of Security Sector Reform*, edited by Mark Sedra, 16–27. Waterloo, Ontario: Centre for International Governance Innovation.

Tommasi, Daniel. 2013. "The Budget Execution Process." In *The International Handbook of Public Financial Management*, edited by Richard Allen, Richard Hemming, and Barry Potter, 285–311. New York: Palgrave Macmillan.

Transparency International U.K., Defence and Security Programme. 2013. "Government Defence Anti-Corruption Index 2013." http://transparency school.org/wp-content/uploads/GI-main-report.pdf.

United Kingdom Ministry of Defense. 2011. "JSP 507: MOD Guide to Investment Appraisal and Evaluation (Version 5.0)." https://www.gov.uk/government/publications/jsp-507-mod-guide-to-investment-appraisal-and-evaluation.

World Bank. 2000. "Measuring Government Employment and Wages." World Bank, Washington, DC.

———. 2003. *World Development Report 2004: Making Services Work for the Poor.* Washington, DC: World Bank.

———. 2005. *Improving Public Financial Management in the Security Sector.* Vol. 5 of *Afghanistan: Managing Public Finances for Development.* Washington, DC: World Bank.

———. 2009. "Report on the Assessment of the Financial Management of the Defense and Security Forces in the Central African Republic." World Bank, Washington, DC.

———. 2011. *World Development Report 2011: Conflict, Security, and Development.* Washington, DC: World Bank.

———. 2012. "Republic of Burundi Public Expenditure Review: Fiscal Challenges, Security, and Growth in Burundi." Report no. ACS3988, World Bank, Washington, DC.

———. 2013a. "Malian Security Forces: Financial Management Assessment Report." World Bank, Washington, DC.

———. 2013b. "Niger Security Sector Public Expenditure Review." Report no. 83526-NE, World Bank, Washington, DC.

———. 2014. "GDP per Capita, PPP (current international $)." http://data.worldbank.org/indicator/NY.GDP.PCAP.PP.CD.

———. n.d. "Country and Lending Groups." http://data.worldbank.org/about/country-and-lending-groups, accessed June 30, 2014.

———. n.d. "CPIA Public Sector Management and Institutions Cluster Average." http://data.worldbank.org/indicator/IQ.CPA.PUBS.XQ, accessed June 30, 2014.

———. n.d. "Governance and Public Sector Management." http://search.worldbank.org/per, accessed June 30, 2014.

————. n.d. "Harmonized List of Fragile Situations FY16." http://
pubdocs.worldbank.org/pubdocs/publicdoc/2015/7/700521437416355449
/FCSlist-FY16-Final-712015.pdf, accessed June 30, 2014.

————. n.d. "International Development Association (IDA)—Country Policy
and Institutional Assessment." http://go.worldbank.org/EEAIU81ZG0,
accessed June 30, 2014.

————. n.d. "International Development Association Resource Allocation
Index—2011." http://www.worldbank.org/ida/IRAI-2011.html.

————. n.d. "World Development Indicators." CPIA cluster averages. http://
data.worldbank.org/indicator, accessed June 30, 2014.

————. n.d. "World Development Indicators Database." http://data.worldbank
.org/data-catalog/world-development-indicators, accessed June 30, 2014.

World Bank and United Nations. 2012. "Liberia Public Expenditure Review
Note: Meeting the Challenges of the UNMIL Security Transition."
World Bank, Washington, DC.

CHAPTER 4

Public Expenditure Reviews of Policing Services

Introduction

This chapter provides guidance to economists, governance specialists, and security sector practitioners tasked to carry out Public Expenditure Reviews (PERs) and public financial management (PFM) assessments of policing. The purpose of such exercises is to answer critical budgetary questions about the affordability and sustainability of resourcing of policing institutions, and about whether those resources are being used efficiently and effectively.

The chapter starts by discussing the role of the police in providing security. It first examines policy options for delivering public safety, approaches to policing and typical police functions, institutional arrangements, and oversight mechanisms. (These are further detailed in annex 4A.) The chapter then focuses on police financing within the broader budget cycle, linking strategic issues of resource allocation to cost drivers, expenditure management of personnel and assets, and to budget controls. Last, the chapter surveys the ways to measure police performance, including statistical methods and indicators such as due process, officer conduct, and policing outputs and outcomes. Annexes present some international data comparisons on criminal justice resources (annex 4B) and address special considerations for donors (annex 4C).

Policing is an inextricable component of the criminal justice system in any setting; but it has been treated separately in this sourcebook because it is such a large and usually expensive component of the system. This chapter and the chapter on criminal justice form a pair and should be read together when undertaking a review of the criminal justice sector.

In any country, region, city, or community, the capacity to maintain security is a precondition for effective governance. Indeed, while levels of insecurity vary enormously across societies, all states, regardless of income level, devote significant resources to preserving law and order. The only study to date that has measured expenditures in criminal justice worldwide found that in 1997, global criminal justice expenditure was $362 billion, of which 62 percent was allocated to policing, 3 percent to prosecutions, 18 percent to courts, and 17 percent to prisons.[1] Another study using data from the United Nations Office on Drugs and Crime (UNODC) Surveys on Crime Trends and the Operations of Criminal Justice Systems from 2000 found that on average, countries spent just under 1 percent of their gross domestic product (GDP) on policing, with some countries spending significantly more than that (see figure 4.1).[2]

Policing services are thus a pillar of the security sector. Their role in safeguarding development is becoming even more essential, as the most recent global trends show an increase in deaths due to interpersonal violence. According to the Geneva Declaration on Armed Violence and Development, at least 526,000 people die violently every year, and roughly 75 percent of these deaths occur in nonconflict settings. One-quarter of all violent deaths occur in just 14 countries, seven of which are in the Americas. Research on femicide also reveals that about 66,000 women and girls are violently killed around the world each year.[3] In fragile and conflict-affected states (FCS), where peace settlements are often weak and the risk of sliding back into civil war persists well beyond the formal cessation of hostilities, data on deaths due to violence are less reliable. But the size of the United Nations Police (UNPOL) deployment worldwide shows that stabilization and law and order remain prime concerns: as of April 2016, the UN had deployed more than 12,000 police units to help build the capacity of weak police agencies in 16 missions.[4]

These figures demonstrate that whether in FCS or in middle-income countries affected by high levels of violence, analysis of the security sector is incomplete without an assessment of police finances.

Understanding the Police in the Security Sector

Upon embarking on a PER, the first task of the team is to understand the challenges concerning crime, violence, and social disorder and the various institutions engaged in addressing those challenges, including the police. What is recommended is a six-step process in which the PER team examines (i) the security context, (ii) policy options to deliver safety and security, (iii) institutional functions, (iv) institutions and organizational structure, (v) management and oversight mechanisms, and (vi) any special issues pertaining to policing services that emerge out of the previous steps. These steps are shown in table 4.1 and discussed in the pages that follow.

Figure 4.1   Expenditure on Policing as a Percentage of GDP in Selected Economies, 1988–2000

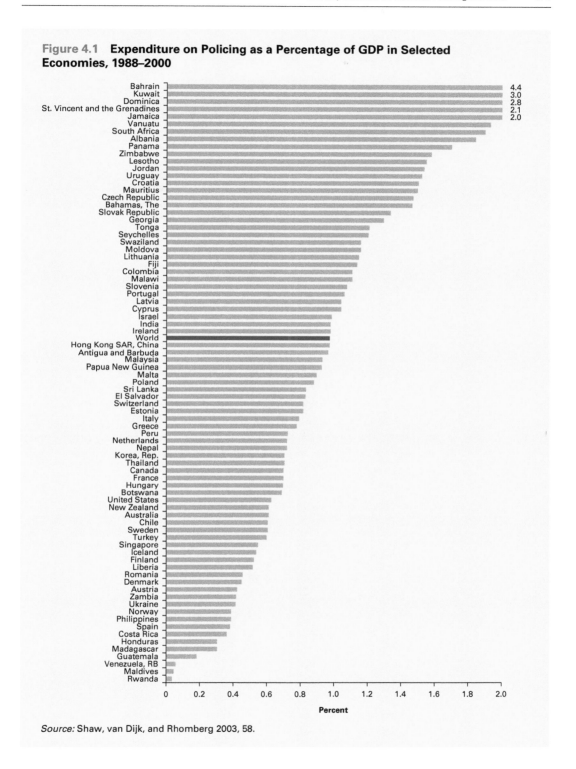

Source: Shaw, van Dijk, and Rhomberg 2003, 58.

Table 4.1   **Steps to Understanding Policing Services**

Step	Analytical focus	Questions
1	Context	What are the main types and key drivers of crime? How are crime and violence geographically distributed?
2	Policy	What are the policy options for delivering safety and security?
3	Functions	What are the main functions performed by police, including public order management, investigative services, patrols?
4	Institutions	What are the key police services, and how are they organized?
5	Management and oversight	How are police services managed and supervised?
6	Special issues (e.g., corruption)	What forms does police corruption take and what are the key causes?

Context Analysis

The team conducting a PER analysis needs to understand both the macro-fiscal context and the particular sector concerned. Thus a PER of policing requires the team to examine crime and violence trends, as well as to understand the underlying drivers of these trends. The latter is an immensely complex and contested task. Crime and violence are multicausal phenomena, and (as outlined in annex 4A) there are many (often ideological) theories about their origins.

To obtain an overview of the crime and violence challenge, the PER team must address a number of key questions:

- What is the magnitude and typology of crime and violence (e.g., homicides, assaults, crimes against property, domestic violence, public disorder)?
- Who are the perpetrators? What is the average age and socioeconomic profile of the perpetrators? To what extent is organized crime an issue?
- Who are the victims? What is the average age and socioeconomic profile of the victims?
- What is the geographical distribution of criminal activity? Are there high differences between urban and rural areas and among different neighborhoods in cities? What accounts for these differences?
- What factors drive crime and violence? Examples include high youth unemployment, poverty, inequality, and social exclusion; drug trafficking and the availability of firearms; youth gangs used for extortion and protection rackets tied to organized crime cartels; high levels of corruption; legacies of conflict; cross-border spillovers of violence; and cultural norms.

The World Bank and the United Nations have also produced some diagnostic tools for practitioners seeking to analyze drivers of crime and violence. These include World Bank studies of the costs of crime and assessments of fragility; transnational and organized crime assessments produced by UNODC; and UNODC manuals and training materials on criminal intelligence analysis and case studies.[5]

Policy Options for Public Safety and Approaches to Policing

The next step for the PER team is to comprehend the policy approach taken by the government (and in certain circumstances, such as in FCS, by non-state actors) through which the sector delivers safety and security for citizens. The main policy options include:[6]

- *Suppression.* The suppression of crime and violence can sometimes be achieved through the direct exercise of force in response to instances of crime or violence. This set of approaches includes a diverse array of activities, such as direct engagement by the military and/or police with persons deemed a threat to peace, and the deployment of the military/police into areas where crime or violence is thought to be likely in order to intimidate and discourage potential perpetrators. A key question that confronts policy makers in the security agencies is the extent to which the successful suppression of crime and violence simply displaces it through time and/or space. For example, intensified street patrols by police officers can result in crime being shifted to areas that are less densely patrolled (see box 4.1). The suppression of crime can also result in the diversification of criminal methods. Thus a heavy police presence in an area in which street-level drug dealing is common could result in changes to the methods suppliers use to access their customers.
- *Deterrence.* Framed simply, the degree of deterrence delivered by the police is a function of (i) the likelihood that an offender will be identified, arrested, and successfully prosecuted; and (ii) the severity of his likely punishment in the event of conviction. In general, the empirical evidence suggests that, at the margin, the deterrent effect of increasing the likelihood of punishment is usually greater than the deterrent effect of increasing the severity of punishment.[7] This point is significant because responses to crime—not just crime itself—are costly, and the opportunity costs of devoting resources to some of the more expensive strategies (such as mass incarceration of offenders) are significant.
- *Incapacitation.* This can be understood as the degree to which security is improved by the mere fact that offenders are "off the street"; it is a function of the severity of sentences imposed by courts, and the volume of crimes prevented by such sentences. One complication of this approach is the possibility that offenders' experience in prison could make them more likely to reoffend on release and to commit more serious crimes.

- *Rehabilitation.* Many states devote resources to reforming offenders under the general rubric of rehabilitation. These programs vary greatly and include skills-building (e.g. "life skills" such as conflict or anger management), as well as drug and alcohol rehabilitation. If these programs are offered in prison, then the prison infrastructure and skill sets of prison officials have to be aligned with the needs of the programs.
- *Prevention.* The notion of crime prevention covers a vast array of initiatives, many of which fall outside the authority and competence of institutions in the security sector. Interventions might include programs aimed at reducing the level of inequality in a society (since there is evidence that crime rates are correlated with levels of inequality)[8] or aimed at increasing employment or incomes in crime-ridden areas and/or among communities or demographic groups thought most likely to engage in criminality. Commonly, crime prevention is separated into primary, secondary, and tertiary approaches:
  - *Primary prevention* focuses on factors that increase the risk of people in the population falling into criminality (e.g., by addressing income or gender inequality).
  - *Secondary prevention* focuses on communities where significant proportions of the target group are already involved in criminality.
  - *Tertiary prevention* focuses on known offenders and might include rehabilitation inside or outside of prison and programs aimed at reducing gangsterism.

Box 4.1   The Challenge of Crime Displacement

One of the most difficult challenges policy makers face in dealing with crime is that even successful interventions can generate offsetting problems. One example is documented by Altbeker, who sought to apply some work done in the United States on the consequences of dramatically improved vehicle-tracking technology to car theft and hijacking in South Africa.[a] In the original study, the authors found that the level of car crime declined dramatically following the introduction of vehicle-tracking technology, and that this reduction was not accompanied by a rise in other forms of criminality.[b]

But the results in South Africa were different. The penetration of vehicle-tracking technology led to a decline in car theft and robbery as large as it had been in the United States, but in South Africa there was a corresponding increase in robberies, especially home invasions and muggings. This comparison suggests that displacement may offset gains from successful interventions—and further shows that results achieved in one jurisdiction will not necessarily be achieved by similar interventions in other places.

a. Altbeker 2006.
b. Ayers and Levitt 1997.

An analysis of public sector approaches to law and order will in turn define the requisite skills and resources. Suppression approaches often rely on high numbers of low-skilled personnel, including military personnel; investigation requires more-educated personnel with more training. Similarly, prisons that simply warehouse inmates may not be adequate to carry out rehabilitation: they may be too overcrowded or too violent, prison staff may lack the appropriate skills, or the facility may lack the space and infrastructure for rehabilitation. The link between the skill set and the type of police strategy matters for PERs, given that the skills and resources available to security institutions often do not match the strategies those institutions are pursuing, claim to pursue, or would like to pursue.

Another challenge for the PER team will be to trace the link between the particular public safety/law and order strategy, the resources assigned to it, and the attributed results. The challenge is that "public safety," like public health or public education, is contingent upon many agencies, institutions, and exogenous entities that lie outside the security sector, such as schools, municipal authorities, and religious and community-based organizations. Thus many of the efforts by cities around the world to increase safety and security do not require the participation of agencies in the security sector (for example, reshaping of public spaces, increasing natural levels of surveillance, or provision of lighting). In some cases, these initiatives might require the deployment of resources by the police—for increased foot patrols, for example, or to staff CCTV (closed-circuit television) control rooms; in other cases, it is institutions and officials in the security sector who identify the need for these strategies—such as the development of drug rehabilitation programs in high-drug-use communities. But it is often agencies that are not considered part of the security sector whose activities are most central to the implementation and effectiveness of these strategies.[9]

Once the PER team has understood the mix of policy options chosen by a country to deliver public safety, the next step is to determine what approaches to policing are being employed within this broader strategy. In recent years, policing approaches have evolved into more specialized types, which are premised upon different relationships between police services and communities, as well as different paths to providing services as effectively, efficiently, and legitimately as possible. Importantly, these approaches are not mutually exclusive, and police agencies can use all or some of them in response to different (or changing) circumstances.

- *Professional policing.* This paradigm was dominant for a long time in much of the developed world. Professional policing emerged in the United States in the late 19th and early 20th centuries, when corrupt local governments were reorganized and reformed.[10]

Under this model, the primary (and even exclusive) goal of the police is to reduce crime by arresting (and/or threatening to arrest) those who break the law. Police officers patrol the streets (to deter or detect crime), respond to calls for service, and investigate crimes that have been committed. The police in this model are thought of primarily in relation to their role in the criminal justice system, and in particular as instigators of processes that could culminate in some form of sanction for an offender.

- *Community policing.* Community policing has evolved in reaction to professional policing and specifically the sense that the professional model is not able to deliver improved safety. The community policing model emphasizes the role of the police in building or reproducing social capital through strong relationships with the communities in which they serve.

- *Problem-solving policing.* In contrast to professional and community policing, problem-solving policing casts the police less as gatekeepers to the criminal justice system or architects of social capital, and more as pragmatists tasked with solving concrete problems that arise in communities and reduce public safety. Police in this model solve problems directly or by mobilizing the efforts of other parties, such as local government and community organizations.[11] Problem-solving policing is largely a response to the fact that the demand upon the police derive from a minority of addresses and citizens. The idea is that the dedicated application of police resources to these areas could reduce crime substantially.

- *Zero-tolerance policing.* Zero-tolerance policing is premised on the idea that crime is a function of social disorganization and that even the most minor manifestation of social disorder—e.g., a broken window or an unpainted fence—invites further decay. Within this framework, the police respond to even the most minor infraction and to technically legal acts of "incivility"—which are seen as forms of disorder[12]—in order to prevent the emergence of more serious problems.

- *Intelligence-led policing.* This approach, which has grown considerably in recent decades, gathers, collates, and analyzes information in order to prevent crime or to identify offenders. It tends to rely heavily on covert police activities, and the desirability of using these techniques in democracies has occasioned much debate. The rise of this approach is associated with advances in technology that facilitate improved surveillance; a growing perception that reactive policing is ineffective (especially against some kinds of threats, such as organized crime and terrorism); and increased legal constraints that make confessions and interviews less useful in court.[13]

Police and Policing: Definitions and Functions

Police and Policing Defined

The next task is to demarcate the institutional scope of the analysis. Will the focus be on "police," or on "policing" services? The distinction here is between a narrow set of functions performed by one or more public sector agencies, and the wider understanding of "policing" as a social function performed by many entities that do not necessarily possess any formal role in the regulation of social life.[14] In spite of expectations to the contrary, increasing socioeconomic development has not always led to an increase in formal responses to insecurity. Indeed, many developing societies continue to respond to crime and insecurity with very strong informal, nonstate systems,[15] such as the burgeoning private security companies in many parts of the world.[16]

Equally, in developed, middle-income, or low-income countries, the PER team may find a variety of institutions undertaking "policing" functions. This is particularly likely in FCS, where institutions that are not funded through public revenues may also be involved in the delivery of public security. Such formal or informal institutions include (i) traditional, nonstatutory police and courts whose operations might not be codified in law, and which are not funded through the tax system; (ii) militias and paramilitary groups; (iii) private security companies (see box 4.2); and (iv) community responses to criminality that are not institutionalized.

Furthermore, while the activities of these entities may complement those of public institutions and may therefore improve the overall security situation, in some cases these entities compete with (or are even in conflict with) public institutions. The PER team may need to consider the following issues:

- The clarity of jurisdictional boundaries between various entities and the definition of their roles, including in relation to command and control over non-national forces
- The extent to which these nonstate entities exist because of failures (real or perceived) of the public bodies or the lack of social and political legitimacy of those bodies
- The extent to which their operational ethos accords with the legal restrictions placed on the conduct of statutory institutions (e.g., in relation to the use of force and the securing of due process rights for suspects and accused persons).

Even if customary institutions are not present, police functions may be undertaken by other security actors; because key elements of security are interrelated, all agencies in the sector may be involved in joint responses to security threats. Thus the military may be deployed to assist the police in some operations that do not address external threats, and the police may be seen as assisting in the management of the country's borders—a task often assigned to the military or to specialized border agencies—when they identify and arrest undocumented immigrants.

Box 4.2   How Big Is the Private Security Industry?

The private security sector is a growing business, with a global annual turnaround of $100 billion to $165 billion per year.[a] Obtaining a detailed analysis is extremely difficult; data generally exist only for "contractual" private security industry personnel (especially if these need to be registered, trained, and accredited) rather than for "proprietary" personnel (e.g., those guarding private property). Even within these constraints, it is clear that the private security industry is substantial.

In 2004, the member states of the European Union employed nearly 1.3 million police officers and nearly 1.1 million private security guards, at a ratio of nearly 1 to 0.9 (see figure B4.2.1). The ratio of private security officers to police officers varies considerably across countries, however. Private security personnel in Latin America outnumber police officers by a ratio of 1.8 to 1. In Brazil and Mexico there are estimated to be some 470,000 and 450,000 private security personnel, respectively.

Figure B4.2.1   Ratio of Private Security Officers to Police Officers, European Union Members (Except Italy), 2004

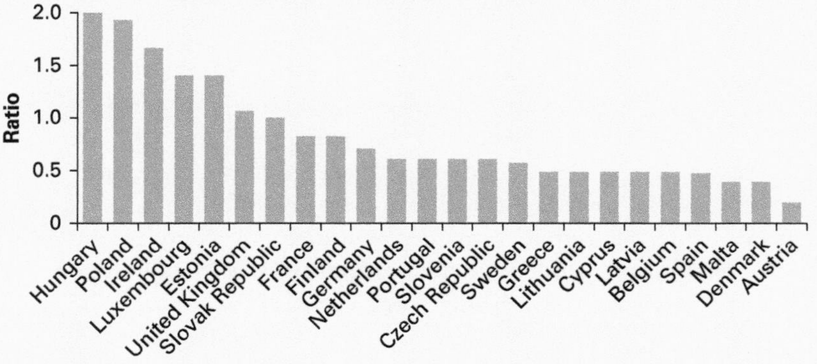

Source: Morre 2004.

a. Small Arms Survey 2011.

It will thus be essential for the PER team to map formal and informal security actors with policing functions (further explained below) in order to understand their organizational structure. This step is a precursor to financial, expenditure, and performance analysis.

Police Functions

The police play multiple roles in the security sector and outside of it. Formally, they can be defined as a cadre of public officials who are charged in conjunction with other criminal justice actors (such as courts and prosecutors) with enforcing some (but not all) domestic law. Such enforcement includes the following:

- Crimes against the person (assaults, rapes, and murders) and crimes against property (theft, fraud, robbery), as well as some crimes against the state (treason, terrorism, and sedition)
- A broader set of responsibilities related to maintenance of public order, controlling large crowds, and responding to emergencies

- A category of incidents that Bittner calls "something-ought-not-to-be-happening-and-about-which-something-ought-to-be-done-now!" situations[17]—that is, circumstances where it is not clear that a crime has been committed or a law broken, but where intervention, mediation, or some other response is needed.

The unique characteristic of these functions is that they are accompanied by a range of statutory powers that allow the police to undertake their work. Police are given the power to use force in the exercise of their functions, and hence hold related powers that significantly intrude on the rights of individuals, including the power to (i) stop pedestrians and motorists and to search them and their vehicles, (ii) search premises, (iii) intercept communications, (iv) arrest and detain individuals suspected of breaking the law, and (v) impose spot fines.

The power to use force, which is enjoyed only by police officers (as opposed to financial regulators, health and safety inspectors, and others who enforce aspects of a society's laws), is sometimes described as the *defining power of the police*, the power that distinguishes them from all other officials. This power is usually regulated by law, although standards and constraints governing the use of force vary considerably between jurisdictions. Such distinctions can play themselves out at the level of standard police equipment: British police officers, for example, are generally unarmed, while in some countries police have access to weapons more usually associated with the military. Overseeing police officers' use of force, and holding them accountable for excesses, is a key requirement for accountable policing, though it is often difficult to effect.

Framed this way, policing might be understood as a state's capacity to respond to the frictions of everyday life, some of which involve criminal acts, but many of which do not (or are not known to at the time that the police are called). More precisely, police work can be divided into the following activities and capabilities, not all of which will be present in all police forces, but any of which may appear in any given force:

- *Police patrols.* Patrol work is often justified by the belief that officers on patrol prevent crime; but patrolling also involves the response of police to incidents, whether criminal or not. Patrolling is supported by *rapid response* services that are usually centralized and that can be deployed following calls for service from members of the public. A subcategory of rapid response services that is often established separately is *highway patrol* units.
- *Public order management.* Police manage crowds and ensure that the public peace is maintained. Because large gatherings are not all alike—they range from riots to sports events, from political rallies to religious festivals—they may require very different sets of skills, tactics, and equipment. The ability to manage crowds is a specialized activity, and trained units may exist for these operations. In addition to managing crowds, police often have the capacity to reduce the risk of politically motivated violence, including potential attacks on VIPs

and acts of terrorism, and they may deploy specialist bomb squads and SWAT teams to deal with these low-frequency threats to public order.

- *Investigative services.* Identification and prosecution of offenders is a universal function of the police. Such a task may be organized differently from one force to another, but usually involves some units that investigate a broad range of common, high-volume crimes, along with units dedicated to more complex, more serious, or less frequent crime (such as computer crime, political crime, high-level corruption, money laundering, and commercial crime). Some forms of criminality require more proactive investigative work—undercover operations, buy-busts and infiltration operations, and long-term surveillance. These operations require both specialized skills and heightened secrecy and security. In addition to the investigating officers themselves, police forces often provide a range of complementary services to assist investigators, such as forensic laboratories, DNA and fingerprint databases, and surveillance operations.

- *Other specialized services.* Some police agencies retain additional capacities for a range of activities including the ceremonial (police bands, protocol officers, public relations), strategic management and analysis, community outreach, border policing, and the protection of key installations. The necessity for these depends on strategic priorities and the distribution of responsibility across agencies in the security sector.

The distribution of police functions is summarized in figure 4.2.

Figure 4.2　Distribution of Police Functions and Operations

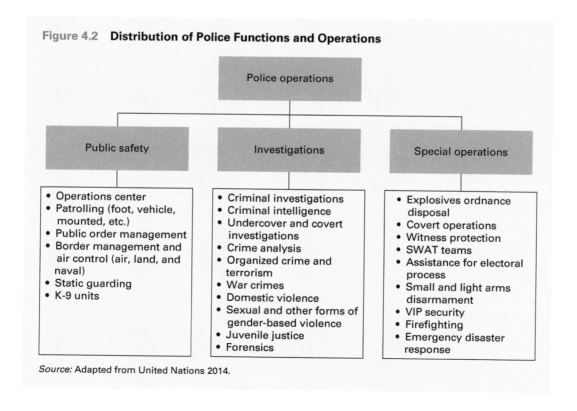

Source: Adapted from United Nations 2014.

The Diversity of Police Structures

Countries differ considerably in how they structure the police and allocate police functions to different levels of government. The most extreme example of decentralization can be found in the United States, where local governments at city and county levels all have police agencies of varying size and jurisdictional authority. These agencies are funded by and accountable to local governments, though they may also receive funds from other levels of government, and there are many federal and state programs intended to subsidize policing at the local level. Some of these simply fund increased staffing, while others offer funding conditional on its being used in pursuit of certain goals.

Even in the United States, however, state and federal police agencies (such as the Federal Bureau of Investigation, FBI) play a role in responding to some kinds of crime (defined either by its seriousness or by its crossing of jurisdictional boundaries). In addition to the thousands of police agencies whose jurisdictions are spatially defined, numerous police agencies exist with more specific functions such as border control, the policing of public transport, or the policing of strategic institutions (such as ports and railways). This classification of police agencies by function is not only found in the United States, it can also include those focused on tax offenses, on political activity and/or threats against the state. By contrast, many FCS countries have a centralized police force, and one police agency performs tasks at the national, state, and local levels. For middle-income countries like Argentina, Brazil, Colombia, and Mexico, the underlying trend is to proliferate police forces.

In more centralized states, policing tends to be a more centralized function, with significant variation apparent in structure and financing. In the United Kingdom, for example, policing is decentralized to 45 territorial police forces that are responsible for the bulk of policing activity, but also includes a number of national police agencies, such as the British Transport Police and the Serious Fraud Office. Though paid for largely through a grant from the Home Office (with some local contribution), the territorial forces were until recently accountable to respective police authorities composed of locally elected officials, magistrates, and senior police officials. Since 2012, the territorial forces have been accountable to a locally elected Police and Crime Commissioner, though almost all funding is still received from central government.

In some countries, such as Mexico and the United States, local governments, especially cities, retain a substantial amount of control over policing (and, in some cases, other components of the justice system). In other countries—Ireland, Nigeria, and South Africa, for example—all policing services are delivered by a single national force (although in South Africa's case, traffic policing is the responsibility of local authorities in the cities and of provincial governments elsewhere). In yet other countries—many of them in Latin America—state and provincial governments play the primary role in delivering policing. Finally, in countries like France and Spain, the degree of decentralization varies by the nature of the

Table 4.2   Classification of Police Structures, with Sample Countries

Number of operating forces	Dispersal of command within forces	
	Centralized	Decentralized
Single	Ireland, Israel, Nigeria, Poland, Saudi Arabia	Japan
Multiple, coordinated	France, England and Wales	Austria, Canada, Germany, India, Italy, Spain, United States
Multiple, uncoordinated	Belgium, Switzerland	Mexico

municipality concerned: local governments in urban areas are responsible for policing, but a national police force delivers services in rural areas where communities may be too small to achieve the fiscal and institutional mass required for efficient delivery of services.

One way to classify police structures is by the number of forces (whether one or many) operating and by the dispersal of command (whether centralized or decentralized).[18] Among those countries with multiple forces, the PER team must further distinguish whether the operations of different police forces are aligned with one another or not. The result is a six-way division of approaches, as shown in table 4.2.

Even where the authority to provide policing services vests in levels of government other than the local, there may be separate local forces that provide limited (and sometimes more or less informal) patrol, prevention, and point-duty services. In some countries, these services are also delivered by more informal institutions on the basis of customary laws and tradition. Such police forces are often unarmed, and vary greatly in terms of their structure and role.

An important distinction between police forces relates to the extent to which they might be described as paramilitary in character. All police agencies exhibit some paramilitary characteristics in that they tend to be hierarchical, rank-based institutions with clear lines of command and control. But the extent to which they rely on military-style operational strategies, tactics, equipment, and weaponry varies considerably. As a general rule, developing countries are more likely to deploy concentrated groups of police officers, often in military formation and equipped with high-caliber weapons, than are developed countries (where police officers work alone or in small groups, often in civilian clothes and armed with much lighter weapons).

One of the underlying reasons for this trend is that in many developing countries, the police forces were created out of the military. Both in El Salvador and Guatemala, for example, the National Police Force was created after peace accords were signed. Similarly, the recently formed South Sudan National Police Service mixes sworn police officers and former combatants, and it still employs military strategies for policing.

The key drivers for paramilitary-style police forces relate to the nature of the disorder and security challenges in different societies, the skill and training of individual police officers (or lack thereof), and the political necessity of employing a large group of former combatants.

A final element in the organization of police services is their link to the broader criminal justice system. The justice system—covering the investigation and prosecution of crime, the adjudicating of criminal cases, and the punishment and/or rehabilitation of offenders—can be pictured as a production line, one formulating a systemwide strategy that can lead to improved effectiveness and efficiency in policing. This was the approach taken by the World Bank in El Salvador, detailed in box 4.3. The chapter

Box 4.3   Police and Criminal Justice Institutions in El Salvador

In June 2012, the World Bank completed a Public Expenditure Review of the security and justice sector in El Salvador. This was the first comprehensive assessment of the sector's resource allocation, efficiency, and effectiveness. The analysis divided the security and justice institutions according to the main tasks they fulfill, and sought to evaluate the allocation of inputs (resources), outputs (specific services), and outcomes (citizen security). In El Salvador, several state institutions that are located under different branches of government execute five main tasks: (i) crime and violence prevention; (ii) police patrolling; (iii) crime investigation and formal indictment; (iv) presentation to court and judicial resolution; and (v) sentencing, supervision, imprisonment, and rehabilitation (see figure B4.3.1).

Figure B4.3.1   Security and Justice Sectors: Tasks and Institutions

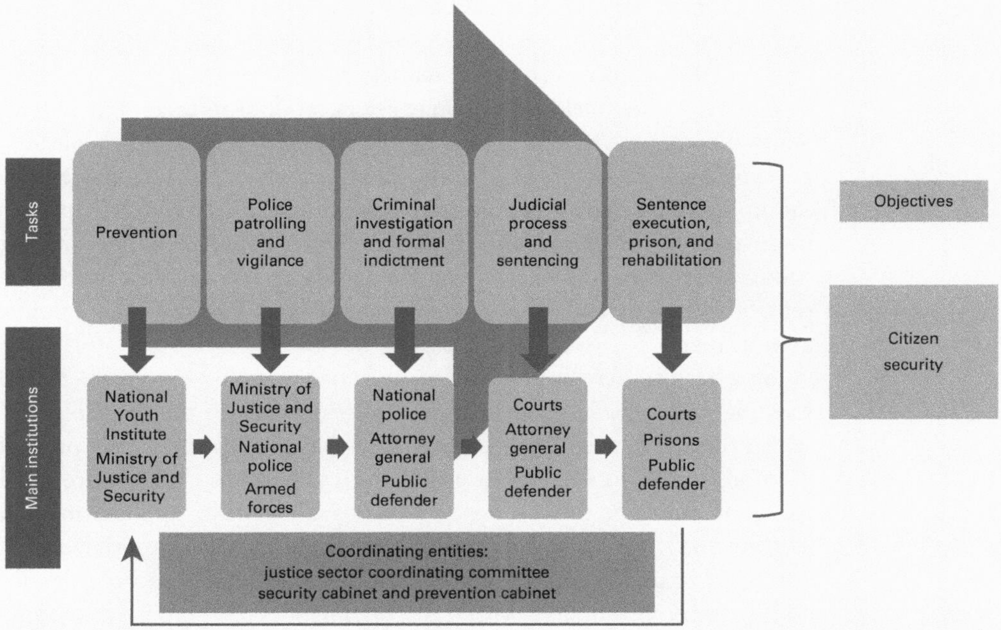

Source: World Bank 2012.

on conducting PERs in the criminal justice system addresses these interconnections in greater depth.

Management and Oversight

Management and oversight are key aspects of policing for several reasons: (i) policing requires effective command and control, (ii) it is unique in its statutory power to use force, and (iii) policing is expensive.

Police managers aim to allocate resources so that the organization achieves its goals. The goals of policing are complex, however, and the link between police activity and some of its goals—notably the prevention of crime—is ambiguous. Thus evaluating the quality of police management is difficult. Nevertheless, police forces need to be accountable for their actions:

> Accountability carries two basic connotations: *answerability*, the obligation of public officials to inform about and to explain what they are doing; and *enforcement*, the capacity of accounting agencies to impose sanctions on power holders who have violated their public duties. This two-dimensional structure of meaning makes the concept a broad and inclusive one that, within its wide and loose boundaries, embraces (or at least overlaps with) lots of other terms—surveillance, monitoring, oversight, control, checks, restraint, public exposure, punishment—that we may employ to describe efforts to ensure that the exercise of power is a ruled-guided enterprise.[19]

Whatever the difficulties entailed in assessment, the performance of police organizations depends heavily on the quality of police leadership and management. As in many organizations, particularly militarized and uniformed organizations, police management is drawn almost exclusively from career personnel (though there are exceptions to this rule). There are many advantages to this trend: familiarity with the complex nature of policing and police organizations, the peculiar organizational ethos of the police, and experience in applying the law as it relates to policing. Importantly, police organizations are often suspicious of outsiders brought into their ranks, and will frequently resist outsiders' attempts to reform them (particularly if the new manager is perceived to be a political appointment).[20]

As a result, changing police organizations can be extremely difficult. Existing police leaders are imbued with the ethos of the organization in which they have spent their careers, and they are invested in its practices. They also tend to have been appointed by managers who share similar views of policing; these existing leaders will in turn appoint managers beneath them who also reflect and perpetuate the same approaches. The effect is to entrench and reproduce existing strategic approaches to policing and managerial practices within the organization. Where policing is relatively well managed (and has been for a time), this creates a virtuous, self-reinforcing cycle; where policing is poorly managed, the opposite can occur.

Overseeing a Wide Dispersion of Activity

A key challenge faced by managers of police organizations is the difficulty of supervising police officers' activities. Police officers perform many tasks (among them patrolling the streets, engaging with members of the public, attempting to halt crimes in progress, attending crime scenes, interviewing witnesses, searching for suspects, serving summonses), and their most important tasks are fulfilled outside of the police station, usually by a single officer or by officers working in small groups. Typically these officers also happen to be the lowest ranking, least experienced, least trained, and lowest paid. Typically, too, they are engaging with people—victims, witnesses, suspects—who know very little about the legal regime governing policing, or about what the police are expected to do, what they are legally empowered to do, and what they are forbidden to do. For the most part, in other words, the performance of policing's most important functions is among the hardest for police managers (and anyone else) to observe directly. It is also difficult for these actions to be assessed retroactively because they involve engagement with people who are not in a position to demand that police officers act (or refrain from acting) in particular ways. In addition, police officers generally have very wide discretion about how to act in any given situation. This is one of the key characteristics of policing as a public service.[21]

To an extent, the challenge of supervising officers depends on the type and the size of the police agency. Larger organizations will have a more decentralized structure, as well as more task differentiation among police personnel. In small police organizations, managers may even participate actively in police beats and general everyday functions, in addition to management. More task differentiation in large police organizations is likely to add more bureaucracy in order to increase control.

Supply and Demand for Policing Services

A defining characteristic of policing is the profound mismatch between the volume of incidents that the police could potentially provide services for and the more limited set of resources available. Because policing is used to respond to very diverse situations, demand for policing services can far outstrip the supply of resources. As a result, most police services apply implicit and explicit rules to prioritize what services to provide, to whom, and in what circumstances. This approach can be controversial because demand is often "managed" by providing limited (or no) services to some members of the public or in response to some kinds of crime.

Police Malpractice

As policing is so difficult to supervise, police organizations run the risk of a variety of malpractices. These include denial of service, abuse of the use of force, torture, corruption, and poor or reluctant service delivery. Preventing these practices (or reducing their number) is a complex task requiring investments in training (for police officers and managers alike), interventions into organizational culture, and the building of an ethos of professionalism and service delivery. For example, in light of the high levels of corruption among U.S. police agencies in the 1980s, the police adopted a "professional" model, in which managerial efficiency and more controls of police personnel became the norm.

Given the risk of abuse, there should be channels through which complaints can be lodged, investigated, and acted upon. Such channels are not always effective, however: the very people who might be victimized by the police—those who are vulnerable because of poverty or lack of education—are often unable to claim or enforce their rights. In addition, their own conduct may be criminal, or they may belong to marginalized groups that are in conflict with the law or the wider community, such as prostitutes, undocumented migrants, ethnic/religious minorities, or members of local gangs.

Levels of abuse vary greatly across police organizations. In U.S. policing in the early decades of the 20th century, for example, the major political movement of the time, Progressivism, drove a cleanup of government (especially local government), and professionalized and depoliticized policing, particularly in relation to appointments and promotions.[22] This also appears to have taken place during the 1970s and 1980s in Hong Kong, where the police service was once famously corrupt: determined leaders reconfigured organizational rules and norms, in part through legislative innovations that created "reverse onus" provisions in the law (police officers with unexplained wealth were presumed by the law to be corrupt, though this presumption could be rebutted in court).[23] In New York, randomly selected police officers were subjected to a range of integrity tests and lifestyle audits to assess whether they might either be engaged in suspicious activities or have access to unexplained income.[24] Independent internal units responsible for investigating allegations of corruption are widely regarded as essential to managing risks.

Oversight Measures

Ensuring that a police organization delivers on its core mandates while minimizing the abuses that emerge is the essential challenge of police managers and the political authorities to whom they report. Efforts to meet this challenge have taken diverse approaches to structuring lines of authority, accountability, and oversight. Among the critical variables are the following:

- The degree to which (elected) civilians oversee police management, and the extent and range of their powers (as well as the statutory limitations thereof)
- The nature, extent, powers, and degree of independence of agencies tasked with investigating complaints of police abuse of authority, abuse of force, and corruption
- The degree to which policing is centralized or decentralized across different levels of government

- The role, if any, played by local communities in the management or oversight of policing in the stations that serve them
- The degree to which appointments in the police, especially of top leadership, are made by political officeholders, and the processes and procedures governing the replacement of police leadership.

These variables create a vast matrix of possible organizational configurations for the management of the police organization, and there are sound arguments for and against any particular configuration. In practice, a great many configurations can likely be made to work in some circumstances, while for a few configurations, almost no set of institutions (or institutional reforms) will significantly improve the quality and accountability of policing in the short term.[25] It is, however, important to recognize the benefits and difficulties associated with the various models, all of which can be effective or ineffective depending largely on the degree of political will, the degree of independence of mind and professionalism in the police and the associated agencies themselves, and, importantly, aspects of police organizational culture and the norms these create for police conduct and performance.

Civilian management of the police is common in both democracies and authoritarian societies, but has quite different connotations in each. Thus it is common for democratically elected governments to require that the policing agencies under their control report to civilians—but the same is true in authoritarian states. A key difference between the two is that democratic states are able to ensure that this approach does not politicize policing or influence the subsequent deployment of police resources in ways that violate democratic norms. More democratic systems of policing can be distinguished from less democratic systems by the degree to which the police regard themselves as accountable to the requirements of the law rather than the expectations of politicians. In reality, however, police in even the most well-established democracies are probably not able to resist every demand placed on them by political leaders. Nor is this resistance always desirable. Once again, established norms will differ across societies, even those at similar levels of development and with apparently similar systems of government. Norms relating to the degree to which the use of police resources and powers are politicized may also change over time. Efforts are underway in FCS to standardize norms and measures of progress (see box 4.4).

Complaint mechanisms in the police are tasked with ensuring that officers do not abuse the powers that they are assigned by law, and that allegations of abuse are investigated. A key consideration here is the degree to which the complaint mechanism is independent of the police; the public suspicion is widespread—and often justified—that police officers will not rigorously investigate their colleagues. While the independence of the complaint mechanism is clearly important, however, it may discourage police management from seeing itself as responsible for the conduct of officers.

Box 4.4   The g7+ Indicators for the Security Sector in Fragile States

Under the g7+ New Deal process, which aims to strengthen country ownership and increase the effectiveness of aid, the g7+ countries[a] have produced a number of indicators to facilitate more rigorous monitoring of security sector accountability. Particularly for actors working with embryonic policing services, these indicators help to support oversight and management capacity. Indicators include the following:

1. Police capacity and accountability:
   * The ratio of prosecutions of police misconduct to the total number of cases taken to an independent commission
   * The capacity to monitor, investigate, and prosecute police misconduct
2. Police performance and responsiveness:
   * The level of public confidence in police
   * Average response times
   * Perceptions of corruption.

Source: International Alert 2013.
a. The g7+ countries are Afghanistan, Burundi, Central African Republic, Chad, the Comoros, the Democratic Republic of Congo, Côte d'Ivoire, Guinea, Guinea-Bissau, Haiti, Liberia, Papua New Guinea, São Tomé and Príncipe, Sierra Leone, the Solomon Islands, Somalia, South Sudan, Togo, and the Republic of Yemen.

(This is a particular problem when complaint mechanisms are weak, owing either to a lack of capacity, a lack of political support, or poor resourcing.) Thus a critical variable in determining the efficacy of complaint mechanisms is the degree to which the commanding officers of the personnel accused of misconduct are held accountable for the actions and inactions of their subordinates and/or for the decision to investigate and discipline them.

Decentralization and Policing

The decentralization of policing is widely believed to increase its responsiveness to local conditions. Precisely how decentralization is effected depends heavily on the country's basic structures of governance, with more centralized states generally having more centralized police forces (see table 4.2). One important concern, however, is that decentralization can result in significant differences in the volume or quality of policing services provided across the country. These differences may also exist in more centralized agencies, but equalizing service delivery in centralized structures is somewhat easier than in decentralized ones.

Local community involvement is generally helpful for ensuring the alignment of police services with the expectations of the community. Structures that facilitate such involvement can also increase local police legitimacy and ensure that processes of community outreach and feedback help the police identify challenges in police-community relations. A critical challenge, however, is to ensure that no voices in the community are overrepresented at the expense of others, that the construction of local priorities reflects the whole community's needs, and that community consultation is reasonably democratic and representative. Meeting this challenge is particularly important when communities are fractured.

The appointment of senior police commanders is one of the main ways in which governments assert control over the police force and help shape its priorities and strategic approach. In this regard, the critical questions relate to the degree to which the leadership of a police force is politicized and the effects that this might have on the conduct of the police; this variable depends as much on the state of the organization that an appointee inherits as on any more universal considerations or the individual's particular qualities and skills.

Managing Police Corruption

For police forces, the challenge of connecting the right skills to the right strategies is exacerbated by corruption. In many countries, police corruption is one of the most serious challenges facing managers and reformers. As the police are among the most visible representatives of the state, high levels of police corruption affect popular perceptions about the quality of governance (to say nothing of the other types of harm they may do). Some likely causes of police corruption are listed in box 4.5.

Police corruption comes in many forms. One distinction—made originally by the Knapp Commission, which investigated corruption in the

---

Box 4.5 The Causes of Police Corruption

Much has been written about the causes of police corruption, with a useful summary provided by Tim Newburn. In identifying causes of corruption, Newburn distinguishes between constant and variable factors. The constant factors are these:

- Police work allows wide *discretion*, which can easily be misused.
- Police work has *low managerial visibility* and *low public visibility*—that is, much of it is done outside the view of either management or the public.
- The culture of policing is one of *peer group secrecy* and *managerial secrecy*—police officers and those who manage them feel a high degree of internal solidarity.
- Police work entails *status problems* to the extent that officers are poorly paid.
- Police work, by its nature, requires *association with lawbreakers/contact with temptation*.

The variable factors are these:

- Specific aspects of the *community structure* and the *organizational structure*—e.g., the political ethos of the former, the levels of bureaucracy in the latter—can contribute to corruption.
- Police officers may be tempted by *legal opportunities for corruption* (in their contact with prostitution, gambling, and other crimes of vice, or in their dealing with licensing, fines, and other regulations).
- The efficacy of *corruption controls* and countermeasures influences the likelihood of corrupt activity, as does the *social organization of corruption*—that is, whether corruption is ongoing or a one-time event.
- The inevitable association with lawbreakers and contact with temptation may produce *moral cynicism* among the police.

Source: Newburn 1999.

New York Police Department (NYPD) starting in 1970[26]—is between "grass eaters" and "meat eaters," that is, between police officers who take bribes when they are offered or engage in other petty corrupt acts, and the police officers who more actively extort money on a larger scale. Knapp found that "grass eating" was common, even pervasive, and was learned on the job from peers, who regarded with suspicion those who resisted participating in the practice. "Meat eaters" actively sought out opportunities to profit from their occupation, though they sometimes rationalized what they did as a means of punishing the guilty.

In contrast to an individual act of criminality that happens to be committed by someone employed by the police, police corruption involves the abuse of the officer's position.[27] There are numerous ways in which police officers can abuse their positions, with one much-cited typology[28] listing nine forms of corruption:

1. *Corruption of authority:* receipt of some material gain by virtue of holding a position as a police officer, without violating the law per se (e.g., free drinks, meals, services)
2. *Kickbacks:* receipt of goods, services, or money for referring business to particular individuals or companies
3. *Opportunistic theft:* stealing from arrestees, traffic accident victims, crime victims, and the dead
4. *Shakedowns:* acceptance of a bribe for agreeing to ignore a criminal violation (e.g., not making an arrest, filing a complaint, or impounding property)
5. *Protection of illegal activities:* protection of those engaged in illegal activities (prostitution, drugs, pornography) so that the business can continue operating
6. *The fix:* undermining of criminal investigations or proceedings (e.g., by "losing" traffic tickets)
7. *Direct criminal activities:* commission of a crime against person or property for personal gain
8. *Internal payoffs:* purchase, barter, or sale of prerogatives available to police officers (holidays, shift allocations, promotion)
9. *Flaking or padding:* planting of or adding to evidence.

An important aspect of the corruption problem in some agencies is the expectation among senior police officers that more junior colleagues will filter some of the rents they extract up the chain of command. For obvious reasons, managing corruption is considerably more difficult when senior officers are implicated in this manner.

The extent of police corruption is a critical variable in determining public confidence in the police, and corruption, as opposed to weak performance along other dimensions, is often the catalyst for demands for reform in policing. There is, in addition, a strong relationship between the extent of corruption in a police organization and its ability to deliver on its core mandates. Causality between high levels of corruption and low levels of performance flows in both directions, suggesting that anticorruption strategies may help to improve police performance. Apart from anything else, rooting out corruption would increase police legitimacy and credibility, facilitating increased cooperation from the public. It should be noted that although corruption and poor performance may drive police organizations to adapt or modify their organizational structure, pressure "sovereigns" such as the legal system, politics, and demographics may also drive structural adaptations.

Police organizations need to deploy a range of strategies to guard against the emergence of significant levels of corruption and, equally important, to roll back corruption once it has become prevalent. Such strategies might involve recruitment and minimum qualifications of new members, level (and, in some cases, regularity) of pay, the creation of anticorruption hotlines to facilitate public cooperation, the creation (and resourcing) of anticorruption investigative units, the deployment of proactive investigative strategies (e.g., attempts to entrap suspect officers), the encouragement of whistle-blowing, and the replacement of suspect managers.

It is also important to be aware of the perception of corruption. The Global Corruption Barometer produced by Transparency International (2013) asked about the extent of corruption in eight different state institutions. Respondents in 36 countries ranked the police as the most corrupt (see map 4.1). Only political parties were identified more often. As a general

Map 4.1   Perception of Police Corruption, 2013

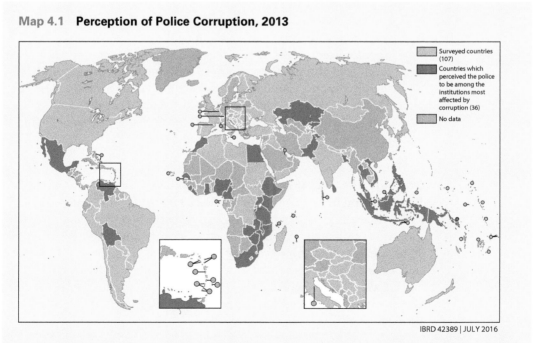

IBRD 42389 | JULY 2016

Source: Transparency International 2013. © 2016 by Transparency International. Licensed under CC-BY-ND 4.0.

rule, the police were rated most corrupt in societies in which levels of overall corruption were perceived to be high.

Analysis of Policing and the Budget Cycle

Once the PER team has an overview of the security and public order context and the institutional arrangements of policing services, the next step is to examine the nexus with the government budget cycle. Specifically, the team needs to understand the key expenditure policy questions and systems as well as the processes in place for managing public finances.[29] This part of the analysis is in some respects no different from what it would be for other sectors. But there are some signature differences in policing:

- *High personnel expenditures.* It is not uncommon to see expenditures on police personnel ranging between 70 and 90 percent of the total police budget. The critical questions facing policy makers concern how and where to deploy personnel, and what services those personnel are expected to deliver. The most significant budget constraint on policy makers and operational commanders is the number of person-hours of police officers available for deployment, qualified by the available profile of skills and equipment.
- *Political, security, and corruption risks.* Police personnel are widely distributed across areas in which banking infrastructure may be absent or poorly developed. Under these circumstances, the need to pay officers creates the potential for administrative failure and corruption. At worst, particularly in fragile settings, political-security risks may arise if personnel are not paid.
- *Standardized assets.* Much of the spending on physical assets (buildings and other installations), equipment (vehicles, uniforms, light weaponry, and IT infrastructure), and consumables (fuel, electricity, food, paper) is devoted to standardized commodities that present few intrinsic difficulties for sound public financial management.

Budget Preparation
Strategy and Sector-Based Budgeting
During the preparation phase of the budget cycle, the PER team examining police expenditures should determine whether the budget request of the line ministry is submitted against an existing security and justice strategy that states clear sectoral objectives for public safety. The strategy should be underpinned by an assessment of the main threats to public safety, which should also show whether these threats justify the level of recurrent and capital expenditures requested by police services. The PER team could look for the following:

- *Clear articulation of country objectives for public safety and security.* The objectives should be reflected in both the national and sector strategy, and should be internally consistent. They should be framed in clear language, rather than set out as broad aspirations.

- *Alignment of objectives across the sector.* Because the functions of the police service form part of a wider chain of criminal justice services (including those provided by prosecutors, judicial officers, prisons, and probation services), aligning the objectives and strategies of the other key institutions can create gains in efficiency and effectiveness. Importantly, budget allocations to related agencies may need to be aligned so that growth in upstream departments' allocations is matched by growth in the capacity of downstream agencies, whose workflows will be affected. The team should also consider what the police components of the national or sector strategy are, whether they can easily be translated into public spending plans, and what strategic choices (trade-offs) the government has made to achieve its objectives.

- *The role of government in providing citizen security and public order.* Particularly in FCS, but in many other developing countries as well, significant justice/policing services are provided by non-statutory institutions (which can range from traditional institutions of authority to foreign-owned private security and military companies), whose functions may have both positive and negative implications for wider objectives of social policy (national reconciliation and integration, modernization, democratic consolidation, and conflict prevention). Policy makers may need to make hard choices about the degree to which they can and should seek to replace the services provided by these companies with those provided through the national budget.

Most important, the team should determine the coherence of the strategy and the institutional arrangements that exist for its implementation (see for example box 4.6). Toward this end, it should review any documented performance of the sector strategy over recent years. Several kinds of information will be required:

- The national security strategy or the strategy for justice and security (which covers policing)
- The threat assessment informing the strategy, which will shed light on the main cost drivers for security and justice services
- The results of a rapid analysis of strengths, weaknesses, opportunities, and threats, which can serve as a basis for assessing the alignment of public spending in cases where sector strategies do not exist
- The national resource envelope, and specifically whether there are sources of revenue for the police or justice sector that do not form part of the national budget (e.g., fines or the proceeds of asset forfeiture operations); how these sources of revenue are budgeted and accounted for; whether these processes are optimal; and how they shape the incentives of the relevant agencies.

Box 4.6   **The Role of Police in Liberia's National Security Strategy**

The World Bank and the United Nations jointly conducted a Public Expenditure Review (PER) of the security sector in Liberia in 2012 to pave the way for the drawdown of the United Nations Mission in Liberia (UNMIL). The first issue examined in the study was the country's security context and the main threats to peace and security. The PER found that Liberia's 2008 National Security Strategy understands national security holistically—that is, it accounts for a range of factors, including democracy, rule of law, human rights, political and economic stability, civic duty, regional dimensions, reconciliation, professionalism of security actors, and the environment. The PER identified the following internal threats: lack of respect for the rule of law, poverty, poor national resource management, deactivated ex-servicemen (17,000), ex-combatants (103,019 demobilized, and about 9,000 not helped by reintegration programs), corruption, robbery, drug abuse and trafficking, illegally held arms, land and property disputes, ethnic hatred and tensions, illiteracy, fire occurrences, overcrowded prisons, and HIV/AIDS.

As the UNMIL drawdown proceeds, the most critical security agencies are the Liberia National Police (LNP) and the border police (the Bureau for Immigration and Naturalization). The PER estimated that the number of LNP cadres—currently 4,200—should be increased incrementally to 8,000 in order to ensure adequate public security and prevent Liberia from sliding back into conflict.

Source: World Bank and United Nations 2012.

Analyzing Resource Allocation

Once budget requests have been submitted, line ministries negotiate resource allocations within the parameters of the ministry of finance ceilings or the spending projections of a medium-term expenditure framework. This phase provides an opportunity for policy makers to examine the sustainability of financing for public safety. The PER team will need to determine how much is spent on public safety by the government as a share of its total spending and as a percentage of GDP. Key questions are:

- Have these shares changed over time? How do these shares differ from those in other countries?
- What are the sources of funds for the police? How much is from the national budget? How much is from other sources? And what are the trends in this regard?
- How much is spent on police by donors as a share of government spending, and as a share of overall donor spending in the country?
- To what extent are these expenditures incorporated into the public budget and reflected in public spending numbers, and how much do private sector companies spend on security services?

An important issue for the PER to examine is the relationship between changes in spending on policing (and/or the number of police officers deployed) and the level of safety and security. The issues here are complex, and very careful analysis is required to assess claims about how changing levels of police capacity have affected (or will affect) public safety. This analysis requires attention to the following:

- *Functional and economic composition of spending.* The composition of public spending at the national level (from both government and donors) should be determined. The analysis could include decomposition by functional area, economic area, current versus capital expenditures, and personnel versus nonpersonnel spending. It should consider how spending compositions have changed over the last 5–10 years and make use of any available country comparisons. As will be discussed, levels of spending on policing are driven overwhelmingly by spending on personnel. Changes in spending levels (up or down) in absolute terms will generally be driven either by changes in the personnel establishment or by changes in the average level of remuneration (itself determined by changes in basic salaries and changes in rank structure) in the police. Analysts need to determine as far as possible what the sources of changes in spending may be, and whether any trends identified are sustainable. In this regard, analysts should be aware that reducing the numbers of police officers and/or members of security forces is often difficult; the public tends to oppose such moves because they perceive retrenched personnel as a threat, and officials see members of the security services as an important political constituency. Thus the PER team should flag spending trends that imply a necessity to reduce staffing to politically untenable or unsustainable levels.
- *National and subnational composition of spending on public safety and criminal justice.* Whereas in FCS the institutions providing policing services are often nascent, in middle-income countries the institutional architecture may be more established. At the same time, this architecture can vary considerably from national to subnational levels. For this reason, it may be important to examine (i) spending trends at all levels and (ii) the spatial allocation of expenditures across provinces, districts, and counties where police are deployed.
- *Sources of public spending.* In analyzing expenditures for the police, the PER team should look at the sources of finance along with associated funding and revenue-generating mechanisms, modalities, and processes. The team should determine the extent to which service fees and levies (e.g., customs fees, fines) are used (see box 4.7). Specifically, they should determine the amounts, trends, and relative importance of these revenues; the ministry of finance's rules for reporting, using, and transferring these revenues; the extent to which these rules are followed; and the effect of these revenues on the incentive structure of the relevant agencies. Raising of revenues is an especially critical issue for FCS, where security services have a privileged position in using force or threat of force to raise both formal and informal revenues (such as "taxation" via checkpoints and licensing).

Box 4.7   **Managing Police Revenues in Mali**

According to a public financial management study conducted by the World Bank, the Malian security forces (and particularly the police) formally collect two main types of revenue for the Treasury, totaling around $10 million per year: taxes due when identification cards and passports are prepared, and fines paid when violations are detected by controls. In practice, the management of these processes was found to be poor: the police had as many revenue accounts as police stations. All these revenues went into the general government budget, with the exception of fines from traffic violations, which are ring-fenced for the National Road Safety Agency. Unlike this agency, the security forces received no budget returns (in the form of contributions or recovered appropriations) from the revenues that they collect.

In theory, reports were to be prepared for all violations and, based on these reports, the security forces would collect fines for the Treasury. In practice, however, reports were frequently not prepared, and fines were not deposited into the relevant accounts—to the detriment of road users. The West African Economic and Monetary Union (WAEMU) and the Economic Community of West African States (ECOWAS) set up a watchdog agency (Observatoire des Pratiques Anormales, OPA) to monitor the scope of abuses and police irregularities along main roads in the subregion. In 2011, the OPA tested the system to see whether trucks that were in full compliance with regulations would nonetheless be fined. The results showed that illicit fines were second highest in Mali (after Côte d'Ivoire), with fines totaling more than $10 per 100 km.

Source: World Bank 2013a.

Once these analyses are performed, the PER team can use several techniques to determine the efficiency and effectiveness of sectoral allocations:

- *Estimation of how much public spending is enough.* This estimation involves determining whether the sectoral budget is consistent with the government's stated priority for public safety and citizen security and with the sector's role in the national security and development strategies. The PER team should also identify trends in spending that have implications for the medium- or long-term sustainability of the budget, and determine the trade-offs with other sectors entailed by increased spending.
- *Analysis of what has led to current levels of allocative efficiency.* The team should identify the factors that led to the current spending patterns and to recent changes at the national and subnational levels. It should also assess the strengths and weaknesses in budget preparation processes at the national and subnational levels, including (i) efforts to align the budget with the sector's objectives and the associated strategy for achieving the objectives, (ii) the mechanism for assessing trade-offs, and (iii) the level of transparency and participation. Where relevant, it should consider sector ceilings established through medium-term expenditure frameworks, annual plans, mid-year budget reviews, and audits. Too narrow a focus on policing is

not desirable; assessing the degree to which decisions about the police affect spending elsewhere in the justice sector (e.g., the population of prisoners awaiting trial) can spur improvements to sectorwide efficiencies. The team should seek to assess levels of interagency cooperation and alignment in budgetary processes. Allocative efficiency can be measured using a wide range of performance measurement methods.

- *Creation of a budgetary flowchart and timetable of the current system, with strengths and weaknesses.* The PER team could assess compliance with budgetary processes and the adequacy of institutional coordination among government agencies involved in providing policing services and criminal justice.

The Political Economy of Public Spending

A critical aspect of the PER process is to understand the political economy of public spending: pressures on the state to deliver public goods and services vary across countries, but high levels of crime and insecurity (and/or widespread fear of crime) can lead to very significant pressures to devote resources to the criminal justice sector. This is especially so for justice agencies considered integral to ensuring public safety (such as the police and, sometimes, the military).

As a general rule, the more unstable and fragile a society, the greater the pressure on (and incentive for) incumbent governments to devote significant proportions of public funds to the security sector. These pressures can come from the public, from incumbent political elites, and from members of the security forces themselves. Judging the merits of agencies' claims to need more resources is not easy; the team should be cautious about recommending large changes to allocations and/or to personnel and other policies that could affect the long-run sustainability of allocations to this sector or to competing sectors. The PER team should also be aware that pressure to align budget allocations to downstream agencies may be significantly lower than pressure to increase allocations to more visible components of the security sector.

External Financing

The PER team will need to assess off-budget spending and to examine (i) the factors that have kept donor finances from being integrated into the budget process, (ii) existing mechanisms for aligning donor support with the sector objectives and strategy, and (iii) the role of these mechanisms in reducing the distortionary effects of donor support to the subnational government relative to their subnational public budgets.

Allocation Trends

Among the main issues to be examined in any PER are trends both in annual allocations across spending categories and in the level of sector spending. Issues to consider include changes in functional, economic, and subnational allocations; changes to policies (e.g., personnel remuneration and promotion policies) that may have implications for budget sustainability; the degree to which these changes are aligned with changes in medium-term allocations across spending categories as reflected in the medium-term expenditure framework (if used); changes that seek to improve consistency, predictability, and alignment of the source of public financing; and changes to improve institutional coordination for more effective implementation of programs influencing public safety outcomes.

In addition, it is important to ascertain whether these trends in annual allocations have had the expected impacts on crime and security. As budgetary allocations to the security sector continue to increase, policy makers and operational managers need to know whether these changes have the expected impact on outputs and outcomes and whether the budget has been spent efficiently. This information would allow police managers to allocate their resources more efficiently—and thus combat crime more effectively.[30]

Budget Execution

In the budget execution phase of the budget cycle, resources are used to implement the policies incorporated in the budget. A well-formulated budget can be implemented poorly; but a badly formulated budget cannot be implemented well.

Three particularly important issues in budget execution are (i) the management of payables and arrears, (ii) budgeting and control of personnel costs, and (iii) managing the procurement process. In all these areas, misuse and mismanagement of public funds are possible, and strong management control is required. Rules are also needed to govern other important technical issues, such as the treatment of requests by spending agencies to transfer funds from one program or chapter of the budget to another during the fiscal year ("virement"), procedures for carrying unspent funds forward at the end of the year to the next fiscal year ("end-year flexibility"), and the use of supplementary budgets and contingency reserves.

While most developing countries continue to rely on cash-based manual systems for processing accounting transactions, many developed and middle-income countries rely on sophisticated accrual-based accounting systems. These systems make use of a computerized financial management information system (FMIS, see box 4.8) that not only processes accounting data but is linked through interfaces to financial systems for payroll, procurement, debt management, revenue collection, etc. The development of accrual-based accounting and reporting systems is supported by international bodies such as the International Public Sector Accounting Standards Board (IPSASB), which has prepared multiple accrual standards but only one cash-basis standard, and by the accrual-based financial reporting framework prepared by the International Monetary Fund.[31]

Analyses of budget execution focus on how to improve the technical efficiency of public spending in the sector (e.g., the efficiency of budget

---

Box 4.8   Financial Management Information Systems

A World Bank study of financial management information systems (FMIS) explains what these systems are and how they are used.

- An FMIS is "a set of computerized solutions that enable governments to plan, execute, and monitor the budget by assisting in the prioritization, execution, and reporting of expenditures, as well as the custodianship and reporting of revenues" (1).
- "A core FMIS generally refers to automating the financial operations of both the budget and treasury units. The system tracks financial events and records all transactions; summarizes information; supports reporting and policy decisions; and incorporates the elements of ICT [information and communication technology], personnel, procedures, controls, and data" (3).
- "An FMIS is usually built around a core treasury system that supports key budget execution functions, such as accounts payable and receivables, commitment and cash management, and the general ledger and financial reporting, combined with budget formulation (multi-year), debt management, and public investment management modules. The non-core systems sometimes linked with FMIS solutions are personnel management/payroll, revenue administrations (tax and customs), public procurement, inventory and property management, and performance management information" (3).
- "Financial control is not the only reason for developing FMIS. More importantly, FMIS solutions are used to support informed decisions on policies and programs, and publish reliable information on budget performance" (3–4).

Typical components of a core FMIS include systems for budget formulation and execution, such as planning and formulation, public investment management, management of budget authorizations/releases, commitment of funds, and payment/revenue management (mostly based on treasury, single accounts, cash forecasting and management, and accounting and reporting).

Source: Dener, Watkins, and Dorotinsky 2011.

---

system implementation and programs). The deeper the coverage is of a PER (of the flow of funds and impact, for example), the greater the scope for analysis of technical efficiency. This section highlights a range of questions and analytical approaches that could be helpful in guiding recommendations on technical efficiency.

A PER team examining budget execution could address the following questions:

- *Budgeted versus actual expenditures.* How do actually spent, allocated, and approved expenditures differ at the overall sectoral level? How do they differ for major programs at both the national and subnational levels? How have these figures changed over the last 5–10 years? What has been driving trends in this regard?
- *Timing of budget releases.* What are the budget release dates for the ministry of justice or interior and subordinate agencies (police, prosecutors, courts, independent investigation agencies, etc.) and/or subnational governments? How predictable have these been? How has this predictability influenced agency planning, operations, and budget

execution? The PER team may find it useful to distinguish between recurrent and development budgets and between donor and government funds.

An essential part of the analysis is to understand what has led to current levels of technical efficiency. If actual spending is lower than budgeted amounts, where did the money go? Were readjustments to allocations made after budget approval? Or was budget approval retrospectively sought? Were budgeted funds not released because of revenue shortfalls? Or was there simply a low use of funds by ministries, so subsequent releases were not made? Answering these questions will require understanding the budget implementation process (budget releases, reporting, cash budgeting).

If the timing of budget releases was not as planned, why was that the case? Is cash budgeting the reason? Was it simply a delay in the fund transfer system? Are any of these factors unique to the criminal justice sector, or are they prevalent across other sectors in the country? To what extent did the quality of financial management and procurement of implementing agencies impact technical efficiency? (This question could be addressed through broader country assessments of national and subnational capacities.) How timely and complete are financial management reports? How transparent is the procurement process? The assessments should identify ways to strengthen financial management.

Main Cost Drivers

The costs of policing services are overwhelmingly direct, current costs of police salaries and benefits. These costs typically consume 70–90 percent of police budgets, and much of the remainder of the budget is also heavily driven by personnel numbers; for example, the vehicle fleet, uniforms, and equipment are all contingent upon personnel numbers. It is therefore quite possible to calculate what a fully equipped and appropriately resourced police officer costs a particular police service, and in principle possible to determine how many police officers can be employed for any given budget.

Five drivers of cost are considered: (i) personnel expenditures and their composition, (ii) management of personnel expenditures, (iii) personnel expenditures in FCS, (iv) nonpersonnel costs, and (v) confidential spending.

Personnel Expenditures. Personnel expenditures frequently account for 70 percent or more of police spending. In South Africa, for instance, personnel expenditure accounted for 75 percent of police spending in 2003/2004.[32] In South Sudan, the police force allocates more than 90 percent of its budget to pay personnel.[33] Colombia allocates up to 70 percent of its police budget to salaries; in Chile and in El Salvador, the share is 80 percent.[34] Although some aspects of investigative support have been automated (e.g., fingerprint searches), others are likely to remain labor-intensive (e.g., forensic investigation and testifying in court).

Map 4.2 shows the number of police officers per 100,000 people worldwide (see also annex 4B for more data). This is an important measure of

Map 4.2   **Police per 100,000 Inhabitants, 2012 or Most Recent Year**

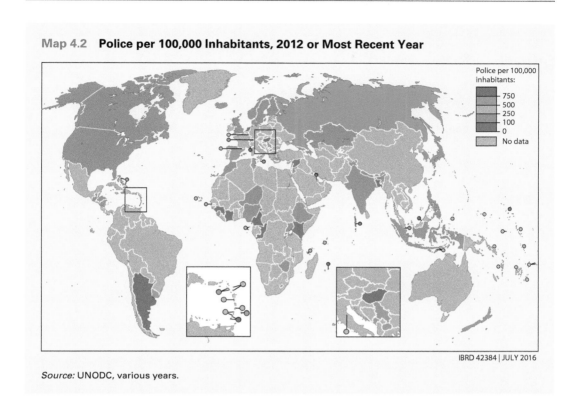

Source: UNODC, various years.

the level of policing in a society. Jurisdictions and policing typologies count "sworn" police officers differently,[35] however, so that no universally accepted definition of a sworn police officer exists. For this reason, administrative surveys (such as those of the UNODC) might not report or might misreport the real number of sworn officers. As with other data presented here, then, these comparative data should be used with a certain degree of caution.[36]

Table 4.3 shows selected data on police personnel, defined by UNODC as personnel in public agencies whose principal functions are preventing, detecting, and investigating crime and apprehending offenders. A comparison of intentional homicide rates (last column) with the ratio of police officers per 100,000 people (second-to-last column) suggests there is no clear link between the personnel strength of a country's police services and rates of violence: in countries with a high ratio of police officers to population, such as Colombia, El Salvador, and Mexico, the homicide rate exceeds the World Health Organization (WHO) threshold for violence epidemics of 9.8 homicides per 100,000 people.

The two factors that determine personnel expenditure in the police—the number of people employed by the police and the average cost of their employment—depend on a variety of policy considerations, some of which are not in the direct control of police management (e.g., salary and benefits policies affecting government as a whole).

Table 4.3   Police Personnel in Countries with Crime, Violence, or Conflict-Related History, 2012 or Most Recent Year

Region	Country	Total number of police officers	Police officers per 100,000 people	Homicides per 100,000 people
Africa	Kenya	42,586	98.6	6.4
	Côte d'Ivoire	15,770	86.4	13.6
	Nigeria	369,438	218.8	20.0
East Asia and Pacific	Indonesia	389,341	161.8	0.6
	Philippines	147,190	152.2	8.8
Central America	El Salvador	21,642	343.7	41.2
	Honduras	12,201	153.7	90.4
	Mexico	429,003	355.0	21.5
Europe and Central Asia	Bosnia and Herzegovina	16,733	436.4	1.3
	Russian Federation	746,996	520.8	9.2
	Ukraine	176,705	383.7	4.3
Latin America	Brazil	487,255	245.3	25.2
	Colombia	165,300	346.5	30.8
Middle East and North Africa	Algeria	155,170	403.2	0.7
	Morocco	55,975	171.1	1.4

Source: United Nations Office on Drugs and Crime statistics, http://www.unodc.org/unodc/en/data-and-analysis/statistics/data.html.

Governments should formulate such policies only after assessing their likely impact on large public sector employers (such as the police), but they often neglect to do so.

Key factors that determine the number of personnel to be employed in any given financial year include the following:

- The extent to which government prioritizes policing and increases budgetary allocations for the police
- The degree to which budgetary resources can be allocated to the employment of personnel and are not ring-fenced for some other purpose
- The extent to which retrenching police officers is politically sustainable
- The capacity of the relevant training institutions to supply new personnel in response to decisions to increase personnel numbers.

In turn, the average cost of employing police officers is determined by these factors:

- Remuneration policies, including basic pay, overtime policies, pension contributions, and nonsalary benefits (such as subsidized health insurance, housing allowances, and deployment allowances)

- The distribution of officers by rank/pay grade
- Promotion policies
- The extent to which relatively expensive officers can be substituted by less expensive personnel.

The critical policy decisions revolve around how many police officers are to be employed and at what levels of remuneration; the critical constraints framing these decisions are affordability and sustainability (see box 4.9 for some differences in police remuneration structures). Furthermore, two factors—the legal framework and the selection and conditions of service—are relevant here.

The Legal Framework. The conditions of employment for police officers are often governed by a range of laws that also frame their roles and responsibilities as well as standards of conduct and professionalism. Ideally there should be legal certainty relating to personnel management, labor relations, control over staffing levels, and the structure and levels of remuneration, overtime pay, bonuses, and awards; in practice, however, these legal frameworks can be absent, weak, or deficient.

There is significant variation across public service systems in how closely officers' conditions of service match those of other civil servants, and in the reasons why the conditions of service differ. Depending on the circumstances, differences may be resented or jealously guarded, and they can affect the dynamics of salary negotiations in the police and/or in the civil service generally.

Box 4.9   How Police Services Differ on the Structure of Remuneration

A 1993 study[a] reviews the rank and pay systems of police services in 20 developed countries and identifies the key differences in approach relating to:

- The number of ranks
- The number of entry points into the police for new recruits
- The extent to which salaries are determined by rank alone or differ on the basis of position (e.g., whether the commander of a police station in a large precinct receives the same salary as a commander in a smaller one)
- The extent to which within-rank pay progression is permitted, and whether this is based on length of service or on performance
- Whether performance-based bonuses are paid periodically.

There is limited empirical work on the impact of police pay on levels of productivity. But an interesting finding on pay and productivity concerns police officers in New Jersey: when final arbitration resulted in pay increases that were lower than what police officers had been led to expect—or lower than what they had demanded through collective bargaining—significant declines in productivity could be detected in the months following the award of the (disappointing) pay increase.[b]

a. Webb 1993.
b. Mas 2006.

Selection and Conditions of Service. Recruitment should be based on merit and objective minimum standards, but often it is not (see box 4.10). Selection is often politicized or discriminatory and in some cases reflects corruption or nepotism. Undue politicization of senior positions can result in costly and unnecessarily high levels of staff turnover and a lack of managerial continuity, which can in turn hurt the quality of budget and performance management.

Promotion is generally a key route to higher salaries for individual police officers. Ideally, promotion policies should reward merit and performance, but they are often dominated by considerations of service-related seniority. Worse still than policies based on seniority are those based on patronage, which can have harmful consequences for performance. Finally, while academic and training qualifications can be a useful signal of candidates' suitability for promotion, excessive reliance on these can also have adverse consequences.

Where police salaries are low, many officers seek additional sources of income ("moonlighting"). Even when it involves legitimate employment, this practice must be carefully regulated to avoid distorting the delivery of police services (e.g., by police officers prioritizing activities that improve economic prospects disproportionately in areas in which they have a vested interest).

Box 4.10   Recruitment and Training Standards for Police Officers

One of the biggest differences between police agencies across the world is their various recruitment and training standards, which reflect key differences in the distribution of skills in the population. Thus developed countries (where much of the population has tertiary education) tend to expect their police officers to be relatively more educated than do developing countries (where tertiary qualifications in the workforce are considerably scarcer). This means that there are also differences in the average length of basic training in different countries; countries whose recruits are less qualified before entering police training institutions typically impose a longer period of basic training on their recruits. Here are some relevant data:[a]

Qualifications required for new recruits

Some tertiary:	Canada, Denmark, United States
Some high school:	Austria, Bulgaria, China, Costa Rica, Germany, Hungary, India, Ireland, Israel, Italy, Kenya, Malta, Netherlands, Nigeria, Poland, Romania, Russian Federation, Singapore, Slovak Republic, South Africa, Spain, Sri Lanka, Sweden, República Bolivariana de Venezuela
Elementary school:	Ghana, Slovenia

Length of training for recruits

Two years plus:	Albania, Denmark, Finland, Germany, Ireland, New Zealand, Poland, Romania, Slovenia, Sweden, United Kingdom

(Box continues on next page)

Box 4.10   **Recruitment and Training Standards for Police Officers** *(continued)*

One year plus: Australia, Bulgaria, Japan, Malta, Netherlands, Spain
Under one year: Canada, China, Costa Rica, Ghana, India, Israel, Republic of Korea, Nigeria,
                    Papua New Guinea, Russian Federation, Singapore, Slovak Republic, South
                    Africa, United States

An important caveat is the absence of rigorous data on the substance of police training—how much training is devoted to legal questions, to police skills of various kinds (such as weapons use, search-and-seizure protocols, interviewing witnesses, victim support, and crowd management techniques), and to physical fitness. It is very likely that variations in the substance of training are greater than variations in the qualifications requirements for recruits and in the length of basic training, with some police agencies emphasizing physical fitness and weapons training and others emphasizing legal training and other "professional" policing skills. In addition, countries will have different approaches to training middle and senior officers and managers, which will require different qualifications and emphasize different skills.

Above a reasonable minimum, higher recruitment standards have less impact than might be expected a priori. Thus a recent review of U.S. evidence concluded, "The two groups that have the most to gain by promoting higher education for police are the police themselves—who enjoy the increased status and material rewards that accompany a college degree—and the academics who are in the business of higher education. What is not clear is how much and what kind of benefit is to be gained by policies that encourage, reward, or require a college education of our sworn officers."[b]

While recruitment policies governing the qualifications of police officers are important, so too may be policies governing the recruitment of police officers from the racial, ethnic, and language groups that are to be policed. This is of particular importance in more fractured societies, where communities may mistrust political authorities who are from particular communities, and where these communities may be overrepresented in the police. Deliberately recruiting officers from otherwise underrepresented communities has also been a strategy used by police forces in the developed world in an effort to improve police-community relations and police legitimacy in some communities.

a. Newman and Howard 1999.
b. Mastrofski 2006.

In some systems, police agencies have no autonomy in determining pay scales and must follow general civil service guidelines. In others, they do have some autonomy. Where police agencies follow the norms and standards of the rest of the civil service, police ranks must be graded against civil service ranks. Where the police have no autonomy in determining remuneration levels, across-the-board pay raises that are not accompanied by increases to personnel budgets will almost always lead to staffing cuts. On the other hand, when police agencies have a larger degree of autonomy in determining remuneration, care must be taken to design appropriate incentives for police managers, who are often sympathetic to rank-and-file officers' claims of financial hardship.

Management and Control of Personnel Expenditure

The most direct way to manage police expenditure is through the personnel establishment. When the resource envelope of the police is increased, personnel numbers can be allowed to rise; when resources are reduced, personnel numbers must usually fall. These processes are driven by police management's ability on the one hand to hire (and train) officers, and on the other to retrench when necessary. With the exception of certain specialized skills areas, the hiring of police officers is seldom constrained by supply; the exceptions are if new hires must meet onerous qualifications or if the capacity of the relevant training institutions limits the number of new hires who can be absorbed.

As already suggested, reducing police numbers can be politically and organizationally complex. Police officers are often a reasonably well organized interest group, enjoy significant political and social traction, and may also be an important constituency for some politicians. In some countries, especially fragile states, the public may fear that retrenching members of the security sector induces instability. Labor market regulation and the specific rules governing the retrenchment of public servants may also reduce the capacity of a police organization to retrench in the face of declining resources.

Remuneration policies have a great impact on police personnel expenditure, and changes to these can greatly increase the cost of policing. In contrast to the management of police numbers, remuneration policies only rarely provide much potential for reducing personnel costs, though they can also increase those costs. The reasons for this are obvious: it is seldom possible (for political and/or labor relations reasons) to reduce civil servant pay scales except in the face of particularly severe, widely recognized fiscal crises. Exceptions to this general rule apply to (i) the variable components of police pay and remuneration, particularly overtime pay and bonuses for merit, long service, hardship postings, or other reasons; and (ii) some aspects of nonsalary remuneration (e.g., health care benefits), expenditure on which might be reduced through policy interventions that limit those benefits.

While reducing officer remuneration in absolute terms may be difficult, it is often possible (and may be essential) to reduce real (i.e., inflation-adjusted) remuneration levels over the medium and long term—or at a minimum to "bend the curve" if remuneration is rising at an unsustainable rate. In assessing the relative importance of reducing police remuneration, it will be essential to test whether a strategy exists for managing trends in remuneration across the civil service and the applicability of this strategy to the police.

Ranking Systems. The distribution of officers by rank varies considerably across police organizations, and it is difficult to generalize about the appropriate ratio of senior to junior officers (see box 4.11). As in other uniformed branches of government, sound command and control is

Box 4.11   Comparing Police Rank Structures

A rank system plays a number of different roles: (i) it defines relative authority, (ii) it allocates personnel to particular functions, and (iii) it determines pay levels. Different rank systems lay different emphases on these roles. In the United States, for example, ranks play an important role in determining pay, but their primary function relates to job descriptions. Thus a patrol officer is more a job description than a salary grade, and officers may remain in that rank for their entire career. Pay, on the other hand, is determined by seniority within that rank. It is possible, therefore, for a long-serving patrol officer to have a higher salary than officers with more senior rank titles.

This is not the case in the South African police, where (until a recent name change), there were 11 ranks, from student constable to national commissioner, each representing a higher level of authority. As pay levels are determined solely by rank, increasing rank is the sole mechanism through which remuneration rises. Promotion is therefore more or less automatic and amounts to a recognition of years served; and an individual's rank says very little about his or her job description and authority (this is especially true at relatively junior levels). This policy can have perverse effects, however: there have been periods when, because of financial constraints, the number of new recruits has fallen, so that the proportion of constables to sergeants and inspectors seemed the opposite of what one would expect.

In the current structure of the South Sudan National Police Service, for example, there are 10 ranks and 6 noncommissioned ranks. The salaries are determined by rank, and there is a significant degree of vertical differentiation between the top rank in the police and the lowest. One of the main issues here is the sizable percentage of ex-combatants who were allocated as rank officers to different security sector institutions. This practice swells up the middle and upper ranks of the police because of the older age of former combatants, and significantly strains the budget. The combination of incoming police graduates and the lack of a retirement plan for former combatants further strains the budget. It also creates a structural bottleneck in the upper ranks that prevents the promotion of lower-rank officers.

Sources: Leggett 2003; Home Office 2013.

essential in the police. Depending on how the police are deployed—whether the basic units are large or small, and whether they are geographically dispersed or highly concentrated—strong cases could be made for force designs that are flat (less hierarchical) or more steeply sloped (more hierarchical). The argument for flatter structures composed of more-evenly trained officers seems to be the preferred approach in the developed world, and particularly among police services that have embraced community policing and problem-solving policing as organizational philosophies.

These same institutions, however, tend also to be those whose officers have the highest skill levels—in Canada, for example, all police recruits must now have tertiary qualifications—and the highest degree of professionalism. In organizations where average skills levels are lower, a plausible case can be made for command-and-control structures that more closely resemble those of the military, with more ranks and a higher proportion of more senior officers commanding large numbers of more junior officers.

Promotions. Promotion policies have a significant effect on medium- and long-term personnel expenditure trends, and these policies must not entail commitments that exceed the organization's likely resource envelope over reasonable time frames. These policies will generally contain provisions governing the following:

- The rate at which remuneration rises as a result of length of service in a particular rank
- The extent to which promotions depend on the accumulation of particular qualifications
- Whether promotions can be made only when appropriate posts are vacant or are more or less automatic
- The remunerative consequences of promotion.

In many police organizations, promotions at the start of a career are more or less automatic, reflecting increasing length of service (together with growing experience), with promotions to higher ranks depending on the availability of vacant posts. Under this model, the automatic promotions of low-ranked officers acknowledge "on-the-job training" and the accumulation of productivity-enhancing experience; officers are to be thought of as fully trained only after they have completed a certain number of years of service. Promotions to higher ranks, by contrast, may depend on the acquisition of additional training and qualifications. Whatever the rationale for promotions, assessing the long-run financial implications of a change in promotion policies may be critically important for managing police budgets over time.

Budgeting and budget execution for personnel expenditure should be relatively straightforward, but data-poor environments, fragile states, and states beset with administrative challenges may struggle to generate the data necessary to make relevant informed decisions. While there is no reason in principle why security agencies and the police should confront greater challenges than other agencies and institutions in managing personnel budgets and expenditures, the challenges they face may be very severe. In countries like the Central African Republic, where data are almost totally nonexistent, the PER may itself be the platform for gathering this information (see box 4.12).

Civilianization. One strategy commonly advocated for lowering the unit personnel costs of police organizations is "civilianization." This approach presumes a differential between the costs of employing police officers and those of employing civilians, due either to differences in pay structure or to the lower cost of training civilians (who have a narrow set of administrative roles). Where such a differential exists, expanding personnel budgets may be better spent on recruiting civilians to play organizational roles in order to free up police officers for police functions. Such roles might include a variety of back-office functions, as well as some administrative functions associated with serving members of the public.

Box 4.12   **Managing Police Personnel in the Central African Republic**

In 2009, the World Bank undertook an assessment of the public financial management of the Central African Republic's armed forces. The inability of police services to grasp the full extent of the staff complement (around 1,400 people) and the payroll was a critical challenge identified by the study. The problem was rooted in overlapping institutional arrangements: the management of National Police personnel, which had been undertaken by the Ministry of Civil Service, was to be transferred to the Central African Republic Police, but the two agencies did not have consolidated data on the actual size of the establishment.

On the basis of existing numbers, further analysis revealed that the pyramid of police ranks was very unbalanced (table B4.12.1). The personnel census of the police showed that noncommissioned officers represented a very large part of the staff (6 percent for the superintendents and *contrôleurs généraux* and 33 percent for commanding officers, 42 percent for inspectors), while the enforcement officers (police officers) constituted only a small minority (18 percent). The last recruitment of inspectors and police officers took place in 1974, and no promotion of chief constables, superintendents, and police officers took place between 2004 and 2007.

Table B4.12.1   **Police Staff in the Central African Republic, by Corps**

Corps	Staff census (February 2009)	
	Number	Percentage
General superintendent	7	
Chief superintendent	11	6
Principal superintendent	35	
Superintendent	28	
Principal commanding officer	17	
Commanding officer	50	33
Chief constable	177	
Officer	217	
Detective inspector	112	
Detective constable	14	42
Sergeant	171	
Sous-brigadier	269	
Police officer	251	18
Civilian and unranked	14	1
Total active employees	**1, 373**	**100**

The payment of salaries was also complicated by the recording system used in the budget: all salary expenses were aggregated together under a single heading, "Salary expenditure not distributed between the departments," which made it impossible to separate the salaries paid to the police from those paid to the other employees of the ministry.

Source: World Bank 2009.

Pensions. Police agency pension commitments (including postretirement medical aid) will generally be similar to those in other parts of the civil service. In some cases, however, police pensions are somewhat more generous to reflect the greater danger that police officers face.

Trade-Offs between Numbers and Professionalization. The trade-off between police officers' average remuneration and the number of officers employed by the agency raises an important policy question. Is it more effective to have fewer police officers who are better trained and better paid, or to have more police officers with less training and less pay? There are no simple answers to this question, but it does touch on some key issues:

- The relationship between police pay, morale, and performance
- The relationship between police pay and the level of corruption
- The relationship between the number of police officers deployed, the level of crime, and the public's fear of crime
- Whether higher pay is needed to attract and retain better-trained and better-performing police officers (the state of the labor market and the likely outcomes confronting potential recruits if they pursue alternative career paths are relevant here).

There is very little information on these questions, and much of what does exist relates to developed world settings[37] and may apply only in those countries. It is likely, however, that below a particular skills threshold, the marginal contribution of individual police officers to public safety may be negligible and even negative. To the extent that a police organization requires individuals with skill sets that are above this threshold, it will need to design pay and promotion policies that attract and retain appropriate individuals.

Financial Management Controls

Giving the weight of the budget to personnel costs offers fewer control risks than giving it (for example) to high-cost procurement of goods and services. Nonetheless, budgetary and spending irregularities are possible; the most important of these include nepotism or corruption in appointments and promotions, the existence of "ghost" employees, and irregular promotions.

Some areas of personnel spending are more likely than others to generate irregular or wasteful spending. One of these is overtime, which is needed in policing to accommodate the aspects of police work that are not easily confined to standard working hours. The payment of overtime may be a legal necessity in these instances, but it also creates some perverse incentives for police officers, who can often determine the pace and timing of their work. While managers play a key role in monitoring abuse, organizational norms may mean that many managers are complicit in gaming the system.

Leave allowances, too, may lead to wasteful spending. If leave is not fully utilized every year, police officers may accumulate substantial credits of unused leave that can result in significant payments in retirement.

Like overtime, the leave system can create incentives for gaming the system, and here again managers might be complicit in the abuses if organizational norms permit (or even encourage) them.

Because decisions relating to personnel numbers and remuneration have effects on police budgets that cannot generally be offset by changes in non-personnel spending, all decisions that affect personnel policies must be properly costed. In addition, to the extent that future budget envelopes are uncertain, decisions with significant budgetary implications should be taken in consultation with the ministry of finance. The following are areas in which clarity about budgetary implications and consultation with the ministry are most desirable:

- Staffing levels
- Financial implications of retrenchment policies, including the costs of paying out accumulated leave allowances and any salary arrears that may exist, and the manner in which years of service are recognized for pension purposes
- Financial implications of changes to remuneration levels (basic pay, supplementary remuneration), promotion policies, and pensions.

In some countries, the allocation of personnel budgets is grouped together with allocations for other goods and services expenditures, and agency managers have a high degree of autonomy to reallocate funds between these categories. While potential efficiency gains might accrue from increased managerial flexibility, there is also a danger that managers will increase personnel funding by imposing undue cuts on nonpersonnel spending. There is also a danger that such reallocations can create long-term commitments to personnel that may be difficult to unwind. Specific limits on personnel spending (and even hard limits on staffing numbers) are often desirable, as are limits on the freedom of agency managers to reallocate budgets from personnel to nonpersonnel spending.

The Challenges of Personnel Expenditures in FCS

In FCS, ensuring full and regular payment of security personnel may be one of the most critical practical reforms needed to secure peace and create the conditions for state building and development (including the building of new security sector institutions). It is also one of the most difficult (see box 4.13).

A 2013 World Bank study of public financial management in postconflict contexts[38] reveals that public financial management reforms have progressed fastest in countries where there were high levels of external support, and where the technical assistance, policy dialogue, and system investments made by donors were more synchronized. From the perspective of security sector reform, it is essential for security sector and finance officials to communicate at the onset of the transition to ensure that investments in FMIS include both civilian and military personnel. It is highly likely, though, that

Box 4.13   **Personnel Expenditure and Police Corruption in the Democratic Republic of Congo**

Baaz and Olsson analyzed the manner in which "unofficial earnings" were accrued and distributed by police officers in the Democratic Republic of Congo. They concluded that policy proposals aimed at reducing corruption by raising the salaries of low-ranking officers failed to recognize the degree to which these illicit activities were organized within the force, and the extent to which senior officers benefited from the upward flow of bribes and extorted income. Absent that recognition, improving salaries for lower-ranked officers was unlikely to reduce corruption.

The highly organized nature of the income flows meant that "officers occupying financially lucrative posts in the field are under constant pressure to deliver upward in the system. Failure to deliver is connected to various punishments such as redeployment, losing the job, forced vacation, and incarceration. However, while a large proportion of the collected resources flow upward in the chain of command and while the incomes are irregular and extremely unevenly distributed (depending on your posts), the levels of income that even lower level officers in the field can gain from these activities are quite substantive, ranging from between three to twelve times higher than the official salary (of approximately forty-five U.S. dollars)."

Intriguingly, Baaz and Olsson argue that "despite predation and exploitation, unofficial economic activities and property violations are also characterized by norms that discourage excesses." They argue that "there is a demand among civilians not only for the formal services provided by the police but also for the informal"; civilians, they assert, understand that the poor working conditions of police officers necessitate a level of corruption if these services are to be delivered at all.

Source: Baaz and Olsson 2011.

resources will be limited; in some cases, the budget, including payment to security sector personnel, will be done in cash transfers, and human resources data will be inaccurate.

According to World Bank experience, cash transfers in turn lead to several sources of risk:

- Disbursement of excessive cash advances for police operations, using weak logistics as a pretext, and with no clarity on accountability lines
- Failure to carry out manual reconciliations between separate personnel and payroll systems to ensure consistency of data and to identify discrepancies such as duplicate entries, ghost employees on the payroll, or ineligible recipients
- No specific access controls and log records for changes to the payroll and staff roster databases
- Insufficient backup for roster and payroll files maintained on the local site
- Infrequent audit of roster registrants' eligibility
- No ex post examination of payroll reports to identify anomalies.

Table 4.4 summarizes recommendations emerging from past World Bank PERs that FCS could implement to ensure better payment of security

Table 4.4 Improving Security Sector Personnel Payment in Fragile and Conflict-Affected States (FCS)

1. Risk reduction: control of specific sources of risk	• Assess cash management needs. • Reduce cash advances. The Public Expenditure Review team should weigh this goal against possible effects on operational efficiency, and should involve an integrated team comprising security sector specialists in making the decision. While in middle-income countries reducing cash advances may take three to six months to achieve through government directives, in FCS the time horizon is likely to be more extended. • Strengthen reconciliation between different databases used for payment. In the short run, cash will likely be used, but databases with the number of employees may be unclear. Data reconciliation should include monthly reconciliations between different systems holding the same information, especially the reconciliation between the personnel database and the roster on the payment system. If these data systems have been destroyed by conflict, significant investments may be needed to build them from scratch in preparation for a more advanced financial management information system (FMIS).
2. Foundation: stronger accountability and transparency structure	• Simplify and accelerate authorization procedures. In many countries (fragile and nonfragile alike), financial transactions largely follow authorization procedures, which tend to be both excessively cumbersome (e.g., requiring 15 signatures and five weeks for a purchase order of a basic consumable) and ultimately ineffective in establishing accountability (given that each signatory is responsible for only a small portion of the process and no one is responsible for the entire process). • Train and appoint financial officers in the police and relevant line ministries.
3. Modernization and improvement	• Increase staff capacity. • Simplify financial management procedures. • Plan and implement adequate FMIS.

sector personnel. Recommendations are divided into three components, which can be phased in the following stages:

1. *Risk reduction:* reduction of high-risk areas and weak internal controls
2. *Foundation:* correction of priority systemic weaknesses that compromise essential financial management foundations
3. *Modernization:* implementation of widespread modernization of security sector financial management.

The length of each stage (three to six months or one year) would be agreed on with the partner government on the basis of the PER team's assessment of local capacities.

Nonpersonnel Expenditures

The bulk of nonpersonnel expenditure in police organizations goes to infrastructure, transportation, equipment, and various consumables (such as fuel, office supplies, and communications equipment). As a general rule, the transport needs of police organizations will consist largely of soft-skinned and hard-skinned vehicles of various kinds (depending, in principle at least, on strategy and risk management). Some police agencies also use helicopters and fixed-wing aircraft for various functions.

Other equipment needs in police organizations are more varied, but include the following:

- Information technology of varying levels of sophistication
- Communications systems (radios and telephones)
- Office equipment and consumables
- Uniforms, nonlethal/compliance weapons, firearms, and other personal equipment for individual officers.

The mix of infrastructure and transportation resources provided to police officers should be determined by strategic priorities and will depend on the population density, the density of police officers per kilometer, the location of police stations, and the spatial distribution of crime. In many jurisdictions, resources may be best deployed in making the police more accessible to members of the community. At the most local level, police stations should have the equipment necessary to ensure that officers can patrol the streets with reasonable continuity and density, though in some circumstances considerations of officer safety may militate against deploying police officers singly, in pairs, or even in relatively small groups. A related question is the location of police stations and the degree to which the public can access them.

Procurement processes in the police, like those in other state agencies, are subject to a wide range of well-known vulnerabilities. A large proportion of assets and consumables typically procured by police agencies are standardized commodities, which ought to make procurement and contract management less vulnerable than might be the case in other public functions. As in other public functions, however, vulnerabilities are greatest for large, nonstandard, one-off procurements. Examples might include uniforms ordered in bulk, physical infrastructure and IT, new communications systems, and lease agreements for accommodation.

Confidential Spending

Some aspects of police procurement processes can present challenges for sound public financial management because they are deemed to be confidential. Keeping the use of certain police assets or resources secret may help achieve legitimate public policy goals. Examples might include (i) the purchase of some kinds of equipment (e.g., specialized surveillance equipment), which could provide forewarning about police capabilities (though systems in which trials are conducted in open court can seldom keep these kinds of capabilities secret for long); and (ii) the establishment of facilities such as safe houses for witnesses in need of protection.

An area of spending that police organizations say necessitates heightened secrecy is the procurement of informers. As a matter of principle, the identity of those who provide confidential information to the police must be protected—even from officers elsewhere in the organization. The nature of the information they provide and the price paid (or reward offered) must usually be kept secret as well. In addition, it is not generally possible to procure information of this nature through open tenders. For all these reasons, heightened secrecy is needed, even at the expense of transparency in budgetary and procurement processes. The need for secrecy is part of what makes it very difficult to establish an appropriate pricing policy for confidential information (for which there is, for obvious reasons, no market price) and next to impossible to assess value for money.

Given the difficulties enumerated here, there is an increased risk of irregularities in expenditure on confidential information. Examples of irregularities include the following:

- Collusion by police officers and informers to defraud the police organization (by falsely claiming that the information provided was essential or by overstating the value of the information)
- Registration (and payment) of "ghost" informers
- Embezzlement of portions of informer fees by police officers who know that even legitimate informers cannot complain to other officers for fear of their identities becoming known.

It is not possible to eliminate these risks entirely, but they should be managed to the extent possible. Precisely how these procedures should operate, the role of police managers and civilian overseers within them, and the authority of the audit institutions to assess them must be aligned with the rules of budget management and oversight of the organization as a whole. In general, however, sound public financial management rules would do the following:

- Ensure that the proportion of the overall budget subject to secrecy is as small as possible given the organization's strategic priorities and threat assessment
- Centralize the administration of these funds under the command of an officer with the highest possible security clearance
- Facilitate investigations into possible misuse of these funds (e.g., through the requirement that officers undergo lie detector tests and possibly disclose assets).

Budget Controls

There are two main models that define the structure of internal control: (i) a centralized system characterized by ex ante control of expenditures by ministry of finance officials; and (ii) a decentralized system in which officials from the ministry of justice or interior (or other ministry overseeing the police) control expenditures subject to ex post monitoring. These systems are generally referred to as the Francophone and Westminster systems, respectively. The preferred system depends on the country's level of institutional development or historical tradition. In less-developed countries, the centralized Francophone approach, with its ex ante controls, may make sense until the line ministry has established sufficient capacity to efficiently manage its own finances, and there is greater trust, transparency, and accountability in the management of public finances overall. Decisions in this regard are likely to be made for the civil service as a whole, but it is plausible to imagine mixed systems in which some institutions and agencies have more authority to manage their budgets than others.

While universal rules are impossible to identify, police agencies are generally thought to have larger skills deficits in managing budgets than other departments and institutions, if only because policing tends not to attract or retain personnel with the relevant skills. As police budgets are relatively straightforward, relatively less intensive management is required in their control. For reasons that should be clear, however, human resource administration is critically important if budgets are to be realistic and if spending is to be managed effectively.

Certain characteristics of police services—their large staffs, their organizational complexity, and their geographic span across the state—create challenges in efficient resource management and effective internal control, especially for staffs with limited expertise in financial and administrative functions. Financial risks may be even greater in the short run if the staff assigned to internal control tasks is poorly trained, and greater still if the accounting is cash-based and police are paid in cash rather than by electronic transfer.

Control activities refer to a broad collection of specific policies and procedures that help ensure policy directives are implemented in a cost-effective and efficient way. In general, financial controls seek to:

- Establish responsibility for budget execution decisions to promote accountability
- Segregate duties related to authorization, payment, and recordkeeping to reduce the risk of fraud or error
- Monitor transactions, either before or after obligations are made, to safeguard funds and ensure they are used for the purposes intended
- Document procedures and retain records so that transactions can be audited and substantiated.

Given the structure of police budgets, control over the bulk of the budget depends on how police salaries and benefits are paid. In data-rich, administratively sound institutions, control over personnel expenditure is not very difficult to exert. Significant challenges exist, however, in poor countries and fragile states, particularly when salaries are paid in cash by senior officers—a practice that is common where banking infrastructure is poorly developed and security personnel are stationed in outlying, underserviced areas. In these circumstances, salaries may be paid late, "taxed" by senior officers, or not paid at all, and the most significant reforms are those that ensure that personnel are paid on time and in full. Regular payment of salaries is critically important for ensuring the stability of security institutions and for the success of any other reforms that may be attempted or proposed.

Though financial control for police services targets salaries (the bulk of the spending), a number of general questions (shown in table 4.5) can be used to guide PER analysis of broader categories of expenditures, marked by each stage of the budget execution process.

Table 4.5   Budget Controls, by Stage of Budget Execution

Stage 1. Apportionment	• Are there sufficient funds available? • Was money appropriated for the purpose stated in the budget? • Does spending reflect a prearranged schedule?
Stage 2. Commitment	• Was the expenditure approved by an authorizing agent? • Is the proposed expenditure provided for in the appropriation? • Are there sufficient funds remaining in the relevant budget category? • Is the expenditure classified correctly?
Stage 3. Acquisition	• Were the goods and services received by an authorizing agent? • Were the goods and services delivered as expected? • Is there documentary evidence of satisfactory delivery?
Stage 4. Payment	• Was the expenditure properly committed? • Did a competent person verify that goods and services were received? • Are the invoice and other documents requesting payment complete, correct, and suitable for payment? • Is the creditor identified correctly?

A well-functioning FMIS can be useful for monitoring and reporting budget implementation if the underlying systems of budget classification and accounting are in place. As noted, an FMIS is a set of automation solutions that enable governments to plan, execute, and monitor the budget. Information typically captured by an FMIS includes:

• Approved budget allocations for both recurrent and capital expenditures
• Sources of financing for programs and projects
• Budget transfers
• Supplementary allocations
• Funds released against budgetary allocations
• Data on commitments and actual expenditures against budgeted allocations.[39]

If the FMIS is integrated with other management systems, such as payroll, the database can be used to generate consolidated, daily reports on transactions and the line ministry's financial standing.

In many police agencies, operational managers have very little control over the bulk of the budget and associated spending from which they derive their operational capability; these are driven overwhelmingly by staff numbers and remuneration. As one expert frames it, expenditure-related decision making by police managers is really about where and how personnel are deployed:

> By and large, police managers do not use resources to achieve desired ends; instead they supervise expenditures according to inflexible rules and traditions. Because police are given resources primarily to hire and support personnel, key resource decisions involve assignments. Allocations are made initially to functional commands (patrol, criminal investigation, traffic, and so forth) and later to geographical areas.[40]

Although deployment decisions are often made on the assumption that personnel used are costless resources (their salaries are treated as already-committed overheads), in practice different kinds of deployment can have different cost implications. Where police officers are deployed outside their usual jurisdiction, for example, allowances may have to be paid for accommodation, subsistence, and hardship posting. Different kinds of operation may also use overtime or transportation more or less intensively. While operational managers may not be responsible for managing basic personnel costs, they may well be responsible for managing these more variable costs associated with the intensity of the use of police personnel.

Budget variations are also highly likely for police operations and maintenance costs. Policing is a local matter and requires a high level of operational flexibility to address location-specific crime patterns and other threats to law and order. But policing budgets are often planned top down, and this approach can create financial tensions and lead to lapses in control when local policing challenges are not as anticipated. Where the need for flexible local response and the desire for strategic coherence clash, one possible solution is to relax input control and hold the front line units accountable for preagreed outputs and outcomes as performance measures. As the next section suggests, however, performance targets in policing are no easy matter; internal and external reporting on resource management as well as inventory control needs to be particularly robust to minimize improper use of assets and resources.

The quality of budget management and execution in a police agency depends above all on the quality of the administrative and financial personnel. Managers have little capacity to influence savings on significant proportions of personnel expenditure, since these are determined by existing contractual commitments that specify both the number of officers and the bulk of their remuneration. Managers can exert a degree of control over some aspects of supplementary remuneration, particularly overtime pay, bonuses, allowances, awards, and the like. Generally, however, these account for only a small proportion of total personnel spending. For this reason, budget discipline depends fundamentally on budget realism.

Although it is relatively straightforward for budget officers to estimate the costs of existing contractual salary commitments, it is more complicated to account for the supplementary remuneration police may receive; formally this type of remuneration may be discretionary and subject to budgetary availability, but in fact it may be governed by various more or less explicit norms and practices. These practices can be difficult to change because operational managers (who often have little control over spending) have little incentive to address organizational practices that they themselves may benefit from and that may affect morale and productivity.

In these circumstances, unrealistic budgets tend to lead to three different outcomes, all of which should be avoided:

1. Arrears owing to officers are accrued and carried over from one financial year to the next.
2. "Savings" are effected to pay for the supplementary remuneration either by leaving empty posts unfilled or by reallocating spending from other budget lines.
3. Budgets are overspent.

A precondition for accurate long-run forecasting is that the current costs are established accurately. The starting point is estimating current personnel expenditure (see box 4.14); but since it is possible that that expenditure masks the full cost of the establishment because arrears are being accumulated, it is important to establish whether current expenditure accurately measures total personnel costs.

If arrears are allowed to accumulate, or false savings have been used to finance obligations, actual spending levels may understate the true costs. In these cases, budget realism may require recognition of the excess spending even when it is not formally apparent in financial statements.

Box 4.14   Managing Police Personnel in South Sudan

A 2014 World Bank study of crime and violence in South Sudan provided a brief institutional analysis of the criminal justice system, including the police force. In terms of human resource capacity, the South Sudan National Police Service (SSNPS) faces a formidable challenge. According to the Comprehensive Institutional Needs Assessment commissioned by SSNPS in September 2013, the SSNPS staff totals a little over 35,000, including 3,272 officers, 14,739 noncommissioned officers, and 17,638 employees who do not perform policing duties. The current size of the SSNPS results in a police/citizen ratio of 1:305, which is well below the internationally accepted standard of 1:450.[a]

In addition to having a lower than average police/citizen ratio, approximately 80 percent of the police force in the SSNPS is functionally illiterate, according to a recent report examining the challenges and opportunities of police reform in South Sudan.[b] This high percentage stems from the fact that many SSNPS personnel came from the phased-out Sudan People's Liberation Army, which had many long-serving, elderly officers. As a result, the SSNPS has a bulged force many of whose members cannot fulfill basic safety and security duties.

The SSNPS is trying to devise a strategy to shed excess personnel, but budgetary constraints are making this difficult; the nonexistent pension system makes it impossible for some to retire even though their capacity to work effectively is limited. This excess manpower exerts significant pressure on annual budgets, which have been capped in recent years and in which salaries account for 90–95 percent.

The personnel issues described here have led to inefficiency and ineffectiveness in the SSNPS, and have made combating crime a serious challenge.

Source: World Bank 2014.
a. Ajwang 2006; Loh 2010.
b. North-South Institute 2012.

Reforms designed to ensure that personnel spending does not exceed budget appropriations are important, but their success may depend upon the extent to which appropriations address the accumulated shortfall between actual personnel spending and budgets. It is not easy to take this step without softening the budget constraint on managers, which may reinforce the problems that the reforms seek to address. In practice, chronic underbudgeting on personnel spending will tend to result in posts going unfilled, in falling staff numbers, or in underspending on complementary inputs into policing.

In the long run, the successful management of personnel budgets will depend on the ability to forecast spending levels accurately. While it is in principle possible to estimate the costs of a police agency's current establishment and future personnel-related plans, in practice there are uncertainties that affect the accuracy of such estimates. A key issue in estimating budgets is how civil service pay levels are determined, since decisions about pay play a significant role in determining trends in long-run personnel costs. Most police agencies have little or no direct control over decisions relating to increases in basic pay in the civil service, though the degree to which these decisions affect budget execution depends on the extent to which allocations made to the police accurately reflect the costs of any increases. It should not be assumed that the allocations made to agencies in response to civil service–wide remuneration policies fully cover the costs of such changes. In personnel-intensive budgets such as the police, any difference between actual costs, changes, and supplementary budgets allocated may have significant implications for budget execution.

Apart from determining the full costs of the existing establishment, long-term forecasting of personnel expenditure necessitates a range of more or less complex processes. These include assessing:

- The numbers and skills of existing police personnel; the extent to which they match the existing (or changing) police strategy; and the extent to which changes to police numbers or skills would necessitate changes to personnel spending (e.g., by requiring a growing number of highly skilled personnel)
- The training-cost implications of changes to strategy and/or establishment size (an assessment that may first have to establish whether the training infrastructure exists to deliver the changes proposed)
- The impact of future salary/benefits negotiations, which might be guided by provisions for government agencies as a whole, albeit moderated by assessments of the credibility of those guidelines (e.g., whether they propose a smaller rise in remuneration than is likely to occur in reality)
- The impact of current (and, if necessary, changing) promotions policies on the distribution of ranks across the establishment in the police agencies
- Staff turnover rates (which can moderate the effect of rising salaries by facilitating a more or less rapid reduction in head count)

- The long-term implications of supplementary personnel costs, particularly those associated with changing policies.

All assessments of future personnel costs need to be based on an accurate estimate of current costs and the evolution of those costs over the preceding period. As suggested earlier, such an assessment will be accurate to the extent that the data are reliable and available, that they cover all costs (including supplementary forms of remuneration and any arrears/deferred spending), and that they cover all relevant personnel. None of these requirements should be assumed to hold.

Measuring Police Performance

One of the key objectives of the PER process is to better understand effectiveness in a particular sector and explore how the public sector can achieve better value for money in meeting sectoral objectives. Although crime and insecurity clearly impose costs on society, it can be difficult to evaluate the benefits of policing (see box 4.15). As a general matter, the benefits of policing include the following:

- Reduced crime and reduced fear of crime
- Management of public order
- Preservation of the security and legitimacy of the state.

Assessing the value of policing, even in relation to its principal objectives and outputs, is difficult. This is both because the direct impact of policing on crime is uncertain (due to the exogenous factors affecting crime rates), and because crime may be displaced spatially or intertemporally. The result is that police management can seldom—if ever—justify current practices (or, indeed, proposed changes) on the basis of objective, verifiable, and replicable studies, since these generally do not exist. Investments in policing are more driven by normative and political exigencies than by empirical evidence of what works and what does not.

Box 4.15   The Kansas City Patrol Experiment

One of the most well-known and important pieces of empirical work on policing was an experiment conducted by the Kansas City police in the early 1970s in which large parts of the city were divided into three categories for distinct "treatments": in one set of areas patrol officers were essentially withdrawn; in a second set of areas patrols were doubled; and a third set was designated a control group and saw no change to patrol intensity.[a] Over the course of more than a year, crime levels, arrest rates, and the public's fear of crime were monitored. A major conclusion was that varying the strength of random mobile patrols made no difference to any of the three measures of performance.[b]

a. Kelling et al. 1974.
b. Bayley 1998.

While quantifying the impact of policing on crime levels is difficult, an initial step involves examining the value of reducing a range of direct costs imposed on society by crime and insecurity. These include:

- The costs of lost income and lost or damaged property associated with crime, including the loss of future income incurred as a result of injury and death
- The costs associated with fear of crime, including estimates of lost income, increased security expenditure, and changes in activity patterns
- The health care costs associated with injuries, both for victims themselves and for health systems
- The costs of insuring against loss, injury, and death.

There are reasonably standard economic and actuarial approaches to valuing these effects, and it is possible to deploy them in order to try to quantify the value of the benefits from the reduction of crime associated with a particular intervention. As suggested already, however, it can be difficult to quantify the impact of policing on crime levels, making the subsequent step of estimating the value of those benefits (net of the costs of the policing interventions themselves) a difficult one.

Overview of Main Challenges to Performance Measurement
The Reduction of Crime and Fear of Crime

Reducing the level of crime is usually expected to reduce fear of crime, but only after a time lag. Yet this relationship is not well established (see box 4.16). The fear of criminality is not determined solely by the current level of crime, but is also influenced by individual and societal factors. Over time, however, a positive correlation can usually be found between the absolute and per capita levels of crime committed each year on the one hand, and the measured level of public fear of crime on the other. Even so, this relationship is not linear, with reductions in the fear of crime typically lagging declines in crime levels and falling less quickly than crime levels.

One reason for this effect is that even as the absolute and/or per capita level of crime committed in each period falls, the total proportion of people who have been victimized rises. Each of those victims, along with members of their immediate social network, will tend to experience increased levels of fear, which could well persist for longer than the period over which the rate of victimization is usually measured. Thus, the decline in crime usually has to be significant and has to last for a sustained period before it will manifest in a marked reduction in the fear of crime. Even with declines in the levels of crime victimization, fear of crime may persist if there is not a corresponding perception that social disorder has also declined.[41] Scholars have suggested potential solutions to the problem of fear of crime, such as more police on foot patrols, reduction of incivility and disorder (the "broken windows" theory), and improved police-community relations. However, the evidence that these solutions have been effective is still inconclusive.

Whatever its source, the fear of crime creates socioeconomic costs. When levels of fear fall, these costs fall, too: expenditures on services like private

Box 4.16   **Relationship between Crime and the Fear of Crime in U.S. Cities**

Reported levels of fear of crime track actual levels of crime imprecisely. This is evident in a simple snapshot of data that maps survey responses about feelings of safety ("Do you feel safe walking alone at night?") against levels of reported crime in cities across the United States (figure B4.16.1). The data show that "people have a rough sense of the risk of crime, but they don't calibrate it very well." One reason why the risk is hard to calibrate is that the odds of becoming a victim of violent crime are generally very low; thus changes in the likelihood of becoming a victim are hard to evaluate precisely.

Figure B4.16.1   **Correlation of Feelings of Safety with Levels of Crime: Percentage of People in U.S. Cities Who Feel Safe versus Violent Crimes per 100,000 Residents, 2012**

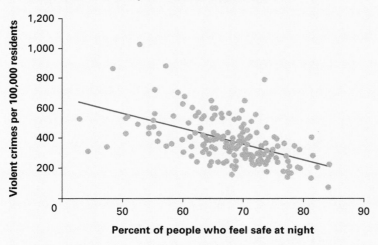

Source: Enten 2014; based on data from the Federal Bureau of Investigation and Gallup.

security, some of which are of marginal socioeconomic value, often decrease; some forms of economic activity, such as informal trade, may increase; and certain transaction costs may decrease. But quantifying the economic value of policing's effect on declining levels of fear of crime is difficult, not only because it is hard to assess the relationship between policing and the fear of crime, but also because it is unclear how to quantify the value of the changes induced, even if those changes could be measured accurately (see box 4.17). An important consideration noted in one study is that the fear of crime might affect the level and pattern of investment, reducing growth or distorting the path of economic development.[42]

Impact of Policing on State Legitimacy

Effective policing may increase the legitimacy of the state, but quantifying the value of this effect is even more difficult than assigning a value to the

> ### Box 4.17 Crime and GDP
>
> The relationship between gross domestic product (GDP) and levels of crime
> and insecurity is a controversial one. It is widely accepted that high levels of
> crime can reduce GDP and GDP growth through various transmission mech-
> anisms, including the costs of death, injury, and the loss of property; the
> opportunity costs associated with expenditure on (low-productivity) security
> services, both public and private; raised costs of doing business; and the
> dynamic losses that crime may generate by increasing risk, changing expec-
> tations of the future, and reducing savings and investment.
>
> It is worth noting, however, that for some crimes, the first-order effect on
> GDP is distributional; income/assets are lost by some and gained by others.
> Other crimes can actually increase national income to the extent that the flow
> of goods and services in an economy is higher than it would be otherwise.
> This second scenario holds, for example, with regard to certain voluntary
> actions and transactions that are criminalized. Thus prostitution (a service)
> and drug manufacture and distribution might increase the value of a society's
> GDP, albeit in unmeasured and generally undesirable sectors, most of which
> are thought to have large negative externalities.

impact of policing on declining levels of crime or of fear of crime (see
box 4.18). Police officers are among the most visible and important points
of day-to-day contact between the state and members of the public; in states
lacking support and legitimacy, good policing can manifest and reflect
improving governance. This improvement, in turn, can have implications
for the costs (or perceived costs) of doing business, and the readiness of
businesses and consumers to save, spend, and invest. Improving the performance of the police, therefore, might be thought of as coinciding with, and
reflecting, the process of state building itself. Manifestly poor policing, on
the other hand, can have the opposite effect on a society, imposing economic costs that are greater than the direct costs of both crime and policing
itself. In other words, there is a strong degree of complementarity between
improved policing and greater state legitimacy. For obvious reasons, valuing the impact of policing is complicated by the impact of improving or
deteriorating policing on perceptions (and the reality) of the quality of
governance.

Legitimacy and Effectiveness

The techniques used by the police and the legitimacy of these techniques can
also have implications for the long-run costs of policing itself. Effective
policing depends heavily on the quantity and quality of the information
provided by members of the public (whether victims, witnesses, or simply
people with information about criminal activity). Information is costly to
procure, and those costs are strongly correlated with police legitimacy,
especially perceptions of competence and integrity. It is therefore no

Box 4.18   Police Strategy, Crime, and the Value of Homes in Rio de Janeiro

Beginning in 2008, a new police strategy was introduced to reduce crime in the *favelas* of Rio de Janeiro. As in many metropolitan areas in developing countries, a significant part of the population of Rio lives in very low-income communities, with a high concentration of substandard, informal housing. Over the past three decades, the city has been plagued by conflicts over territory between drug gangs and militias, with many *favelas* effectively being occupied and governed by the drug gangs. The Unidade Pacificadora da Policia ("Pacifying Police Unit," UPP) program reoccupies specific *favelas* by force using elite police units, drives out the drug gangs, roots out caches of weapons and drugs, and then installs permanent police stations staffed by highly trained, well-paid, and newly recruited officers; 18 such stations have been installed since 2008. The basic objective of reoccupation is the renewed assertion of the rule of law and the reduction of drug gang–related crimes.

Frischtak and Mandel sought to estimate the impact of falling levels of crime as a result of the UPP on the rise in the value of houses in areas adjacent to the new stations.[a] They demonstrated that (i) the police strategy worked (in that crime levels fell faster in areas where UPP was implemented than it did in other areas); and that (ii) one consequence of the declining high levels of crime was a faster-than-average rise in the value of homes in the area. As a significant proportion of household wealth is tied up in housing assets, the decline in crime simultaneously raised household wealth.

a. Frischtak and Mandel 2012.

accident that illegitimate police services need to rely more heavily on the most costly means for obtaining information (informers, surveillance, interception of communications, detention without trial, and coercion or torture). These techniques frequently have the effect of further undermining police legitimacy and further raising the costs of reliable information. For this reason, techniques that appear cost-effective in the short run may make it harder (and more costly) to provide effective policing (reduce crime) in the medium and long run.

Aggressive policing runs the risk of lowering police legitimacy, but it can sometimes reduce levels of crime and insecurity. In other words, overly aggressive tactics can harm the legitimacy of the police while also generating suppressive effects whose impact might persist over time. Indeed, where crime and violence are endemic (and where police lack the capacity to deploy more moderate tactics or where there is significant public support for aggressive policing), the impact of these strategies on police legitimacy may even be positive. That is, an aggressive, "tough on crime" approach may be judged favorably by the public and so may increase the legitimacy of the police, at least in the short term. In the longer term, however, it may reduce it—and may also reduce citizens' willingness to comply with the police. This appears to have been the case with the stop-and-search strategies in New York City.[43]

In developing countries, aggressive policing practices are generally more widely accepted. For example, public opinion surveys in Latin America and the Caribbean reveal that citizens tend to support more aggressive policing practices to tackle crime.[44] Hence there appears to be an association between endemic levels of crime and fear of crime on the one hand, and more aggressive policing practices on the other.

What is much less clear, however, is whether an aggressive approach is sustainable. Two factors suggest it may not be. The first is that the success of these measures (assuming they are successful in their own terms) can reduce the perceived need for such tactics among members of the public, making their continued use less legitimate. The second is that there is a significant risk of overreach and error in executing tactics of this kind, sometimes leading to crises in police legitimacy that can impose different kinds of direct and indirect costs on the police and on the government to which they are accountable. It is important to recognize here that police actions will always offend some members of the community; so policing to a greater or lesser extent is always engaged in the pursuit of legitimacy and consent.

Approaches to Measuring Police Performance

Measuring performance—developing a set of reliable indicators of activity, output, or outcome that can be easily collected and unambiguously understood—has proved harder for policing than for most other public service institutions. As already described, it can be difficult to assess the relationship between policing and the key policy goals associated with it: the prevention or reduction of crime and the maintenance of public safety. Crime levels are determined by a very wide variety of factors, the majority of which are likely more important than the volume or quality of policing services. A second challenge, one that is not inherently insurmountable but is still significant, is that the police organization itself usually collects the key data used in assessing its impact. This role can create problems of incentives that raise doubts about the reliability of crime statistics.

One approach to this problem is to have independent agencies conduct *victimization surveys*. Such surveys, however, tend to be expensive, difficult to conduct, and fraught with methodological challenges of their own. They may also be conducted unevenly across police jurisdictions and focus on potentially unrepresentative cities and regions. More important, most victimization surveys are not conducted regularly enough to be used as a basis for assessing changes in police performance, even if they do provide important insights both into levels of public safety and into the reliability of police crime statistics. The upshot, however, is that the crime information provided by police organizations is often its own master set, and its accuracy cannot be easily assessed.

Measuring police performance is also hard because it has been difficult to generate an academic and practitioner-wide consensus about *how* to measure policing. Police agencies offer a range of services, and for each one, performance can depend on how it is delivered. One way to summarize the challenge of achieving value for money in policing is this: (i) policing is a complex set of tasks that cannot easily be reduced to a single measure, and (ii) policing is most cost-effective when the police are legitimate and when they conduct their duties with the consent of those who are being policed. The difficulty is that in cases where policing is not legitimate and is not conducted with the consent of the policed, achieving legitimacy and public consent is time-consuming and expensive. To the extent possible, performance measures should not only assess what services are delivered and how; they should also measure how police activity affects legitimacy and public consent. To this end, experts have proposed a variety of alternative approaches to framing the elements of policing that need to be measured in order to holistically assess how well the police are delivering on their multidimensional mandate.

While multidimensional (or "balanced scorecard") approaches to measuring police performance complicate the process, there is broad (if not complete) consensus that too narrow a construal of key performance areas creates perverse and untenable outcomes when applied to a service as complex and diverse as policing. As Davis suggests, "performance measurement systems should capture the complex set of expectations that modern society has of the police, including service to citizens who request assistance and humane treatment of persons detained or held in custody."[45] One approach recommended as the basis of international best practice involves measurement of seven dimensions of performance[46]:

1. *Reducing crime and victimization.* Although some experts have argued that crime is beyond the control of the police, reducing crime is the single most important contribution that police make to the well-being of society and must therefore be a critical element of police organizations' assessments, both internally and externally.

2. *Holding offenders accountable (clearance and conviction rates).* Calling offenders to account is desirable for several reasons: it serves as punishment, can prevent and deter offenders from committing future crimes, and helps to mete out justice and restore equity.

3. *Reducing fear and enhancing a feeling of personal security.* Fear of victimization is one of the principal costs of crime. It is linked to victimization rates, but it is also influenced by other factors, including disorder and "incivility" conditions.

4. *Increasing safety and order in public spaces.* In today's anonymous cities, the police help ensure that strangers interact with each other appropriately in public spaces (parks, roads, etc.).

5. *Using force sparingly and fairly.* In pursuit of greater public safety, society gives the police special powers that they must use judiciously and equitably.

6. *Using public funds efficiently and fairly.* Society expects the police to operate economically and to control costs in a responsible manner (e.g., deploy officers fairly, keep costs down).

7. *Enhancing public satisfaction.* The police provide many services to the public above and beyond crime fighting. Providing good service to citizens increases police legitimacy.

A survey of the literature of police performance indicators is outlined in box 4.19.

Box 4.19   Dimensions of Police Performance

Ideas about how to measure police performance have evolved over time. They were first proposed during the emergence of the professional policing model in the 1930s, when the key performance indicators for the police were (i) the number of cases cleared (generally through arrest), and (ii) the value of stolen property recovered.[a] Subsequently these measures evolved to include proposals for community surveys about impressions of the police. For most scholars, there is no single "bottom line" for policing (see below), although some practitioners (most famously William Bratton, who has run both the Los Angeles and New York police departments) insist that crime rates are the single bottom line. Other areas that have attracted attention include the number of arrests and/or citations; clearance rates, which measure the rate of crimes cleared in relation to the crimes recorded; and response times to calls for service.

Numerous concerns about the efficacy and desirability of these measurements of police performance have led to the development of broader measures that seek to assess (i) what communities want from the police, and (ii) what police officers actually do. These in turn have led to the development of multidimensional measurements of police performance defined by a variety of approaches (as described in Maguire[b]):

- O'Neill, Needle, and Galvin (1980)[c] proposed 46 individual key performance indicators grouped around
  - Crime prevention
  - Crime control
  - Conflict resolution
  - General service
  - Police administration.
- Hatry et al. (1992)[d] focused on
  - Crime prevention
  - Apprehension of offenders
  - Responsiveness of the police
  - Feeling of security
  - Fairness, courtesy, helpfulness, honesty.
- Mastrofski (1999)[e] focused on
  - Attentiveness—visible police presence
  - Reliability—predictable response
  - Responsiveness—effort to satisfy people's requests and explain actions/inactions
  - Competence—knowledge of how to handle victims, witnesses, offenders, and the public
  - Manners—respectful treatment of all people
  - Fairness—equitable treatment of all people/groups in society.
- Moore (2002)[f] focused on
  - Reducing criminal victimization
  - Calling offenders to account
  - Reducing fear and enhancing personal security
  - Guaranteeing safety in public spaces
  - Using resources fairly, efficiently, and effectively
  - Using force fairly, efficiently, and effectively
  - Satisfying customer demands and achieving legitimacy with those policed.

As this brief survey shows, approaches to defining the dimensions along which police performance can and should be measured are diverse and divergent. The key commonality is that policing needs to be evaluated across a spectrum of indicators.

a. Maguire 2003.
b. Ibid.
c. O'Neill, Needle, and Galvin 1980.
d. Hatry et al. 1992.
e. Mastrofski 1999.
f. Moore 2002.

Measuring Police Performance in Relation to Crime Rates

The impact of policing on crime levels is the subject of intense academic and policy debate, partly because of methodological challenges. One of the most important of these is a problem of endogeneity: levels of crime in a particular area may be the consequence of the level of policing in that area, but may also be the reason for variations in the level of resourcing available. Thus if police resources are deployed to areas in which crime levels are believed by policy makers to be high, studies may underestimate the effect of policing on crime.

When resourcing decisions are made on the basis of factors other than crime levels—social and political dynamics, for example, that prioritize the need of some communities over that of others—assessing the impact of policing is complicated further. This is because police carry out very complex and varied tasks in addition to law enforcement that increase the difficulty of measuring impact. Even further complications arise if crime levels are measured using police crime statistics, since these may be poor measures of actual levels of crime and may be strongly influenced by the availability, accessibility, and legitimacy of the police as well as by police recording practices.

Another important complication, critical for security sector reform, is that the effectiveness of the police depends on the level of legitimacy they enjoy (see box 4.20). Increased policing may have measurably positive impacts in an area where police are seen as legitimate; but these results will

---

Box 4.20 Building Police Legitimacy

At a 2013 United Nations Police (UNPOL) conference of global police practitioners, David Bayley argued that legitimate policing was a critical building block for legitimate government. Because ensuring public safety is so central to the expectations that citizens have of their states, legitimate government cannot be built without legitimate policing. Bayley suggested that police legitimacy requires four elements:

1. Respect for the rule of law
2. A commitment to human rights
3. Accountability to external authorities
4. Responsiveness to the public.

Of these four, only the last was fully in the control of the police agency itself; the others require active commitment from other parts of the state. In relation to police responsiveness, Bayley suggested that there were three priorities for building the requisite performance to secure legitimacy:

1. Availability to the public (i.e., ability to answer calls for service, be present in the streets)
2. Helpfulness (i.e., ability to provide services that actually improve the situation)
3. Fairness to and respect for those with whom police officers engage.

Each of these elements of the police responsiveness agenda could be broken down further, but together they offer a useful frame for thinking about the challenges of police reform.

Source: David Bayley, keynote address at UNPOL conference of global police practitioners, Oslo, March 2013.

be hard to replicate in areas where they are not. As already discussed, police legitimacy is critically important for police performance: police are much better able to fulfill their functions if they enjoy public support and if members of the public are willing to provide them with information and evidence. Importantly, levels of legitimacy can vary across socioeconomic or ethnic groups (who often have different experiences of law enforcement).

Gender mainstreaming can also play an important role, both institutionally and operationally, in good policing and in building public legitimacy, particularly in the security sector reform context. The UN Department of Peacekeeping Operations' Integrated Technical Guidance Note emphasizes that gender-responsive security sector reform "can serve as a model for the inclusion of marginalized and excluded groups in the security sector."[47] In turn, institutions reflective of all members of society are more likely to be trusted and seen as legitimate. Better gender balance in policing not only improves access by all citizens to the law, but also increases the efficacy of policing itself via a "broader range of police skills, approaches, and perspectives."[48] Greater gender inclusiveness involves building ties with women's civil society groups, having both men and women present on patrols, training both male and female officers to respond to sexual and gender-based violence, and having female officers speak with female victims of crime.

Reporting of Crime Rates and Public Perceptions

Even in the best-resourced, best-managed police agencies, crime levels as recorded by the police usually understate the level of victimization in a community. One reason why police crime statistics may be inaccurate is the underreporting of crime by victims, which could be a consequence of various factors:

- Victims are unaware or do not believe that a crime has been committed, because they are unaware of the incident, do not view the incident as criminal, or think the incident should not be deemed criminal (as may be the case with some kinds of gender violence, for example).
- The police are inaccessible.
- There is a lack of faith in policing and the courts among citizens, particularly among socially marginalized groups (such as ethnic minorities, undocumented migrants, prostitutes, etc.), who see going to the police to lay a criminal complaint as undesirable (see box 4.21 and box 4.22).
- The police lack legitimacy.

A second important reason why crime statistics might be inaccurate is the underrecording or misreporting of crime by police officers. This is a particularly pervasive issue in fragile countries, where it occurs for these reasons:

- Police data management infrastructure and systems (including the skills of data handlers) may be inadequate to the task of accurate reporting.

- The police may deliberately understate the level of reported crime (or the level of particular crimes about which there is particular political pressure) in order to satisfy their superiors or the public.

For example, the International Crime Victims Survey showed that in the year 2000, more than 50 percent of victims did not report the crime to the police.[49]

Box 4.21   Police-Citizen Relations in Africa

Afrobarometer, a research organization that conducts regular surveys across a range of African states, has asked respondents about their relationship with the police. Majorities or large minorities of respondents say that they do not trust the police at all or trust them only "a little" (figures B4.21.1 and B4.21.2). One reason for this mistrust may be the fact that large majorities in most countries—especially in rural areas—do not see police or police vehicles frequently.

When asked whether they report crimes to the police, only a fifth of respondents said that they did. They offered a wide range of reasons for not doing so.

Figure B4.21.1   Proportion of Citizens in African Countries Who Do Not See Police or Police Vehicles Frequently, 2011–2012

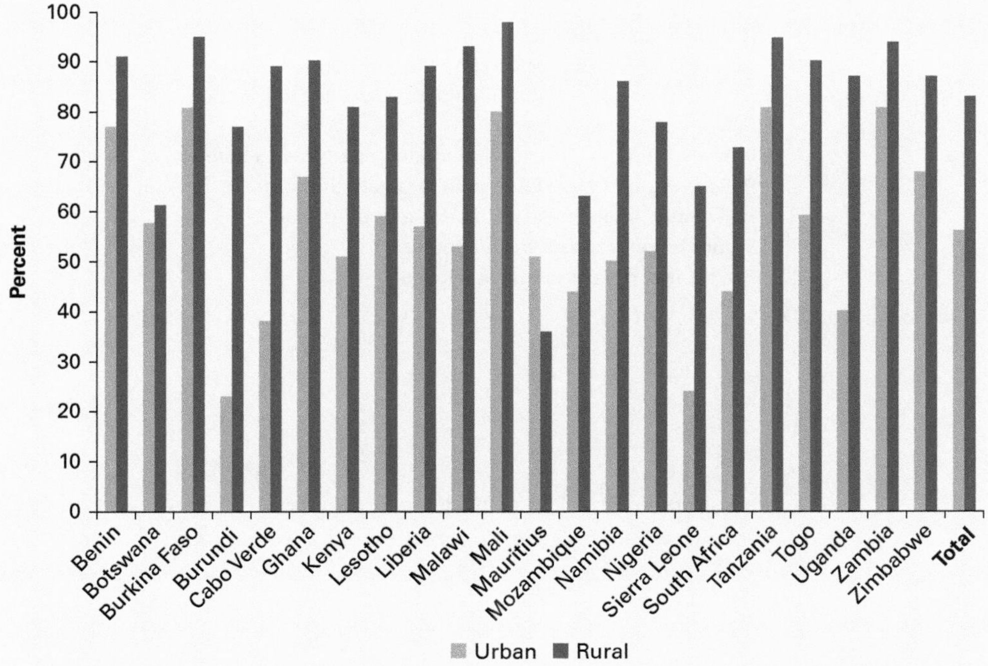

Urban ■ *Rural*

(Box continues on next page)

Box 4.21   **Police-Citizen Relations in Africa** *(continued)*

Figure B4.21.2   Frequency of Top Reasons for Not Reporting Crimes to Police in African Countries, 2011–2012

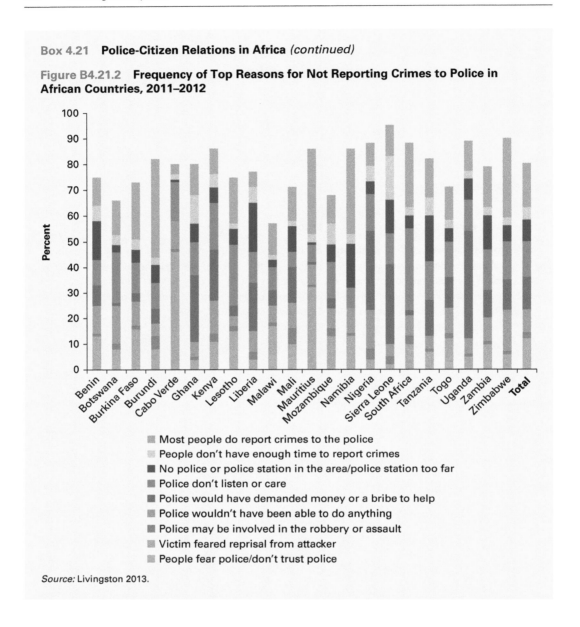

■ Most people do report crimes to the police
▨ People don't have enough time to report crimes
■ No police or police station in the area/police station too far
■ Police don't listen or care
■ Police would have demanded money or a bribe to help
▨ Police wouldn't have been able to do anything
■ Police may be involved in the robbery or assault
▨ Victim feared reprisal from attacker
▨ People fear police/don't trust police

Source: Livingston 2013.

The opposite problem to underrecording is overrecording of crime; this may occur when police organizations seek to increase the pressure on political authorities in an effort to increase their resourcing. Such tactics are rare, however, given that security sector budgetary allocations are on average fairly constant. Indirect overrecording of crimes, which may take place when crimes are misclassified or downgraded to reduce the number of more serious crimes recorded, is more likely than direct overrecording of crimes.

Box 4.22   Police-Citizen Relations in Latin America

The Latin American Public Opinion Survey (LAPOP) conducts regular surveys across Latin America and the Caribbean on citizens' perceptions of a range of issues, including safety and security. One of the questions addresses the relationship between citizens and the police. Trust in the police appears to be a major issue in the region (figure B4.22.1). During the past decade, opinion surveys have shown that 20 percent of the population does not trust the police forces at all, compared to 10 percent who trust the police a lot (LAPOP survey, 2000–2012). However, there is substantial variation across countries. For example, data show that in Argentina and the Dominican Republic, a significantly higher percentage of people do not trust the police than in Nicaragua, where the percentage of people who trust the police a lot is slightly higher than the percentage of people who don't trust the police at all.

Figure B4.22.1   Trust in the Police in Latin American Countries, 2000–2012

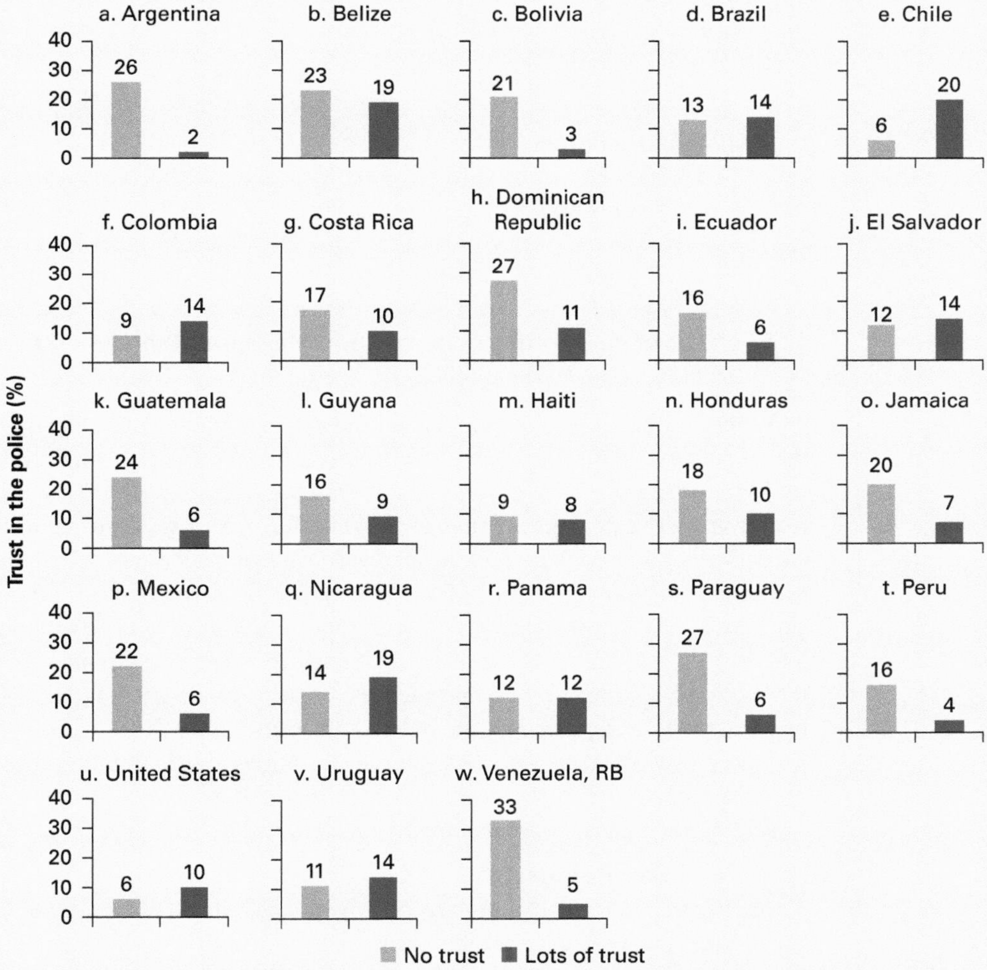

Source: Vanderbilt University 2012.

(Box continues on next page)

Box 4.22   **Police-Citizen Relations in Latin America** *(continued)*

The public's levels of trust in the police likely affect reporting of crimes: people are less likely to report crime when they have less trust in the police, more likely to report crime when they have more trust. Using the LAPOP survey for the 2000–2012 period, a simple correlation analysis shows on average a positive and statistically significant correlation—albeit weak—between trust in the police and the reporting of crime. This weak correlation is likely due to the fact that levels of trust in the police are generally low.

Source: Vanderbilt University 2012.

The recording of crime involves five different steps, any one of which may introduce bias into police crime statistics and lead to underestimation. These steps include the following:

1. The recognition by a victim that a crime has occurred and that it should be reported
2. The decision by the victim to report the crime to the police and then actually doing so
3. The accurate recording of the crime by the police officer to whom it is reported
4. The existence of a comprehensive process for aggregating crime data
5. The accurate reporting of the results of those to authorities outside of the police (and to the public).

Where police organizations are undergoing significant reform—or where society as a whole is experiencing significant changes—the level of underreporting of police crime statistics can vary. If the police reform is a response to the perception that levels of safety are low, then reformers consciously and explicitly seek to increase levels of police accessibility and legitimacy so that reporting rates will increase. Reformers might also be consciously aiming to increase the accuracy of police recording practices. Similarly, social changes that disrupt established patterns of civilian-police interaction have important consequences for the probability that particular incidents will be reported to the police and recorded by them. Thus while changes in police crime statistics can reflect underlying changes in the level of public safety (as in the first example), this is not always the case and should be kept in mind when statistics are interpreted.

Police and Self-Reporting

As previously mentioned, a key reason why police crime data are difficult to use for the purposes of assessing performance is that they are collected by the police. There are a number of important consequences of this fact:

- Assessing the level of public safety purely on the basis of police crime statistics can increase the incentives of the police—and the institutions they report to—to manipulate the data.

- The existence of a "dark number" (defined as those crimes not reported to the police) and a "gray number" (defined as those crimes reported to the police but not recorded or not properly recorded) means that increases or decreases in recorded crime statistics might simply reflect changing reporting practices rather than changes in the underlying trend. If increasing levels of recorded crime are the result of increased reporting, they might reflect the police force's increased legitimacy and accessibility. In this case, the appropriate interpretation of an increase in recorded crime might be that police performance has improved—so that more people feel it worthwhile to report crime—or might be that social values are changing.

- The difficulty of assessing the level of public safety can be mitigated by conducting victimization surveys, but these tend to be expensive and of limited utility unless they use extremely large samples. As already mentioned, they must also be repeated regularly to be of any value in assessing either changing levels of safety and security or police performance. Finally, they, too, are subject to a wide range of methodological and interpretive challenges relating to how respondents understand and define events.

- Because crime statistics cannot be audited independently, their use as performance indicators—of individuals, of police units, or of the police organization as a whole—can generate perverse incentives. A corollary is that the greater the emphasis on crime and safety in public debate and political contestation, and the greater the emphasis on the police's responsibility for crime, the greater the incentive to manipulate the data. It is possible to manage these processes effectively, as demonstrated by the success that the NYPD (and others) have had in using Compstat and other statistics-based systems for monitoring the performance of individual precinct and beat commanders and the deployment of resources (see box 4.23). It is unclear, however, whether this success is replicable in institutions where managerial skills are less developed, human and IT capabilities are less sophisticated, and police officers (and managers) may not be very numerate.

- Following the apparent success of Compstat-based approaches in some large cities (see box 4.23), similar systems have been adopted by large municipal forces in Latin America. The city of São Paulo and the state of Minas Gerais, for example, credit Compstat-like strategies for their success in reducing levels of violence. Other countries in the region, including Colombia and Mexico, have adopted similar platforms to tackle crime more effectively.[50]

- A final consequence relates to so-called "victimless crimes," where the criminal conduct is voluntary and consensual. Since there is no obvious "victim" to report crimes like drunk driving, drug dealing, corruption, and prostitution, they are recorded only as a result of police-initiated activity (e.g., roadblocks, buy-bust operations,

---

Box 4.23   Compstat

The term "Compstat" is often used to refer to two distinguishable systems. The first is a strategic management system that generates and maps crime data much more rapidly than was historically possible for police data-gathering and aggregation processes. The second is a set of internal management processes, established in the New York Police Department (NYPD) in 1994 by its then commissioner, William Bratton, when the IT system underpinning those processes was implemented. As one study notes, Compstat has also become shorthand for the full range of strategic, problem-solving activities in the NYPD, including the institution's twice-weekly Compstat "Crime-Control Strategy Meetings," where precinct commanders appear before several of the department's most senior managers to report on crime problems in their precincts and their responses to them, and where new data generated by Compstat are assessed.[a]

Compstat's main contribution to management seems to be speed: crime data are now available to precinct commanders for the previous week (compared to a lag of three to six months before Compstat). The data include a full range of operational statistics as well as sophisticated crime maps, helping to identify trends in crime in close to real time, and forcing commanders to account for how they have adjusted deployments or how they will do so in the future. Compstat also facilitates coordination across organizational boundaries.

In recent years, however, Compstat has been subject to increased scrutiny because some precincts have allegedly mismanaged the program to suggest the police were more effective than they actually were. For example, some serious crimes appear to have been deliberately downgraded and the number of stop-and-frisks increased.[b]

a. Weisburd et al. 2004.
b. Eterno and Silverman 2012.

---

surveillance operations, and stings). Any increases or decreases in these crimes may therefore say more about police activity than about the underlying trends.

Apart from the possibility that using crime statistics as performance indicators may create perverse incentives, the extent to which crime levels are affected by policing is unclear. Debate about the relationship of policing to levels of security is ongoing, unresolved, and possibly unresolvable. For this reason alone, using crime statistics to measure the performance of the police—and in particular the performance of individual officers and groups of officers—may be undesirable; premised on the assumption that crime levels are strongly affected by police action (or inaction), this approach distorts debate about the legitimate role of the police and about the proportion of public resources to be expended on policing. That is, police organizations, units, and individual officers will have reason to expect higher levels of resourcing when crime levels are factored into reviews of police performance.

Crime statistics are often the only data available for monitoring and assessing policing, and there is obvious utility in examining what they reflect about levels of safety and security. But they need to be used very carefully and with clear recognition of their limits.

Alternative Ways to Measure Performance

Alternative measures of police performance are available, though each has its own weaknesses. Some common alternatives to crime statistics include:

- Activity-based measures, such as patrol intensity, emergency response times, and the number of activities such as stop-and-search or road-blocks conducted
- Output-based measures such as seizures of contraband
- Output measures on arrest and clearance rates.

Like activity-based measures in other domains, measurements of police activity can provide data on the efficiency with which police resources are being used, but may not convey any information about the impact of their use on levels of safety and security. Indeed, the activity-based approach is beset by weaknesses; the most obvious is that little data exist on the relationship between particular activities and levels of safety and security. At the same time, where there is at least some evidence that a particular police strategy is useful for some goals—e.g., that stop-and-search may reduce the carrying of illegal weapons, or that police roadblocks may reduce the incidence of drunk driving—measurements of police activity can be assumed to reflect something about the effectiveness of the use of police resources. (For some significant problems with the stop-and-search strategy, see box 4.24.)

A more difficult problem with activity-based measurements, however, is their tendency to encourage misallocation of police resources and energy. If police officers or units are measured on the number of roadblocks they conduct and the number of vehicles they search, they may expend fewer resources and less energy on other kinds of activities or strategies. Crimes that require these other approaches are likely to go relatively under-resourced precisely because they are not being measured in the same way and with the same degree of rigor.

Measuring Outputs

Using measurements of police output (as opposed to activities) has potential problems, but it is often more easily justified even when the link between a particular output and the level of crime is ambiguous. Key output measures include the volume of contraband seized by the police, the number of arrests made, and the conversion of those arrests into prosecutions and convictions (i.e., arrest rates and clearance rates).

One key police output is the seizure of contraband and the recovery of stolen goods. Police agencies often dedicate significant resources to the seizure of illegal goods (e.g., narcotics and illegal weapons), legal goods being traded illegally (e.g., unlicensed or untaxed liquor or cigarettes; intellectual property traded without the payment of royalties), and stolen goods.

There is contradictory evidence about the impact of these activities even on the kinds of crime they seem most likely to affect. For instance, the prices charged for narcotics have been falling consistently for decades,[51] suggesting that police activity has made little impact on supply even as demand has

---

Box 4.24   Controversies Surrounding Stop-and-Search

One of the most common police activities across the world is the stop-and-search, in which officers stop pedestrians (and sometimes motorists) and search them. In some jurisdictions this is often the premise for a "shakedown" (when an officer threatens to arrest a member of the public unless paid off) or outright theft or robbery. Yet even when officers are not abusing their authority in this way, the practice is controversial because of who tends to be targeted. Consider the chapter titles of a recent edited collection on stop-and-search practices across the world[a]:

- The Formation of Suspicions: Police Stop and Search Practices in England and Wales
- Stop and Search in London: Counter-terrorist or Counter-productive?
- Ethnic Profiling in ID Checks by the Hungarian Police
- The Usual Suspects: Police Stop and Search Practices in Canada
- The Fantastical World of South Africa's Roadblocks: Dilemmas of a Ubiquitous Police Strategy
- "War on Illegal Immigrants," National Narratives, and Globalization: Japanese Policy and Practice of Police Stop and Question in Global Perspective
- Ethnic Profiling in the Netherlands? A Reflection on Expanding Preventive Powers, Ethnic Profiling and a Changing Social and Political Context
- "It Sounds Like They Shouldn't Be Here": Immigration Checks on the Streets of Sydney
- Suspecting Immigrants: Exploring Links between Racialised Anxieties and Expanded Police Powers in Arizona.

These titles suggest the essentially political nature of active police patrols and, hence, their potential for promoting controversy and perceptions of unfairness. There is, of course, some evidence that in some contexts, these patrols can play a big role in increasing public safety and/or public perceptions of police and government effectiveness. They are credited for playing a role in reducing crime in many American cities over the past two decades. Nevertheless, it should also be clear that, unless levels of police professionalism are high, use of these strategies in some societies might have more to do with social and political dynamics than managing public safety.

a. Weber and Bowling 2012.

---

remained essentially static.[52] At the same time, it seems implausible that police resources devoted to the seizure of contraband and recovery of stolen goods would fail to disrupt the markets for some kinds of goods (e.g., stolen cars, drugs sold at street level).

Another important output measure is the number of suspects identified and arrested, and the conversion of those arrests into prosecutions and convictions. It should be stressed that the link between arrest, prosecution, and conviction (to say nothing of incarceration), on the one hand, and crime levels, on the other, is contested in the theoretical and empirical literature; for every study suggesting that crime levels are affected by police productivity in this sphere, there is another casting doubt on the relationship. Nevertheless, if the mandate of the police is understood to include the delivery of justice to offenders (or if the needs and desires of victims of crime have political salience in setting criminal justice policy), then the arrest, prosecution, and conviction of offenders is a legitimate public policy goal, even if it has only an ambiguous effect on the level of crime. From this point of view, the commission of a crime is not a measure of the failure of policing (as it might be if crime prevention were the sole goal of the police), but the event that instigates the delivery of police services, and, indeed, the services of the rest of the justice system.

Data on arrests, prosecutions, and convictions convey important information about how police (and justice system) resources are being used. However, relying on these data entails certain caveats, which are listed here (and discussed further in box 4.25):

- The *volume* of arrests may be unrelated to the *quality* of those arrests. There are recorded instances, for example, of police officers seeking to clear unsolved cases by charging suspects in one crime with other (similar) crimes even when evidence for this link is absent or weak. Thus data on arrest and clearance rates ought to be qualified by data

---

Box 4.25   Two Cautionary Notes on Measuring the Performance of the Criminal Justice System

At a 1993 Bureau of Justice Assistance conference on performance measures for the criminal justice system, James Q. Wilson argued that the utility of police performance measures is limited, because the effect of police behavior on public safety is limited:

> Most of the efforts to improve performance measures for policing have concentrated on finding either real measures of overall effectiveness or plausible proxy measures. Not much has come of these efforts for reasons that should be obvious. There are no "real" measures of overall success; what is measurable about the level of public order, safety and amenity in a given large city can only be partially, if at all, affected by police behavior. (For example, if the murder or robbery rates go up, one cannot assume that this is the fault of the police; if they go down we should not necessarily allow the police to take credit for it.) Proxy measures almost always turn out to be process measures—response times, arrest rates or clearance rates—that may or may not have any relationship to crime rates or levels of public order.[a]

Speaking at the same conference, Alpert and Moore criticized the use of standard measures of police performance—crime levels, arrest rates, clearance rates, response times—for a different reason: they don't facilitate the deployment of community police strategies and in fact result in resources being misdirected:

> These measures remain critical as part of an overall system for measuring police performance. As currently used, however, they reflect an increasingly outmoded model of police tasks and fail to capture many important contributions that the police make to the quality of life. More important, these measures may misguide police managers and lead them and their organizations towards purposes and activities that are less valuable than others that can be achieved with limited and diminishing resources.[b]

a. Wilson 1993, 159.
b. Alpert and Moore 1993, 109.

on the nature of the cases in which the arrests were made, the number of cases prosecutors take to court, and the proportion of cases that result in convictions. Since prosecution and conviction may occur sometime after arrests are made, it may be difficult to assess the quality of arrests when the number varies significantly from period to period. In addition, given that making arrests is easier for some kinds of crime than for others, it may be important to assess the distribution of arrests across categories of criminal activity.

- Prosecution and conviction rates can be helpful in assessing the quality of arrests—but only when the prosecution services and courts are sufficiently independent and professional to render these data meaningful. One potential (perverse) consequence of using these data, however, is that they may encourage the deployment of police (and justice system) resources to the simplest cases (those in which it is relatively easy to identify suspects, produce evidence, and achieve convictions). Some kinds of cases—particularly those committed by strangers (e.g., robbery) or committed surreptitiously (e.g., burglary)—are notoriously difficult to solve[53] and may be deprioritized in a justice system that uses prosecution and conviction rates to assess police productivity and effectiveness. In addition, police officers often contend that inadequate skills and resources in the prosecution services (or judiciary) account for the failure of cases in courts, so that low prosecution and conviction rates do not necessarily reflect the quality of police work. Incentives in the prosecution services may also have an influence here: if prosecutors' performance is judged on the rate of convictions for the cases they actually take to court, they may choose to prosecute only the cases in which a conviction is very likely.[54]

Measuring Response Times

One frequently used set of performance data, which falls somewhere between measuring activity and measuring outputs, relates to police responsiveness and reaction time. Rapid response times from the police are highly valued by communities and politicians, and overall perceptions of police quality are often partly based on the speed of police response to calls for service. To the extent that this is so, the rapidity of response might be deemed an output of policing rather than an activity. Yet for most "ordinary criminality," the rapidity of police response has little relation to the likelihood that a suspect will be arrested or successfully prosecuted. (Of course in some circumstances—e.g., incidents of public violence—ranging from barroom brawls to community conflict to political protests to mass shootings—response time is potentially important.) Response time tends to be comparatively unimportant because by the time the police are called, the crime has usually been completed and the offender is no longer present. For this reason, police organizations need graduated responses to different kinds of calls for service, and should seek to manage public expectations in this regard. The absence of this kind of triage—a situation sometimes dubbed the "tyranny of 911"—can result in the inefficient allocation of resources within a police agency.

Professional Supervision and Data Collection

The difficulties of measuring police performance suggest the importance of highly professional management of the police; with less skilled or well-trained managers, it is difficult to ensure that resources are deployed in a way that maximizes value for money. Building a professional management cadre where one does not exist is a complex task, however. Where management is weak or inadequate, systems based on quantifiable indicators can be useful, in spite of their numerous difficulties. In other words, a well-designed system of performance indicators may substitute for some of the weaknesses in managerial capabilities—although instituting such a system is itself not easy, and its impact on performance will depend partly on the quality of police managers. Simply providing and making transparent some performance data, however, can ensure an improved debate about the need for—and direction of—police reform. In this regard, a critical challenge is designing a data collection process that ensures accurate data: because the police may be the sole source of the data, there may be no way to assess its accuracy and no independently gathered data against which to measure it.

Measuring the Use of Force

The use of force, including the risk that force will be used inappropriately or disproportionately, is a key element in understanding policing, and several institutions recommend using performance indicators that focus on this issue. The Vera Institute of Justice, for example, suggests using the rate of death and injury of people in contact with the justice/security sector (police, military, and prisons, in particular) as a measure of the performance of the system as a whole, and also recommends using measures of perceived safety when people are in contact with the system.[55]

Community Surveys

Because policing services can be delivered unequally to politically or socially marginalized communities, many experts also recommend measuring police performance by means of community surveys that focus on the experience of these groups. Victimization surveys and surveys of public perception are both useful tools, whether for a performance evaluation system being designed from scratch or for those using existing sources of data. They tend to be expensive (and, therefore, generally infrequent), but they can provide important data for policy makers and operational managers. Analysis of the surveys should recognize, however, that public perceptions—particularly when measured in general surveys—tend to be affected by factors over which the police may have little control. These might include general political dynamics, levels of media coverage, how community leaders position themselves in relation to the police, etc. These surveys often find that members of different communities have quite distinct impressions of the police and their performance, with negative views being more common among people from socially and politically marginalized communities. Contact surveys (which interview people who have had recent contact with the police) can often provide more accurate data on individual experiences of policing, and results tend to be less differentiated for distinct social groups; but they may miss important aspects of group-based public perception.

Measuring Police Performance: Two Proposed Frameworks

Given the complexities associated with performance measurement in the police, attempts to measure performance must respect the limitations of the data. An appropriate strategy depends largely on the extent to which a particular environment is rich or poor in data. In data-rich environments, it is appropriate to use all the available data to build as nuanced a picture as possible of the performance of the police and justice sector, all the while recognizing the limits of the data and the potential systemic biases that may affect the data's accuracy and interpretation. Davis argues that "it is important not to rely on individual measures, but rather to examine a set of indicators. Individual measures may be misleading, but looking for patterns in a set of indicators is likely to give a better picture of an agency's level of professionalism."[56] Or, as the Vera Institute of Justice notes, "an indicator should rarely be used on its own. To interpret changes in ambiguous indicators, you should always use a group or 'basket' of indicators relating to the same policy objective. Baskets of indicators provide a more valid, reliable, and rounded view of policy progress."[57]

When crime statistics (however derived) are used to evaluate the quality of policing across different jurisdictions, results must be adjusted to reflect differences in the jurisdictions. It would, for example, be unfair to use crime levels alone in comparing the performance of inner-city police with police in a quiet country district. How to make these adjustments is controversial precisely because it is not clear what causes crime or what risk factors ought to be used to make the adjustment. Two approaches are possible: one is to simply compare changes in indicators over time for the same police station; the second is to define peer groups of police stations and assess performance of individual stations against more or less comparable peers.

It is also always desirable to test police crime data against other sources, in particular the results of victimization surveys and data from other departments in the justice system that might point to trends in the throughput of cases and suspects to court. In general, initial interpretation should focus on trends revealed by the data and should assume that any systemic weaknesses have not changed over the period under review. At the same time, it may be worth assessing whether this assumption still holds, since the relationship between the data and the underlying reality might have changed as a result of changes in policy or practices. It is also useful to obtain data on prisoners awaiting trial (numbers and average length of incarceration), which can suggest the efficiency of the justice system as a whole.

In data-poor environments, the most critical interventions may be (i) to obtain organizational buy-in for building the systems needed to gather data, and (ii) to ensure that requisite systems and skills are in place to use such a system (see box 4.26). The most important data to attempt to capture are police data on criminal activity. This information will probably not be comprehensive and may not even cover the whole country. It will, however, offer at least some insight into some aspects of police workload. This should be supplemented with victimization survey data, which are often the only feasible way to get a clear picture of the level of insecurity in the short term. In addition, data on throughput of cases, prisoner numbers, and the number (and average length of incarceration) of prisoners awaiting trial should be obtained wherever possible.

Measuring Police Performance: Technical, Allocative, and Overall Efficiency

Police forces, like other public institutions, use inputs to produce outputs and outcomes. Examples of police outputs include clearance rates, which use inputs such as the number of police officers, computers, and vehicles, among others. Put simply, the resources put forth by the police force should increase the number of crimes cleared.

However, the impact of the work of the police goes beyond the clearing of a certain number of crimes. For example, it can change, for better or worse, the overall crime rate, quality of life of citizens, and citizens' perceptions of the police. These are considered outcomes, and they measure the effectiveness of the police force in actually reducing the crime rate or increasing the perception of safety in communities.

Box 4.26   Strengthening Crime Data Collection Systems in South Sudan

One of the key areas for sound policy making on crime and violence prevention is the collection, systematization, and analysis of data on crime and violence. After decades of civil war, the newly formed South Sudan National Police Service (SSNPS) did not have the installed capacity to collect and analyze crime data. Following a directive issued by the inspector general of the SSNPS, and with the assistance of the United Nations Development Programme, there has been a comprehensive effort to install the institutional capacity to collect and analyze data on crime and violence. The objective is to develop a better understanding of the levels and nature of crime in South Sudan. The collection of crime statistics is aimed at assisting the South Sudan police administration to analyze the trends and patterns of crime across the counties and states, which in turn will assist the police administration in formulating important policy-level decisions regarding deployment of police personnel, establishing or reinforcing police stations, recruitment, transfers, special police measures, increasing patrolling, mobile patrolling, searching and community policing.[a]

Seven quarterly reports have been issued since December 2011. These reports provide statistics on crime and violence and a brief analysis of the trends and crime situation. While the statistics suffer from weaknesses in terms of measurement, they still make it possible to approximate the police workload and capacity to collect and measure data.

a. South Sudan National Police Services 2011–2013.

In assessments of the efficiency and effectiveness of spending, the World Bank has used frontier analysis to estimate technical, allocative, and overall efficiency.[58] Statistical frontier techniques like data envelopment analysis permit the measurement of efficiency in public sector institutions like the police and allow police managers and policy makers to identify top- and worse-performing stations and adjust budgets accordingly. In order to assess efficiency and effectiveness, each police station can be treated as a decision-making unit (DMU). For the sake of this example, we assume a total of five DMUs, and assume further that each DMU uses two inputs (number of police officers and vehicles) to produce one output, crimes cleared (of which a percentage is being calculated over total number of crimes recorded). Efficiency is simply defined as the ratio of outputs to inputs.[59] In other words, a DMU is efficient if it maximizes the outputs produced utilizing the smallest amount of inputs. Efficiency can be illustrated with a simple example: if each police station has the same resources allocated to it, but police station A produces a higher amount of outputs (percentage of crimes cleared), it can be argued that police station A is relatively more efficient than the rest of the stations.

Technical efficiency—referred to simply as "efficiency" in the example above—is the simplest and most commonly used measure of efficiency in performance analysis. As noted before, a DMU is deemed technically efficient if it produces the maximum amount of outputs using the smallest amount of inputs. An example (shown in table 4.6) can help illustrate this relationship.[60] For the five DMUs, there is one input, 25 police officers; and there is one output, 100 crimes cleared. (For the purposes of this example, we assume that this is the maximum capacity of the DMU given its current organizational structure and budgetary allocations.)

The results indicate that police station D cleared 90 crimes out of the 100 possible for each police station in this example. The best achievable efficiency score was 100/100 (if inputs are used efficiently to produce the maximum output), and the current efficiency score was 90/100. Thus police station D can be assessed as operating at 90 percent efficiency. On the other

Table 4.6 **Technical Efficiency Scores per Decision-Making Unit (DMU)**

DMU	Actual output	Maximum technical efficiency	Actual technical efficiency
A	30	100	30
B	80	100	80
C	10	100	10
D	90	100	90
E	60	100	60

hand, police station C cleared 10 crimes, and its technical efficiency is only 10 percent. Police station C can be assessed as very inefficient; it would have to increase its outputs by 90 percent to become efficient.

In order to measure allocative efficiency, the input prices must be known.[61] Allocative efficiency can be defined as the optimal use of inputs given their prices. Given the difficulty of determining accurate input prices for public sector institutions, this measure is generally not employed in efficiency studies of police forces. However, if prices are known, the allocative efficiency could be measured.

Overall (economic) efficiency is measured as the combination of technical efficiency and allocative efficiency.[62] As noted before, however, because accurate input prices for public institutions like the police are difficult to obtain, this measure is generally not reported in performance studies.

A Nonquantitative Alternative

One framework that attempts to organize some of the complexities involved in measuring police performance is offered by Davis, who identifies three distinguishable kinds of performance measures: process measures, officer conduct measures, and outcome measures.[63]

Process measures are essentially "checklist" measures indicating whether the agency has adopted policies governing a particular issue. Examples are given in table 4.7.

Officer conduct measures are a set of indicators that address the degree of professionalism in officers' conduct, the volume and nature of citizen complaints about officers, etc. Examples are in table 4.8.

Outcome measures are a set of indicators that relate to the outputs and outcomes of policing, including crime rates, response times, clearance rates, etc. Examples are in tables 4.9 and 4.10.

Table 4.7 **Process Measures for Performance**

Indicator	Definition	Source
Police policies	Policies on use of force and traffic/pedestrian stops conform to national best practices	Analysis of written policies
Training programs	Hours of academy and in-service training on use of force, stops, ethnic sensitivity	Analysis of training curriculum
Early warning system	Databases to (for example) track citizen complaints received by officers, use of force, stops	Analysis of early warning system specifications
Transparency	Publication of data on (for example) crime complaints, arrests, stops, use of force, citizen complaints	Analysis of departmental reports, website
Community interface	Establishment of citizen advisory council, public attendance at open district meetings, citizen participation in anticrime activities	Analysis of data from departmental records, observation of meetings

Source: Davis 2012. © RAND Corporation. Reproduced with permission from RAND Corporation; further permission required for reuse.

Table 4.8   **Performance Measures for Officer Conduct**

Indicator	Definition	Source
Handling of routine incidents	Professionalism of officers when interacting with persons requesting assistance or stopped by the police	Brief surveys to assess satisfaction of "consumers" of police services
Citizen complaints	Number of citizen complaints, rate at which complaints are sustained, proportion of officers disciplined	Analysis of annual reports of complaint agency
Officer morale and ethics	Officer job satisfaction and "climate of integrity"	Surveys of police officers

Source: Davis 2012. © RAND Corporation. Reproduced with permission from RAND Corporation; further permission required for reuse.

Table 4.9   **Performance Measures Based on Policing Outputs**

Indicator	Definition	Source
Crime rates	Rates of reported crime and criminal victimization, adjusted for community demographics	Analysis of records management system data and/or surveys of randomly selected community members
Response times	Time to respond to emergency and nonemergency calls for service	Analysis of data from departmental records
Clearance rates	Proportion of crime reports cleared by arrest	Analysis of data from departmental records

Source: Davis 2012. © RAND Corporation. Reproduced with permission from RAND Corporation; further permission required for reuse.

Table 4.10   **Performance Measures Based on Policing Outcomes**

Indicator	Definition	Source
Community opinion	Public opinions of police effectiveness and police misconduct	Surveys of randomly selected community members
Citizen cooperation with the police	Willingness of citizens to report crimes and noncrime problems to the police	Surveys of randomly selected community members

Source: Davis 2012. © RAND Corporation. Reproduced with permission from RAND Corporation; further permission required for reuse.

Conclusion

This chapter has outlined the complexities of policing for the purposes of conducting a PER, including the security sector context, the strategic and institutional responses, and the nexus to expenditure policy, financial management, and performance measurement. The particular focus or comprehensiveness of any particular PER will be contingent on the request of the client government, the resources available, and the time frame provided.

To cover the ground envisaged, the PER team should ideally comprise at least a country specialist, an expert on policing, and an expert on economic policy and financial issues. The team makeup will be resource contingent, but the multidimensional aspects of the task require a multidisciplinary team to support the government and relevant stakeholders in providing the necessary analysis.

Finally, given the many contextual and data challenges of undertaking a PER on policing, the PER should launch a process of engagement with the relevant stakeholders. Save for in exceptionally high-capacity environments, it is doubtful that a one-off PER would be sufficiently rigorous to be useful. In weaker capacity environments, the PER should take some steps toward better informing financial and policy decision makers but should be considered as a part of a longer-term trend analysis and capacity-building agenda.

Annex 4A: An In-Depth Review of Policy Options for Delivering Safety and Security

Managing budgets and expenditures of the security sector (outside of the military) presents few intrinsic difficulties for public financial management (apart from some areas of budget secrecy). But defining a strategy for the sector, and deploying resources to execute it, are profoundly difficult tasks. The sources of a society's insecurity are complex, and relationships of causality are notoriously difficult to define. This is particularly true of "ordinary crime" (as opposed to some forms of conflict), which plays a large role in insecurity in much of the world. Precisely why some countries, regions, cities, and neighborhoods are less safe than others is a highly contentious question (see box 4A.1). Prescriptions and remedies are equally contentious. What is clear is that many of the key factors that drive increases or decreases in security are not in the control of the security sector.

It is generally accepted that socioeconomic conditions (such as levels of employment, poverty, and inequality), as well as some historical/cultural factors (such as social attitudes to violence, recent experience of episodes of violence and insecurity, the degree of social cohesion), play a role in shaping a society's overall level of security. Usually, however, the security sector can do little to ameliorate those conditions. Nor is it likely to have much influence on aspects of youth culture, and in particular the attitudes of young men to the use of violence that play a critical role in shaping levels of security. Indeed, confrontation with law enforcement authorities is actively celebrated among young men, while in others adverse contact with the criminal justice system is seen as a rite of passage.

Norms and attitudes of this kind affect the extent to which the activities of the security sector will affect the level of safety and security, and, at the extreme, may mean that police activity actually helps consolidate gangs and gang culture. Similarly, a wide literature suggests that the effect of

Box 4A.1   The Contest over the Causes of (and Solutions to) Crime

There is a wide literature—both theoretical and empirical—on the causes of crime and the role of law enforcement in reducing crime; and within this literature there is ample disagreement. It is therefore not possible to summarize the arguments succinctly or in a way that does not reveal conscious and unconscious biases. Some of the more notable contributions to this debate, however, include the following:

- Becker (1968) applies the framework and logic of neoclassical economics to the supply and demand of criminality and emphasizes the role of deterrence—the likelihood and severity of punishment—in determining the level of crime.[a] He concludes that, at the margin, crime rates are more responsive to improvements in the likelihood of detection than in the increase in the severity of punishment.
- Wilson (1985) argues, in part, that the rapid rise in the level of crime in the United States in the early 1960s was a direct consequence of changing demographics—in particular, the age structure of the population—and that the failure to adapt to the changing ratio of young people to adults resulted in weakening patterns of socialization.[b]
- Wilson and Petersilia (1995) collect essays by America's leading criminologists seeking to answer the question of what role public policy can play in reducing crime.[c] A key essay in the collection is by Lawrence Sherman, who describes the limited knowledge about the relationship between policing and crime levels.
- Since the publication of Lott (1998),[d] a heavily contested literature about the relationship between gun ownership and crime levels has emerged, with evidence and counterevidence appearing in an ever-growing bibliography.
- Blumstein and Wallman (2006) gather a collection of essays on the reasons for the rapid decline in crime in the United States in the 1990s.[e] The contributions suggest that the main driver of the rapid decline in homicide was the decline of the crack market, since virtually the entire reduction in murder rates (and, indeed, the preceding rise) could be accounted for by the reduction in murders of young African American men killed by handguns—(i.e., the kind of murders associated with competition among street-level drug dealers).
- Fajnzylber, Lederman, and Loayza (2002) find a strong and significant statistical relationship between levels of inequality, on the one hand, and per capita levels of violent crime, on the other.[f]
- Donohue and Levitt (2001 and 2003) argue that legalized abortion in the United States played a large role in the decline in crime starting in the late 1990s.[g] They suggest that because the legislation made it easier for mothers to choose not to have children, fewer children were born into distressed and disorganized households, resulting in less crime a few decades later.
- Stretesky and Lynch (2001) link the level of violence in a society to the level of exposure to lead and to the concentration of lead in the atmosphere (confirmed by other studies such as Wolpaw Reyes [2007]).[h]
- Levitt (2004) discusses a range of possible explanations for the decline in crime in the United States, dismissing six (the strong economy of the 1990s, changing demographics, better policing strategies, gun control laws, concealed weapons laws, and increased use of the death penalty) and highlighting four (increases in the number of police, the rising prison population, the waning crack epidemic, and the legalization of abortion).[i]

(Box continues on next page)

Box 4A.1   The Contest over the Causes of (and Solutions to) Crime *(continued)*

- Altbeker (2008) explores the reasons for high levels of violent crime in South Africa.[j] He emphasizes both the socioeconomic origins of the problem and the degree to which high levels of crime have become self-perpetuating through their impact on opportunity structures and social culture. He suggests that weaknesses in the criminal justice system's response to crime allowed a "culture of crime" to take root.

a. Becker 1968.
b. Wilson 1985.
c. Wilson and Petersilia 1995.
d. Lott 1998.
e. Blumstein and Wallman 2006.
f. Fajnzylber, Lederman, and Loayza 2002a, 2002b.
g. Donohue and Levitt 2001, 2003.
h. Stretesky and Lynch 2001; Wolpaw Reyes 2007.
i. Levitt 2004; Spelman 2006.
j. Altbeker 2008; Stone 2006.

imprisonment on crime levels can be quite ambiguous. Some studies even suggest that in spite of incapacitating offenders for the duration of their sentence, incarceration may lead to little if any change to the lifetime number of offenses that prisoners commit. This is because many people who are eventually imprisoned have committed numerous previous offenses (many of which may not have been detected by the police) and may be likely to continue to offend on their release. In turn, the experience of prison can increase offenders' postincarceration propensity to commit crime, either by "hardening" them by or by limiting their choices and so making them less able to build a life outside of crime.

Although some countries have made efforts to assess the relative impact and cost of different approaches to improving safety and security, these assessments may not translate easily from one context to another (see also annex 4B). More specifically, it is not clear whether and to what extent results from assessments by developed countries and countries with relatively low crime levels can be applied to different contexts. To understand why formulating policing strategies is so difficult and so dependent on context, it is helpful to look at a more straightforward process, the formulation of strategies for improving health outcomes. While social and cultural dynamics are implicated in health outcomes (particularly in relation to sexually transmitted diseases, but also in relation to diet, smoking, and alcohol), and while there are legitimate arguments about the cost-effectiveness of different approaches to dealing with health challenges, ultimately the effectiveness of these approaches is governed by biomedical relationships that can be known with some certainty and that apply universally. This is not the case with safety and security, where social and historical dynamics play an overwhelmingly important role in outcomes. Thus it is not possible to construct a "production function" for security that could be plausibly applied across different societies, and it may not even be possible to construct one for the same society over time.

In general terms, the main vehicles through which the security sector delivers safety to citizens relate to five broad categories of response to insecurity: suppression, deterrence, incapacitation, rehabilitation, and prevention.

Suppression

Crime and violence can sometimes be suppressed through the direct exercise of force, or the deployment of personnel empowered and equipped to use force, in response to instances of crime or violence. This set of approaches includes a diverse array of activities, such as direct engagement by the military and/or police with those who are deemed a threat to peace, and the deployment of the military/police into areas where crime or violence is thought to be likely; in both cases the goal is to intimidate and discourage potential perpetrators.

In general, these kinds of tactics are deployed when (i) threats to the state's monopoly on the legitimate use of force or to the safety of individuals and communities are particularly serious; (ii) threats to public safety are highly concentrated in a particular location; and (iii) threats are strongly linked to more-or-less readily identifiable organized groups of criminals, particularly street gangs and heavily armed organized crime groups. Still other circumstances in which this kind of law enforcement activity might be applied include operations that flood identified areas with police and military personnel for short periods in order to temporarily increase security, often to ensure safety for visiting dignitaries or to ensure the security of elections, sporting events, religious and cultural festivals, etc.

Ordinary police street patrols and beat policing are another version of suppressive tactics, though on a smaller scale. These tasks are the services most readily associated with urban policing in the developed world, and, while they may be accompanied by aggressive stop-and-search activities, they are often associated with a reasonably passive model of policing in which the mere presence of the police officer makes citizens feel safer and discourages the commission of crime. The presence of police officers in these contexts often generates activities that are not directly related to the prevention of crime—providing advice and directions, helping to resolve noncriminal disputes, directing traffic, managing accident scenes, etc.—but that are still socially valuable; these activities may reduce crime (although not necessarily explicitly or directly) and also create public confidence in the police and the state they represent.

A key question that confronts policy makers and operational managers in the security agencies is the extent to which the suppression of crime and violence simply displaces it through time and/or space. It is possible, for example, that intensified street patrols result in crime either being shifted to areas that are less densely patrolled or to times when patrols are less active. The suppression of crime can also result in changes in criminal method. Thus a heavy police presence where street-level drug dealing is common could result in changes to the methods suppliers use to access their customers. It is unlikely, however, that all crimes suppressed in this way are displaced, meaning that there is usually some net benefit. But it is critically important to acknowledge the full consequences of suppression initiatives rather than the apparent successes in the area in which they are applied in order to accurately assess the costs and net benefits of such operations.

Scott examines the role of police "crackdowns" in police strategies, and considers both the benefits and potential costs of such interventions.[64] Defining crackdowns as "sudden and dramatic increases in police officer presence, sanctions, and threats of apprehension either for specific offenses or for all offenses in specific places," he suggests that they can be used to combat a variety of types of crime, including (i) robbery and burglary, (ii) gun-related crime, (iii) gang-related crime, (iv) street-level drug dealing, (v) street-level prostitution, and (vi) drunk driving. Scott argues that the benefits of these strategies derive from increasing (albeit temporarily) the certainty of detection or the severity of punishment. These benefits might not last long, but the perception of increased risk might persist. Naturally, these interventions might also result in the arrest of offenders, thereby reducing the likelihood of their committing offenses. These strategies also have some drawbacks, including (i) the limited temporal effect, (ii) potential displacement through time or space, (iii) the cost of the operations, (iv) the risk of police abuses, (v) negative community responses, (vi) overload of the rest of the justice system, and (vii) the opportunity costs.

Deterrence

Although an element of deterrence inheres in the state's capacity to execute suppressive operations, deterrence is more usually thought to consist of the state's capacity to identify, prosecute, and punish people involved in crime or violence. These processes are normally used against criminal threats to safety and security, and are normally governed by a set of legal rules and norms (some of them potentially not codified) relating to the rights of suspects and accused people as well as the powers of the police. These legal norms vary across jurisdictions, change over time (especially during transitions from authoritarian rule), and are often ignored or violated by police officers, prosecutors, and judicial officers. They may also enjoy varying and uncertain levels of legitimacy and support both among ordinary citizens and the political elite. Nevertheless, the expansion of democracy around the world has usually been accompanied by a broadening of the public legitimacy enjoyed by due process rules.

The degree of deterrence delivered by a security sector is a function of (i) the likelihood that an offender will be identified, arrested, and successfully prosecuted; and (ii) the severity of his likely punishment in the event of conviction. Both of these elements are themselves functions of a variety of determinants, such as (i) the number and quality of police officers; (ii) the nature and quality of complementary inputs (such as fingerprint and DNA databases, capacities for forensic investigation, and surveillance equipment); (iii) the degree of corruption in the police, prosecution, and judiciary; (iv) sentencing policies and their interpretation and application by the judiciary; and (v) the quality of life in prison (levels of overcrowding, violence, access to visitors, quality of food).

Various studies find that, at the margin, the deterrent effect of increasing the likelihood of punishment is usually greater than the deterrent effect of increasing the severity of punishment.[65] This point is significant because responses to crime—not just crime itself—are costly, and the opportunity costs of devoting resources to some of the more expensive strategies (such as mass incarceration of offenders) are significant. Optimizing social welfare requires minimizing the sum of the costs of crime and the costs of the responses to criminality. Cook and Ludwig review evidence accumulated in the United States in an effort to describe a "golden portfolio" of responses that would minimize the full social cost of crime.[66] They conclude that "the push for longer prison sentences . . . is likely to have sharply diminishing returns" (7) and suggest that the current approach allocates too many resources to raising the severity of punishment and too few to raising its certainty.

For a brief look at deterrence in South Africa, see box 4A.2.

A distinction is sometimes drawn between deterrence in general and "specific deterrence," which aims to deter specific classes of individuals from specific offenses. An example of specific deterrence is mandatory arrest for spousal assault. Under ordinary circumstances, cases of spousal assault often do not involve arrest, but when policy experiments required police officers called to the scene to make an arrest, the rate of subsequent offending declined. (Further studies suggest, however that this effect may hold true only in some socioeconomic circumstances, and that the effect is greatest in communities with high employment rates and income.[67])

Box 4A.2   Crime Deterrence in South Africa

South Africa is widely believed to have one of the highest crime rates in the world.[a] Between 2000 and 2010, it instituted a number of measures intended to lower the crime rate, including passage of a law mandating severe minimum sentences for a wide range of offenses. This has led to a very rapid increase in the average sentence length of prisoners (see figure B4A.2.1).

While this approach might be expected to increase the level of deterrence, this effect has probably been offset by a marked decline in the number of convictions being handed down by the courts in South Africa; there were roughly 340,000 in 2004, compared to 188,000 in 2010.

(Box continues on next page)

Box 4A.2   **Crime Deterrence in South Africa** *(continued)*

Figure B4A.2.1   **Profile of Sentence Lengths in South Africa, February 1995–December 2010**

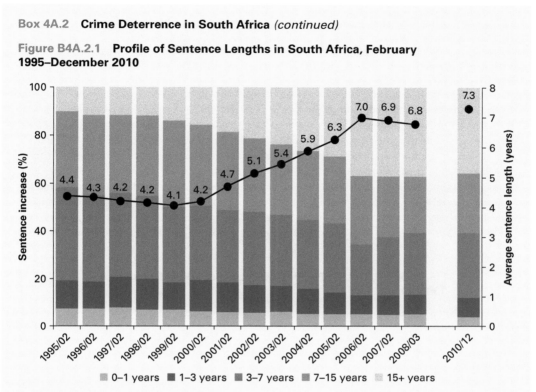

Source: Institute for Security Studies 2011.

It is unclear to what extent these trends help explain trends in the level of crime (which may have been affected by a wide range of other factors, including incapacitative effects of incarceration), but over the same period, levels of recorded crime have tended to decline. Thus, in 2004–2005, some 18,800 murders were recorded by the police, compared to 15,600 in 2011–2012. Figures for aggravated robberies recorded by the police tracked a similar course, falling from over 126,000 to less than 102,000.[b]

a. See Altbeker 2008; and Stone 2006.
b. South African Police Service 2015.

Incapacitation

Incapacitation can be understood as the degree to which security is improved by the mere fact that offenders are "off the street." (See box 4A.3 for a discussion on incarceration levels in the United States.) It is a function of the severity of sentences imposed by courts and the volume of crimes committed by the typical offender subjected to that process over the period that he would otherwise be free to commit crimes. In turn, the experience of offenders in prison might make them more likely to reoffend on release and to commit more serious crimes. Where prison has the effect of increasing the postincarceration levels of criminality, it offsets the "incapacitated" effect of sentencing practices.

Box 4A.3   Data on U.S. Incarceration Rates

Although it is well known that the United States has one of the highest rates of incarceration in the world, less well appreciated is the fact that the level of incarceration has risen rapidly over the past three decades (figure B4A.3.1).

These figures, it should be noted, exclude prisoners held in county and state prisons; including them would raise the incarceration rate to nearly 1,000 per 100,000 people. More data on incarceration rates around the world are offered in annex 4B. Although it seems plausible that the "incapacitated" effect would rise with rising incarceration rates, this is somewhat controversial in the literature. Thus Levitt argues that rising prisoner populations explain a significant proportion of the fall in crime in America, while Spelman suggests the opposite.[a] An important issue relates to cost-effectiveness, since growing prisoner populations can be extremely expensive. An influential study compared the number of crimes prevented per million dollars spent on various noncarceral interventions against the likely impact on crime of California's "three strikes and you're out" sentencing policy (see figure B4A.3.2).[b] It found that programs combining social worker visits to the homes of

Figure B4A.3.1   U.S. Federal Prisoners per 100,000 People, 1980–2008

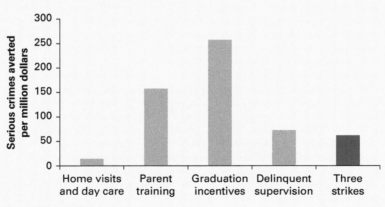

Source: Bureau of Justice Statistics.

Figure B4A.3.2   Cost-Effectiveness of Early Interventions versus California's Three-Strikes Law

Source: Greenwood et al. 1998.

(Box continues on next page)

Rehabilitation

Many states devote resources to attempting to reform offenders. A great variety of initiatives fall under the general rubric of rehabilitation, including skills-building programs ("life skills," conflict and anger management, etc.) as well as drug and alcohol rehabilitation programs (see box 4A.4). Although these initiatives usually focus on individual offenders, some also require engagement with families or communities, and, potentially, even with victims. If these programs are offered in prison, then the prison infrastructure and the skills of officials running prisons must be aligned with the needs of the rehabilitation programs. If programs are run as alternatives to prison (i.e., the offender either participates in the program or is incarcerated), then resources (human and/or technological) are needed to monitor probationers and to enforce conditions of probation.

Prevention

Crime prevention covers a vast array of initiatives, many of which fall outside the authority, mandate, and competence of institutions in the security sector.

To the extent that crime levels are a function of socioeconomic factors, programs that address those factors directly might be seen as seeking to reduce crime. Indeed, in some cases they will also be motivated and resourced precisely because of their possible impact on levels of criminality. Interventions of this kind include initiatives aimed at reducing levels of inequality (since some evidence suggests that crime rates are correlated with levels of inequality) or aimed at increasing employment or incomes in crime-ridden areas and/or among communities or demographic groups considered most likely to engage in criminality. They can also include programs aimed at providing young people with activities that engage them and reduce opportunities for offending, such as inner-city "midnight basketball" programs in the United States.

Crime prevention is often divided into a range of conceptual categories. One common approach is to distinguish between primary, secondary, and tertiary crime prevention, with each level focused on a narrower, riskier portion of the population.

- *Primary prevention* seeks to reduce crime by diminishing the risk that sectors of the population will fall into criminality. Programs often focus on reducing future criminality, so assessments of their economic benefit must discount the value of those benefits that accrue in the more or less distant future. Thus programs that help young families cope with the demands of parenting so that their children are less likely to commit crime might fall into this category. So too might certain publicity campaigns, school-based programs on conflict management, and initiatives aimed at reducing domestic violence.
- *Secondary prevention* focuses on communities or groups of people where significant proportions of the target population are already involved in criminality. Community-level initiatives in high-crime areas or programs that involve "at-risk" or similar youth in activities that reduce the likelihood of their committing crime might fall into this category. Police patrols in high-crime areas might also be considered forms of secondary prevention. Finally, it might be argued that the deterrence effect of effective criminal justice systems is a variant of secondary crime prevention, though some would call this an illegitimate expansion of the definition of prevention.
- *Tertiary prevention* focuses on known offenders and might include rehabilitation programs inside or outside of prison and programs aimed at reducing gangsterism. Arguably, the incapacitative effects of incarceration might also be counted as a form of tertiary crime prevention. Other initiatives include forms of restorative justice and efforts to reduce the trauma experienced by victims that can sometimes metastasize into later criminality.

Other relevant terms and categories include *social crime prevention* (which is sometimes used to describe all programs/activities aimed at reducing crime that do not involve institutions in the security sector) and *spatial crime prevention* (which aims to alter spatial design and use in ways that reduce the opportunity for criminality).

Because interventions are often interrelated in complex ways, they are not always easy to categorize. For example, the capacity of the police to respond rapidly to emergencies and calls for service (such as 911 lines) can be understood under the rubric of *prevention* (in the sense that dispatching police officers might *prevent* a crime that is about to be committed or is being committed). Yet, this capacity can also be understood as a form of *deterrence* because 911 lines increase the likelihood that offenders will be caught—either because the police will arrive while the offender is on or near the scene, or because they will be more likely to secure valuable evidence if they arrive on the scene soon after the departure of the offender. Or these responses can be viewed as an element in the *investigation* of crime. Disagreements about how to categorize rapid-response interventions are often based on disagreement about whether rapid response does in fact increase the likelihood that a crime-in-progress will be disrupted or result in an arrest, whether at the scene or later.

However the various interventions are defined, they involve distinct approaches to the challenge of reducing crime and require different kinds of physical and human resources. To achieve their goals, many of these strategies involve agencies and institutions outside of the security sector as primary actors. Thus the many initiatives that cities have taken to increase safety and security by reshaping public spaces, such as increasing natural levels of surveillance or providing lighting, do not always require the participation of agencies in the security sector. In some cases, these initiatives might require the deployment of resources by the police (for increased foot patrols, for example, or to staff closed-circuit television control rooms), while in others institutions and officials in the security sector identify the need for these strategies (as might be the case, for example, in the development of drug rehabilitation programs in high-drug-use communities). But it is often other agencies whose activities are most central to the implementation and effectiveness of these strategies.[68]

Even where security sector institutions are directly involved, however, different strategies will require different sets of skills and resources. A police strategy premised on suppressive tactics requires different skills and resources from those needed for strategies premised on criminal investigation and prosecution. Similarly, prisons that simply warehouse prisoners may not have adequate resources for rehabilitating them: they may be too overcrowded, prison staff may lack the appropriate skills, and the institutions may be too violent. It is important for PER teams to be aware that skills and resources available to security institutions often do not match the strategies that those institutions are pursuing, claim to be pursuing, or would like to pursue. This mismatch can result in ineffective and inefficient implementation—or in the need to develop a resourcing plan to match the strategic approach of the institutions concerned.

Annex 4B: International Comparisons of Criminal Justice Resources

Decision making on allocating resources to criminal justice can be assisted by comparative international data. Great care must be taken in using such data, however, because a range of methodological problems beset comparisons of spending levels and of actual resource deployment. In addition, even in the absence of such methodological challenges, comparing spending and resource levels across jurisdictions remains difficult, because the resourcing of the criminal justice system depends heavily on levels of safety and security in individual contexts.

The problem of international comparisons is still further complicated by differences in the structure and functions of justice systems in different jurisdictions. These include differences in (i) the legal systems they are designed to uphold; (ii) the functions allocated to various institutions (e.g., the police in the United Kingdom are responsible for traffic control and regulation); and (iii) the structure of those systems (e.g., the United States has 17,000 law enforcement agencies organized at federal, state, and local levels, making the accumulation of data difficult, and marking it with a degree of internal variation).

The result is that rigorous international comparisons of criminal justice systems have been few and far between. However, the United Nations Office on Drugs and Crime conducts a periodic survey of world criminal justice systems. This annex builds on the data presented in the UN report.[69]

Crime Levels

The starting point of any assessment of a criminal justice system must be the level of crime in the country in which it operates—not because the quality of the criminal justice system is seen as the sole determinant of crime levels, but because developing a properly resourced and functioning criminal justice system is an appropriate policy goal.

Comparing countries' crime levels is fraught with difficulty. Apart from the difficulty that not all crimes are defined in the same way in all jurisdictions, crime statistics provided by the police are subject to underreporting, underrecording, and misrecording. Many countries also lack the requisite administrative systems to collate crime statistics, which tend to be accumulated in a highly decentralized system. This is one reason why considerable effort has gone into collecting survey data on crime levels (though as will become apparent these too present challenges).

One response to the challenges of incompatible definitions of crime, underreporting, and underrecording is to focus on the murder rate. The rationale is that such a serious crime, and one whose definition is generally comparable across jurisdictions, would likely be included in official statistics. But this may not be the case: when the per capita murder rate as derived from official statistics provided to UNODC is compared to the estimated

Figure 4B.1 Homicide Rates from Police/Criminal Justice Sources Compared with Those from the World Health Organization, by 10-Year Period

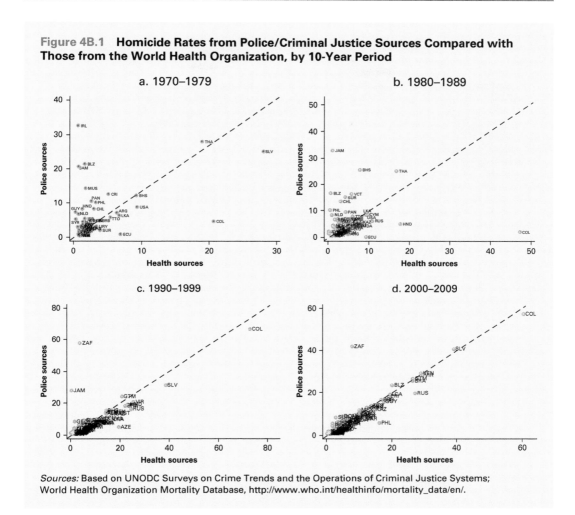

Sources: Based on UNODC Surveys on Crime Trends and the Operations of Criminal Justice Systems; World Health Organization Mortality Database, http://www.who.int/healthinfo/mortality_data/en/.

figures calculated by WHO using epidemiological models, significant disparities in the report levels are evident. In recent years, however, the number of homicides reported by criminal justice institutions and the number reported by health sources have converged (see figure 4B.1). Regressions disaggregated by time periods and regions also show very high correlations between criminal justice and health data. Nevertheless, there are still significant challenges to reconciling the two sources of data.[70]

The Offender Population

Although both the per capita level of crime and the per capita prisoner population reveal something about the state of a society and the nature of its response to crime and violence, an underappreciated measure of the policy response to criminality is the extent to which the incidence of crime results in capture, conviction, and incarceration of offenders. This measurement is difficult not least because (i) crime levels are poorly measured, and

Map 4B.1   Prison Population per 100,000 Inhabitants, 2013 or Most Recent Year

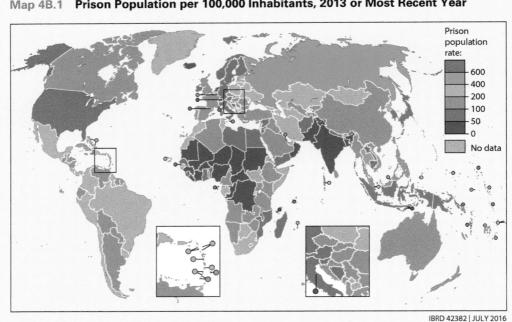

IBRD 42382 | JULY 2016

Source: International Centre for Prison Studies 2014.

(ii) some societies' incarceration rates are driven by policies not directly related to levels of crime and violence. Nevertheless, the result offers a somewhat different measure of comparative punitiveness and of the comparative workloads of different justice systems.

The nature of a society's response to crime is generally first measured by levels of incarceration. The data for 2013 show that the use of incarceration in response to criminality varies widely across countries (map 4B.1).

The proportion of prisoners who are awaiting trial is often used as a measure of the efficiency of the criminal justice system (that is, more efficient systems resolve cases more quickly), though it might also be thought of as a measure of fairness. Though delays in bringing prisoners to trial are an issue in all countries, some systemic differences between developed and developing countries are apparent (figure 4B.2 and map 4B.2).

As shown in these depictions, there are roughly 10 percent more prisoners awaiting trial in developing countries than in developed countries; Africa and South America are the regions with the largest number of prisoners awaiting trial.

Resources in the Justice System

An important measure of the level of policing in a society is the number of police officers per 100,000 people (map 4B.3). Unfortunately, there is

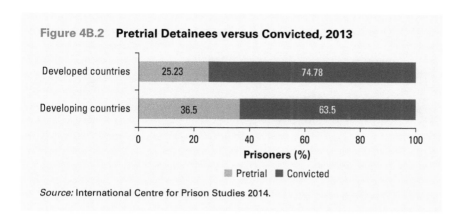

Figure 4B.2 Pretrial Detainees versus Convicted, 2013

Source: International Centre for Prison Studies 2014.

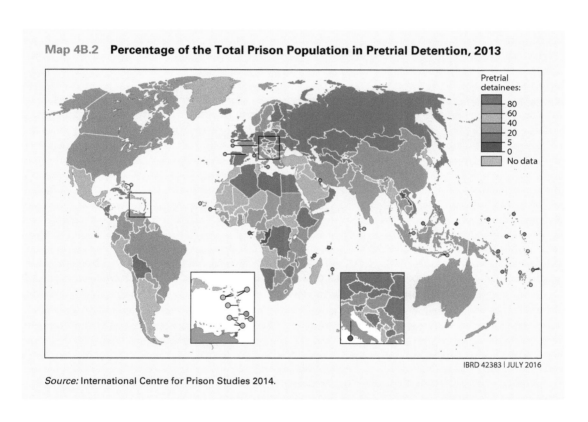

Map 4B.2 Percentage of the Total Prison Population in Pretrial Detention, 2013

IBRD 42383 | JULY 2016

Source: International Centre for Prison Studies 2014.

not a universally accepted definition of a "sworn" police officer, so this measure may not be entirely accurate. Administrative surveys such as those conducted by the UNODC may not accurately report the real number of sworn officers because the data provided by respondents may not conform to the definitions provided. For example, research in the United States on the specialized police units questions the data provided by police

Map 4B.3   Police per 100,000 Inhabitants, 2012 or Most Recent Year

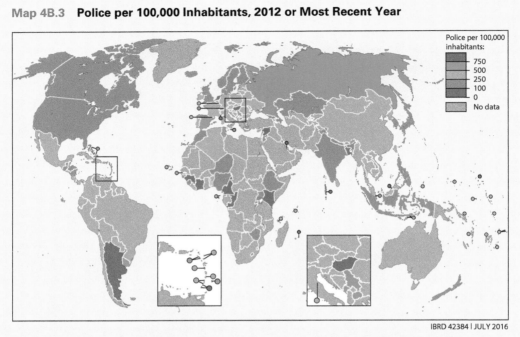

IBRD 42384 | JULY 2016

Sources: UNODC, Surveys on Crime Trends and the Operations of Criminal Justice Systems, various years.

agencies on the number of officers who perform specialized anti-gang activities.[71] Thus a certain degree of caution is warranted in using comparative sources.[72]

An alternative approach to evaluating the resourcing of the police is to compare the level of policing to the level of crime. Given the difficulties of defining whom to count as police officers and of reporting and recording crime, caution must be exercised in taking this approach. A simple cross-country bivariate regression analysis (not reported here) shows no correlation between the numbers of police per capita as a result of higher murder rates, higher burglary rates, or higher theft rates. Not surprisingly, the correlation between property crimes like theft and burglary is positive but not statistically significant at conventional levels, which suggests that the higher volume of property crimes compared to homicides, for example, may drive this relationship.[73]

Other measures of resourcing in criminal justice systems concern the number of prosecutors per 100,000 inhabitants (map 4B.4), the number of prosecutors per homicide (which gives a sense of the adequacy of resources relative to the level of crime; map 4B.5), and prison occupancy rates (that is, the percentage of prison capacity in use; map 4B.6). The available data indicate wide differences across countries for all these measures.

Map 4B.4   Prosecutors per 100,000 Inhabitants, Most Recent Year

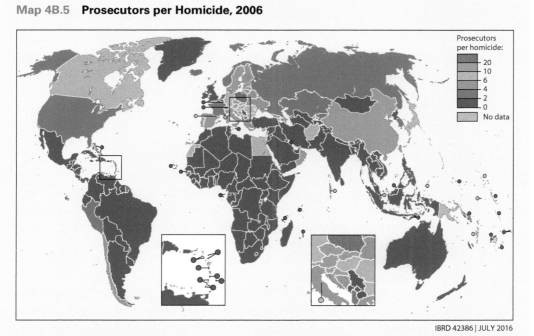

IBRD 42385 | JULY 2016

Sources: UNODC, Surveys on Crime Trends and the Operations of Criminal Justice Systems, various years.

Map 4B.5   Prosecutors per Homicide, 2006

IBRD 42386 | JULY 2016

Sources: UNODC, Surveys on Crime Trends and the Operations of Criminal Justice Systems, various years.

Map 4B.6   **Prison Occupancy Rates Based on Official Capacity**

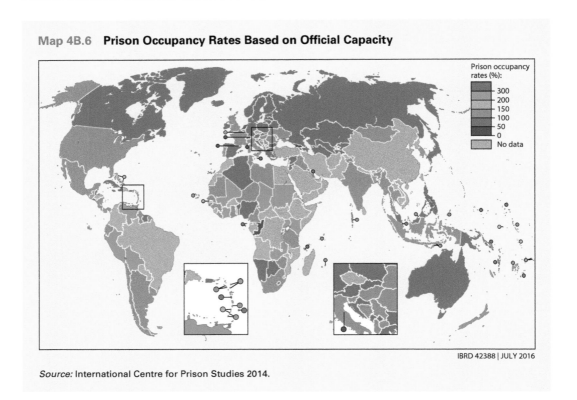

Source: International Centre for Prison Studies 2014.

Annex 4C: Donor Approaches to Police Assistance in Fragile and Conflict-Affected States

The purpose of this annex is to review some of the main donor approaches to police reform in countries affected by fragility, conflict, and violence. Without undertaking an extensive literature review on the topic, it (i) typologizes the essential components of donor programs, (ii) illustrates them with two examples, and (iii) highlights some main challenges noted either in project implementation or in relevant academic and policy writings.

Overview: Funding and Typology of Approaches

Global data on police expenditures are difficult to compile due to complex institutional arrangements and methodological difficulties. First, law enforcement structures differ significantly from country to country, depending on the type of criminal justice system and on the role played by informal institutions in delivering public safety. Second, approaches that compare single monetary values representing the whole police budget are questionable because of differences in budget entries and possible extreme variations in exchange rates.[74] A study attempting to overcome this challenge through econometric models—and the only study to date that has measured expenditures in criminal justice worldwide (Farrell and Clark 2004)—found that in 1997, global criminal justice expenditure was $362 billion, of which

62 percent was allocated to policing, 3 percent to prosecutions, 18 percent to courts, and 17 percent to prisons. [75]

Estimating the value of donor assistance to police reform is similarly difficult. Using publicly reported amounts of official development aid, the Development Assistance Committee of the Organisation for Economic Co-operation and Development (OECD) and the Center for International Cooperation at New York University found that assistance to the security sector comprises a small amount of all sectorally allocated aid. In 2012, aid allocated to building the security sector in fragile states, including police, totaled just $858 million. Security support (1.4 percent) and justice support (3.1 percent) represented a single-digit percentage of all assistance in fragile situations for the year. When spending in Afghanistan and Iraq is removed, the investment in other fragile states is even smaller—less than 1 percent of total,[76] as shown in table 4C.1.

Even though resources are few, it is possible to classify donor approaches according to several distinct perspectives, which in practice overlap as complementary program components.[77] They are discussed below and summarized in table 4C.2.

- *Human rights*. This approach focuses on protecting internationally recognized rights, especially freedom from torture. The terminology is that of improving police conduct. The approach seeks to remove rights violators from police ranks, update police doctrine to include human rights standards, and establish internal and external mechanisms of accountability.
- *Gender*. Mainstreaming gender has become an essential element of donor approaches to security sector reform. This perspective assesses the implications for women and men of any planned action of police reform, including legislation, policies, programs, and staffing. A key feature is the attempt to address gender-based violence.[78]
- *Democratization*. Built on the human rights approach, this perspective emphasizes the rule of law and long-term justice and security, rather than short-term order. It uses terminology such as police reform

Table 4C.1 Official Development Assistance (ODA) to Security Financing in Fragile and Conflict-Affected Countries

ODA sector allocation	Total—all fragile countries		Fragile countries excluding Afghanistan and Iraq	
	Amount distributed (million $)	Percentage of all sectorally allocated ODA	Amount distributed (million $)	Percentage of all sectorally allocated ODA
Security	858	1.40	528	0.99
Justice	1,912	3.13	836	1.57

Source: OECD 2015.

Table 4C.2   Approaches to Police Assistance

Perspective	Human rights/ democratization	Gender	Peacekeeping	Law enforcement	Economic development
Main concerns	• Human rights • Building democratic institutions	• Gender equality • Gender-based violence	• Public order management • Capacity building	• Crime control	• Governance • "Securing development" • Expenditures and planning
Key concepts	• Police conduct • Accountability • Justice reform	• Gender main-streaming • Access to justice	• Police restructuring • Police reorganization • Training	• Professional policing	• Security sector reform • Citizen security
Sponsoring institutions	• NGOs • Bilateral donor agencies • International organizations	• NGOs • Bilateral donors • International organizations	• Donor governments • UNPOL	• UNPOL officers • Donor police agencies	• United Nations • World Bank • Inter-American Development Bank

Source: Call 2002.
Note: NGOs = nongovernmental organizations; UNPOL = United Nations Police.

and rule of law, and is common among donor agencies dedicated to judicial reform.

• *Peacekeeping.* This perspective prioritizes ensuring law and order immediately after the termination of war and preventing a reversion to conflict. In recent years, the terminology has evolved from technical aspects of police restructuring, reorganization, and capacity building to broader concepts of police reform, which include financial sustainability. A separate concern, particularly for agencies charged with peacekeeping tasks, is the incorporation of former combatants into police forces.

• *Law enforcement.* This perspective emphasizes the strengthening of local and external capabilities in order to control crime. It uses a language of crime control and professionalization, and tends to favor strengthening of law enforcement organizations' capabilities over restructuring or democratization approaches.

• *Economic development.* International financial institutions and some development agencies have overcome long-standing resistance to involvement with security actors to support disarmament, demobilization, and reintegration projects (especially in Africa), as well as citizen security initiatives in Latin America and the Caribbean. To various degrees, police are part of these projects, which reflect interest in enhancing the environment for economic development, removing impediments to foreign investment, and reducing the costs of crime and violence. The terminology is often that of security sector reform, and the governance lens implies that the security sector, like other economic sectors such as health, education, or agriculture, should be subject to the same standards of accountability, effectiveness, and efficiency.

The next section reviews in brief how these perspectives interact in practice in two specific countries, the Democratic Republic of Congo and Bosnia and Herzegovina.

Examples of Donor Engagements

Security Sector Accountability and Police Reform Program in the Democratic Republic of Congo (2015)

Context. The U.K. Department for International Development (DFID) initiated the Security Sector Accountability and Police Reform Program (SSAPR) in January 2010. By this time key aspects of police reform had been planned and publicly announced, but they had not been implemented by Congolese authorities due to institutional and human capacity challenges, lack of resources, and integrity issues. Multiple institutions with different mandates were involved in the reform process, leading to confusion about how to enact police reform. Meanwhile, violent conflict and instability had persisted in the east of the country, despite a UN peacekeeping mission that was attempting to provide some measure of civilian protection.[79]

Intervention. DFID provided roughly $80 million to achieve a dual goal: strengthening accountability of the security and justice sectors in the Democratic Republic of Congo and supporting long-term police reform, including the immediate provision of improved security and access to justice for poor people. The project thus aimed to build the capacity of key sector institutions, including the Ministry of Interior and Security, Decentralization and Customary Affairs; the Congolese National Police (PNC); the Inspectorate General of Audit; the Committee for the Reform of the Police Secretariat; Parliament; and civil society organizations. SSAPR was to be delivered in four components:

1. *Community policing.* This approach was implemented in three pilot provinces: Bas Congo, Western Kasai, and South Kivu.
2. *Control and coordination of the security sector.* This component supported cross-government coordination, accountability, and internal oversight of security sector institutions. It also built capacity to monitor and evaluate service delivery in the security and justice sectors, and to ensure the financial sustainability of the police reform process by assessing the future budgetary needs of the PNC.
3. *External accountability.* This component concentrated on strengthening civilian participation, oversight, and control mechanisms and providing support for Parliament and the Security and Justice Commission as well as the media, civil society, and academics.
4. *Monitoring and evaluation.* Beyond M&E activities, this component aimed to facilitate lesson learning and risk management.[80]

Expected Results. The intervention was expected to improve safety, security, and rule of law for Congolese citizens, and to strengthen the capacity and accountability of the PNC to respond to the needs of local communities. The following results were expected at the output level:

- Improved collaboration between state and nonstate actors on security and justice policy and service delivery
- Enhanced oversight and accountability of security and justice policy and service delivery (internal and external accountability)
- Improved PNC service delivery (prevention, problem solving, respect for human rights) in pilot provinces to inform the development of a national policing strategy that reflects key principles of community policing
- Improved capacity, coordination, and collaboration in and between key state institutions on security, and improved justice policy and decision making that promotes effective crime and violence prevention and improved respect for human rights
- Enhanced capacity of the key stakeholders to manage resources and manage change
- Increased likelihood of sustainability of reforms (national ownership, affordability/resources, policy, legal frameworks).[81]

Impact. According to the 2014 annual program review, SSAPR was making substantial progress toward its goals; it had moved beyond anecdotal evidence of positive impact to more robust proof of value for money. Direct feedback from beneficiaries showed that the community policing element had proved effective in reducing crime and violence in pilot areas, leading to higher levels of public trust in the PNC. Perception studies also showed that police trained under the project were more likely to adhere to human rights standards than peers. However, as of February 2014, two concerns remained: (i) whether the current level of investment and focus on police reform was appropriate for DFID's future program in the country; and (ii) whether shortcomings at the political level, particularly those related to the development of a sectorwide approach to internal security, could be overcome.[82]

The same sense of ambivalence emerges in a broader review of U.K.-sponsored security and justice interventions in a range of other countries. According to the Independent Commission for Aid Impact, many of the activities in DFID's security and justice programs were not appreciably improving the lives of the poor because program objectives were unclear and program implementers were poorly supervised.[83] One consequence of the lack of an overall strategy is that certain interventions are repeated, including (for the police) community policing; pilot police stations; victim support services; training in forensics and criminal investigations, public order management, and leadership; training academies and curricula; human resources and budgeting; and election security.

One central problem identified by the review was the tendency to view policing solely through a service delivery lens. Part of this perspective was the assumption that capacity building and institutional strengthening were the proper way to provide greater security and justice for the poor. An alternative approach was to regard these challenges as a set of social issues (related to land tenure, labor rights, or urban insecurity), which would require broad, multipronged interventions to address. The review posited that poor people's experiences of insecurity and injustice had more to do with surrounding socioeconomic conditions and cultural norms than with the quality of or accessibility to services.[84]

Community Policing Project in Bosnia and Herzegovina (2005–2008)

Context. Police reforms had been ongoing in Bosnia and Herzegovina since 1996, first through the United Nations mission and subsequently through the United States and European Union (EU), which offered equipment and training for dealing with organized crime, terrorism, and border control. In 2003, the EU established the European Union Police Mission to provide an overview of various aspects of policing, including public order management and community policing, though the latter element was phased out in 2005. Earlier (in 1999) a regional program (Police Reforms in South Eastern Europe) had been launched by the Swiss Federal Department of Justice and Police, and in 2000 this was handed over to the Swiss Agency for Development and Cooperation (SDC). A number of projects and pilots in Bosnia and Herzegovina fell within the remit of this program, including support to juvenile justice, the State Investigation and Protection Agency, and the Organized Crime Training Network. SDC also supported the police academies in Bosnia and Herzegovina with technical assistance in organizational development, training, facilitation of professional exchange between the academies and international police services, and refurbishment of academy facilities.[85]

Intervention. In 2004, SDC began a pilot community policing project in the district of Zenica, which was ultimately deemed to be successful, and the pilot was scaled up to cover the canton level. Phase 10 of this program (March 2005–December 2007) was budgeted at roughly $4 million. The program had two objectives: (i) to help law enforcement agencies improve their ability to fight transnational organized crime, and (ii) to promote community policing as a means of conflict prevention. Initially, the program faced considerable resistance due to its link to EU accession conditions, which included the formation of a unitary police force and the redrawing of police districts. By mid-2006, the Ministry of Security (a cross-entity body) convened a working group comprising officers and ministry officials from across the country, which with support from SDC was mandated to develop the first countrywide strategy for community policing. The strategy was based on a recognition that previous efforts, including various pilots or internationally supervised reforms, had been fragmented, inconsistent, and at times overly theoretical. The strategy was adopted in 2007 and provided a common framework around which the country's several policing agencies, ministries, donors, and interested NGOs could align their efforts. The working group was established as an official structure in January 2008 and tasked with developing the means of implementing the strategy. This effort constituted an essential part of phase 11 of the SDC-sponsored project.[86]

Expected Results. According to the logical framework of phase 11, the project aimed to improve the quality of security in Bosnia and Herzegovina as measured through the following:

- Better police presence
- Visible preventive police work
- Transparency regarding public order police work
- Execution of three prevention campaigns between 2007 and 2010
- Opinion polls suggesting a more favorable perception of the police.

Impact. The program's higher-level indicators were vague, and it was unclear how progress toward them was to be achieved. An evaluation conducted in 2009 noted that breaking indicators down into more specific elements would be helpful—for example, the police presence indicator should indicate how police presence is measured quantitatively and qualitatively (number of police on the streets, percentage of population regarding the police presence as having a positive impact on the public security).[87] Another weakness is that the program addressed gender only marginally.[88] Thus while a program evaluation found that most outputs were accomplished, whether the desired outcomes were achieved remains open to interpretation.

These examples underscore the various challenges encountered by donors assisting police reform in fragile states, which are discussed in greater detail in the following section.

Challenges
Navigating the Political Economy of Fragility, Conflict, and Violence
Police in FCS play pivotal roles in the broader political economy of conflict—they often perpetrate violence during war, but as strife subsides, they must become guardians of public order. This background means that purely technical approaches—those that focus on train-and-equip programs without analyzing the implications of local conflict dynamics—risk failing. Donors need to understand, for example, that the lines between the military and police may be blurred in the initial stages of a peacekeeping intervention, affecting the development of indigenous police services. Strong donor assistance thus requires investing in knowledge of local circumstances, and in expert discussions about how those circumstances may affect implementation.[89]

Complex Institutional Arrangements
It is important for donors to understand the complex arrangement of security and justice institutions. Unlike health or education institutions,

for example, which are organized within a single sector under a lead ministry, these institutions form a cluster of systems that includes multiple independent agencies (courts, prosecutors, police, corrections) with their own agendas, priorities, and cultures. Given this arrangement, there is little to induce justice and security institutions to work collaboratively or cooperatively. A further complexity for donors is the high degree of legal pluralism exhibited in FCS: these countries often have traditional or informal justice and security institutions as well as formal institutions. Poor residents generally have better access to the former, and consider them more legitimate.[90]

Effective Risk Management

The challenges of navigating such diverse political terrain make risk assessment and risk management essential elements of donor support. Two questions arise: (i) under what circumstances should donors deliver aid to local police, and (ii) how should that aid be delivered? These dilemmas require both policy and operational responses—that is, intervention criteria and an intervention delivery plan.

- *Intervention criteria.* The U.S. Agency for International Development (USAID) has offered policy guidance for assisting civilian policing since 2005. The guidance stipulates that no assistance can be provided for civilian police authorities that are not under the control of democratic authorities or, in transition situations, that are not demonstrably moving toward being under this control. If the human rights situation in a country is poor, assistance to civilian police authorities requires careful risk assessment. USAID missions should also avoid situations where pervasive corruption makes attaining assistance objectives doubtful. Lastly, civilian police assistance excludes commodity support for lethal technology and weapons, as well as supplies or training for their use; it also excludes commodity support for, or assistance in the carrying out of, internal intelligence or surveillance operations.[91]

- *Intervention delivery.* Evidence from DFID's security and justice operations underscores the importance of effective supervision as a prerequisite to success. Among other things, supervision requires challenging implementing partners on overambitious reporting; ensuring that program components are well integrated and that staff in charge of various activities communicate; taking extra precautions to verify that fungible funds are used for their intended purpose, e.g., multiple asset check spots; and using effective procurement systems that allow timely submissions of bids and proper specifications.[92]

The Relationship between Crime, Violence, and Police Reform

Police reform requires donors to balance the claims of public order with those of human rights. On the one hand, high levels of criminality, violence, and public insecurity (whether due to organized crime or collapse of law and order) demand donor support for police reform. On the other hand, if the support focuses too much on law enforcement or peacekeeping, it may neglect democratic norms, human rights, or gender mainstreaming; under these circumstances, the police become effective at reducing crime, but not more accountable or more respectful of human rights.[93] Thus, donors must weigh whether enhancing police reform is more urgent than enhancing police capacity. The decision often depends on how donor governments relate to the internal constituencies pressuring them to offer support, and on donors' need to buttress foreign law enforcement agencies whose effectiveness is essential in countering terrorism or transnational organized crime.[94]

Organizational Change in Police Cadres

The powerful esprit de corps among police officers means that the success of reform initiatives may depend more on the attitude of senior leaders and word of mouth among staff than on formal procedures, training, and personnel recruitment measures. Police officers tend to be skeptical about new programs, especially when they result from frequent changes in leadership. This skepticism reflects in part their experience with training as recruits, which is regarded almost universally as irrelevant to what they encounter on the job.[95]

Measuring Police Performance

The prevalence of indicators focused on outputs versus outcomes inhibits police reform. Excessive focus on outputs means that police officers pay more attention to reporting what they do than to what they actually achieve. This encourages them to become preoccupied with meeting norms of activity rather than adapting their activity to produce desired results, which in turn discourages innovation and reduces operational flexibility.[96]

Little Evidence Base for Success

An analysis of DFID's security and justice portfolio found little evidence that the three most common approaches to police assistance—model police stations, training, and community policing—have improved police performance or increased levels and perceptions of security. Monitoring, evaluation, and learning were broadly inadequate. Similarly, a review of EU-led assistance to the security and justice sector in the Democratic Republic of Congo found that programs were likely unsustainable and had not significantly improved operational capacity. EU support had been overly ambitious, the review found, and did not take into consideration the Congolese political context.[97]

Long-Term Commitments

The focus on outcomes rather than outputs and the need for flexibility in delivering assistance requires a greater awareness of how governance issues affect donor support efforts. For instance, in the Dutch-sponsored Security Sector Development (SSD) project in Burundi, the program has no logical framework, results framework, or business case at the outset. Rather, it adopted a highly flexible problem-solving approach, taking conditions on the ground as its starting point and building on them to progressively achieve the shared vision and objectives. At the end of each two-year phase, the program has evaluated its progress and adjusted accordingly. To this end, the SSD program began with concrete activities during phase 1 (2009–2011) to build the trust and relationships that would later be necessary to tackle the thorny governance issues involved in security sector reform. For example, the SSD helped build the capacity of the police to maintain their communications equipment, and also supported activities that enhanced the operational effectiveness of the military and the police. Priorities between 2014 and 2017 include, among other things, improving the vehicle maintenance system for the police and building the police's counterterrorism capacity.[98]

Notes

1. Graham Farrell and Ken Clark, "What Does the World Spend on Criminal Justice?"(HEUNI Paper 20, European Institute of Crime Prevention and Control, affiliated with the United Nations, Helsinki, 2004).
2. Mark Shaw, Jan van Dijk, and Wolfgang Rhomberg, "Determining Trends in Global Crime and Justice: An Overview of Results from the United Nations Surveys on Crime Trends and the Operations of Criminal Justice Systems," *Forum on Crime and Society* 3, nos. 1–2 (December 2003): 35–63, http://www.unodc.org/pdf/crime/forum /forum3_Art2.pdf.
3. Geneva Declaration on Armed Violence and Development, "Executive Summary," in *Global Burden of Armed Violence 2011,* http://www .genevadeclaration.org/fileadmin/docs/GBAV2/GBAV2011 -Ex-summary-ENG.pdf.
4. United Nations Peacekeeping, "Troop and Police Contributors," April 2016, http://www.un.org/en/peacekeeping/documents/Yearly.pdf.
5. The training manuals and resources include *Guidance on the Use and Preparation of Serious Organized Crime Threat Assessments: The SOCTA Handbook* (New York: United Nations, 2010); https://www .unodc.org/documents/afghanistan/Organized_Crime/SOCTA _Manual_2010.pdf; and *Digest of Organized Crime Case Studies* (New York: United Nations, 2012), https://www.unodc.org/documents /organized-crime/EnglishDigest_Final301012_30102012.pdf.
6. This typology of policy approaches is not rigid; for more on this point see annex 4A.
7. G. Becker, "Crime and Punishment: An Economic Approach," *Journal of Political Economy* 76, no. 2 (1968): 169–217.
8. See for example Richard Wilkinson and Kate Pickett, *The Spirit Level: Why More Equal Societies Almost Always Do Better* (London: Allen Lane, 2009).
9. See UNODC and UN-HABITAT, *Introductory Handbook on Policing Urban Space* (Nairobi: United Nations, 2011), http://www.unodc.org

/documents/justice-and-prison-reform/crimeprevention/11-80387 _ebook.pdf) for a review of the ways in which cities can mobilize diverse agencies to combat urban criminality.

10. R. M. Fogelson, *Big City Police* (Cambridge, MA: Harvard University Press, 1977).

11. H. Goldstein, *Problem-Oriented Policing* (McGraw-Hill: New York, 1990).

12. G. L. Kelling and C. M. Coles, *Fixing Broken Windows: Restoring Order and Reducing Crime in Our Communities* (New York: Free Press, 1998).

13. T. John and M. Maguire, "Criminal Intelligence and the National Intelligence Model," in *Handbook of Criminal Investigation,* ed. T. Newburn, T. Williamson, and A. Wright (Portland, OR: Willan Publishing, 2007), 199–225.

14. Michael Rowe, *Introduction to Policing,* 2nd ed. (London: Sage Publishing, 2014).

15. A. A. Adeyemi, "Crime and Development in Africa: A Case Study on Nigeria," in *Essays on Crime and Development,* ed. U. Zvekic (Rome: United Nations Interregional Crime and Justice Research Institute, 1990).

16. Rita Abrahamsen and Michael C. Williams, *Security beyond the State: Private Security in International Politics* (Cambridge, U.K.: Cambridge University Press, 2011).

17. E. Bittner, *Aspects of Police Work* (Boston: Northeastern University Press, 1990), 249.

18. See P. L. Reichel, *Comparative Criminal Justice Systems: A Topical Approach*, 3rd ed. (Upper Saddle River, NJ: Prentice Hall, 2002).

19. Andreas Schedler, "Conceptualizing Accountability," in *The Self-Restraining State: Power and Accountability in New Democracies,* ed. Andreas Schedler, Larry Diamond, and Marc F. Plattner (Boulder, CO: Lynne Reinner Publishers, 1999), 14.

20. A relevant example is offered by the experience of the South African Police Service's civilian appointees to the position of national police commissioner; see Mandy Weiner, *Killing Kebble: An Underworld Exposed* (Johannesburg: Pan Macmillan South Africa, 2012).

21. The recent attention on U.S. policing is an example of this issue and the increase in use of body-worn cameras. See for example: B. Ariel, W. Farrar, and A. Sutherland, "The Effect of Police Body-Worn Cameras on Use of Force and Citizens' Complaints against the Police: A Randomized Controlled Trial," *Journal of Quantitative Criminology,* 31, no. 3 (2015): 509–35.

22. R. M. Fogelson, *Big City Police* (Cambridge, MA: Harvard University Press, 1977).

23. R. Klitgaard, *Controlling Corruption* (Berkeley: University of California Press, 1988).

24. Gareth Newham and Lulama Gomomo, "Bad Cops Get a Break: The Closure of the SAPS Anti-Corruption Unit," *South African Crime*

Quarterly 4 (2003), http://journals.assaf.org.za/index.php/sacq/article/view/1065.

25. For a review of police accountability mechanisms in Africa, see African Policing Civilian Oversight Forum, "An Audit of Police Oversight in Africa" (APCOF, Cape Town, 2008).

26. Michael Armstrong, *They Wished They Were Honest: The Knapp Commission and New York City Police Corruption* (New York: Columbia University Press, 2013).

27. C. B. Klockars, "The Dirty Harry Problem," in *Moral Issues in Police Work*, ed. F. A. Elliston and M. Feldberg (Totowa, NJ: Rowan and Allanheld, 1985); cited by T. Newburn, "Understanding and Preventing Police Corruption: Lessons from the Literature" (Police Research Series Paper 110, Home Office, London, 1999), http://www.popcenter.org/problems/street_prostitution/pdfs/newburn_1999.pdf.

28. Julian B. Roebuck and Thomas Barker, "A Typology of Police Corruption," *Social Problems* 21, no. 3 (1974): 423–37.

29. Generic information on the budget cycle was drawn or adapted from the World Bank's internal public financial management training program manual, as well as from sectoral work such as *Practitioners' Toolkit for Agriculture Expenditure Analysis* (Washington, DC: World Bank, 2011).

30. An improvement in the efficiency of outputs does not necessarily indicate a reduction in crime, which is the final outcome of police forces. Similarly, a reduction in the levels of crime does not necessarily indicate that the police are spending resources efficiently to combat crime.

31. International Monetary Fund, *Government Finance Statistics Manual 2001*, https://www.imf.org/external/pubs/ft/gfs/manual/.

32. Antony Altbeker, "Puzzling Statistics: Is South Africa Really the World's Crime Capital?" *South African Crime Quarterly* 11 (2005).

33. Based on quarterly crime statistics for 2011–2013 issued by the South Sudan National Police Services.

34. Data for Colombia and El Salvador are calculated using approved budgets for 2014. For Chile, the data are from the executed budget in 2013. Data for the accumulated budget expenditures in July 2014 showed that salaries made up 85 percent of total budgetary allocations to the police. For South Sudan, calculations used the approved budget for 2013.

35. Charles M. Katz, Edward R. Maguire, and Dennis W. Roncek, "The Creation of Specialized Police Gang Units: A Macro-Level Analysis of Contingency, Social Threat and Resource Dependency Explanations," *Policing: An International Journal of Police Strategies and Management* 25, no. 3 (2002): 472–506.

36. See Gregory J. Howard, Graeme Newman, and William Alex Pridemore, "Theory, Method, and Data in Comparative Criminology," *Criminal Justice* 4, no. 4 (2000): 139–211.

37. See for example Alexandre Mas, "Pay, Reference Points, and Police Performance" (NBER Working Paper 12202, National Bureau of Economic Research, Cambridge, MA, 2006).

38. World Bank, "Public Financial Management Reforms in Post-Conflict Countries: Synthesis Report" (World Bank, Washington, DC, 2013), http://documents.worldbank.org/curated/en/2012/01/16380099 /public-financial-management-reforms-post-conflict-countries -synthesis-report.

39. This account is adapted from World Bank internal training materials and the defense chapter of the current work.

40. David H. Bayley, *Police for the Future* (New York: Oxford University Press, 1994), 50.

41. Mark H. Moore and Robert C. Trojanowicz, "Policing and the Fear of Crime" (*Perspectives on Policing* no. 3, U.S. Department of Justice, National Institute of Justice, Washington, DC, 1988), https://www. ncjrs.gov/pdffiles1/nij/111459.pdf.

42. Christopher Stone, "Crime, Justice, and Growth in South Africa: Toward a Plausible Contribution from Criminal Justice to Economic Growth" (CID Working Paper 131, Center for International Development at Harvard University, Cambridge, MA, 2006).

43. Jeffrey Fagan, Amanda Geller, Garth Davies, and Valerie West, "Street Stops and Broken Windows Revisited: The Demography and Logic of Proactive Policing in a Safe and Changing City," in *Race, Ethnicity, and Policing: New and Essential Readings,* ed. Stephen K. Rice and Michael D. White (New York: New York University Press, 2009), 309–48.

44. United Nations Development Programme, "Human Development Report for Latin America 2013–2014. Citizen Security with a Human Face: Evidence and Proposals for Latin America," in *Human Development Report* (New York: United Nations Development Programme, 2013).

45. Robert C. Davis, "Selected International Best Practices in Police Performance Measurement" (RAND Center on Quality Policing, RAND Corporation, Santa Monica, CA, 2012), 3.

46. Ibid., 4.

47. United Nations Department of Peacekeeping Operations, "Gender-Responsive Security Sector Reform," 2012, 39, http://asset-ssr.org /images/pdf_file/english/GenderResponsiveSSR.pdf.

48. See United Nations Department of Peacekeeping Operations, "Guidelines for Integrating Gender Perspectives in National Police and Law Enforcement Agencies" (United Nations, New York, 2008), 10.

49. United Nations Interregional Crime and Justice Research Institute (UNICRI), International Crime Victims Survey (Turin: UNICRI, 2000), http://www.unicri.it/services/library_documentation/publications/icvs /statistics/17-icvs-app4.pdf.

50. Robert Muggah and Gustavo Diniz, "Digitally Enhanced Violence Prevention in the Americas," *Stability: International Journal of Security and Development* 2, no. 3 (2013).

51. Jonathan P. Caulkins and Peter Reuter, "How Drug Enforcement Affects Drug Prices," in *Crime and Justice* vol. 39, ed. Michael Tonry (Chicago: University of Chicago Press, 2010).

52. National Institute of Drug Abuse, "DrugFacts: Nationwide Trends," 2012, http://www.drugabuse.gov/publications/drugfacts/nationwide -trends.

53. P. W. Greenwood and J. Petersilia, *Summary and Policy Implications*, vol. 1 of *The Criminal Investigation Process* (Santa Monica, CA: RAND Corporation, 1975).

54. Jean Redpath, "Unsustainable and Unjust: Criminal Justice Policy and Remand Detention since 1994," *South African Crime Quarterly* 48 (2014): 25–37.

55. Vera Institute of Justice, "Measuring Progress toward Safety and Justice: A Global Guide to the Design of Performance Indicators across the Justice Sector" (Vera Institute, New York, 2003).

56. Robert C. Davis, "Selected International Best Practices in Police Performance Measurement" (RAND Center on Quality Policing, RAND Corporation, Santa Monica, CA, 2012), 4.

57. Vera Institute of Justice, "Measuring Progress toward Safety and Justice: A Global Guide to the Design of Performance Indicators across the Justice Sector" (Vera Institute, New York, 2003), 4.

58. This was done in work completed in 2015 in Mexico for a multisectoral public expenditure review, which included a citizen security chapter.

59. A. Charnes, W. W. Cooper, and E. Rhodes, "Measuring the Efficiency of Decision Making Units," *European Journal of Operational Research* 2, no. 6 (1978): 429–44.

60. Yasar A. Ozcan, *Health Care Benchmarking and Performance Evaluation: An Assessment Using Data Envelopment Analysis (DEA)* (Berlin: Springer, 2008).

61. Time Coelli, "A Computer Program for Frontier Production Function Estimation: Frontier Version 2.0," *Economics Letters* 39, no. 1 (1992): 29–32.

62. Leigh Drake and Richard Simper, "X-efficiency and Scale Economies in Policing: A Comparative Study Using the Distribution Free Approach and DEA," *Applied Economics* 34, no. 15 (2002): 1859–70.

63. Robert C. Davis, "Selected International Best Practices in Police Performance Measurement" (RAND Center on Quality Policing, RAND Corporation, Santa Monica, CA, 2012).

64. Michael Scott, "The Benefits and Consequences of Police Crackdowns" (Response Guide no. 1, Center for Problem-Oriented Policing, 2004), http://www.popcenter.org/responses/police_crackdowns/.

65. See for example G. Becker, "Crime and Punishment: An Economic Approach," *Journal of Political Economy* 76, no. 2 (1968): 169–217.

66. P. Cook and J. Ludwig, "Economical Crime Control" (NBER Working Paper 16513, National Bureau of Economic Research, Cambridge, MA, 2010).

67. David H. Bayley, *What Works in Policing* (New York: Oxford University Press, 1998).

68. See UNODC and UN-HABITAT, *Introductory Handbook on Policing Urban Space* (Nairobi: United Nations, 2011), http://www.unodc.org /documents/justice-and-prison-reform/crimeprevention/11-80387 _ebook.pdf) for a review of the ways in which cities can mobilize diverse agencies to combat urban criminality.

69. See the UNODC website at https://www.unodc.org/unodc/en/data -and-analysis/crimedata.html.

70. J. P. Stamatel, "Using Mortality Data to Refine Our Understanding of Homicide Patterns in Select Postcommunist Countries," *Homicide Studies* 12, no. 1 (2008): 117–35.

71. Charles M. Katz, Edward R. Maguire, and Dennis W. Roncek, "The Creation of Specialized Police Gang Units: A Macro-Level Analysis of Contingency, Social Threat and Resource Dependency Explanations," *Policing: An International Journal of Police Strategies and Management* 25, no. 3 (2002): 472–506.

72. Graeme Newman and Gregory J. Howard, "Introduction: Data Sources and Their Use," in *Global Report on Crime and Justice*, ed. Graeme Newman and Gregory J. Howard (Oxford, U.K.: Oxford University Press, 1999), 1–23.

73. Nonetheless, further research on this issue is needed. This would include controlling for other covariates—socioeconomic measures— that may help ascertain what drives increases in police personnel.

74. Graham Farrell and Ken Clark, "What Does the World Spend on Criminal Justice?" (HEUNI Paper 20, European Institute of Crime Prevention and Control, affiliated with the United Nations, Helsinki, 2004).

75. S. Harrendorf, M. Heiskanen, and S. Malby, eds., *International Statistics on Crime and Justice* (Helsinki: European Institute for Crime Prevention and Control, affiliated with the United Nations [HEUNI], 2010).

76. New York University Center for International Cooperation, "OECD States of Fragility Report: Meeting Post-2015 Ambitions" (Presentation prepared for World Bank Fragility, Conflict, and Violence Forum, Washington, DC, February 11–13, 2015), http://cic.nyu.edu/sites /default/files/wb_fragility_forum_cic_hearn_2.pdf.

77. Charles T. Call, "Competing Donor Approaches to Post-Conflict Police Reform," *Conflict, Security and Development* 2, no. 1 (2002): 100–09.

78. United Nations SSR Task Force, "Security Sector Reform Integrated Technical Guidance Notes" (United Nations, New York, 2012), http:// unssr.unlb.org/Portals/UNSSR/UN%20Integrated%20Technical%20 Guidance%20Notes%20on%20SSR.PDF.

79. Development Alternatives Incorporated, "Annual Review: Security Sector Accountability and Police Reform Program," 2013, http://iati .dfid.gov.uk/iati_documents/4130456.docx.

80. Ibid.

81. Ibid.

82. Development Alternatives Incorporated, "Annual Review: Security Sector Accountability and Police Reform Program," 2014, http://iati .dfid.gov.uk/iati_documents/4382748.

83. Independent Commission for Aid Impact (ICAI), "Review of U.K. Development Assistance to Security and Justice" (Report 42, ICAI, 2015), http://icai.independent.gov.uk/reports/uk-development-assistance -for-security-and-justice/.

84. Ibid.

85. Dorte Hvidemose and Jerome Mellon, "Monitoring and Evaluation Arrangements for the Implementation of Community Policing in Bosnia and Herzegovina: A Case Study" (Saferworld Research Report, 2009), http://www.saferworld.org.uk/resources/view-resource/382-bosnia -case-study.

86. Ibid.

87. Ibid.

88. Ibid.

89. Adapted from David H. Bayley, "Democratizing Police Abroad: What to Do and How to Do It," in *Issues in International Crime* (Washington, DC: U.S. Department of Justice, National Institute of Justice, 2001).

90. ICAI, "Review of U.K. Development Assistance to Security and Justice" (Report 42, ICAI, 2015), http://icai.independent.gov.uk /reports/uk-development-assistance-for-security-and-justice/.

91. U.S. Agency for International Development (USAID), *Assistance to Civilian Policing: USAID Policy Guidance,* 2005, http://www.usaid .gov/sites/default/files/documents/1866/200mbf.pdf.

92. Adapted from ICAI, "Review of U.K. Development Assistance to Security and Justice" (Report 42, ICAI, 2015), http://icai.independent .gov.uk/reports/uk-development-assistance-for-security-and -justice/.

93. David H. Bayley, "Democratizing Police Abroad: What to Do and How to Do It," in *Issues in International Crime* (Washington, DC: U.S. Department of Justice, National Institute of Justice, 2001).

94. Ibid.

95. Ibid.

96. Ibid.

97. Antoine Vandemoortele, *Learning from Failure? British and European Approaches to Security and Justice Programming,* 2015, http://www .ssrresourcecentre.org/2015/03/13/learning-from-failure-british-and -european-approaches-to-security-and-justice-programming/.

98. Nicole Ball, "Lessons from Burundi's Security Sector Reform Process" (Africa Security Brief no. 29, Africa Center for Strategic Studies, Washington, DC, 2014), http://www.ciponline.org/images/uploads /publications/Lessons-from-Burundis-SSR-Process.pdf.

References

Abrahamsen, Rita, and Michael C. Williams. 2011. *Security beyond the State: Private Security in International Politics*. Cambridge, U.K.: Cambridge University Press.

Adeyemi, A. A. 1990. "Crime and Development in Africa: A Case Study on Nigeria." In *Essays on Crime and Development*, edited by U. Zvekic. Rome: United Nations Interregional Crime and Justice Research Institute.

African Policing Civilian Oversight Forum. 2008. "An Audit of Police Oversight in Africa." APCOF, Cape Town.

Ajwang, Debra. 2006. "Police Accountability in Kenya." Presentation at a roundtable facilitated by the Commonwealth Human Rights Initiative, in collaboration with the East Africa Law Society, "The Police, the People, the Politics: Police Accountability in East Africa." Arusha, Tanzania, June 12–13. http://www.humanrightsinitiative.org/programs/aj/police/ea/conference_2006/police_accountability_in_kenya_debra_ajwang.pdf.

Alpert, G. P., and M. H. Moore. 1993. "Measuring Police Performance in the New Paradigm of Policing." In *Performance Measures for the Criminal Justice System*, discussion papers from the Bureau of Justice Statistics-Princeton Project, edited by J. DiIulio, G. Alpert, M. Moore, G. Cole, J. Petersilia, C. Logan, and J. Wilson, 109–41.

Altbeker, Antony. 2005. "Puzzling Statistics: Is South Africa Really the World's Crime Capital?" *South African Crime Quarterly* 11.

———. 2006. "Cars and Robbers: Has Car Theft Crime Prevention Worked Too Well?" ISS Working Paper 124, Institute for Security Studies, Pretoria. www.issafrica.org.

———. 2008. *A Country at War with Itself: South Africa's Crisis of Crime*. Cape Town: Jonathan Ball Publishers.

Ariel, B., W. Farrar, and A. Sutherland. 2015. "The Effect of Police Body-Worn Cameras on Use of Force and Citizens' Complaints against the Police: A Randomized Controlled Trial." *Journal of Quantitative Criminology* 31 (3): 509–35.

Armstrong, Michael. 2013. *They Wished They Were Honest: The Knapp Commission and New York City Police Corruption*. New York: Columbia University Press.

Ayers, Ian, and Steven D. Levitt. 1997. "Measuring Positive Externalities from Unobservable Victim Precaution: An Empirical Analysis of Lojack." NBER Working Paper 5928, National Bureau of Economic Research, Cambridge, MA.

Baaz, Maria Eriksson, and Ola Olsson. 2011. "Feeding the Horse: Unofficial Economic Activities within the Police Force in the Democratic Republic of the Congo." *African Security* 4: 223–41.

Ball, Nicole. 2014. "Lessons from Burundi's Security Sector Reform Process." Africa Security Brief no. 29, Africa Center for Strategic Studies,

Washington, DC. http://www.ciponline.org/images/uploads/publications /Lessons-from-Burundis-SSR-Process.pdf.

Bayley, David H. 1994. *Police for the Future*. New York: Oxford University Press.

———. 1998. *What Works in Policing*. New York: Oxford University Press.

———. 2001. "Democratizing Police Abroad: What to Do and How to Do It." In *Issues in International Crime*. Washington, DC: U.S. Department of Justice, National Institute of Justice.

Becker, G. 1968. "Crime and Punishment: An Economic Approach." *Journal of Political Economy* 76 (2): 169–217.

Bittner, E. 1990. *Aspects of Police Work*. Boston: Northeastern University Press.

Blumstein, Alfred, and Joel Wallman, eds. 2006. *The Crime Drop in America*. Rev. ed. New York: Cambridge University Press.

Bureau of Justice Statistics. n.d. http://www.bjs.gov/, accessed 2013.

Call, Charles T. 2002. "Competing Donor Approaches to Post-Conflict Police Reform." *Conflict, Security and Development* 2 (1): 100–09.

Caulkins, Jonathan P., and Peter Reuter. 2010. "How Drug Enforcement Affects Drug Prices." In *Crime and Justice*, vol. 39, edited by M. Tonry. Chicago: University of Chicago Press.

Caulkins, Jonathan P., C. Peter Rydell, William L. Schwabe, and James Chiesa. 1997. "Mandatory Minimum Drug Sentences: Throwing Away the Key or the Taxpayers' Money?" MR-827-DPRC, RAND Corporation, Santa Monica, CA.

Charnes, A., W. W. Cooper, and E. Rhodes. 1978. "Measuring the Efficiency of Decision Making Units." *European Journal of Operational Research* 2 (6): 429–44.

Coelli, Time. 1992. "A Computer Program for Frontier Production Function Estimation: Frontier Version 2.0." *Economics Letters* 39 (1): 29–32.

Cook, P., and J. Ludwig. 2010. "Economical Crime Control." NBER Working Paper 16513, National Bureau of Economic Research, Cambridge, MA.

Davis, Robert C. 2012. "Selected International Best Practices in Police Performance Measurement." RAND Center on Quality Policing, RAND Corporation, Santa Monica, CA.

Dener, C., J. A. Watkins, and W. L. Dorotinsky. 2011. *Financial Management Information Systems: 25 Years of World Bank Experience on What Works and What Doesn't*. Washington, DC: World Bank.

Development Alternatives Incorporated. 2013. "Annual Review: Security Sector Accountability and Police Reform Program." http://iati.dfid.gov .uk/iati_documents/4130456.docx.

———. 2014. "Annual Review: Security Sector Accountability and Police Reform Program." http://iati.dfid.gov.uk/iati_documents/4382748.

Donohue, J. J., and S. D. Levitt. 2001. "The Impact of Legalized Abortion on Crime." *Quarterly Journal of Economics* 116 (May): 379–420.

———. 2003. "Further Evidence That Legalized Abortion Lowered Crime: A Reply to Joyce." NBER Working Paper 9532, National Bureau of Economic Research, Cambridge, MA. http://www.nber.org/papers /w9532.pdf.

Drake, Leigh, and Richard Simper. 2002. "X-efficiency and Scale Economies in Policing: A Comparative Study Using the Distribution Free Approach and DEA." *Applied Economics* 34 (15): 1859–70.

Enten, Harry. 2014. "Where People Feel Safe, and Where They Are Safe." FiveThirtyEight (website), April 17. http://fivethirtyeight.com/datalab /where-people-feel-safe-and-where-they-are-safe/.

Eterno, J., and E. Silverman. 2012. *The Crime Numbers Game: Management by Manipulation*. New York: Taylor and Francis.

Fagan, Jeffrey, Amanda Geller, Garth Davies, and Valerie West. 2009. "Street Stops and Broken Windows Revisited: The Demography and Logic of Proactive Policing in a Safe and Changing City." In *Race, Ethnicity, and Policing: New and Essential Readings*, edited by Stephen K. Rice and Michael D. White, 309–48. New York: New York University Press.

Fajnzylber, P., D. Lederman, and N. Loayza. 2002a. "Inequality and Violent Crime." *Journal of Law and Economics* 45 (1): 1–40.

———. 2002b. "What Causes Violent Crime?" *European Economic Review* 46: 1323–57.

Farrell, Graham, and Ken Clark. 2004. "What Does the World Spend on Criminal Justice?" HEUNI Paper 20, European Institute of Crime Prevention and Control, affiliated with the United Nations, Helsinki.

Fogelson, R. M. 1977. *Big City Police*. Cambridge, MA: Harvard University Press.

Frischtak, Claudio, and Benjamin R. Mandel. 2012. *Crime, House Prices, and Inequality: The Effect of UPPs in Rio*. Staff Report no. 542. Federal Reserve Bank of New York.

Geneva Declaration on Armed Violence and Development. 2011. "Executive Summary." In *Global Burden of Armed Violence 2011*. http://www .genevadeclaration.org/fileadmin/docs/GBAV2/GBAV2011-Ex-summary -ENG.pdf.

Goldstein, H. 1990. *Problem-Oriented Policing*. New York: McGraw-Hill.

Greenwood, Peter W., Karyn Model, Peter Rydell, and James Chiesa. 1998. *Diverting Children from a Life of Crime: Measuring Costs and Benefits*. Santa Monica, CA: RAND Corporation.

Greenwood, P. W., and J. Petersilia. 1975. *Summary and Policy Implications*. Vol. 1 of *The Criminal Investigation Process*. Santa Monica, CA: RAND Corporation.

Harrendorf, S., M. Heiskanen, and S. Malby, eds. 2010. *International Statistics on Crime and Justice*. Helsinki: European Institute for Crime Prevention and Control, affiliated with the United Nations [HEUNI].

Hatry, H. P., L. H. Blair, D. M. Fisk, J. M. Greiner, J. R. Hall Jr., and P. S. Schaenman. 1992. "How Effective Are Your Community Services? Procedures for Measuring Their Quality." Urban Institute and International City/County Management Association, Washington, DC.

Home Office. 2013. "National Statistics: Police Workforce, England and Wales, 31 March 2013." https://www.gov.uk/government/publications /police-workforce-england-and-wales-31-march-2013/police-workforce -england-and-wales-31-march-2013.

Howard, Gregory J., Graeme Newman, and William Alex Pridemore. 2000. "Theory, Method, and Data in Comparative Criminology." *Criminal Justice* 4 (4): 139–211.

Hvidemose, Dorte, and Jerome Mellon. 2009. "Monitoring and Evaluation Arrangements for the Implementation of Community Policing in Bosnia and Herzegovina: A Case Study." Saferworld Research Report. http:// www.saferworld.org.uk/resources/view-resource/382-bosnia-case-study.

ICAI (Independent Commission for Aid Impact). 2015. "Review of U.K. Development Assistance to Security and Justice." Report 42, ICAI. http:// icai.independent.gov.uk/reports/uk-development-assistance-for-security -and-justice/.

Institute for Security Studies. 2011. "Expenditure Trends and Spending Priorities of the Department of Correctional Services." Institute for Security Studies, Pretoria. http://www.issafrica.org/crimehub/uploads /DCS_budget_revised_final_4_May2011.pdf.

International Alert. 2013. "The New Deal's Peacebuilding and Statebuilding Goals and Organized Crime." http://www.international-alert.org/sites /default/files/DVC_PSGsOrganisedCrime_EN_2013.pdf.

International Centre for Prison Studies. 2014. "World Prison Brief." http:// www.prisonstudies.org.

International Monetary Fund. 2001. *Government Finance Statistics Manual 2001*. https://www.imf.org/external/pubs/ft/gfs/manual/.

John, T., and M. Maguire. 2007. "Criminal Intelligence and the National Intelligence Model." In *Handbook of Criminal Investigation*, edited by T. Newburn, T. Williamson, and A. Wright, 199–225. Portland, OR: Willan Publishing.

Katz, Charles M., Edward R. Maguire, and Dennis W. Roncek. 2002. "The Creation of Specialized Police Gang Units: A Macro-Level Analysis of Contingency, Social Threat and Resource Dependency Explanations." *Policing: An International Journal of Police Strategies and Management* 25 (3): 472–506.

Kelling, G. L., and C. M. Coles. 1998. *Fixing Broken Windows: Restoring Order and Reducing Crime in Our Communities*. New York: Free Press.

Kelling, G. L., A. M. Pate, D. Dieckman, and C. Brown. 1974. *The Kansas City Preventive Patrol Experiment: Technical Report.* Washington, DC: Police Foundation.

Klitgaard, R. 1988. *Controlling Corruption.* Berkeley: University of California Press.

Klockars, C. B. 1985. "The Dirty Harry Problem." In *Moral Issues in Police Work*, edited by F. A. Elliston and M. Feldberg. Totowa, NJ: Rowan and Allanheld.

Leggett, Ted. 2003. "What Do the Police Do? Performance Measurement and the SAPS." ISS Paper 66, Institute for Security Studies, Pretoria.

Levitt, Steven D. 2004. "Understanding Why Crime Fell in the 1990s: Four Factors That Explain the Decline and Six That Do Not." *Journal of Economic Perspectives* 18 (1): 163–90.

Livingston, Steven. 2013. "Africa's Information Revolution: Implications for Crime, Policing, and Citizen Security." Research Paper 3, Africa Center for Strategic Studies, Washington, DC.

Loh, Johannes. 2010. "Success Factors for Police Reform in Post-Conflict Situations." Hertie School of Governance Working Paper 57, Berlin. http://edoc.vifapol.de/opus/volltexte/2013/4270/pdf/57.pdf.

Lott, J. 1998. *More Guns, Less Crime: Understanding Crime and Gun Control Laws.* Chicago: University of Chicago Press.

Maguire, E. R. 2003. "Measuring the Performance of Law Enforcement Agencies." Parts 1 and 2, *CALEA Update Magazine* 83. http://www.calea.org/calea-update-magazine/issue-83/measuring-performance-law-enforcement-agencies-part-1of-2-oart-articl.

Mas, Alexandre. 2006. "Pay, Reference Points, and Police Performance." NBER Working Paper 12202, National Bureau of Economic Research, Cambridge, MA.

Mastrofski, S. D. 1999. "Policing for People." Police Foundation, Washington, DC. http://www.policefoundation.org/wp-content/uploads/2015/06/Mastrofski-1999-Policing-For-People.pdf.

———. 2006. "Police Organization and Management Issues for the Next Decade." Paper presented at the National Institute of Justice Policing Research Workshop "Planning for the Future." Washington, DC, November 28–29. https://www.ncjrs.gov/pdffiles1/nij/grants/218584.pdf.

Moore, M. H. 2002. "Recognizing Value in Policing: The Challenge of Measuring Police Performance." Police Executive Research Forum, Washington, DC.

Moore, Mark H., and Robert C. Trojanowicz. 1988. "Policing and the Fear of Crime." *Perspectives on Policing,* no. 3, U.S. Department of Justice, National Institute of Justice, Washington, DC. https://www.ncjrs.gov/pdffiles1/nij/111459.pdf.

Morre, L. 2004. "Panoramic Overview of Private Security Industry in the 25 Member States of the EU." http://psm.du.edu/media/documents/reports _and_stats/global_data_and_statistics/coess_facts-figures_2004.pdf.

Muggah, Robert, and Gustavo Diniz. 2013. "Digitally Enhanced Violence Prevention in the Americas." *Stability: International Journal of Security and Development* 2 (3).

National Institute of Drug Abuse. 2012. "DrugFacts: Nationwide Trends." http://www.drugabuse.gov/publications/drugfacts/nationwide-trends.

Newburn, T. 1999. "Understanding and Preventing Police Corruption: Lessons from the Literature." Police Research Series Paper 110, Home Office, London. http://www.popcenter.org/problems/street_prostitution /pdfs/newburn_1999.pdf.

Newham, Gareth, and Lulama Gomomo. 2003. "Bad Cops Get a Break: The Closure of the SAPS Anti-Corruption Unit." *South African Crime Quarterly* 4. http://journals.assaf.org.za/index.php/sacq/article/view/1065.

Newman, Graeme, and Gregory J. Howard. 1999. "Introduction: Data Sources and Their Use." In *Global Report on Crime and Justice*, edited by Graeme Newman and Gregory J. Howard, 1–23. Oxford, U.K.: Oxford University Press.

New York University Center for International Cooperation. 2015. "OECD States of Fragility Report: Meeting Post-2015 Ambitions." Presentation prepared for World Bank Fragility, Conflict, and Violence Forum, Washington, DC, February 11–13. http://cic.nyu.edu/sites/default/files /wb_fragility_forum_cic_hearn_2.pdf.

North-South Institute. 2012. "Police Reform in an Independent South Sudan." Policy Brief, Spring. http://www.nsi-ins.ca/publications/police -reform-in-an-independent-south-sudan/.

OECD (Organisation for Economic Co-operation and Development). 2015. *States of Fragility 2015: Meeting Post-2015 Ambitions.* Paris: OECD Publishing. http://dx.doi.org/10.1787/9789264227699-en.

O'Neill, M. W., J. A. Needle, and R. T. Galvin. 1980. "Appraising the Performance of Police Agencies: The PPPM (Police Program Performance Measures) System." *Journal of Police Science and Administration* 8 (3): 253–64.

Ozcan, Yasar A. 2008. *Health Care Benchmarking and Performance Evaluation: An Assessment Using Data Envelopment Analysis (DEA).* Berlin: Springer.

Redpath, Jean. 2014. "Unsustainable and Unjust: Criminal Justice Policy and Remand Detention since 1994." *South African Crime Quarterly* 48: 25–37.

Reichel, P. L. 2002. *Comparative Criminal Justice Systems: A Topical Approach.* 3rd ed. Upper Saddle River, NJ: Prentice Hall.

Roebuck, Julian B., and Thomas Barker. 1974. "A Typology of Police Corruption." *Social Problems* 21 (3): 423–37.

Rowe, Michael. 2014. *Introduction to Policing.* 2nd ed. London: Sage Publishing.

Schedler, Andreas. 1999. "Conceptualizing Accountability." In *The Self-Restraining State: Power and Accountability in New Democracies,* edited by Andreas Schedler, Larry Diamond, and Marc F. Plattner, 13–28. Boulder, CO: Lynne Reinner Publishers.

Scott, Michael. 2004. "The Benefits and Consequences of Police Crackdowns." Response Guide no. 1, Center for Problem-Oriented Policing. http://www.popcenter.org/responses/police_crackdowns/.

Shaw, Mark, Jan van Dijk, and Wolfgang Rhomberg. 2003. "Determining Trends in Global Crime and Justice: An Overview of Results from the United Nations Surveys on Crime Trends and the Operations of Criminal Justice Systems." *Forum on Crime and Society* 3 (1–2): 35–63. http://www.unodc.org/pdf/crime/forum/forum3_Art2.pdf.

Small Arms Survey. 2011. *Small Arms Survey: States of Security.* Geneva: Small Arms Survey.

South African Police Service. 2015. "Crime Statistics of Republic of South Africa." http://www.saps.gov.za/resource_centre/publications/statistics/crimestats/2015/crime_stats.php.

South Sudan National Police Services. 2011–2013. *Quarterly Crime Statistics.* Government of South Sudan, Juba.

Spelman, William. 2006. "The Limited Importance of Prison Expansion." In *The Crime Drop in America,* rev. ed., edited by Alfred Blumstein and Joel Wallman, 97–129. New York: Cambridge University Press.

Stamatel, J. P. 2008. "Using Mortality Data to Refine Our Understanding of Homicide Patterns in Select Postcommunist Countries." *Homicide Studies* 12 (1): 117–35.

Stone, Christopher. 2006. "Crime, Justice, and Growth in South Africa: Toward a Plausible Contribution from Criminal Justice to Economic Growth." CID Working Paper 131, Center for International Development at Harvard University, Cambridge, MA.

Stretesky, P. B., and M. J. Lynch. 2001. "The Relationship between Lead Exposure and Homicide." *Archives of Pediatric Adolescent Medicine* 155: 579–82.

Transparency International. 2013. Global Corruption Barometer. http://www.transparency.org/gcb2013/results.

UNICRI (United Nations Interregional Crime and Justice Research Institute). 2000. International Crime Victims Survey. Turin: UNICRI. http://www.unicri.it/services/library_documentation/publications/icvs/statistics/17-icvs-app4.pdf.

United Nations. 2010. *Guidance on the Use and Preparation of Serious Organized Crime Threat Assessments: The SOCTA Handbook.* New York: United Nations. https://www.unodc.org/documents/afghanistan/Organized_Crime/SOCTA_Manual_2010.pdf.

———. 2014. *Police Peacekeeping Strategic Guidance Framework*. http://www.un.org/en/peacekeeping/sites/police/initiatives/guidelines-police-command.shtml.

United Nations Department of Peacekeeping Operations. 2008. "Guidelines for Integrating Gender Perspectives in National Police and Law Enforcement Agencies." United Nations, New York.

———. 2012. "Gender-Responsive Security Sector Reform."http://asset-ssr.org/images/pdf_file/english/GenderResponsiveSSR.pdf.

United Nations Development Programme. 2013. "Human Development Report for Latin America 2013–2014. Citizen Security with a Human Face: Evidence and Proposals for Latin America." In *Human Development Report,* edited by Khalid Malik. New York: United Nations Development Programme.

United Nations Peacekeeping. 2016. "Troop and Police Contributors." http://www.un.org/en/peacekeeping/documents/Yearly.pdf.

United Nations SSR Task Force. 2012. "Security Sector Reform Integrated Technical Guidance Notes." United Nations, New York. http://unssr.unlb.org/Portals/UNSSR/UN%20Integrated%20Technical%20Guidance%20Notes%20on%20SSR.PDF.

UNODC (UN Office on Drugs and Crime). 2012. *Digest of Organized Crime Case Studies.* New York: United Nations. https://www.unodc.org/documents/organized-crime/EnglishDigest_Final301012_30102012.pdf.

———. Various years. Surveys on Crime Trends and the Operations of Criminal Justice Systems (UN-CTS). https://www.unodc.org/unodc/en/data-and-analysis/United-Nations-Surveys-on-Crime-Trends-and-the-Operations-of-Criminal-Justice-Systems.html.

UNODC and UN-HABITAT. 2011. *Introductory Handbook on Policing Urban Space.* Nairobi: United Nations. http://www.unodc.org/documents/justice-and-prison-reform/crimeprevention/11-80387_ebook.pdf.

USAID (U.S. Agency for International Development). 2005. *Assistance to Civilian Policing: USAID Policy Guidance.* http://www.usaid.gov/sites/default/files/documents/1866/200mbf.pdf.

Vandemoortele, Antoine. 2015. *Learning from Failure? British and European Approaches to Security and Justice Programming.* http://www.ssrresourcecentre.org/2015/03/13/learning-from-failure-british-and-european-approaches-to-security-and-justice-programming/.

Vanderbilt University. n.d. Latin American Public Opinion Project database (accessed October 2012), http://lapop.ccp.ucr.ac.cr/Lapop_English.html.

Vera Institute of Justice. 2003. "Measuring Progress toward Safety and Justice: A Global Guide to the Design of Performance Indicators across the Justice Sector." Vera Institute, New York.

Webb, Barry. 1993. *Approaches to Rank Structure and Pay in Police Services: An International Survey.* London: Home Office.

Weber, Leanne, and Ben Bowling, eds. 2012. *Stop and Search: Police Power in a Global Context*. Abingdon, U.K.: Routledge.

Weiner, Mandy. 2012. *Killing Kebble: An Underworld Exposed*. Johannesburg: Pan Macmillan South Africa.

Weisburd, D., S. D. Mastrofski, R. Greenspan, and J. J. Willis. 2004. "The Growth of Compstat in American Policing." *Police Foundation Reports* (April). http://assets.lapdonline.org/assets/pdf/growthofcompstat.pdf.

Wilkinson, Richard, and Kate Pickett. 2009. *The Spirit Level: Why More Equal Societies Almost Always Do Better*. London: Allen Lane.

Wilson, James Q. 1985. *Thinking about Crime*. New York: Random House.

———. 1993. "The Problem of Defining Agency Success." In *Performance Measures for the Criminal Justice System*, 156–166. Washington, DC: Bureau of Justice Assistance. http://www.bjs.gov/content/pub/pdf/pmcjs.pdf.

Wilson, James Q., and Joan Petersilia. 1995. *Crime: Twenty-Eight Leading Experts Look at the Most Pressing Problem of Our Time*. San Francisco: ICS Press.

Wolpaw Reyes, Jessica. 2007. "Environmental Policy as Social Policy? The Impact of Childhood Lead Exposure on Crime." NBER Working Paper 13097, National Bureau of Economic Research, Cambridge, MA. http://www.nber.org/papers/w13097.

World Bank. 2009. "Report on the Assessment of the Financial Management of the Defense and Security Forces in the Central African Republic." World Bank, Washington, DC.

———. 2011. *Practitioners' Toolkit for Agriculture Public Expenditure Analysis*. Washington, DC: World Bank.

———. 2012. "El Salvador Security and Justice Public Expenditure and Institutional Review." World Bank, Washington, DC.

———. 2013a. "Malian Security Forces: Financial Management Assessment Report." World Bank, Washington, DC.

———. 2013b. "Public Financial Management Reforms in Post-Conflict Countries: Synthesis Report." World Bank, Washington, DC. http://documents.worldbank.org/curated/en/2012/01/16380099/public-financial-management-reforms-post-conflict-countries-synthesis-report.

———. 2014. *Report on Crime and Violence in South Sudan*. Washington, DC: World Bank (unpublished manuscript).

World Bank and United Nations. 2012. "Liberia Public Expenditure Review Note: Meeting the Challenges of the UNMIL Security Transition." World Bank, Washington, DC.

CHAPTER 5

Public Expenditure Reviews in the Criminal Justice Sector

Introduction

The criminal justice system is responsible for delivering justice services to communities across a nation. How to increase access to justice for citizens and make criminal justice institutions more effective and efficient is often at the heart of policy debates. For governments faced with the combined challenges of fiscal constraint and rising crime and insecurity, the key policy questions involve what is adequate, affordable, and effective budgeting for the criminal justice system.

When the interest in quality management in government institutions grew worldwide about three decades ago, criminal justice sector institutions too started to focus more on setting performance goals, regularly assessing their operations, and translating good practices into management systems. Internationally, there is now an extensive global network of institutions and organizations involved in training, setting standards, and producing accompanying tools and research to assist criminal justice sector agencies in assessing and improving their services.[1] Given the growth of these networks, policy makers and practitioners can call upon assessment toolkits as well as comprehensive evidence-based evaluations of criminal justice reform to support their work.[2] The identified gap in this support, however, is an examination of criminal justice through a public finance lens, which offers guidance on how allocations may be prioritized against national plans and strategies, how funds may be used more efficiently and effectively, and what accountable and transparent expenditures may look like.

The instrument for providing such guidance is a Public Expenditure Review (PER). Sectoral PERs in general are used to analyze both the allocation and disbursement of public funds to a specific sector over a given period of time in the context of the sector's performance. A criminal justice sector PER is used in the same way. A PER can also include a review of the budgetary process and may assess the institutional arrangements within the sector. Often PERs are termed Public Expenditure and Institutional Reviews to indicate that they review not only funding flows but also institutional performance.

This chapter provides an overview of how the PER has been used to support reform efforts by governments and organizations within the criminal justice system. More specifically, the chapter (i) outlines the rationale for undertaking a PER in the criminal justice sector, (ii) describes how to map the criminal justice sector in terms of functions and institutions, (iii) examines the criminal justice chain and inter-sector coordination, (iv) describes how to measure performance, and (v) lists the steps involved in undertaking a PER and the expected outcomes.

Annexes to this chapter offer guidance for assessing core criminal justice institutions (excluding the police): prosecution agencies (annex 5A); the criminal courts (annex 5B); corrections (annex 5C); and other criminal justice institutions (annex 5D). One annex also deals with carrying out a criminal justice sector PER in fragile and conflict-affected states, or FCS (annex 5E); and a final annex deals with assessing criminal justice sector data (annex 5F).

The Rationale for a PER

PERs inform decisions about resource needs to support efficient operations and meet policy goals. They provide answers to questions about what a particular approach costs and what is affordable; they can also highlight uneven distribution of resources and performance across and within agencies. This type of information is essential not only in conflict-affected countries where a functioning system has to be (re)established, but also for governments seeking to improve the performance of their criminal justice system, especially when they are challenged by shrinking budgets.

A sound PER should therefore help the criminal justice system in the critical task of "choosing priorities among goals and objectives, since there will never be sufficient funding to do everything that might reasonably be thought necessary in an ideal system of justice."[3] Adequate financing of the criminal justice system, based on well-assessed capacities and needs, will ultimately improve not only the performance and accountability of the system, but also its independence.

How and when to launch a PER process will vary according to context. Examples of PERs undertaken by governments and the World Bank to address particular issues in different country settings include the following:

A PER in Serbia clarified the link between resources and potential reform.[4] In 2010, data collected by the European Commission for the Efficiency of Justice showed that over 75 percent of the budget of Serbia's courts came from fees and fines. This was the highest percentage among European courts; most did not reach 40 percent, and close to one-third reached only about 20 percent. This finding showed a low overall spending allocation from government to the criminal justice sector historically, and indicated the judiciary's extensive involvement in registration of property and business. The outcome of the review was two key policy options: either take away these functions and supplement revenue from the national budget, or strengthen the courts' administrative staff to execute these administrative functions (rather than have them undertaken by more expensive judicial staff).

In El Salvador, a PER promoted a policy dialogue and started a process to obtain better data.[5] In 2012, in response to ever increasing rates of crime and violence, the government of El Salvador requested World Bank assistance in undertaking a PER. The review process achieved two objectives: it brought together different stakeholders within the criminal justice system to provide a sector review; and it fostered a coordinated policy dialogue based on data and evidence. The conclusions of the PER were used in a series of workshops with the key actors to develop an action plan for a more efficient allocation of resources in the sector.

In two African countries, a PER examined the links between international support and national service provision: for Liberia in 2012 and Somalia in 2016, the PER shed light on domestic budget resources and expenditure flows with the aim of informing budget needs for future system development and operations.[6] These reviews were important because a significant portion of criminal justice servicing in these countries is externally financed, and in some instances (e.g., where there is a large police peacekeeping contingent), externally implemented. The policy expectation was a gradual reduction in peacekeeping presence over time as the two war-affected countries built up their own system capacities.

In Morocco, a PER furthered reform efforts and helped in standard-setting.[7] In 2013, Morocco undertook a justice sector PER to determine opportunities and challenges for the judiciary in reaching the strategic goals of the reform process under way in the country. The review focused on four key areas relevant to the reform process: (i) access to justice, (ii) the judiciary's caseload and performance, (iii) the judiciary's human resources and management, and (iv) the evolution and management of the sector's public expenditures. This review included a detailed analysis of variations in court performance across the country and provided a data set for future benchmarking of all courts in Morocco.

As these examples show, the country context will drive the objectives and expected outcomes of a PER; these are not template exercises. In turn, particularly where there may be a paucity of data,[8] a PER can simply be a useful exercise to launch a sectorwide process aimed at improving effectiveness, even where the necessary data to match policy with budgeting only arrive some years the later.

The Fiscal Framework and Criminal Justice

Given that a PER examines government expenditure, criminal justice spending and budget reviews must from the outset be linked in some way with the country's fiscal framework.[9] Generally, the portion of the overall national budget that goes to the criminal justice system tends to be small, especially when it comes to the budget for prosecutor services, legal aid, and the judiciary. Not surprisingly, the criminal justice budget (excluding the police) is frequently not a critical priority for ministries of finance.

For example, according to the European Commission for the Efficiency of Justice, in 2012, the average proportion of the total public expenditure allocated to the courts, prosecutors, and legal aid in European states was 2.2 percent.[10] The criminal justice part is just a fraction of this allocation. The call upon the national budget for criminal justice services tends to be small in most countries, but there are exceptions. In some countries where there is a high incidence of crime and violence, spending on criminal justice tends to be higher; in Central America, for example, the average public expenditure allocation in 2008 was 4 percent of the national budget.[11] Spending also tends to be higher in conflict-affected countries where governments and international partners are attempting to rebuild criminal justice systems (assuming the international contributions are reflected in the national budget).

The largest claimant in the system is often the police; a 2004 global survey of spending on criminal justice (the only study of its kind) estimated that 62 percent of spending goes to the police, 3 percent to prosecution, 18 percent to courts, and 17 percent to corrections.[12]

Police budgets and expenditures were covered in the previous chapter, so the focus here is on the judiciary, prosecution, legal aid, and corrections. Allocations to the third branch of government, the judicial branch (which sometimes includes an independent prosecution agency), tend to be small. Nevertheless, reviews related to spending may be a particularly contested task for a number of reasons:

- There can be sensitivity within the judiciary when the executive branch insists on aligning budgets to judicial performance and imposes managerial accountability. It is not always clear how the third branch of government should be measured (especially if no performance measures are to be established for the first branch of government, the legislature). Nor is it always clear who should have the authority and capability to monitor, compare, and comment on the effectiveness of court operations, not to speak of judicial performance.
- System incentives for more efficient judicial performance cannot focus on crime reduction alone, since criminal cases are just one part of the courts' responsibility.[13] Furthermore, economic criteria, including

quantitative measures, have an important part to play in determining what levels of funding enable courts and other criminal justice system agencies to carry out their functions; but for many criminal justice system functions, an economic justification for adequate funding is not only difficult but counterintuitive.[14]

- The provision of public financing to the courts is necessarily founded upon difficult-to-quantify value judgments about their functions in the maintenance of constitutional arrangements, the rule of law, and the provision of access to justice for individuals, organizations, and governments.[15]

- The judicial branch tends to lack a strong constituency, which places it at a disadvantage when competing with executive branch agencies for resources. Elected officials often have little incentive to divert resources to the judicial branch at the expense of projects where the benefit to their constituents is more directly visible.[16]

Factors in Undertaking a PER

Undertaking a PER for the criminal justice system entails some factors that are not normally part of PERs in others sectors. In particular, a criminal justice PER often involves more than one ministry and several government agencies under each ministry, plus the judicial branch, making the required data collection and analysis especially complex. These somewhat distinctive factors are described below.

Independent Funding

One of the salient characteristics of the criminal justice system is the judiciary's (and sometimes the prosecution service's) position as the third branch of government. The usual considerations regarding budgeting and public financial management for agencies of the executive branch need to be qualified when applied to the judiciary. The main reason for this is the need to guarantee the judiciary's independence from the executive and the legislative branches. Such guarantee may take the form of constitutional or statutory rules providing a minimum level of budget allocation to courts or keeping the resourcing process of the courts outside of the usual budget process. A number of judiciaries in Latin America, for example, are constitutionally guaranteed a set percentage of the government's annual budget— irrespective of need or performance.

Criminal Justice within an Overall Justice System

While determining the level of public resources spent on the public prosecution and corrections service in a country may be a relatively straightforward exercise, the same may not be as easy for police and other law enforcement agencies or the criminal courts. Because these agencies tend to be responsible for a broader range of law and order and regulatory enforcement actions, discerning the percentage of their budget that is or should be attributed to criminal enforcement actions is often difficult. Similarly, in most countries the judiciary—sometimes also the prosecution service—deals with different case types (civil, administrative, criminal, commercial, and so forth). The budget for the judiciary (or even for individual courts), on the other hand, rarely specifies the resources that are allocated to different case types. Courts often handle a mix of cases and even when specialized chambers are created they tend to share buildings, services, and personnel (in many small first-instance courts the same judge may be responsible for both civil and criminal cases). To quantify the concrete budget dedicated to criminal courts may therefore be a difficult task.

Multiple Sources of Funding

In some countries funding for criminal justice system agencies comes from different government levels (national, regional, and local). Otherwise independent court and prosecution services are funded through a combination of judicial and nonjudicial budgets.[17] For example, building construction, operation, and maintenance may not be within the judicial budget. The same may be the case for salaries for employees other than judges. In addition, courts may use their own revenues (collected through court fees and fines) to fund their operations and may use external aid (which is not always reflected in the budget) to finance investments.

Linking Inputs to Outputs and Outcomes

Most countries' budgetary documents do not follow a functional or program-activity classification of public expenditures. The general rule is that information on public expenditures for the criminal justice system will be recorded in an economic classification, which makes it difficult to assess if such expenditures are allowing the justice system to achieve its goals. A budget with an economic classification can give a sense of how much is being spent on (for example) performance-enhancing items such as information technology systems. But it will not indicate where these investments are being made (geographic locations, prosecution offices/ courts/corrections with higher workloads or specific needs, and so forth), or how they are affecting the performance of the institutions where they are being implemented. Ideally, to properly link expenditures to activities, budgets should be program or activity based, and expenditure data should be available at local administrative levels and comparable to any performance data available or to be developed.[18] Yet many developing countries do not use such a budgeting method, which requires a wealth of detailed data by location.[19]

Mapping the Criminal Justice Sector

The criminal justice system is generally "understood by scholars and practitioners to comprise all of the institutions, processes and services responsible for the prevention, investigation, adjudication, treatment and response to illegal behaviors. The sector includes the institutions traditionally associated with it, such as police, prosecutors, public defenders, courts and corrections, as well as a wide range of other institutions such as private police, victim services, private lawyers and bar associations, human rights and ombudsman's offices, addiction and other treatment programs as well as community engagement and services programs."[20]

The system also must be understood as an important constituent of the public sector. The public sector "comprises upstream core ministries and central agencies, downstream bodies including sector ministries, and non-executive state institutions. . . . Downstream bodies include both sector ministries and agencies, including education and health care providers which deliver and fund services under the policy direction of the government."[21] The place of the criminal justice system institutions in this "downstream/upstream" conceptual framework is not always easy to determine and varies across countries. On the one hand, these institutions deliver specific services and thus have direct contact with citizens. On the other hand, they are also involved in ensuring executive accountability, not only through maintaining oversight of administrative procedures,[22] but also through holding public officials accountable for criminal activities such as corruption.

The traditional functions of the core criminal justice system institutions are to investigate and prosecute criminal activities, adjudicate criminal cases, and incapacitate and/or rehabilitate offenders. Depending on country context these can be broader and can include protecting witnesses and victims, preventing crime and public disorder, and informing criminal justice system policy development.

Importantly, the judiciary (including those members working within the criminal justice system) is the third branch of government and considered independent in most countries. The criminal justice system's role as guarantor of the executive's accountability is an indirect outcome when courts judge criminal cases involving government decisions or members of the government.[23] This essential accountability function of the judiciary also implies that courts cannot be treated as any other executive agency in the context of interagency competition for resources. Of course the courts' funding will be affected by the overall budget situation of the government, but decisions about their funding level should always take into account their central role as one of the three powers of the state.

Criminal justice agencies have the dominant government role and responsibility for community safety and security within a country, but what exactly this role is and which agency is involved depends on the country context. The respective roles and responsibilities of the various agencies tasked with different aspects of safety and security are generally outlined in the country's legal framework (where it exists) which establishes mandates, jurisdiction, powers and responsibilities, organizational structures, and operational framework and funding sources. Hence these systems vary significantly across nations: decentralization of the structures and functions of the criminal justice agencies is generally greatest in federal nations; military and intelligence services may have a substantial or highly limited role; roles and responsibilities of individual criminal justice agencies differ across countries and may go beyond what is expected; and agencies that are generally not considered a part of the criminal justice system, such as schools, health departments, or housing agencies, may be highly engaged in addressing crime and violence.

The criminal justice system includes various institutions. The police,[24] prosecution service, criminal courts, and corrections are the core agencies of the institutional framework that most countries have adopted to respond to crime through investigation and prosecution of criminal activities, adjudication of criminal cases, and incapacitation and/or rehabilitation of offenders. At the same time, a range of other entities deliver important criminal justice services that have to be funded from the government's budget. Legal aid and criminal defense services are among the more costly of these services—and they often remain underfunded, with serious consequences for individual rights and justice system operations. Particularly as societies increasingly recognize the importance of crime prevention, additional institutions join the criminal justice sector, such as services for youth at risk, school crime prevention services, employment and treatment services for offenders, child protective services, and a range of public education efforts along with research and evaluation efforts—and all require funding.

Examining this complex institutional terrain will require an inventory of the organizations and actors involved. There is no standard institutional typology, and there will be variation between common and civil law systems, depending on the legal framework. The United Nations Office on Drugs and Crime (UNODC) provides a useful graphic (figure 5.1) that offers some guidance as to the range of institutions that could be covered, as well as the respective functions and different steps in the criminal justice chain.

The Legal Framework

How a country's legal framework evolves is influenced by the country's history. Thus history—more than deliberate choice of a best-fit model based on a solid assessment—influences issues like levels of decentralization, division of roles, accountability and governance structures, agency independence, and the sources for funding the criminal justice system. These influences are important for understanding why many different types of law enforcement agencies operate and why they are under the authority of such a broad range of local, regional, and national agencies. For example, the justice systems of former colonies tend to resemble those of the former colonial power, and often include the very structures that existed under the colonial powers decades or even a century before. Even for a nation state establishing itself after the prior regime has collapsed, creating optimal governance structures is difficult; history and current politics will still influence choices and can lead to changes over time that result in less efficient structures. At the same time, nations committed to delivering high-quality government services with existing resources will undertake the

Figure 5.1   Example of Case Flow and Decision Points in the Criminal Justice Sector

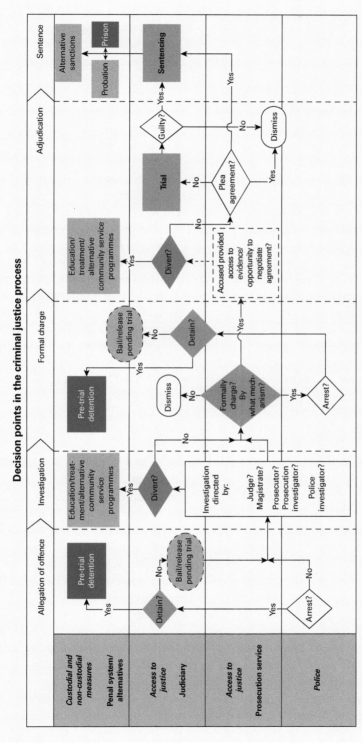

Decision points in the criminal justice process

Source: United Nations Office on Drugs and Crime, "Decision Points Map in the Criminal Justice System," in "Criminal Justice Assessment Toolkit," © 2006 United Nations, reproduced with permission from United Nations; further permission required for reuse. https://www.unodc.org/documents/justice-and-prison-reform /cjat_eng/Decision_Points.pdf.

needed changes to develop more appropriate structures. The United Kingdom, for instance, created the Crown Prosecution Service in the mid-1980s, shifting prosecutorial responsibilities away from the police, and in 2000 the Netherlands shifted most management responsibilities for the courts, especially most budgetary responsibilities, away from the Ministry of Justice to a judicial council.

The combined agencies comprising the criminal justice system are generally granted constitutional powers to carry out some of the essential functions needed to create safe communities and ensure the state's security. These functions include (i) implementing their monopoly on the legitimate use of state force within the territory; (ii) maintaining public order and preventing crime; (iii) responding to public disorder and criminality; (iv) providing a fair, legitimate, and expeditious process of trial and adjudication for criminal cases; and (v) incapacitating and/or rehabilitating offenders. These are significant powers and require adequate controls and supervision—another reason why criminal justice agencies are often parts of different decentralized powers (national, state, local), respond to different ministries (ministry of justice, ministry of interior, ministry of home affairs, etc.), and represent at least two branches of government (i.e., the executive and the judiciary). Further, such agencies not infrequently require presidential and/or parliamentary approval of key appointments as well as annual reports or other reporting or oversight arrangements (e.g., ombudsman offices, human rights commissions, nongovernmental organizations [NGOs]).

Traditional/Informal Institutions and the Public Sector

Another important consideration in mapping the criminal justice sector is the role of traditional institutions, whether in developed countries (the aristocracy in the House of Lords in the United Kingdom) or in developing countries (tribal elders in Sub-Saharan Africa). Where formal institutions are weak and have limited reach, it is important to consider the justice services that traditional or informal actors may provide. In Rwanda, for example, the *gacaca* courts—existing traditional tribunals—were adjusted to try the overwhelmingly large number of genocide cases that the weak formal system could not be expected to handle. While the choice—and ultimate success—of these courts is frequently questioned, they offered one of the few options available for addressing these cases at all.[25]

Building upon existing traditional systems—after understanding how they function and who they can serve—is an option that has been recognized in many countries across the globe. But it is still often overlooked, especially when the urgent need to create viable formal institutions distracts decision makers from the possibility of investing in a nongovernment option. Understanding these options and alternatives is actually quite important as part of the effort to understand priorities for investments in the formal sector and choices for the future scope of the public sector. If traditional systems address at least some disputes reasonably well, then there is no need to invest in creating these capacities in the formal sector, particularly when resources are already scarce.

Beyond customary courts, other institutions not formally part of the public sector include private security services, as well as legal aid services provided pro bono or supported by international donors. The relationship of these organizations with those funded through public revenues can vary from cooperation to competition and even conflict. Because these institutions are not funded by public revenues, they are by definition excluded from the criminal justice system PER. However, in certain countries the analysis of the scope of these other activities may help to clarify the performance of the criminal justice system and may help to identify whether actual service gaps exist. This analysis may include a review of the clarity of jurisdictional boundaries and role definition (or its absence). It may also seek to determine the extent to which these entities exist because of failures (real or perceived) of the public bodies or their lack of legitimacy, and the extent to which their operational ethos accords with the legal restrictions placed on the conduct of statutory institutions (e.g., in relation to the use of force and the securing of due process rights for suspects and accused persons).

The Criminal Justice Chain and Interagency Coordination

A Criminal Justice Architecture

Although criminal justice responsibilities are divided among a range of government agencies across all government levels, there rarely exists a national-level structure to effectively coordinate different agency responses or develop and implement a comprehensive national criminal justice policy. As a result, governance of the criminal justice system is dispersed across agencies, and policies to address crime and security are rarely created to guide the entire system. At the same time, the reason that the chain of criminal justice agencies is referred to as a *system* is because the actions or nonactions of one agency tend to affect the workload and operations of the others. If police arrest more people, then prosecutors and possibly courts have to respond to increasing numbers of detentions and investigative requests, pretrial detention numbers will increase unless courts have alternatives, and so on. If prosecutors have broad discretion, office policy may allow them to dismiss or defer prosecution of misdemeanor and other cases, especially when high arrest numbers are overwhelming their capacities to respond within legal time limits. Such policy decisions by the prosecutor's office may be justifiable, but they render increased police efforts ineffective. This outcome is not only likely to contribute to interagency difficulties but also would mean that police resources were wasted. This example—which is just one of many—highlights the need for good cooperation and a systemwide policy (both of which are lacking in many countries) and makes clear why a systemwide review of resource allocations, policies, and performance is important.

Coordination of the Criminal Justice Chain

In chainlike systems such as the criminal justice system, consistent, coordinated systemwide improvements in the interconnected work flow from one entity to another are where many long-term changes can have their biggest impact. Nevertheless, criminal justice institutions have a high degree of autonomy and they tend to work in silos. Interventions in one part of the criminal justice system can have little or no effect in another, or may trigger unintended consequences that cause inefficiencies—not just for agency operations and resource needs but for people, victims, offenders, and communities alike.[26] It is not unusual for criminal justice system institutions to blame each other for the systems' inefficiencies and bottlenecks, with each considering itself the most underfunded. In addition, even if the relationship among institutions is cooperative, no institution has the ability to compel the others to change internal operations, staffing, business processes, or organizational configurations.[27]

Given the interconnectedness of the criminal justice system, one of the first issues to review is whether any coordination mechanisms are in place to align strategies and pool resources. Several countries have experimented with different types of coordination mechanisms, yet such mechanisms continue to be the exception rather than the rule. For example, in some countries large ministries coordinate management and budgeting of criminal justice. New ministries of public safety or justice have emerged in countries such as Chile, El Salvador, Mexico, and New Zealand (see box 5.1), blending the boundaries between ministries of justice, prosecutors' offices, and the ministry of interior. On a smaller scale, Kosovo and other countries have consolidated certain functions such as training academies in order to pool resources and allow criminal justice actors to become more knowledgeable

---

Box 5.1   Coordinating the Justice Sector in New Zealand

Coordinating the justice sector in New Zealand entails recognizing the "pipeline" across the criminal justice system—that is, the flow of responsibilities across the sector, from investigating crime and carrying out arrests, to prosecution and sentencing, and finally to sentence management and rehabilitation. Actions and decisions at any one part of the pipeline can substantially influence other parts.

Coordinating the justice sector also involves a specific approach to leadership. The Sector Leadership Board was formed in 2011 and is made up of the chief executives of Police, Justice, and Corrections, with the secretary of Justice acting as chair and a sector group in the Ministry of Justice providing support. The board has charge of the justice system's overall performance; more specifically, it coordinates major changes in the sector and handles improvements (modernization, cost reduction, service enhancement, etc.).

The Justice Sector Fund, a funding pool established in 2012, further facilitates coordination across the sector. The fund makes it possible to transfer savings between agencies and across years, and thus allows direction of funds to the highest-priority concerns.

Source: Based on Ministry of Justice of New Zealand n.d.

about the entire system and related agencies. In countries as diverse as Albania, Mexico, South Africa, and Uganda, multi-agency task forces have been established to respond to specific crime problems, such as gender-based violence, corruption, prison overcrowding, or drug crimes. Although these examples show a very positive trend, such coordination mechanisms are the exception, and even when they exist they do not necessarily translate into adequate resourcing of the criminal justice system. While a well-coordinated system can result in various benefits, a poorly coordinated one increases fragmentation, augments costs and time, reduces accountability, and creates barriers to access to services.[28]

Coordination beyond the Criminal Justice System: Experiences from Drug Policy Coordination Mechanisms

Effectively combating drug use and trafficking requires significant coordination among different institutions beyond the justice sector. In particular, public and even private agencies from the health, education, and social services need to collaborate closely with law enforcement institutions to tackle the multifaceted aspects of drug use and trafficking. The governments of Australia, Mexico, the United States, and several European Union countries have established different nationwide strategies and coordination mechanisms in an effort to reduce the illicit drug market.[29] In addition, because drug trafficking regularly requires coordination across jurisdictional borders and often has a transnational dimension, effective counternarcotics efforts involve coordination at the international level. Regional bodies such as the Caribbean Community Secretariat (CARICOM) and the Andean Community have set up several international agreements and multilateral action plans to coordinate efforts to combat the abuse and trafficking of illicit narcotics and psychotropic substances. Other regional organizations such as the African Union or the Economic Community of West African States (ECOWAS) have promoted similar initiatives.[30] The type of arrangements and degree of coordination vary from country to country, and depend largely on contextual factors and political elements such as political leadership, government priorities, and the degree of influence of certain interest groups.[31] Such mechanisms have facilitated information sharing, fostered agreement on core issues and directions, and minimized duplication, among other benefits.[32] Yet these arrangements have not necessarily resulted in the better-coordinated allocation of resources. At the same time, as some observers have argued, common budgeting is one of the most effective coordination mechanisms, and it provides the necessary support to implement new organizations and policies.[33]

Executive-Judiciary Coordination Arrangements

Any coordination mechanism among criminal justice system institutions will be affected by the arrangements between the judiciary and the executive. From the executive side this relationship is mainly articulated through three ministries or agencies: (i) the ministry of justice (or equivalent), (ii) the ministry of interior (or equivalent), and (iii) the ministry of finance (or equivalent).

- *Ministry of justice.* The PER should review the responsibilities of the ministry of justice in relation to the judiciary. In some countries, it is responsible for the administration of courts; often it is also responsible for the prosecution services and corrections. A particular question is the ministry of justice's role regarding the judicial budget. In countries based on the Westminster system of government and in many civil law countries, the executive plays the dominant role in seeking the necessary appropriation for the judiciary, but in other countries (e.g., the United States) the courts negotiate their budget directly with the legislature (see annex 5B for a typology of judicial budget negotiation arrangements).
- *Ministry of interior.* The ministry of interior or its equivalent may be responsible for the police, and sometimes also for the corrections services. In such cases, the PER should also include this ministry in its analysis of issues such as the following: resource allocation; the number and salaries of corrections agency officials; appointment or promotion of officials; the number and salaries of support staff; drafting of the strategies, policies, or guidelines for the corrections services; investment in IT, new buildings, and infrastructure; and operations and maintenance (see the policing chapter for details).
- *Ministry of finance.* In most countries, the ministry of finance is responsible for the management of the public finances and the government's budget. It is usually in charge of negotiating and assigning budget allocations to line ministries. The ministry of finance can also be responsible (through the treasury) for managing appropriations and transfers, collecting and spending revenues from court fees and fines, and coordinating and managing the external financing of investments of criminal justice system institutions.

The Role of Judicial Councils

The PER team should also identify whether there is any judicial council (JC) or similar institution, what its role and authorities are, and how it is funded. Some countries split the responsibility for approving and managing judicial resources between the JC and the ministry of justice. For example, the JC may be responsible for determining the salaries and number of judges in the courts and the day-to-day court operating expenses, while the ministry of justice maintains the authority for determining the salaries and number of support staff, as well as for capital investments in courts. Box 5.2 provides a typology of JCs in Europe, which could be useful in guiding the analysis of these institutions. In addition, the PER should assess the governance structure of the JC (members, appointment rules, government branches responsible for member appointments, etc.), which will have important implications for its authority and position within the budget process.

Box 5.2   Major Governance Models of Judicial Councils in Europe

A World Bank study identifies two models for governance by European judicial councils (JCs):

The *northern European model* (seen in Denmark, Ireland, the Netherlands, and Sweden):

- JCs have an extensive role in the administration of justice and also budgetary powers.
- The main focus is on strengthening judicial resource management and efficiency without compromising judicial independence.
- JCs handle administrative provision of the courts; monitor caseloads and quality standards; and manage judicial facilities, court automation, and public information—but courts have substantial operational autonomy.
- JCs have authority for budget preparation, resource allocation to judicial bodies, and accounting for expenditure; budgets are prepared in close consultation with the ministry of finance.
- Some JCs contract with individual courts for "delivery of justice"—courts agree to decide on a certain number of cases and can allocate agreed-upon resources as they see fit.
- JCs act as consultants to the ministry of justice or other executive agency responsible for developing justice sector policy.

The *southern European model* (seen in most European Union jurisdictions, including Belgium, France, Italy, Portugal, and Spain as well as some post-communist countries, including Poland, Romania, and the Slovak Republic):

- JCs make decisions about personnel in the judiciary and in some countries carry out judicial inspection and handle quality standards.
- The main goal is to protect and strengthen guarantees of judicial independence as enshrined in the constitution.
- The ministry of justice or other executive agency manages resources.

Source: World Bank 2008.

Coordination and Territorial Organization of the State

In addition to addressing the overall criminal justice coordination mechanisms and institutional arrangements between the judiciary, the executive, and the legislature, the PER has to reflect the territorial organization of the state and how it translates into the structure and financing of the criminal justice system. In some countries the prosecutors, courts, and prisons are national institutions and centrally managed and financed. In other countries the criminal justice system's organization, management, and funding may be divided among federal, state, and local government levels. In these cases, the PER will need to look at the institutional arrangements linking the criminal justice system and the executive and the legislature at each level (as well as the arrangements among government levels—federal/national, state/provincial, and local). Different structures will have different funding and operational consequences that will need to be assessed. For example, decentralized funding of courts may have positive or negative consequences; courts funded in this way may be able to better reflect local needs for justice services, but they may also be exposed to greater pressures from local authorities. Especially in regions with more limited government resources, funding may be insufficient to deliver even minimal services, and local executives/legislatures may exert more pressure on courts to raise money via fines and fees—a possibly unrealistic requirement in poor districts and one that exposes the courts to greater corruption risks.[34]

Coordination across Borders

Global flows of people, goods, money, and ideas mean that crime is no longer restricted within national borders. Examples of transnational crimes include terrorism, cybercrime, art crime, trafficking in drugs or antiquities, human trafficking, organ trafficking, nuclear material trafficking, illegal logging and other environmental crime, child pornography, kidnapping, extortion, pharmaceutical fraud, migrant smuggling, sea piracy, identity theft, and money laundering.[35] Even where the majority of crimes are domestically contained, governments may have limited capacities to address crimes occurring across their borders, making them unable to tackle some criminal behaviors that harm their territory and citizens. In these cases, cooperation, coordination, and information sharing among countries become essential. Where the analysis of the typology of crime in the country indicates important cross-border criminal activity, the PER should include existing international cooperation mechanisms and their funding to understand how these may be affecting the criminal justice system's ability to address cross-border crimes.

In reviewing these different aspects of coordination, a PER should assess the key elements that may in turn affect criminal justice performance. Once it has been established that a coordinating mechanism exits, some of the key guiding questions for the review are these:

- How long has the coordination mechanism existed?
- Which institutions participate in this mechanism? Are any key agencies not represented?
- Is this an informal or formal arrangement?
- What are the areas (e.g., budget allocations, human resources, policy coordination, data gathering, information exchanges) that fall under the coordination mechanism's responsibility?
- Are its decisions binding for the participating institutions?
- How often does it hold its meetings? How are decisions made?
- Does it have the material and human resources to fulfill its tasks?
- Do performance measures for assessing the impact of coordination exist? Are data available to measure performance, and is coordination informed by data?

A checklist for the ministry of justice includes the following:

- Which criminal justice institutions is the ministry of justice responsible for?

- Does the ministry of justice have any responsibility for the following: resource allocation; the number and salaries of judges, prosecutors, corrections officials, or support staff; appointment or promotion of court presidents, court administrators, chief prosecutors, or corrections officials; legal aid and defense service provision; drafting of the strategies, policies, or guidelines for prosecutors' offices, courts, or corrections; investment in IT, new buildings, and infrastructure; operation and maintenance; and training of judges, prosecutors, or other staff?
- Does it negotiate the budget with the ministry of finance (or legislature), or does the judiciary/prosecutions office negotiate it directly?
- Does it (or other executive agency) have power over the establishment, collection, regulation, and use of court and other criminal justice agency fees?

Measuring Criminal Justice System Performance

The ultimate objective of a PER is to match expenditures against stated policy objectives; hence the importance of measuring criminal justice system outcomes. Measurement is no easy task, however, given that the common public policy yardstick will be crime rates. The drivers of crime are multiple, complex, and ingrained in demographic, sociological, behavioral, economic, and geographical elements. The implications of this reality are twofold: (i) the typology of crime needs to be understood for any policy choices to have the desired impact, and (ii) the achievement of outcomes will not depend solely on the good performance of the criminal justice system. Other interventions, such as crime prevention programs, education, employment, and welfare mechanisms, will play into the causal chain, making it impossible to single out one cause for the increase or decrease in crime and citizen security, or to clearly identify the impact of a particular criminal justice system response.

Efforts to measure criminal justice system performance need to make a clear distinction between performances at two levels: (i) the *end-goals level*, and (ii) the *criminal justice system or agency level*.

Performance at the End-Goal Level

The reduction of crime and the increase of citizen security are the two main end goals of the criminal justice system. One core indicator to track the achievement of those goals will be a decrease in crime as recorded by police (e.g., a decrease in homicides per 100,000 inhabitants), possibly a decrease in the severity of crime (e.g., a shift from violent to nonviolent crime). One issue with this indicator is that it cannot account for unreported crimes, which can be significant in number depending on the type of crime and country context. Whether victims report a crime is greatly influenced by public trust in the police, public perception of investigative success, public perception of the criminal justice system's overall effectiveness, and certain cultural norms. In addition, in some cases authorities may not be willing to release numbers or, worse, they may manipulate them for political reasons.

End-goal analysis needs a sensitive reading of data. One result of successful reforms can be that public trust increases, resulting in higher rates of reported crimes; thus this positive result translates into higher official crime rates. To better understand the influence of public trust on crime rates, it is helpful to use reported crime data in combination with victimization and safety perception surveys and self-report data.[36] These surveys distinguish between reported and unreported offenses, and they also allow for the inclusion of explanatory variables in the survey. While such surveys have their challenges,[37] they can also measure citizens' level of trust in the criminal justice system, both by inquiring about trust directly and by comparing the numbers of victims of crime with the numbers of officially reported crimes. Public perception surveys are also the primary tool for measuring citizens' perception of safety.

Performance at the Criminal Justice System Level

Assessing performance at the criminal justice system level involves two areas: (i) the performance of individual institutions of the criminal justice system in carrying out their functions, and (ii) the effectiveness of their interinstitutional cooperation in delivering services. Agency performance reviews should assess the performance of core functions (for police: patrol, investigation, etc.; for prosecution: investigation, prosecution, victim services, etc.; for courts: pretrial hearings, trials, posttrial actions, etc.; for corrections: pretrial detention, offender screening and classification, prison management, treatment management, probation and parole, etc.). For understanding how the criminal justice system performs overall, information and measures for the combined core functions are needed. For example, the entire investigative process may be the responsibility of multiple agencies, and the combined processes should be reviewed and the combined outcome measured.

Looking at performance of core criminal justice system functions and services across all relevant agencies is rarely attempted. (To our knowledge, first steps have been taken via a very few criminal justice case flow studies in developing countries and evolving states, including Mongolia and most recently Serbia.[38]) Still, a review of criminal justice system functions across agencies would provide for a way to better understand systemic challenges and resource impacts. Since functions vary depending on country context, this approach would involve a range of different agencies and processes. Beyond the main police functions that are covered in a separate chapter, at a minimum the following three main functions across criminal justice system agencies would need to be assessed: (i) investigation and prosecution, (ii) adjudication, and (iii) incapacitation and rehabilitation.

Investigation and Prosecution

Investigation is usually the responsibility of the police or other law enforcement agency; but in many jurisdictions it may also involve the prosecution service and the judiciary (for example, investigative judges in civil law). These processes and how they are applied within each agency are governed by a set of legal rules and norms relating to the rights of suspects and the powers of the criminal justice system's institutions, and they greatly influence how well each agency can perform. These legal norms vary across jurisdictions, change over time (especially during transitions from authoritarian rule), and may be ignored or violated. They may also enjoy more or less legitimacy both among ordinary citizens and among the political elite.[39] International performance guidelines and national standards (where they exist) for both functions and agencies focus on organizational performance measures (such as timeliness, processing efficiency, cost-effectiveness, and reasonable transparency and accountability), as well as quality measures (such as quality of the investigation/prosecution in terms of rate of successful filings). They also comprise specific measures related to protection of human rights, "user" satisfaction (users being victims, witnesses, offenders, defense attorneys, and other counterparts), and public perceptions.[40] Box 5.3 lists some examples of performance measures in investigation and prosecution functions.

Adjudication

Adjudication is the process, regulated by a set of rules and norms, by which the state exercises its power to determine if a suspected offender is innocent or guilty. Cases are typically brought to the criminal court by a prosecutor (some systems still allow police prosecutions, and sometimes private parties can prosecute cases), who presents the case to the court based on a previous investigation and conclusion that the defendant should be convicted for a criminal activity. The judicial proceeding is normally structured to guarantee the rights of the defendant, in particular the right to a proper defense, and it may require that the state provide a defense attorney.

Box 5.3   Sample Performance Measures in Investigation and Prosecution Functions

- Percentage of reported crimes that are successfully prosecuted and sentenced
- Number of pretrial detainees waiting for completion of investigation and prosecution
- Average time of pretrial detention due to delays in investigation and prosecution
- Percentage of citizens feeling that most crimes are successfully investigated and prosecuted
- Percentage of victims/witnesses satisfied with the way the investigation and prosecution were conducted
- Number of crimes dropped due to lack of coordination or understanding among investigation and prosecution agencies.

How this process is structured, who has what roles and responsibilities, how interim decisions are handled, and how many hearings are held all greatly depend on country context and case type—and all naturally have significant resource implications. Performance measures for the adjudication process—and the relevant agencies/institutions involved (i.e., not just the judiciary, but the prosecution and defense, possibly also police and corrections) generally focus on organizational performance measures and certain quality measures (i.e., overall quality of decisions, procedural fairness), in combination with specific measures related to judicial independence and public perceptions.[41]

Adjudication is one of several functional criminal justice system areas where shared goals and cooperation among all institutions involved are essential for system outcomes (as well as for agency performance and end-goal outcomes). At the same time, this cooperation is not easy to achieve, since the players involved may not have the same process outcomes in mind. Defense attorneys may consider a prolonged process beneficial to their client, given that witnesses' memories can fade; their client might need some form of intervention or treatment, but the system does not offer such an option unless the client is found guilty, and of course the defense attorney cannot seek a guilty verdict. Or certain pressures—unrefined agency performance measures, such as successful prosecution and adjudication rates or arrest/conviction ratios, along with intra-agency or public pressures—may push police, prosecutors, and judges to aim for convictions and long sentences and to ignore exculpating evidence and alternative treatment or sentencing options. While the differing interests in individual cases are part of the reason for the balanced structure that the justice system provides, they are also among the challenges for setting goals and realistic performance metrics.

The criminal justice system is different from other sectors, where there may be more general agreement about what a "good" service comprises, such as access to potable water or adequate education and health services. Agreeing upon performance measures is significantly more challenging in the criminal justice system, not only because multiple agencies need to agree but because the private sector as well as affected citizens play a major role in achieving these outcomes. Box 5.4 lists some examples of performance measures for adjudication functions.

Incapacitation and Rehabilitation

Incapacitation can be understood as the degree to which crime is reduced and security is improved by the mere fact that offenders are "off the street." Considering that incarceration or other forms of detainment (such as in secure treatment facilities, strict and controlled house arrest, even strictly supervised probation) present a severe limitation of personal freedom, it can only follow a court decision (unless, for example, an offender voluntarily enters treatment early in the process).

Box 5.4   Sample Performance Measures for Adjudication Functions

- Clearance rate of criminal cases
- Average time to disposition (disaggregating by type of disposition)
- Criminal case turnover ratios
- Average time of pretrial detention due to delays in adjudication
- Percentage of citizens/users believing that crimes are adjudicated effectively and promptly
- Percentage of citizens/users believing that crimes are adjudicated with fairness
- Percentage of defendants saying they have not received adequate defense because of costs, unavailability of legal assistance, distrust, distance, or other reasons.

A great variety of programs and initiatives fall under the general rubric of rehabilitation, including schooling and vocational skills–building programs, drug and alcohol rehabilitation programs, behavior change programs and anger management interventions, etc. Where these programs are offered in secure or semisecure corrections facilities, the corrections agency infrastructure and the skill set of administrators need to be aligned with the needs of the rehabilitation programs. Where such programs are a condition of probation or deferred sentencing, resources (human and/or technological) are needed to monitor probationers, enforce conditions of probation, and deliver rehabilitative services in the communities where probationers live.[42] Many of these services are provided by noncriminal justice system agencies and private providers. Considering this diversity of services and goals, performance measures can be complex; like other criminal justice system functions, these center around organizational performance but with a more pronounced focus on quality measures and outcomes, such as timely access to and provision of services, quality of assessments and services, cost-effectiveness, and different measures of intervention success and recidivism rates (i.e., length of time an offender remains drug free, reduction in relapse rates, no crimes committed for a year or two—possibly excluding simple parole violations).[43] Box 5.5 lists some examples of performance measures for incapacitation and rehabilitation.

Box 5.5   Sample Performance Measures for Incapacitation and Rehabilitation

- Recidivism rates
- Employment rates of past offenders
- Percentage of offenders who have completed sentence and are awaiting release
- Reduction in the number of corrections population
- Increase in the number of alternative measures to incarceration
- Reduction in the number of crimes committed in or from corrections
- Number of drug-addicted inmates successfully rehabilitated
- Percentage of citizens believing that corrections are effective in reducing criminal behavior and rehabilitating offenders.

The performance of the sector-related functions depends on well-run processes and cooperation. Even at the agency level, institutions may not have the power to improve low performance in some of these indicators. For example, high numbers of individuals in and overly long periods of pretrial detention may be caused by any of the following: (i) delay in adjudicating cases by criminal courts, (ii) delay in the prosecution by the prosecutor's office, (iii) insufficient defense attorney capacities or purposeful delay tactics by the defense, (iv) inability of the courts to ensure that needed witnesses are available at the time of hearings, or (v) insufficient coordination between the criminal courts and corrections authorities to track pretrial duration and ensure the accused is brought to hearings in time.

Poor performance can also be caused by weaknesses in "upstream" functions of the public sector (e.g., treasury) by transfer financing mechanisms that allow funds to dissipate before they reach criminal justice system institutions.[44] The indicators in box 5.5 (data permitting) can point to key measures in criminal justice performance. A more in-depth analysis that combines quantitative data collection with some qualitative methods (focus groups, in-depth interviews, etc.) might be needed to shed light on the potential reasons for weak performance, time and resources permitting.

Undertaking a PER and Potential Outcomes

This section outlines the practical steps included in undertaking a PER and then considers some of the potential outcomes and what a PER can achieve. A number of international actors, including the World Bank and the UN, have undertaken institutional reviews and PERs, and these offer valuable lessons for new initiatives that governments or international practitioners may undertake.[45] Considerations for new initiatives include the following:

Scope and Government Ownership

Key stakeholders should be engaged from the beginning, and the PER exercise should be synchronized with relevant government and stakeholder cycles, including for budget, policy reform, and/or external assistance consultation. Important questions about the scope and objectives of the PER should be posed up front in order to determine feasibility and timelines.

Objectives and Key Questions

It is essential to know clearly what the government expects from the PER, and it is equally important for stakeholders to understand what the PER can and cannot produce. The PER team needs to explain that results will depend on the availability of both data and resources (time, personnel, and costs). Many governments may be willing to receive a value-for-money analysis of the resources they spend in providing criminal justice system services. However, stakeholders should understand from the outset that without a performance-based budget and data disaggregated by service delivery unit, it becomes difficult to directly link budget allocations to outputs and outcomes.[46]

Fundamental questions to be posed by a standard PER include the following:

- Is the system appropriately funded to achieve key policy goals?
- How is the budget allocated across agencies? What are agencies spending on, and does this spending reflect and support performance goals?
- Does the budget support "right-sizing" of each agency?
- What would a reformed system look like? What budget would be needed, and can the country afford this now and in the future?
- Are resources being used in the most cost-efficient manner?

Analysis of Context

Within a relatively short time, a PER should (i) obtain a good grasp of crime and violence trends, including spatial variations; (ii) conduct a political economy analysis of justice service provision; and (iii) make macroeconomic projections of expected revenues and expenditures for the duration of the PER period.

It is useful to start the PER with a good understanding of the crime and citizen security context within which the system should deliver. "Demand" for criminal justice services cannot be characterized the same way as for civil and administrative justice, where citizens "choose" whether or not to bring a case before a court. Where criminal cases are concerned, citizens may or may not choose to report a crime or cooperate in the investigation and prosecution proceedings. With some exceptions, however, police and prosecutors are required to actively address crime, and those suspected of having committed a crime are mandatorily brought before the justice system. The term "demand" in this case would refer to the need for criminal justice system services in a certain country, and it will be determined by the levels and features of crime impacting different locations and parts of society, by the public's need and demand for protection, and by criminal justice system response in different locations. Understanding demand in this sense requires a review of crime rates, trends, and typology (e.g., gang or drug related, domestic violence, etc.) as well as drivers of crime, socioeconomic characteristics of offenders and victims, etc.

Crime levels vary by location so "demand" will vary geographically. Further, demand is affected when a society prefers not to give petty crimes the full weight of the criminal justice system, or when victims of certain crimes do not trust the system enough to come forward. In the latter case, actual crime rates may be high but demand for a criminal justice response low. It is important to understand the crime "map" across a country—where demand exists, where demand is effectively met otherwise, and why demand may be lacking—to fully understand criminal justice system service needs, resource requirements, and gaps.

Political economy considerations are important, particularly with regard to the potential impact of policy reform recommendations and guidance on issues like building a consensus for reform, sequencing reforms, and grand-fathering existing arrangements into new procedures.[47]

Data Availability

Closely linked to the analysis of context is a thorough assessment of the quantity and quality of the data that a PER team will be able to gather. These depend on (i) what data are readily available or can be created, and (ii) the willingness of the owner to release the data. In some countries, concerns about protecting the independence of the judiciary mean that the executive does not have access to relevant data (on performance, actual expenditures, allocations at the court level, etc.). The PER team should therefore make sure that it is granted access by the institutions with author-ity to release that data (such as the JC or the supreme court).

Typically, data are collected and analyzed to help prioritize spending and align public resources with stated national policy objectives, strategies, and programs.[48] An initial data collection chart (annex 5F) provides sample data-gathering scenarios that will influence the type of analysis that can be carried out.

Stakeholder Consultation

The PER team should attempt to consult with the broadest possible range of stakeholders in order to obtain information and data on budgets, revenue, expenditure, policy, and performance. The consultation should not be limited to the standard ministry teams if certain types of data are required—for example, budget allocations to subnational-level government or estimates of external development assistance.[49] For the institutional review component, the team should conduct direct interviews and observations in key agencies, including a small sample outside of the capital city if time and resources allow.

Team Composition

A good PER team generally needs a mix of people who together have (i) in-depth experience in the sector and the country, (ii) deep understand-ing of the public expenditure management system, (iii) solid economic analysis skills, and (iv) requisite international sectoral expertise. Since the quality of the public expenditure work hinges on sectoral inputs, it is important to ensure that staff with the required sector expertise are mobi-lized and committed.[50]

Costs

To date, no study has truly covered all criminal justice system compo-nents. For the few PER reports that have been developed in the justice sector, the estimated cost reportedly ranged from approximately $50,000 to over $400,000.[51] The average cost of a report that covers the standard topics—analysis of level and composition of the budget, institutional

arrangements, detailed assessments of organizational and budgetary information, and performance indicators—is likely to be around $250,000,
including all sources of financing. More resources are required in countries
where language is a constraint and translators are needed for consultations
and discussion sessions, or where the data are poor and a reasonable
amount of information must be collected for analysis.[52]

Outline of a PER

The outline of a PER will vary according to the context, the specific focus,
and the key questions raised by the government and the stakeholders in the
criminal justice system. An outline of a standard PER may be along the following lines:

1. Objectives and scope; key areas of focus
2. Methodology; team and data access
3. Context; crime trends, political economy analysis, and macroeconomic projections
4. Systemwide institutional and governance arrangements, service
   delivery structures, reforms, and existence of national and sectorwide policies
5. Institutional review of the core delivery agencies (including their
   management, organization, operations, capacities, workloads, and
   performance)
6. Human resource allocation reviews by agencies and functions; workload and staff allocation and management by agency performance
   outcomes
7. Budget and finance processes and management; expenditure and
   revenue streams
8. Policy options.

Policy Options and Potential Outcomes

As of 2016, the World Bank has undertaken nine PERs that have entirely or
partly focused on criminal justice or the wider justice sector.[53] That these
have had different outcomes reinforces the point that context and government direction determine PER results.

The principle lesson suggested by these reviews is that, given the complexity of the sector and its sensitive nature in the public policy realm, PERs
should not be prescriptive and ideally should not be a one-off event or
report. Rather, PERs should be used to inject data and analysis into the
public policy dialogue in order to facilitate opportunities for reform. This
was done in El Salvador, for example, where the process started with a PER
identifying the key institutions and stakeholders within the criminal justice
chain along with their priorities and respective expenditures. Subsequently,
however, the data and analysis that were part of the PER enabled the
government to launch a more in-depth strategy process (see figure 5.2)
which examined ways to strengthen the overall criminal justice system and

Figure 5.2   El Salvador PER-Based Policy Dialogue Working Groups

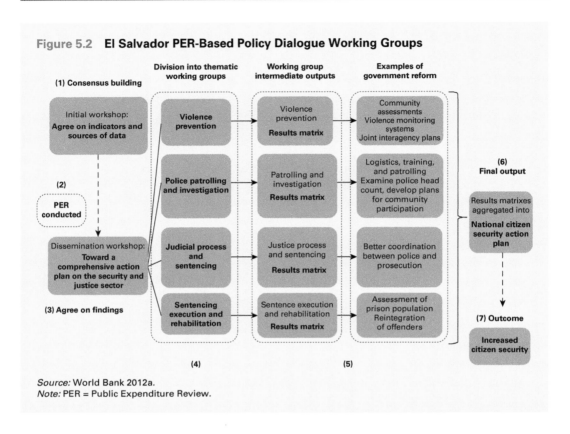

Source: World Bank 2012a.
Note: PER = Public Expenditure Review.

in turn ways to use public resources more efficiently and effectively. Like many countries, El Salvador remains some way off from having an effective and efficient criminal justice system. Yet the PER instrument provided a neutral basis for presenting data and information to the key stakeholders and thus offered an opportunity for incremental reform.

Annex 5A: Prosecution Agency Assessment

Overall Agency Assessment

In most countries, the main role of prosecutors in the criminal justice system is to provide legal guidance to the investigation, review its results, translate them into a charge to be filed in court, and prosecute the criminal case on behalf of the state. In this last role, they exercise the sovereign power of the state and represent the best interests of the community, which include honoring the rights of the accused.[54] Prosecutors are essential not only for keeping communities safe, but also for holding public institutions, private sector companies, and indeed government officials to account.[55]

In spite of this overall similarity, prosecutors in different countries have different roles and authorities, both in the investigation and prosecution stage and during the court hearings. They may also have responsibilities for representing the state in cases filed against the state, including serving as attorney in cases involving public companies; they may have responsibilities for providing victim and witness services; and they may have responsibility for supervising the execution of the sentence, which sometimes translates into supervision of prisons. Considering this broad scope of potential responsibilities, the first step in assessing the prosecution agency is to analyze the full range of prosecutorial responsibilities and identify what they actually mean in terms of prosecutor and support staff actions and resource requirements. For example: supervision of the investigation can mean being available to the investigative agency for legal advice or guidance; it can mean being physically present during investigative agency search and arrest operations to clear actions; it can mean that dedicated investigators working for the prosecutors' office conduct the investigations; or it can mean that prosecutors attend parole hearings or visit corrections facilities monthly to conduct different levels of supervision activities.[56]

Traditionally, common law countries have established a clear separation between the investigation stage (in charge of the police) and the prosecution stage (in charge of the prosecutor's office). By contrast, in many civil law countries, the prosecutor was conceived as the head of the investigation phase, directing and supervising police activities during the investigation process. These differences have increasingly become blurred,[57] and the criminal justice system PER team must begin by assessing actual responsibilities, since these impact resource allocation needs. The often significant range of responsibilities also means that international resource allocation comparisons are rarely useful. Within-country comparison, on the other hand, can detect performance variations.

Another important difference among systems that the PER must consider is the degree of flexibility that prosecutors (and investigative agencies) have in pursuing criminal cases. Civil law countries follow the "legality principle," meaning prosecutors have to pursue every criminal case brought to them, can only dismiss a case after insufficient evidence is developed, and have no room to negotiate charges. Most common law countries, on the other hand, follow the "opportunity principle," meaning that prosecutors have considerable discretion as to the type of case to pursue. It is generally the chief prosecutor—who may be an elected official—who sets the policy for when to pursue prosecution, when to drop a case, and when to seek other alternatives, such as deferred prosecution. The chief prosecutor also sets the policy on conditions for plea negotiations. This broad scope of policy discretion means greater control over the workload (including the flexibility to adjust to resource availability).[58] For example, prosecutors can decide to prioritize the prosecution of some cases on grounds of their severity, relevance for community safety, costs involved, and likelihood of success. Without this discretion, staff capacities may be overwhelmed by the number of cases, especially minor cases or those with a problematic evidentiary base; timely and careful processing of more serious cases will likely suffer under these circumstances, and costs will go up.[59]

Even in countries with the legality principle such as France, the function of the prosecutor has been expanded to include some discretion in order to reduce the delay and expense associated with an increasing criminal caseload.[60]

The existence of different discretionary tools has a significant impact on the prosecutor's ability to manage resources and also affects the court caseload, the number of offenders sent to correctional services, and eventually police charging decisions.

Prosecutors' Position in the Overall State Structure

State structure impacts responsibilities and funding streams. In some countries, the prosecutor's office is part of the executive branch under the ministry of justice. In others, it is considered an independent agency and a quasi-judicial branch entity with similar independent budget authorities. Internationally it is recognized that aside from their location within the overall government, prosecutorial agencies should be designed as independent institutions in order to insulate prosecutors from undue influence and thereby assure fair and impartial criminal trials.[61] In the United Sates, voters elect most prosecutors at the local level; thus prosecutor accountability is built on electoral accountability. Yet, in many countries prosecutors join a centralized bureaucracy and comply with internal guidelines and rules that are enforced by regular internal review.[62] Understanding these factors is important when assessing accountability mechanisms and incentives in prosecutors' agencies, which in turn affect performance and resourcing.

Main Organizational Aspects of the Prosecution Service

In some countries, such as the United States, prosecution services are decentralized and funded by state or local governments, while in others, the services are centralized at the national level and funded from the national budget. In the United States, the prosecutor's office may receive funds from the county or city general budget, the state's general budget, and (for special projects) the federal government; in addition, these offices may generate revenue in the form of fees or via forfeiture funds. There have even been occasions when private funding contributed to the budget in the form of funding for community-based activities or for special investigative units focusing on insurance fraud.

Some of the key guiding questions for the PER include the following:[63]

- How is the prosecution service organized? Does the office handle noncriminal cases? Can budget and expenditure data be allocated to criminal cases only?
- Is criminal prosecution a centralized or decentralized function?
- What is the distribution of competences among different levels of prosecutors (by case type, relevance of the case, etc.)?
- Does legislation authorize a specific number of prosecutors?
- What is the geographical distribution of prosecutor offices and of prosecutors and support staff?

- What is the human resources structure of the prosecution service?
  - How are staffing requirements estimated?
  - How are prosecutors selected and assigned? Do prosecutors rotate regularly?
  - What performance management system is used for prosecutors and staff?
  - How are tasks divided among prosecutorial staff (prosecutors, investigators, assistants, etc.)?
  - How are cases assigned among prosecutors?
- To what extent are chief prosecutors accountable for results, and, if they are accountable, to what extent do they have the managerial autonomy to achieve those results?
- Who is responsible for the IT systems, office space, their management and maintenance, and other capital expenses? What type of IT system supports prosecution functions, and who uses it?
- How is training provided, and what are the training needs?

The question of training is an especially important one. Countries emerging from crisis or undergoing significant political and societal changes tend to have the largest needs for training and education, but the needs vary significantly even in these conditions. Especially where general education and law school education are underdeveloped, these training needs will be significant and require large investments over time—investments that can rarely be assured without significant financial support from the international community. The scope of training to be provided not only must reflect the actual and future knowledge and skill levels desired for prosecutors and judges and their support staff; it also must build upon current capacity levels. A country like Afghanistan, where schooling is limited and many sitting judges have not had even much basic education, will have training needs quite different from those of a country like Croatia, where there have been changes in many of the fundamental laws, in the demands on the judiciary, and in society, but where every judge has had tertiary education. Understanding the needed scope and level of training requires solid assessments with long-term needs projections. Any assessment of the adequacy of budget allocation to the training function will need to be informed by this detailed understanding of training needs.

Data Collection and Assessment of Work Volume and Human Resources Allocation

Services provided by prosecution offices are personnel-intensive; services are basically carried out by people (the prosecutors, their aides, and support staff) who direct investigations, study evidence, prepare cases, and appear before courts. There is no heavy equipment or machinery involved in the performance of these tasks. Thus personnel costs account for the biggest share of the prosecution budget, and staff resource allocation significantly impacts performance. In assessing the adequacy and efficiency of resource allocation, the PER should focus on human

---

Box 5A.1   Activity-Based Costing in the Crown Prosecution Service

The Crown Prosecution Service (CPS), the main prosecuting authority for England and Wales, makes use of the activity-based costing (ABC) method, which bases costs on the activity of a person, group, or institution. This approach breaks an activity down into its constituent components and then calculates the work effort involved in each one. In this way, the CPS can attribute staff costs to specific activities and can measure the resources needed for particular elements of work.

The CPS applies the following formula to determine total cost of staff time spent on the CPS prosecution process: number of files handled multiplied by staff time and staff salary costs. As practiced by the CPS, ABC includes only staff time, not accommodation or other ancillary costs.

The CPS has used ABC for about 15 years. Currently, it is used for core prosecution process work (including legal and administrative staff). It is not used for staff who are not directly involved in the casework process, or for national headquarters staff, business support center staff, or staff in counterterrorism and similar units.

Source: U.K. Crown Prosecution Service 2014.

---

resources structures and policies and their impact on current and future expenditures. The PER should also assess any tools or approaches in place to estimate the staffing needs.[64] In addition, the team may want to analyze the personnel costs by different programs. An example of such an activity- or program-based costing, carried out for the Crown Prosecution Service in the United Kingdom, can be found in box 5A.1.

The study team should seek to collect data on human resource management in order to answer the following questions:[65]

- How many prosecutors, investigators, and other support staff (by type) are currently employed by the prosecution service, both agencywide and by location? What are their functions and ranks (by gender, minority representation)? How many positions are not filled (by location)? What is the average number of days prosecutors and staff work, and what are the working hours?
- Does the prosecution service hire, promote, discipline, and fire its own staff? If so, how are prosecution staff, including prosecutors, recruited? What selection process does the prosecution service use?
- How are prosecution service support staff evaluated, promoted, disciplined, demoted or terminated? Is there a written procedure for each potential step?
- Does the prosecution service have civil service status or other such protections? Are prosecutors or any of the staff unionized?
- Are the terms of service, compensation, etc., determined for prosecutors by law or regulation?
- What is the range of salary for prosecutors and staff? Are the salaries regularly paid?
- Is their remuneration consistent with their position? Is their salary reasonable when compared to the local cost and standards of living? Do they receive benefits, such as housing, other than salary as part of their compensation?

Understanding the Workload

As in all criminal justice system agencies, staffing and other resource needs are driven not simply by the caseload, but also by the workload—i.e., the effort required to efficiently and fairly process the different types of cases in a timely manner and provide other services mandated. This distinction is fundamental. A prosecutor or judge may be able to handle and decide 20 simple theft cases in a day, but covering a complex fraud case, one with possibly hundreds of victims from across the country or even abroad, is significantly more time-consuming and costly. Understanding the different resource needs of at least the major case types is at the core of understanding resource requirements. Unfortunately, few prosecutor agencies collect case data by case complexity or develop estimates of resource requirements for different case types. In the United States, workload studies aimed at developing formulas to support budget requests have been conducted for prosecutors' offices, courts, and defense services in several states, but such studies are scarce in developing countries.[66] The lack of such information is a major challenge for meaningful performance and expenditure reviews in many countries; often, case types must be at least generally categorized to reflect a meaningful complexity level before workloads and resource requirements can be assessed.

Workload data should be collected in order to answer the following questions:

- How many cases are handled (i.e., investigated, prosecuted, etc.) by case type and location? What is the median time from receiving the case to completion? What are the case results (i.e., dismissal, prosecution by court decision, etc.)?
- How many cases does a prosecutor generally handle, by location and case type? To what extent does the allocation of prosecutors and support staff reflect the criminal workload and other services? At all levels? In different regions/rural/impoverished areas?

Analyzing Prosecutors' Budgets

Once the prosecution services' functions, organizational features, workloads, and revenue sources are well understood and data availability has been established, it will be easier to understand the prosecution services' funding requirements and structures. At that point, various aspects of funding have to be reviewed.

The first aspect of funding concerns general expenditures, specifically the following:

- Annual total expenditure on prosecutor services in real (inflation-adjusted) terms over time, and as a proportion of total public expenditure and GDP per capita[67]
- Annual expenditure on prosecutors by programs or main areas of activity[68]

- Annual expenditure on prosecutors disaggregated between capital/development and recurrent spending streams (to show whether trends in sector spending apply equally to capital and recurrent budgets)
- Salaries (scale and compression) and benefits (current and future commitments)
- Expenditure disaggregated by the different functions of the prosecutors (the "functional classification" of expenditure)
- Executed budget (or "releases") as a proportion of the amount budgeted each year (e.g., budget execution, execution rate, burn rate, disbursement rate) disaggregated (i) between recurrent and capital spending, and (ii) by individual prosecution offices[69]
- The spatial distribution of prosecutors' expenditures across the country[70]
- Expenditures related to training or special programmatic efforts, such as victim and witness services and protection, community outreach, and others
- Projects and amounts funded by external donors, if any.[71]

The second aspect of funding to be reviewed concerns budget cycle information, specifically the following:

- The process for the formulation and approval of prosecutor offices budgets
  - Who or what body determines the distribution of prosecutorial resources regionally and nationally?
  - How does the budget formulation process fit into the overall state budget process?
  - Are there any off-budget expenditures or contingency funds?
  - Which prosecutor offices, if any, are required to prepare a budget? Who participates in this process (chief prosecutor, financial staff)?
- Policies applicable to the actual level of funding and allocations
  - Are there strategic priorities established for the prosecution service? Are these translated into more specific policies and targets?
  - Are resources being allocated in accordance with the priorities of the prosecution service?
  - What percentage of the budget is mandated by law/constitution and therefore cannot be changed by the legislature/executive?
  - What is the basis for calculating prosecutors' budgets?
- The management of allocated funds (including own revenues)
  - Concerning the tracking of expenditures, do the prosecutor offices have a bank account, or do they just submit a payment order to the treasury?
  - What are the procurement policies (competition, value for money, and controls) applicable to the prosecution?
  - What information is available regarding costs (e.g., cost of operating the prosecution services or activity-based costing)?

- To what extent do chief prosecutors have reliable budgets necessary to deliver the results required of them?
- Oversight and accountability
  - What is the reporting line and frequency of revenue and expenditure accounting and monitoring throughout the year?
  - Is there an effective internal audit system?
  - To what extent are good procurement practices observed?
  - To what extent is financial information reliable and timely?
  - What mechanisms exist to improve expenditure performance and reduce nonperformance (e.g., public disclosure on expenditure allocations, client satisfaction surveys, expenditure tracking surveys, effective external audit)?
  - Are prosecutor offices audited by an internal auditor, an external auditor, or both?

Assessment of the revenues collected by the prosecution service needs to recognize that some of these revenues may result from law enforcement and criminal justice activities, such as fines, forfeitures, and program fees. Such revenues may be designated for the prosecutors' general budget, for special prosecution programs, or for a targeted criminal justice fund; or they can go directly to the general government budget. Although they can be a useful complement for resourcing the prosecutors' budget, these revenues are not predictable, and increasing them may not be a realistic or ethical option.[72] It is essential to assess the sources of these revenues, the amounts involved, and their management (see the example in box 5A.2). Some of the guiding questions for the assessment team to answer are these:

- Who is responsible for regulating, collecting, managing, and spending fines, forfeitures, and program fees?
- Are these revenues used to fund prosecutors' budgets?

Box 5A.2 Canada's National Fine Recovery Program

The Public Prosecution Service of Canada (PPSC) is responsible for overseeing Canada's National Fine Recovery Program (NFRP), which seeks to recover court-ordered fines owed by individuals and companies convicted under federal statutes. Eight fine-recovery units, located in PPSC regional offices, carry out this mission.

A range of methods is used to recover the fines: letter, telephone, set-off of income tax refunds or certain tax credits (through an agreement entered into with the Canada Revenue Agency in 2008), payment negotiations, seizure of assets, registration of liens on property, and income garnishment. Between 2002, when the program was first established, and 2012, the program recovered more than Can$63 million in fines, including almost Can$7.3 million in 2011–2012.

Source: Public Prosecution Service of Canada 2012.

- If so, what percentage of the prosecutors' budget is financed through these sources?
- To what extent, if any, are revenues earmarked to fund specific budget items or programs?

Nonpersonnel Expenditures in the Prosecution Budget

Nonpersonnel expenditures make up a much smaller share of the total prosecutor's office budget than personnel expenditures, but they are also essential for the provision of prosecutor services. Major nonpersonnel expenditures include the following:

- *Services and supplies.* This category includes costs of office furniture, supplies, telecommunications, and contractual services such as cleaning, translation, and printing.
- *Investments.* These comprise the budget allocated to equipment and office or IT infrastructure.
- *Scientific and forensic work.* These expenditures are required by many criminal cases for such things as drug analysis, fingerprint identification, or ballistics analysis. This scientific work may be performed by a government crime laboratory, with the costs being paid by the budget of that laboratory, but in other cases these (substantial) costs may need to be covered by the prosecutor's budget.
- *Victims and witnesses.* The cost of providing the needed expert witness expertise, victim support, and witness protection programs can be significant for the prosecutors' offices. Sometimes these costs are funded under the ministry of justice budget, but the prosecution services may still have to cover part of the costs.
- *Security.* Protecting prosecutors (or their families) from threats is key to ensuring their integrity and independence. While few prosecution agencies in the developing world make budget allocations for security measures, every agency needs the capacity to at least assess the threat risks endured by individual prosecutors, other agency staff, and their families, and the review may provide an opportunity to assess needed security budget allocations.[73]

Assessing and Understanding Prosecutorial Performance

Agency performance in relation to resource allocation may be assessed on the institutional level, but rarely in relation to system and crime reduction outcomes. The core performance measures used by prosecution agencies internationally are shown in table 5A.1. Some prosecution agencies may also include "programmatic" indicators related to a particular public safety goal, such as obtaining restitution orders for victims or participation in community crime prevention activities, but this is rare in developing countries.[74]

Table 5A.1   Sample Indicators to Measure Performance of the Prosecutor's Office

Measurement category	Indicators
Efficiency and timeliness	• Clearance rate of criminal reports (claims filed with the criminal court/crime reports received), by case type
	• Average time to disposition of criminal reports, by case type
	• Percentage of cases resolved through alternatives to prosecution
	• Backlog of criminal reports, by case type
	• Cost per criminal report: average of distributed expenditures/ dispositions by crime report, disaggregated by case type
	• Average and geographical distribution of caseload per prosecutor (or office)
	• Average elapsed time criminal defendants are jailed awaiting trial
Quality	• Conviction rates of prosecuted crimes, by case type
	• Consistency in applying policy to cases
	• Percentage of victims and witnesses satisfied with prosecution services
	• Number of citizens stating they have faith in the prosecutors and believe that they will get fair treatment
Transparency and accountability	• Number of ethics complaints received and handled concerning poor treatment, corruption, and other problems encountered with prosecutors
	• Percentage of prosecutors who publish financial or asset disclosure reports
	• Number of citizens expressing their belief that the prosecutor's office is transparent and accountable
Independence	• Percentage of citizen/user and staff survey respondents indicating that in practice, decisions and powers accorded to prosecutors are not usurped by other government actors
	• Indication by agency data that criminal acts by other officials are investigated and prosecuted successfully
	• Existence in law of prosecutor career and secure tenure
	• Indication by staff surveys that the selection, evaluation, promotion, and retention of prosecutors occurs through transparent, merit-based procedures
	• Number of citizens expressing their belief that the prosecutor's office is independent

Annex 5B: Criminal Court Assessments

Overall Agency Assessment

Separating the Criminal Court Functions from the Larger Court System

In most countries, courts handle a range of case types, most typically comprising civil, criminal, and administrative cases. The budget for the judiciary (or even for individual courts) may not specify the resources that are allocated to criminal case handling; and even where specialized benches or courts are established, these often share buildings, services, and personnel (in many small first-instance courts the same judge may be responsible for both civil and criminal cases). Hence the criminal justice system PER team may need to calculate the proportions of resources that are spent specifically on criminal justice, both by asking officials and making their own estimations. This step will increase the costs and difficulties of the study.

The Interconnection between Court Organization, Functions, and Court Budgeting

The way a country's courts are organized in terms of management structures and operations will largely determine the courts' financing mechanisms. Some observers even conclude that court finance is just the fiscal counterpart of court administration: "When a court system is administratively and functionally integrated, the budget expresses the means by which the various activities of the system are to be carried out. When a system is not administratively integrated, its budget is a formal, but not functional, document: It simply aggregates expenditures for activities that are only nominally related to each other."[75] Courts in developed countries have budgets that allow for linking resources to functions, even some level of performance, but many courts in developing countries do not.

Analyzing the Court Organization

The next step is to understand what functions and services are administered by criminal courts at the different court levels. The formal criminal justice system courts and prosecution service in most countries are generally structured to include three (more rarely two or four) levels of appeal. In some countries, courts that serve as the first level of appeal for simple cases may also be the first level of court for complex cases. In addition, many countries have created small-claims courts below that first-instance level in order to increase efficiency in processing and reduce costs for both the court and the litigant; some of these small-claims courts handle cases that had before been handled in first-instance criminal courts, mainly simple traffic violations. Depending on the severity or complexity of the cases to be judged, courts may be composed of professional or lay judges or a combination thereof; hearings may need to be held by one judge or a bench of three or more judges. Trials may involve juries and expert witnesses, both of which have significant budget implications. In some countries, certain types of disputes may make up the core of a court's workload, while in other countries the same kinds of disputes may not be resolved by the courts at all.[76] In terms of courts' internal organizational arrangements, courts' auxiliary and support services may be placed outside or inside the court system's administrative domain. These arrangements too (in addition to other coordination and management issues that may affect performance) have budgetary consequences that need to be considered.

Some of the questions that the PER should focus on include the following:

- What are the functions and services administered by criminal courts at various levels?
- What is the geographical distribution (court map) of criminal courts, and what is their workload by level and location?
- What are the sizes of criminal courts in terms of staff and workloads (average, variation, largest, smallest, etc.), and are there efficiency correlations?[77]
- To what extent are court managers (court presidents/court administrators) accountable for results, and to what extent do they have the managerial autonomy to achieve those results?
- What is the human resources structure of the criminal courts?
  - How are staff requirements estimated?
  - How are tasks divided among court staff (judges, clerks, assistants, etc.)?
  - What is the support staff/judge ratio across different locations, court levels?
  - What is the prosecutor/staff ratio?
- Who owns the court buildings and is responsible for maintenance and capital investments?
- Who manages and funds the administrative support structure of criminal courts?
- Who is responsible for the IT systems and operation and management of criminal court buildings and equipment?
- Who if anyone in the criminal courts is responsible for regulating, collecting, and managing court fees (including registries) and fines?

Data Collection and Assessment of Work Volume and Human Resources Allocation

Understanding Workloads

The volume of cases that enter the courts is a driving factor for determining resource needs. However, aggregated caseload data that do not distinguish case type, court type, level, or location are not a good indicator for resource needs. Disaggregated data are important for three reasons:

1. Different case types require different levels of work from judges, court staff, and other participants in the adjudication process.
2. Different court types tend to have different procedural requirements that require different levels of effort.
3. Processing requirements can differ among locations for good reasons (e.g., additional travel time in rural areas, influence of local court support structures and user attitudes on work effort needed).

Thus to distinguish case complexity and differences in case mix, both of which may influence overall work effort required, court case data should be broken down at least by major case types (minor and major civil, criminal, administrative, etc.), and ideally by court type and level (general jurisdiction, specialized court, first instance, appeal) and by location. If significant other tasks are handled by judges and court staff, these should also be captured.

The core court case data to be collected therefore include the following:

- Number of cases filed by case type, court type, location
- Number of cases disposed by case type, court type, location (and by disposition type)
- Number of cases pending at the end of the year by case type, court type, location (median age of pending cases, if available).

Understanding Court Staffing

Judges decide cases, but much of the administrative work required to process a case is—or should be—conducted by support staff. Judicial resources should not be focused on activities that can be more efficiently provided by specialized support staff. In addition, some procedural decisions, even simple judicial decisions in simple cases, are better assigned to nonjudicial staff, and the workload of judges can be significantly reduced if they have support for legal research and decision drafting from junior lawyers or paralegal staff. It is important to understand the different staff positions' roles and functions to assess staff requirements and budget implications in light of different workloads.[78]

The core court staff data to be collected should include the following:

- Number of judges by location, court level and type (case type, if possible), and position
- Number of court administrative and other support staff by location, court level and type (case type, if possible), and position.

To understand the appropriate resource allocations, case and staffing data should be available for at least three years. Case and staff development trends provide insight into what may be needed in the future. Other types of projections will be needed to determine resource needs under policy changes, or in cases where no data or only unreliable data are available.[79]

Analyzing Court Budgets

The elements involved in reviewing court budgets do not generally differ from those outlined for prosecution services. What is important is to capture the different funding sources and to reflect that the judicial branch budget may include several independent budgets. Naturally this is the case where courts are decentralized, but even where this is not the case, the supreme or constitutional court may have a budget separate from all other courts, and so may a judicial council and a judicial training institute.

Traditionally, criminal courts have been funded through two major sources: (i) an allocation from the general public budget, and (ii) own revenues collected mainly through court fees. In addition, courts have increasingly expanded their funding sources and sought new ways to obtain the resources needed to provide their justice services. For example,

> **Box 5B.1   Criminal Fines, Illicit Property, and Gains Linked to Criminal Activity: Who Collects?**
>
> Paying criminal fines and seizing property and funds linked to criminal activity are an important part of criminal sentences. In imposing a criminal fine, the state holds offenders accountable but does not undermine their ability to prove that they can be productive members of society. This punishment is particularly appropriate for nonviolent first-time offenders, especially when financial gain was a motivating factor.
>
> Which agency is responsible for the collection of criminal fines, property, and illicit gains varies greatly from one country to the next, and sometimes even within a country depending on the level of government and the location. How the revenues from these efforts are used also differs. For example, at the federal level in the United States, seizure and forfeiture of property is in the hands of the U.S. Marshals, while collection of fines is the responsibility of the Executive Office of the U.S. Attorneys. At the state level, a range of mostly executive agencies are responsible, but sometimes the prosecution service is responsible for seizures and forfeitures, or there is a combined forfeiture task force. It may also be the court that is responsible for collection of criminal fines, or, as in one county in Pennsylvania, the office of court records, which is a combined court/county entity.
>
> The funds can go to the general budget, to one or several agencies, or to a special fund that may or may not support criminal justice system activities.

in several countries, the ministry of justice or similar agency provides seed funding for pilot programs, new approaches to case management, and projects to support better case management through improved operations and training.

Other countries have established specific funds, such as legal aid or compensation of crime victims, to directly finance key services provided by the courts. In some countries, private funds are established by concerned citizens, prominent lawyers, and leaders of the business community to support particular court services or provide resources to improve the courts' performance. Finally, other sources of funding of the criminal courts include sale of official bulletins and publications, sale of seized assets, donations, interest, bonds, sale of official forms and seals, and rental of court property. Box 5B.1 outlines the potentially different ways that courts may deal with fines and seized assets.

All these different financial resources need to be analyzed to determine their sustainability and predictability, and to clarify whether funds from these sources are earmarked for one specific service or provide general budget support to the court.

Allocation of Other Court Funding and Revenues

As mentioned, courts may collect their own revenues through court fees and fines. For many countries in Europe, revenues from court fees represent around 30 percent of the total budget allocated to courts.[80] Especially in countries where courts operate registries, fees related to registries' activities can be an important source of funding and can offer an attractive solution to financial shortfalls. Most of such fees come from civil cases, however, and it needs to be understood how they are allocated and if they actually support criminal court activities. Such revenues, fees, and fines can be used by the courts, or they can go directly to the general government (ministry of justice or finance) budget. When used to fund courts' budgets, they might be earmarked for specific line items or programs. According to some observers, if own revenues are used as a direct source of courts' budget support, they may motivate the courts to raise fees and fines at the expense of access to justice and may make the courts less accountable about their spending.[81] In the United Kingdom, for example, the government established "full-cost pricing" in the civil courts. This obliged courts to set fees such that court services would be self-funded. Various judges protested, arguing that this approach impeded access to justice.[82] Although such concern is less relevant in the domain of criminal justice, where an exemption to court fees usually applies, access to justice considerations need to be added when evaluating court fee policies.

Some of the guiding questions that the PER team should answer to understand the criminal justice system's own resource structures are these:

- Do courts operate registries?
- Who is responsible for regulating, collecting, managing, and spending court fees (including registries) and fines?
- Are these revenues used to fund criminal courts' budgets? If so, what percentage of the budget do they finance?
- To what extent are revenues earmarked to fund specific budget items or programs?

Criminal Courts' Funding Requirements

Once the court organization, operations, workload, staffing, and funding sources have been properly mapped, it will be easier to understand the funding requirements of criminal courts. At this point, the review will focus on (i) general expenditures information, (ii) budget cycle information, (iii) personnel expenditures, and (iv) nonpersonnel expenditures.

General Expenditures Information

General expenditures information includes the following:

- Annual total expenditure on criminal courts in real (inflation-adjusted) terms over time, and as a proportion of total public expenditure and GDP per capita
- Annual expenditure on criminal courts by programs or main areas of activity
- "Economic classification" of expenditure—i.e., annual expenditure on criminal courts disaggregated between capital/development and recurrent spending streams (to show whether trends in sector spending apply equally to capital and recurrent budgets)
- Salaries (given that services provided by criminal courts tend to be personnel-intensive and to depend heavily on the number and quality of staff and their distribution across the relevant jurisdiction)

- "Functional classification" of expenditure—i.e., expenditure disaggregated between the different functions of the criminal courts
- Executed budget (or "releases") as a proportion of the amount budgeted each year (e.g., budget execution, execution rate, burn rate, disbursement rate) disaggregated (i) between recurrent and capital spending, and (ii) by individual criminal courts
- The spatial distribution of criminal courts' expenditures across the country
- Projects and amounts funded by external donors.

Budget Cycle Information

Budget cycle information includes the following:

- The process for the formulation and approval of criminal courts' budgets
  - How does the budget formulation process fit into the overall state budget process?
  - Are there any off-budget expenditures or contingency funds?
  - Which criminal courts are required to prepare a separate budget? Who participates in this process?
- Policies applicable to the actual level of funding and allocations
  - Are there strategic priorities established for the criminal justice system (and criminal courts)? Are these translated into more specific policies and targets?
  - To what extent are resources being allocated in accordance with the priorities of the criminal justice system?
  - What percentage of the budget is mandated by law/constitution and therefore cannot be changed by the legislature/executive?
  - What is the basis for calculating the criminal courts' budgets?
  - Could alternative transfer formulas be established to promote greater efficiency and effectiveness in resource use?
  - Are line-item restrictions used by the legislature/executive to constrain courts' budgetary discretion?
- The management of allocated funds (including own revenues)
  - Concerning the tracking of expenditures, do the criminal courts have a bank account or do they just submit a payment order to the treasury? Is there data on actual expenditures, or do the courts operate as a black box?[83]
  - What are the procurement policies (competition, value for money, and controls) applicable to the criminal courts?
  - What information is available regarding costs (e.g., cost of operating the criminal courts or average cost of each case disposed)?
  - To what extent do court managers (court presidents/court administrators) have reliable budgets necessary to deliver the results required of them?
  - What is the amount of the budget funded through court fees?
  - Are there pressures to collect certain amounts?

- Are these court fees collected by the criminal court, other courts or divisions of the court, or by the executive for redistribution among courts?
- Are there restrictions regarding how these own revenues can be used?
- Oversight and accountability
  - What is the reporting line and frequency of revenue and expenditure accounting and monitoring throughout the year?
  - Is there an effective internal audit system?
  - To what extent are good procurement practices observed?
  - To what extent is financial information reliable and timely?
  - What mechanisms exist to improve expenditure performance and reduce nonperformance (e.g., public disclosure on expenditure allocations, client satisfaction surveys, expenditure tracking surveys, effective external audit)?
  - Are courts audited by an internal auditor, an external auditor, or both?

Personnel Expenditures

Personnel expenditures are the biggest percentage of courts' budget, and are therefore a key element of any criminal justice system PER.

In many countries, salaries of judges and other court personnel account by far for the largest percentage of the budget. In Europe, for example, salaries for judges and court staff represent 66.1 percent of the budget allocated to courts.[84] This situation is perfectly understandable in a sector in which the major service or output is the delivery of decisions (judgments) made by qualified state representatives (judges) with the aim of resolving disputes and implementing the law. The major implication is that effective human resource management will be central to cost-effective operations and high-quality outcomes. How adequate staffing levels can best be assessed has been outlined above. Other relevant areas to review include the following:

Recruitment. While recruitment of court staff will be similar to recruitment of other government employees, policies for recruiting judges are quite specific and have important financial consequences. In general terms, two systems for recruiting judges are used: (i) judges are appointed from a pool of lawyers with sound professional and ethical records at the later stages of their careers, often serving for a set term of years; and (ii) relatively young law graduates become entry-level judges after passing state examinations and receiving judicial training. In this second system, judges normally are appointed for life, and they gradually move up in the judicial hierarchy, often as a result of their length of service. The systems have different implications for initial training and continuing education (and related cost), as well as different implications for the courts' pension system and flexibility when it comes to judicial positions. The rationale for lifetime appointments is to protect the independence of judges, which could be undermined if selection and retrenchment were used with political purposes. Under this type of system, it is difficult to reduce the number of judges as a way of reducing expenditures; and because of the long-term budget implications, it may be difficult to increase the number of judges if workloads rise. This limited flexibility can lead to inefficient operations when workloads change, unless alternative processing or staffing options have been established, such as early retirement offers, the temporary use of retired judges, or increased use of law clerks or other court staff with legal education to handle simple cases and provide judicial legal support.

Promotion. As with recruitment policies, rules for promoting judges are usually designed to prevent undue influence of the judiciary. Modern judiciaries implement a system of performance reviews and clear and transparent promotion rules based on merit. In countries where the judiciary is undergoing significant reforms, performance reviews of judges may still be understood as interfering with judicial independence, so that promotions follow traditional seniority structures, or even worse are made in an opaque manner based on personal alliances. Both these methods of promotion undermine efficiency and public trust and tend to disregard the courts' budget situation.

Training. Training of judges and court staff is an important function that is not always under the administrative, content, or budget control of the judiciary. As mentioned before, how judges are appointed (i.e. shortly after graduating from law school or later in their career) has an impact on the entry-level and continuing training requirements.

Different training models have different budget implications. Some models of training development will be more cost-effective than others, but the most effective training model may not be a feasible option initially. One important lesson learned from years of donor-supported judicial education across the globe is that while countries may wish to develop a large, state-of-the-art training facility for the judiciary, such an approach is rarely feasible and is very costly. A central institute, possibly even a dedicated facility, is important for ensuring that judicial training can be developed and delivered strategically and uniformly for all judges (and court staff) across the country, ideally in coordination with other criminal justice system institutions. But this facility need not provide all training. Effective models include a central training management unit that coordinates and organizes the different training services and coordinates monitoring and evaluation as well as co-training with other criminal justice system agencies using contract staff, experienced judges, other staff, and government as trainers, and outsourcing logistics, housing, material development, and other tasks if that is a cost-effective option.

Any criminal justice system PER will need to review structure, cost, and performance of the different training entities that each of the criminal justice system agencies has in place. Beyond what has been said above, there are many issues that need to be considered in relation to all criminal justice system training efforts. There have been few attempts to align training across different institutions, and for good reasons: each agency has very different training and education needs, and it is important to preserve some distance between them since each not only needs to coordinate with others but also may need to provide some control function over others. At the same time, there are training areas where cooperation, sharing of trainers and material, sharing of equipment, and even co-training are not only cost-effective but essential to ensuring that the criminal justice system chain and needed cooperation work well.

Remuneration and Benefits (Including Retirement). The PER team should conduct a detailed analysis of different salary levels, evolution, scales, and components for judges, including comparisons to the average wage and the wage of similar professionals (other public servants, lawyers, notaries, prosecutors) as well as for support staff. Like recruitment and promotion policies, remuneration policies try to ring-fence judges' independence, but they may also make for an inflexible system that has trouble adapting to changes in the availability of resources. The PER should also identify the benefits provided. Not only does the combined salary and benefits package influence both recruitment and retention figures, but in some countries benefits packages can be significant (adding up to more than the base salary). Beyond the traditional medical, vacation, and sick leave benefits, they may include housing, transportation, security, schooling for children, tuition reimbursement, entertainment, and a range of other benefits. These benefits may be more extensive than in other public sector agencies because the judicial agencies aim to attract the best candidates.

Nonpersonnel Expenditures

Although a substantially smaller percentage of the total court budget in most countries, the following nonpersonnel expenditures should be assessed:

- *Services and supplies.* This category includes costs of office furniture, supplies, telecommunications, and contractual services such as cleaning, interpretation and translation,[85] court hearing transcriptions, and printing services. Included here or as a separate budget line may be funding for special service programs, such as witness/victim services, expert witnesses, child care, pro se assistance, and public education.
- *Investments.* These comprise the budget allocated to equipment, office, communication, and IT infrastructure. Buildings may be included if they are not rented, as well as some transportation vehicles.[86]
- *Operation and maintenance.* These costs apply to both physical and technological infrastructure and equipment and involve the materials for refurbishment, spare parts, or software updates, as well as associated labor costs.
- *Legal aid.* This can be a significant cost element in countries where it is provided directly by the courts (see also annex 5D).

- *Security.* This may include costs for salaries and equipment for security personnel on the ministry of justice's payroll, or payments to external providers such as the ministry of interior or private companies.
- *Other court expenses.* These may be covered under "services and supplies" or as a separate budget line.

Assessing and Understanding Court Performance

Due process rules and requirements and the performance of other criminal justice system actors greatly influence the ability of the criminal courts to manage criminal cases and provide other related justice services. Since criminal cases tend to be just one part of the courts' overall caseload, the performance measures that apply to the overall court operations tend to be used for the criminal caseload as well—with adjustments as needed to reflect the special situation of criminal caseloads and occasionally with added quality measures related to the protection of human rights or even treatment outcomes (such as compliance with treatment orders or recidivism rates, even though these are only partially a result of the courts' interventions). Several sets of internationally accepted measures for court performance have been developed: trial court standards specific for criminal courts (by the United States), a set of CourTools that applies to all case types (by the National Center for State Courts), and measures to assess European courts (by the European Commission for the Efficiency of Justice). In addition, the International Framework for Court Excellence links court management to performance measurement.[87]

Measures generally relate to core performance areas that reflect the purpose of the courts, specifically access to justice; expedition and timeliness; equality, fairness, and integrity; independence and accountability; and public trust and confidence. The sample measures indicated in table 5B.1 provide an overview of different measures applied by courts in different countries.

Table 5B.1 Sample Indicators to Measure Performance of Criminal Courts

Measurement category	Indicators
Expedition and timeliness	• Clearance rate of criminal cases (cases disposed/new filings), by case type
	• Average time to dispose of or suspend criminal cases, by case type
	• Backlog of criminal cases
	• Average of distributed expenditures/dispositions, disaggregated by case type
	• Average and geographical distribution of caseload per judge (or criminal court)
	• Average elapsed time criminal defendants are jailed awaiting trial

(Table continues on next page)

Table 5B.1   Sample Indicators to Measure Performance of Criminal Courts *(continued)*

Measurement category	Indicators
Equality, fairness, and integrity	• Like outcome for like cases
	• Rate of overturns on appeal
	• Number of citizens stating they have faith in the courts and believe that they will get fair treatment
	• Number of positive responses to user satisfaction survey
Transparency, accountability, and independence	• Whether by law the judiciary has an "independent status" as regards noninterference by other branches of government, and whether in practice, decisions and powers accorded to the judiciary are not usurped by other government actors
	• Ability of judges to review government acts for conformity with the law, and laws (and actions) for conformity with the constitution; actual passing of judgment against the government
	• Whether judicial career and secure tenure exist in law, and whether in practice, the selection, evaluation, promotion, and retention of judges and administrative staff occurs through transparent, merit-based procedures
	• Number of citizens expressing their belief that the judiciary is independent
	• Publication of judgments
	• Availability to parties to a case of all information on its current status and past history
	• Number of ethics complaints received and handled concerning poor treatment, corruption, and other problems encountered with judges and courtroom staff
	• Number of court users who report satisfaction in terms of transparency
Access	• Population saying they have not taken a case to court or to alternative services because of costs, unavailability of legal assistance, distrust, distance, or other barriers
	• Number of legal aid providers per 100,000 population and geographic distribution of same
	• Number of judges per 100,000 inhabitants
	• Geographic distribution of both judges and criminal court units
Public trust and confidence	• Number of citizens reporting they trust and have confidence in the judiciary

Annex 5C: Corrections and Rehabilitative Services Assessment

Overall Agency Assessment

Corrections (and related rehabilitative services) are generally considered the last stage of the criminal justice system chain. At the same time, these agencies are often in charge of pretrial detention and may provide a range of services before an offender is found guilty. At their core, corrections are the prison service in its many variations. The performance of this part of the criminal justice system tends to be measured more in relation to end goals—to punish, incapacitate, deter, and rehabilitate the offender—than in relation to institutional measures.[88]

Responsibility for corrections may fall under different ministries, but in most countries the responsible agency is the ministry of justice or the ministry of interior. Placing responsibility with the ministry of justice is considered good practice by the United Nations Office on Drugs and Crime.[89] The ministry of justice is responsible for corrections in all 47 countries of the Council of Europe except Spain; it also tends to be responsible for corrections in most of the Americas, much of Africa, and some of Asia. In the Middle East, corrections are more commonly part of the ministry of interior, and among former Soviet countries either one can be responsible.[90] In many countries, there may be additional detention facilities run by the military, the ministry of health and social welfare, or education departments.[91]

The organization of the corrections system varies significantly across countries. Some countries, such as China, the Philippines, and the United States, have a number of corrections systems reflecting state structures, e.g., federal, state, county, and district corrections systems. Others have a nationally organized corrections system.[92] Both structures have advantages and disadvantages. While decentralized systems make it harder to articulate a clear mission statement and set common standards across the country, centralized systems limit opportunities to reflect local needs and often impede efforts by local managers to explore innovative initiatives (including alternatives to imprisonment and reform programs).[93]

The structure, management, focus, and budget of the corrections services, as well as which institutions are involved in the punishment or rehabilitative processes, further depend on the overall criminal justice system policies and are highly affected by the size of the offender population. In countries where the focus is on strict punishment, corrections have to manage a large population in secure facilities and may have few options for early interventions, treatment, and release. Research across the globe has shown that a purely punitive approach is not only very costly, it is also ineffective in deterring crime or rehabilitating offenders. For all corrections and rehabilitation services, it is also important to understand that resource requirements are determined by two quantitative factors, the number of admissions and length of stay, in addition to the quality (effectiveness and cost) of the services provided. Not surprisingly, the largest impact on the cost of corrections comes from changes in policies regarding sentencing and releases.[94]

Corrections services face a myriad of challenges, in particular in developing countries or fragile and conflict-affected states (FCS); overcrowding of often outdated facilities is one of the most predominant. Other common challenges include very poor facilities, few resources, poorly trained staff, and widespread corruption. There also tends to be little information about actual corrections populations, current issues, and trends; registries and data are often inadequate, have been destroyed during conflict, or never existed. Poor conditions alone generally result in human rights abuses: long-neglected and undersourced facilities frequently have to house many times the number of people they were built for decades before. Corrections overcrowding is often a result of (i) outdated sentencing policies that do not allow for alternatives to secure detention and prison or for early release and (ii) inefficient criminal proceedings and detention and prison management, which lead to overly long pretrial detention and to holding of prisoners beyond their court-set time of release. Construction of new facilities is one solution where existing facilities are dilapidated, inappropriate for holding offenders, and not designed for providing rehabilitative services. But over-crowding is not a problem for developing nations alone. In May 2011, the U.S. Supreme Court ordered the state of California to release 40,000 inmates, not because they had served their sentences, but because prison overcrowding had reached unacceptable levels.[95]

Building larger facilities and maintaining them is costly, and often not the solution to a larger policy problem. Instead, alternative measures (e.g., ratio-nalization in sentencing policy, wider use of alternatives to imprisonment) should be explored.[96] One growing trend in many middle-income and even low-income countries (though unlikely in FCS) is to outsource prison man-agement to the private sector as a cost-saving option. But a review of other options to reduce the number of individuals in secure facilities and the length of time they are incarcerated is generally more effective than out-sourcing.[97] Cooperating with other government services and private provid-ers of treatment, along with streamlining and automating operations and using modern IT solutions, represents a more promising option, and not just in the developed world. The use of video hearings is among the most prom-ising. Arraignments, cross-jurisdictional hearings, and other pretrial hear-ings can be held via video collaboration, saving costs for prisoner transport, reducing time in court, and freeing up police and court staff time. In India, where about 75 percent of the prison population is awaiting trial, video hearings are beginning to be used for pretrial proceedings. A major reason why such a large share of India's jails is occupied by individuals who have been accused but not tried is the lack of police officers and vehicles to trans-port them to court for hearings. Video collaboration is speeding up the pro-cess while saving money. The Bangalore Central Prison, which is using video for some processes, estimates that more than 900,000 rupees—about $20,000—is saved each month as a result, not counting the benefit to the individuals involved.[98]

While secure corrections services play a key role in an effective criminal justice system by holding offenders accountable and ensuring safety, the degree of causality between the use of imprisonment and reduction of crime is contested. On the one hand, studies in the United States estimated that the quadrupling of the prison population since the 1980s accounted for between 25 and 30 percent of the fall in crime, while other more recent research in New York City, for example, has shown that reductions in crime can be achieved together with reductions in the prison population.[99] Today, there is ample research that has found no clear link between crime and violence on the one hand and incarceration on the other.[100]

Research has further shown that incarceration has a detrimental effect on individuals, families, and even some communities, especially those living in poverty, mainly serving the purpose of retribution and often failing to deter crime. There is no question that those who break the law, especially those who harm others, have to be held accountable. Imprisonment, however, may not be the best response in every case, especially if it is not combined with rehabilitative service and reentry programs. The negative impact of secure imprisonment on offenders' lives and the likely substantial consequences for their own and their families' well-being (economic and otherwise) are well established. As the UNODC notes: "The impact can be especially severe in poor, developing countries where the state does not provide financial assistance to the indigent and where it is not unusual for one breadwinner to financially support an extended family network." In these cases, the family's financial loss is "exacerbated by the new expenses that must be met—such as the cost of a lawyer, food for the imprisoned person, transport to prison for visits and so on." Release from prison brings its own problems: "Former prisoners are generally subject to socio-economic exclusion and are thus vulnerable to an endless cycle of poverty, marginalization, criminality and imprisonment." The UNODC concludes: "Imprisonment contributes directly to the impoverishment of the prisoner, of his family (with a significant cross-generational effect) and of society by creating future victims and reducing future potential economic performance."[101]

Incarceration may also not be in the interest of the victims, their family, or their community—and in developing nations and among indigenous communities it may not be a response that reflects customary mechanisms for settling conflicts (see box 5C.1). Incarcerating the offender

---

Box 5C.1 Why Did the Judge Incarcerate the Rapist? A Story from the Arid Lands in Kenya

Among communities in the arid lands in Kenya, not all acts considered criminal under the law are seen as crimes. If a sexual offense is committed, for example, the families try to work out an informal solution rather than seeking redress through the formal legal system. In the event that a report is made to the police, however—even if the report is meant as a tool in the families' private negotiations—the case must be filed in court if it involves a crime under the law.

One Kenyan magistrate hearing a case of a rape imposed a sentence of life imprisonment. The decision shocked the local Tugen community, who had expected to negotiate compensation and arrange a marriage between the girl and her attacker. Given the community norms, incarceration perhaps served no one's interests, and many considered it was not the optimal response to what took place.

Source: Chopra 2009.

may meet the victim's and community's need for retribution and increase the feeling of safety, but it does not address the victim's need for compensation or desire for an honest apology and active engagement by the offender to make things right. Particularly in societies where customary rules call for specific types of compensation (such as restitution in the form of payment in cattle or even working for victims and their families), incarceration is not the desired outcome. Victim and community expectations must be considered in designing sentences that are both in line with international human rights standards and responsive to customary approaches. Some developed countries, such as the Netherlands, offer offenders a range of options to work off the debt to the victim and society, and these same options should be available in the developing world. Under special programs in Australia, Canada, and the United States, community circles or elders lead proceedings and agree on active restitution for crimes, including violent crimes; the government then supports these rulings as official responses.[102] Such options can be structured to protect human rights and address community and victim needs in a way that is not only cost-effective, but also effective in restoring the offender to a productive place in society and in limiting conflict resulting from unfulfilled revenge.

Institutional Analysis

In addition to mapping the system's organizational and management structures on all government levels, the PER should also be guided by these questions:[103]

- How are the different institutions comprising corrections structured? How are they staffed, resourced, and funded? What services exist in each, and what are their responsibilities?
- Is the system centralized or decentralized with regard to its governance or delivery of services? If decentralized, how much autonomy do regional or local systems have?
- Is there a policy and clear statement of principles to guide the management of the corrections system (i.e., statement of purpose, mission statement, or value statement), and does it apply to all corrections facilities and programs? Does it involve rehabilitation and preventive services, including those outside the criminal justice system?
- Does the corrections service have a strategy document or plan to systematically address the main challenges in corrections, such as overcrowding, health concerns, and lack of corrections treatment?
- Is there a national development plan for the corrections system? Who is responsible specifically for planning? What is the planning capacity? How are plans developed? What is included in the plans?
- What is the number of staff positions in corrections? What is the actual number? What percentage are women (or minorities, where appropriate)? How does the situation vary geographically?

- What services exist in corrections? How many staff positions are in each service? What is the actual number? How does the situation vary geographically?
- To what extent is there a standard and proper recruitment procedure for corrections staff?
- To what extent is remuneration consistent with employees' positions? Are salaries reasonable when compared to the local cost and standards of living? Do employees receive benefits other than salary as part of their compensation?
- Do corrections staff receive in-service training to improve their qualifications?
- Where are secure and other corrections services located, especially in relation to population and crime centers? How accessible are nonsecure and treatment options? Do they have the capacity to respond to the needs? How accessible are the facilities to family members?
- To what extent are the facilities designed to respect human rights standards? To accommodate modern offender management and treatment?
- How much of the corrections services—secure and nonsecure—is outsourced? How is the quality of service delivery monitored and measured?
- What data are available across all facility and program types to assess workloads, efficiency, and cost-effectiveness in management, quality of service delivery, and outcomes? If such data are available, how reliable are they? How are they used? Are any published?

In order to deliver the desired outcomes, all related corrections functions should be designed not just with institutional measures but also with the end goals in mind, and the review should aim to collect information accordingly. The core areas to review may include the following:

- Management of pretrial detention and diversion services
- Offender assessment, sentencing recommendations, and offender classification
- Management of nonsecure alternatives, halfway houses, and treatment options/facilities
- Management of the corrections population
- Management of offenders on probation, parole, and work release; management of family visitation programs
- Management of reentry programs.

For each of these areas, the following should be reviewed:

- Institutional arrangements, including admissions, records management, classification, tracking, services and treatment, status reviews, issues identification and responses, release, and aftercare. This category also includes staffing and staff management, key processes, policies, equipment, IT (especially for case management), and IT support in light of workloads across programs, key offender groups, and locations.[104]

- Organizational arrangement and management of complaints, overall data collections, and performance management, as well as general organizational management, including facilities, human resources, supplies, equipment, security, and transportation, by facility and program type across locations.[105]

Data Collection and Assessment of Work Volume and Human Resources Allocation

Considering that corrections systems in many countries do not simply focus on holding offenders but rather seek to facilitate their reentry into society, related programs and other services need to be accounted for. The scope of rehabilitative services provided will determine exactly what data are needed, but the core data to be collected are listed here:

- Number of facilities/programs by type and location
- Number of inmates/clients by offense type, sentence type, location, age group, and gender
- Number of inmates by 100,000 population (by offense type, sentence type, location, age group, and gender)
- Median time in facility/program.

As in other criminal justice agencies, human resource data also need to be collected by staff type and function. The core human resources data to be collected include:

- Number of staff by type, function, location, program (and gender)
- Staff/offender ratio by type, function, location, program (and gender).

Analyzing Corrections System Budgets and Funding Streams

Once overall structures, functions, and responsibilities are mapped and workload and human resource data are collected for all corrections entities involved, the various aspects of corrections funding can be assessed:[106]

General Expenditures Information

The review should seek the following information on general expenditures:

- Annual total expenditure on corrections in real (inflation-adjusted) terms over time, and as a proportion of total public expenditure and GDP per capita
- Annual expenditure on corrections by program or main area of activity
- Annual expenditure on corrections disaggregated between capital/development and recurrent spending streams
- Salaries (scale and compression) and benefits (current and future commitments)
- Executed budget (or "releases") as a proportion of the amount budgeted each year (e.g., budget execution, execution rate, burn rate,

disbursement rate) disaggregated (i) between recurrent and capital spending, and (ii) by individual corrections
- Expenditures by corrections across the country
- Projects and amounts funded by external donors, if any
- Industries in place and their annual profits, along with disposition of profits
- Whether prisons are allowed to reinvest these profits, and whether offenders receive payment
- Availability of correction land for agricultural purposes, and amount of land farmed (in hectares or acres); agricultural production figures and budget
- Contribution of land to the food service; disposition of agricultural profits.

Budget Cycle Information
The review should seek the following information on budget cycles:

- The process for the formulation and approval of corrections' budgets
  - Who or what body determines the distribution of corrections' resources nationally and regionally?
  - How does the budget formulation process fit into the overall state budget process?
  - Who prepares and submits the operating budget? Are individual corrections administrations involved in budget planning? To what extent?
  - Are there any off-budget expenditures or contingency funds?
- Policies applicable to the actual level of funding and allocations
  - Are there strategic priorities established for corrections? Are these translated into more specific policies and targets?
  - To what extent are resources being allocated in accordance with the priorities of the corrections service?
  - What is the basis for the calculation of corrections budgets?
- The management of allocated funds (including own revenues)
  - Who manages the budget? Who oversees its spending?
  - Did the corrections service receive the funds allocated in its budget? Are there normally delays, fiscal constraints, or other obstacles to gaining access to these funds? Where are the funds held? Who authorizes their disbursement?
  - What are the procurement policies (competition, value for money, and controls) applicable to the corrections services?
  - How is procurement organized? Who is responsible for procurement? Is it centralized or decentralized? How does the system work, especially for food and medication?
  - Is procurement formalized? Is it based on competitive bidding? Is the bidding process transparent? Is there integrity of process? Are there allegations of favoritism, profiteering, or corruption in the

procurement of goods and services? What plans, if any, exist to improve the procurement and distribution process?

- What information is available regarding costs (e.g., cost of operating the corrections or activity-based costing)?
- To what extent do corrections managers have reliable budgets necessary to deliver the results required of them?

- Oversight and accountability
  - What is the reporting line and frequency of revenue and expenditure accounting and monitoring throughout the year?
  - Is there an effective internal audit system?
  - To what extent are good procurement practices observed?
  - To what extent is financial information reliable and timely?
  - What mechanisms exist to improve expenditure performance and reduce nonperformance (e.g., public disclosure on expenditure allocations, client satisfaction surveys, expenditure tracking surveys, effective external audit)?
  - Are corrections audited by an internal auditor, an external auditor, or both?

Expenditures within the Corrections Budget

The main categories of corrections expenditures are the following:

- *Salaries.* The salaries of staff who perform the core functions (registering, managing, and overseeing inmates, maintaining order, etc.) are a significant part of corrections expenditures.
- *Services and supplies.* This category includes costs of food, clothes, uniforms, other supplies, telecommunications, and core services such as cleaning and transportation.
- *Capital expenditures.* This category comprises budget allocated to purchasing and rehabilitating the capital assets that support the corrections system, such as buildings, equipment, and land.[107]
- *Education and vocational services.* This category includes all the costs associated with providing education and vocational training to the correctional population.
- *Health care.* Expenditures related to health care services are one of the biggest allocations of corrections budgets in certain countries.
- *Security.* This category includes expenditures on technology and other devices to ensure security in corrections. It may also include the costs of contracting personnel (including military) to carry out security tasks. The criminal justice system PER team should be mindful not to count as security expenditures other expenses that may be accounted under salaries or capital expenditures.

Expenditures outside the Corrections Budget

In some countries, the costs of some services provided by corrections may not be reflected in the corrections budget. The criminal justice system PER team should be aware of these in order to fully understand the extent of the corrections operations, performance, and expenditures. Some of the main costs that may fall outside the corrections budget are these:[108]

- *Employee benefits and taxes.* Although the salaries for corrections employees should be included in the department's budget, funding for some personnel costs (such as health insurance or the employer share of social security taxes) may be provided by a central administrative fund.
- *Pension contributions and retiree health care contributions.* Certain administrations may make contributions to pension plans and retiree health care for all their employees through a central fund.
- *Capital costs.* In some countries, funding for capital projects to construct and renovate corrections is provided outside the corrections budget.
- *Legal judgments and claims.* The costs of corrections-related legal judgments and claims may be provided through a central account of the state, the ministry of justice, etc.
- *Statewide administrative costs.* In certain cases, central agencies provide administrative services related to corrections operations.[109]
- *Hospital care.* In some countries, a portion of the costs for inmate hospital care is funded outside the corrections department.[110]
- *Education and training.* Departments other than corrections sometimes pay for some costs of education and training for men and women in detention.
- *Various treatment options and other programs.* While some treatment and corrections program options may be outsourced but still part of the agency's budget, others may be included in health department, education department, or municipal agency budgets. Where NGOs, charities, or religious organizations provide such services free of charge, the study should at least establish a sense of their scope to identify their potential resource contribution.

A cautionary note should be sounded regarding the use of per-inmate costs, which are among the most widely used measures for analyzing corrections spending and comparing it with that of other countries or jurisdictions. As already explained, the corrections budget may not include all the expenditures related to the services being provided; what budgets include varies widely across countries. In some instances, this figure is also used as a measure of spending efficiency, but this can be misleading as well: low per-inmate costs may be due to factors that have collateral costs to society or other jurisdictions. For example, per-inmate cost will likely be lower in countries where prisons are overcrowded or where many prisoners are low-level offenders who do not require high security or safety expenditures. The comparison based on per-inmate costs should therefore be avoided, as low per-inmate costs may invite poorer outcomes in terms of safety and recidivism.[111]

A useful measure for assessing the financial impact of the increase or decrease in the corrections population is the marginal cost of incarceration. This indicator distinguishes between *fixed costs*, which do not change with an increase of workload (e.g., facility operations and administration); *step fixed costs*, which remain stable until there is a certain level of change in the workload (e.g., security personnel); and *variable costs*, which directly relate to workload (e.g., food and clothing).[112] The marginal cost of incarceration will therefore depend on the costs affected by a change in the size of the workload, and the budget should be readjusted in response to that change.

Understanding Funding Streams

Correctional services may receive funding from different ministries and other government agencies. Treatment programs and alternatives are often supported by other agencies, even private sources. Especially in developing countries, these often attract funding from the international development community, an aspect of funding that needs to be considered but is not always easy to track.

Outsourcing and Competitive Service Delivery

Increasingly, outsourcing is used to reduce cost in corrections and other criminal justice system functions. Starting in countries such as the United Kingdom and the United States, the private sector has assumed a greater role in the criminal justice system. To date, private security companies have provided security services and have constructed and managed prisons in Brazil, Chile, Israel, and South Africa. Treatment services also have been provided for years by specialized and experienced private sector providers. In the United Kingdom, this trend was recently complemented with innovative payment-by-results pilots in local criminal justice settings (see box 5C.2). Although such mechanisms are still a quite nascent trend and much debated, their impact on the performance and finances of the system should be reviewed.

Assessing and Understanding Corrections Performance

As mentioned before, the performance of the corrections service is measured by institutional effectiveness measures as well as by end-goal criminal justice system measures. Indicators that measure performance in corrections are listed in table 5C.1.

Box 5C.2   Innovative Funding Approaches in the U.K. Criminal Justice System

Competitive selection for service provision

The U.K. government has come out strongly in favor of competition in policing and criminal justice. In response, the new Competition Strategy for Offender Services sets out as a guiding principle that "competition will apply to all services not bound to the public sector by statute." Among others it is envisaged that the majority of services currently provided by public Probation Trusts will be opened up to competition, including corporate services such as central IT and facilities contracts. The Probation

(Box continues on next page)

Box 5C.2   Innovative Funding Approaches in the U.K. Criminal Justice System *(continued)*

Trusts will retain responsibility for managing higher-risk offenders and will provide advice to court and public interest decisions such as initial assessments of risk for all offenders.

The expansion of payment by results

Since 2010, the U.K. government has launched a variety of innovative payment-by-results pilots in local criminal justice settings, introducing a strong performance focus into criminal justice for the first time. Under these pilots, providers receive a proportion of their contract value if they succeed in rehabilitating offenders. There are currently payment-by-results pilots under way across a number of criminal justice areas, including prisons, probation, youth justice, offender welfare, and drug and alcohol treatment services.

Source: Haldenby, Majumdar, and Tanner 2012.

Table 5C.1   Indicators to Measure Performance of Corrections

Measurement category	Indicators
Rehabilitation	• Recidivism rates
	• Employment rates of past offenders
	• Percentage of offenders who have completed sentence and are awaiting release
Security, safety, and order	• Number of prison escapes
	• Number of violent incidents in the corrections facility
	• Number of attacks on corrections staff
	• Number of violent deaths per 1,000 inmates
	• Number of corrections staff per 100 inmates
Health and welfare	• Average waiting time to receive medical treatment
	• Number of inmates infected by HIV or tuberculosis during stay in corrections
	• Number of nonviolent deaths per 1,000 inmates
	• Number of average family visits per inmate per month or year
	• Percentage of inmates enrolled in training, sport, or other activities
	• Number of inmates per square meter
Transparency and accountability	• Number of published inspection reports by nongovernmental organizations or other independent bodies
	• Publicly available information on deaths in custody
	• Number of complaints received and handled concerning poor treatment, corruption, and other problems encountered with corrections officials
Operational effectiveness and efficiency	• Percentage of inmates classified according to risk levels
	• Percentage of inmates who could have received an alternative to incarceration
	• Per-inmate costs (fixed, step fixed, and variable)

Annex 5D: Other Criminal Justice Institutions and Services Assessment

In addition to police and the three core criminal justice system institutions already outlined (prosecutor's office, criminal courts, and corrections), various other agencies play a key role in the criminal justice system. Among the most important are pretrial services, victim and witness services, public defenders and legal aid services, and research and data centers; these are briefly described in this annex. Where these entities are located differs across countries: they may be part of the core criminal justice system agencies, including the ministry of justice, or they may be separate institutions. Collecting detailed data on each of these institutions may be beyond the scope of a PER, but some kind of sectorwide review is important in order to understand their relationship with the core institutions and the resource implications.

Especially in FCS, traditional institutions such as tribal leaders may play important roles in the criminal justice system; they need to be taken into account because they form part of the context for how the community understands and responds to crime. Understanding what role these institutions play, what justice sector services they actually provide for different parts of the population, and how well they function is important for assessing if and how formal institutions should be adjusted and linked. It is also important for determining whether to support investment in traditional and other informal mechanisms (e.g., community paralegals, mediation, and other conflict resolution mechanisms). See annex 5E for a more detailed look at PERs that include traditional institutions and approaches to crime.

Pretrial Services

Pretrial detention refers to the period between arrest and sentence of a suspected offender. It comprises the time spent in the custody of police or other criminal justice system agencies, and the time between the suspect's remand into custody and the court delivery of a sentence. The custody under the police normally takes place in sites of temporary detention such as police cells and should not last long. The court may decide that the detainee should remain in custody until he or she is adjudicated, normally due to the serious nature of the offence, or due to the risk of evasion, reoffending, or obstructing the investigation. In such cases, the suspect should be transferred from police custody centers to pretrial (or remand) detention centers.[113] The latter are usually managed by the corrections service.

International standards require that untried inmates be held separately from convicted ones. Those held in pretrial detention are considered innocent (unless they admit guilt) and have to be treated as such. They should receive health and other basic services and generally have the right to receive food and other items privately, if desired and feasible. In many countries, however, pretrial detention is overly lengthy, and delays in court proceedings sometimes contribute to pretrial detention periods beyond even the maximum possible prison term. Overcrowding, generally poor holding conditions, and cohabitation with tried offenders can pose significant risks to individuals and may entail human rights violations. In some countries, the decision on pretrial release mainly depends on whether defendants can make bail and not on the risks they may pose,[114] a practice that discriminates against the poor and that may potentially release dangerous individuals back into the community. Pretrial detention that provides the required conditions and services to suspects presents a significant cost to the state and is one area where more efficient processes, policies, and coordination along with the creation of effective alternatives would not only improve operations and better protect human rights but could also significantly reduce costs.

Victim and Witness Services

Victims—and often their families—are directly affected by crime. They suffer physically, emotionally, and economically, and often experience further distress and disruption (attending hearings, losing time at work) as they contribute to the investigation and court process. Some may even be threatened by the offender and his accomplices or gang. Yet in many countries, state institutions do not provide victims with the most basic supports, such as protection, assistance with managing the criminal process, reimbursement for expenses, medical and other support, and compensation for the damages they have suffered. Witnesses, too, may be in need of certain services and supports—for example, protection from gangs or authorities. To ensure that victims and witnesses cooperate and remain safe, supporting them with necessary services is essential. Such interventions may also be needed to prevent social tension in particular communities and prevent further crimes, including acts of revenge.

The United Nations has issued guidelines for responding to victims' needs, and an increasing number of countries have introduced legislation (victims' bill of rights, victim protection related to evidentiary requirements, procedural law, victim assistance programs and funds, and so forth) to protect victims' rights. Some governments have introduced programs—often funded from criminal fines—to assist, compensate, and protect victims and witnesses.[115] Since many offenders tend to have limited resources to pay for even partial compensation, the responsibility for addressing the victims' needs falls to the state. Less affluent countries may have fewer options for providing such financial compensation, but they can still seek to reduce the burden and stress on the victim or witness, to provide at least protection and in certain cases anonymity, and to link victims to other needed government services. These options cost little, are of great help to the victim or witness, and contribute greatly to the criminal process, which is essential to achieving conviction. It is in the interest of the state, the victim, and the general public to provide at least these conditions.

Public Defender Offices and Legal Aid Services

Where criminal defendants cannot afford to hire their own private attorney, they may be entitled to have publicly financed counsel. This is a fundamental human right, but it is often limited to the most serious cases or to those involving a long prison sentence. Few countries have the financial resources to offer more. The way such legal aid is provided can vary widely among countries. Most often, criminal defense services are provided by private attorneys appointed and contracted by the court. This may sound like a flexible and cost-effective solution, but depending on defense needs, access to qualified attorneys may be limited, and costs can be driven up when there is little competition.

In order to control cost while at the same time assuring adequate defense services, jurisdictions in some countries have chosen to establish a public defenders' office. Such public defender systems can be in charge of a combination of tasks in addition to providing defense services: (i) implementing and informing government policy, and reporting on service delivery to the government; (ii) developing the scope of state-sponsored services; (iii) identifying resource needs and allocating funding; (iv) certifying service providers; (v) monitoring and evaluating services; and (vi) compiling data and conducting research on services.[116] Alternatively, the state may simply subcontract the provision of services with private lawyers, bar associations, or other legal aid organizations. Considering the high cost of good defense services, most criminal justice systems rely on other nonstate options, such as legal aid provided by NGOs, law school legal clinics, or lawyers acting pro bono. Ensuring adequate services and equal access to defense attorneys is a significant challenge for many countries, and it is often only through good relationships, the willingness to cooperate with private providers, and a systematic coordination approach that services can be provided.

Research and Data Centers

Collecting, analyzing, and disseminating data on crime, offenders, and the operation of criminal justice institutions are key to moving from intuition-based to evidence-based policy making for the entire sector. Various countries have established agencies dedicated to improving knowledge and understanding of crime patterns and justice institutions through quantitative and qualitative analysis. Some of the most prominent ones, such as the National Institute of Justice in the United States, the Research and Documentation Center in the Netherlands (WODC), and the Research Department of the Home Office in the United Kingdom, are part of the executive branch. Some countries, such as Australia, Honduras, Jamaica, and South Africa, have created crime observatories that collect and analyze crime and offender trends across different locations to inform criminal justice system strategies and policies. These observatories, which may be public bodies, NGOs, or university affiliates, differ significantly in scope, responsibility, and experience. The rise of such observatories and similar entities is due to a growing recognition that crime can be effectively countered only if proper information is available.[117] Modern technology, especially GIS software, greatly aids in this process.

These organizations may include multidisciplinary teams and represent a true systemwide approach. Others are supported by academic institutions with limited funding or may have limited regional scope. Although funding for such data collection may not be seen as a priority in poor countries or those that are just emerging from conflict, data are essential to developing effective operations, strategies, and policies. Investment in a coordinated data collection effort may therefore be a wise and cost-effective choice, one that will be especially helpful if it builds upon and feeds into agency systems.

Annex 5E: Assessing Criminal Justice Institutions in Fragile and Conflict-Affected Situations

The role of justice institutions in supporting development is especially relevant in fragile and conflict-affected situations. The 2011 *World Development Report* showed that injustice (perceived or actual) fuels inequality, insecurity, conflict, and violence, and it recommended investment in justice institutions as a credible signal of commitment to and stabilizer of reform. Effective and legitimate justice institutions underpin transitions from conflict and fragility by enhancing citizen security, enabling economic activity and access to government services, and helping to resolve grievances and conflicts before they escalate toward (further) violence.[118]

In crisis and immediate postconflict environments, a PER should seek information about the crime and violence context, about informal criminal justice mechanisms, about the funding needs of a rebuilt justice system, and about the role of donors and external assistance.

A PER therefore can be an important component of the evidence base needed to achieve consensus about the direction, scope, and priorities of justice sector development in a particular country. The PER encourages fiscal realism in policies and plans, and supports more effective coordination among donors and stakeholders. A growing body of PER work in the criminal justice sector in FCS points to four considerations that are particularly relevant to these contexts:

First, the PER should be informed by an understanding of the most salient criminal justice needs and the institutions (formal and informal) that address those needs. In situations where seemingly everything is a priority, a problem-driven approach makes it possible to assess the most pressing disputes that fuel conflict. Understanding grievances and the parties involved is one step toward understanding how such disputes are handled and what capacities exist to address these disputes. In such settings, the formal criminal justice system may be identified with the state and therefore not be seen as legitimate in resolving disputes; hence communities may rely on informal and traditional institutions.

Second, the PER should include analysis of the political economy dynamics that shape justice service delivery overall. Justice institutions in any context reflect the balance of power, nature of agreements and settlements, and processes of contestation among political actors, but in FCS the dynamics that inhibit fair and effective justice services are often closely related to the sources of conflict and fragility. Informed by an understanding of broad patterns of authority, the PER can shed light on the economic dimensions of prevailing political settlements, and point to both obstacles to reform and entry points for institutional change.

Third, any review of expenditures in the criminal justice system should bear in mind that significant parts of the criminal justice services in FCS are often funded through external sources, especially donor aid. Since these funding streams are not necessarily included in the regular budget process and documentation, tracking them may be difficult. In addition and perhaps more important, the heavy involvement of these external actors in financing the criminal justice system, particularly at the early stages of transition and peace, poses sustainability challenges that the PER could address directly.

Fourth, the PER should be seen as part of the process of policy dialogue and change in the context of transitions from fragility and violence. Since a common challenge in FCS is the lack of consensus or even knowledge regarding the reality of justice service delivery, the local variations of conflict sources, and the definition of what constitutes "crime," the PER can play a role in enabling an informed policy dialogue and decision-making process.

Key Questions for a PER in FCS

A nonexhaustive list of key questions for a PER in FCS is outlined here.

Crime Context

What are the criminal justice needs that are most related to conflict and insecurity across the country/region? What are the underlying reasons for and main drivers of key conflict and insecurity issues across the country/region? Which of these needs is being or can realistically be addressed by the criminal justice system?

Institutional Arrangements

Which institutions and actors—state and nonstate—currently provide criminal justice services? How accessible are these different institutions to different potential user groups? How well are they accepted by different groups? How does the performance of these institutions reflect the political economy dynamics, including prevailing political settlements, economic interests, normative commitments, and other factors? How do current justice arrangements reflect or fuel fragility and conflict? Are there risks that assistance may be exacerbating sources of conflict?

Budget and Financial Flows

What are the current budget sources and expenditure flows, including donor funds, on and off budget? What public financial management and accountability systems are in place, and how effectively are these being implemented in practice? Is there a discrepancy between what is officially in place, how funds are spent, and what is actually working?

Human Resources Capacities and Resource Allocation

What are the current arrangements for hiring, appointing, training, and disciplining personnel? How do these arrangements reflect both formal and informal rules, networks, and power relations? What are the actual current human resource capacities in terms of numbers and knowledge/skills? How is funding for positions determined? Does the number of positions budgeted for match with those actually filled? What are the greatest challenges for developing a professional workforce? Do other sectors face similar challenges, and are there options for collaboration? What support is needed and available for strengthening capacities in the informal justice sector?

Overall Analysis

What are the most appropriate mechanisms for addressing priority justice needs? What budget is needed to fund such a system, and can the country afford this now and in the future? Are there lower cost/more sustainable alternatives to comprehensive institutional strengthening? What trade-offs are involved?

Practical Challenges for a Criminal Justice System PER in FCS

Criminal justice system PERs are challenging exercises, especially in FCS. A careful up-front desk review, along with early policy dialogue with government officials, key stakeholders, and other donors, will be necessary to achieve consensus on the PER's focus. Practical steps toward completion include the following:

- *Responding to competing motives and interests.* The motives for conducting a PER often vary, sometimes reflecting competing priorities of domestic and external actors. Donors might look to PERs to inform the cost of implementing provisions of a peace agreement, of beginning a donor engagement, or of planning for the transition from a peacekeeping force. Recipient governments might want the PER to help address a particular justice challenge, to identify innovative approaches, or merely to secure donor funds.
- *Addressing donor-driven funding and lack of transparency.* In FCS, a significant proportion of criminal justice system funding often comes from external sources, mainly multilateral and bilateral donors who may also provide significant human resources to "run" criminal justice agencies. In addition to creating a sustainability dilemma, this funding also poses a practical challenge to the PER team. In order to get a full picture of the available resources (and their permanence in the medium and long term), the team will need to collect data that may not be recorded in the budgets and expenditure information systems of ministries and institutions.

- *Incorporating nonstate justice mechanisms in analysis of service delivery and costs.* Services delivered by nonstate institutions are an important consideration in conflict-affected contexts. Although it may not be possible to conduct a fiscal analysis of the full range of state and nonstate mechanisms, understanding their role can clarify how criminal justice institutions fit into a broader institutional landscape; in turn, this understanding can be the basis for prioritizing investments and making choices regarding the potential scope of a formal criminal justice system. Where a range of nonstate institutions deals with alternative dispute resolution, restorative justice, family law and land issues, reconciliation, and victim support, and meets the demand with reasonable quality, funding to the state institutions can be used to complement this service provision, and not to substitute it. Because of the nature of these mechanisms, incorporating them in the analysis poses additional data and methodological challenges. The PER team will need to understand this issue and address it as early as the design stage.
- *Compensating for limited absorptive capacity/policy space for conducting PERs and acting on recommendations.* Shortages in human capacity caused by flight and destruction, combined with a multitude of reform priorities and development programs, can complicate PER exercises in FCS. Government counterparts may have limited time or capacity, and may be stretched thin by the numerous priorities competing for their attention. Justice reform may not receive sufficient attention from policy makers, or there may be active resistance to increasing transparency. At the same time, a PER can serve to build capacity among donor counterparts to collect and analyze data and use it for decision making, and can also serve to open the space for policy change. Ensuring that the PER can benefit donor counterparts will require deliberate planning and thought about how to involve counterparts, how to disseminate PER results, and how to apply them so as to inform policy.
- *Dealing with data scarcity.* Data are particularly difficult to collect in these contexts. If data and files were collected in the past, they have likely been destroyed, and many of the criminal justice institutions lack the most basic information collection systems. For these reasons, the team will need to plan ahead and design data collection methodologies (needs surveys, institutional mappings, public expenditure tracking surveys, ethnographic research, etc.) to produce the necessary information.
- *Handling security threats to the team.* From a more pragmatic perspective, these exercises can be jeopardized by the security conditions on the ground. In FCS, unlike other countries, it may be difficult to collect needed information from public ministries and agencies in the capital city. Data collection may involve fieldwork in areas where the security situation is more unstable. The team's knowledge of the region, risks, cultural patterns, and language is especially important for conducting criminal justice PERs in FCS.

Annex 5F: Assessment of Data: Sample Collection Scheme

Table 5F.1   Assessment of Data: Sample Collection Scheme

	Ideal scenario	Average scenario	Acceptable scenario
Expenditure data	• Data from integrated financial management information system (IFMIS) in electronic format, including both national and subnational service delivery units[a] • Expenditure data from IFMIS disaggregated by economic, functional, and programmatic classification • Data on staff expenses, investment, and purchases of goods and services disaggregated at the service delivery unit level as well as for headquarters • Information on allocations for judges and prosecutors assigned to each case category and type, by position and rank and by location • Data from donor-funded projects • Information on allocated and executed expenditures • Information (law and actual practice) on budget management and oversight *[Data will be consistent throughout the analyzed period.]*	• Data from IFMIS in electronic format • Expenditure data by economic classification only • Regionally disaggregated data as well as data on expenditures from headquarters • Data from donor-funded projects • Information on allocated and executed expenditures • Information (law and actual practice) on budget management and oversight *[Data should be consistent throughout the analyzed period.]*	• Data from IFMIS in electronic format without geographic disaggregation • Information only on allocated expenditures • Legal framework of budget management and oversight

(Table continues on next page)

Table 5F.1   Assessment of Data: Sample Collection Scheme *(continued)*

	Ideal scenario	Average scenario	Acceptable scenario
Activity data	• Demand-side information by case type[b] and service delivery unit location • Caseload (including case mix and complexity),[c] workload, and average time devoted to each type of case, by service delivery unit and by staff[d] • Average cost of proceedings of each case type, by service delivery unit and by staff • Performance indicators such as case clearance rates, adjusted clearance rates (taking into account the backlog), average age of backlog cases, case turnover ratios, minimum-average-maximum disposition time, and case enforcement rates by service delivery unit and staff, and disaggregated by case type • Recidivism rates and safety indicators by corrections and offense type • User satisfaction data (access, quality, fairness, trust), ideally by service delivery unit and case type *[Ideally, data will be obtained from an automated case management system, and they will be consistent throughout the analyzed period.]*	• Demand-side information by service delivery unit but without disaggregation by case type[b]—just by major category of cases • Performance indicators such as case clearance rates, adjusted clearance rates (taking into account the backlog), average age of backlog cases, case turnover ratios, minimum-average-maximum disposition time, and case enforcement rates by service delivery unit, but without disaggregation by staff or case type • Recidivism rates and safety indicators at the national level *[Data should be recorded electronically, although not necessarily through an integrated case management system. They should be consistent throughout the analyzed period.]*	• Only national aggregated information on caseload • Basic performance measures (clearance rate, backlog) at the national level

(Table continues on next page)

Table 5F.1 Assessment of Data: Sample Collection Scheme *(continued)*

	Ideal scenario	Average scenario	Acceptable scenario
Counterparts involved	• Ministry of finance (IFMIS unit) • Ministry of justice • Prosecutor's office • Courts • Corrections directorate/department • Judicial branch (supreme court, judicial council, or others) • Ministry of interior • Bureau of statistics • Audit office • NGOs and research and data centers (if public)	• Ministry of finance (IFMIS unit) • Ministry of justice • Prosecutor's office • Courts • Corrections directorate/department • Ministry of interior • Judicial branch • Audit office • NGOs (if public)	• Ministry of finance (IFMIS unit) • Ministry of justice • Courts • Ministry of interior • Audit office

Note: NGOs = nongovernmental organizations.

a. The term "service delivery unit" refers to prosecution offices, criminal courts, and corrections. In the case of criminal courts, these should also include appeals courts, and the case categorization and recording system should be homogenous to monitor the appeals rates and the entire duration and costs of cases.

b. Ideally this typology would be in line with international standards to allow cross-country comparisons.

c. In the case of prosecutors and criminal courts, such information should distinguish between litigious and nonlitigious cases and count separately process steps in substantive cases, in those requiring prosecutorial/judicial action, and in those currently counted as separate cases.

d. The term "staff" refers to prosecutors, judges, and corrections managers as well as their supporting personnel.

Notes

1. Examples include the Commission on Accreditation for Law Enforcement, the International Association of Prosecutors, the International Consortium for Court Excellence, the European Commission for the Efficiency of Justice, the International Association of Penal Law, the International Institute for the Sociology of Law, the European Institute for Crime Prevention and Control, the Academy of Criminal Justice Sciences, and the Justice Research and Statistics Association.

2. For toolkits, see for example United Nations Office on Drugs and Crime (UNODC), "Criminal Justice Assessment Toolkit," 2006, https://www.unodc.org/unodc/en/justice-and-prison-reform/Criminal -Justice-Toolkit.html; for evidence-based evaluations, see Open Society Institute, "Towards a New Consensus on Justice Reform: Mapping the Criminal Justice Sector," 2008, https://www.opensocietyfoundations .org/sites/default/files/justice_20081124c_0.pdf.

3. Geoffrey C. Hazard Jr., Martin B. McNamara, and Irwin F. Sentilles III, "Court Finance and Unitary Budgeting" (Yale Law School Faculty Scholarship Series, Paper 2412, New Haven, CT, 1972), http:// digitalcommons.law.yale.edu/fss_papers/2412/.

4. World Bank, "Serbia Justice Public Expenditure Review" (World Bank, Washington, DC, 2010).

5. World Bank, "El Salvador Public Expenditure Review" (World Bank, Washington, DC, 2012).

6. World Bank, "Liberia Public Expenditure Review" (World Bank, Washington, DC, 2012); World Bank, "Somalia Security and Justice Public Expenditure Review" (World Bank, Washington, DC, 2016).

7. World Bank, "Morocco Justice Public Expenditure Review" (World Bank, Washington, DC, 2013).

8. World Bank, "The Impact of Public Expenditure Reviews: An Evaluation" (World Bank, Washington, DC, 1998).

9. The fiscal framework comprises the parameters on public spending fixed by a government accounting for revenues, debts, and expenditures.

10. European Commission for the Efficiency of Justice, "Report on European Judicial Systems—Edition 2014 (2012 Data): Efficiency and Quality of Justice," 2014, http://www.coe.int/t/dghl/cooperation/cepej /evaluation/2014/Rapport_2014_en.pdf.

11. The figure is from the United Nations Development Programme and is cited in H. Noé, *Gasto público en seguridad y justicia en Centroamérica* (Mexico City: United Nations, 2011).

12. Graham Farrell and Ken Clark, "What Does the World Spend on Criminal Justice?" (HEUNI Paper 20, European Institute of Crime Prevention and Control, affiliated with the United Nations, Helsinki, 2004).

13. D. Webber, "Good Budgeting, Better Justice: Modern Budget Practices for the Judicial Sector" (Law and Development Working Paper 3, World Bank, Washington, DC, 2007).

14. Chief Justice R. S. French, "Boundary Conditions: The Funding of Courts within a Constitutional Framework" (paper prepared for the Australian Court Administrators' Group Conference of the Australian Institute of Judicial Administration, Melbourne, May 15, 2009).

15. Ibid.

16. J. W. Douglas and R. E. Hartley, "The Politics of Court Budgeting in the States: Is Judicial Independence Threatened by the Budgetary Process?" *Public Administration Review* 63, no. 4 (July/August 2003): 441–54.

17. Geoffrey C. Hazard Jr., Martin B. McNamara, and Irwin F. Sentilles III, "Court Finance and Unitary Budgeting" (Yale Law School Faculty Scholarship Series, Paper 2412, New Haven, CT, 1972), http://digital commons.law.yale.edu/fss_papers/2412/.

18. For example, if performance data are not collected or are unrealizable, a sample case file review may be used to establish basic performance information, such as timeliness.

19. M. Fowler, P. Abbott, S. Akroyd, J. Channon, and S. Dodd, "Forest Sector Public Expenditure Reviews: Review and Guidance Note" (Program on Forests [PROFOR], Washington, DC, 2011).

20. Anne-Marie Leroy, "Legal Note on Bank Involvement in the Criminal Justice Sector" (World Bank, Washington, DC, 2012), 2, http://siteresources.worldbank.org/INTLAWJUSTINST/Resources/CriminalJusticeLegalNote.pdf.

21. World Bank, "The World Bank Approach to Public Sector Management 2011–2020: Better Results from Public Sector Institutions" (Public Sector and Governance Board, Poverty Reduction and Economic Management, World Bank, Washington, DC, 2012), 1, http://siteresources.worldbank.org/EXTGOVANTICORR/Resources/3035863-1285601351606/PSM-Approach.pdf.

22. Ibid.

23. The judiciary also holds the executive accountable for the provision of services such as health and education to citizens, as well as for compliance with administrative and other laws in its activity. Yet this oversight function is carried out by administrative courts and not criminal ones.

24. Because the police play a central role in the criminal justice system and also can comprise a significant proportion of the national budget, they are treated in a separate chapter.

25. See for example Paul Christoph Bornkamm, *Rwanda's Gacaca Courts: Between Retribution and Reparation* (Oxford, U.K.: Oxford University Press, 2012).

26. National Center for State Courts, "Innovations and Efficiency Study: Phoenix Justice System," 2012, http://cdm16501.contentdm.oclc.org/cdm/ref/collection/ctadmin/id/1995.

27. Ibid.

28. Caitlin Hughes, Michael Lodge, and Alison Ritter, *The Coordination of Australian Illicit Drug Policy: A Governance Perspective* (Drug Policy Modelling Program Monograph 18, National Drug and Alcohol Research Centre, Sydney, 2010).

29. For Europe, see European Monitoring Centre for Drugs and Drug Addiction (EMCDDA), *Drug Coordination Arrangements in the EU Member States* (Luxembourg: Office for Official Publications of European Communities, 2001). For Mexico, see David A. Shirk, "The State of Security in Mexico" (Wilson Center Mexico Institute, 2013), http://www.wilsoncenter.org/sites/default/files/security_2013_mexico_shirk.pdf.

30. See for example CARICOM, "Regional Drug Control Activities," December 2000, http://www.caricom.org/jsp/community_organs/regional_drug.jsp?menu=cob; and ECOWAS, "Final Communique, Forty Second Ordinary Session of the ECOWAS Authority of Heads of State and Government," February 27–28, 2013, http://www.ecowas.int/wp-content/uploads/2015/02/42nd-ECOWAS-Summit-Yamoussoukro-27-28-Feb-20131.pdf.

31. Caitlin Hughes, Michael Lodge, and Alison Ritter, *The Coordination of Australian Illicit Drug Policy: A Governance Perspective* (Drug Policy Modelling Program Monograph 18, National Drug and Alcohol Research Centre, Sydney, 2010).

32. Ibid.

33. Ibid.

34. J. W. Douglas and R. E. Hartley, "The Politics of Court Budgeting in the States: Is Judicial Independence Threatened by the Budgetary Process?" *Public Administration Review* 63, no. 4 (July/August 2003): 441–54.

35. R. Barberet, *Criminal Justice Backgound Note* (World Bank, unpublished report, 2013).

36. The International Crime Victim Survey has been administered in six waves; see J. van Kesteren, J. van Dijk, and P. Mayhew, "The International Crime Victimization Survey: A Retrospective," *International Review of Victimology* 20, no. 1 (2014): 49–69. Sampled countries and cities vary per wave. New methods to access uncounted victimization are emerging. For example, Mexico's Índice de Víctimas Visibles e Invisibles attempts to measure the many unknown or indirect victims of crime (kidnapping, extortion, families of victims, etc.).

37. R. Barberet, *Criminal Justice Backgound Note* (World Bank, unpublished report, 2013).

38. See for example National Center for State Courts, *Mongolia Judicial Reform Program: Annual Report* (Washington, DC: USAID, 2005); and World Bank, "Serbia Criminal Chain Review" (World Bank, Washington, DC: USAID, forthcoming).

39. See the police chapter for more detail.
40. Relevant sets of norms include Office of the United Nations High Commissioner for Human Rights, "Guidelines on the Role of Prosecutors," 1990, http://www.ohchr.org/Documents/Professional Interest/prosecutors.pdf; International Association of Prosecutors, "Standards of Professional Responsibility and Statement of the Essential Duties and Rights of Prosecutors," 1999, http://www.iap -association.org/getattachment/34e49dfe-d5db-4598-91da-16183bb 12418/Standards_English.aspx; and the "European Guidelines on Ethics and Conduct for Public Prosecutors," 2005.
41. See for example the standards and measures developed by the European Commission for the Efficiency of Justice; those developed by the International Framework for Court Excellence; the Trial Court Performance Measures (CourTools) developed by the National Center for State Courts; and the UNODC's "Criminal Justice Assessment Toolkit."
42. See the police chapter for more detail.
43. Relevant examples are measures developed by the Federal Bureau of Prisons, Penal Reform International, and the Open Society Institute, among others.
44. World Bank, "The World Bank Approach to Public Sector Management 2011–2020: Better Results from Public Sector Institutions" (Public Sector and Governance Board, Poverty Reduction and Economic Management, World Bank, Washington, DC, 2012), http:// siteresources.worldbank.org/EXTGOVANTICORR/Resources /3035863-1285601351606/PSM-Approach.pdf.
45. World Bank, "The Impact of Public Expenditure Reviews: An Evaluation" (World Bank, Washington, DC, 1998).
46. M. Fowler, P. Abbott, S. Akroyd, J. Channon, and S. Dodd, "Forest Sector Public Expenditure Reviews: Review and Guidance Note" (Program on Forests [PROFOR], Washington, DC, 2011).
47. World Bank, "The Impact of Public Expenditure Reviews: An Evaluation" (World Bank, Washington, DC, 1998).
48. M. Fowler, P. Abbott, S. Akroyd, J. Channon, and S. Dodd, "Forest Sector Public Expenditure Reviews: Review and Guidance Note" (Program on Forests [PROFOR], Washington, DC, 2011).
49. Ibid.
50. World Bank, "Guidelines for the World Bank's Work on Public Expenditure Analysis and Support (including PERs)" (World Bank, Washington, DC, 2001 [draft]).
51. Estimates are based on communications with relevant task team leaders.
52. World Bank, "Guidelines for the World Bank's Work on Public Expenditure Analysis and Support (including PERs)" (World Bank, Washington, DC, 2001 [draft]).

53. The nine were as follows: Bulgaria (2008), Serbia (2010), El Salvador (2012), Guatemala (2012), Croatia (2013), Morocco (2013), Romania (2013), Mexico (2016), and Somalia (2016).

54. Lisa D. Williams, "Sizing Up the Prosecution: A Quick Guide to Local Prosecution" (Harvard Law School, Cambridge, MA, 2010), http:// hls.harvard.edu/content/uploads/2008/07/prosecution2010.pdf.

55. H. Gramckow, "Preventing Corruption in Prosecution Offices: Understanding and Managing for Integrity" (Justice and Development Working Paper 15/2011, World Bank, Washington, DC, 2011).

56. UNODC, "Access to Justice: The Prosecution Service," in "Criminal Justice Assessment Toolkit," 2006, https://www.unodc.org/documents /justice-and-prison-reform/cjat_eng/3_Prosecution_Service.pdf.

57. "Comparative analysis in relation to prosecution systems reveals that both adversarial and inquisitorial systems either in theory or in practice have moved away from their traditional models." Despina Kyprianou, "Comparative Analysis of Prosecution Systems (Part II): The Role of Prosecution Services in Investigation and Prosecution Principles and Policies," *Cyprus and European Law Review* 7 (2008).

58. Ibid.

59. Ronald F. Wright and Marc L. Miller, "The Worldwide Accountability Deficit for Prosecutors," *Washington and Lee Law Review* 67 (2010): 1587–620.

60. Jacqueline S. Hodgson, "The French Prosecutor in Question," *Washington and Lee Law Review* 67 (2010): 1361–411.

61. H. Gramckow, "Preventing Corruption in Prosecution Offices: Understanding and Managing for Integrity" (Justice and Development Working Paper 15/2011, World Bank, Washington, DC, 2011). According to Artem Anyshchenko, "the creation of the separate system of prosecution service has been one of the cornerstones of the political system of the Soviet Union. That separation, extensive prerogatives and lack of judicial control made the prosecutor's office one of the principal instruments of repression." "Transformation of the Ukrainian Public Prosecution According to the European Democratic Standards in Comparison with the Baltic States" (master's thesis, University of Twente, Enschede, the Netherlands, 2010).

62. Ronald F. Wright and Marc L. Miller, "The Worldwide Accountability Deficit for Prosecutors," *Washington and Lee Law Review* 67 (2010): 1587–620.

63. Some of these questions are based on UNODC, "Access to Justice: The Prosecution Service," in "Criminal Justice Assessment Toolkit," 2006, https://www.unodc.org/unodc/en/justice-and-prison-reform /Criminal-Justice-Toolkit.html.

64. For a review of the wide range of methods for estimating staffing needs in the justice sector see H. Gramckow, "Estimating Staffing Needs in the Justice Sector" (Justice and Development Working Paper

19/2012, World Bank, 2012), https://openknowledge.worldbank.org /handle/10986/18404.

65. These questions are based on UNODC, "Access to Justice: The Prosecution Service," in "Criminal Justice Assessment Toolkit," 2006, https://www.unodc.org/documents/justice-and-prison-reform/cjat _eng/CJAT_Toolkit_full_version23Mar10all.pdf.

66. H. Gramckow, "Estimating Staffing Needs in the Justice Sector" (Justice and Development Working Paper 19/2012, World Bank, Washington, DC, 2012), https://openknowledge.worldbank.org /handle/10986/18404.

67. If data and comparable concepts exist—which is not often the case— they allow international comparisons.

68. Analysts will be able to assess which programs appear underresourced.

69. This figure is an important indicator of the credibility of the budget in allowing criminal courts to plan activities and delivering the services outlined in their policy statements and work plans.

70. Such analysis provides information regarding geographical disparities (and potential inequities). Such information may be compared with performance indicators for criminal courts.

71. M. Fowler, P. Abbott, S. Akroyd, J. Channon, and S. Dodd, "Forest Sector Public Expenditure Reviews: Review and Guidance Note" (Program on Forests [PROFOR], Washington, DC, 2011).

72. National District Attorneys Association, *National Prosecution Standards*, 3rd ed., 2009, http://www.ndaa.org/pdf/NDAA%20 NPS%203rd%20Ed.%20w%20Revised%20Commentary.pdf.

73. H. Gramckow, "Preventing Corruption in Prosecution Offices: Understanding and Managing for Integrity" (Justice and Development Working Paper 15/2011, World Bank, Washington, DC, 2011).

74. See for example Santa Barbara County District Attorney's Office, *Annual Report 2011*, https://www.countyofsb.org/ceo/budgetresearch /documents/budget1011/District-attorney.pdf.

75. Geoffrey C. Hazard Jr., Martin B. McNamara, and Irwin F. Sentilles III, "Court Finance and Unitary Budgeting" (Yale Law School Faculty Scholarship Series, Paper 2412, New Haven, CT, 1972).

76. International Consortium for Court Excellence, *International Framework for Court Excellence*, 2nd ed., 2013, http://www.courtexcellence.com /~/media/Microsites/Files/ICCE/The%20International%20 Framework%202E%202014%20V3.ashx.

77. On this subject, P. Albers writes: "The maintenance and operating costs of small courts, i.e. courts with a relatively low workload, can be relatively high in comparison to larger jurisdictions and can [place] a high financial burden on the total budget for the judiciary. Merging small court locations into larger court buildings is often recommended, to achieve more efficiency and lower operating costs for the courts. At the same time local conditions may mean that access to the court is severely limited if court stations are concentrated in a few centers.

The benefit of cost reduction has to be carefully weighed against access to the courts and implications for public trust and confidence." "The Budgetary Situation of the Judiciary in Europe and Central Asia: Challenges and Solutions" (paper prepared for the Justice Sector Budget Professionals Community of Practice of JUSTPAL, The Hague, June 7, 2012).

78. For a short discussion of the implications of different support staff functions and proper task assignment between judges and other staff see World Bank, "Morocco Justice Public Expenditure Review" (World Bank, Washington, DC, 2013, unpublished).

79. Different approaches to estimating staffing needs and making related projections are addressed in H. Gramckow, "Estimating Staffing Needs in the Justice Sector" (Justice and Development Working Paper 19/2012, World Bank, Washington, DC, 2012), https://openknowledge .worldbank.org/handle/10986/18404.

80. European Commission for the Efficiency of Justice, "Evaluation of European Judicial Systems," 2014, http://www.coe.int/T/dghl /cooperation/cepej/evaluation/2014/Synthese_Version_fi nale_en.pdf.

81. J. K. Hudzik, "Court Budgeting: Judicial Branch Independence and Accountability," in *Encyclopedia of Public Administration and Public Policy*, 2nd ed. (CRC Press, 2007); and R. Barberet, *Criminal Justice Backgound Note* (World Bank, Washington, DC, unpublished report, 2013).

82. K. Decker, C. Molhen, and D. Varela, "Improving the Performance of Justice Institutions" (World Bank, Washington, DC, 2011).

83. This information will (i) give a sense of the potential controls on expenditures by criminal courts, and (ii) tell the PER team where the executed expenditure information can be found. In those countries where administrative data are scarce (or not available), other instruments such as public expenditure tracking surveys can provide useful information on the supply side of service delivery (e.g., courts). Such tools have been used by the World Bank—for example, in the education and health sectors in Uganda. See Ritva Reinikka, "Using Surveys for Public Sector Reform" (PREM Notes no. 23, World Bank, Washington, DC, 1999), http://siteresources.worldbank.org/INTPEAM /Resources/premnote23.pdf.

84. This figure represents the average of the 29 states for which data are available. European Commission for the Efficiency of Justice, "Evaluation of European Judicial Systems," 2012, http://www.coe.int/T/dghl /cooperation/cepej/evaluation/2012/Synthese_Version_finale_en.pdf.

85. In locations with a very diverse population base, this can be a significant cost item. One confidential report found that in Abu Dhabi in the United Arab Emirates, for example, 80 percent of the criminal hearings require interpretation.

86. Judges and staff may be required to visit crime locations for on-site evidence hearings, to "ride circuits" (i.e., hold court in different

outlying areas), or to facilitate "community or mobile justice" via cars, motorcycles, boats, and buses. If the court has enforcement responsibilities, the relevant staff will need to have transportation even when many of the enforcement actions are outsourced.

87. For an overview of these and other court performance indicators and measures, see H. Gramckow and O. Ebeid, "Good Practices for Courts: Elements of the Doing Business Quality of Process Index" (World Bank, Washington, DC, 2016).

88. Penal Reform International, "The Use and Practice of Imprisonment: Current Trends and Future Challenges" (paper prepared for the 22nd session of the Commission on Crime Prevention and Criminal Justice, Vienna, April 22–26, 2013).

89. UNODC, "Custodial and Non-custodial Measures: The Prison System," in "Criminal Justice Assessment Toolkit," 2006, https://www .unodc.org/unodc/en/justice-and-prison-reform/Criminal-Justice-Toolkit.html.

90. Penal Reform International, "The Use and Practice of Imprisonment: Current Trends and Future Challenges" (paper prepared for the 22nd session of the Commission on Crime Prevention and Criminal Justice, Vienna, April 22–26, 2013).

91. Ibid.

92. M. Bastick, "The Role of Penal Reform in Security Sector Reform" (Occasional Paper 18, Geneva Centre for the Democratic Control of Armed Forces, 2010).

93. UNODC, "Custodial and Non-custodial Measures: The Prison System," in "Criminal Justice Assessment Toolkit," 2006, https://www .unodc.org/unodc/en/justice-and-prison-reform/Criminal-Justice -Toolkit.html.

94. C. Henrichson and R. Delaney, "The Price of Prisons: What Incarceration Costs Taxpayers" (Center on Sentencing and Corrections, Vera Institute of Justice, 2012), 21, http://www.vera .org/sites/default/files/resources/downloads/price-of-prisons -updated-version-021914.pdf.

95. Center for Digital Government, "Collaborative Justice: Transforming Criminal Justice Services through Unified Collaboration" (Issue Brief, Center for Digital Government, 2013).

96. UNODC, *Handbook for Prison Leaders*, Criminal Justice Handbook Series (New York: United Nations, 2010).

97. For more information about experiences with outsourcing and public-private partnerships in corrections, see P. English and R. Allen, "Public-Private Partnerships in Prison Construction and Management" (Justice and Development Working Paper 25, World Bank, Washington, DC, 2013).

98. Center for Digital Government, "Collaborative Justice: Transforming Criminal Justice Services through Unified Collaboration" (Issue Brief, Center for Digital Government, 2013).

99. Alfred Blumstein and Joel Wallman, eds., *The Crime Drop in America* (New York: Cambridge University Press, 2000); and Michael Jacobsen, *Downsizing Prisons: How to Reduce Crime and End Mass Incarceration* (New York: New York University Press, 2005).

100. Penal Reform International, "The Use and Practice of Imprisonment: Current Trends and Future Challenges" (paper prepared for the 22nd session of the Commission on Crime Prevention and Criminal Justice, Vienna, April 22–26, 2013).

101. UNODC, "Prison Reform and Alternatives to Imprisonment: Concept Note" (UNODC, 2011), 9–10, https://www.unodc.org /documents/justice-and-prison-reform/UNODC_Prison_reform _concept_note.pdf.

102. See for example Tribal Law and Policy Institute, "Tribal Domestic Violence Case Law: Annotations for Selected Tribal Court Cases" (Tribal Law and Policy Institute, 2011), http://www.tribal -institute.org/download/TribalDVCaseLaw-06-15-2011.pdf; and Elena Marchetti and Kathleen Daly, "Indigenous Courts and Justice Practices in Australia" (*Trends and Issues in Crime and Criminal Justice* no. 277, Australian Institute of Criminology, Canberra, 2004).

103. Some of these questions are based on UNODC, "Custodial and Non-custodial Measures: The Prison System," in "Criminal Justice Assessment Toolkit," 2006, https://www.unodc.org/unodc/en/justice -and-prison-reform/Criminal-Justice-Toolkit.html.

104. UNODC, *Handbook for Prison Leaders*, Criminal Justice Handbook Series (New York: United Nations, 2010).

105. UNODC "Custodial and Non-custodial Measures: The Prison System," in "Criminal Justice Assessment Toolkit," 2006, https:// www.unodc.org/unodc/en/justice-and-prison-reform/Criminal -Justice-Toolkit.html.

106. Some of these areas for assessment are based on UNODC, "Custodial and Non-custodial Measures: The Prison System," in "Criminal Justice Assessment Toolkit," 2006, https://www.unodc.org/unodc/en /justice-and-prison-reform/Criminal-Justice-Toolkit.html.

107. Comparisons of different countries' capital costs should take into account lessons from interstate comparisons in the United States: "States often borrow from the public by issuing bonds to provide the funding necessary for large projects and then pay off this debt over a period of years. This payment is called debt service and consists of regular payments of principal and interest in a manner similar to a home mortgage. The payment period usually coincides with the useful life of the asset. Although most states finance capital purchases though debt (which they repay through debt service after a prison is built), some capital costs are paid with current revenues, meaning that the entire cost of the project is paid up front (the 'pay-as-you-go' approach).

In states that finance capital assets with current revenues—whether these costs are inside or outside the corrections department—the total cost of prisons in 2010 is understated in this report because prior capital investment appears to be 'free' in the current period even though the assets remain in use. Similarly, capital costs will be overstated in years when states make new investments, because the cost of an asset, which will have a useful life of many years, will be erroneously attributed to only one year of use. Thus capital costs cannot be compared between states that finance capital costs through debt and current revenues." C. Henrichson and R. Delaney, "The Price of Prisons: What Incarceration Costs Taxpayers" (Center on Sentencing and Corrections, Vera Institute of Justice, 2012), 21, http://www.vera.org/sites/default/files/resources/downloads/price-of-prisons-updated-version-021914.pdf.

108. Ibid.

109. Sometimes these services are billed to corrections, and therefore costs are included in the budget.

110. "While in most countries health in prisons is still under the authority of the Ministry responsible for the prison administration, there is currently a trend to shift this responsibility to the Ministry of Health. Indeed placing health under the responsibility of the Ministry of Health has shown to bring positive results in terms of access to health care in prisons and in terms of continuity of care (through care). This is the case for example in France, Australia, and more recently in the United Kingdom. International norms also make it clear that medical care in prison should be of an equivalent nature to that in the community—best achieved by making prison health care part of the responsibility of the Ministry of Health rather than the prison system." Penal Reform International, "The Use and Practice of Imprisonment: Current Trends and Future Challenges" (paper prepared for the 22nd session of the Commission on Crime Prevention and Criminal Justice, Vienna, April 22–26, 2013).

111. C. Henrichson and R. Delaney, "The Price of Prisons: What Incarceration Costs Taxpayers" (Center on Sentencing and Corrections, Vera Institute of Justice, 2012), http://www.vera.org/sites/default/files/resources/downloads/price-of-prisons-updated-version-021914.pdf.

112. C. Henrichson and S. Galgano, "A Guide to Calculating Justice-System Marginal Costs" (Cost Benefit Analysis Unit, Vera Institute of Justice, 2013), http://www.vera.org/pubs/marginal-costs.

113. UNODC, "Custodial and Non-custodial Measures: Detention Prior to Adjudication," in "Criminal Justice Assessment Toolkit," 2006, https://www.unodc.org/unodc/en/justice-and-prison-reform/Criminal-Justice-Toolkit.html.

114. S. Aungst, "Pretrial Detention and Community Supervision: Best Practices and Resources for California Counties" (Partnership for

Community Excellence, California Forward, 2012), http://caforward.3cdn.net/7a60c47c7329a4abd7_2am6iyh9s.pdf.

115. UNODC, "Cross-Cutting Issues: Victims and Witnesses," in "Criminal Justice Assessment Toolkit," 2006, https://www.unodc.org/unodc/en/justice-and-prison-reform/Criminal-Justice-Toolkit.html.

116. P. Prettitore, "Delivery of Justice Sector Services to the Poor: How Are Middle East Governments Addressing the Gaps?" (World Bank, Washington, DC, 2013).

117. Joanie Prince, Stéphanie Ferland, Serges Bruneau, Jean Carrière, and Valérie Sagant, "Crime Observatories: International Experience Directory" (International Center for the Prevention of Crime, 2009), http://www.crime-prevention-intl.org/fileadmin/user_upload/Publications/Crime_Observatories_ANG.pdf.

118. World Bank, *World Development Report 2011: Conflict, Security, and Development* (Washington, DC: World Bank, 2011). See also other general references on work in fragile states, e.g., UNODC and U.S. Institute of Peace, *Criminal Justice Reform in Post-Conflict States: A Guide for Practitioners* (Vienna: United Nations, 2011).

References

Albers, P. 2012. "The Budgetary Situation of the Judiciary in Europe and Central Asia: Challenges and Solutions." Paper prepared for the Justice Sector Budget Professionals Community of Practice of JUSTPAL, The Hague, June 7.

Anyshchenko, Artem. 2010. "Transformation of the Ukrainian Public Prosecution According to the European Democratic Standards in Comparison with the Baltic States." Master's thesis, University of Twente, Enschede, the Netherlands.

Aungst, S. 2012. "Pretrial Detention and Community Supervision: Best Practices and Resources for California Counties." Partnership for Community Excellence, California Forward. http://caforward.3cdn.net/7a60c47c7329a4abd7_2am6iyh9s.pdf.

Barberet, R. 2013. *Criminal Justice Background Note.* Unpublished report, World Bank, Washington, DC.

Bastick, M. 2010. "The Role of Penal Reform in Security Sector Reform." Occasional Paper 18, Geneva Centre for the Democratic Control of Armed Forces.

Blumstein, Alfred, and Joel Wallman, eds. 2000. *The Crime Drop in America.* New York: Cambridge University Press.

Bornkamm, Paul Christoph. 2012. *Rwanda's Gacaca Courts: Between Retribution and Reparation.* Oxford, U.K.: Oxford University Press.

CARICOM (Caribbean Community Secretariat). 2000. "Regional Drug Control Activities." December. http://www.caricom.org/jsp/community _organs/regional_drug.jsp?menu=cob.

Center for Digital Government. 2013. "Collaborative Justice: Transforming Criminal Justice Services through Unified Collaboration." Issue Brief, Center for Digital Government.

Chopra, T. 2009. "Justice versus Peace in Northern Kenya." Justice and Development Working Paper 2, World Bank, Washington, DC.

Council of Europe. 2005. "European Guidelines on Ethics and Conduct for Public Prosecutors (or the Budapest Guidelines)," Conference of Prosecutors General of Europe.

Decker, K., C. Molhen, and D. Varela. 2011. "Improving the Performance of Justice Institutions." World Bank, Washington, DC.

Douglas, J. W., and R. E. Hartley. 2003. "The Politics of Court Budgeting in the States: Is Judicial Independence Threatened by the Budgetary Process?" *Public Administration Review* 63 (4): 441–54.

ECOWAS (Economic Community of West African States). 2013. "Final Communique, Forty Second Ordinary Session of the ECOWAS Authority of Heads of State and Government." February 27–28. http:// www.ecowas.int/wp-content/uploads/2015/02/42nd-ECOWAS-Summit -Yamoussoukro-27-28-Feb-20131.pdf.

English, P., and R. Allen. 2013. "Public-Private Partnerships in Prison Construction and Management." Justice and Development Working Paper 25, World Bank, Washington, DC.

European Commission for the Efficiency of Justice. 2012. "Evaluation of European Judicial Systems." http://www.coe.int/T/dghl/cooperation /cepej/evaluation/2012/Synthese_Version_finale_en.pdf.

———. 2014. "Report on European Judicial Systems—Edition 2014 (2012 Data): Efficiency and Quality of Justice." http://www.coe.int/t/dghl /cooperation/cepej/evaluation/2014/Rapport_2014_en.pdf.

European Monitoring Centre for Drugs and Drug Addiction (EMCDDA). 2001. *Drug Coordination Arrangements in the EU Member States.* Luxembourg: Office for Official Publications of European Communities.

Farrell, Graham, and Ken Clark. 2004. "What Does the World Spend on Criminal Justice?" HEUNI Paper 20, European Institute of Crime Prevention and Control, affiliated with the United Nations, Helsinki.

Fowler, M., P. Abbott, S. Akroyd, J. Channon, and S. Dodd. 2011. "Forest Sector Public Expenditure Reviews: Review and Guidance Note." Program on Forests [PROFOR], Washington, DC.

French, R. S. 2009. "Boundary Conditions: The Funding of Courts within a Constitutional Framework." Paper prepared for the Australian Court

Administrators' Group Conference of the Australian Institute of Judicial Administration, Melbourne, May 15.

Gramckow, H. 2011. "Preventing Corruption in Prosecution Offices: Understanding and Managing for Integrity." Justice and Development Working Paper 15/2011, World Bank, Washington, DC.

———. 2012. "Estimating Staffing Needs in the Justice Sector." Justice and Development Working Paper 19/2012, World Bank, Washington, DC. https://openknowledge.worldbank.org/handle/10986/18404.

Gramckow, H., and O. Ebeid. 2016. "Good Practices for Courts: Elements of the Doing Business Quality of Process Index." World Bank, Washington, DC.

Haldenby, Andrew, Tara Majumdar, and Will Tanner. 2012. "Doing It Justice: Integrating Criminal Justice and Emergency Services through Police and Crime Commissioners." *Reform* (October). http://www.reform.uk/wp-content/uploads/2012/10/DoingItJustice.pdf.

Hazard, Geoffrey C., Jr., Martin B. McNamara, and Irwin F. Sentilles III. 1972. "Court Finance and Unitary Budgeting." Yale Law School Faculty Scholarship Series, Paper 2412, New Haven, CT. http://digitalcommons.law.yale.edu/fss_papers/2412/.

Henrichson, C., and R. Delaney. 2012. "The Price of Prisons: What Incarceration Costs Taxpayers." Center on Sentencing and Corrections, Vera Institute of Justice. http://www.vera.org/sites/default/files/resources/downloads/price-of-prisons-updated-version-021914.pdf.

Henrichson, C., and S. Galgano. 2013. "A Guide to Calculating Justice-System Marginal Costs." Cost Benefit Analysis Unit, Vera Institute of Justice. http://www.vera.org/pubs/marginal-costs.

Hodgson, Jacqueline S. 2010. "The French Prosecutor in Question." *Washington and Lee Law Review* 67: 1361–411.

Hudzik, J. K. 2007. "Court Budgeting: Judicial Branch Independence and Accountability." In D. Bearfield and M. Dubnick, eds., *Encyclopedia of Public Administration and Public Policy*. 2nd ed. CRC Press.

Hughes, Caitlin, Michael Lodge, and Alison Ritter. 2010. *The Coordination of Australian Illicit Drug Policy: A Governance Perspective*. Drug Policy Modelling Program Monograph 18, National Drug and Alcohol Research Centre, Sydney.

International Association of Prosecutors. 1999. "Standards of Professional Responsibility and Statement of the Essential Duties and Rights of Prosecutors." http://www.iap-association.org/getattachment/34e49dfe-d5db-4598-91da-16183bb12418/Standards_English.aspx.

International Consortium for Court Excellence. 2013. *International Framework for Court Excellence*. 2nd ed. http://www.courtexcellence.com/~/media/Microsites/Files/ICCE/The%20International%20Framework%202E%202014%20V3.ashx.

Jacobsen, Michael. 2005. *Downsizing Prisons: How to Reduce Crime and End Mass Incarceration.* New York: New York University Press.

Kyprianou, Despina. 2008. "Comparative Analysis of Prosecution Systems (Part II): The Role of Prosecution Services in Investigation and Prosecution Principles and Policies." *Cyprus and European Law Review* 7.

Leroy, Anne-Marie. 2012. "Legal Note on Bank Involvement in the Criminal Justice Sector." World Bank, Washington, DC. http://siteresources.worldbank.org/INTLAWJUSTINST/Resources /CriminalJusticeLegalNote.pdf.

Marchetti, Elena, and Kathleen Daly. 2004. "Indigenous Courts and Justice Practices in Australia." *Trends and Issues in Crime and Criminal Justice* 277, Australian Institute of Criminology, Canberra.

Ministry of Justice of New Zealand. n.d. "About the Justice Sector." http:// www.justice.govt.nz/justice-sector/about-the-justice-sector, last updated September 19, 2016.

National Center for State Courts. 2005. *Mongolia Judicial Reform Program: Annual Report.* Washington, DC: USAID.

———. 2012. "Innovations and Efficiency Study: Phoenix Justice System." http://cdm16501.contentdm.oclc.org/cdm/ref/collection/ctadmin/id/1995.

National District Attorneys Association. 2009. *National Prosecution Standards.* 3rd ed. http://www.ndaa.org/pdf/NDAA%20NPS%20 3rd%20Ed.%20w%20Revised%20Commentary.pdf.

Noé, H. 2011. *Gasto público en seguridad y justicia en Centroamérica.* Mexico City: United Nations.

Office of the United Nations High Commissioner for Human Rights. 1990. "Guidelines on the Role of Prosecutors." http://www.ohchr.org /Documents/ProfessionalInterest/prosecutors.pdf.

Open Society Institute. 2008. "Towards a New Consensus on Justice Reform: Mapping the Criminal Justice Sector." https://www.open societyfoundations.org/sites/default/files/justice_20081124c_0.pdf.

Penal Reform International. 2013. "The Use and Practice of Imprisonment: Current Trends and Future Challenges." Paper prepared for the 22nd session of the Commission on Crime Prevention and Criminal Justice, Vienna, April 22–26.

Prettitore, P. 2013. "Delivery of Justice Sector Services to the Poor: How Are Middle East Governments Addressing the Gaps?" World Bank, Washington, DC.

Prince, Joanie, Stéphanie Ferland, Serges Bruneau, Jean Carrière, and Valérie Sagant. 2009. "Crime Observatories: International Experience Directory." International Center for the Prevention of Crime. http:// www.crime-prevention-intl.org/fileadmin/user_upload/Publications /Crime_Observatories_ANG.pdf.

Public Prosecution Service of Canada. 2012. *Annual Report 2011–2012*. Ottawa: Public Prosecution Service of Canada. http://www.ppsc-sppc.gc .ca/eng/pub/ar10-ra10/index.html.

Reinikka, Ritva. 1999. "Using Surveys for Public Sector Reform." PREM Notes 23, World Bank, Washington, DC. http://siteresources.worldbank .org/INTPEAM/Resources/premnote23.pdf.

Santa Barbara County District Attorney's Office. 2011. *Annual Report 2011*. https://www.countyofsb.org/ceo/budgetresearch/documents/budget1011 /District-attorney.pdf.

Shirk, David A. 2013. "The State of Security in Mexico." Wilson Center Mexico Institute. http://www.wilsoncenter.org/sites/default/files/security _2013_mexico_shirk.pdf.

Tribal Law and Policy Institute. 2011. "Tribal Domestic Violence Case Law: Annotations for Selected Tribal Court Cases." Tribal Law and Policy Institute. http://www.tribal-institute.org/download /TribalDVCaseLaw-06-15-2011.pdf.

U.K. Crown Prosecution Service. 2014. "A Guide to Activity Based Costing." https://www.cps.gov.uk/publications/finance/abc_guide_2014.pdf.

UNODC (United Nations Office on Drugs and Crime). 2006a. "Access to Justice: The Prosecution Service." In "Criminal Justice Assessment Toolkit." https://www.unodc.org/documents/justice-and-prison-reform /cjat_eng/3_Prosecution_Service.pdf.

———. 2006b. "Criminal Justice Assessment Toolkit." https://www.unodc. org/unodc/en/justice-and-prison-reform/Criminal-Justice-Toolkit.html.

———. 2006c. "Cross-Cutting Issues: Victims and Witnesses." In "Criminal Justice Assessment Toolkit." https://www.unodc.org/unodc/en/justice -and-prison-reform/Criminal-Justice-Toolkit.html.

———. 2006d. "Custodial and Non-Custodial Measures: Detention Prior to Adjudication." In "Criminal Justice Assessment Toolkit." https:// www.unodc.org/unodc/en/justice-and-prison-reform/Criminal-Justice -Toolkit.html.

———. 2006e. "Custodial and Non-Custodial Measures: The Prison System." In "Criminal Justice Assessment Toolkit." https://www.unodc .org/unodc/en/justice-and-prison-reform/Criminal-Justice-Toolkit.html.

———. 2006f. "Decision Points Map in the Criminal Justice System." In "Criminal Justice Assessment Toolkit." https://www.unodc.org /documents/justice-and-prison-reform/cjat_eng/Decision_Points.pdf.

———. 2010. *Handbook for Prison Leaders*. Criminal Justice Handbook Series. New York: United Nations.

———. 2011. "Prison Reform and Alternatives to Imprisonment: Concept Note." UNODC, 9–10. https://www.unodc.org/documents/justice-and -prison-reform/UNODC_Prison_reform_concept_note.pdf.

UNODC and U.S. Institute of Peace. 2011. *Criminal Justice Reform in Post-Conflict States: A Guide for Practitioners*. Vienna: United Nations.

van Kesteren, J., J. van Dijk, and P. Mayhew. 2014. "The International Crime Victimization Survey: A Retrospective." *International Review of Victimology* 20 (1): 49–69.

Webber, D. 2007. "Good Budgeting, Better Justice: Modern Budget Practices for the Judicial Sector." Law and Development Working Paper 3, World Bank, Washington, DC.

Williams, Lisa D. 2010. "Sizing Up the Prosecution: A Quick Guide to Local Prosecution." Harvard Law School, Cambridge, MA. http://hls.harvard.edu/content/uploads/2008/07/prosecution2010.pdf.

World Bank. 1998. "The Impact of Public Expenditure Reviews: An Evaluation." World Bank, Washington, DC.

———. 2001. "Guidelines for the World Bank's Work on Public Expenditure Analysis and Support (including PERs)." World Bank, Washington, DC.

———. 2008. "Bulgaria: Resourcing the Judiciary for Performance and Accountability." Report no. 42159-BG, World Bank, Washington, DC.

———. 2010. "Serbia Justice Public Expenditure Review." World Bank, Washington, DC.

———. 2011. *World Development Report 2011: Conflict, Security, and Development*. Washington, DC: World Bank.

———. 2012a. "El Salvador Public Expenditure Review." World Bank, Washington, DC.

———. 2012b. "Liberia Public Expenditure Review." World Bank, Washington, DC.

———. 2012c. "The World Bank Approach to Public Sector Management 2011–2020: Better Results from Public Sector Institutions." Public Sector and Governance Board, Poverty Reduction and Economic Management, World Bank, Washington, DC. http://siteresources.worldbank.org/EXTGOVANTICORR/Resources/3035863-1285601351606/PSM-Approach.pdf.

———. 2013. "Morocco Justice Public Expenditure Review." World Bank, Washington, DC.

———. 2016. "Somalia Security and Justice Public Expenditure Review." World Bank, Washington, DC.

———. Forthcoming. "Serbia Criminal Chain Review." World Bank, Washington, DC.

Wright, Ronald F., and Marc L. Miller. 2010. "The Worldwide Accountability Deficit for Prosecutors." *Washington and Lee Law Review* 67: 1587–620.

Selected Bibliography

Security and Development

Books

Jackson, Paul, ed. 2015. *Handbook of International Security and Development*. Northampton, MA: Edward Elgar Publishing.

Mueller, John, and Mark Stewart. 2011. *Terror, Security, and Money: Balancing the Risks, Benefits, and Costs of Homeland Security*. New York: Oxford University Press.

Picciotto, Robert, and Rachel Weaving, eds. 2006. *Security and Development: Investing in Peace and Prosperity*. New York: Routledge.

Pinker, Stephen. 2011. *The Better Angels of Our Nature: Why Violence Has Declined*. New York: Penguin.

Spear, Joanna, and Paul D. Williams, eds. 2012. *Security and Development in Global Politics: A Critical Comparison*. Washington, DC: Georgetown University Press.

Tschirgi, Necla, Michael Lund, and Francesco Mancini, eds. 2010. *Security and Development: Searching for Critical Connections*. Boulder, CO: Lynne Rienner.

Williams, Paul D. 2013. *Security Studies: An Introduction*. 2nd ed. New York: Routledge.

World Bank. 2003. *Breaking the Conflict Trap: Civil War and Development Policy*. Washington, DC: World Bank and Oxford University Press.

———. 2011. *World Development Report 2011: Conflict, Security, and Development*. Washington, DC: World Bank.

Zvekic, U., ed. 1990. *Essays on Crime and Development*. Turin, Italy: UN Interregional Crime and Justice Research Institute.

Reports

Petesch, Patti. 2014. "How Communities Manage Risks of Crime and Violence." *World Development Report 2014* background paper, World Bank, Washington, DC.

World Bank. 2011. "Crime and Violence in Central America: A Development Challenge." World Bank, Washington, DC.

Security Sector Reform

Article

Jackson, Paul. 2011. "Security Sector Reform and State Building." *Third World Quarterly* 32, no. 10: 1803–22.

Books

Ball, Nicole, and Jay Kayode Fayemi, eds. 2003. *Security Sector Governance in Africa: A Handbook*. Lagos: Centre for Democracy and Development.

Born, Hans, and Albrecht Schnabel, eds. 2009. *Security Sector Reform in Challenging Environments*. Geneva Centre for the Democratic Control of Armed Forces.

Nathan, Laurie, ed. 2007. *Local Ownership of Security Sector Reform: A Guide for Donors*. U.K. Global Conflict Pool.

Sedra, Mark, ed. 2010. *The Future of Security Sector Reform*. Waterloo, Ontario: Centre for International Governance Innovation.

Guidelines

OECD (Organisation for Economic Co-operation and Development). 2004. "Security System Reform and Governance: Policy and Good Practice." OECD, Paris.

———. 2007. *OECD DAC Handbook on Security System Reform: Supporting Security and Justice*. Paris: OECD Publishing.

United Nations SSR Task Force. 2012. "Security Sector Reform Integrated Technical Guidance Notes." United Nations, New York. http://unssr .unlb.org/Portals/UNSSR/UN%20Integrated%20Technical%20 Guidance%20Notes%20on%20SSR.PDF.

Reports

Andersen, Louise. 2011. "Security Sector Reform and the Dilemmas of Liberal Peacebuilding." DIIS Working Paper 2011:31, Danish Institute for International Studies, Copenhagen.

Ball, Nicole. 1998. "Spreading Good Practices in SSR: Policy Options for the British Government." Saferworld. http://www.ciponline.org /images/uploads/publications/Spreading_Good_Practices_in_SSR_NB _Saferworld_1998.pdf.

———. 2014. "Lessons from Burundi's Security Sector Reform Process." Africa Security Brief no. 29, Africa Center for Strategic Studies, Washington, DC. http://www.ciponline.org/images/uploads/publications/Lessons-from-Burundis-SSR-Process.pdf.

Reports of the United Nations Secretary General

United Nations Secretary General. 2005. *In Larger Freedom: Towards Development, Security and Human Rights for All*. United Nations, A/59/2005, March 21.

———. 2008. *Securing Peace and Development: The Role of the United Nations in Supporting Security Sector Reform*. United Nations, A/62/659; S/2008/39, January.

———. 2009. *Peacebuilding in the Immediate Aftermath of Conflict*. United Nations, A/63/881-S/2009/304, June.

———. 2012. *Civilian Capacity in the Aftermath of Conflict*. United Nations, A/67/312–S/2012/645, August.

Security Sector Public Expenditure Reviews

World Bank. 2005. *Improving Public Financial Management in the Security Sector*, vol. 5 of *Afghanistan: Managing Public Finances for Development*. Washington, DC: World Bank.

———. 2009. "Report on the Assessment of the Financial Management of the Defense and Security Forces in the Central African Republic." World Bank, Washington, DC.

———. 2012. "El Salvador Security and Justice Public Expenditure and Institutional Review." World Bank, Washington, DC.

———. 2012. "Republic of Burundi Public Expenditure Review: Fiscal Challenges, Security, and Growth in Burundi." Report no. ACS3988, World Bank, Washington, DC.

———. 2013. "Malian Security Forces: Financial Management Assessment Report." World Bank, Washington, DC.

———. 2013. "Niger Security Sector Public Expenditure Review." Report no. 83526-NE, World Bank, Washington, DC.

World Bank and United Nations. 2012. "Liberia Public Expenditure Review Note: Meeting the Challenges of the UNMIL Security Transition." World Bank, Washington, DC.

Public Expenditure and Financial Management

Books

Allen, Richard, Richard Hemming, and Barry Potter, eds. 2013. *The International Handbook of Public Financial Management*. New York: Palgrave Macmillan.

Allen, Richard, Salvatore Schiavo-Campo, and Thomas Columkill Garrity. 2004. *Assessing and Reforming Public Financial Management: A New Approach.* Washington, DC: World Bank.

Allen, Richard, and Daniel Tommasi. 2001. *Managing Public Expenditure: A Reference Book for Transition Countries.* Paris: Organisation for Economic Co-operation and Development.

Dener, C., J. A. Watkins, and W. L. Dorotinsky. 2011. *Financial Management Information Systems: 25 Years of World Bank Experience on What Works and What Doesn't.* Washington, DC: World Bank.

Klitgaard, R. 1988. *Controlling Corruption.* Berkeley: University of California Press.

Schick, Allen. 1998. *A Contemporary Approach to Public Expenditure Management.* Washington, DC: World Bank.

World Bank. 1998. *Public Expenditure Management Handbook.* World Bank: Washington, DC.

Reports

Byrd, William, and Stephane Guimbert. 2009. "Public Finance, Security, and Development: A Framework and an Application to Afghanistan." Policy Research Working Paper, World Bank, Washington, DC.

Fowler, M., P. Abbott, S. Akroyd, J. Channon, and S. Dodd. 2011. "Forest Sector Public Expenditure Reviews: Review and Guidance Note." Program on Forests [PROFOR], Washington, DC.

Reinikka, Ritva. 1999. "Using Surveys for Public Sector Reform." PREM Notes no. 23, World Bank, Washington, DC. http://siteresources.worldbank .org/INTPEAM/Resources/premnote23.pdf.

World Bank. 1998. "The Impact of Public Expenditure Reviews: An Evaluation." World Bank, Washington, DC.

———. 2012. "The World Bank Approach to Public Sector Management 2011–2020: Better Results from Public Sector Institutions." Public Sector and Governance Board, Poverty Reduction and Economic Management, World Bank, Washington, DC. http://siteresources.worldbank.org /EXTGOVANTICORR/Resources/3035863-1285601351606/PSM -Approach.pdf.

———. 2013. "Public Financial Management Reforms in Post-Conflict Countries: Synthesis Report." World Bank, Washington, DC. http:// documents.worldbank.org/curated/en/2012/01/16380099/public-financial -management-reforms-post-conflict-countries-synthesis-report.

Tools

IMF (International Monetary Fund). 2014. *Government Finance Statistics Manual 2014.* Washington, DC: IMF. http://www.imf.org/external/np /sta/gfsm/index.htm.

PEFA (Public Expenditure and Financial Accountability). 2016. "Framework for Assessing Public Financial Management." PEFA Secretariat, Washington, DC. http://www.pefa.org/en/content/pefa-2016-framework.

World Bank. 2010. "Tools for Evaluating Public Expenditures: Benefit Incidence Analysis." World Bank, Washington, DC. http://wbi.worldbank .org/boost/tools-resources/topics/sector-analysis/benefit-incidence -analysis.

Defense

Articles

Antonakis, Nicholas. 1997. "Military Expenditure and Economic Growth in Greece, 1960–1990." *Journal of Peace Research* 34, no. 1: 89–100.

Ball, Nicole. 1983. "Defense and Development: A Critique of the Benoit Study." *Economic Development and Cultural Change* 31, no. 3: 507–24.

Benoit, Emile. 1978. "Growth and Defense in Developing Countries." *Economic Development and Cultural Change* 26, no. 2: 271–80.

Caruso, Raul, and Addesa Francesco. 2012. "Country Survey: Military Expenditure and Its Impact on Productivity in Italy, 1988–2008." *Defence and Peace Economics* 23, no. 5: 471–84.

Chang, Tsangyao, Chien-Chiang Lee, Ken Hung, and Kuo-Hao Lee. 2014. "Does Military Spending Really Matter for Economic Growth in China and G7 Countries: The Roles of Dependency and Heterogeneity." *Defence and Peace Economics* 25, no. 2: 177–91.

Dunne, John Paul. 2012. "Military Spending, Growth, Development, and Conflict." *Defence and Peace Economics* 23, no. 6: 549–57.

Gray, Colin S. 2010. "Strategic Thoughts for Defence Planners." *Survival: Global Politics and Strategy* 52, no. 3: 159–78.

Kusi, N. K. 1994. "Economic Growth and Defense Spending in Developing Countries: A Causal Analysis." *Journal of Conflict Resolution* 38, no. 1: 152–59.

McNamara, Robert S. 1991. "Reducing Military Expenditures in the Third World." *Finance and Development* 28, no. 3: 26–30.

Smaldone, J. 2006. "African Military Spending: Defence versus Development?" *African Security Review* 15, no. 4: 17–32.

Books

Bebler, Anton. 1997. *Civil-Military Relations in Post-Communist States: Central and Eastern Europe in Transition.* Abingdon, U.K.: Routledge.

Brauer, J., and J. P. Dunne. 2002. *Arming the South: The Economics of Military Expenditure, Arms Production and Arms Trade in Developing Countries.* New York: Palgrave Macmillan.

Brewer, John. 1989. *The Sinews of Power: War, Money, and the English State, 1688–1783.* Abingdon, U.K.: Routledge.

Fitch, John S. 1998. *The Armed Forces and Democracy in Latin America.* Baltimore: Johns Hopkins University Press.

Gleditsch, Nils Petter, Naima Mouhleb, Göran Lindgren, Sjoerd Smit, and Indra De Soysa, eds. 2000. *Making Peace Pay: A Bibliography on Disarmament and Conversion.* Claremont, CA: Regina Books.

Hartley, Keith, and Todd Sandler, eds. 1995. *Handbook of Defence Economics.* Amsterdam: Elsevier.

Jones, L. R., Philip J. Candreva, and Marc R. Devore. 2012. *Financing National Defense: Policy and Process.* Charlotte, NC: Information Age Publishing.

Omitoogun, Wuyi, and Eboe Hutchful, eds. 2006. *Budgeting for the Military Sector in Africa.* Oxford, U.K.: Oxford University Press.

Tan, Andrew T. H., ed. 2010. *The Global Arms Trade: A Handbook.* London: Routledge.

Database

Stockholm International Peace Research Institute. Military Expenditures Database. http://www.sipri.org/research/armaments/milex/milex_database.

Reports

Ball, Nicole, and Malcolm Holmes. 2002. "Integrating Defense into Public Expenditure Work." U.K. Department for International Development. http://www.gsdrc.org/document-library/integrating-defence-into-public -expenditure-work/.

Hendrickson, Dylan, and Nicole Ball. 2002. "Off-Budget Military Expenditure and Revenue: Issues and Policy Perspectives for Donors." CSDG Occasional Paper 1, International Policy Institute, King's College, London. https://www.ciponline.org/images/uploads/publications/OP1_Off Budget_Military_Expenditure.pdf.

Knight, Malcolm, Norman Loayza, and Delano Villanueva. 1996. "The Peace Dividend: Military Spending Cuts and Economic Growth." Policy Research Working Paper 1577, World Bank, Washington, DC.

Transparency International U.K. Defence and Security Programme. 2013. "Government Defence Anti-Corruption Index 2013." http:// transparencyschool.org/wp-content/uploads/GI-main-report.pdf.

Policing

Articles

Altbeker, Antony. 2005. "Puzzling Statistics: Is South Africa Really the World's Crime Capital?" *South African Crime Quarterly* 11.

Call, Charles T. 2002. "Competing Donor Approaches to Post-Conflict Police Reform." *Conflict, Security and Development* 2, no. 1: 100–09.

Katz, Charles M., Edward R. Maguire, and Dennis W. Roncek. 2002. "The Creation of Specialized Police Gang Units: A Macro-Level Analysis of Contingency, Social Threat and Resource Dependency Explanations." *Policing: An International Journal of Police Strategies and Management* 25, no. 3: 472–506.

Muggah, Robert, and Gustavo Diniz. 2013. "Digitally Enhanced Violence Prevention in the Americas." *Stability: International Journal of Security and Development* 2, no. 3: 57, 1–23.

O'Neill, M. W., J. A. Needle, and R. T. Galvin. 1980. "Appraising the Performance of Police Agencies: The PPPM (Police Program Performance Measures) System." *Journal of Police Science and Administration* 8, no. 3: 253–64.

Roebuck, Julian B., and Thomas Barker. 1974. "A Typology of Police Corruption." *Social Problems* 21, no. 3: 423–37.

Stamatel, J. P. 2008. "Using Mortality Data to Refine Our Understanding of Homicide Patterns in Select Postcommunist Countries." *Homicide Studies* 12, no. 1: 117–35.

Books

Bayley, David H. 1994. *Police for the Future*. New York: Oxford University Press.

———. 1998. *What Works in Policing*. New York: Oxford University Press.

Bittner, E. 1990. *Aspects of Police Work*. Boston: Northeastern University Press.

Fogelson, R. M. 1977. *Big City Police*. Cambridge, MA: Harvard University Press.

Goldstein, H. 1990. *Problem-Oriented Policing*. New York: McGraw-Hill.

Kelling, G. L., and C. M. Coles. 1998. *Fixing Broken Windows: Restoring Order and Reducing Crime in Our Communities*. New York: Free Press.

Newburn, T., T. Williamson, and A. Wright, eds. 2007. *Handbook of Criminal Investigation*. Portland, OR: Willan Publishing.

Rice, Stephen K., and Michael D. White, eds. 2009. *Race, Ethnicity, and Policing: New and Essential Readings*. New York: New York University Press.

Rowe, Michael. 2014. *Introduction to Policing*. 2nd ed. London: Sage Publishing.

Weber, Leanne, and Ben Bowling, eds. 2012. *Stop and Search: Police Power in a Global Context*. Abingdon, U.K.: Routledge.

Reports

Bayley, David H. 2001. "Democratizing Police Abroad: What to Do and How to Do It." In *Issues in International Crime*. Washington, DC: U.S. Department of Justice, National Institute of Justice.

Davis, Robert C. 2012. "Selected International Best Practices in Police Performance Measurement." RAND Center on Quality Policing, RAND Corporation, Santa Monica, CA.

Hatry, H. P., L. H. Blair, D. M. Fisk, J. M. Greiner, J. R. Hall Jr., and P. S. Schaenman. 1992. "How Effective Are Your Community Services? Procedures for Measuring Their Quality." Urban Institute and International City/County Management Association, Washington, DC.

Kelling, G. L., A. M. Pate, D. Dieckman, and C. Brown. 1974. *The Kansas City Preventive Patrol Experiment: Technical Report.* Washington, DC: Police Foundation.

Mastrofski, S. D. 1999. "Policing for People." Police Foundation, Washington, DC. http://www.policefoundation.org/wp-content/uploads /2015/06/Mastrofski-1999-Policing-For-People.pdf.

Moore, M. H. 2002. "Recognizing Value in Policing: The Challenge of Measuring Police Performance." Police Executive Research Forum, Washington, DC.

Newburn, T. 1999. "Understanding and Preventing Police Corruption: Lessons from the Literature." Police Research Series Paper 110, Home Office, London.

Vera Institute of Justice. 2003. "Measuring Progress toward Safety and Justice: A Global Guide to the Design of Performance Indicators across the Justice Sector." Vera Institute, New York.

United Nations Tools and Reports

United Nations. 2010. *Guidance on the Use and Preparation of Serious Organized Crime Threat Assessments: The SOCTA Handbook.* New York: United Nations. https://www.unodc.org/documents/afghanistan /Organized_Crime/SOCTA_Manual_2010.pdf.

United Nations Development Programme. 2013. "Human Development Report for Latin America 2013–2014. Citizen Security with a Human Face: Evidence and Proposals for Latin America." In *Human Development Report.* New York: United Nations Development Programme.

United Nations Office on Drugs and Crime. 2012. *Digest of Organized Crime Case Studies.* New York: United Nations. https://www.unodc.org /documents/organized-crime/EnglishDigest_Final301012_30102012.pdf.

United Nations Office on Drugs and Crime and UN-HABITAT. 2011. *Introductory Handbook on Policing Urban Space.* Nairobi: United Nations. http://www.unodc.org/documents/justice-and-prison-reform /crimeprevention/11-80387_ebook.pdf.

United Nations Police Division. 2015. "Strategic Guidance Framework for International Police Peacekeeping." United Nations. http://www.un.org /en/peacekeeping/sites/police/initiatives/policy.shtml.

Criminal Justice

Articles

Douglas, J. W., and R. E. Hartley. 2003. "The Politics of Court Budgeting in the States: Is Judicial Independence Threatened by the Budgetary Process?" *Public Administration Review* 63, no. 4: 441–54.

Hazard, Geoffrey C., Jr., Martin B. McNamara, and Irwin F. Sentilles III. 1972. "Court Finance and Unitary Budgeting." Yale Law School Faculty Scholarship Series, Paper 2412, New Haven, CT. http://digitalcommons.law.yale.edu/fss_papers/2412/.

Hudzik, J. K. 2007. "Court Budgeting: Judicial Branch Independence and Accountability." In D. Bearfield and M. Dubnick, eds, *Encyclopedia of Public Administration and Public Policy*, 2nd ed. CRC Press.

van Kesteren, J., J. van Dijk, and P. Mayhew. 2014. "The International Crime Victimization Survey: A Retrospective." *International Review of Victimology* 20, no. 1: 49–69.

Webber, D. 2007. "Good Budgeting, Better Justice: Modern Budget Practices for the Judicial Sector." Law and Development Working Paper 3, World Bank, Washington, DC.

Wright, Ronald F., and Marc L. Miller. 2010. "The Worldwide Accountability Deficit for Prosecutors." *Washington and Lee Law Review* 67: 1587–620.

Books

Blumstein, Alfred, and Joel Wallman, eds. 2006. *The Crime Drop in America*. Rev. ed. New York: Cambridge University Press.

Jacobsen, Michael. 2005. *Downsizing Prisons: How to Reduce Crime and End Mass Incarceration*. New York: New York University Press.

Reichel, P. L. 2002. *Comparative Criminal Justice Systems: A Topical Approach*. 3rd ed. Upper Saddle River, NJ: Prentice Hall.

Guidance from International Organizations and Bilateral Donors

European Commission for the Efficiency of Justice. 2012. "Evaluation of European Judicial Systems." http://www.coe.int/T/dghl/cooperation/cepej/evaluation/2012/Synthese_Version_finale_en.pdf.

———. 2014. "Report on European Judicial Systems—Edition 2014 (2012 Data): Efficiency and Quality of Justice." http://www.coe.int/t/dghl/cooperation/cepej/evaluation/2014/Rapport_2014_en.pdf.

International Association of Prosecutors. 1999. "Standards of Professional Responsibility and Statement of the Essential Duties and Rights of Prosecutors." http://www.iap-association.org/getattachment/34e49dfe-d5db-4598-91da-16183bb12418/Standards_English.aspx.

U.K. Crown Prosecution Service. 2014. "A Guide to Activity Based Costing." https://www.cps.gov.uk/publications/finance/abc_guide_2014.pdf.

Reports

Bastick, M. 2010. "The Role of Penal Reform in Security Sector Reform." Occasional Paper 18, Geneva Centre for the Democratic Control of Armed Forces.

Center for Digital Government. 2013. "Collaborative Justice: Transforming Criminal Justice Services through Unified Collaboration." Center for Digital Government.

Chopra, T. 2009. "Justice versus Peace in Northern Kenya." Justice and Development Working Paper 2, no. 1, World Bank, Washington, DC.

Decker, K., C. Molhen, and D. Varela. 2011. "Improving the Performance of Justice Institutions." World Bank, Washington, DC.

Farrell, Graham, and Ken Clark. 2004. "What Does the World Spend on Criminal Justice?" HEUNI Paper 20, European Institute of Crime Prevention and Control, affiliated with the United Nations, Helsinki.

Gramckow, H. 2011. "Preventing Corruption in Prosecution Offices: Understanding and Managing for Integrity." Justice and Development Working Paper 15/2011, World Bank, Washington, DC.

————. 2012. "Estimating Staffing Needs in the Justice Sector." Justice and Development Working Paper 19/2012, World Bank, Washington, DC. https://openknowledge.worldbank.org/handle/10986/18404.

Gramckow, H., and O. Ebeid. 2016. "Good Practices for Courts: Elements of the Doing Business Quality of Process Index." World Bank, Washington, DC.

Henrichson, C., and R. Delaney. 2012. "The Price of Prisons: What Incarceration Costs Taxpayers." Center on Sentencing and Corrections, Vera Institute of Justice. http://www.vera.org/sites/default/files/resources/downloads/price-of-prisons-updated-version-021914.pdf.

Open Society Institute. 2008. "Towards a New Consensus on Justice Reform: Mapping the Criminal Justice Sector." https://www.opensocietyfoundations.org/sites/default/files/justice_20081124c_0.pdf.

Prettitore, P. 2013. "Delivery of Justice Sector Services to the Poor: How Are Middle East Governments Addressing the Gaps?" World Bank, Washington, DC.

United Nations Tools and Reports

Office of the United Nations High Commissioner for Human Rights. 1990. "Guidelines on the Role of Prosecutors." http://www.ohchr.org/Documents/ProfessionalInterest/prosecutors.pdf.

United Nations Office on Drugs and Crime. 2006. "Criminal Justice Assessment Toolkit." https://www.unodc.org/unodc/en/justice-and-prison-reform/Criminal-Justice-Toolkit.html.

———. 2006. "Custodial and Non-custodial Measures: The Prison System." In "Criminal Justice Assessment Toolkit." https://www.unodc.org/unodc/en/justice-and-prison-reform/Criminal-Justice-Toolkit.html.

———. 2010. *Handbook for Prison Leaders*. Criminal Justice Handbook Series. New York: United Nations.

United Nations Office on Drugs and Crime and U.S. Institute of Peace. 2011. *Criminal Justice Reform in Post-Conflict States: A Guide for Practitioners*. Vienna: United Nations.

World Bank Justice Expenditure Reviews and Legal Guidance

Leroy, Anne-Marie. 2012. "Legal Note on Bank Involvement in the Criminal Justice Sector." World Bank, Washington, DC. http://siteresources.worldbank.org/INTLAWJUSTINST/Resources/CriminalJusticeLegalNote.pdf.

World Bank. 2010. "Serbia Justice Public Expenditure Review." World Bank, Washington, DC.

———. 2013. "Morocco Justice Public Expenditure Review." World Bank, Washington, DC.

Image Credits

Page 1: © UN Photo/Mark Garten. Used with the permission of UN Photo/ Mark Garten. Further permission required for reuse.

Page 61: © UN Photo/Stuart Price. Used with the permission of UN Photo/ Stuart Price. Further permission required for reuse.

Page 105: © Andrew McConnell/Panos. Used with the permission of Andrew McConnell/Panos. Further permission required for reuse.

Page 143: © UN Photo/Martine Perret. Used with the permission of UN Photo/Martine Perret. Further permission required for reuse.

Page 273: © UN Photo/Christopher Herwig. Used with the permission of UN Photo/Christopher Herwig. Further permission required for reuse.

Page 393: © UN Photo/Staton Winter. Used with the permission of UN Photo/Staton Winter. Further permission required for reuse.